Praise for NAPA

"A book about wine, money, power, and land that reads like a novel . . . A great story . . . *in vino veritas* indeed." — **International Herald Tribune**

"A very lively book . . . James Conaway got into places and activities that most native westerners never even get close to, and he reports them with verve, wit, irony, and a very sharp eye." — **Wallace Stegner**

"A luscious chronicle [that] mixes love affairs and family feuds with corporate buyouts—a sort of *Falcon Crest* meets *Barbarians at the Gate*."
— **Business Week**

"Thoughtful and provocative . . . compelling and intimate . . . candid, flowing, and dramatic . . . Conaway has barged out of the wine cellar and gone sniffing through attic and closet, discovering more than a few family skeletons." — *Sacramento Bee*

"A wonderful and well-considered evocation of the new West, all the better because it reads like a fine novel. It is all the more scathing in its quiet, poignant, elegant way than any of the other indictments of the predators of our government." — **Jim Harrison**

"Lively . . . a full-bodied work." — *USA Today*

"*Napa* is the story of an extraordinary American success, of family feuds and corporate intrigue, and of warfare over the beautiful Napa Valley itself. This is more than a 'wine book'—it is a fascinating and closely reported social history that illuminates the continuing struggle over the destiny of our open land." — **Tracy Kidder**

"[A] lively history . . . Conaway relates the stories of those colorful individuals who settled in the California valley for its beauty and quiet, but were drawn by the favorable conditions into the competition to make a better wine." — *Publishers Weekly*

Books by James Conaway

The Big Easy
(fiction)

*Judge: The Life and Times
of Leander Perez*

The Texans

World's End
(fiction)

The Kingdom in the Country

Napa

Memphis Afternoons
(memoir)

The Smithsonian

America's Library

The Far Side of Eden

Napa

*James
Conaway*

A MARINER BOOK
Houghton Mifflin Company
BOSTON · NEW YORK

First Mariner Books edition 2002

Copyright © 1990 by James Conaway
ALL RIGHTS RESERVED

Visit our Web site: www.houghtonmifflinbooks.com.

Library of Congress Cataloging-in-Publication Data
Conaway, James, date.
Napa / James Conaway.
p.   cm.
"A Richard Todd book."
Includes bibliographical references and index.
ISBN 0-395-46880-9
ISBN 0-618-25798-5 (pbk.)
1. Napa River Valley (Calif.)—History. 2. Wine industry—
California—Napa River Valley—History. I. Title.
F868.N2C66 1990   90-4708
979.4'19—dc20   CIP

Book design by Robert Overholtzer
Map by Jacques Chazaud

QUM 10 9 8 7 6 5 4 3 2 1

The author is grateful for permission to quote lines
from the poem "November: In Passing" by Marky Daniel,
from her book *Discovery Passage*.

For Susanna

And Noah, a husbandman, began to till the ground, and planted a vineyard, and drinking of the wine was made drunk, and lay naked in his tent.

Genesis 9:20–21

The Americans, then, have not required to extract their philosophical method from books; they have found it in themselves.

Alexis de Tocqueville,
Democracy in America

CONTENTS

I · *Terra Incognita* · 1

II · *Leviathan* · 101

III · *As Good As the Best* · 161

IV · *Deluge* · 203

V · *In the Eye of the Beholder* · 261

VI · *Noah's Children* · 333

VII · *The Tragedy of the Commons* · 393

Epilogue · 505

Acknowledgments and Sources · 507

Index · 512

Photographs follow pages 178 and 370

FOUNDERS

Charles Krug (Charles Krug Winery, 1860)
Jacob Schram (Schramsberg Vineyard, 1862)
Gustave Niebaum (Inglenook Vineyards, 1879)
Georges de Latour (Beaulieu Vineyard, 1899)
Louis Michael Martini (Louis M. Martini Winery, 1933)
Cesare Mondavi (Sunny St. Helena, 1937; Charles Krug Winery, 1943)

INHERITORS

John Daniel (Inglenook)
Hélène de Latour de Pins (Beaulieu)
Louis Peter Martini (Martini)
Robert Mondavi (Robert Mondavi Winery; Opus One)
Mary Mondavi (Krug)
Helen Mondavi (Krug)
Peter Mondavi (Krug)

THIRD GENERATION

Marcia Daniel Smith (Napanook/Dominus)
Robin Daniel Lail (Napanook/Dominus)
Dagmar de Pins Sullivan (Beaulieu)
Carolyn Martini (Martini)
Michael Martini (Martini)
Peter Martini (Martini)
Patricia Martini (Martini)
Michael Mondavi (Mondavi; Opus One)
Marcia Mondavi (Mondavi; Opus One)
Timothy Mondavi (Mondavi; Opus One)
Peter Mondavi, Jr. (Krug)
Marc Mondavi (Krug)

VINTNERS

Stan Anderson (S. Anderson Vineyard)
Gary Andrus (Pine Ridge Winery)
James Barrett (Château Montelena)
Sam Bronfman (Sterling Vineyards; Domaine Mumm)
Tom Burgess (Burgess Cellars)
Jack Cakebread (Cakebread Cellars)
Chuck Carpy (Freemark Abbey)
Donn Chappellet (Chappellet Vineyard)
Francis Ford Coppola (Niebaum-Coppola Estate)
Jay Corley (Monticello Cellars)
Jack Davies (Schramsberg Vineyard)
Carl Doumani (Stags' Leap Winery)
Dan Duckhorn (Duckhorn Vineyards)
Randy Dunn (Dunn Vineyards)
Tom Ferrell (Sterling)
Dennis Fife (Inglenook)
Ric Forman (Forman Winery)
Steve Girard (Girard Winery)
Miljenko ("Mike") Grgich (Grgich Hills Cellar)
Dennis Groth (Groth Vineyard and Winery)
Bill Harlan (Sunny St. Helena Winery)
Joe Heitz (Heitz Cellars)
William Hill (William Hill Winery)
Agustin Huneeus (Franciscan Vineyards)
William Jaeger (Rutherford Hill Winery)
Reverdy Johnson (Johnson-Turnbull Vineyards)
Guy Kay (Beringer Vineyards)
Legh Knowles (Beaulieu)
Hanns Kornell (Hanns Kornell Champagne Cellars)
Fred McCrea (Stony Hill Vineyard)
Dick Maher (Christian Brothers Winery)
Justin Meyer (Silver Oak Cellars)
Christian Moueix (Château Pétrus; Dominus)
Michael Moone (Beringer)
Peter Newton (Newton Vineyard)
Gil Nickel (Far Niente Winery)
Dick Peterson (Atlas Peak Vineyards)
Joseph Phelps (Joseph Phelps Vineyards)
Bernard Portet (Clos du Val Wine Company)
Mike Robbins (Spring Mountain Vineyards/Falcon Crest)
Koerner Rombauer (Rombauer Vineyards)

Baron Philippe de Rothschild (Château Mouton-Rothschild;
  Opus One)
Tom Selfridge (Beaulieu)
John Shafer (Shafer Vineyards)
Jan Shrem (Clos Pegase)
Stuart Smith (Smith-Madrone Vineyards)
J. Leland Stewart (Souverain Cellars)
John Trefethen (Trefethen Vineyards)
Bob Trinchero (Sutter Home Winery)
Charles Wagner (Caymus Vineyard)
John Williams (Frog's Leap Wine Cellars)
Warren Winiarski (Stag's Leap Wine Cellars)
John Wright (Domaine Chandon)

GROWERS

Andy Beckstoffer
René di Rosa
Volker Eisele
Andy Pelissa
Bob Phillips

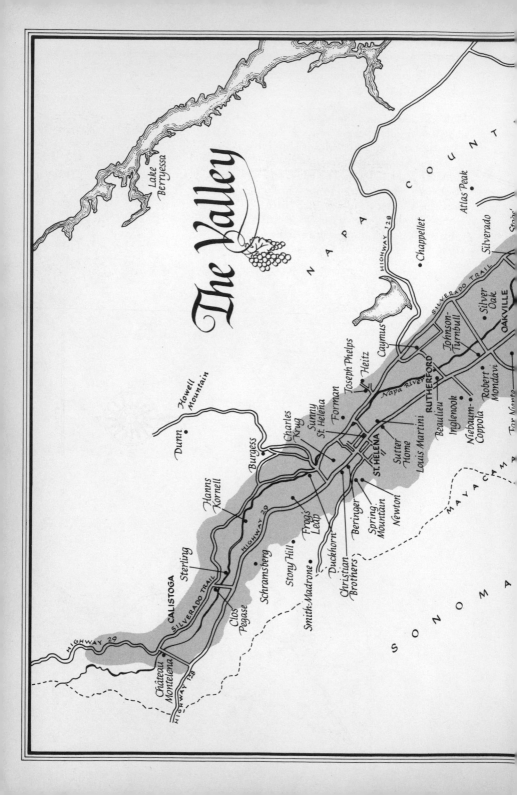

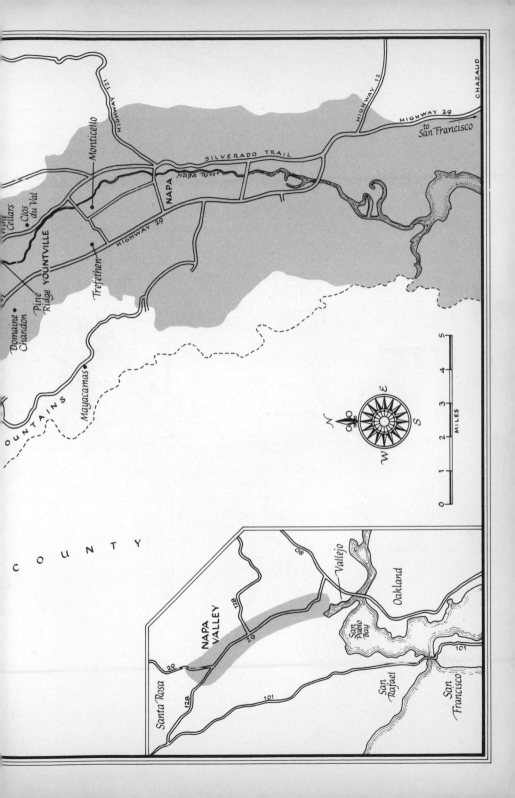

I

Terra Incognita

I

FOR MORE THAN a year now they had been searching: on the highway, near the river, atop oaky knolls that rose abruptly from the valley floor, up wild canyons, and along the spines and scarps of two rugged coastal ranges. What they were looking for was not easily put into words, but the quality of the ideal was absolute and unassailable in their minds. They were searching for . . . They would know it when they found it.

They didn't want a hut in the woods. They didn't want a roadside attraction. They didn't want one of those Victorian piles built in homage to Europe, with too many rooms and too much view (views could be just as pretentious as architecture) and strange names like Château Montelena, Château Chevalier, Freemark Abbey — white elephants all, and all for sale, with weeds in the yards and blank windows staring back into the illusions of the founders.

The couple's name was Davies, and the fact that these near-ruins existed in an agricultural backwater given over to prune and walnut trees, pastures and some vines, intrigued them. The valley, named for the Napa River that flowed through it, was still tenuously connected to a process going back thousands of years and halfway round the world, to the Transcaucasus, south of the Caspian Sea, where similar vines clung to rocky ledges and the grapes were once placed in earthen pots, and the substance that came of them, wine, made its way down the Euphrates, through Egypt, Greece, imperial Rome, and France, to arrive at this redoubt in northern California sometime in the previous century.

Now, in the spring of 1964, Napa Valley was about to achieve something unique in America — again. Wine, lately considered the dubious beverage of immigrants, made in basements, would soon be transformed into a symbol of high culture, and winemakers would be heralded as artists. The owners of wineries themselves would be celebrated as a new class. These self-made baronets — formerly real estate speculators, developers, academics, brokers, dentists, oilmen, and purveyors of products as varied as frozen food and feature films — would put their names on bottles, tacitly associating themselves with an older order and an endeavor above ordinary commerce. They would invite the public into a romantic association not unlike that involving movie idols and real royalty.

The children of these "vintners" would grow up on little fiefdoms, accustomed to the sight of workers among the vines and to the pleasures of life far from the raucous cities and suburbs their parents had left behind. They would reject the unsavory methods of earning the money required to have brought about such a change in their families' fortunes. Some would seek to turn the land into tourist attractions, increasingly urged to exploit the place. Finally, the valley would take on a gloss that had more to do with money than with the product for which it became famous; it would be transformed into a paradigm of material ambition and dissent, threatened by the very brilliance of the imprint it left on the world.

No one had yet thought of these things in 1964. The Davieses — he of the quizzical smile, she of the pale green, catlike eyes — had more immediate concerns. They would, of course, be influenced by history and the natural beauty, but also by practical considerations like sufficient living space, plantable land, a decent barn, good water — all part of a daring, maybe harebrained scheme to get out of Los Angeles.

The Davieses, like many people in the country at that time, sought to change their way of life. The dim notions of freedom they brought with them to Napa Valley, and many of the problems they encountered, were representative of a broader exodus. Jack was the vice president of acquisitions for a large, privately held metals distributor. At forty-two, he had a solid reputation as a businessman; he was methodical and judicious. Those qualities augured against the scheme for escaping, and if it became reality, he was going to have some very surprised associates.

His wife, Jamie, thirty, wore her blond hair short. The breadth of her smile left people with the impression that they were talking to a taller person. To her, the vineyards of Napa Valley, the parched hills against the deep green of oak and conifer and the arching blue sky, seemed timeless and dense with promise.

•

The house had been vacant for quite a while, the real estate agent warned them as they drove up a narrow defile on the eastern slope of the Mayacamas Mountains. It was spring, and hot. The riven road jarred the car and offered up its dust. Jamie Davies could no longer see the thrust of Mount St. Helena off to the right, at the top of Napa Valley, but she could see water running in the streambed — a good sign — and big eucalyptus, redwoods, madroña, and oak trees leaning into one another. Wild vines grew in tangles in the branches, their canes extending clear across the road. The property had once belonged to a German barber in San Francisco named Schram, who came up a century before and fell in love with the setting. He had made wine there but the vineyards had gone to seed since Prohibition, overrun by the same wild vines, poison oak, and impenetrable red-stalked manzanita.

The land was steep, but then the Davieses wanted hillside property. To the south lay a state park, another plus. Then Jamie saw the house. It was made partially of stone and commanded a kind of courtyard, with an old winery on one side, a mountain on the other, and a porch that turned the corner. Victorian, all right, but not a pile. Robert Louis Stevenson had stayed there, the real estate agent said, and had written about the place in a book called *Silverado Squatters.*

He led them up the steps and into the old house. Drapes blocked the light from tall windows; covered furniture stood mutely in the shadows. Jamie felt a palpable tug from a previous age and knew that Jack felt it, too.

They were shown tunnels in the mountain, full of bats. Schram's tunnels had been dug by hand. Jamie could see old bottles lying about in the gloom, and collapsed barrels that had once held aging wine. Schram had wandered the valley with razor and shears, shaving frontiersmen and cutting hair to support his nineteenth-century obsession.

They talked about it all the way back to L.A. Their excitement seemed a bit irrational to Jamie. For starters, the property was too big. They would have to invite friends in as investors, lots of friends, if they tackled it. The house was only half painted; none of the rooms was fit to live in. Animals romped in the walls. The plumbing was a disaster and rain came through the ceiling. The winery needed a new roof. There were no vineyards. And those tunnels! A wonder of individual human industry, full of junk.

Jamie found a copy of Stevenson's *Silverado Squatters.* The writer had visited Napa with his new wife in 1880. Jamie lingered over his description of the approach to the Schram place. "A rude trail rapidly mounting; a little stream tinkling by on the one hand, big enough perhaps after the rains, but already yielding up its life; overhead and on all sides a bower of green and tangled thicket, still fragrant and still flower-bespangled." The Schram house was "the picture of prosperity: stuffed birds in the veranda, cellars dug far into the hillside, and resting on pillars like a bandit's cave: all trimness, varnish, flowers, and sunshine, among the tangled wildwood. Stout, smiling Mrs. Schram . . . entertained Fanny in the veranda, while I was tasting wines in the cellar. To Mr. Schram this was a solemn office . . . he followed every sip and read my face with proud anxiety."

Apparently Stevenson liked what he tasted. He wrote, "The smack of California earth shall linger on the palate of your grandson."

It was sheer luck that had led the Davieses to the same house, Jamie thought. Blind passage.

When the time came to move, she was again eight months pregnant. Her father, a lawyer, jokingly said she never did anything really challenging unless she was about to have a baby. Like the time she and Jack had sailed from San Francisco to L.A. aboard a thirty-seven-foot yawl. Now her father thought she was acting irresponsibly, moving to Napa. He had helped raise Jamie in Pasadena, with what was commonly referred to as all the advantages. She and Jack were turning their backs on a nice, comfortable southern California existence and moving to the ends of the earth — they were acting like beatniks!

Jamie loved her father. He had introduced her to the wonders of the California wilds, both desert and mountain. She told him that it was for *her* children that they were moving. She wanted them to know more than pavement, freeways, transience, and a present dimmed by the recent murder of the President and by an expanding war in Vietnam. At the same time, Jamie felt good about the future, encouraged by the success of America's space program and the coming of a new age that it implied. She and Jack were going to be part of something new and audacious.

Usually she heeded her father's advice. At the University of California at Berkeley she had studied political science because he didn't want her to major in art. He saw her as a schoolteacher, and she tried that for a while, but in Carmel she fell in love with art all over again, quit teaching, and started selling paintings out of a van.

Someone took her to a party at Jack's place, in San Francisco. She saw original art and that surprised her. Jack Davies didn't seem like the type to invest in works of the imagination. His words came out flat, without affect, his eyebrows rising and falling behind his glasses, like semaphore. He seemed remarkably straightforward. Later, after they were married, Jack told her that his grandfather had mined coal in Wales. Jamie thought that probably explained some things. Jack had studied economics and business management at Stanford and at Harvard; his career was eclectic — paper packaging, furniture manufacturing, management consulting. He criticized American business in general for talking down to the consumer and for growing fat and lazy.

When Jack announced that he was moving to the Napa Valley, his boss couldn't believe it. He begged Jack to remain in southern California. They were just getting in on the aerospace play! All Jack's associates said he was wrecking a fine career, and for what? *Winemaking?* Get serious. Where was the security? Americans didn't drink wine, they drank Coke. When they did drink wine, it was out of a bottle with a handle on it, produced by people whose last names ended in vowels.

Jack and Jamie knew people who drank wine, including good California wine, and some who made it, people whose names did not end in vowels. The most celebrated was Martin Ray, a former stockbroker who lived in Saratoga, near San Jose. The Davieses had been taken to lunch there by friends and had left twelve hours later, rocked by the experience. They had seen that another way of life was indeed possible. Ray was inspiring and argumentative; his stunning technical recitations were followed by displays of guile and charm, and sometimes anger. He popped corks from bottles of Dom Pérignon and fine Bordeaux and dared you to compare them with his own creations. He was, in short, a wild man, but one committed to making something rare and unequivocal, and absolutely convinced it could be done in California. They could make wine there as good as the French.

Jack drove north with their four-year-old son in an old International pickup, followed by the moving van. He had bought the Schram place with savings and with the proceeds of the sale of their house in L.A. He had bought 51 percent of it, that is. Investors had bought the other 49 percent. Jack had run the numbers on a start-up winery and figured he would need eight years to make it profitable. Of course the figures that went into the equation didn't necessarily mean anything, but they were the best he could find.

Jamie flew up from L.A. with the two-year-old and an Argentine live-in mother's helper, who brought her own television set. Jack insisted that the family spend the first night in the Calistoga Inn while he cleaned out a couple of rooms. The following morning they showed up early; the mother's helper told Jack, "Any man who would bring his wife and children to a place like this should be ashamed."

They had thirty days to render it livable. Jack and Jamie worked constantly. At night, they listened to mice, rats, and other creatures coursing through the walls and across the attic floor. Every day the Argentine nurse, her television set barely functioning in this crease in the Mayacamas range, stood in the doorway and told Jack, "You'll never make it."

Jamie delivered in the hospital in Vallejo, another boy. Jack finished painting the bedroom. After Jamie and the baby came home, he took the nurse and her television set to the airport and put them both on a plane.

There began a procession of "help" up their dirt road: housekeepers who wouldn't, handymen who weren't. Some came just to gander at the city slickers. The Davieses had social and financial advantages not shared by most of the natives, who had changed appreciably since Robert Louis Stevenson's time, when he described them as "rebellious to all labour, and pettily thievish . . . rustically ignorant, but with a touch of woodlore and the dexterity of the savage. . . . Loutish, but not ill-looking, they will sit all day, swinging their legs on a field fence."

One of the early babysitters tried to steal Jack's dime collection, but in the neighborhood Jack and Jamie soon came to know people they liked and trusted, on all levels.

Jack hired a man to help him put a redwood shingle roof on the winery, and cleaned out the tunnels himself, disturbing the bats. Often he had to turn his back on the demands of the tunnels, winery, and house, and fly down to L.A. to deal with an employer reluctant to let him go. Then Jamie took over the jobs, doing what she could while attending to three small children.

Jack would come home at night and see the fog blowing off the cold water of San Francisco Bay. The fog would follow him north from the airport, through the city of Napa and little hamlets named for dead and forgotten heroes — Yountville, Rutherford, St. Helena — and then stars would appear in the narrow wedge of sky at the head of the valley.

The dinner invitation came from the McCreas, up the mountain. The Davieses had met them at a wine tasting. Fred McCrea was from Minneapolis, Eleanor from Buffalo; they had courted in Napa Valley in the thirties, and Fred had gone into advertising in San Francisco. They had purchased an old 160-acre homestead during World War II for $7,500, planted a vineyard, and called it, appropriately, Stony Hill.

The McCreas made Chardonnay, a sign in the valley that they were a little strange. They had also planted Riesling and Pinot Blanc, at the insistence of professors at the University of California at Davis, the campus for viticulture. The professors disapproved of amateurs pretending they were in Burgundy, where Chardonnay was grown, when they were in northern California, where white wine was made out of French Colombard, Chenin Blanc, and other white grapes better able to withstand frost. The McCreas' wine had won medals and considerable notoriety, however.

Jamie was surprised to discover that Fred drank gin, and Eleanor bourbon. Fred told her, "White wine before dinner is an affectation."

The Davieses and the McCreas hit it off. Fred had opinions about how to set up the sort of small winery the Davieses had in mind. He talked about "position" and "image." His wife gave off a kind of radiance. The McCreas were older than the Davieses, but they were all in this together — Anglo-Saxons with Mediterranean delusions, if truth be told. What a glorious thing it would be if the delusions ever became real!

There were others in the valley like them, refugees from business, academia, and totalitarianism, and some colorful misfits. J. Leland Stewart, owner of an upgraded hovel on Howell Mountain called Souverain Cellars, had left the meat-packing business to write a novel but had turned to making wine back in the forties. Lee Stewart had been a great help to the McCreas. So had Joe Heitz, who had worked for Gallo over in the Central Valley and for Beaulieu Vineyard before buying his own winery on Highway 29. Heitz knew a lot about winemaking and was notoriously abrupt; more than once he had reduced Eleanor McCrea to tears.

Stony Hill, Souverain, Heitz, Mayacamas Vineyards — these

were the only creditable small producers in the valley. A couple of the Victorian piles, Beaulieu and Inglenook Vineyards, were also making good wine. There were a few graduates of UC Davis and Fresno State employed as cellar rats around the valley, but most of the grape growing and winemaking was done by people who had done it for years and whose names really did end in a vowel: the Martinis, the Mondavis, and others, all friends of the McCreas.

The phone book was full of names like Rossini, Solari, Forni, Pelissa, Trinchero, Stralla. A lot of coarse grape varieties were grown by families who depended on farming and had for generations. Their ancestors had been refugees not from corporate America but from the older tyrannies of politics and poverty. They didn't care as much for quality in wine as for quantity; their product was sold in jugs. They drove wagons, and their descendants pickups, over dirt roads, raising dust that hung in the air over the tangled waysides, fields, woodlots, and the occasional house. The dust, like the wine, had figured in Napa's reputation for a century.

The fog had always found its way up the valley or through the gaps in the Mayacamas from neighboring Sonoma Valley. The dawn view from the side of Mount St. Helena had not diminished in its most dramatic features from that encountered by Stevenson, who awoke one morning roughly a century before to find that Napa Valley "was gone; gone were all the lower slopes and the woody foot-hills of the range; and in their place, not a thousand feet below me, rolled a great level ocean. It was as though I had gone to bed the night before, safe in a nook of inland mountains, and had awakened in a bay upon the coast. . . . To sit aloft one's self in the pure air and under the unclouded dome of heaven, and thus look down on the submergence of the valley, was strangely different and even delightful to the eyes."

That fog, like the fogs encountered by Jack and Jamie Davies, was usually gone by midmorning. Mount St. Helena still dominated the northern horizon, yet the mountain's solidity was a comfort, devoid of Alpine dramatics. The view from the north of the valley, at lower elevations, retained the beauty and sense of isolation. On a clear day the Davieses could see the wild barriers of the Palisades, the ridge of Howell Mountain, and the southward sweep of low mountains. There was gentle human industry in the foreground, or no industry at all. The domestic clusters of Calistoga, St. Helena, Rutherford, and other hamlets dwindled into pasture, orchards, and the tumbled greenery of conifer forests and valley oak on eastern and western slopes.

The Silverado Trail was just that in 1965: a two-lane road connecting narrow tracks feeding in from the canyons, each with its share of struggling calf-and-cow operations, prune farmers, and even vineyardists. During "crush," the grape harvest, the valley took on the antic quality of a community with a single purpose, but even then the pace was measured. There were few tourists. Life seemed balanced, on the whole, by family and the assumption — mistaken — that things were not going to change much.

A few thousand souls lived in the valley, most of them down in Napa city, the historic river port. Up-valley life was unremittingly rural, though there were pockets of transplanted gentility, the names recalling colder climes: Ramsey, Hart, Daniel, de Latour. The society crowd was connected to wine only incidentally in most cases. Weekending in the valley had been a correct endeavor for a century, lending Napa an aura of respectability lacking in neighboring Sonoma, which was still associated with hideaways where, during Prohibition, San Franciscans had retreated from the strictures of polite society and the law. Napa's probity, by contrast, could be read in the façades of old edifices like Inglenook and Beaulieu.

San Francisco's finest, including some displaced royalty, still owned "ranches" in Napa devoted to vineyards as well as cows. The owners took part in an ongoing celebration, with lunch at someone's ranch and dinner at someone else's, and cocktails in between. The men talked about investments and the harvest; the women discussed cooking schools. Occasionally someone got into bed with someone else's mate, but bridge was the preferred activity.

The Davieses wondered where they fit in. Were they mavericks or colorful misfits? Should they aspire to society? All they knew for certain was that they weren't Italian.

Jack flew to L.A. one last time. Jamie left the windows open that night and woke up to a house full of bats. She called the St. Helena Police Department. The sergeant came up after work with his son; they asked for brooms and began to knock bats off the moldings, out of the draperies, out of the air. Jamie got her tennis racket and reluctantly joined them, going from room to room smashing the intruders.

2

VOLCANIC, PRECIPITOUS yet assailable by the casual hiker, touched with green in winter when the rains came and burned to burlap by the summer sun, the mountains hung in the near distance as a reminder of the valley's violent past. Once it lay beneath a vast inland sea extending from the Sierra Nevada on the east to what are now the Farallon Islands off the West Coast. Sediments miles deep depressed and broke apart the ocean floor, releasing molten rock that eventually lifted above the brine, a process repeated many times in the collisions of vast plates beneath the earth's surface that created California quite apart from the rest of the continent.

The emergence of the coast range and the torrential rains of the Pleistocene sent torrents down the west slope of the Sierras. Thousands of converging streams broke through at the Carquinez Strait and then at the Golden Gate, flooding into the Pacific. Melting glaciers later elevated the earth's oceans. Napa lay above the water line, a narrow valley drowned in the south and pinched in the north between two converging lines of tortured rock.

The soil, over a plain of gray shale, was composed of volcanic ash and the remains of ancient marine life deposited during long-term erosion that can still be read in the alluvial fans and washes on opposing slopes. For millennia the river wandered back and forth across the valley floor, mixing the soils, providing water in the driest years for a dark-skinned trans-Siberian people living in this wrinkle in the coast ranges and called, for convenience, the Wappo. They fashioned tools and weapons from obsidian and abandoned the river each spring to throngs of grizzlies that came down to feed on spawning steelhead.

The Wappo and their ancestors had lived in the valley for four thousand years before the arrival of Europeans. The word Napa, attributed to them, remains the subject of some confusion. Various meanings ascribed by early settlers and ethnographers to "Napa" do have a common theme in the resources of nature. Napa means grizzly, or harpoon point, or fish, or bounteous place.

By the time of the Civil War the Wappo had been variously indentured by the Spanish who had established missions between San Diego and Sonoma, and by Anglo invaders who set loose cattle on the sprawling Caymus and Carne Humana ranchos. The Wappo were displaced, massacred, and ensnared by their own inability to resist the products of civilization: gunpowder, disease, whiskey. Ever dwindling, they took part in harvests in the valley until the end of the century, coming down from their redoubts in Lake County, farther north, and camping near Bale Mill and south of St. Helena. By then they were a pitiful remnant that today has no survivors.

Vineyards thrived in southern California as early as 1818. Wine was made from grapes called Mission, or Criolla, brought north by the Franciscan monks and generally ascribed to Father Junípero Serra. George Calvert Yount, a trapper from North Carolina and the first white settler in Napa Valley, planted Mission vines bought from General Mariano Vallejo in Sonoma in 1838, but by midcentury the Mission was being replaced throughout California by better European varieties.

California enjoys unblinkered sunlight many months of the year; all along the North Coast, gaps in the mountains admit cooling fogs from the Pacific. These qualities were recognized by Agoston Haraszthy, a Balkan immigrant who started a winery in Sonoma, called Buena Vista, in 1856. Haraszthy traveled to Europe in search of good wine grape varieties and brought back thousands of vine cuttings, possibly including Zinfandel, and claimed the state of California owed him money for the effort. The state disagreed. Controversy hung about Haraszthy, but he is commonly recognized as the inspiration behind California's early enological successes. And his son's sparkling wine, Eclipse, was the toast of San Francisco for a time. His Sonoma winery eventually failed and the flamboyant, questing Haraszthy perished in pursuit of other prospects, in Nicaragua.

Wine was made commercially in Napa in 1858 by John Patchett.

The river port drew various sorts of adventurers, romantics, and idealists. The traveler to Napa from San Francisco had in those days to take a steamer north to Vallejo, where the broad mouth of the valley touched the tide-washed bay. Mountains funneled northward toward the brooding lump of Mount St. Helena, supposedly named by members of an expedition from Fort Ross forty years before that had included Princess Helena de Gagarin, the niece of the czar. The valley floor sustained pastures and fields that broke against the slopes of the Mayacamas. The roads were daunting. A member of the geologic survey team sent to California in 1860, William H. Brewer, commented on Napa's "dust, *dust!* DUST! . . . from fence to fence the dust is from two to six inches deep, fine as the liveliest plaster of Paris . . . into which the mules sink to the fetlock, raising a cloud out of which you often cannot see."

A Prussian immigrant and freethinker, Charles Krug, made wine in Napa three years after Patchett, first in Patchett's winery and then in a twelve-foot hole dug in the ground for that purpose. But Krug's methods improved. He made wine for the family of Dr. Edward Bale, an English settler who had built the gristmill near St. Helena on his ten-thousand-acre section of the old Carne Humana grant, then married Bale's daughter, Carolina, and set himself up as Napa's foremost vintner.

The Beringer brothers — more Germans — worked for Krug and in the late 1870s constructed their winery, tunneled into the mountain, and eventually built an elaborate seventeen-room mansion, Rhine House. Their friend, Tiburcio Parrott, bastard son of a San Francisco banker and one of the city's early millionaires, owned a vineyard in the hills above the Beringers and had a home built there on the scale of Rhine House. Other men, and some women, attempted to make fine wine, like Hamilton Crabb, owner of the To Kalon vineyard in Oakville, and Gustave Niebaum, a Finnish sea captain who created an architectural wonder, Inglenook.

Napa wine received its accolades in various expositions around the world; even the French recognized that the valley might someday provide real competition.

The wineries were hard hit by the depression of the 1870s, when the price of wine went down to ten cents a gallon. But Napa continued to produce more wine than any county in California, and despite the threat of a strange, otherworldly disease called phylloxera and the national financial panic, the wine business boomed in Napa during the 1880s. Land under vines increased sixfold, to eighteen thousand acres, and the number of wineries grew from a few dozen to 166.

Napa experienced two early disasters. The first was phylloxera, an insect that had devastated most of the French vineyards and was likened in catastrophic force to the defeat of France by the Prussians in 1870. A microscopic, voracious aphid usually hidden beneath the soil, phylloxera had first been carried across the Atlantic Ocean inadvertently from the American East Coast on the roots of native American vines intended for collectors and experimental use in Europe. The American vines were immune to phylloxera because of thousands of years of exposure, but the disease attacked the European species, *Vitis vinifera,* and eventually swept the Continent.

Diseased vine cuttings and rootstock of *vinifera* were brought from Europe by enterprising men like Haraszthy, Krug, and Niebaum, who did not know they were vectors. Sonoma was struck first, then the aphid made its way to Napa on the feet of animals, or on wooden boxes used for transporting grapes, or on ocean winds lifting over the Mayacamas.

Later, European grape varieties were grafted onto phylloxeraresistant American rootstock and planted in the ravaged vineyards, which proved to be their salvation, but phylloxera had already wiped out most of the vineyards on the Napa Valley floor. By the turn of the century it would have destroyed all but three thousand acres of vineyards and driven many vineyardists to plant grain and fruit trees. They were predominantly white, Anglo-Saxon, Protestant. The Chinese in pigtails, carrying gourds of tea to their labors, almost disappeared after the passing of the Chinese Exclusion Act of 1892 and the open racial hostility of the locals. The Chinese had built the wineries and picked the fruit, but their language was already being replaced in fields and vineyards by Italian.

Old man Krug died a tragic figure whose wife had gone insane and who was himself paralytic and cancer-ridden. The Beringers were little better off, the grand schemes originating in the Rheingau largely abandoned; Rhine House with its tunnels and massive, ornate cooperage had become a curiosity. Jacob Schram's vineyards were devastated by phylloxera and he lacked the means and the inspiration to replant. Schram was often seen in the valley, in the early years of the twentieth century, wearing a black suit and traveling in a black spring wagon.

The second disaster, from which the valley was just recovering in 1964 when Jack and Jamie Davies arrived, was Prohibition.

At the beginning of World War I, more than thirty states had been declared dry, and Congress, driven by a combination of wartime zeal and a century's worth of proclaimed guilt over the use of alcohol, passed the War Prohibition Act in 1918. Then came the Eighteenth Amendment and the Volstead National Prohibition Act of 1920 — the end of a long era of legitimacy. During the thirteen years of Prohibition, Americans spent an estimated $36 billion on booze, and the illegal profits created an organization of crime that was to endure. Worse, Prohibition fostered cynicism because the laws were unenforceable and universally contravened.

In Napa a few wineries, most notably Beaulieu, prospered by producing sacramental and kosher wine, but most went under. Wine and brandy did find their way out of Napa and Sonoma in considerable quantities, shipped ingeniously: coffins were filled with jugs and stacked at railway depots, for instance, to be sent to the city. Federal agents raided some homes in St. Helena and turned up a brandy still. One bootlegger equipped his car with a wooden bumper for pushing his way past government agents and other hindrances, but illegal wine and booze made few fortunes in the valley. Vineyards were yanked out and replaced with prune trees and walnuts, or the vines simply left to grow in a wild proliferation of canes, and eventually to die amidst the weeds, in the celebrated California sun.

3

T HE DAVIESES weren't the only hopefuls arriving in the valley in the mid-1960s. There was a blossoming after the dog years that trailed Prohibition for three decades, although the blossoming was gradual and sometimes almost imperceptible. People paid for good wine now; others put money into good grapes, into French oak barrels in which to age the wine. Strangers appeared in the valley, eager to talk about things like malolactic fermentation and other academic subjects related to wine and its appreciation. Something stirred.

In what he later considered a great act of imprudence, Warren Winiarski left the University of Chicago, where he taught political science and sat on the Committee on Social Thought, and headed west. He was not returning to the land, for he had never been on it. But the forces of social discontent and a turbulent Aquarian dream were sweeping the country in the 1960s, and he was to be part of it.

While stopping in the Rio Grande Valley in New Mexico to consider the prospect of apple farming, he thought he heard censure in the wind. *Your ancestors did not have this in mind,* the voice said. *They will curse you, and so will your children.*

He had two children and a wife of roughly his age, which was thirty-five. That was a bit late to be starting over. Her name was Barbara and they had met at St. John's, in Annapolis, where they had read the great books and developed a propensity for considering all ramifications of any single act. The single act that had indirectly propelled Winiarski westward across the continent was the fermenting of Baco Noir grapes in a crock in the back of a station wagon being driven from Maryland to Chicago.

He had begun to read books — always books — about wine and

to write letters. The first went to Martin Ray, about whom Warren had read. Ray was doing something special in the arcane, essentially un-American art of winemaking. To his surprise, Ray wrote back. Warren went to see him in California and stayed a week. Ray judged the success of an evening by the number of empty bottles left; he was imperious, volatile, his wines had a grandeur, and Warren could have learned all he needed to know from him but feared he and his family would become indentured in the process.

He wandered north from Saratoga into the Napa Valley. The stark, sere hills contrasted sharply with the reassuring green of the vines. He made his way up to Mayacamas Vineyards, atop the mountain range of the same name, one of the highest vineyards in the county — beautiful, romantic, what he imagined as suitable topography for a Winiarski. Starlings streaked in to get at the ripening fruit, and inky Cabernet lay in bottles in the old stone winery.

Maynard Amerine, professor of enology at UC Davis, suggested that Warren try Souverain Cellars. Warren asked Lee Stewart for a job there, and Stewart hired him because he couldn't afford to hire a trained technician. Warren showed up on Howell Mountain in black-rimmed glasses, a professor soon pulling hoses, moving barrels, and shoveling muck out of fermenters. He rented a cabin on Crystal Springs Road, down the mountain in what was known as Dago Valley, owned by the Rossinis, the family that had sold sixty acres to Stewart twenty-five years before.

Barbara Winiarski came out with the children and was appalled by the parched brown hillsides. Fires burned all that fall, then it rained for a month. The house had a wood-burning stove and some secondhand furniture. At night not a light could be seen in their narrow valley. They had no friends. Even in the sixties, it was difficult to appear socially at ease when you were broke, buying your clothes in thrift shops and eating so many potatoes.

People called Stewart "the Stone." If he was interested in literature, he gave no indication of it to Warren. The name of his makeshift winery had been suggested by his daughter, who was studying French at St. Helena High and had made a list of French nouns for her father's consideration. Stewart thought a winery should have a French name. Humorless, hard working, and meticulous, he had learned winemaking from a Russian émigré named André Tchelistcheff and had trained several young, hungry dreamers who helped

Stewart make acclaimed wine. He bought Riesling from Stony Hill, across the valley, and other good grapes where he could find them. He fermented in metal tanks, a brash new concept, and used something called a heat exchanger to keep the temperature down during fermentation, to preserve the wine's freshness. Most of the equipment was second- and thirdhand. When Stewart was fined $50 by the Bureau of Alcohol, Tobacco and Firearms for a small infraction, he didn't have the cash to pay.

Warren dug up books about winemaking and took a short course at UC Davis, sixty miles to the east. He once asked Stewart if he thought a wine had *tournée,* a microbial spoilage he had read about. "How the hell do you know about that?" Stewart asked. He didn't know if the wine had *tournée,* and didn't care.

In the spring, Barbara saw her first big steelhead in the Napa River, come all the way from the bay to spawn.

That fall Warren made the first Winiarski vintage from Stewart's second crop of Cabernet grapes, so small and undernourished that Stewart wouldn't put them into Souverain wine. Stewart gave Warren an old barrel to ferment in, and the Rossinis let him put the barrel in their stone shed across the road.

The wine turned out much better than the Baco Noir fermented in his station wagon a few years before. Now Warren wanted his own winery, something small and prestigious, but there were four or five of those in the valley already. Lee Stewart said there might be room for one more.

Stewart sold some old puncheons to Joe Heitz, and Warren helped deliver them. Heitz was skinny, irreverent, cocksure; he inspected every stave, amused by some private joke. He had bought an old grape press that wasn't working properly but he wouldn't admit this. Instead, he talked in a general way about improving the performance of wine presses, hoping Stewart would give him advice. Stewart, a Scot, didn't give anything away, so the conversation didn't go far. Warren had an opinion, but they considered him a Young Turk, full of theory.

The Army had gotten Joe Heitz out of Illinois. He had spent World War II in beautiful Fresno — foggy in winter, baked in summer. When he needed more beer money he had walked down the street knocking on doors, he said, looking for part-time work.

Italian Swiss Colony, which made wine from fruit concentrate, hired him to run an evaporator; later, he worked for the Gallo brothers. He liked to say he was vaccinated by the wine needle, meaning that there was nothing romantic about wine for Joe Heitz.

After the war he went to UC Davis and majored in horticulture. The school offered no viticultural or enological degrees in those days. He studied apple trees, then grapes and winemaking. After graduate school he went down to Modesto — hot and flat — to work for Ernest and Julio. The Gallos were making headway in the bulk-wine business, and they put Joe in the laboratory. Quality control. He set up tastings for the Gallos and kept his mouth shut.

Beaulieu Vineyard, in Napa, hired Joe as an assistant winemaker for $325 a month — better than beer money — in 1951. He went back for another stint in the Central Valley, to help set up Fresno State's enology department. Then Hanns Kornell, a German immigrant who had gotten out of a concentration camp in Nazi Germany and walked and hitchhiked across North America, told Joe about a place for sale on Highway 29 south of St. Helena. Eight acres and a winery, Italian-owned, with an annual gross of $4,500.

Joe had a wife and three children to feed. He could buy wine and increase the volume; he could make the place pay even if he had to sell to the "crows" — tourists. The banks wouldn't touch him so he borrowed five grand from an old friend and was in business. He bought wine made from Chardonnay and Pinot Noir from Hanzell Winery over in Sonoma County, aged in Limousin barrels. At Beaulieu, they kept the wine in American oak barrels, but the French oak seemed to give it more complex flavors, so Joe bought some old French barrels from Hanzell. He liked the taste of the wine that came out of them. Apparently his customers did, too.

Within four years he needed to expand. There were plenty of places for sale in Napa, but nothing he wanted and little he could afford. One day he drove to the end of a dirt road on the east side of the valley, where there was a farmhouse and a big empty stone barn. An old man came out to talk. He had 160 acres; during Prohibition Italians had come up to play bocce on the grass and drink red wine, and now he was selling out.

Joe scraped together the $50,000 deposit from investors. The day he put the money down he danced in celebration.

The Davieses would call their wine Schramsberg, after the estate. There had once been a "Schramsberger" wine, made by the nineteenth-century barber. The name sounded grand and established, but in fact wine was a risky endeavor, always had been. A few old families had managed to hang on, like the de Latours, owners of Beaulieu, and the Daniels, inheritors of Inglenook. There were a few descendants of the Beringers around, although that family had gone downhill, like the Krugs.

Louis Martini was making a go of it. So was Christian Brothers, supporting the order's school system with money made from the sale of brandy and wine. The small, quality-minded mavericks like Stewart, McCrea, and Heitz scraped by. Most of the Italians stayed solvent by selling their wine to other wineries or to the Gallos, who had it trucked down to Modesto to add some verve to their jugs. Jack made contacts as he had in the metals business, going around and introducing himself to the mavericks, the establishment, the Italians.

Stewart turned out to be blunt but approachable. He liked boozy meals in the steak houses, and Jack and Jamie joined him and the McCreas on these jaunts. Jack already knew that Schramsberg would have to be different. No point trying to compete with these people, or with Inglenook or Beaulieu, with Martini, Krug, or even Beringer. Schramsberg needed its own niche, what Fred McCrea called position.

That position would be . . . bubbles! No one in California made only sparkling wine as it was made in Champagne, by the so-called *méthode champenoise,* fermented in the bottle, and using fine grapes of the classic varieties. The Davieses would do that. Jack would grow them himself and, in the meantime, buy the grapes he needed from others.

When word got around that Jack Davies wanted to make sparkling wine, people laughed at him. He intended to make it out of Chardonnay and Pinot Noir, they said, instead of the much cheaper French Colombard. Where did he think he would find Chardonnay? The McCreas didn't have enough to sell; the few growers crazy enough to plant a little Chardonnay already had contracts to sell it elsewhere.

Jack went to see Joe Heitz, mindful that Joe had reduced Eleanor McCrea to tears. Heitz asked what Jack had in mind and listened skeptically. When Jack asked if he would sell him some unbottled Chardonnay, Joe said, "Now why would I want to do that?"

Jack was invited to breakfast in St. Helena by Robert Mondavi, the member of the family who was running the Krug winery. Robert showed up with his older son, the handsome, black-haired Michael, just out of college and eager to get into the business. Robert was balding and broad-shouldered, with a nose straight off a Roman coin and frank, friendly eyes. He stammered slightly but that in no way interfered with what he had to say about the valley, its glorious future, and the Mondavis' role in it. He liked Jack's idea for making sparkling wine.

A grower, a friend of Jack's named Jerry Draper, suggested that Jack buy good Riesling grapes from him and then trade them to a winery for Chardonnay wine. Jack could take the wine back to Schramsberg and do whatever it was he intended to do to turn it into champagne.

Jack telephoned Robert Mondavi and proposed such a deal. Mondavi agreed to trade Jack five hundred gallons of Chardonnay wine for the Riesling grapes Jack intended to buy from Jerry Draper.

Connections, Jack thought.

Then Robert Mondavi and his younger brother, Peter, had a fistfight that threatened to undo it all. Peter had gotten the worst of the fight, Jack heard, and Robert had been banished from Krug. Jack assumed his deal was dead but when he telephoned the winery, Peter told him, "If Bob said you could have Chardonnay, you can have it."

Jack made a shopping list of what he needed: an air compressor, a refrigration unit, eventually a wine press. He had so much to learn about chemistry (acidity and pH), electricity (one- and two-phase), and motors (strokes and horsepower). He experimented with the siphon filler and the hand capper. He actually replaced the diaphragm in a pump, a mystery to a man who might someday have been president of the Fiberboard Corporation.

He strapped an old metal tank on a flatbed truck and took it down to Krug. An hour later, he drove home with the five hundred gallons of potential sparkler sloshing around in his tank, as nervous as he had ever been and utterly, ridiculously happy.

4

I N 1965, after thirty years in the wine business, Robert Mondavi — general manager of Charles Krug Winery, voice of the valley, apostle of California wine — had no job. He had no savings, either, and no house of his own and three children in private school. His father was dead, his mother had turned against him, and the life he loved threatened to evaporate.

He had argued with his brother, Peter, over the family business, a common occurrence. As the older son, Robert was accustomed to having his way. The fairer, slighter Peter, Krug's winemaker — known in the family as Babe — his mother's boy and his sisters' favorite, resented what he considered Robert's highhanded, spendthrift ways.

Robert told Peter that he was sick of Peter's criticism, sick of Peter's acting behind his back to gain influence over the winery staff, sick of his working through their mother to block the path of Robert's older son, Michael, to the top. Robert was sick, in short, of Babe's thwarting Robert's dreams.

Peter accused Robert of stealing from the company, and Robert hit him, backing Peter up.

Peter said, "You can hit me all you want, Bob, but it's not going to change anything."

Robert had played rugby at Stanford. He was a forceful man, frustrated for years, and he wrestled with Peter and hit him some more.

Peter later told his mother, Rosa, "I ran into a door."

She knew better. Rosa was famous in the Italian community of northern California for her cooking and the bounty of her table. Rosa knew how to work, and she knew the folly of men driven by goals other than those of family. She summoned Robert to her house in St. Helena. Peter had told his older sister, Mary, about the fight, and she had told Rosa. Neither woman could bear the sight of the bruises on Babe's face.

Robert found them all waiting: Rosa, Peter, Mary, and Helen, Robert's other sister. Also Fred Ferroggiaro, a family friend and business consultant with whom Robert had never had good relations. Ferroggiaro received no money for his services to the family, but he loved Rosa's cooking and availed himself of as much of it as possible.

Robert expected a discussion; he hoped for resolution of the dispute between him and Peter. Robert was an optimist. In fiscal year 1965, Krug had a pretax profit of $200,000, ten times what the winery had earned the year before. This was due primarily to Robert's salesmanship, and the family could not overlook that fact.

There was to be no discussion of what had happened, however. Rosa, ashen, stood up and left the room, followed by everyone but Robert and Fred Ferroggiaro. After a pause, Ferroggiaro told Robert that he was being given a six-month leave of absence with pay for the sake of family harmony. Robert was no longer Krug's general manager.

Robert asked, "What does this mean? Who will prepare for the future?"

Ferroggiaro said, "You talk too much about the future, Bob."

He felt betrayed. His father, Cesare, would not have dismissed Robert like this; Cesare Mondavi had not been a vengeful man.

"Is this the thanks I get?" Robert asked Rosa later. He wanted to know what would happen after his leave was up.

Rosa said, "Be a good boy, then we'll see."

So he went to Joe Alioto, lawyer, family friend, San Francisco politician, and another addict of Rosa's cooking. Alioto had nothing to say. It took days and some pleading by Robert finally to be able to piece together an explanation: Robert's son Michael would not be allowed to work at Krug for ten years, thereby giving Peter's two sons a clear shot at the top.

That Christmas looked pretty bleak. Robert and his wife, Marge, sat down with Michael and Tim, Robert's younger son, and their sister, Marcia, home from school. They discussed the future. Robert said, "If you're willing to sacrifice, we'll start a small winery and compete with the best in the world."

He had two partners willing to put up $50,000 apiece, and friends willing to loan him another $100,000. They all agreed he should push on.

Robert asked Rosa to invest in his new winery, but she said, "We already own a winery."

Robert was reaching too far, she added. Others in the family agreed that he was a dreamer. He would be back at the end of his leave, begging for a place at Krug.

Robert used the borrowed funds to buy a plot in Oakville next to the old To Kalon vineyard Krug had purchased a few years earlier. He lined up two consulting jobs to support himself and started cutting deals. An insurance company gave him a construction loan; he got another from a glass company for the bottling line by agreeing to use their bottles. He borrowed wherever he could, and was further helped by a gifted wine distributor who got Mondavi wine into many West Coast restaurants.

Meanwhile, Peter moved into Robert's old office at Krug. He proposed a salary increase for board members that was approved by the family. He told Alioto, now Krug's attorney, to write a formal letter to Robert and to sign it.

"I made a considerable effort to ameliorate the unfortunate situation that developed in your family," Alioto wrote. "I did tell you, however, that the moment you went ahead to a point of no return on the construction of a winery in the Napa Valley that all chances of success in restoring family unity would be gone. . . . Your employment by Charles Krug, in these circumstances, is terminated."

Robert still owned a considerable percentage of Krug. Alioto told him, man to man, "Get the best attorney you can find — you're going to need him."

Robert thought, So be it.

His father, Cesare, had grown up in Marches, a part of central Italy bordering the Adriatic, where vineyards compete with olive groves for the heat of a sun that sets behind the Apennines. By the time Robert saw his ancestral country, an autostrada glided with ease through a dozen tunnels along the crimped, rocky coast, but when his father was a boy, Marches was isolated and bucolic.

Cesare came to the United States to work in the iron mines of Minnesota in 1906. Two years later he was back in Ancona looking for a bride. He chose Rosa Grassi, barely literate but a fine cook, and Cesare took her to Minnesota with him. He had bought a saloon, and Rosa turned their home into a boarding house, an institution later celebrated in family palaver and even in the press. Rosa's tenants were all Italian men accustomed to a certain style of cooking, a certain manner of living. For years she rose every day before dawn and worked until midnight, cooking, washing, scrubbing, and darning for fifteen men, and delivering hot lunches to the mine. She reasoned that these poor men were separated by thousands of miles from their own wives, sweethearts, and, most cruel, from their mothers.

Rosa talked very little about those days, and Cesare talked less. He preferred to communicate through a series of shrugs, nods, winks, and Marchesan hand motions. Not once in his life would Robert have with his father what most people thought of as a conversation.

Cesare belonged to the Italian Club. Wine was the staple of every table, and when Prohibition threatened to cut off access to wine, Cesare was chosen by his friends to travel to California in search of grapes. The law allowed families in America to make two hundred gallons of fruit juice a year, juice that with a little encouragement became wine. So fruit was shipped east from California in vast quantities, much of it rotting on the rail lines, but there was money to be made.

Cesare went to Lodi, north of Fresno in the northern San Joaquin Valley, where grapes grew black, sweet, and profuse — Zinfandel, Carignan, Muscat, Alicante Bouschet. Cesare sent grapes back to Minnesota. He realized that there must be a market for grapes all over, and eventually set up his own shipping business. He resettled in Lodi, where he earned a reputation for reliability and extreme taciturnity. He was known jocularly as "the Phantom." In a broad-brimmed Italian hat pushed to one side, he would lean against the door of his car as he drove through town, the window cracked to emit the smoke from his eternal *toscano*.

Lodi was a farm town with more than its share of Italians. Robert first tasted wine as an infant, from a spoon. Families gathered for picnics and football games and long Sunday meals where young and old mixed as equals. The Mondavis moved from a little clapboard bungalow on a side street to a proper two-story house. "Look, Mom," Robert cried on first viewing the bathroom, "tiles!"

Cesare bought a new Studebaker and put Robert behind the

wheel when he was thirteen. He served as the family chauffeur, without a license, taking his mother to the market, his sisters to the movies, himself and his kid brother, Peter, to the shed on the outskirts of town where they nailed together wooden produce boxes for their father's shipping business. When a cop stopped him, Robert would say, "I'm Cesare's boy."

Prohibition came to an end with Robert still at Stanford. His father began making bulk wine and told Robert there was a future in the business. So Robert took a chemistry course before graduating. Cesare bought a small bulk winery in Napa Valley, Sunny St. Helena, where he planned to use grapes grown in Napa and Sonoma counties to be made into wine a bit better than that from Central Valley grapes, scorched by the sun.

St. Helena was two hours west and north of Lodi. Robert moved there after graduating, to protect his position in his father's eyes, knowing that Peter would also need a job when he got out of the University of California at Berkeley. Robert lived in a room outside town and learned to make bulk wine in an old stone building next to the railroad tracks. He bought "Zin" (Zinfandel), "Pets" (Petit Sirah), and Carignan — the workhorse grapes. With a couple of helpers he built up Sunny St. Helena's production to a million gallons, which he stored in a dozen different cellars in the neighborhood.

Robert went regularly to Lodi to report to Cesare, who would wink and nod and gesture, and then Bob would drive back to St. Helena.

Peter studied the cold fermentation of wines — keeping the temperature down to preserve freshness — before he went into the Army. Robert put that theory into practice. The wines sold well, being lighter and fruitier than the competition's. At that time, right after Prohibition, 80 percent of the wine made in California was sweet, but Robert was more interested in dry wine, the kind you drank with food. The sort of wine that had made estates like Inglenook and Beaulieu famous.

In the evenings Robert would pump wine into an overhead tank and, while it ran down through the filter, stroll to a friend's for dinner or to the kitchen at the Hotel St. Helena, run by an old Italian. There were several good Italian restaurants: Bruni's, the Bossettis' Madrone Restaurant in Rutherford, the Mount View Hotel in Calistoga. The Depression had been keenly felt in the wine industry, but people still ate and drank well. With meals they opened a bottle of Larkmead, from the winery owned by the Salmina brothers.

Sunny St. Helena joined the Wine Institute. Robert went to the meetings in San Francisco, where he met Ernest Gallo and Louis Petri, both slugging it out in the bulk-wine market, trying to take over. Robert knew he could never compete with these guys. He was drawn not to the warring Italians but to the soft-spoken, articulate scion of an old San Francisco family, John Daniel, owner of Inglenook. Robert followed him around like a puppy. When Daniel presented the minority view of the small, quality producers, he spoke with conviction: good wine was beneficial to all, Daniel said. It should be promoted, even if it took some small part of the market away from Gallo, Petri, and the Cellas, owners of the huge Roma Wine Company.

When Robert passed trucks from Inglenook and Beaulieu on the highway in Napa Valley, he bowed his head in homage to quality, to what people called class.

In 1943 a banker in St. Helena told him that Charles Krug Winery could be had for $87,000. There were already two prospective buyers. "If you want it," the banker said, "you'll have to hurry."

Sunny St. Helena was a cottage industry compared to the legendary Krug. Robert drove straight to Lodi, devising as he went a plan to present to Cesare. The price of bulk wine had been frozen by the government at twenty-eight cents a gallon. The Mondavis might be able to buy Krug and sell some Sunny St. Helena wine under the Krug label. They could have two lines of wine: a quality line for prestige and a jug line to finance it. Gradually they could expand until the Mondavis sat up there with the de Latours and the Daniels.

Cesare heard him out, and said, "I'm happy the way things are. I don't want to be as big as Cella." Exhausted by so much conversation, he went to bed.

Desperate, Robert appealed to Rosa. The idea was not to compete with the big boys, he said. They would do something entirely different, something better. The family would never get another chance to acquire a landmark so prestigious so cheaply. There would be room for the grandchildren once things got rolling.

Rosa didn't commit herself — Robert knew better than to expect that — but in the morning Cesare came downstairs, and asked, "When do we go to St. Helena?"

Peter was home on leave and the three men drove over together, Peter in his Army uniform. The Krug property sprawled on the northern outskirts of town — vineyards, a towering carriage house of regal design, big oaks shading a collection of houses where the Krugs had once lived, lawns gone to seed, a winery of heroic proportions. The railroad ran between the winery and some other buildings, but the property was so extensive that even this intrusion seemed minimal. The Mondavis walked through the cavernous fermenting room, inspecting the old cooperage. Robert had to admit that the winery was a mess; it had been leased for years as a factory for bulk wine. Cesare asked the boys how much money it would take to get the place in shape.

Robert said, "Sixty thousand."

"More," said Peter.

Cesare said he would buy Krug if his sons would work together. They agreed, and the three drove to San Francisco, to the Bank of America. Cesare put up $25,000 in cash and signed the agreement of sale. Robert couldn't believe his father was doing this — the conservative Cesare Mondavi — and giving each of them 12 percent of the business, and his daughters each 8 percent.

Cesare retained the rest for himself and Rosa. They came often to St. Helena and stayed on the property, where Cesare tossed bocce balls in the soft Napa evenings, or played cards, winking and shrugging and leaving the work to the boys. Robert moved into one of the houses on the property with Marge, his high school sweetheart and now his wife, and became general manager of Krug.

Peter was to be the winemaker when he got out of the Army, an arrangement like the Gallos', out in the Central Valley, that enabled brothers to work together. *I'll sell all the wine you can make if you'll make all the wine I can sell.* That was the idea.

Peter — Babe — was supposedly like his father: cautious and quiet compared to Robert, who had more in common with Rosa. Her fare kept a circle of faces around the Mondavi dinner table for decades and took on the proportions of legend. Somewhere in all that conviviality was the future, Robert thought: putting people and wine together, talking and tasting and generally letting the juices intermingle.

The old vines were torn out of the Krug vineyards and replaced with some Cabernet Sauvignon, Chardonnay, Riesling, and Sauvignon

Blanc. Robert bought the usual bulk grapes, fermented the juice, put the wine into gallon and half-gallon jugs and called it CK Mondavi (Charles Krug's initials) and shipped it east. The jugs would pay for the improvements in the better wines, sold in restaurants and quality shops under the Krug label.

Robert asked for some winemaking advice from Louis Martini, and got it. He wanted the same from Beaulieu's enologist, André Tchelistcheff, whose name was almost unpronounceable. It sounded like steam escaping from a pressure cooker — *Cellist-chef* — and the spelling was even worse. Robert invited the little Russian to dinner. John Daniel had given Robert a bottle of Inglenook Cabernet and one of Pinot Noir, made in the previous century, to show him how good Napa Valley wine could be, and Robert opened the Cabernet. A wonderful fragrance filled the room, and Tchelistcheff began to loosen up. Robert also served some Krug wines. They discussed oak cooperage, winemaking and vineyard practices, and Robert invited Tchelistcheff to be his consultant.

Robert bought 1,300 old brandy barrels, hoping that would make a difference in the wines. It was still the forties and French barrels weren't available. First the CK Mondavi went into the brandy barrels, to remove the rough edges, then the good stuff went in. The bottled wines didn't turn out as well as the Bordeaux and Burgundies Robert had tasted, they weren't as impressive as Inglenook's best, but they began to win medals at the state fairs.

Robert publicized his Krug wines in a newsletter he sent to anyone who would have it. He talked about the medals when he traveled east, which he did with increasing frequency, developing what he saw as the most salable aspect of Krug: prestige. He began to open Krug wines alongside the Bordeaux and Burgundies, in the company of liquor distributors, retailers, restaurateurs, journalists — talking, talking, talking about wine and Napa Valley, its past and its glorious future. Those people ate the meals that Robert paid for, and drank the fancy French wine, and put Krug wines on their lists. Robert Mondavi was so different from other Italians coming out of California, they said, with their tank cars full of dago red.

He even opened a public tasting room in St. Helena. He displayed the medals Krug had won to passers-by who stopped to sip Krug wine and wonder why a big old barn in the middle of nowhere would give the stuff away.

The trouble had started, Peter thought, when he got out of the Army. Robert seemed to resent his coming to the winery, and their sister Mary agreed. So did Peter's wife, Blanche. She said Robert even resented the fact that Peter had married her — he didn't want another voice in the family, another competitor.

It hadn't always been like that, Blanche reminded Peter. In the old days, whenever Blanche went to dinner at the Mondavis' house in Lodi, she was amazed that they were so nice to one another. Blanche would go home and tell her mother, "They never argue!"

Robert had his problems in 1946: he had bought too many grapes. Cesare thought so, too. There was a big crop that year and then the price of bulk dropped to fifty cents a gallon. Peter figured they lost close to half a million dollars, since Robert insisted on paying the growers full price.

Robert paid off some of the debt with Krug inventory. As soon as the bank took off the clamps, Robert was flying again, creating new demand for Krug wine that had yet to be produced. Peter wanted them to get their feet on the ground, to get profitable before they started expanding. But Robert wouldn't wait for anybody. He always wanted more wine.

Robert insisted on blind tastings — matching one wine with another and judging which was best, and why — and bringing in people with advice about how to ferment this wine, how to age another one. Theirs was a family business, Peter thought. They didn't need a lot of outsiders. He knew how to make wine without constant discussion of bacteria, acidity, oxidation. After listening to all the theories, Peter was the one who had to *do* it.

Cesare had asked them to work together, and Peter tried. He turned down a raise Robert offered, while insisting that Robert get more pay. Robert was on the road a lot, Peter said. He was the family's personal salesman and deserved a raise. That made Blanche angry and didn't help Peter's relationship with his brother; it just went to Robert's head, Peter thought.

Then he noticed Robert being very particular about things, not just wine. Like the table Rosa had given Robert and Marge. It was a nice table with a lamp attached, but Robert wasn't satisfied. He took it back to Rosa several times and asked her to exchange it for a different style, a different color, a different shade. Robert was putting on airs, in Peter's opinion.

"Know what I mean?" he asked his sisters, asked his mother, just to make sure he wasn't misjudging Robert. They told Peter they knew what he meant.

He and Robert argued over money, sales promotion, and quality, their voices echoing in the old office across the tracks from the winery. Neither was very good with words, but Robert got his out faster. Peter didn't mind — he wasn't trying to get the best of anybody. Peter wasn't a stinker! But Robert was never satisfied. He pushed for more and more production. You aren't making all the wine I can sell, Robert said. There was no place to put the product but into railroad tank cars; the wine was released before it was properly aged. Then Robert came home from a promotion trip and gave Peter hell because somebody in New York or Minneapolis had told him the wine didn't taste quite right.

Finally Peter told him, "Stop chewing me out!"

Robert told Peter to delegate authority, keep up the technical tastings, follow through on the expert advice he was getting. At the same time Peter needed to experiment, to loosen up. It seemed contradictory but it wasn't, not in Robert's mind.

He and Peter belonged to the Napa Valley Technical Group, a loose coalition of winemakers suspicious of one another but eager for information about their little-understood profession. Robert and Peter attended the meetings together; Peter never said a word. He would tell family members what he was doing in the winery, but not outsiders. Robert wanted to tell everybody.

Peter tried to keep a lid on production, while Robert wanted to expand. Expansion meant money for the finest equipment, the finest grapes, the finest everything. Robert was trying to find out exactly *what* he wanted. Meanwhile Krug wines started to get worse. Reports from the field — Robert's intelligence — told him they were losing customers because the wine was oxidized and unappealing. Peter was making all the wine Robert could sell, but Robert couldn't sell all the wine Peter made.

Robert went to his father. Cesare might be conservative but he understood lost accounts and declining returns and he put Robert in full control. Peter was relegated to blending wine already made, a less responsible position. Peter left the winery for a few months, to go on the road and sell. He hung out there in limbo for a while, and then Cesare died.

Underlying the collective grief in Lodi was the uneasy state of family affairs. Cesare had left everything in trust to Rosa; Robert assumed that she and his sisters would put him in charge at the next board meeting, since Krug was ailing. But Peter urged his mother to be president, and his sisters agreed.

Robert couldn't believe it. He asked them all, "Is this the thanks I get?"

He called a meeting at his lawyer's office in San Francisco. Peter went, sure that Robert had a sponsor and was trying to buy Krug for book value only — ten cents on the dollar! Peter walked right out of the office. He told Rosa and his sisters that Robert was acting like an egomaniac. He wouldn't listen to anyone. He wanted his own son to take over when Robert was gone, cutting out Peter's younger boys. Criticism just made Robert more aggressive.

The sales department dominated the picture at Krug, but no amount of sales could justify all Robert's traveling and entertainment. Robert spent money like water. Of course, the winery was making money — Peter would give Robert some credit for that. Nobody could promote like Robert Mondavi. But Peter wondered aloud where all the money went. Something had happened to Robert, something related to all the attention he had received. Everything had to be just right. After one of Marge's dinner parties that Peter attended, Robert went back into the kitchen and criticized everything from the soup to the dessert. Marge took it because she idolized Robert, but Peter and Blanche thought it a shame.

Robert went to Burgundy for the first time in 1962 and tasted dozens of wines, and thought he understood, really understood, the difference that good oak barrels could make. Different woods imparted wholly different flavors. He ordered some barrels, then went to Bordeaux and ordered some more. He went to Germany. Everywhere he talked to people, learned things; there was so much more they could be doing at Krug, would do, in fact. But when he returned to Napa and tried to convey these things to Rosa and his sisters, the words and the inspiration slipped away.

Peter had turned them against him, Robert thought. Peter was telling the winery staff that he and Rosa were running things now, at a time when profits were starting to soar.

❧

Blanche Mondavi, Peter's wife, liked to think she was the first to notice. It was 1965, or maybe 1966. As the wife of Peter Mondavi, she had a certain responsibility at Krug. What she noticed before anyone else noticed — or so she imagined — was a connection between her brother-in-law, Robert Mondavi, and Margrit Biever, the pretty blond Swiss.

Margrit had shown up at Krug before the family split; Blanche had always liked her. Margrit was lively, with a thickly braided pigtail draped over one shoulder and what Blanche described as a divine accent. An artist with a husband and children, Margrit had attended a Christmas party at Krug in 1964, where Robert danced with all the women, including Margrit. Not that Blanche noticed anything then. Margrit and her husband had tangential contacts with the older, more social crowd; her husband reputedly drank too much, and Margrit had her charity, working with children and music. Margrit wanted to stage a concert at Krug to raise money for her cause, and Robert agreed to supply some wine, since any promotional event appealed to him. Margrit held a reception and Robert and Peter took over a mixed case of wine — sherry, rosé, Zinfandel, and Chenin Blanc.

Margrit worked at Krug, giving tours. She was quite competent. She took a short course in winemaking at UC Davis and stood up to the cellar workers at Krug who didn't think a woman could learn; she also sold a lot of wine. In the tasting room she would write the names of the wines to be tasted each day on a blackboard, like hymns to be sung in church.

Not long after Margrit came to Krug, Robert and Peter fought with their fists, and Robert was sent away from the winery. Margrit also left. She had children and a husband to attend to, she said. Blanche still hadn't noticed anything. After Robert started his own winery in Oakville, Blanche heard that Margrit Biever had gone to work there, and then Blanche thought, Ah-ha!

5

WHILE THE FIRST vintage of Jack and Jamie Davies's Schramsberg sparkling wine was fermenting, the assistant winemaker at Beaulieu offered to run the necessary tests to measure its progress. The son of Beaulieu's winemaker, a vineyard consultant, agreed to visit Schramsberg once a month and advise the Davieses on everything from winemaking to grape planting. And when the time came to bottle, the hose puller for Lee Stewart at Souverain, Warren Winiarski, explained to Jack by telephone how to filter his new wine through pads coated with diatomaceous earth, a task Jack performed with the receiver cradled against his shoulder.

More connections, Jack thought.

He had bought a secondhand device for freezing the necks of the bottles, so he could "disgorge" — shoot the sediment out of the bottle before the cork went in, just as they did in Champagne. Jack disgorged into an old beer keg with a hole cut in the side, then he, Jamie, and some friends corked by hand, and labeled the same way.

Beaulieu's cellar man came up to Schramsberg and showed them how to stack two thousand bottles in the tunnels. The foreman employed by the friend who had sold Jack the Riesling to trade to the Mondavis for Chardonnay showed the Davieses how to graft young vines. Jack and Jamie practiced on willow boughs. They bought rootstock and cleansed, pruned, and buried it in sand, bottoms up, to slow budding until it could be planted. A rumor went through the valley that the Davieses were putting in a new vineyard upside down.

They belonged to the Exciting Wave. Jack and Jamie didn't think of themselves and the other newcomers to the valley in the late sixties as part of anything so dramatic. It was only later that the description came to light, when another of its members was able to look back, and say, "That's when it changed, when the exciting wave arrived and people stopped going around with the old boring crowd."

It wouldn't have been thought of as the Exciting Wave if the contrast between the new people and the Boring Crowd had not been so pronounced. The Boring Crowd continued to move between cocktails and bridge rubbers at various ranches. Money, lineage, and making a debut in San Francisco were the sole measures of worth. As one observer put it, "If anybody in that boring crowd had an original thought, it would crack his skull."

The Exciting Wave wore less jewelry and was concerned about the future. Their floating dinner parties were much more fun, the people more aware — not just of vineyards and wine but also of new political forces on the march in America. In some ways Napa more closely resembled Iowa than California. The occasional bearded enology student arriving from UC Davis or Fresno State was considered as exotic as a Mongolian herdsman and usually treated like one. The valley was still isolated, with its shallow bay in the south and two bracketing mountain ranges. Beyond them, the turmoil of the sixties rattled like retreating drums, and some of the valley's citizens never heard them at all.

Jack and Jamie got to know Belle and Barney Rhodes and Tom and Martha May. Tom, a du Pont, bought a vineyard from the Rhodeses and named it Martha's Vineyard, in honor of his wife. Martha's Vineyard produced some fine Napa Valley Cabernet grapes, which were sold to Joe Heitz, who would turn them into a wine to make him famous. Joe and his wife, Alice, joined the Exciting Wave's potluck circuit; occasionally the Martinis and the Carpys, from Freemark Abbey, were seen there.

Members of the Exciting Wave attended square dances at the Lodi Farm Center, along with the cellar rats and electricians. There were others: McNeely, Deetert, Peters, a Crocker, the Phillipses — she was an heir to the famous Hawaiian sugar fortune — the Floods, Stones, Newtons, Hills, and Trefethens. They didn't talk about what they did; they talked about *life*.

Then the formation of a second, more exclusive square dancing group became the unofficial watershed between a more egalitarian valley and one where social rank was again important.

Jack carried the bottle in a brown paper bag toward Cosmo Place. In his former life as a corporate executive he had made many presentations before groups and assumed the responsibility for moving millions of dollars' worth of goods. He had never lost much sleep over those things, but wine was different. Now that he had made his own wine and risked his family's financial well-being, he worried about the reception of his wine, his creation.

He was bound for Trader Vic's, the famous San Francisco restaurant. In the paper bag was the '65 Schramsberg Blanc de Blancs, white sparkling wine made from white grapes, the winery's first vintage. He and Jamie had not only corked it, they had put on the wire cage, the foil, and the label. Now he had to sell it.

Good retail shelf position did not come easily, but restaurants were even tougher, and just as important. A wine in a good restaurant took on the aura of the establishment, adding prestige to the actual benefit of the sale; it became a living advertisement. Nothing could be better than inclusion on Trader Vic's wine list.

Jack did not know the Trader but had heard that he was an abrupt person who did not suffer fools. His restaurant was filled with between-meals clamor, the cooks prepping and the waiters suiting up. The woman in the foyer directed Jack to the office in the back, but he found it empty. Then he saw a man coming out of the kitchen, carrying a plate of shrimp — Trader Vic.

"Hello," said Jack. "I'm Jack Davies. I . . ."

The Trader kept walking, forking shrimp into his mouth. Jack followed him into the cramped office, where the Trader sank into a chair behind his desk. He continued to eat. Jack started to tell him about the wine, and the Trader stopped eating long enough to interrupt him. "Leave the bottle and I'll try it," he said.

Jack went back to Napa feeling depressed. He told Jamie that Trader Vic's was one restaurant that would not be selling Schramsberg.

Driving up and down Highway 29, Jack often looked westward across some of the valley's best Cabernet vineyards, at the massive cellar of Inglenook, with its red roof and yellow gables, brooding in the lee of a knoll covered with eucalyptus. Only Inglenook could be described as a château. It was founded a century before, dedicated to making wine equal to that of France; it had passed on to Gustave Niebaum's grandnephew, John Daniel. The Daniels might be part of the Boring Crowd, but if there was a representative of the valley's illustrious past, one who took part in politics and occasionally in society, who advanced the notion of great wine from a great valley, it had to be John Daniel.

Jack had heard that people loved Daniel for his gentleness, his depth of character, and his very good manners. Family history and a difficult wife lent him an air of sadness — some said of tragedy. Jack had met Daniel at a gathering of the San Francisco Wine and Food Society, and had telephoned Daniel when he and Jamie were looking for property. Jack had been surprised by Daniel's reaction: he thought it was silly for city people to come up to the valley and attempt to get into the wine business. Perhaps Daniel foresaw that the Davieses and others like them were destined to clash with tradition in ways not limited to winemaking. Whatever the reason for John Daniel's coolness, Jack realized that they would never be friends.

A week after Jack had traveled to San Francisco, he received a letter from Trader Vic. The Trader had tasted the Schramsberg sparkling wine and was putting it on his list.

6

INGLENOOK EMBODIED the past in Napa Valley. Everything that had transpired — the dreams of estate wines equal to those of Europe, the ravages of phylloxera and Prohibition, the slow renaissance of the 1960s — was reflected in the massive structure on Highway 29 put up so long ago by the mysterious Finnish sea captain. In a curious way Inglenook would continue to absorb the forces brought to play in what was still an isolated place. Inglenook was the key to understanding what had gone before and what lay unsuspected on the horizon.

John Daniel, owner of Inglenook and a certified member of the valley's *noblesse,* had dreamed not of wine but of flying. He had grown up with stories of aerial combat during World War I and the exploits of brave, patriotic pilots. Charles Lindbergh flew the Atlantic for the first time while John was at Stanford. He was soon taking flying lessons himself. Being a pilot might not have been as likely a profession for him as that of doctor, lawyer, or stockbroker, but what flying lacked in social acceptability it more than made up for in the offer of freedom: flying would take him away, regularly and honorably, from the Victorian precepts that had been drummed into him as a child, and from a father who insisted that he major in engineering.

That father, John Daniel, Sr., a successful San Francisco contractor and noted rake, was said to be the only man to sleep through the 1906 San Francisco earthquake. His young wife died of diphtheria, though some said of a broken heart, leaving her two small children, John junior and his sister, Suzanne. John senior had no talent for dealing with his own offspring and no inclination to do so, and gave them up to his wife's aunt, the widow Niebaum, to raise according to her own notions of right and wrong. She was known as Tante, a kind but unyielding woman firmly rooted in the previous century. Her descendants came to think of her as a steel rod in black bombazine.

Tante took her grandnephew and grandniece to the big white Victorian in Rutherford, built by her and her husband among ancient oaks at the point where Navalle Creek emerged from the narrow, wooded valley under Mount St. John. The house had a broad wraparound porch and a view of rolling vineyards, stables, and oak and eucalyptus trees. The rooms, smallish but exquisitely appointed, suggested the elegant confines of a ship. There were sliding doors, tall windows, mantels of polished chestnut, and a richly paneled ceiling in the dining room.

Tante Niebaum navigated the house as the embodiment of old-fashioned morality and family duty. Only the winery, out of sight beyond the knoll at the far end of the meadow, harbored a hint of the illicit. Prohibition came into effect when John was twelve. The vineyards at Inglenook were maintained during those dozen difficult years as much out of a sense of decorum as out of an enduring family preoccupation with wine. Yet wine was to be John Daniel's life and, some said, his undoing.

While at Stanford, he met the dark-haired, hazel-eyed Elizabeth Naylor, known as Betty, the daughter of an English professor and his moderately wealthy wife who lived in the Claremont Hotel in Berkeley. Betty's mother belonged to a big Mormon clan in Utah, and most of her money went to the upbringing of her beautiful daughters. Betty had already arrived at the end of an impressive career by the time John Daniel found her. Spectacular looking at sixteen, she had been sent to the riding academy in Lausanne, Switzerland, where she became not just an accomplished horsewoman but also a formidable tennis player and the object of desire of young men with titles. They courted her in various European capitals, in style. Betty gained a level of experience beyond that of most girls her age and returned to California after several years barely able to speak her native English.

Betty's sophistication went well beyond that of the prominent, earnest engineering student from San Francisco and Rutherford. She and John had one thing in common: some knowledge of Napa Valley. The Naylors had owned the old Schram place for a time, using it as a retreat and filling the house with noisy children seeking recourse from the pressures of life by the bay. For a time the young Napa rubes had hung around the old Schram place in the summers, ogling the Naylor girls, although John Daniel was not among them. Then the property slipped back into decrepitude and onto the market, to be bought by the Davieses many years later.

A lasting bond between the beautiful equestrienne and the aspiring aviator seemed unlikely, considering their differences. Betty was mercurial, extravagant, sometimes brilliant; John was methodical, thrifty, utterly predictable. Betty expected attention; John did his best to provide it. His idea of a good time involved healthy outdoor activity, usually in the air. Betty's candor could be shocking at times — she said what was on her mind — but John fell thoroughly in love with her and they were married in 1933, the year he graduated and the year of Repeal.

John Daniel was considered quite a catch. Some members of San Francisco society wondered aloud why such an eligible young man would marry an unorthodox, worldly girl from an obscure family. Betty's behavior did not reassure her new family or her new acquaintances among San Francisco's best. Her insights into the character of others could be amusing — Betty read books — but also less than diplomatic. Their honeymoon took them to Hawaii, the pleasuring ground of Californians of means and a place where the Daniels were known, and Betty's wry comments on the local customs and her general demeanor caused some eyebrows to go up.

Despite his degree in engineering, John wanted to be a commercial pilot. But John Daniel, Sr., had another profession in mind for him. With Repeal came the opportunity once again to bring Inglenook into the commercial production of wine, and father informed son that he was to go to work there and eventually take over the management of Inglenook. It didn't matter that John had little knowledge of or interest in wine, or that flying was the only thing, other than Betty, that he really cared about. He had been raised on the horns of duty and family honor and he had no choice in the matter. It was, in his view, a command performance.

After the honeymoon, the young couple was to move into the white Victorian mansion where John had grown up — and where Tante waited.

Riding west on Niebaum Lane, Betty Naylor Daniel must have seen the winery before she saw the house; she didn't like Inglenook, being a Mormon by upbringing and opposed to alcohol. The massive stone façade of the winery dauntingly combined Scandinavian economy with Victorian grandeur, two hundred feet broad and seventy feet in depth. Heavy wooden doors reared under stone arches, and eight smaller portals sat resolutely below east-facing dormers. Leaded glass and finials drew the eye ever upward, for four stories, to the touch of whimsy about the slatted cupola, topped by a ball on a reticulated column. The gravel courtyard could have accommodated several locomotives. Creeper grew between each set of doors, scaling Niebaum's towering dream like some botanical skin — all for the glory of wine.

Napa Valley during the Depression offered the traveler back roads shaded by big oaks, little traffic, and views of vineyards and flowering fruit trees. Life was simple and sometimes perilously close to impoverished, but the natives lived a rural idyll without always realizing it and without any idea that it might someday end. Fresh produce abounded, as did game. A man with a pitchfork could easily kill a steelhead up a creek during spawning season and take it home to be poached for friends and neighbors. Socializing meant dancing at St. Helena High, and ham and eggs afterward. Diehard revelers swam in the Napa River at midnight and went home in time to get up with the sun.

Betty became disillusioned with Rutherford almost as soon as the starch was off the nuptial sheets. She had known excitement and glamour in Europe and had expected some of the same from John. Instead, she found herself living in a rural backwater with a husband who, rather than flying airplanes to distant cities with her, wallowed in the odoriferous activities of Inglenook's vast cellar.

The workers at Inglenook in 1933 became accustomed to the sight of the handsome, matter-of-fact young Daniel armed with the slide rule he had used at Stanford, his dark hair parted as if with a knife, his shirt sleeves rolled up neatly above the elbows. He earnestly tasted all the Inglenook wines and listened to treatises on winery management from Carl Bundschu, who had been hired to get Inglenook back into operation. Bundschu, from an established Sonoma Valley winemaking family, was at fifty-five the antithesis of the novice Daniel. Stocky and balding, with a large red nose that signaled an interest in drinks stronger than wine, Bundschu would every afternoon disappear into the bar across the highway. But he understood winemaking, and he knew how to market the product. He wrote florid promotional letters and organized a party at Inglenook to celebrate Repeal and, incidentally, the arrival of the Niebaum heir.

Within a year John Daniel was representing Inglenook at professional conferences. At home, he pressed for more investment in Inglenook's facilities. He sought advice from the renowned viticulturist Albert Winkler and a brilliant student of enology, Maynard Amerine, both at the University of California. What became the Department of Viticulture and Enology was in the process of moving from Berkeley to Davis. John and Bundschu hired two new winemakers. Inglenook wines took first- and second-place medals in the 1934 California State Fair, and Bundschu promoted this relentlessly, conducting tastings and more hospitality events at Inglenook.

He and John attended meetings of the Wine Institute, an organization of California winemakers dedicated to keeping bad wine off the market. John stood up among the older members and attempted to explain the needs of the handful of quality producers, radiating decency and concern for the future.

In the valley, John tried to make it plain that he was not a dilettante and rich boy in a manufactured job. People found him to be forthright, charming, even "sweet," with an underlying sadness. His wife didn't care for his profession, and Tante Niebaum didn't approve of Betty any more than Betty approved of Inglenook. Betty was too outspoken, too demanding, too well dressed, and a Mormon. Her affiliation with the Church of Jesus Christ of Latter-day Saints was tenuous at best, but Betty sensed Tante's disapproval and emphasized the very traits of which Tante disapproved.

John showed sympathy for what he considered her weaker sex. He promised that their lives would be easier and richer once he made Inglenook a success. That didn't alleviate Betty's feeling of isolation or her faltering sense of her own place in the broader scheme of the valley.

John Daniel had no real peers. His and Betty's restricted social life pained her considerably more than it did him. The distractions of the city lay hours away. John could have had a place in San Francisco society but didn't want one; Betty wanted a place but didn't belong and thought that those who did looked down on her. She was just the woman who had married a very eligible bachelor and so was torn between resentment of the established families and a desire for company that suited her style and expectations.

Napa contained many unlikely people, in her estimation. There were pockets of sophistication, best represented by Beaulieu, but the family who owned it, the de Latours, had been largely ignored by the Niebaums. So the de Latours and their heirs, the de Pinses, were little more than neighbors to John and Betty. There were a few other acceptable families — mostly members of the Boring Crowd — and a great many Italians.

Betty found no ready diversion during the long sunny days and little distraction at night other than the occasional cocktail party and dinners at the Miramonte in St. Helena. From there she and John would drive home through Napa's pervasive darkness, the valley practically empty of lights. In summer, the air did not move, reverberating with the sound of insects, smelling of flowers that Betty loved, of crops and the wild tangles behind the Niebaum house and the mysterious processes of a beautiful, breathless land.

Then John Daniel met Louie Stralla, himself a recent arrival in the valley. Stralla was older than John and, it would seem, the last person likely to become his friend. Stralla had grown up in Los Gatos delivering his mother's bread, and later moved to San Francisco, where he worked for the *Call-Bulletin*. Uneducated, gregarious, he had drifted around the country working for newspapers until he arrived in Las Vegas in the early thirties. He became a partner in a hotel venture that catered to men working on Boulder Dam. Stralla patronized a restaurant known for the blondes from little western towns who worked there. He would later tell people that one named Fontaine had been barefoot when he met her, and that he chased her all over the desert in his sand-colored Chrysler Imperial convertible with red upholstery before he finally caught and married her.

Louie's half-brother owned a gambling ship anchored off the California coast beyond the three-mile limit. After it was shut down by the authorities, Stralla brought furniture from the ship to St. Helena, and linoleum from the decks to cover his floors, but otherwise he tried to obscure his kinship to a half-brother rumored to be a gangster, a thick-necked, impatient man who owned an interest in a Las Vegas casino and who was later shot to death.

Louie and "Fon" had left the desert with Stralla owing money. Napa offered refuge, from just what people were never sure. They stayed for the first few weeks in Calistoga, an old resort town with hot springs and spas that was founded in 1860 by Samuel Brannon, a real estate promoter. The town's name reportedly sprang from Brannon's inebriated enthusiasm over the prospect of making the place the Saratoga of California, but instead he had muddled the comparison, calling it "the Calistoga of Sarifornia." The name and the town's carny atmosphere had endured.

The Strallas holed up in the Mount View Hotel. It belonged to an old Italian who talked to Louie about wine in the valley and introduced him to Adam Bianchi, a partner of Charles Forni's and a shipper of grapes. Bianchi told Louie there was a future in bulk wine and suggested that Stralla go down to St. Helena and see if he could rent the empty Krug winery, owned by a banking family in San Francisco, the Moffitts, who later sold the winery to the Mondavis. They leased it to Stralla, no money down, and he found a man named Joe Ponti, who made wine for Beaulieu, to advise him. Stralla told Ponti, "You don't know me from a load of hay. I want to go into the wine business, and I'm looking for somebody who might know something about how to make wine."

Ponti sent him to another winemaker, who told Stralla how to clean the redwood tanks; he told Stralla who to hire to do the work, then stayed to make sure it was done right. Stralla borrowed to pay for it all, and by November 1933 he owned 400,000 gallons of red wine.

Stralla had no idea how to move it. He went to New York and talked to some Italian wholesalers, and met another young Italian from California doing the same thing; his name was Ernest Gallo. On subsequent trips Stralla ran into Gallo on the New York–bound airplane, which also bumped down in Sacramento, Reno, Lincoln (Nebraska), and Chicago. Gallo would never tell Stralla who he was going to see.

At ten cents a gallon for the wine, shipped east in railway tank cars, Stralla made a profit of $12,000. Each year the price rose a few cents a gallon. He sold some to Gallo and some to the Cellas. Gradually Louie paid his debts and lost the hangdog look he had brought to Napa from Vegas. He had fallen in love with the valley and would have bought Krug if he had had the money. Italians owned the monumental Greystone Cellars across Highway 29, and Fred Abruzzini was managing Beringer. Holy piastras, Stralla told Fon, the Italians have taken over!

His exuberance touched a chord in John. They began to have lunch together almost every day in St. Helena, a ritual that often included the local doctor and the bank president. At night, the Strallas and the Daniels would meet for dinner at the Miramonte. Fon's striking fair hair and complexion provided a foil for Betty's darker good looks; they were both newcomers to Napa, and a friendship sprung up between the women.

The workers at Inglenook regularly began to see Mrs. Daniel riding horseback with an attractive blonde, heading down the drive lined with almond trees on sunny mornings. The women in the bottling line remarked on the riders' "beautiful shapes" and their enviable lack of worries. Betty and Fon would turn south toward Yountville, where they would be joined by Carolyn Stelling, another beauty, the wife of Martin Stelling, who owned large tracts of vineyardland. The three women would ride for hours through these vineyards and along the eastern base of the Mayacamas where there were few fences to impede their progress.

Fon found Betty amusing and bright. Betty often gave her presents and invited the Strallas to the house for dinner. Fon noticed that Betty never drank wine, although there was plenty available at meals.

John struck her as proud but without pretense. He had strong opinions about things like government interference in private or business affairs, and yet he talked around a subject rather than going directly for it, as her husband would have. Sometimes Fon wanted to say, "Come on, John, out with it!"

Betty liked to boss him, but there was a limit to what John would take. She was always complaining, after the death of Tante, of the ugly old furniture left by the Niebaums, but John was too practical to toss it out. Despite his Scots temperament, he occasionally lent money. He didn't want to be taken for a sucker but had difficulty asking for repayment, so kept a record of debts on scraps of paper carried for years in his wallet.

Fon and Louie often talked on the way home about how different John and Betty were; Fon would say, "Opposites attract."

John Daniel received an invitation to have lunch with Louis Martini, who had emerged from Prohibition as one of the best winemakers in the state. Martini was a founder of the Wine Institute; he owned vineyards high on the western side of the Mayacamas Mountains in Sonoma County, as well as in Napa Valley. A volatile man who liked to argue, who wore a pinky ring and drove his big car at speed, Martini had arrived in the United States from Genoa in steerage, alone, at the age of thirteen. The railroad authorities in New York pinned a card on him stating who he was and where he was going and shipped him west to join his father in San Francisco, where he owned boats and brought in clams, mussels, and smelts to the fish market on Merchant Street. Louis drove the fish wagon and was almost killed in 1906 when half the market collapsed in the earthquake and he raced up to Kearny Street, people clinging to the wagon, begging him to take them to the waterfront so they could escape. But Louis Martini had a load of clams to deliver.

Martini had moved to Napa in 1933. He bought ten acres for $3,000, tore out the prune trees, and started planting vines, including Cabernet Sauvignon and Zinfandel, considered sheer exotica. He loved the valley but was not bound by it, and also bought a three-hundred-acre vineyard in the Mayacamas and named it Monte Rosso for its red soil. He planted more Cabernet and Zinfandel. Years later, he bought a ranch in Carneros called La Loma, south of the city of Napa and close by the bay. "Carneros" meant sheep, but some people doubted that the land was fit for even that dubious animal. Carneros certainly didn't seem suited to grapes. Low lying, barren, swept with wind from San Pablo Bay, it was chilly even on summer nights. Few people lived in Carneros. Those who did grew vetch, if they grew anything, and when Martini put in Pinot Noir and Chardonnay, people said he was crazy.

John Daniel was not the only man to accept Martini's luncheon invitation. There was Charles Forni, Fred Abruzzini, and some other Italians. Martini told them over lobster at his house in the Monte Rosso vineyard that they should all gather regularly to discuss common problems and, more importantly, to eat and drink. That was the beginning of the Napa Valley Vintners Association — in Sonoma County — with Martini as president and John as vice president.

The young Daniel might have been a Scot, but he could appreciate a joke and liked to pun. He had a satirical label printed for a

wine he called Mole Hill Red ("It's a wine you'll gopher"), a parody
of Louis Martini's claims to superior mountain-grown grapes.

Subsequent meetings of the nascent Napa Valley Vintners Association were held at the St. Gothard Tavern, and then at the Miramonte. The group grew to include other winemakers and representatives of Christian Brothers, Larkmead, Beaulieu. Louie Stralla
joined and rarely missed a meeting. He made it clear he didn't care
for the romance of wine but he liked having lunch with friendly
people.

With the death of Tante Niebaum in 1937, John and his sister had
become the sole owners of Inglenook. She took no interest in the
place, preferring to raise dogs and horses out beyond Lodi. John took
over the management of the entire estate. He had learned all he could
from Bundschu, who was increasingly showing the effects of alcohol, and hired a new winemaker, George Deuer, a temperamental
German from Rottenburg. Deuer had learned winemaking as an ap-
prentice but had come to America and worked on the Studebaker
assembly line in South Bend and in the Ford plant in San Francisco.
Then he returned to his real profession in Napa Valley, first at Christian Brothers, then at Beringer, and finally Inglenook, one of six
cellar men.

By the end of Bundschu's reign Deuer was already making the
Inglenook wine. He was not an intellectual, but meticulous and a
hard worker. In overalls, he performed much of the physical labor
himself. He had no interest in customers; winemaking was his business. For a while he managed to keep two of his habits hidden from
Daniel. One was an appetite for Scotch — whiskey was becoming a tradition among Inglenook winemasters — which he indulged
throughout the day. Sometimes the habit would overcome the man
and Deuer would disappear for days. The other habit was less disruptive to the winemaking process but caused concern and some ri-
bald amusement at Inglenook. Deuer's amorous overtures earned
him the nickname "Fast-hand George." The young women knew
better than to climb the stairs at the winery ahead of him; even worse
was to be cornered by Deuer back among the oak ovals. If Fast-hand
George had been drinking, his advances could turn exceedingly ar-
duous.

Deuer made good wine under conditions that had changed little
since Niebaum's day, and John learned from him. The winery was a

relic, but it had a certain logic. A carriageway had originally been cut high into the hillside to provide access for wagons at harvest time. The grapes could then be crushed on the third floor and the juice delivered by gravity to huge fermenters below; later, gravity would again move the wine to lower levels for aging and bottling. The floors were of poured, vaulted concrete stressed with steel cable from San Francisco's original cable car system, with gutters built into the surfaces to carry off spillage and water. The hydraulic wine press and other heavy machinery were confined to the center tower, while scores of 1,000- and 500-gallon oval redwood and oak tanks occupied the two identical wings.

Crush now took place on the ground level, outside the north doors. The "must" — juice and skins — was moved upstairs with piston pumps and the stems were carted away. Inglenook used not just Cabernet and Pinot Noir but also Johannisberg Riesling, Semillon, a bit of Chardonnay, Gamay Beaujolais, Charbono, and other good varieties preserved during Prohibition, which put the winery in a fine position at the time of Repeal.

Owner and winemaker tasted the wines together in the Captain's Room just inside the front door of the winery. It had been fitted during the previous century with stained glass from Holland, an ornate lamp, crystal goblets, pressed oak chairs, wine-related antiques, and open racks on paneled walls containing Inglenook wine. The effect was proper, Germanic, not particularly comfortable. A winery required an elegant tasting room, but John's granduncle had not used it much.

John concentrated on those wines from the best casks, going through as many as a hundred at a session. Sometimes he would disqualify all but a quarter of them and sell the rest off under a different label — extraordinarily expensive quality control, unequaled anywhere in California. The "cask wines" that emerged from the process were not only fine but also wildly underpriced. Marketing and sales were not John's talents.

He hired an expansive Portuguese, Joe Sousa, to supervise the vineyards. Sousa moved into a house on the property with his wife and shortly became friends with John. When John was in the valley, Sousa would come to him to describe what would be taking place in the vineyards during the day, and soon the pale blue Daniel convertible would be seen easing to a halt at the edge of the vines. The importance of the vineyards had become apparent to John early on, when many winery owners still took their grape supplies for granted and paid little attention to the vineyards. Sousa taught him much about individual climates. As always, Daniel subjected vine-spacing plans and predicted tonnage to trial by slide rule.

He hired a promoter named Jimmy Blumen to perform the more blatant commercial functions. Inglenook wines began to appear on lists in prestigious dining rooms on both coasts. John belonged to the Pacific Union Club in San Francisco and so prevented Inglenook wines from being promoted there, to avoid any possible breach of etiquette, but he did present the wines at dinners given by the Wine and Food Society, usually at the French Club, organized by Jimmy Blumen. His pre-Prohibition bottles of Inglenook impressed the membership. Half a century later Maynard Amerine would remember a 1906 Inglenook Semillon served at a dinner where John stood up and spoke proudly of its provenance.

John joined the board of the Wine Institute in 1941 and continued his efforts to promote fine wine, often in opposition to the interests of the Central Valley. He donated to UC Davis the library that had been collected by Niebaum, probably the most extensive private wine library in the world. Most of the books were written in foreign languages — including some in Gothic script — and stored in the cellar of the house.

Inglenook was one of the first wineries to put "Napa Valley" on its labels; Inglenook's practice of vintage dating was also uncommon. The best wines continued to win medals in competition and the rest were sold off in bulk, in half-barrels or by the tank car load, for as little as fifteen cents a gallon. Inglenook was a far from profitable enterprise. The scale of the operation, and what John saw as his historic mission, prevented him from putting the Inglenook name on any wine that failed to meet his expectations.

The grapes came from four different vineyards, including the one on the hill north of the Daniels' house, and were all "dry farmed." No one irrigated in those days. The Cabernet was usually picked in the first week of October without measuring the sugar content; it was done on instinct alone, Sousa breaking the grapes in his fingers to feel the stickiness of the juice.

The doors in the winery were kept open to allow air to pass through, but heat remained a problem, threatening to stop the fermentation in the big redwood tanks. Inglenook had one 5,000-gallon tank for cold water, and a standing order with the Union Ice Company. The cold water was circulated by a "snake" around different batches of fermenting wine, keeping it from bubbling over. Fermentation lasted for only five days, in contrast to the much longer regime next door at Beaulieu. The wine was not pumped over the "cap" — the mass of skins and pips floating on top of the fermentation tank — but the cap was punched back down into the wine once a day. The wine went into mostly German oak casks and eventually into any bottles Daniel could find; they were corked and labeled by women working in the old stable.

The Cabernet sold for an impressive $2 a bottle before World War II. It was shipped to San Francisco and Los Angeles, and some wine found its way to New York, Washington, D.C., Boston, New Orleans, and Minneapolis, mostly because of Jimmy Blumen. At one point there were seven Inglenook wines on the list of the Waldorf-Astoria.

The war stopped the flow of European wine to America. Then California Cabernet jumped to $3.50 a bottle. The demand for drinkable bulk wine turned clamorous — another upturn in a notoriously unstable business. In New York on a selling trip, John wired to ask if Deuer could get ten carloads ready for shipment the following week, but Inglenook didn't have the wine or the equipment to meet such a demand. Inglenook's strength lay in quality, not quantity.

John was introduced to another man with whom he would become good friends, a man very different from Louie Stralla. Alexis Klotz described himself as a brass-assed long-range pilot. He had flown for TWA, the Air Corps, and before that lifted the night mail out of Pasadena. Klotz flew Wendell Willkie around the world and Cordell Hull to Russia, where Klotz lunched with Stalin. Klotz's brother and John Daniel had been fraternity brothers at Stanford, and John and Alexis became instant buddies, the way aviators often did. Klotz used his influence to obtain for John a job in the Air Corps as Klotz's copilot; they were to fly dignitaries to wherever the government wanted them flown. It was the thing John had dreamed of all his life, and to Klotz's disgust John turned it down because he didn't want to be separated from Betty.

John was a good pilot, Klotz thought, but possessed an old-school propriety. Honor was everything. When Herb Caen wrote an unflattering piece about John in the *San Francisco Chronicle*, John hired a boxer to teach him to fight, so he could knock Caen down if he ever encountered him.

John and Alexis teamed up to buy a vineyard on the outskirts of Yountville that John had bought from Louie Stralla, called Napa-nook. It produced some fine grapes and provided Klotz with something to do besides play bridge when he was on the ground in Napa Valley, where wine and grapes were frequent topics of conversation, but flying was the men's passion. When the Air Corps started selling off its surplus AT-6 trainers — real he-man planes with lots of horsepower and maneuverability — John and Alexis went down to the airfield at South Dos Palos together and John bought one for $1,500. John flew it back to a landing strip north of Inglenook that John called Rutherford International. Klotz called the strip the Virgin — "It's hard to get into" — but John wasn't amused.

Klotz bought his own AT-6. He and John had a lot of fun flying the two planes from Rutherford International. Klotz also used the pasture in front of Stag's Leap, a seedy resort hotel that catered to wartime transients, including the wives of servicemen stationed at Mare Island. Louie Stralla decided he had to have an AT-6 too, even though he didn't know how to fly, and John and Klotz returned to South Dos Palos and brought a third AT-6 back to Rutherford International. Louie got in the plane and started up the engine and taxied around, raising the tail off the ground, for the thrill of it.

Klotz didn't know what to make of Louie. Once, as a favor to him, Klotz flew a man and a bag of cash down to southern California, no questions asked. Louie was always involved in something shady, Klotz thought.

Sometimes the Daniels and the Strallas traveled together. John always filed a flight plan first. They would all go down to Carmel. John loved the town and the steep, rocky coastline south of Monterey. The years during the war were a romantic time in California, not yet overrun with people and preserved as if forever in the innocence reflected in Hollywood films made then and in the leisurely quality of life. Occasionally John and Louie flew north to Oregon, to fish for trout. When John returned home after dark and passed low over the house, Betty would drive out and direct the headlights onto the dirt landing strip so John could set his plane down.

He and Betty now had two young daughters, Marcia and Robin; the engineering student and the equestrienne had assumed all the roles set out for them. The Daniel family should have been a happy one, the girls growing up in the house John had known as a child, but Betty's unhappiness had not abated. Several times she had threatened divorce; gradually a darker story emerged from the house at the end of Niebaum Lane.

cæu

Fon Stralla discovered that Betty broke off relations with an old childhood friend. Then their own friendship faltered. Betty's erratic behavior, her domineering attitude toward John, and what could only be described as grandiose notions of her own importance had distanced her from all her acquaintances. Another source of discord was Betty's infidelity to John. Every winter she spent a month or two skiing in Yosemite and Sun Valley, leaving the children with servants; sometimes she brought men she had met there back to the house in Rutherford. It seemed strange to the Strallas, but John didn't object and tried to make the visitors feel at home. Fon suspected that there was more to Betty's friendships than skiing.

Then she learned that Betty was having an affair with an officer in the Coast Guard. John didn't know about it, or if he knew, he pretended that he didn't.

Betty's behavior didn't square with her moralistic pronouncements; that rubbed Fon the wrong way. Betty insisted that her girls attend church and be raised as Mormons, and would sometimes spend long evenings reading to them from the Bible, and then do things that could hardly be considered Christian. Betty's was a God of wrath, not love. She told her daughters that the world would come to an end before they could grow up to be wicked. Betty impressed the older, Marky, with her severe Old Testament vision; she terrified Robin.

In the beginning Betty had objected to the time John spent away on company business. Now she objected to the business itself. Wine was evil, and John should stop making and selling it. He argued that Inglenook represented a unique tradition in California, and that production of fine wine was in fact a high calling. He intended to make a success of what had for half a century been a costly endeavor for his family.

They entertained at home even less. John used the St. Helena Hotel for promotion when necessary, in sharp contrast to Beaulieu next door, where Mme. de Latour and Mme. de Pins had become an indefatigable team with a public relations expert in Los Angeles, of all places. Ironically, Beaulieu retained the reputation for rigorous Old World integrity, while Inglenook, pursuing a less commercial course, maintained consistent quality and continued to operate at a loss.

The winery became a personal adversary of Betty's. She forbade the girls to enter it. Marky bent before her mother's will, but Robin would slip into the winery on the pretext of using the bathroom and then rush up the stairs before one of the office workers could catch her. Robin adored the place, with its vast storage tanks, heady smells of old wood and fermentation, exotic machinery, deep shadows, and the possibility of finding her father somewhere in the cavernous building, slide rule at his side, smiling at her across the broad concrete floors.

The Daniels seldom quarreled in front of the girls. If an argument arose between Betty and her daughters, it was John who demanded reconciliation. He always took Betty's side. She was, after all, the adult, and adults were infallible in the world in which John Daniel had been raised. Neither of the girls blamed him, but Betty didn't return his allegiance. She criticized his family, saying that the dead Tante had been too rigid, a stifling influence. She suggested that John and his sister were not the only Niebaum heirs, that there was an illegitimate Eskimo fathered by Gustave Niebaum up in Alaska who would someday show up to claim Inglenook.

Alexis Klotz stayed often at the Daniels'; he decided that Betty was the bitch incarnate. She would insist on drinking Coca-Cola at cocktail parties among the valley's small social elite, then go home and get tanked up on Scotch. She would get in bed with anybody she felt like getting in bed with. John seemed defenseless against these things. He had economic muscle in the valley and twice got rid of Betty's lovers by depriving them of jobs, but there was always a replacement.

One day John told Klotz and Louie that Betty was leaving him. Louie checked around and discovered that she was shacked up with an Air Force lieutenant in St. George, Utah. Louie wanted Klotz to fly them over there, and Klotz agreed, but John refused to go.

Later, Klotz came down the stairs to find John crying at the dining room table. John said, "We're getting a divorce."

"Thank God," said Klotz.

"Well, I don't feel that way."

Betty had often threatened divorce. She had left home on several occasions. The general respect and affection for John in the valley, and his own distaste for publicity, always muted the trouble.

Klotz decided that John was downright feudal. He wanted to keep the institution of marriage inviolate but would not deal with the reality of Betty's behavior. He wanted absolute control of his land and crops but wouldn't bend before economic necessities. When Klotz signed a contract to sell Napanook grapes to the St. Helena co-op, John objected for philosophical reasons. The growers were all selling to Gallo, but John didn't want to belong to a co-op or to sell to Gallo. He and Klotz argued, John bought him out, and the threads of their lives separated.

7

URING THE WAR the price for a ton of grapes rose from $15 to $50. The growers of Napa Valley and the rest of California made money and planted more. Field hands who had made only $1.75 for a nine-hour day now received 40 cents an hour at Inglenook and other wineries — an astronomical wage. And there were not enough workers to be found.

Rafael Rodriguez's father sometimes made kitchen shelves in Mexico City from wood salvaged from fruit crates. As a child Rafael had dismantled the crates and had often paused to look at the labels on them showing, in vibrant colors, orchards, lush fields, and hazy mountains in a northern land called California.

Mexico languished in an ongoing depression during the years of the Second World War. The 1910 revolution in Mexico had failed. An ocean of deprivation and cultural heritage still separated rich and poor. Rafael was keenly aware of the difference between the people and the authorities, those well-dressed figures glimpsed in the Zócalo outside the presidential palace. Common men still had to remove their hats when approaching these people; sometimes they knelt and muttered, "In God's name."

His father was an *obregón,* a worker in a textile factory. He was often unemployed. The Rodriguezes lived among the capital's *vecindades,* slum tenements of the barrios of Tepito. Later Oscar Lewis would describe Tepito in *Children of Sanchez* as "a poor area with a few small factories and warehouses, public baths, run-down third class movie theaters, over-crowded schools, saloons, *pulquerias. . . .* This area ranks high in the incidence of homicide, drunkenness and delinquency."

Rafael's father had been part of the mass migration to the capital from the countryside. More than a million and a half impoverished people lived in Mexico City in the early 1940s — a third of the population. Though illiterate, he managed to marry into a family of merchants. Rafael never knew his mother, or even her name, and assumed she died in childbirth. Her mother cared for Rafael as a small child, and he remembered the sweet, musty odor of green bananas smoked in a room off the courtyard, to age them before they were sold.

His father, a handsome man with a mustache and unmistakable Indian features, often came to the house, only to be turned away. "He's a street vendor," Rafael's grandmother would tell Rafael.

His father came and took Rafael away when he was five. His father was jailed for this but eventually Rafael went to live with him, his second wife, and their children in the small house in the barrio. His father belonged to the Confederación Regional Obrero Mexicana, but the textile mill ran intermittently, and then not at all. The family existed by selling clothes from a stall in La Merced, the big market, or on the street. Then Rafael and his father would cross Mexico City on foot, pushing a cart loaded with clothes bought cheaply, including handkerchiefs made by Rafael's stepmother. They sold them to buy beans and tortillas cooked in lard on the roadside.

Rafael's stepmother made soup from tiny fish bought in the market. There was no plumbing in the house; Rafael and his stepbrothers had to walk six blocks to fetch a jar of water. Often there was not enough to eat. Mexico City was in turmoil, with more people arriving daily without money or the prospect of jobs; competition in the markets was fierce. Rafael knew how to read and write, and his father, using union connections, managed to enroll him in technical school when Rafael was thirteen. There he learned to operate the big looms, but he found little or no work.

He had heard of El Norte. He didn't know exactly what it was, only that it lay far north of Mexico City and that there a man could earn more in six months than in five years in Mexico. He also heard that El Norte was the exploiter; he saw thousands of poor people in line outside the Estadio Nacional, fighting to join the braceros. The braceros were promised jobs in El Norte. Rafael couldn't believe their determination. They stood, and slept, in the lines; peddlers sold them food, and others rented them the use of buckets so they could relieve themselves without losing their place in line.

Rafael told his father about this possibility of work and his father said, "If you have to go, be good to the Americano, and he will be good to you."

Rafael was so hungry he ate banana skins off the floor of La Merced. One morning outside the Estadio Nacional, he stepped into the line of braceros. Within hours he was surrounded by people from the provinces — Indios — who spoke a strange Spanish. The man in front of him asked Rafael if he had worked in the fields. Rafael said no, and the man gave him a piece of lead and told him to rub his palms with it, to build up the calluses and to add color to a city boy's hands.

The second day the door opened and hundreds flooded into the building, Rafael among them. There they found more lines, and food in boxes. Each man was given two pieces of bread with a slice of meat, a piece of pie, and an apple. A huge gringo in a khaki uniform, speaking broken Spanish, asked Rafael's name, where he was from, and what farm work he had done. By then Rafael knew the answers the gringos wanted: he had planted rice, he said, in Guanajuato.

The gringo examined his hands and sent him to another line. A gringo told the men to undress. They looked at one another and then complied, and marched into another room carrying their clothes. There gringos in white coats subjected them to degrading examinations, x-rayed and photographed them, and told them to return the following day.

Rafael heard his name called. He was handed an envelope. Inside was a card with a photograph of a slight, dark-haired young man looking confused, a number — 61353 — and words in Americano stipulating that he was to earn no less than 37 cents an hour.

He took the card home and showed it to his father, and the next morning went to the train station with a blanket. He and hundreds of other men boarded old railroad cars that had been fitted with rows of straight-back wooden seats. It was February and there was no heat on the train, and no food other than tortillas and frijoles brought by the lucky ones. Rafael did not know where he was going or how long he would be gone.

Rumors spread that the braceros were sold into slavery, that they would never see Mexico or their families again. The crowd on the railroad siding shouted, *"No vayas! Bajate!"* Don't go! Jump!

The train lurched northward.

•

Food ran out the second day. For diversion, the men sang, accompanied by a guitar in the hands of a bracero from the state of Hidalgo:

> *"Yo soy como el chile verde llorona,*
> *Picante pero sabroso."*
> I am like a green pepper,
> Very hot but very good.

Rafael trembled with the cold; he was exhausted. The train stopped once at a remote siding outside Durango, where he could see nothing but fields of grain, and took another day to reach the border. There the men sat for three hours before the door was opened and they were ordered across the tracks — into Los Estados Unidos. Rafael sniffed the clean air.

A passenger train waited, shades drawn; inside there were padded seats. Gringos told the braceros where to sit and not to raise the shades. Masses of food appeared on paper plates.

Early the next morning Rafael took a chance and pulled the window shade aside; he saw desert and dry, distant mountains. The rumor was that if the train turned right, they would end up in Chicago. If it turned left, they were bound for California. So far the train had not turned at all. It entered a vast plain of houses and eventually pulled into a cavernous station, where they were allowed out onto the platform. This, he heard, was Los Angeles, but he couldn't be sure. The gringos waved them back into the train and all night they sped north.

At dawn the train stopped in the middle of a flat landscape. Furrows ran off toward infinity. The men left the train and lined up in the bright sunlight. A Mexican woman told them in Spanish that they were not in Chicago but in Watsonville, California, and that they would pick lettuce for a large company in Salinas. A bus took them to the bunkhouse in the Watsonville barrio, known as El Paharo. There were outhouses, a communal shower, and food not as good as that on the train: frijoles, pig's feet, flour tortillas.

At four the next morning they were fed mush called oatmeal, and then packed into buses that took them thirty miles through the dark to the still-frigid fields. There Rafael learned to use the *cortito,* a small hoe for thinning lettuce. The work was hard and the day very hot, and the men arrived back at the bunkhouse after dark, dirty and exhausted.

At the end of two weeks he was given not money but a slip of paper with his name and wages written on it. Rafael didn't know

what to make of this. At the store he was told to sign his name on
the back of the slip of paper and then was handed $75. In Mexico, it
would have taken him two months to earn the same amount of
money. Seven and a half dollars had been taken out of his pay and
sent to the Mexican government; he had the feeling that he and the
other men were being rented to the gringos.

Most of the other men were illiterate. Rafael helped them sign
their checks. He and a friend he had made on the train were still city
boys; despite the real calluses on their hands they felt out of place,
trapped in the bunkhouse, the bus, the endless rows of lettuce. His
only outside contact was the Mexican woman, an American citizen
who worked for a government agency known as the Food Administration. She saw that Rafael and his friend were different and one
Sunday invited them to dinner. They showered, put on their best
clothes, and waited outside the bunkhouse until she picked them
up.

Her mother's house was the first American home Rafael saw; to
him it was luxurious, and the food incredibly abundant. Here were
good Mexicans, he thought, who had accepted El Norte and apparently been accepted by it.

A young Mexican American working for the Food Administration
was assigned to an office in a place called St. Helena; he asked Rafael
and his friend if they wanted to go with him. On impulse they
packed their clothes and left.

Passing through San Francisco, Rafael looked up at the white
buildings, steep hills, and blue bay. Girls on the street wore shorts,
something he had never seen. The car crossed a great bridge, where
fog poured in from the sea. The sun came out again and they crossed
lowlands and headed north through a rich agricultural valley. Rafael
had forgotten about the rural scenes on the fruit box labels back in
Mexico City. Looking out at plum orchards and rows of strange
vines running off at perfect angles from the highway, he was reminded of those visions.

In St. Helena they were met by a taciturn man named Charlie
Wagner. Without ceremony he told them to get into the back of his
pickup and then drove wildly through the dust and potholes to a
ranch near the Napa River. There was a vegetable garden and chickens. To Rafael's surprise, Wagner gave each of the young men a
Coca-Cola and then introduced them to his wife. She took them out

to the shed where they were to live. The beds had been made. That night, at age twenty-two, Rafael lay down between sheets for the first time.

If hoeing lettuce in Salinas had been exhausting, picking plums — what the gringos called prunes — was crippling. Much of the time Rafael spent on his hands and knees. The crew was paid by weight, and the others were used to the work and impatient with the newcomers. Rafael also had to shake prunes loose from the trees by placing a pole against the branches and throwing his weight against it. If the prunes didn't fall immediately, a dozen people screamed at him.

His knees bled and his hands blistered. He cried at night. Wagner turned out to be a kind and fair man — the first real farmer Rafael had ever met. He told Rafael and his friend they would have to find some other work; they didn't have the stamina for prunes.

Rafael went to a nurseryman in Napa named Salvator Emmolo, an Italian who spoke broken Spanish. In Emmolo's nursery were grape vines. They appeared to be dead, but Emmolo taught him how to cut the long canes so new ones would grow in the spring. The canes were piled at the ends of the rows, collected, and burned. All that January smoke rose over the valley, pearl-gray columns against the green mountains and blue sky.

Emmolo taught Rafael to graft new vines onto old rootstock and then to wrap them to assure that the buds survived. The work was not physically hard but demanded concentration, and Rafael found that he liked it. Emmolo was patient. He even put Rafael on the tractor. He had never driven one before and had not been allowed even to approach the tractors in Watsonville. But Rafael knew how to operate the machines in the textile factories at home, and he learned to run this farming machine. The fact that Emmolo let him try raised Rafael's opinion of himself.

Some others in the valley were not kind. When Rafael went to a store, the owner did not want him to touch things he didn't intend to buy. There were many places he could not enter, and girls he could not look at.

He married a Mexican who had become a U.S. citizen, but Rafael had to return to Mexico, as required by law. He left his wife and an infant son behind. Then a change in immigration law gave him the opportunity to return. He went back to work in Napa picking tomatoes, prunes, and walnuts, and gardening. Wineries were few and far between, and what went on in them remained a mystery to Rafael.

One day Emmolo took him to Rutherford and introduced him to a big Portuguese named Sousa. He was the foreman of a vast ranch and vineyard known as Inglenook, with hundreds of acres of vines and a towering stone winery that was the finest thing Rafael had seen in Napa. Mexicans were not allowed to work in the vineyards except to pick up cuttings and to weed and cut brush. Pruning was left to men of Italian and Portuguese descent. Sousa would pay him $1.25 an hour, which seemed like gold to Rafael.

When Sousa discovered that Rafael could drive a tractor, he let him move with his wife and now two young children into the little house between the winery and the Victorian mansion owned by the Daniels.

Sousa taught him how to drive the big D4 Caterpillar and sent him to the cellar when wine needed to be racked or moved. At those times Rafael came under the direction of the winemaker, George Deuer, the rudest man Rafael had ever worked for. He shouted and cursed at those he didn't like, and seemed maniacally jealous of his position. He recorded dates, grape tonnages, and other figures in a notebook he kept in his desk drawer. He didn't want others looking at the notebook, and if Rafael or anyone else entered Deuer's office when he wasn't there, he became enraged. But from Deuer Rafael learned the rudiments of winemaking.

First he punched down the thick crust of grape skins and pips that collected on the top of fermenting wine in the huge redwood casks. Walking along the overhead beams, carrying the wooden punch, he felt intoxicated from the smell of the gas put off by the fermenting grapes. The wine drained through hoses down to settling tanks on the first floor. From there it was pumped into 2,000-gallon upright oak and redwood casks at the south end, beyond the Captain's Room and the sales office. Rafael shoveled the heavy residue of fermentation, known as pomace, out of the presses and onto a primitive conveyor belt. From the winery the pomace was trucked to the fields and vineyards and spread as fertilizer.

He picked grapes during harvest, in the mornings. Rafael and other Mexicans lifted the grape boxes one at a time and dumped them over the side of the crusher — heavy work for small men. Then Deuer would come out of the winery and shout at the men to stop. The winemaker simply couldn't handle any more fruit with

Inglenook's antiquated equipment. One small crusher served the entire winery. Sometimes the electric pump would be overwhelmed by the volume of wine, and Deuer would emerge again from the shadows, shouting, "You damn Mexicans!"

Sousa allowed Rafael to do more than menial work; he taught him to prune, even though the other Portuguese workers were jealous. Rafael learned to distinguish among the twenty-two different grape varieties at Inglenook. The vines, which had always seemed strange to him, took on new life.

Rafael's wife had a weak heart. She died unexpectedly and the children went to live with Rafael's mother-in-law. Rafael was still a young man; he didn't fully comprehend what had happened, or that there might again be an element of happiness in his life. He devoted himself to work and found comfort in the huge, drafty, mostly empty winery, with its gravel floor — cool in summer, clammy in winter — and its powerful, pungent aromas. Rafael scrubbed, and painted, and once climbed to the top of the peeling cupola, from which he could see the fields of Cabernet, the railroad station at Rutherford, and the mountains beyond.

8

A SENSE OF misfortune hung about the Daniel house. Both John and the girls seemed happier out of it. Marky and Robin grew used to the sight of their father in a worn tweed jacket and old slacks, walking in the vineyards with Joe Sousa or in the company of Stralla, whose business interests had grown exponentially. When Daniel had to travel to San Francisco, he put on a business suit and set his hat at a slight angle; he always kissed the girls goodbye, and smiled and tipped the hat to workers in the winery on his way out to the highway.

Marky would go to the Sousas', behind the main house. Whenever she heard her father's plane returning from some far-flung mission, she felt a powerful sense of well-being. Sometimes he would take the girls up in the AT-6. First he would strap them into parachutes and tell them, "If anything goes wrong, dive out. Don't jump — the tail will crack your skull."

One day Betty brought a young soldier to the house. She had met him at Sun Valley, and Marky would always remember the man's uniform and his dark, determined face. Later, her father came into her room at night and sat on the edge of her bed. He told her that her mother had left home with the young man and that she would not be coming back.

Betty's new lover, a Umatilla Indian, took her to Salt Lake City. Some people in Napa said good riddance; others were truly shocked. Running away with another man was not a common or an accepted practice but it sometimes happened. Going off with an Indian was simply unimaginable.

Stories of Betty's new life making their way back to Rutherford told of an existence very different from what she had known. She had no money. Her lover reportedly knocked her to the floor when she attempted to embrace him. He took her into the mountains, where he shot arrows at targets and Betty was forced to retrieve them.

John granted her a divorce but would not give up hope of getting Betty back. Louie Stralla couldn't understand the continuing attraction any more than Alexis Klotz had. Stralla introduced John to various women whom Louie considered acceptable alternatives to Betty, but without success.

John threw himself into the work at Inglenook as a means of coping with his unhappiness. Every afternoon he hiked up Mount St. John behind the house. Sometimes he cut wood with an ax and returned exhausted to dinner. Later, he would read to the girls — *King Arthur* and other romantic tales — sitting in the old stuffed leather chair. He would tuck them in and tell them not to worry.

Betty left her lover after he threatened to fill her body with arrows, and hid out in Las Vegas, supposedly fearing for her life. The story of her escape was never verified and Fon Stralla didn't believe any of it. She was sure the man had kicked Betty out and that Betty was too proud to admit it but not too proud to call John.

When the car drove up in front of the white Victorian in Rutherford in 1950, Robin stood at the upstairs window. She watched her mother take her luggage out of the car, and thought, Here comes trouble.

Inside, Betty took a long look at Marky, and asked, "Do you make good grades?"

Marky said she did.

"I hope you do, because you're never going to be good looking or coordinated."

Marky remained in awe of her mother. She had a vision of Betty as a remote, beautiful woman in the red crepe gown she had worn one New Year's Eve; it was covered with sequins and seemed to absorb all the light around her. Marky's love of literature derived in part from listening to Betty read dramatically from "The Owl and the Pussy Cat" and Robert Louis Stevenson's "The Highwayman." But Betty could be cruel.

She and John decided to remarry immediately — in Seattle. The girls were taken up for the ceremony, which was held sufficiently far from Rutherford and San Francisco not to attract attention. Afterward, the family went on a collective honeymoon in the Pacific Northwest and

Banff National Park, in a big Buick station wagon. For a few days they were a happy, reunited clan. John acted as guide and intrepid stream crosser; Betty was pleased by his exuberance and displayed flashes of the old energy and charm.

At the Calgary Stampede, when Robin fell through a fence and cut her arm, Betty rescued her and solicitously treated the cut, reassuring Robin. She was the mother every ten-year-old wanted. Problems arose when people around Betty were well and not in need. Then some unspoken rivalry and resentment surfaced, frightening in its intensity.

At a dude ranch in the Tetons, Betty threw Robin into a pond and stood watching while she floundered to shore. Robin had never learned to swim and Betty said that now she had. At the hotel at Lake Louise, over dinner, she became infuriated because Marky did not wield a knife and fork to her liking. The fact was, Betty had never taught her daughters table manners.

It didn't matter to the girls, as long as their parents got along. Robin considered them the perfect couple. Marky was old enough to know better but was afraid of her own thoughts.

The preservation of an aura of well-being was important to John. He believed in propriety and the orderly pursuit of business and family objectives; appearances were a large part of reality. Betty wanted to look happy because to seem otherwise would be an admission that her life was less than enviable.

Back in Rutherford, the Daniels picked up where they had left off. None of their friends asked about Betty's experiences; it was as if she had been away at school again and returned in glory. Betty's relatives began to show up, as they always had. They borrowed money from John, and he scribbled the figures on scraps of paper and put them in his wallet.

The Niebaum house on Pacific Avenue in San Francisco was sold and an apartment purchased in the Marina for jaunts into the city. Trips to Carmel became more frequent. Betty took up tennis with a vengeance and was runner-up in the California women's tournament. John would fly down to Carmel occasionally, and the family would go to Point Lobos or Big Sur for picnics. For a time it looked as if the struggle between Betty and Inglenook had abated.

Inglenook's fortunes were a modifying force: it was difficult to argue with success. Before the war, Daniel had come close to begging people to buy his wine. The train running through the valley had to be flagged down on the rare occasions when there was wine to ship from Inglenook. During the war demand rose, so a spur line had to be built. John was forced to allocate Inglenook's vintage selections.

The winery was still far from turning a profit but not so great a drain on John's considerable financial resources. The reputation Inglenook gained in competitions and in fine restaurants in California and elsewhere carried some weight even in Betty's eyes. But she remained an antagonist, one given to fits of pique directed indiscriminately — at Inglenook, friends, and family. At times her resentment seemed to have no bounds. During a luncheon at the house Betty told the guests a story·that Marky had related to her, casting Marky as the butt of the joke. Marky burst out, "I never said such a thing!"

"Don't you ever contradict me," Betty said, her anger sudden and palpable. She stood up, stepped behind Marky's chair, and drove her fist into the back of her daughter's neck. Marky fell face-forward into her bowl, momentarily unconscious. When she revived and sat up, soup streaming onto her dress, Betty was gone and the guests were staring at Marky in horror.

John was ashen. He said, "Go upstairs and apologize to your mother."

◁≈▷

Rafael Rodriguez, happily employed at Inglenook, stood in awe of John Daniel, the tall, handsome *padrone* who owned an airplane. Every year Rafael drove the tractor to the airstrip north of Rutherford and pulled the metal disks through the heavy soil, to smooth it out. Daniel would drive out and inspect the work. Flying seemed to be very important to him. Daniel reminded Rafael of Rock Hudson, the actor who visited Inglenook with Jean Simmons during the making of a film in the valley, causing little stir in such an isolated place.

Every day Daniel came to the winery to taste wine with Deuer and Sousa, a custom that went on for years. He would drive into the vineyards in his blue Corvette, and then return to the house or continue on to the highway. Sometimes Sousa sent Rafael up to the main house, where Mrs. Daniel would tell Rafael what to do — help the gardener or perform some household chores. She usually wore a kimono and lay on her bed with the shades drawn. Often there was a dark mask over her eyes. More than once Rafael saw the doctor there.

When she was well, Mrs. Daniel tried to convert Rafael and other servants to Mormonism. The servants weren't sure exactly what the sect was, but they listened politely. Every year Mrs. Daniel ordered the almonds picked from the trees lining the long drive out to the highway and delivered to the Mormon church in St. Helena, depriving the workers at Inglenook of what had traditionally been a fringe benefit. What the church did with the almonds no one knew.

Rafael heard rumors that Mrs. Daniel did not like the winery and the vineyards, and that she had run away. Sousa had no respect for her and even spoke to her rudely on occasion. The Sousas had become second parents to Marky. After she went off to college, Robin could usually be found at the foreman's house.

Mrs. Daniel had the window in her own bedroom boarded up and spent more and more time in the dark.

John Daniel wrote, "A business is but the lengthened shadow of a man." The words were those of his granduncle, Gustave Niebaum, founder of Inglenook, a solitary, murky figure. John had often wished to know more about him, but the facts were few and had about them a fabulous quality. Research didn't turn up much. John went to Finland with Robin to find some distant kin, without success; it was as if Niebaum had invented himself. However, the trip did provide a tour of European capitals for Robin, now a teenager.

When John returned to Rutherford, he began to write a short biography of his granduncle, using the material available. He hoped that in some way Niebaum's life would add clarity to the Inglenook enterprise and perhaps to Daniel's own life. The research took him far back into California history, before Prohibition and phylloxera, to a time when the state and the city of San Francisco lived in a kind of golden age. Then a broad bay flecked with sails must have confronted the voyager passing through the Golden Gateway, as Captain Niebaum did in 1868. The tugs, assembled in fleets, were for the most part converted steamers, San Francisco being the end of the line for many boiler-driven ships in a fierce coastal competition remarkable for its explosions. Elegant sailing vessels rested in the lee of the southern headlands, and the side-wheel steamers and small launches and lighters passed jauntily under the brow of a city on a succession of hills rising from the deep blue inland sea.

An eastward promontory, Telegraph Hill, displayed a semaphore announcing the arrival of the sacrosanct mail boats and other vessels of strange and unlikely aspect. They moved as if by instinct toward the warehouses, emporiums, and ships' chandlers of all sorts that crowded the docks, along with grog shops, rough hotels, and the varied commerce of a densely thriving port. Gustave Ferdinand Nybom — the spelling was different then — was twenty-six years old and a native of a proud, semiautonomous grand duchy ruled by Czar Nicholas I. He had attended the Nautical Institute and been made captain, at the extraordinary age of twenty-two, of a ship bound for that outermost part of the czar's empire, Russian America. Declining Russian influence in Alaska and the Pribilof and Aleutian islands had created unstable conditions, but Nybom successfully traded in furs for three years, until Alaska was sold to the United States, and then sailed south with half a million dollars' worth of pelts in the hold.

San Francisco promised more than sensory pleasures, although those were considerable in the years following the Civil War. It had grown up on the twin bonanzas of the Gold Rush and the Comstock Lode and was accustomed to sudden fortunes. The silver mines of Nevada alone had pumped a hundred million dollars into the city in the last decade; the transcontinental railroad, still under construction, promised to end the city's isolation, bringing more people and more money through Sacramento to San Francisco. Laying rails had drawn more than a hundred thousand Oriental laborers to California, bound for the passes of the high Sierras, just one note in San Francisco's racial medley. The landscape reflected the prosperity and soaring ambitions of people from various parts of the world who had absorbed the wealth and were in the process of building greater fortunes and more splendid houses to accommodate them. San Francisco had more than twenty millionaires, including Leland Stanford, one of the founders of the Central Pacific Railroad, who was already planning a mansion on Nob Hill that would include singing mechanical birds and rooms devoted to Italian and Chinese artistry.

The Grand Hotel was going up at the corner of Montgomery and Market streets. Horse-drawn railway carriages took passengers around the city, skirting the big hills that were unassailable by public transport, although a fantastic cable system was being talked about that would effortlessly haul cars up even the greatest heights.

California had been part of the United States for almost two decades; the problems posed by the Civil War were resolved, and San Francisco sat on the sunny, crumbling edge of the Gilded Age. A general anticipation was reflected in the city's passion for theater, exotic restaurants, social extravaganzas, and other outlets for money. Celebrities and titled foreigners enjoyed an enthusiastic reception regardless of their credentials, and a young man even from the Scandinavian antipodes had no difficulty finding diversion and enterprise on a number of levels.

Russians and their representatives were no strangers to San Francisco. In the first years of the nineteenth century an emissary of the czar had arrived, searching for supplies; he had married a daughter of the Spanish commandant. A Russian expedition entered Bodega Bay, north of the city, in 1808, and a settlement was established at Fort Ross. Crops were planted and attempts made to trade in furs, but the colony languished until 1841, when the Russians left, having given their name to a river. Before leaving, they sold their livestock and land to an enterprising fellow named John Sutter, who eventually showed up in Napa Valley.

Nybom fell in with investors and with traders he had known in Alaska. They formed a partnership modeled on the old Russian American Company that had functioned in the north for sixty years, aiming for exclusive sealing rights in the Pribilofs. Members included a number of financiers and established fur traders from the East Coast; they called their umbrella the Alaska Commercial Company. Nybom was the youngest member, and the most knowledgeable. He spoke seven languages. A photograph of him seated in the San Francisco office of the company showed a tall man with a formidable nose and full beard seated by an enormous roll-top desk, under a photograph of one of the company's two river steamers, the *Yukon Twins*.

The Alaska Commercial Company received the rights in the Pribilofs and over the next two decades paid more than $12 million in fees to the U.S. government. The proceeds enjoyed by the partners amounted to considerably more. Nybom later changed his name to Niebaum and married the neighbor of one of his partners, a young Shingleberger. Niebaum wasn't satisfied with stylish landlubbering and dreamed of retiring and building a ship — a floating mansion — but his wife did not care for the sea. Her Germanic resolve proved a match for Finnish nautical fantasies, and Niebaum turned to wine.

Inspired by the sight of European châteaux on trips abroad, and the tastes of their industry, Niebaum studied wine and winemaking and decided there was no reason why California couldn't do as well as Europe. He traveled to Napa Valley and found scattered vineyards among fields, orchards, pastures, and halfhearted touristic enterprises built around the geysers and hot springs. Krug, Schram, and the Beringer brothers were already established in the north. In the hamlet of Rutherford — part of the old Caymus Ranch — was a failed sanitarium with some land planted with vines, belonging to a bank official and struggling winemaker who had named the place Inglenook, a Scots term for a hearthside seat. Niebaum bought the makeshift winery and some sixty acres of Black Malvoisie and Zinfandel.

He needed a good man in place and hired the former agent of the Alaska Commercial Company in the Pribilofs, a Vermonter named Hamden McIntyre. Niebaum acquired additional land and had it cleared back to the base of the Mayacamas. A thousand Sauvignon Blanc cuttings were bought from a nursery in San Jose, and eventually dozens of European varieties went into the vineyard, to determine which would prosper and which would not. Niebaum used his connections and his fortune to obtain whatever horticultural and mechanical devices he desired. He hired a score of men to do his bidding in the vineyards.

An elaborate stone stable was built, and a small experimental winery that nonetheless involved fine masonry. His first harvest at Inglenook, in 1882, saw too much rain. Niebaum had the grapes harvested anyway, and then separated them from the leaves and bits of stem before crushing, a fastidiousness that amused his neighbors. Inglenook produced eighty thousand gallons of wine that year, a large fermentation for a hobbyist. Some of it went into the brandy still.

Niebaum traveled to Europe and brought back vine cuttings and soil samples for comparison with Napa's prevailing dust. He imported English and Greek walnut trees, Russian silver birches, and fig, chestnut, olive, and almond trees. He had his vines planted much closer together than those elsewhere in California — emulating the Europeans. He placed standing orders with French and German nurserymen, and studied various aspects of viticulture. Niebaum took notes on the foreign vineyards and collected books on all aspects of wine in a dozen different languages. He instructed a Frankfurt bookseller to buy any relevant volume, old or new, that crossed his desk.

What had begun as an entrepreneur's avocation had to be gener-
ously supported by proceeds from the Alaska Commercial Company. Niebaum would allow no oaks to be cut to make way for
vines. If a young tree was discovered among the rows, a fence was
erected around it and the sapling encouraged to grow. He had cypress
and eucalyptus planted on the grounds, often in holes broken in rock
and filled with soil carried in baskets on the heads of the Chinese
laborers.

Niebaum avoided publicity; he took his own good time in releasing
the wine he thought was drinkable. He hired a marketer and publicist
in San Francisco to deal with the less pleasant adjuncts of the wine
trade: wine sellers and journalists. He attended the state viticultural
convention and lectured winemakers on technical innovations.

Inglenook's stone structure reared above the Rutherford plain.
The eastern slope of the hill in the center of the estate had been ex-
cavated and an enormous masonry archway constructed. This vault
was to draw on the cooling mass of interior basalt, to keep the wine
stored there at an unvarying temperature. Niebaum had studied winery construction and engaged the architect William Mooser, and instructed the Vermonter, McIntyre, to supervise assembly. McIntyre
would later build the monumental Greystone Cellars just north of
St. Helena, Far Niente, and Leland Stanford's winery in Yolo County, part of the largest vineyard in the world and the world's most
stupendous winemaking failure.

The winery's interior reflected Niebaum's concerns. All tools
were nickel-plated, and steam faucets installed. Niebaum had read
Pasteur and was an avowed enemy of the microorganism, in an age
when the connection between cleanliness and quality was not a popular notion. Machinery, bins, and floors were scrubbed with soda
after use. The oak and pine wainscoting was treated with oil to repel
dirt. Niebaum toured his winery wearing white gloves, trailing a
hand over working surfaces. Soiled gloves meant grief for the
workers.

Most California wine at the closing years of the century was
shipped by cask and often blended by the agent at the other end.
Most bulk wine was poorly treated, tampered with, and diluted;
some was not wine at all but spirits and other concoctions appearing
behind highly imaginative labels. Inglenook wine was available only
in bottles corked at the winery, and Inglenook's label — a classic

geometric design with Niebaum's intertwined initials — stated that the bottle contained "pure wine."

Inglenook wines traveled as far as Australia in quest of recognition. In 1889, at the Paris Exposition, medals went to twenty-seven other California wineries, but Inglenook received a special award for overall "excellence and purity." The effect of the judgment was enrapturing. "It means that France," the *San Francisco Merchant and Viticulturist* proclaimed, "our greatest rival, has declared to the world that the products of California's vintages rank with those of her own."

To John Daniel, Niebaum embodied Victorian America's great emphasis on industry and the primacy of the successful enterprise. *A business is but the lengthened shadow of a man.* Niebaum's shadow was embodied in the substance of Inglenook, but what of John Daniel's in the middle years of the 1960s?

9

ROBIN DANIEL remembered the old Alaska Commercial Company building in San Francisco and the Niebaum home on Pacific Avenue, full of the ghosts of relatives she had never known. Although she was part of all that, the man Niebaum was just a name to her. Even her great-grandaunt, Tante, was more symbol than real, and Tante had done much to shape the father Robin loved.

John Daniel had tried to impress on his daughters some of the notions Tante had instilled in him, but less forcefully. He had once told a wine critic visiting Inglenook, "Wines are like children, you know. No matter how much loving attention you give each one of them, some always turn out better than others. We've always followed a policy of gentle guidance rather than rigid regimentation in making our wines."

Robin's and Marky's childhoods had been a bit more complicated than that. The problems of the Daniel household were never discussed, the airing of such things being anathema to John.

The girls had both been sent off to Carmel every summer to play tennis at Pebble Beach; they had otherwise been provided with all the proper exposure. Robin had grown into a willowy blonde with her father's height and some of her mother's good looks. But the Daniels' privileged milieu grated on her. She and most of the people she knew went to the right schools, where they met more of the right people, and made the right marriages. Robin had come to think of this life as a series of horizontal planes: you performed the acceptable activities and received the anticipated rewards and moved on to the next horizontal plane, never going up or down. Not the least of those rewards was security and the avoidance of pain that supposedly came with observing the unwritten rules, for not overreaching and for not thinking too much about alternatives.

Marky — dark like her father, more restrained than her mother or Robin, very studious — attended Brigham Young University in Provo, Utah, for two years to satisfy Betty's demands, and then transferred to Stanford. She wanted to be a writer and studied under the literary critic Malcolm Cowley. After graduation she applied to the University of Edinburgh but did not know the required Latin and Greek and so went to France instead, to sort out her future. There she stayed for a time at the villa in Versailles owned by Betty's aunt. She decided to attend the Sorbonne.

In California, she had become engaged to James Smith, the scion of a wealthy Washington State family, owners of sawmills and other enterprises. Now he insisted that they marry first, and Marky agreed. The Daniels and the Smiths gathered in Rutherford for the ceremony; Marky did not go back to Paris after all. John Daniel hoped his new son-in-law would be interested in the wine business, that he might assist in the management of Inglenook and perhaps take it over someday. But his son-in-law was interested in making money. The idea of taking on an unwieldy, romantic, and generally ruinous enterprise like the Daniels' winery, about which he knew virtually nothing, had no appeal for Jim Smith.

He and Marky moved to Yakima, Washington, a physical and emotional haven in which she could write and, for once, be distanced from the unspoken demands of Daniel family life.

Betty's behavior, insufferable for all but her husband, began to affect him as well. She indulged in what her former friend, Fon Stralla, called dirty tricks: giving away the old leather flight jacket that John loved more than any other possession, telling rumors about the Sousas, who had practically raised her own children, in an attempt to get John to evict them. She tried to break up the friendship between John and Louie Stralla. Apparently Louie's attempts to introduce John to other women, however fruitless, were held against him by Betty, although she pretended still to be friendly with Fon.

Once Betty invited the Strallas to dinner and they arrived to find the house dark — another dirty trick. The Strallas let themselves in, as they often had in the past. Fon walked into the kitchen, where the maid told her that Mrs. Daniel was in bed. Just then Betty appeared on the stairs. "I don't feel well enough to eat dinner," she announced, and went back to her room.

As the Strallas were leaving, Fon saw the maid going up the stairs with a tray for Betty laden with food.

Despite the fights, the divorce, Betty's disappearances, and her railing against the winery, Robin still thought of her parents as the perfect couple, so strong was her belief in her father's cherished image of familial accord. John and Betty Daniel had to be exemplars of taste and decency.

Robin went to Stanford, too — his school. She came home many weekends, and John would slip her ten dollars as she was about to return to Palo Alto. Robin kept the illusion of her parents' perfection alive until Betty took to her bed and began to gain weight. She grew too fat to wear the fine clothes she had collected for thirty years; she became increasingly bitter. Finally Robin began to see her parents as something less than what she had imagined.

Betty's hypochondria was added to the growing list of personality defects. When she wasn't eating she was consuming pills. John continued to struggle for ideals that became more and more remote. He looked older. Inglenook was still losing money despite the fact that the wines were so popular they had to be allocated. Betty's vendetta against the winery continued. Then in the early 1960s George Deuer, the winemaker, decided to retire, placing an added burden on John. He had no sons to take over, and although Robin repeatedly expressed an interest in Inglenook, her father didn't think managing a winery was a suitable position for a woman. It was not one of the horizontal planes.

She went to work for the Bank of America in San Francisco. Napa Valley was a nice place to be from, she decided. She met a young architect from Denver, the product of a banking family with some financial problems. His name was Jon Lail and he had grown up in a mansion with a ballroom and a swimming pool on the ground floor. John Daniel did not approve of Lail. He thought him a mountain version of a surfer, too much interested in the out-of-doors. And architecture was a questionable profession in John Daniel's eyes.

Robin thought her father would eventually come around, and she married Jon. He was interested in the wine business, whereas John Daniel's other son-in-law had not been. But when Robin suggested to her father that he train Jon Lail to take over Inglenook, her father said, "I would give it to you first."

She was the only family member interested in Inglenook. John Daniel began to explain the family's financial affairs to her, reluctantly at first, then with increasing urgency. Robin discovered that the Daniels owned a great deal of real estate in Napa Valley, among other assets. She saw a contract Tante Niebaum had been forced to sign by Robin's grandfather, John Daniel, Sr., before he would let her raise his children, stipulating that Inglenook would be left to John and his sister. That shocked Robin. She wondered what sort of man would have exacted such a bargain, and what would have happened if her great-grandaunt had refused to sign and John Daniel had been allowed to construct a life of his own, out from under the yoke of Niebaum's legacy.

It never occurred to Robin that her father might simply dispose of Inglenook. Selling was simply not in the realm of possibility.

The valley in the mid-1960s had seen the limited success of outsiders like Lee Stewart, the McCreas, and Joe Heitz. More recently it had inspired the Davieses and the Winiarskis. But Napa was still a backwater and the wineries still questionable financial propositions. The idea of owning one appealed mostly to the irrational side of people with money to spend and a romantic vision of rural life where winemaking was more idyll than profession. Wineries and vineyards were not highly sought after, and the money they brought when they did sell was paltry compared to what those properties would bring in a few short years.

The first person to hear of it was Lou Gomberg, a wine prognosticator in San Francisco who published an industry report. Gomberg had a law degree and nine years experience as a newspaper reporter; he had worked for the Wine Institute and had known Ernest Gallo when he was just a peddler of cheap, sweet bulk wine. Gomberg knew the Cellas and Petri from the old days, and Louis Martini.

Gomberg had written a newsletter for something called the Academy of Master Winegrowers in the late fifties, and it was then that John Daniel had first called him up to explore, in strict confidence, the possibility of selling Inglenook. Gomberg could not have been more surprised. Daniel was the last person he expected to hear from, although in retrospect it made sense. Daniel was a different sort of man from most in the industry, not just ethnically but also temperamentally. John was unsuited to the push and shove of marketing. He didn't like to go out there and pitch, and he had problems at home. He asked Gomberg to keep his ears open.

A Beverly Hills banker made an inquiry on behalf of a customer wanting to buy a winery, but nothing came of it. Later, Gomberg got a call from a representative of a pharmaceutical entrepreneur, who was interested in acquiring such a property. Gomberg relayed the information to Daniel, who said, "Let me think about it." He did for a few months, and then said no, adding, "There's no hurry."

Then, in early 1964, he called Gomberg again; there was an urgency in Daniel's voice. He wanted to know if Gomberg was in touch with Louis Petri, founder of the huge cooperative United Vintners. Petri and his associate Larry Solari had expressed an interest in buying Inglenook. Gomberg assumed they had heard that John was looking for a buyer from Louie Stralla, a friend of Solari's as well as a close friend of Daniel's. Stralla had a way of showing up on the edge of deals. Although Daniel did not wish to sell to a giant like United Vintners, and hated cooperatives, he now badly wanted to sell.

Daniel had seen the rise of two big producers of quality wine, Almadén and Paul Masson. Even Beringer had surpassed Inglenook in production. John told Gomberg to pass the word to Petri that he was willing to talk.

The Petri family had been in the wine and cigar business — the twisted Italian *toscanos* — before Prohibition. They had sold grapes back east, using the Cellas as their agents. Together they fueled many a clandestine winery in the basements of big-city tenements, and made contacts through bootlegging that would continue to pay off. After Repeal, Angelo Petri got into winemaking in a big way. He made wine in two leased facilities in Napa, but most of the production came from the Central Valley. His son, Louis, bought four additional wine companies, including Italian Swiss Colony, before Gallo could buy it. He refitted a salvaged World War II tanker to transport two million gallons of wine east, in part to thwart the railroads' exorbitant freight rates. Seven times a year California wine left through the Golden Gate for a depot in Houston by way of the Panama Canal; from Houston the wine was shipped to Chicago and other cities. Once Petri almost lost two million gallons of bulk wine on the beach at San Francisco before tugs brought the disabled tanker to rest.

The Petri Wine Company became the largest California producer for a time and the only big one, other than Gallo, to market and promote table wine actively. Louis lumped all the different wineries into United Vintners, a cooperative that was nevertheless family-owned. He also helped organize a vineyardists' cooperative, Allied Grape Growers, and then in a Modesto motel room talked the members into buying him out for $24 million. He argued that the growers would then own their outlets — his wineries — and would not have to worry about having to sell to people like Ernest Gallo. Gallo, he said, married the growers when the industry was oversupplied, but refused to divorce them after grape prices rose again.

Petri also talked Allied Grape Growers into letting him stay on as chief executive officer of United Vintners after they had bought him out, a shrewd maneuver. He chose as president of United Vintners a tough-talking man with slicked-back hair, Larry Solari, who owned vineyards in Napa. Solari had helped create the Wine Advisory Board after Prohibition, but he had grown increasingly cynical about the wine business. He had no respect for Petri or the other characters in the bulk end; he called them "the money grabbers" but worked for them anyway.

Petri was *the* operator — hotel owner, real estate maven, grape grower, full-time businessman. He held what was known as the Italian seat on the board of the Bank of America, which was also the agricultural seat. His family was strictly North Beach: his grandfather had lived on Telegraph Hill in the old days; Petri's father had never cleaned up his English, but Louis had gone to medical school for a time. He fell in love with one of the Cella girls, married her, and they moved up in San Francisco society together, attending the opera and the charity balls.

Short, freckled, and balding, Petri reveled in the notions of himself as golfer and yachtsman, but what he really liked was making deals. He knew that Ernest Gallo would buy Inglenook if he got the chance. Petri was something Gallo could never be, but he was no John Daniel. Acquiring Inglenook would be more than economic success for him; it would top even the Allied deal, not in money but in prestige.

Louis Petri and John Daniel met for lunch at the Villa Taverna in San Francisco; one of the people who saw them together was Walter Sullivan, the son-in-law of Mme. de Pins, owner of neighboring Beaulieu Vineyard. Sullivan went home and told his wife, "You won't believe this, but John is selling Inglenook."

She laughed at him. John Daniel would never sell — the idea was ludicrous. She told her mother and they both laughed at Sullivan. But he was in the real estate business and could recognize a deal when he saw one, and he *knew*.

The story broke in April 1964. By then, some in the valley had heard that Inglenook was being sold, but few believed it. The announcement, in *Wines and Vines,* shocked and even angered people. The amount of money Inglenook had brought was not disclosed, only that the winery and some vineyards along the access road were included in the sale. Inglenook was not just another Napa Valley winery; it was a château, the exemplar of tradition and purpose. Those who knew John understood why he was selling. Rehabilitation was necessary and very expensive; decent return on the investment lay many years in the future; the winemaker, George Deuer, was leaving. But behind these protestations lay unhappy circumstances that no amount of capital and energy could alter. John was the most decent man in the business, people said; the fact that he was selling out inspired tremors of apprehension among those remaining.

Gomberg and other wine journalists shook their heads. John was not just decent, he was utterly likable even to the most hard-nosed. They didn't fault him for his air of *noblesse oblige,* or even for selling out to Petri and Solari. If they had a criticism it was that John lacked imagination. He seemed bound up in some vision few ordinary wine drinkers could understand, and unwilling to compromise for the sake of greater exposure and sales. Now Inglenook belonged to United Vintners, itself part of Allied Grape Growers. Old Niebaum's dream was just another relatively insignificant piece of a huge cooperative.

At best, John had handed over the keys to a couple of promoters. At worst, he had let the barbarians into the valley.

The sale went through a month later. Solari announced that Daniel was being retained as a consultant and that no rapid expansion was planned for Inglenook. Solari's words dripped with concern for stability, tradition, excellence. He had a four-part plan, he said. Estate bottling — wines made entirely from grapes grown on either Inglenook or Daniel property — would continue. So would vintage dating. The designation of Napa Valley as the origin of all the grapes would still appear on every Inglenook label, automatically limiting rapid expansion, assuring quality. Only varietal wines — those identified by grape variety, rather than cheap generics — would be sold. Solari called Inglenook "the Tiffany of the California wine industry."

Inglenook had been sold for $1.2 million. A few weeks later Lou Gomberg received a letter from Daniel. He opened it and a check fell onto his desk made out for $37,000. Gomberg had not expected to be paid and telephoned Daniel and told him the check wasn't necessary. Daniel told him he was entitled to the fee.

ᏸ

Rafael Rodriguez was typical of those in the valley who were overtaken by the event. Although Rafael worked for Inglenook, he and other employees there were not forewarned. Then came the rumor at Inglenook that the workers would all be fired and replaced by people brought in by the new management.

Rafael had married again — the daughter of migrant pickers, named Domitila but known as Tila. They had two daughters of their own, and this was no time to lose his job and his house. But he had no access to the people running Inglenook. He wasn't even sure who these people might be. There was nothing for him to do but wait and watch.

Some workers did leave, and new faces appeared. The old order slipped away, and many tasks went undone. George Deuer, always stubborn, hung on as winemaker for a bit longer; he and Rafael were among the estate's oldest employees. Rafael had always avoided Deuer, but now he felt that he had no choice but to approach him, to see if he could discover what lay ahead. Rafael asked if Deuer thought he would be able to keep his job. To Rafael's surprise, Deuer asked him if he thought he could manage the entire vineyard.

Rafael said yes.

"The place is yours," Deuer told him.

Rafael couldn't believe it. Vineyard and property managers were usually chosen from the owner's family or, lately, from the university, not from the fields.

He went home to the little house near the Niebaum stable and told Tila of Deuer's offer. She was as stunned as Rafael. She asked if he could handle the job, and where they would live. Rafael told her that Sousa had moved out of the little clapboard house next to the winery and that Deuer had offered the house to the Rodriguezes. It was a real house, one of the prettiest in the valley. This rude German, Fast-hand George, who had often shouted, "You damn Mexicans!" and terrorized the winery staff, had even offered to lend the Rodriguezes his pickup to move their belongings.

10

THE VALLEY IN 1967 remained a quilt of mostly small ranches where walnuts, prunes, and cattle competed with grapes. Rural families would halve parcels to provide a plot for a son or daughter, or quarter them for grandchildren. Individual holdings were shrinking and houses appearing in obvious conflict with the business of the valley, which was growing things. Some people broke up their land into acre parcels and built cheap bungalows and "ranchettes" to sell. Anyone looking closely at the valley while thinking about these things could see a real danger. Some were keenly aware of what was being done to suburban communities down on the peninsula south of San Francisco, where ticky-tacky little houses had inspired the song made famous by Pete Seeger. Walnut Grove, Fremont, and other once-rural towns now looked just the same. From Santa Clara Valley came the phrase "Silicon Valley," ringing with scientific achievement but also with an incipient environmental disaster.

One person who did not want that to happen in Napa Valley was Dorothy Erskine, who lived in San Francisco but who owned a house in the valley. Dorothy was well off and committed to preservation of the natural environment, and had helped start an organization called People for Open Space. She worked persistently but subtly for her cause. Dorothy Erskine would have a dinner party, and you would go and have a good time, and when you left you would have a job.

While Jack and Jamie Davies worked to perfect the second vintage of Schramsberg, they were invited to dinner at Dorothy Erskine's house. They went, and when they left Jack was the head of a citizens' committee for the creation of something called an agricultural preserve. Jack had never been involved in causes and didn't care to be. He knew next to nothing about agriculture and less about politics. The demands of making sparkling wine, seeing to his vineyard, and positioning Schramsberg in good restaurants and wine shops kept him busy. But Dorothy Erskine made him see differently. Before, winemaking had seemed an isolated craft, pursued on but almost indifferent to the land. But now Jack realized that winemaking and the land were inextricably linked.

This effort, this unexpected new enterprise, would greatly affect their chosen land. It was destined to alter Napa Valley so profoundly that even the most imaginative of its residents could only dimly perceive its importance.

Jack drove around the valley talking up the idea of an ag preserve zone — legal protection for productive land. It would mean that no building could be put up on less than twenty acres. Most winery owners liked the idea. It didn't occur to the proponents that their cause would split the valley like a fault line, that they would be called city slickers and worse, and that Jack Davies and others like him might well lose their front teeth while pursuing it.

Lowell Eddington sold a little real estate, but mostly he liked working on county advisory boards. He had served as one of the five county supervisors years back, when he worried, as a lot of people did, about Napa's tax base. Basalt Rock and Kaiser Steel about summed up the valley's industry. Every time a foundation went in for a new house in the valley, there was more demand for services and less productive land to pay for them. The county was slowly digging its own grave.

When Lowell got off the board of supervisors, he helped form a taxpayers' association to protect the rural north end of the valley. A loose coalition of landowners, monied weekenders, and a preservationist or two formed Upper Napa Valley Associates. With some exceptions they hailed neither from the old Boring Crowd nor from the Exciting Wave. Many were retirees, including a Disney cartoonist who feared that Los Angelean pavement might follow him all the way to Calistoga. There was a retired state parks official, and some San Francisco money.

Lowell served as director of UNVA, and they all met at the El Real Restaurant in Rutherford. He would set up a blackboard and chalk out a few goals, like improving the tax base. Agriculture had to be the answer: Napa had the soil and the climate for growing the best grapes in the state. Increasingly, winemaking know-how meant a superior product that the world would buy. Without the land there would be no grapes, and so the land had to be protected.

That was the argument, and the El Real became the site of UNVA dinners, nothing fancy — highballs, roast beef, and baked potatoes in tinfoil, and none of the social climbing that came later. The members had a straightforward good time. Vera Petersen, from a third-generation Napa family, wore a corsage and met people at the door. Once an upended bowl of sour cream landed on her head, but Vera was a good sport and covered it with a napkin and kept talking about conservation.

The California Land Conservation Act, better known as the Williamson Act, was named for the state senator and sponsor. The act allowed counties to tax agricultural land at a lower rate than adjacent residential areas. In other words, the land was to be assessed according to the return on the land, not at market value. To qualify, the owners had to agree not to develop their land for at least ten years, a stringent requirement but still the best alternative to residential development. Built into such a contract was the prohibition on subdividing of family plots. Everyone agreed that would be tricky.

The advocates moved methodically, talking to the Napa County Planning Commission — five citizens appointed by the supervisors to review building and land-use requests — and to individual supervisors. They sought out the county farm advisor. The Agricultural Extension Service rep brought in two economists to discuss the theoretical and real possibilities of an ag preserve. Senator Williamson came all the way to St. Helena from Sacramento to explain how his law would work, and talked about soils and productivity and what would be "the highest and best use of the land." Few others in the county paid attention in the beginning. An agricultural zone was a pipe dream.

The strategy sessions for the conservationist group sometimes took place in the back of the Sweet Shop in St. Helena, home of the Yummy (grilled cheese and deviled egg). On most days a forward table by the door was occupied by the local power structure: Paul Alexander, manager of the St. Helena branch of the Bank of America; John Daniel, former owner of Inglenook and a bank board member; and Louie Stralla, an extrovert with a shadowy past. Lowell Eddington knew them all.

Alexander's father had run the bank before him. If Alexander believed in your business scheme — in your winery, for instance — you got a loan. If not, your prospects for starting up and eventual success were greatly diminished — in most cases, nonexistent. Almost everybody was a customer of the B of A, from Daniel, at the apex of up-valley society, to a bleached blonde who had run an illicit but popular establishment beyond the Pope Street Bridge in St. Helena known as the Pecker Parlor. Every Monday morning she had arrived at the bank with a cloth sack full of bills to be deposited. Paul Alexander would joke with her while patting one of her more marketable commodities.

Daniel had exercised a subtle but pervasive influence over who was admitted to the Napa Valley Vintners Association, and who received a loan from Paul Alexander. Louie Stralla was the unlikely member of the Sweet Shop threesome. He always hailed Lowell, who would stop by the power table. Stralla would say, "Join us. You don't want to eat with a bunch of women and . . ." He didn't know exactly what to call the men.

Lowell would laugh about it later. He and his friends were hatching a plot under the noses of the very men who would most oppose it.

The plan for the ag preserve could not have gone forward without the support of politicians like Dewey Anderson. One of the five members of the Napa County Board of Supervisors. Dewey lived within a few hundred feet of where he grew up, just outside the city limits of Napa. His wife, Joyce, had urged him to run for the board of supervisors and when he did, and won, he had to sell his auto repair shop to handle the county's work.

Dewey Anderson thought of himself as a funny bird: a Republican, a believer in individual rights, and a skeptic when it came to big government. He was dead set against accepting federal grants, and with them federal dictates, but when it came to development in the valley, his politics changed. He believed in protecting the home turf from outside shysters.

The idea of an agricultural preserve had been around for a while. To Dewey, it still sounded radical. The former director of the Planning Commission had proposed it to the board before Dewey's time and the board had laughed at him. They weren't laughing anymore. The Williamson Act had given the idea legitimacy and some influential backers, including Felix Vanderschoot, presently chairman of the Planning Commission. Felix was in the car business too, and was no more likely to go for radical notions than Dewey. His role in drafting the county's first General Plan and the zoning and subdivision regulations had taught Felix something about the politics of development.

A big landowner and grape grower on the Planning Commission, Andy Pelissa, liked the ag preserve concept and was willing to say so. Along with Dewey and Felix Vanderschoot, Andy thought there ought to be limits to what a person could do to his surroundings.

Al Harberger, the county administrator, got some information from the Agricultural Extension Service. He talked to Louis Martini, son of the founder, a giant of a man, better known as Louis Peter. He was slow to join the movement, but one night during a public meeting on the subject, Louis Peter raised himself up to full height and announced that he was in favor of the ag preserve. Most of the new vintners wanted it and many worked for it, but not all.

So there were many people involved. Harberger seized on the ag preserve as an opportunity to make his mark and as a chance to set an example. Nothing existed in California — in the United States — like what they were discussing for Napa Valley. Not only would agricultural land be assessed at a lower rate, but actual zoning laws would have to be enacted preventing building on less than twenty acres in the rural areas. Some people were talking about a forty-acre minimum. Developers, and people wanting to sell to them, complained. The ag preserve contradicted the expansion fanfare heard all around the Bay Area, all over the state.

The county tax assessor, George Abate (pronounced A-*bate*-ee), the man who had to make all this pay, was a secret believer in the plan. That impressed Dewey Anderson. Abate's father had made wine; he loved the smell of grapes fermenting. But he was not about to get himself caught out on a fiscal limb for sentimental reasons. He was predicting that agriculture — particularly grapes, and wine — would provide a better tax base than development. Abate would not say that the creation of an ag preserve would lower taxes. He would say that taxes wouldn't go up *as much* with the ag preserve as they would without it.

Dewey knew that the tax assessor, the county administrator, the Planning Commission, and the environmentalists could make all the recommendations they wanted, but in the end it was the five supervisors who had to say yea or nay. They made the laws. Fortunately they were all friends and all but one Republicans. They were abalone divers and deer hunters. They partied together with their wives and went to conventions together. They regularly had lunch as a group at the Grapevine Inn in Yountville, taking along Harberger, the county engineer, the county health director, and maybe the reporter for the *Napa Register*. They wanted a place where they could shoot the breeze without being heckled, and there they talked about soil samples and wholly owned parcels and eventually came up with twenty-five thousand acres suitable to set aside as an ag preserve, which happened to be most of the valley floor. There would be a lot of gerrymandering around the towns, and transitional zones, but basically it looked doable to Dewey.

First the Planning Commission had to conduct public hearings and take the initial heat. Everyone knew that, but then the press got hold of the story, and no one was prepared for the intensity of the public reaction. At a community clubhouse north of Napa city, men stood up and shouted about the loss of their rights. Felix Vanderschoot had to adjourn that meeting briefly to let the hotheads cool off. And that was just the beginning. So great was the pressure that no one on the board escaped unmarked: more than a year later Dewey would go deer hunting in Sonoma County, shoot a big buck, and be skinning it out when he vomited blood.

Jack Davies drove down Highway 29, turned onto a dirt road, got out of his car, and explained to the owner of the property why the idea of an agricultural preserve was a good one and why he ought to be for it. Then he got back into his car and headed on down the highway, noticing in his rearview mirror that the long, chromed wonder driven by Louie Stralla turned onto the road he had just left.

Later, Jack heard that Stralla had told the same property owner that he would lose his land if the ag preserve went through, and that the people pushing it were outsiders — city people and some lying left-wing sons of bitches. The incident was repeated many times. Stralla didn't understand that the preserve would create scarcity, and that would increase land values, not decrease them. He and his friends viewed the notion of an ag preserve as a personal affront.

Al Harberger, the county administrator, also out on the road selling the cause, told Jack, "They'll hurt you if they can. If you owe money, they'll put the pressure on."

Fortunately Jack didn't owe money in the valley, but he felt another kind of pressure, at the post office, the gas station, the community center. "There's that city boy," someone would say. "Know what he wants to do?"

Schramsberg had no scale with which to weigh grapes, and when Jack took his loads to the little St. Helena co-op to get them weighed, the men gave him a hard time. He was told to move the truck on and off the scales, and finally banished.

The public hearings were worse — movable feasts of resentment. Men stood outside community halls and high schools in small groups and commented on the morals and motivations of UNVA members and others working for the ag preserve. Some small landholders dreamed of a real estate bonanza to rescue them from grape growing, a profession that had never been very profitable and probably never would be. If Napa had a prosperous future, they said, it was as a bedroom community for San Francisco, and only a fool, or worse, would tie up the land in some doomed government scheme.

Others simply wanted to subdivide and build homes for their children, and their anger radiated. Eleanor McCrea felt it. She feared for her physical well-being but attended the hearings anyway.

Jack thought the board of supervisors believed in the ag preserve but needed someone to make a public case for it. He and his friends tracked down every statistic they could find on grapes in Napa Valley. They used a dentist's office for a time as headquarters. People donated the use of telephones and a mimeograph machine. Opponents had charged that no good data existed — a tactic for delaying a decision, and delay meant loss of momentum. Tom May, the owner of Martha's Vineyard, set a box of papers on the table at one public forum and read lengthy statistics about grape production and the prospects for the wine industry, the contributions of grape growing to the economy, all facts that made an impression.

Lowell Eddington had to debate John Daniel and Louie Stralla on television and he worried about that. He asked big Louis Peter Martini to go to the San Francisco studio with him. There were other locals in favor of the ag preserve but few as physically imposing as Martini, who agreed to go. Lowell telephoned the moderator, Caspar Weinberger, a friend, and said, "Cap, if one of those guys gets hold of the microphone, we'll never get it back."

Weinberger assured Lowell that he could interrupt the proceedings at any time: "Just give me the sign."

On television, the proponents made a good case. After the debate, Daniel and Stralla were very angry, and Lowell was glad to have Martini at his side.

Later, Lowell received a call from Paul Alexander at the Bank of America in St. Helena; he went to see him. Alexander threw a letter onto his desk endorsing the ag preserve which had been signed by Lowell and the others, and said, "I'm against this thing." Alexander was accustomed to having his way, and Lowell was glad he did his banking elsewhere.

Things came to a head at the supervisors hearing held in the St. Helena grammar school in that very important year, 1968. Supporters and adversaries sat together, waiting their turn to speak. The two Galleron brothers, old-time growers and the epitome of hard-working, unprivileged, unexciting, and unpretentious farmers, also epitomized the split in the valley. One Galleron stood up and denounced the ag preserve as destructive of private property. The other stood up and praised the idea as a means of keeping productive land out of the grip of speculators and suburbanites.

No one matched the passion of John Daniel, whose granduncle had built Inglenook almost a century before. Daniel had brought a lawyer with him, prepared to fight. Daniel cast about for ways to convey his objections and his outrage. Decorum — the Daniel hallmark — gradually dissolved in a tide of rising vituperation, surprising those who knew him. Dewey Anderson had the impression that Daniel really believed the government sought to confiscate his land, that this would be the end of life as the valley had known it.

Daniel said he didn't believe that the county wanted to protect the valley and the little guy growing a few grapes and making a little wine. Why, he demanded, should he give up his property rights in the interest of some unknown, future third party — in other words, posterity? If the government wanted to control his land, why shouldn't the government fully compensate him? The tax break was a sham, he concluded, and the restrictions on subdividing immoral.

George Abate had to watch himself. As tax assessor he couldn't afford to appear partisan. He had held that job for five very interesting years; he had seen the jump in land values after passage of Assembly Bill 80 in Sacramento, which required all properties to be assessed on 25 percent of market value. Abate knew that would mean the demise of the cow-and-calf outfits — the small working ranches — and probably the end of some prune and walnut operations. Only grapes, in Abate's opinion, had a chance of producing enough income to hang on as "the highest and best use of the land," meaning the most economical.

If Abate had to apply Assembly Bill 80 in one year, it would be traumatic; fortunately there was some leeway. When the movement for the ag preserve came along he saw a way to minimize the jump in assessments.

Al Harberger was so determined to get the ag preserve passed that he spent little time at home, and he and his wife would eventually go their separate ways. Al had latched on to the idea of the ag preserve after the rep from the Extension Service had pointed out some benefits for the county. Big corporations were moving in all over California, buying huge parcels and throwing up cluster-type housing with golf courses and swimming pools. Not one of the state's fifty-eight counties was immune. The assessors had to deal with this, and Abate had gone to Harberger, saying, "Al, we have to control the land."

Al knew that meant controlling development, that the county needed a way to keep farming profitable and to thwart the one-acre bungalow pox. And that meant strong restrictive zoning within the thirty thousand acres on the valley floor. Abate was glad that Harberger and the supervisors liked the preserve plan. It would not make Abate popular if it passed, but it would ease the burden of accelerating assessments.

He had to revalue the land anyway, because the state was on his back, sampling him for intercounty and intracounty equalization. They sapped you one year and then two years down the road they "trended" you. Each county had to keep up. If it hadn't been for this statewide equalization, Napa could have gone on growing anything — cows, prunes, hay, or nothing at all — until the residential real estate boom caught up with it.

Now assessments were going up and the supervisors were getting calls from their constituents: Who is this goddamn assessor who's doubling our tax bill? Well, if the ag preserve didn't pass, the assessments were going to go up a hell of a lot faster! That was the message politicians would understand.

•

Abate remembered some bureaucrat from Sacramento coming into his office and asking how much it would cost to get a right-of-way for a sewer and water line to run from Calistoga to Napa city. Somebody had big plans for residential development. Abate always wished he had said, "That's asinine. Who the hell sent you here?" But he hadn't.

What the county needed was a forty-acre minimum lot, but people were screaming about that at the hearings, so the proponents backed off to twenty acres. Abate wanted to see the land preserved, but preservation wasn't his job, tax assessment was. His father had immigrated to this peaceful rural valley from Italy and Abate did not want to see it turn into another San Jose. He thought grapes could support people; only grapes could compete with houses. Not really compete, maybe, but prove profitable enough to provide a real tax base.

George Abate looked at "the highest and best use of the land" philosophically. The highest and best use was not necessarily what brought in the most money — something he couldn't admit when he traveled around the county. Assessments were going up, he told people. Farmers could get relief by entering into a contractual agreement with the state, under the Williamson Act, not to develop their land for ten years.

Sometimes George Abate and Al Harberger made the pitch together. Mostly they talked about budgets. They knew that if the ag preserve passed and a lot of people signed agricultural contracts, and then the tax revenues didn't come up to expectations, it would be Abate's and Harberger's asses. Then the pressure to spot-zone, or to change the zoning altogether, would be irresistible, and the battle would be lost.

They never talked about it like that. The consensus among county officials was implicit, never stated, which in later years amazed Abate. They were hoping to put this thing together and make it legal, but before it became legal it was, well, moral.

The supervisor who took the most heat was Julius Caiocca, whose district included St. Helena. His family owned the grocery next to the bank, where every day old man Caiocca could be seen sweeping the pavement in his apron and waving to passers-by. "Juli" Caiocca sold insurance and could expect to see his business evaporate if he voted for the preserve. Juli's constituency included Daniel, Stralla, and Paul Alexander. The proponents pushed, the opponents threatened, and Juli — so far undeclared — sat nervously on the edge as the vote approached. At the hearings his hands shook, and he read from the material set before him with a quavering voice.

The vote should have taken place in St. Helena but opponents of the preserve charged that another supervisor had missed a hearing and so should disqualify himself. There was a short delay. The ag preserve needed three votes, a majority of the five supers on the board, and the opposition hoped that by eliminating one favorable vote they might get a tie and be able to further delay action until after the next election, when they hoped to turn it around. Dewey Anderson knew that the valley would not again have a board of supervisors and a Planning Commission willing to take the heat and possibly vote for something that raised such colossal hackles. Not in his lifetime, and maybe never.

When the supervisors convened for the vote in the Napa City Hall, Daniel, Stralla, and some other men circled Juli Caiocca outside, and Stralla wagged a finger in Caiocca's face. Dewey Anderson didn't have to hear the conversation to know that Juli was in trouble.

The meeting convened and Dewey felt a tightness in his own stomach as he cast his vote for the ag preserve. He listened as others did the same. When it came time for Caiocca's decision he was trembling and pasty-faced. He said, "Nobody's gonna shake a finger at me," and voted yea.

That made it unanimous. Outside, Stralla shoved Caiocca up against a wall. Tempers ran high; some men stood close to real violence. The lawyer working against the ag preserve told Felix Vanderschoot that three votes and thirty days would change everything. The lawyer, Daniel, and the others intended to elect three new supervisors and throw out the Planning Commission *and* the ag preserve. "In twenty years," he said, "nobody will even remember this."

In fact, in twenty years the fight would still be going on, with different antagonists. The ag preserve would prove to be one of the most important things to have happened to Napa Valley, as important in its way as the phylloxera epidemic and Prohibition, except that its effects were positive. It would outlast that lawyer and profoundly affect the natural and political landscape for the remainder of the century.

II

THE VOW TO maintain the integrity of Inglenook, made by its purchasers, United Vintners, meant nothing. The actual winemaking was moved to a plant in Oakville and the Rutherford property used only for storage and for impressing tourists. Production shot up, while the quality of Inglenook wines performed a dismaying downward arabesque. Larry Solari introduced a line of cheap generic wines made from Central Valley grapes which was wretched in the critics' eyes and a great threat to Inglenook's long-standing reputation.

When John Daniel bitterly objected, Solari told him, "We are going to show you how to sell, baby."

Ironically, one of the biggest sellers was Navalle, a rosé John had introduced as an afterthought while he still owned the winery, as a means of using up excess Gamay Beaujolais grapes. He named the wine after the creek on the property that Niebuam had cherished, having had the banks reinforced with elaborate stonework done by Chinese laborers. John had intended the wine Navalle to be made in small quantities, but Solari produced rivers of it, using Central Valley grapes and equating Navalle, and Inglenook, in the public mind with inexpensive, slightly sweet pink wine. This drove the now powerless John Daniel wild.

Within two years he had retired as consultant. Shortly after that he heard that United Vintners — including his beloved Inglenook — had been sold to Heublein, the liquor conglomerate.

John's cramped office at the top of the stairs in the house on Niebaum Lane contained an old-fashioned desk and a number of filing cabinets. Two were devoted to nothing but the agricultural preserve. John fought its creation with all the energy he had previously directed toward Inglenook; the subsequent lawsuit brought by him and a few allies against the county was lost, but he still could not accept the reality of the ag preserve. In his view it was one step removed from land reform by government fiat, without regard for the individual's rights. One of his concerns was the third- and fourth-generation families in the valley who would not be able to pass land on to their heirs because they did not own enough of it to subdivide. And he felt that he had lost control of his family's legacy.

Fewer and fewer people listened to his arguments. The issue of the ag preserve separated him from other vintners who had favored the restraints on development; many had already lost sympathy with John for selling Inglenook. He resigned from the various boards of organizations concerned with wine that he served on, which was tolerable, but when he was dropped from the roster of the Napa Valley Vintners Association, John resented it. He had been a founding member and assumed he would be given some sort of emeritus standing. But the rules called for members to be producers, and although John still owned extensive vineyards, he made and sold no wine. So the man who had once heavily influenced admission to the Vintners, who had helped determine what direction the organization took and the face the valley showed the world, was himself rejected. He had no profession and no forum, and he seemed to those who knew him like a ship without a rudder.

A friend encountering John in early 1970, at a promotional dinner at the Grapevine Inn, said, "This is great, eh? Good food, good wine."

John replied, "There's more to life than that."

The friend knew that something was seriously amiss.

Hanns Kornell and his wife, Marilouise, met John at another function, and they talked awhile. On the way home, Marilouise wept silently for John. She had known and respected him for years and he now seemed utterly lost. When she turned to her husband, she saw that his face, too, was streaked with tears.

The Strallas worried about John: his confidence had evaporated. On Louie's increasingly rare visits to the Daniel house, he found his old friend distraught, wracked by doubts and jealousies that had lain dormant for years. Sometimes he seemed irrational, and once he told Louie he had to get rid of his airplane because he was penniless. Louie assured him that this wasn't true. John's sister was at that moment teetering on the edge of bankruptcy, and John felt responsible for her, and increasingly vulnerable.

Fon and Louie suspected that Betty taunted John with references to her former liaisons. He was being treated for high blood pressure at the clinic down at Stanford and taking heavy medication for it. Fon worried about that, knowing that Betty had her own suitcase full of pills.

Robin attended to her father as best she could from the distance of Mill Valley, with frequent visits to Rutherford. Five years after the sale she still had trouble believing that Inglenook was no longer in the family. It had simply never occurred to her to ask her father not to sell the winery, and she wondered what would have happened if she had asked.

Her husband suggested that they move to the valley and get involved in the life there. "Why?" Robin asked. "Inglenook was the best, and it's gone. You can't just start without a building, without history."

Jon Lail said, "I want to do it anyway."

They went to Lake Tahoe over the weekend to discuss it. Robin sat on a rock next to deep, cold, clear water while John sat on another rock. Was it possible to buy Inglenook? she asked. Would Heublein get tired of owning it before Inglenook's reputation was thoroughly destroyed? Was it possible to buy just the Inglenook name? Was there any point in even talking about these things?

Yes, said Jon. There was a point.

Robin went back to Mill Valley determined to raise the subject with her father and to work out some brave new plan. They had been home only a short time when she received a telephone call from an aunt in St. Helena with terrible news.

Marky Smith, in Yakima, had talked to her father by telephone the week before; it was like talking to a complete stranger. The problem, she knew, was the medication. John Daniel didn't have high blood pressure, in her opinion. He had always been nervous around doctors, and when he went for a checkup his heart raced. During one such visit the doctor had left the device on his arm after determining that his blood pressure was too high, only to discover a few minutes later that it had returned to normal. But he was given the medication anyway.

Then his doctor took him off that prescription and put him on a powerful stimulant, to fight the depression. That medicine was so strong it made his legs tremble.

Marky was walking down a street in Yakima when her husband drove up. She got into the car with him, and he told her that her father was dead.

She said instinctively, "He's a suicide."

What followed would always be vivid in Robin's mind, dominated by the desperate sense of loss, the race north to Rutherford, the struggle with her mother, the flood of detail that robbed her of grieving. She found herself helping others in *their* grief while it was her father who lay in state in the funeral home in St. Helena.

Robin, now thirty, felt she had no time to react, unconsciously behaving as John Daniel would have wanted her to — responsibly, soberly, gripped by the demands of the moment, and, in the end, unable even to cry. It would take her a long time to get over that.

John Daniel had reportedly died of a heart attack. But a large dose of barbiturates was discovered in his body, and the county coroner ruled that he had administered it himself. He really died, Robin knew, from the weight of too much nobility and too many secrets. She blamed him for nothing but knew he blamed himself. That was the source of her own, greater unhappiness. Her father would consider the manner of his death a negation of everything he had accomplished in life, when in fact he was not himself when it occurred. Robin loved him, and so did everyone who knew him. His work and effort to maintain certain ideals would survive him. But John Daniel would not have accepted this explanation, and he would have hated the publicity.

The *Napa Register* described Daniel as a "staunch opponent of the agricultural preserve on the valley floor, and the third generation family member to operate the historical, stone Inglenook winery." The writer went on to say that Daniel, "a well-known vintner and aviator, devoted his entire lifetime to improving the quality of the wines, which are widely known throughout the world. . . . The vintner died in his sleep at the family home."

The circumstances of his death, as it turned out, were not made public. A few people knew, and others suspected, that much more lay behind the standard obituary, but the unspoken support that often obscured discord and unhappiness in the valley made itself felt again. There the question remained, unanswered because it was never posed, overshadowed by the genuine shock and sadness his death brought on.

Coming down from Yakima, Marky wept for her father. It was difficult for anyone to live in the world when that figure became an anachronism. John Daniel took personal responsibility for all that had happened to him and to Inglenook; he made no excuses. The buck stopped with him. He had a social conscience and felt that people in the valley had, with the creation of the ag preserve, lost control of their land and their lives, and so had he.

The weight of his death was more than she thought she could bear. She had always told herself, in times of depression and emotional distress, If Daddy can do it, I can do it. Now, it seemed, Daddy couldn't do it.

Marky blamed the medication: John Daniel was not the man who had committed suicide, but someone created by the pills the doctors had prescribed. She blamed her mother for not paying enough attention to her father.

Both she and Robin were surprised by Betty's composure when they arrived in Rutherford. She rose to the occasion as the wife of John Daniel might be expected to do; both daughters were grateful for that, at least. They fought with Betty over one thing only: the viewing of their father's body. Betty insisted that they go to the funeral home while the casket lay open; the young women refused. The argument was acrimonious and a foreshadowing of what was to come, but then the three of them moved shoulder to shoulder in the final outward show of family unity.

Marky went to the cemetery before the funeral. She followed the gravel walkway past the mausoleums where so many Italians lay stacked in marble honeycombs and into the shade of the big conifers. There, more of Napa's diverse cultural history was carved in stone, some simply and others ornately, verses and brief statements about death behind rusting iron fences and vases of dry flowers. It was July, and hot. Her father's grave had been dug, and the sight of raw earth and the severed roots drove home her own mortality.

Rafael had seen the cars driving back and forth from the Daniel house. Later, he heard that John Daniel had died. He had not known Daniel well, despite the fact that he had lived on his property for years and had taken many orders from him indirectly. Daniel's death had about it the same quality that surrounded his life, Rafael thought. Daniel had always been composed, considerate, even generous, but had maintained a distance that Rafael found unbridgeable.

He put on a suit and tie and went to the funeral in St. Helena. Outside the church, he saw Mrs. Daniel and the girls in a large car. He stood for a moment on the pavement, surrounded by other mourners. He wanted to say a few words of appreciation and condolence but in the end said nothing at all.

⁕

Robin found some consolation in the crowd and the obvious sorrow it embodied. Then she overheard a young Heublein executive say that his company intended to buy the old Daniel house, to complete the corporate package. She thought, Please not here. Not now.

The aftermath of the funeral exceeded it not in pain but in emotional wreckage. Betty transformed herself into what Robin thought of as the true Mrs. John Daniel. Thwarted for years, at least in her own mind, by convention, leftover Niebaum probity, and neo-Victorian restraint, Betty began to shed property along with those few personal inhibitions that had somehow endured.

There had been many wills drawn up over the years; the most recent, signed by Daniel shortly before his death, shocked Robin and Marky. They had always been told that the house and possessions would go to them and their children. They expected these and other specific bequests to be spelled out in the will, but they weren't. Betty was the inheritor, and Betty wanted to sell everything. She told the girls that the property and the responsibility for it had ground her husband down and finally killed him. It wasn't going to kill her.

Robin had been designated trustee. A struggle developed between her and the bankers and lawyers in San Francisco who had drawn up the new will. Robin realized that there would be nothing left if Betty had her way.

Her aunt called shortly after the funeral to tell Robin that Betty was giving away all the family possessions. Robin rushed north to the valley, to find Betty's relatives from the Bay Area carrying furniture out of the house and digging up shrubbery. Cars were parked crazily on the broad lawn beneath the ancient oaks, U-Hauls backed up to the steps.

Robin and Marky protested but found they had no legal ground to stand on. Betty was the survivor, armed with the new will and driven by her anger at John Daniel for doing what he had done. The girls watched the objects they had grown up with and adored disappear, sold or given away. They came to think of it as Betty's demolition derby. Marky saw it as final proof that her mother had loved her father and so resented his passing that she inflicted her rage on what was left behind.

Betty was to sell the house as well, she announced; there was nothing the girls could do about it. She sold it not to Heublein but to a couple who intended to develop the mountainside. Then, by Robin's reckoning, Betty went through $4 million in seventeen months. While disposing of heirlooms, she bought continuously from catalogues — jewelry, clothes, assorted junk. She went on a cruise. She bought land and a house in New Zealand. Betty intended to move there and at long last become the person she was meant to be.

At one point she was about to give away Rutherford International to a furniture mover who had been nice to her. Only Robin's entreaties prevented the loss of one more piece of the family's past.

Marky wrote her mother an impassioned letter asking that 240 acres somewhere be spared and left to her and Robin, so they might have something to leave to the four grandchildren. One parcel was the Napanook vineyard in Yountville that Daniel had purchased from Stralla back in 1947. Napanook lay over deep aquifers and produced quality fruit without irrigation.

The vineyard seemed important to Robin, in real as well as sentimental terms. She wrote to the lawyers suggesting that 200 acres be assigned to her and Marky, with 40 acres each going to their children. They refused. But Robin as trustee had influence, and she continued to fight for Napanook.

Marky bought for $350 a cut crystal bowl from her parents' house that an antiques dealer had bought from Betty for $50. Robin went to the house on Niebaum Lane with the express intention of taking *something*, whether or not her mother approved. By then the house was almost bare. In the kitchen Robin found an old clock with a cracked face, not particularly valuable, and ugly — a thing, in fact, she had always disliked — but she took it anyway. As she was walking out with the clock under one arm, it chimed.

Betty appeared at the head of the stairs in a kimono and demanded to know what Robin was doing.

"Nothing, Mother," she said, gently setting the clock down.

⟋⟍

Daniel's death was harder on Louie Stralla than the death of his own brother had been. "There'll never be another John," Louie kept telling Fon.

Several times a week he drove out Kearny Street in St. Helena to the cemetery and stood beside the grave. He was not satisfied with the reported cause of death, and neither was Fon. John had high blood pressure and was always munching on an antacid, but he was no hypochondriac. In the darkest moments, Fon blamed Betty for the demise of John Daniel.

When Marky thought of her father she was reminded of a winter scene from her own childhood. After a long silence, she wrote a poem about it.

> Father, your ghost still comes —
> So thin in the thickening afternoon —
> To stand beyond the light
> Left burning in our cold kitchen . . .
> Did you think we might have options among
>   the nightmares? . . .

Robin sometimes wondered if it might not be possible to sit down with a celestial advisor and map out a plan for life — what you wanted to achieve, what the important decisions would be — and then to be born and follow the plan. At other times she thought of herself as a child at a carnival, riding in a car on a track, turning the steering wheel this way and that, waving to her parents and thinking she was in control while the car went round and round just as it was ordained to do.

She had to resurrect things, that much she knew. She could not allow John Daniel to be forgotten, and she could not give up the family's place in the valley. She would succeed in a way that would make him proud; she would somehow reclaim a piece of what had been lost.

II

Leviathan

12

TODAY THE TRAVELER who turns into a narrow, unmarked lane off Highway 29, just north of the hamlet of Rutherford, passes between two rows of sycamores half a mile long. Vineyards stretch away on both sides, a common sight though these are not common vineyards. The lane leads first to a bank of flowers and shrubs beneath a towering palm. Off to the left stands a stone cellar, and next to it an arbor of trellised trees trained over the years to provide a natural harlequin canopy of branches, broad green leaves and geometric squares of unbroken blue sky. Beyond the canopy stands a house, impressive without the grandeur of palatial stone, a rambling country "cottage" combining the best of Gallic propriety and American ease. A gallery runs the length of it; there are scattered outbuildings for servants and guests, a swimming pool, and proliferating gardens. Despite the fact that they and the orchards have fallen off in productivity since the days of Georges de Latour, who founded Beaulieu Vineyard, the overall, lasting impression of grounds and house is one of decorum and purpose.

Inside, the rambling rooms contain a treasury of French antiques. The heavy guest ledgers are full of jottings of the rich, famous, and powerful who have lingered here. "A moment's halt, a momentary taste," wrote Winston Churchill in September 1929. His son, Randolph, made a more poetic effort: "Here with a book of verse, beneath the bough." Napoleon's grandnephew found it sufficient merely to sign his name.

There are others: Chester Nimitz, Lord Salisbury, John Foster Dulles, Herbert Hoover, Arthur Vandenburg . . . But they came later, after a diminutive Russian émigré named André Tchelistcheff first turned into the lane in 1938 and found himself facing a new life with a family that was already a legend in Napa Valley.

André had known similar rural surroundings as a child in Russia and a member of the petty aristocracy that lost everything in the chaos of the revolution. The Tchelistcheffs had been an old provincial family in Kaluga province, and liberals in the tradition of Tolstoy and Turgenev, who had written about Kaluga in *A Sportsman's Notebook:* "Forests where no timber may be cut stretch for hundreds of versts, the blackcock . . . is not yet extinct, the generous snipe abounds." André's father and uncles hunted with kennels of borzoi hounds and sold horses to the czar's cavalry. André had been born in 1901 and, given the odds, should have died in infancy. He suffered from an inflammation of the abdominal cavity before the days of penicillin; every day the doctor came to extract fluid with a syringe. André was fed a mixture of buckwheat, milk, and chopped raw beef, and would never forget the taste of blood.

His father, a jurist in the Russian court system, advocated an end to absolute monarchy and joined the provisional government after the 1917 revolution. He argued for the creation of a democratic republic like those in Western Europe, but the Bolsheviks declared him an enemy of the people. The Tchelistcheffs were dispossessed of their property and fled south. André fought with other young men in the White Russian army against the Reds, as a first lieutenant. In the frozen Crimea his troops went down in a confused assault on machine-gun emplacements, and André crawled into a hedgerow and lost consciousness.

His family, then in Yalta, received word of his apparent death and held a Russian Orthodox funeral service on the day a Cossack retrieving the dead from the frozen battlefield found the small body of a first lieutenant and threw it over the back of his horse.

After the war, André enrolled at the University of Brno, in Czechoslovakia, under the auspices of the League of Nations. He studied animal science and took a course in general agronomy. His family had moved on to Yugoslavia, in what was to be an unhappy, wandering exile. He joined them in Belgrade and married the daughter of an exiled Siberian lawyer. From Belgrade they moved to Paris. André worked on a farm near Versailles and studied in Paris at the Institut Pasteur and the Institut National Agronomique. In the spring of 1938, André's professor introduced him to a visitor from California, a Frenchman in a tailor-made suit with manicured nails and an impeccable bearing. He was Georges de Latour, the owner of a winery, and he was searching for a trained winemaker. André had already been offered similar jobs in Chile and southern China; he didn't think he could survive in the Wild West, but he was intrigued by this elegant Frenchman prospering in two worlds.

Georges de Latour, he learned, was the product of Jesuit schools. He had inherited an estate in Périgord that was destroyed by phylloxera and left France for the West Coast of America in 1883. San Francisco's French community folded about him at a time when things French, from cuisine to prostitutes, had great cachet, and imported French gowns and perfume were absolute necessities in fashionable San Francisco households. De Latour went to work in the counties north of the city, buying the scrapings from the inside of wine vats, to be made into cream of tartar for baking powder. He married a Franco-German girl and moved to Healdsburg, in Sonoma County, where the de Latours became a familiar sight, traveling by buggy on the dusty roads. In 1899 they bought one hundred acres of fields and orchard in Rutherford, Napa County, on the northern border of Inglenook. Mme. de Latour called their acquisition Beaulieu, "a beauteous place."

De Latour bought inferior lees and press wines from other wineries, and sold them. His first vintage was made in borrowed space. Using French methods and secondhand French equipment, he made acceptable table wine containing relatively little alcohol and sold it briskly at low prices. He bought additional vineyards and returned to France for cuttings of superior grape varieties not yet popular in California. The Mission and other old vines were torn out at Beaulieu and replaced with his transatlantic discoveries. De Latour wanted to make a classic claret — a soft, flavorful Bordeaux-type wine — but he wanted profits, and he saw opportunity in a looming, uniquely American idiocy known as Prohibition.

He bought and put away a huge supply of sweet wine, whose value quickly rose from a few cents a gallon to dollars after the onset of Prohibition. The first three months after alcohol was banned the wineries were allowed to liquidate their stocks, and Beaulieu sold wine twenty-four hours a day at greatly inflated prices. Then, when other wineries were closing their doors and tearing out vineyards, de Latour was catering to another market, the Catholic church.

Wine for mass had originally brought the Mission grape northward from Mexico to California. Now the archbishop of San Francisco, de Latour's personal friend, provided him with the monopoly on sacramental wine. By virtue of this market, de Latour provided what there was of leadership in the wine industry during the unhappiness of Prohibition. He grew wealthier during the process, a result of good fortune and a tribute to his foresight and business acumen. The Sebastiani family in Sonoma and the Wentes in Livermore Valley provided a steady supply of wine that was trucked to Rutherford to be finished, bottled, and sold. Beaulieu also produced kosher wine. A rabbi came to the winery during crush, laughed when he was splashed with wine from the open tanks, and bootlegged some of it to the bar in Rutherford.

For years de Latour coveted the larger Seneca Ewer Winery, which faced Beaulieu across Highway 29. In 1923 he bought it and had a new cellar dug. The de Latours lived in San Francisco, but their house in Napa Valley had rambling gardens and several additions. Their children, Richard and Hélène, grew up in the bucolic summer idylls that were Napa's in the early years of the century.

When de Latour rode up from San Francisco in his Cadillac, driven by a Portuguese chauffeur, he often brought Hélène along. Beautiful, accommodating Hélène was sent off to school in France. There she met Marquis Henri Galcerand de Pins, whose family owned Château de Montbrun in Gascony. The marquis was not only a nobleman but also a French cavalry officer who had graduated from École Militaire du Saumur, founded by Napoleon Bonaparte. He had been wounded by machine-gun fire in World War I. Handsome and charming, de Pins danced, rode horses, and used fine Belgian shotguns well, and owned one hundred pairs of shoes.

His family disapproved of his growing attachment to Hélène de Latour; so did her father. He considered de Pins a product of the aristocracy, as he was, and although de Latour loved the aristocracy, he considered it unsuited to American commerce and American life. He wanted an American businessman for a son-in-law. But Mme. de Latour wanted nobility, and de Pins and Hélène were married in 1924 in San Francisco. They led a peripatetic life of some glamour, divided between California and the Continent, traveling through royal parlors and across the pages of domestic and foreign newspapers.

At the end of Prohibition, Beaulieu was once again in a good position, with a large store of wine on hand, productive vineyards, and an active sales force. Most of the wine being drunk then was sweet — ports and sherries. Table wine was considered "sour" by most American wine drinkers, but that would change, and when it did Beaulieu would be ready.

Wineries run by foreigners — Beringer, Krug, Niebaum, de Latour — had introduced fine wine to Americans, yet all but Beaulieu Vineyard were comatose, or almost so. The de Latours sat at the pinnacle of their world, living sumptuously in Rutherford and San Francisco and enjoying some celebrity. Meanwhile, Beaulieu wines arriving on the new legal market seesawed between good and barely acceptable. Activity at the winery remained so feverish and profit-driven that there was no time for renovation. Then Beaulieu's enologist, Professor Leon Bonnet, announced that he was retiring, and de Latour began to search for the only sort of person who could make truly great wine — another Frenchman.

What he found, in Paris, was the little Russian émigré with an unpronounceable name.

❧

The Tchelistcheffs boarded the ship bound for New York from France in September 1938 — André, his Russian wife, and their six-year-old son, Dimitri. André had great reservations about leaving France. His colleagues did not believe that good wine could be made in America, regardless of the enologist's skill. André had tasted two California wines at the 1937 International Exposition in Paris, an Inglenook Gewürztraminer and a Cresta Blanca Sauvignon Blanc. They were surprisingly good.

They arrived in the midst of the Depression. His wife's brother, a cab driver, took them in. André contacted de Latour, who was also on the East Coast, and they met again at a cellar in midtown Manhattan where some Beaulieu wines were kept, next to the subway. The cellar vibrated, which was bad for the wine, as was the high temperature. But the "burgundy" de Latour poured for him, made of Cabernet Sauvignon, showed promise.

The Tchelistcheffs boarded the train west. The trip took four days and André was stunned by the breadth and diversity of the country. Some of it reminded him of Russia: the forests of the Mississippi Valley and the dun-colored grain fields of the Midwest. He was amazed by the blue intensity of the California sky and the corresponding expanse of the Pacific Ocean. San Francisco smelled of salt air, fresh bread, and the unmistakable fermentation of grapes in home winemakers' cellars.

More of his wife's family lived in the city, and she and Dimitri joined them. André was picked up, in a black Cadillac with a chauffeur, by de Latour and Mme. de Latour, an imposing woman. They crossed the newly constructed Golden Gate Bridge and after many miles turned east across the southern flats of Sonoma and Napa counties. It was fall, the sun hot, the air very dry. The road north followed the railroad line between parched foothills and the low, constricting mountains. André had expected many vineyards, as in Bordeaux, and although some rows of vines did run east and west of the road, this strangely beautiful landscape was dominated by plum orchards and dairy farms, where ruminant cows and men in large hats watched the big car speed past.

Rutherford was nothing more than a whistle stop. They passed the entrance to Inglenook's magnificent château, set far back against the western mountains, and turned into the next road. The surrounding country looked like wilderness even to someone raised in Kaluga province, but the de Latours had created their own oasis. The house was surrounded by gardens tended by an English gardener and six assistants. All the servants in the house wore uniforms and spoke French. The estate produced its own milk, cream, butter, eggs, even its own *écrevisse* — crayfish.

Trout abounded in an artificial stream of aerated well water. "It is Friday," de Latour said, "so we will have trout. You may select your own German brown, or a rainbow."

During lunch, the de Latours spoke of improving conditions at the winery. André could do what he thought necessary, they said, and he and his family would live in the little yellow house on the property.

André was dismayed by Rutherford. People outside the confines of Beaulieu were all compelled to shout at one another. There were Mexicans in sombreros, mustachioed Italians, and Americans with less obvious racial heritages who wore open shirts, enormous boots, and suspenders. When they were not shouting, they were spitting. The day André's son, Dimitri, went to the clapboard one-room schoolhouse wearing short pants and riding a bicycle, as he had in France, the other boys threw tomatoes at him. Then they beat him and sent him home in tears. He told André he wouldn't go back, that the Americans were beasts. André told Dimitri he would have to make his peace with the locals.

The condition of the winery shocked André. He visited it wearing a coat and tie, as was his habit, and a white smock. The "doctor" was shown old and spoiled cooperage reeking of vinegar and years of accumulated filth. There was not even a janitor to sweep up. To a student of the teachings of Pasteur, a disciple of cleanliness, Beaulieu was a vision of microbial hell. The open fermenters released clouds of carbon dioxide that intoxicated birds and mice, which tumbled into the young wine and drowned. In one tank a rat swam contentedly in the Sauvignon Blanc.

The superintendent, an Italian Swiss named Joe Ponti, shrugged off these deficiencies. Ponti had come to Napa as a mason, and had known Mussolini in Italy, a fact that earned him great respect among Rutherford's Italians. He had worked for de Latour for more than thirty years and knew how slow change would be, if it came at all.

André had the tanks cleaned with potassium permanganate, with the help of a Portuguese assistant and several former Swiss Guards retired by the Vatican — further evidence of de Latour's close connections with the Catholic church. The guards made indifferent laborers. André and his assistant constantly urged them to work faster until finally one hulking Swiss seized the two of them by their collars and dangled them over the concrete sump in the winery floor. "You sons of bitches," he said. "If you don't stop, I'll kill you."

André decided to leave California after the harvest. He could not sleep. His son was miserable. There was so much work, and no prospect that it would ever be accomplished. The workers were intractable and the neighbors, with the exception of Inglenook, making unfinished wine from inferior grapes and shipping it off in tank cars.

Much of Beaulieu's wine belonged in the same category. The year before, de Latour had signed a contract with the New York distributor Park and Tilford, agreeing to provide them with twenty-five thousand cases of bottled and labeled wine. But it soon spoiled after arrival on the East Coast, and de Latour had to face the humiliation of a flood of returned bottles. André was not surprised. The grape crusher, pipes, and pumps at Beaulieu were old and made of rusty cast iron, and they regularly released doses of iron oxide. The filters, corroded copper, bled more heavy metal into the product. The bottling procedure was laughable. Wine delivered by gravity from the second floor passed through tiny asbestos filters and then through six little spouts into the bottles; they were corked by one man seated at an antiquated machine. Oxygen, recognized as bad for wine, was introduced at every stage of the process.

Fortunately André had inherited a small laboratory, in which he conducted experiments and furthered his research — a retreat from the near-medieval setting of the working winery.

Georges de Latour was a typical Frenchman, André thought: suspicious and tight-fisted, warm and often generous — a contradiction. Enormously cultured, his conversation was full of philosophical and literary allusion. André had great respect and affection for him. Yet de Latour could be cynically shrewd. He urged his neighbors to continue planting Alicante, a poor wine grape, knowing that varieties like Cabernet and Pinot Noir would eventually be more popular and that he, having planted them, would be in a stronger marketing position.

He insisted on tasting everything in the winery, despite the fact that most of the wines were indistinguishable. De Latour would say, "This is Riesling," or, "This is Sauvignon Blanc," and André would write the solemn incantation on the tank with a piece of chalk. After de Latour had gone away, Ponti would laugh at him. "Why bother?" he asked. "It's all the same."

Reading was almost an obsession with de Latour. It was part Jesuit training, part natural curiosity; his intellect and essential Frenchness surrounded him like the concentrated light in a medieval painting. He would arrive from San Francisco with a book in hand, look up to see the blessed aspect of Beaulieu, step out of the big chauffeured car, and urinate on the same tree in the orchard. The ritual never varied. Then he would tramp around to every part of the estate, exchanging greetings and views with the gardener and the vineyard foreman, the winemakers and cellar rats, the maids and the chef. De Latour was open to all.

André discovered a stock of red wine aging in small oak barrels, the only Beaulieu wine in such expensive cooperage; de Latour shared his enthusiasm for its quality. The wine, the '36 Cabernet, had been left by André's predecessor and was a potentially great wine. André asked for more cellar space for aging Beaulieu wine from the best vineyards, and additional small oak barrels — only sixty from France. De Latour agreed. The new barrels would have to be American, however, since the war had cut off most commerce with the Continent.

•

De Latour's daughter, Hélène, and her husband, the Marquis de Pins, rented a spacious apartment on Powell Street in San Francisco and were given a section of the big house in Rutherford. De Pins had a room paneled with pine and hung with expensive imported shotguns. Shooting was his passion. Accustomed to hunting birds driven by Gascon beaters, he convinced a group of barefoot Rutherford boys to roust fat Napa pheasants out of the fields and vineyards, and gunned them down in awesome displays of marksmanship and sangfroid.

He was made a vice president and sent around the United States and Canada to represent Beaulieu. He found it an onerous chore but brought it off in style, and one year was voted the best dressed man in America. De Pins waited for de Latour to give him more responsibility and for Mme. de Latour to recede from the management of the winery. But he refused to associate the de Pins name with Beaulieu, which would have dramatically increased his influence.

He and André tasted the wines together. De Pins had a good palate and a surprisingly simple nature. Their developing friendship was based on their common Francophilia and occasional unhappiness. Both were exiles by choice; sometimes they felt trapped. André had been miserable the first year but gradually his enthusiasm triumphed over the environment. The marquis, however, did not like American food, American conversation, and American men. The women were tolerable. He generally liked women of all nationalities, and Mme. de Latour complained of being unwilling to hire attractive maids because of the marquis.

André began to correct the problems in the winery. He and the Swiss Guards became friends. André even opened a lab of his own in St. Helena, where he could better conduct the sort of experiments he had done in France, and act as a winemaking consultant.

In 1940 Georges de Latour died in San Francisco. He was buried there, with four archbishops presiding at the ceremony. The next year, Beaulieu released the '36 Cabernet that he and André had so liked. Mme. de Latour suggested that it be called Georges de Latour Private Reserve; the price was an impressive dollar and a half.

Now that the old man was dead, people speculated about the leadership of BV. Mme. de Latour was an old woman now; perhaps she had lost interest in her late husband's enterprise. The marquis was middle-aged and seemed the obvious choice. But his refusal to associate the de Pins name with Beaulieu had permanently disqualified him, and all doubts soon evaporated about who would be running things. Mme. de Latour asserted her authority and was made president by the board; she took over the active management of the estate's affairs. The marquis found himself even more isolated from the decisions.

His behavior didn't improve his position. He thought Beaulieu wines too alcoholic, and said so; he diluted his with water, further offending his mother-in-law. His caustic comments about Beaulieu's wines became legendary. He sometimes ordered beer in restaurants rather than Beaulieu, to show his contempt as much for Mme. de Latour as for the wine itself.

But the marquis had insights. Once he stood up at a Beaulieu board meeting and said, "Ladies and gentlemen, excuse me, but what I am going to say may sound stupid. I believe that the future of Beaulieu is in one wine — Cabernet."

André agreed, but the suggestion was met with amused tolerance by Mme. de Latour. Those dozens of lesser wines, cheaper to make and easier to sell, brought in the revenues needed to keep the estate — herself and the family — afloat. She wasn't interested in giving up anything in her life for the presumed glory of one wine.

The marquis was expected to help entertain Mme. de Latour's guests, and he acquiesced, behaving decently on most occasions. Visitors included members of the clergy and women socialites. In private, the marquis complained of the women bitterly, referring to them as *garces Américaines*, American witches.

He and Hélène quarreled, and lapsed into long silences. They never used the familiar form of address, an aristocratic French habit and one that suited their domestic arrangement. When possible, the marquis would go to his ancestral home in Gascony; the stays grew longer. From there he would write Hélène long letters about his loneliness, and an expectation would grow in both until they came together in Rutherford. Then the old malaise would set in again. The *garces Américaines* would descend, and the marquis's considerable social charms would again come into play.

Mme. de Latour showed as much interest in the quality of the wines as her husband had. Some good wine was necessary, she said, for the good of the de Latour name. She was discerning, sometimes cold-blooded, but also generous. When Martin Ray's cellar burned, she told him he could choose any replacement wines he wanted from hers. She could be imperious as well. The only person who consistently stood up to her was the Japanese cook.

She traveled more after her husband's death. Europe was the favored pleasuring ground, but the Orient was also within reach. She went to Hawaii in the summer of 1947, while renovation was being carried out at Beaulieu. Shredded redwood bark laid under the winery roof as insulation caught fire after one of the workers installing glass lines for transporting wine dropped a cigarette. André was working at the lab in St. Helena when he received word; he drove south toward Rutherford, where he could see smoke rising against the sky.

Inside the winery, fire had crept down one wall. The sherry cooker exploded. Blue flames engulfed the huge wooden tanks full of port, and a wall of flame sprung up, fed by the alcohol. André couldn't believe the suddenness of it. One by one the tanks burst like bombs, and a surge of wine and spirits three feet deep burned with an incredible intensity. Firemen arrived from St. Helena, then Napa, and finally Vallejo; there wasn't enough water to put out the flames. The fermenting room and the cellar constructed for the special small cooperage burned along with the rest. André watched a decade's worth of work billow up in smoke. What wine did not burn flowed in a torrent into the little Napa River, turning it a dark purple and eventually polluting every well for miles around.

Ironically, André made the best Sauvignon Blanc of his life that year — and developed an ulcer.

In the 1950s "BV" — Beaulieu — wines occupied lists in the Waldorf-Astoria and Le Pavillon in New York, the Blackstone in Chicago, the Brown Derby in Denver, the Ritz-Carlton in Boston, and the Jockey Club and Hôtel Georges V in Paris. Beaulieu was celebrated as the subject of a Broadway hit, *The Most Happy Fella,* and Georges de Latour inspired the hero in a best-selling novel, *The Cup and the Sword.* A similar character was portrayed by Claude Rains in a film shot partially in Rutherford, a hamlet that now drew celebrities from all over the world.

Hélène de Pins took over the supervision of Beaulieu after the death of Mme. de Latour. Hélène was a good businesswoman — meticulous, obsessed with detail. She demanded the perfection she had known as a child, when her father upheld such standards, and even went so far as to make André pick up his cigarette butts from her gravel drive. She insisted that chairs sit exactly three inches from the dining room table. Like her father, Hélène was contradictory. She ignored the deteriorating cooperage in the winery but allowed expansion into the Carneros region in southern Napa County — expensive and far-sighted viticultural pioneering.

For Hélène de Latour de Pins, Beaulieu Vineyard was locked into the moment of her father's death. Georges de Latour had told her that everything had been taken care of, that nothing could go wrong at Beaulieu, and she had believed him. She lived in another century and would not adapt; everything revolved around tradition. André found that he, who had been raised in similar circumstances in Russia, had come to value the opposite. The silverware used at the Tchelistcheff dinner table, for instance, had been worn down by the teeth of his ancestors. He never wanted to see another heirloom and wondered why Hélène, with deeper roots in America than he, felt so bound by the past.

Her daughter, Dagmar, an only child, had grown up with a more egalitarian nature; for a time she resisted speaking French at home. Crippled slightly by polio, Dagmar found a retreat in the vineyards and the activity associated with them. She had inherited the simple nature of her father, the marquis; André admired her passionate view of life. As a young woman she seemed in search of a suitable object for her affections, and in revolt against her parents.

Dagmar was reintroduced during her debut in San Francisco to the son of a banker named Walter Sullivan. They had met in Rutherford when Dagmar was thirteen and Sullivan's parents were visiting the de Pins. Walter was a Stanford graduate, a former polo player with a second lieutenant's commission in the Army. Hélène de Pins and the marquis wanted a French aristocrat for their daughter, but Dagmar and Walter Sullivan were married right after the war.

The marquis remained contemptuous of Beaulieu and of America. The de Pinses' lives were glamorous by most standards, but ultimately unsatisfying. Hélène insisted on perfection and never found it. She and the marquis visited France often, and began packing two months in advance. Hélène would have the servants send cartons of toilet paper, facial tissues, aluminum foil, and plastic wrapping paper on ahead. Most of it would not be needed, and to prevent it from being used in her absence, or stolen, she would order it shipped back again when their stay was over.

The marquis became obsessed with his father's admonition to die in the family home. He would go back to Gascony determined to die there, but he would not die and couldn't wait to return to Rutherford. In Rutherford, he began to worry about a proper grave site in Gascony. Burial in the family chapel was mandatory. The marquis ordered the family crypt opened on his next trip to Montbrun, to see if there was room for him. What he saw was a hole flooded with spring water. He told André, "I don't want to spend the next million years bobbing around like a bottle."

André went to Gascony to locate a suitable resting place in the chapel wall for him. He called in a builder from Toulouse and the two of them, accompanied by the family retainer, went around tapping the ancient masonry. The man found a narrow, unoccupied place, but the retainer objected. "The marquis must be sitting," he said. The remains of a distant relative were removed from the wall so the marquis could be accommodated when the time came.

Hélène's secretary regularly sent Teletype messages from the Rutherford office to the one in San Francisco, with detailed instructions for purchases to be made in the city. Not just tomatoes, but *firm, red* tomatoes. Hélène would read the messages to make sure her exact words had been used, then order them delivered to the grocers, butchers, poultry and seafood merchants. The food and other purchases were packed into boxes and driven up to Napa by the chauffeur or an employee who had been assigned the task.

Mme. de Pins kept an egg timer by the telephone to limit the duration of business calls. One year she gave some employees a 14-cent raise. When the gardener spoke of the need to transplant a shrub or cut one of the beautifully trellised sycamores on the family estate, Hélène de Pins would ask, "How can this be?" Hadn't her father, Georges de Latour, told her that everything had been taken care of?

Many adored her, however, among them André. Her hospitality was famous, yet she would allow no one outside the family on the property to harvest excess vegetables and fruit. People accepted this as part of the nature of the valley's well born, and the produce rotted where it lay.

André's working relationship with Hélène was argumentative. Beaulieu existed to finance family activities, so money was put into the winery with great reluctance and in amounts only fractionally related to the true needs. André threatened to quit, and retired twice, yet he always came back, trying to keep up standards while pressing for additional tanks, barrels, and equipment.

There was never enough revenue to suit Hélène. The Fabrini

brothers had handled Beaulieu's sales for years, but Mme. des Pins and Aldo Fabrini never got along. He once told her, "You are the queen and I am the prime minister." Aldo preferred daiquiris to wine.

In the early 1960s Hélène de Pins began to look around for a new sales manager. Her husband had no interest in the winery now, and Dagmar, the third generation to own Beaulieu, had no business experience. Hélène needed sound advice.

She had heard of an attractive young man working for the Gallo brothers, of all people, out in the Central Valley, as removed from the graciousness of BV as the lunar plains. The young man, a former trumpet player named Legh Knowles, seemed an unlikely candidate for manager of the most prestigious winery in America. But he came highly recommended. Hélène invited him to San Francisco for an interview, after talking to him by telephone for the prescribed three minutes.

13

L EGH (pronounced *Lee*) Knowles had come to Gallo from the Wine Advisory Board, a promotional adjunct of the California wine industry. But he told people that he was really a trumpeter, that he had joined the musicians' union at age twelve and was playing in Glenn Miller's band when he was eighteen. Whenever he talked about Miller, Red Norvo, or Charlie Spivak, people listened. He would talk about the Glenn Miller sound — the clarinet and tenor sax playing an octave apart, the voices all in harmony — and people would eat it up.

During the war he joined the Air Force, and afterward the Wine Advisory Board hired him. They needed someone accustomed to standing up in front of crowds; Knowles told them he had appeared on stages before thousands. He had a mellifluous voice, a cherubic face, and energy, but he drank gin.

One day in New York, he met a stocky wine merchandiser from California who had little respect for industry boards or wine appreciation. "Why are you guys running around talking about wine?" he asked Knowles. "That's a lot of bullshit. The important thing is, who's first in sales in Connecticut?"

His name was Ernest Gallo.

In 1958 Knowles went out to Modesto to talk to Gallo about a job. Modesto was a dog of a town, all railroad tracks and sun-baked pavement, but Gallo was a serious guy. He made all his bottles so he wouldn't have to depend on a supplier; he owned a trucking firm and didn't have to worry about unions. His warehouse looked like a city under one roof.

Gallo told Knowles, "I'm going to take over Cincinnati."

He had gone there unannounced and surveyed the stores, traveling with a driver so he could jump out of the car, check the displays and shelf position, ask a few questions, and jump back in. When Gallo left Cincinnati, he knew more about availability than the people living there. He had asked a dozen black men about wine; they had told him, "Gallo, the little ol' winemaker."

The little ol' winemaker was Italian Swiss Colony, not Gallo. The fact that people were still buying Gallo wine meant they liked it, even though it was being confused with a competitor's. And that meant the Gallo advertising campaigns cooked up in New York were useless.

Gallo got on the telephone to the ad agency and told them they didn't know what they were doing, that the ad guys had better get off their butts and go to Cincinnati and talk to some of the same people Gallo had talked to. Then they'd better get their butts out to Modesto.

Gallo and an assistant grilled Knowles. What would he do to increase sales of Gallo wine?

"Print some recipes," said Knowles.

That broke them up. Recipes! In Cincinnati!

Gallo sent Knowles there and had him put on the payroll of Gallo's distributor. Ernie wanted to see what the kid from the Glenn Miller band could do; he told Knowles, "Sell wine with your hands, not just your mouth."

Gallo wines went onto the shelves at eye level. The sales force worked like slaves, setting up displays and stroking every liquor store owner in town. Knowles was just a grunt in the war that won Cincinnati. He went on to become the national table-wine brand man, every month selling 200,000 cases just in New York of what he thought of as burgundy with the built-in heartburn. From there he moved up to rosé brand manager.

Gallo wrote to him, "Remember what John Paul Jones said, 'I have just begun to fight.'"

⟡

Ernest Gallo's father killed his wife with a shotgun in Fresno back in 1933, and then killed himself. His grape-shipping business had failed and, as an immigrant from Piedmont, he saw his future fatally circumscribed by the Depression. Twenty-five years later, few in the trade knew the story; those who did kept it to themselves.

One of those who knew was Leon Adams, a reporter who began

covering Prohibition in 1923 for the *San Francisco News*. Adams thought the violent deaths of the older Gallos left Ernest with a deep-seated mistrust of the world and a determination to succeed where his father had failed. In Adams's opinion, Ernest kept his younger brother, Julio, around because he considered Julio the only person who wouldn't someday stab him in the back.

Adams had decided after Repeal to help educate Americans about wine drinking. He worked for the Wine Institute, the trade association under contract to the state's Wine Advisory Board that promoted California wine. The board was funded by California wineries, each required by law to contribute a percentage of its sales. When Gallo refused to pay its share, Adams began to gather information that would change Ernest's mind. He went to the *Sacramento Bee* and put together a file heavy with details about the double shotgun slaying in Fresno, among other things. Meanwhile, Ernest decided he couldn't beat the requirements of the California Marketing Order for Wine and paid his dues, and Adams put his file in a drawer.

Adams's zeal for wine and what he saw as the civilizing of America had taken him from journalism to advocacy. Wine became a mission. By exposing the public to it, he, Leon Adams — short, pipe sucking, tenacious — might help fulfill Thomas Jefferson's dream of a sober nation soberly employed, drinking wine with its meals and avoiding whiskey and other gross intoxicants. Adams decided that Ernest Gallo was the single greatest threat to that possibility in America.

Adams quit the Wine Institute and went to work for Gallo as a consultant, one with a secret agenda: to mitigate the harm this man might do. He settled down to write a booklet about wine appreciation, and some training manuals for which Gallo would become famous, hoping to influence America's drinking habits and thereby the course of history. Adams would leave Gallo and go on to write *The Wines of America* and to be hailed as the dean of American wine writers, but he would never abandon his agenda.

Ernest Gallo had gotten into the wine business with Julio by using pamphlets about winemaking from the Modesto Public Library. They had divided the duties, with Julio making the wine and Ernest selling it, but Ernest clearly dominated. As far as Adams could tell, Ernest had pushed the concept of penny pinching into another stratosphere. He had picked up some social graces at the junior college in

Modesto, but mostly he interviewed people; he served his guests the competition's wine and then asked for an analysis. Leon Adams had never met a more suspicious man, nor one who went through colleagues as quickly.

Ernest's utter efficiency dominated an industry noted for inefficiency. His jugs sold well enough, but it was the sweet dessert wines that pushed the E. & J. Gallo Company past Roma, owned by Schenley, and up to the portals of Italian Swiss Colony, the biggest producer in California. Ernest wanted to buy Italian Swiss Colony but didn't want another brand, so he bided his time while Louis Petri bought and later sold Italian Swiss to a growers' cooperative. Then Gallo pulled ahead.

Ernest's evolving system of brand management and guerrilla sales tactics provided half the company's success; the other half came from the lab in Modesto where flavor-enhanced, highly alcoholic concoctions rolled off the Bunsen burners by the number. One of these, a lemon-flavored white port called Thunderbird, launched itself on the big-city radio waves:

> "What's the word?"
> "Thunderbird."
> "How's it sold?"
> "Good and cold."
> "What's the jive?"
> "Bird's alive!"
> "What's the price?"
> "Thirty twice."

The unprecedented success of Thunderbird turned a flourishing business into something more and whetted Ernest's appetite for alchemy. It also gave rise to stories of uninhibited sales techniques: strewing selected skid rows with empty Thunderbird bottles as a unique route to product awareness, and the destruction of the competition's aluminum screw-on caps by bands of men roving the liquor stores. Thunderbird's alleged low road bothered few at the time other than Leon Adams. Later, Gallo would be pressured to take Thunderbird off the market, on grounds that the company was profiting from the misery and addiction of impoverished alcoholics.

A year after taking over Cincinnati, Gallo brought Knowles west to be the district manager in Los Angeles. Knowles saw himself as a musician. He was still young. "I'm not tough enough," he told Gallo plaintively.

"When you depend on people," Gallo said, "and they let you down, then you'll get tough."

Knowles and his team sold 100,000 cases the first month, and Gallo asked him to move to Modesto, to be in charge of recruiting and training the sales force. Knowles said he would move if Ernest would get him into the country club and his kids into the Catholic school. The country club was no problem, Gallo said, but Knowles would have to work things out with the priest himself.

Of Knowles's new job, Ernest told him, "Remember, people aren't led — they're driven!"

You needed a sense of humor in Modesto, and thick skin. Knowles couldn't believe how Gallo roughed up his people at the daily meetings. Visiting admen got the same treatment. One would begin a dissertation on sales strategy, and Gallo would interrupt him. "Who's first in New York?" he would ask.

"You are," the adman would say and start to explain. But Gallo would interrupt him again.

"Who's first in New Jersey?"

"You are."

"None of you guys know what you're talking about. We're first because of quality."

Afterward, the admen and the salesmen would go to the bar across the highway. They called it the decompression chamber.

No one could con Ernest. Knowles lost track of the number of times someone said, "He's never wrong." Ernest would sit in his office or in a plane seat and go over every possible scenario for the future of Gallo, the future of the wine industry in California, the future of a product. Then he would say, "Give me the cases, give me the card, give me the new color, and be ready to go."

When he had the numbers, the price, and the blend, he wanted it on the market . . . now! Once, when the Bureau of Alcohol, Tobacco and Firearms rejected a label, on impulse Ernest changed the name of the new wine to Mountain Red. That was on a Thursday. The product had to be on the shelves by the following Monday. New labels had to be printed and applied, and the wine shipped. Mountain Red had been made just to knock a Franzia wine out of the market. The Franzia family happened to be Gallo's in-laws, but he knocked them out anyway.

A technician named Charles Crawford kept an eye on the details at the winery. Table wine had priority. Gallo bought grapes all over the state, using those from the Central Valley for their copious juice and those from the more prestigious North Coast for taste and balance. Napa Valley fruit gave some edge to his jugs. Gallo dominated the co-ops and set the terms. Growers found they had no recourse if their grapes fell short of Gallo standards, or if they crossed Julio or annoyed one of the quality controllers standing by the crushers, ruling over the harvest like padishahs.

Three Ph.D.'s in the research department looked into such things as "the mechanism of isoamyl alcohol formation" and "copper casse formation in white table wine," but they also made the concoctions. Vinous rocket scientists, these men were kept separate from the winemaking staff, the analytical lab, and the quality control people. They devised, among other drinks, a nitrogen-free wine using ion exchange, so it didn't matter if yeast or bacteria were left in the wine, since they couldn't grow. Too bad the wine was barely palatable.

The rocket scientists tried oak chip extraction to give wine character. Aging it in oak barrels was too expensive, so Gallo bought boxcars full of oak chips and blew them into the blends, to give the impression of age and complexity. This improved the sweet ports and cream sherry but didn't do much for the table wines.

One rocket scientist, Dick Peterson, a bright, fresh-faced midwesterner with a Ph.D. in chemistry from Berkeley, was told to create a whiskey sour that contained no whiskey but had a real kick, and could be sold as a cheap version of that very popular drink. It would be called Sporting Wine. Using brandy, port, and strong lemon and oak flavoring, Peterson made a concoction that was a dead ringer for a whiskey sour. Ernest decided to introduce it in Memphis, where people knew something about whiskey sours — one of his few marketing mistakes. It bombed. They changed the name to Champion's Belt and tried again in Toledo, and bombed again.

Gallo was the first big winery to use a centrifuge to separate juice and solids, and a diffuser to recover alcohol and sugar from the residue in the bottom of the press. Gallo's huge tonnage made it profitable. Ernest was out to make money any way possible. He decided to market a new pink wine and this time went to the winemakers, known as blenders. They mixed Gallo's standard rosé with a white Muscat and called it Rhinegarten; it flopped. More sugar was added, and carbon dioxide, which lofted the aroma as soon as the top came off the bottle. This one they called Pink Chablis, and it rolled over the competition.

Knowles became another "first pencil" for Ernest, revising the training manual that spelled out every aspect of wine salesmanship, almost every word suggested and then scrutinized by Ernest. Knowles
knew by now that nothing happened until somebody sold something
to somebody; that was the key. But Ernest took no chances. Salesmen were charged with the responsibility for Gallo's future, and then
instructed on how to manage this frightening prospect, from intro-
ductory remarks for retailers to bottle display. The highly advertised
items were to go in at eye level, the inspirational buys just above the
belt, the jugs to the right of the smaller bottles. Gallo reps were to
fight — artfully — for ever more floor space. They were to think of
customers as belonging to one of six categories of human being,
starting with the silent type and concluding with the aggressor. They
were not to tell dirty jokes. They were to fill up retailers' cold boxes
and shelves with Gallo bottles, and to visit and revisit stores until
Gallo dominated the landscape.

The young men who pored over the sales manual were recruited
from Harvard and Stanford business schools, from Procter & Gamble, Carnation, or some other company good at marketing. The pay
was fine and the ability to say you had worked for Gallo invaluable,
but the work was lousy. The recruits went to Los Angeles, the Fort
Bragg of Gallo's sales force. The regulars were to reduce them to
rubble, their only crack at the company's elite, and they took obvious pleasure in doing so. Many a hotshot M.B.A. quit after working fourteen-hour days and six-day weeks, and then building a demo
in some remote store until 2 A.M.

The survivors went into marketing; by then they knew the system from the bottom up. After a few years in Modesto, the inevitable happened: they needed or wanted more information about the
company and could not get it. For a time they beat their heads
against the ceiling of statistical availability, until it became clear that
that ceiling would never rise unless they happened to be Gallos. Ultimately, there were no survivors.

Gallo made his early distributors millionaires; they *expected* him
or his minions to check the stores for the company line. Ernest
worked as hard as anyone and ran the business like a regent, his day
one long conference during which he reduced decisions to obvious
imperatives and his staff to different consistencies of jelly. He was
always calling long-distance. Area managers had to stay informed
right up to the brink of the immediate; no one knew where the tel-

ephonic ax might fall. At night Ernest went home with books of
sales figures.

Once someone asked him the secret of his success; he said, "I
always assumed I would work hard. And I was always loyal."

An admonition. Ernest *was* the company, and Gallo employees a
polyglot version of Caesar's wife.

Julio seemed more human, a similarly stout Gallo in linen pants and
a Panama who spent his time in the vineyards when he wasn't in the
winery. Every afternoon at four o'clock he came bounding up the
stairs and into the tasting room, where the blenders waited. They
went through the wines, and woe be he who didn't have a trenchant
remark for the products at hand. Julio spat winemakers out the door
every day, it seemed. One made the mistake of shooting pool on a
hot Saturday afternoon with an assistant winemaker from a competing winery, and on Monday found that he had no job.

Once a month Julio had a party for the staff. He would bring
shrimp and cook them in the lab, the long, garlicky trail extending
the length of the building, drawing everyone in, from lab workers
to production people. They gathered in the break room downstairs,
where for an hour they could eat bagna calda, drink Paisano, and
cuss the decisions and even the decision makers. No one could imagine Ernest tolerating such ribaldry.

Julio went to Rotary once a month — the public glimpse of the
otherwise closed Gallo face. The few times he invited people out to
the compound just over the Modesto city line, where big old houses
stood surrounded by palms, oaks, and olive trees, Julio served them
fresh lettuce and tomatoes from his garden. Vineyards ran right up
to the lawns. The agricultural sprawl suggested the commodious estates of northern Italy, without walls or fences, just shrubs and ragged borders and an easy accommodation of nature and human arti-
fice rare among America's wealthiest families.

Just to the east began the ambiguity of Modesto: clapboard bungalows, squat concrete buildings, warehouses, machine shops, and
railroad tracks meeting the broad, near-empty streets baking in the
summer sun. There was no epicenter, but there was the Gallo industrial complex. No sign marked its location: if you had to ask, you
didn't belong. In what was once two hundred acres of alfalfa had
sprung up a stainless steel tank farm. Thirty-odd acres of warehouse
under a single roof contained avenues of stacked crates converging

in the great distances and a battalion of forklifts. While Angelo Petri had been shipping wine east through the Panama Canal in a tanker, in the 1950s, Ernest Gallo put profits into a plant that would reduce all his competitors to names in obscure texts at the University of California at Davis.

This was the world's largest winery. Enough wine rested in steel and 4,000-gallon oak tanks to float an ocean liner. Five furnaces fed from silos of sand spat globs of molten glass into molds that shaped them into bottles and sent them trundling through the shadows to cool and then be filled on conveyors with one of dozens of alcoholic liquids — 500,000 bottles a day, then a million, then a million and a half. The glass plant never shut down.

When Ernest decided he wanted a cellar capacious enough for a million gallons of wine, he simply built a concrete bunker the size of two football fields and covered it with dirt. That prominence provided an ideal landing pad for the eventual six-seat Jet Ranger helicopter. The administration of it all took place in a neoclassic temple, with peacocks and guinea fowl on the manicured lawn guarded by uniformed security agents with Gallo arm patches. Inside, across the palm court and the pond in which ten-pound koi lolled, was Julio's office, expansive, heavily furnished — and directly under that of Ernest, who was no stranger to strategic position, autocratic, and utterly inviolable.

Legh Knowles realized early that you could admire it all, you could learn and profit from it, but you couldn't join. That was for family. But the main thing he learned was that *nothing happens until somebody sells something to somebody.*

☙

In her San Francisco apartment, Hélène de Pins and her daughter, Dagmar, and Dagmar's husband, Walter Sullivan, listened to Legh Knowles's suggestions for the running of Beaulieu Vineyard. They should concentrate on Cabernet Sauvignon, Knowles said, Cabernet being BV's most renowned wine. They should cut out the discounts to distributors. Since Beaulieu was a prestige item, they should also limit production. Then the price of the wine could be raised.

"Wine's made out of grapes," Knowles added. "There are only so many fine ones."

Walter Sullivan was impressed. He made real estate deals —

Sullivan had seen John Daniel having lunch with Louis Petri and thereby knew that Inglenook was being sold — and he prided himself on good business sense, picked up at Stanford and in the comfortable chairs of the Pacific Union Club in San Francisco. Sullivan had nothing to do with the management of Beaulieu. That was his mother-in-law's and, incidentally, his wife's baby. But Sullivan maintained a keen interest in the subject.

Sullivan liked Legh Knowles. He seemed bright and energetic and had an appealing, homespun business ethic, learned in the Gallo school of hard knocks. Modesto was the antithesis of Rutherford, where Knowles would be working if Mme. de Pins hired him.

She did, and Knowles was duly invited to Rutherford in high summer. The family gathered at the long dining room table, Mme. de Pins at one end, the marquis at the other. Dagmar and Walter Sullivan joined them, as did the company lawyer. The French-speaking Japanese butler poured Beaulieu wines while Hélène told stories about the house and the winery, dropping names of foreign dignitaries and certifiable wine personages with links to Beaulieu. Eight times the marquis cleared his throat; finally his wife said, "Yes, Galcerand?"

He rang for the butler, who brought him a cold bottle of Coors. "You Americans are crazy to drink wine on a hot day," said the marquis.

Hélène, unruffled, went on talking. Knowles thought, This woman has class.

André Tchelistcheff drove him down to the new vineyard in Carneros. André had recommended that the family buy it. "In fifteen years," he told Knowles, "people will be drinking marvelous wine from here."

Knowles was accustomed to thinking of people drinking wine the day after tomorrow but didn't say so.

Not long afterward, while in Beaulieu's San Francisco office, Knowles received a Teletype from Mme. de Pins in Rutherford. Before returning to the valley, the message said, would he be so kind as to pick up six avocados? Six *very nice* avocados . . .

Dick Peterson, the Gallo rocket scientist who had put the bubbles in Pink Chablis and invented Sporting Wine/Champion's Belt and now headed the technical division in Modesto, received a call in late 1968 from André Tchelistcheff, the winemaker at BV. André told Peterson that he was expanding his consulting business and would not be devoting much time to Beaulieu's wines. "I've chosen you to replace me," he said.

The California wine business was a small pond. Everyone in it belonged to the American Society of Enologists and went to the same meetings; everyone knew what everyone else was doing. Peterson was the only Ph.D. in chemistry making wine; he and Tchelistcheff's son, Dimitri, had been colleagues at Gallo. They had considered buying the old Schram place a few years earlier, and Freemark Abbey, and had flown up together in a National Guard observation plane — both men were pilots and reservists — and landed at Rutherford International. They hadn't been able to put together the money to buy their own winery, however, and Dimitri had gone off to Mexico to make wine for someone else.

Dimitri had grown up in the presence of wine and Pasteur's maxims, passed along by his father. Maynard Amerine had urged Dimitri to stay in the enology department at UC Davis. "We need your palate," Amerine had said, but Dimitri preferred the real world. And although he was the obvious successor to his father at Beaulieu, he refused to pick up cigarette butts for Mme. de Pins.

The idea of working at Beaulieu thrilled Peterson. He drove to San Francisco to meet the daughter of the famous Georges de Latour. Once there, he felt like a midwestern farmer in the presence of royalty. Mme. de Pins considered him capable of making superior wine but was bothered by the Gallo association. Beaulieu had already hired one Gallo alumnus, Legh Knowles. She didn't want the foremost winery in California to be thought of as an extension of the largest.

Peterson pointed out that Gallo was the only winery doing technical research, and biochemistry was the future of wine in California. The people at Gallo were not all alike, he added. That seemed to reassure her — and the fact that he didn't look and sound like an Italian producer of bulk wine.

Peterson went to work in Rutherford in the spring. André, who stayed on as Beaulieu's consultant, showed him around. Peterson was shocked by the state of the equipment. They were still fermenting white wines in old-fashioned redwood tanks — even aging them in redwood, which caused oxidation, discoloration, and a loss of freshness and complexity. Peterson realized that André had been making great wine at Beaulieu for years using the enological equivalent of baling wire.

After Peterson blurted this out, André said, "My dear sir, after you get to know Mme. de Pins a little better, you will understand that she does not, of her own free will, put money into the winery. After all, the winery is here to support her."

Still, Mme. de Pins often asked why Beaulieu's white wines weren't better. Peterson told her bluntly that stainless steel tanks were absolutely necessary. She said, "Well, you know, I suspected that might be true. If I'm not mistaken, André mentioned that once or twice."

14

BEAULIEU'S new winemaker, Dick Peterson, got his stainless steel fermentation tanks, but that wasn't the end of the problem. Wineries required more capital than other businesses, and Beaulieu required more than most. Peterson told the members of the Beaulieu board that the winery needed an immediate infusion of half a million dollars just to stay operative — a proverbial finger in the dike. That need would change Beaulieu's future and Peterson's, as well as the futures of people only tangentially connected to the legacy of old Georges de Latour, by introducing a new, dominant species to the valley's fauna: the corporation man.

Andy Beckstoffer grew up in Richmond, Virginia, thinking he wanted to be an engineer and spend his adulthood tooling around the Tidewater in some vaguely successful manner. He didn't see himself as particularly ambitious; that came later. He graduated from Virginia Tech and joined the Army, although he didn't have to. He was already married, but young men in Richmond joined the Army.

He found himself a lieutenant at the Presidio in San Francisco, not a bad billet. On weekends the Beckstoffers would sometimes drive up to Napa to check out the wineries. Ordinarily Andy Beckstoffer drank milk, but Napa was pretty. The wineries looked so traditional and romantic.

In 1963 something happened that would change Beckstoffer's life: he heard Jack Kennedy speak at Berkeley. Until then, Beckstoffer had thought of himself simply as a boy from Richmond. But the President spoke forcefully and eloquently about courage, the courage to be a man, the courage to be whatever you wanted to be, even in California. The words touched something in Beckstoffer. He later told people, "I decided then not to be just a boy from Richmond."

He decided to be a capitalist. When he got out of the Army he applied to Stanford but was rejected. He ended up at the Amos Tuck School of Business at Dartmouth College in faraway New Hampshire. He still drank milk, although now it was powdered milk because money was short. By the time he graduated he had further decided, as he put it, "to go as far into the free enterprise system as possible."

Beckstoffer joined the Heublein Corporation, a large producer of spirits with headquarters in Hartford. The notion of taking something nearly worthless — in Heublein's case, raw spirits — and creating vast amounts of capital with it appealed to him. Alcohol cost about five cents a gallon to make. The federal government got twenty-one times that amount in tax on the gallon, and the maker sold it for one hundred times what it cost to make. Now that was real value added!

He had a soft southern accent, large brown eyes, and a nose that gave him a slightly clownish look. Older men tended to trust the boy from Richmond. Beckstoffer moved to the Hartford suburbs and into Heublein's acquisitions department; he became director of "acquisition analysis," a vague position that allowed him to search for companies that might mesh with Heublein's disposable product line, which included Smirnoff vodka, one of the great value-added commodities of all time.

Beckstoffer wasn't interested in snowmobiles for Heublein; he was interested in dog food and wine. He remembered Charles Krug in the Napa Valley and wanted to buy it, but Krug wasn't for sale and was too small to turn the corporate head.

Heublein had already acquired a company called Vintage Wine Merchants, which included Lancers, the sweet Portuguese rosé. More good value added. The supply was vast, the cost of producing Lancers low, and the price disproportionately high. Better still, consumers thought it was good. In the years before the quality wine boom, when people were tired of Gallo's Paisano but uncertain where to go, they started taking Lancers's terra-cotta flasks out of the refrigerator and pouring rosé with spaghetti or chicken breasts. Heublein raised the price even higher.

Lancers was to the budding red wine market what Cold Duck was to champagne. Vintage Wine Merchants sold Cold Duck, too — cheap, purple, fizzy — and moved it by the tanker load. Vintage

Wine Merchants also owned the rights to a line known as Harvey's Classics — cognac, champagne, and some ranked Bordeaux that cost a lot but were unknown to most Americans. They had been imported and warehoused all over America, and it fell to Beckstoffer to get this stuff "under control," collect it in some central location. Getting control, he discovered that many of the labels had been damaged in shipment and storage; the wine didn't look sufficiently "up-market." It could have been sold easily enough through special channels, but the Heublein brass had Lancers and Cold Duck on its mind when it wasn't concerned with Smirnoff. What were a few cases of first- and second-growth Bordeaux compared to three million cases of sweet pink-and-bubbly?

Heublein had a problem, and the boy from Richmond could solve it — not the last time he would find himself in the right place at the right time. Beckstoffer gave some of the precious wine away; warehousemen and forklift drivers were treated to bottles of Lafite and Mouton-Rothschild with scruffy labels and long corks that, once popped, revealed a dense, flavorful wine beyond the appreciation of most Americans, and most Frenchmen. Many bottles went into what became the movable Beckstoffer cellar. He had not been particularly adept at drinking fine wine before, but with a supply that now included '45 Latours to practice on, he improved.

In 1967 Beckstoffer learned that Allied Grape Growers, in California, might consider selling. It was an attractive prospect, but baffling. No one had ever bought an agricultural cooperative before. Allied produced mostly bulk wines. Since it was a cooperative, there were no shares. Where's the equity? Beckstoffer asked. His question was repeated by some of the brass at Heublein, and Beckstoffer took off for the West Coast to find out.

California was pleasant; he enjoyed being back in the place where he and his wife had been so happy. But understanding a co-op was no easy matter, he discovered. For instance, a co-op didn't have stated profits as such, but something called retains — excess returns on the tons of grapes crushed that went into a grower's account. What kind of a bottom line was that? And those farmers bore no resemblance to the executives he was accustomed to dealing with. They just wanted a home for their crops — in this case, grapes — whereas businessmen wanted profits. Of course, they wanted as high a price as they could get for their grapes, and Heublein would be paying if it acquired Allied.

Beckstoffer started spending a day or two a week in California. Some of the data he collected were suspect, like the claim that Allied's sales were equal to Gallo's. That year, Gallo outsold Italian Swiss Colony for the first time, and dry wine outsold sweet. Italian Swiss Colony, owned by Allied, did bring in millions, but the jug-wine business was a jungle where all the trails had changed, with dry wine coming up and the big producers, used to selling sweet, scrambling for new market share. Italian Swiss Colony was in a good position, Heublein decided, to take advantage of this shift.

Heublein would have to buy the parent, Allied, to get the subsidiary, United Vintners, and with it Italian Swiss Colony and what Beckstoffer considered the jewel, Inglenook. Inglenook's production was tiny compared with United Vintners' other respectable performers, including the Petri and Lejon lines, but Inglenook made what was called premium wine. Presumably the labels were in better shape than those on the Harvey's Classics Bordeaux bottles, and even if they weren't, the buyer would get the Inglenook cellar, land, and name.

United Vintners had picked up Inglenook for a paltry $1.2 million. Word that United might now sell everything came from Lou Gomberg, the industry analyst out of San Francisco, who had gotten in touch with the Heublein brass in Hartford. The chief executive officer at Heublein, Stuart Watson, wanted Inglenook. He had a vision of owning this choice Napa Valley estate, but Watson's visions were sometimes problematical. He had evolved from the world of advertising and lacked management skills, in the opinion of some of his underlings.

Lou Gomberg had been approached by Larry Solari, the chairman of United Vintners and a Napa grape grower in his own right, who told him that the whole package, including Inglenook, might be had. United Vintners was really run by Louis Petri. It took Beckstoffer a while to figure it all out. Solari theoretically worked for Allied Grape Growers, since Allied owned United Vintners. But Solari had contempt for Allied's director and paid no attention to him, despite the fact that the director's ego was as big as Solari's. Solari did pay attention to Petri, who was, at least in theory, also answerable to the head of Allied Grape Growers. But Petri was the ranking member of the Allied co-op because the grape production from his own vineyards was larger than anyone else's. In the end, it was Petri who called the shots.

Beckstoffer figured Allied was worth upwards of $35 million. He wanted to buy it without bothering with a financial analysis first. Watson agreed, but one of his underlings pointed out that this made little sense. So Watson farmed out the analysis to a consulting company but stayed with his plan to buy Allied. He had already made two dubious purchases for Heublein, Kentucky Fried Chicken and Hamm beer, and Allied had the potential to be a third. The growers obviously wanted to sell because the trend toward dry wine meant that less grapes were needed, and Allied had a surplus.

Some people later said that the farmers took the eastern city slickers to the cleaners. It didn't look that way then to Andy Beckstoffer. The director of Allied seemed reluctant to sell, so Beckstoffer worked through Solari. He went to Solari's house on Larkmead Lane in Napa. They had a drink and Beckstoffer provided information that Solari could use on Allied's director: Allied had no means of promoting and marketing its wines; drinking had moved from sweet to dry and sparkling, and Allied lacked the capital to convert its operations. Heublein could handle both problems. "You guys have the grapes and the brands," Beckstoffer told Solari. "We have the cash and the marketing expertise. Let us carry you into the new world."

The director of Allied Grape Growers tentatively agreed to a sale that would give the co-op members a chunk of Heublein stock. But first the members had to approve. The director traveled around California pitching the deal, accompanied by Beckstoffer and Stuart Watson, whom Beckstoffer got to know very well. Watson loved Napa Valley, with its comely estates, and hated the little central California farm towns. He raised Charolais cattle on a picture-book plot in New England and saw himself as a gentleman farmer. The irony was that he thought he was buying quaint little Napa Valley when he bought Allied; in fact, he was buying the dusty roads and gritty vistas of the Central Valley, and only incidentally getting Inglenook.

Beckstoffer smoothed things out as best he could and made sure Allied's director didn't screw up the presentations. The growers went for the deal. Heublein had to pay an additional $65 million for Allied's inventory from the upcoming harvest, and then Beckstoffer and Watson flew off to Caesars Palace in Las Vegas for a little R & R.

Heublein was now in the wine business in a big way. It had to use all Allied grapes, but nobody was worried about that. Grapes were grapes, after all. The production of Navalle, which had never topped five thousand cases when John Daniel owned Inglenook, would reach *eight million* cases under Heublein and essentially bail the company out. And by owning Inglenook, Heublein could make a quality claim — that the corporation was serious about wine when actually the opposite was true.

The Inglenook deal was the first of many that would radically alter Napa Valley. It nudged Walter Sullivan over the edge. As Mme. de Pins's son-in-law and the husband of Dagmar, Sullivan had to listen to a lot of complaining about the costs of running Beaulieu Vineyard. The family he had married into was a typical French matriarchy: the "girls" — his word — consulted, and Mme. de Pins made all the decisions. She didn't want to borrow the capital needed to keep BV going; neither did she want to sell the considerable stock left by old man de Latour and use that money for refurbishing. She didn't want all the eggs in one basket.

Yet the refurbishing had to be done. The girls knew it, and at the same time they didn't know it. Only someone in the family could understand how that might be, someone like Walter Sullivan. He understood the limitations of privilege. He enjoyed the pleasures of life and had grown stout after his polo-playing days, but he could still *act*.

Sullivan reasoned — to himself — that if Heublein had been interested in Inglenook, then it might also be interested in BV. Beaulieu's lawyer, Ted Kolb, was a friend of his, as well as a friend of Louis Petri's, and Sullivan secretly discussed with Kolb the possibility of selling Beaulieu. Sullivan knew that word would reach Petri and, through Petri, the people at Heublein, that Beaulieu might be had. Discretion was mandatory, Sullivan told Kolb. He did not want Mme. de Pins or Dagmar to know what he was up to until it was a done deal.

The message was delivered, and the drums began to beat. Sullivan then suggested that Kolb tell Petri to bring Stuart Watson to lunch in Rutherford the next time Heublein's CEO found himself on the West Coast. There was nothing like a tour of the grounds and good French cuisine to impress visitors. Sullivan posed the idea to Mme. de Pins and Dagmar as well, casting it as a simple gesture of hospitality. "After all," he told them, "they're our neighbors."

The group grew to include Legh Knowles and one of Heublein's attorneys. Larry Solari might have been a luncheon guest as well, but there Mme. de Pins drew the line: she could abide Petri but not his egregiously Italian sidekick.

What Watson saw when the car turned west off Highway 29 was a corridor of sycamores, BV's choice vineyards, and the spectacle of the de Latour home. Walter Sullivan was aware of the impact of the grounds on an easterner. The de Latour place was not for sale, of course, only the winery and some other vineyards, but the estate lent a regal air to BV, just across the road.

Sullivan knew what the Heublein executives did not: that premium wineries were capital-intensive businesses that paid back nothing in the short run and sometimes nothing forever. People owned them for the style of life they offered, not the return, and that style would be impossible to reproduce in 1968 with Beaulieu's problems. And even if it could be reproduced, it could not be enjoyed from Hartford, Connecticut.

During lunch Watson said, "Now that we own Inglenook, we're trying to be good neighbors."

The right words, certainly. Mme. des Pins and Dagmar did not suspect that the words obscured a very real assessment, not of the property but of the disposition of the owners.

Sullivan took Watson and Petri aside, on the pretext of touring the gardens. He told them, "If you make an unsolicited offer for Beaulieu, it will receive favorable consideration."

Andy Beckstoffer pushed the idea of buying Beaulieu while aboard Heublein's Falcon, flying from Hartford to Reston, Virginia, to buy Virginia Gentleman, the bourbon distillers. Also on the plane were Stuart Watson and John Martin, the chairman. Beckstoffer argued that Beaulieu was possibly the best winery in Napa Valley, had more production than Inglenook and, most important, a national distribution system. In short, Beaulieu was a better property from a public relations point of view, and had a better portfolio.

Watson was already convinced, and Martin didn't seem to care much one way or the other. An international playboy and a friend of Howard Hughes's, Martin was part of the family that had started Heublein, which had gotten unwieldy. But Smirnoff's profits could cover a lot of bad deals. Martin said that any property they acquired ought to be able to produce two million cases of wine a year, and left it at that.

They agreed, on the way back to Hartford, to buy Beaulieu anyway. They would go as high as $8 million.

Walter Sullivan decided that Heublein's first offer, whatever it was, would be too low. He had no doubt that Heublein would come back; what he feared was a leak. Any kind of public speculation about the sale of fabulous Beaulieu would alarm his mother-in-law, and the deal — if there was to be a deal — would certainly fall through.

When the Heublein offer came, it was for a stock swap. Sullivan wasn't interested in stock; he wanted cash. Then Hartford sent young Andy Beckstoffer out to negotiate, accompanied by a couple of lawyers. They all met in Kolb's office. Sullivan had a tax man there as well. They hammered away at one another until 3 A.M.

A few hours later Sullivan went to the girls. He told Mme. de Pins and Dagmar that he had an agreement of sale for $8.4 million. He showed them a document signed by Heublein's representatives. All they had to do was agree, he said, and Beaulieu would be off their hands forever.

Dagmar broke down. Mme. de Pins demanded, "How could you do this?"

"Better to sell when you can," Walter said — the old argument — "than when you have to."

Slowly Mme. de Pins's resolve ran out; so did Dagmar's. She loved the winery and had spent many hours there. She had been afraid of her grandmother, Mme. de Latour, who woke everyone up at 8:30 A.M. and insisted on their eating breakfast, and had cleared out of the house as soon as possible. As angry as Dagmar now was, she knew she couldn't stop the sale. She felt that it was a fait accompli. She and her mother were, after all, just women.

It took them a week to come around to Walter's point of view. Meanwhile, he kept the sale under wraps. Publicity was distasteful in most cases, and certainly now, when an heirloom was being sold to a corporation, and an eastern one at that. Walter didn't discuss the prospect with his wife again. In his opinion she had swept it and her emotions under the rug, where they would smolder for decades.

The day the sale went through, Sullivan met Beckstoffer for a drink in the opulence of the Pacific Union Club. Beckstoffer had the necessary checks in his pocket, but no crass business could be transacted in those rooms, so he and Sullivan went outside and sat in Beckstoffer's rented car to exchange the checks and sign the papers.

Legh Knowles was one of the last BV executives to hear about it. He had set up good distribution for Beaulieu's wines, with low commissions and coverage as broad as the nation. The allocation was working, creating the impression of scarcity. Beaulieu's luster kept attracting the moths. Heublein wanted to buy it, and so did Budweiser and Bacardi. Also Georgia-Pacific. An agent of Kobrand had contacted Knowles on behalf of Louis Latour of Burgundy. Knowles kept saying no, no, no. All the while he tried to get the family to spend some money.

He received a call from Ted Kolb's secretary in San Francisco. Would Mr. Knowles come by the office? Knowles walked in and found Mme. de Pins and Dagmar there, in tears, Walter Sullivan and their lawyer, looking appropriately glum, and Heublein's West Coast representative. That tipped off Knowles to what had happened.

Mme. de Pins was a strong woman, but she cried out, "We have to sell!"

Knowles knew she didn't have to and also that there was nothing he could do about the decision. Heublein's representative offered Knowles a job on the spot, that of general manager, at a better salary. But Knowles was suspicious. Petri was involved, and Larry Solari, chairman of United Vintners, who was not a pleasant person. In five years United Vintners had had five presidents because no one could get along with Solari. And Solari didn't like Knowles and claimed that he played golf every day at the Silverado Country Club.

Knowles said, "I've got to talk to Masson and Gallo first." He knew he could get a job with either if things didn't work out.

What had happened, with remarkable suddenness, was the transformation of Beaulieu from an independent, highly regarded Napa Valley château into a piece of corporate property. When the Federal Trade Commission filed an antitrust suit against Heublein for allegedly destroying competition in the wine market, Heublein would put Beaulieu and Inglenook under the Smirnoff umbrella. Knowles now realized that if he stayed, he would again be working for a big company, with all the headaches and corporate infighting he thought he had left behind in Modesto.

Walter Sullivan could barely wait to get him out into the corridor, where Walter shed his solemnity, and said, "Guess how much we got? Eight and a half million dollars!"

•

It didn't take Knowles long to find out what Larry Solari thought of the deal. Solari danced through the halls of United Vintners, shouting, "Only eight and a half million! . . . They got it for *only eight and a half million dollars!*"

Then he passed along a message to Knowles: "I'll give Legh three months to clean up that goddamn country club."

If the announcement of the Inglenook sale had surprised the valley, the sale of Beaulieu brought consternation and some fear. The irony was lost on most people, but not on André Tchelistcheff. He remembered that Georges de Latour had wanted his daughter, Hélène, to marry an American businessman, thereby assuring the survival of Beaulieu as a family enterprise. Hélène married Marquis de Pins instead, and Beaulieu proved more enduring than he.

Hélène and the marquis had wanted their daughter, Dagmar, to marry a French aristocrat, but she chose an American businessman. And he had delivered Beaulieu into the jaws of the whale.

15

"NOW WE OWN Napa Valley," Andy Beckstoffer said in 1969. He was twenty-nine years old and vice president of planning. If he had a problem with one of the Heublein reps — somebody in Allied, United Vintners, anywhere — he could go over his head to Stuart Watson in Hartford.

The workers at Inglenook grew accustomed to the sight of a brash young man in a coat and tie marching around giving orders. Some thought Beckstoffer lacked a proper appreciation of Inglenook's heritage; others found him downright obnoxious. He did not seem interested in the views of locals if they happened to be contrary to his own. He acted as if he owned Niebaum's creation, from the cupola to the ornate chairs in the Captain's Room.

His least tolerable activity, in the eyes of what was left of the original office staff, involved the cases of old Inglenook Cabernet and Pinot Noir that Beckstoffer ordered removed from the cellar, wine with great emotional resonance. The employees watched John Daniel deal reverently with these heirlooms from Inglenook's wine collection, and one of the women had the temerity to tell the boy from Richmond, "You're not supposed to do that," as he ordered up more wine. Beckstoffer just signed a piece of paper and carted off the dusty bottles.

Inglenook belonged to a giant concern in distant Connecticut, apparently without concern. Beckstoffer was its de facto representative and presumably had good reason, and certainly the power, to open priceless bottles.

One of those having the most trouble with Beckstoffer's *modus* was Robin Lail, John Daniel's daughter and the unofficial guardian of Niebaum's legacy. Robin didn't think of herself as appointed; afflicted would be a better word. She was interested in working at

Inglenook but couldn't stand by and watch what she considered an inexcusable waste of resources and a flouting of tradition. She complained to Beckstoffer and was finally banished from the winery.

Solari and Beckstoffer together had pushed for the sale of Allied Grape Growers to Heublein. As the head of United Vintners, which now included Inglenook and Beaulieu, as well as Italian Swiss Colony, Solari had to deal with the gargantuan supply of Allied fruit from the Central Valley. He was committed to using it, so Heublein began to produce an ocean of pop wine, not just Cold Duck and the standby sweeties but also Bali Hai, Zapple (made of apples), and a cola-flavored creation called I Love You. The brand managers for these were Dick Maher and a man hired by Maher, both of whom would rise curiously through the ranks of Heublein long after I Love You was forgotten.

Beckstoffer decided that Beaulieu, too, had potential for growth. Value added. Two weeks after the sale, he set up a breakfast meeting with Dick Peterson, Beaulieu's enologist, at the Silverado Country Club, a suitable site, he thought, for impressing a chemist from Iowa.

They met in the plush solarium, over a white tablecloth. Before the eggs arrived Beckstoffer said, "Dick, I'd like to know why you're using Chenin Blanc to make champagne."

Peterson, tall and thin, gazed intently through steel-rimmed spectacles. He was touchy on this subject. Beaulieu's champagne was usually made from Chardonnay and Pinot Noir, the traditional blend, but shortages had forced him to use some Chenin Blanc that year. He thought Beckstoffer was worried about quality, as Peterson was. He said defensively, "I didn't have enough Chardonnay."

"I don't mean that. I mean, you can get Thompson seedless for eighty dollars a ton, and you're paying a lot more than that for Chenin."

Thompson seedless was primarily a raisin grape from the Central Valley. But Beckstoffer made no distinction between it and the classic Napa Valley varietals. Cold Duck and Beaulieu champagne, the bottom and the top of the market, were apparently the same to him. Peterson told Beckstoffer, "Andy, let's just eat our breakfast. There's nothing you could do to make me use Thompson seedless in Beaulieu wines."

"Dick," Beckstoffer said, "you'll never make a million dollars."

Two weeks later a Heublein financial expert showed up to look Beaulieu over. He recommended grafting all Beaulieu vines to Gamay Beaujolais, another less-than-stellar grape, to increase "turnover" and cash flow. He wanted to get rid of Beaulieu's Cabernet, Pinot Noir, and Chardonnay, the strengths of the company for thirty years — the things that set Beaulieu apart from everybody else. He wanted 140,000 cases of Gamay Beaujolais!

Peterson made no secret of his contempt for these new guys. It was only Legh Knowles's diplomatic talents that postponed Peterson's departure from Beaulieu. Knowles told the corporate officers that wine is made from fresh grapes, not from long-range plans, and that running a quality operation was not a part-time job that could be done from the other side of the continent.

Peterson had already begun to formulate his "janitor's theory." Corporations, he decided, automatically presume that the janitor in the office is better informed than the Ph.D. in the field, and that the greater the distance between corporate headquarters and industrial production, the dumber the people out there.

Heublein's vice president in charge of manufacturing proved it. He came to Rutherford, learned that Beaulieu needed ten new 8,000-gallon fermenting tanks, and told Knowles, "Legh, you're in the big time now. Just ask for one eighty-thousand-gallon tank."

Knowles said gently, "We like to ferment our red and white wines separately."

The breakfast meeting had not gone off quite as Beckstoffer had expected. Peterson was dangerously independent. But if Beaulieu needed good grapes — better than Thompson seedless — then Beckstoffer would find them. It wasn't easy. For one thing, Robert Mondavi, who had a new winery down the road in Oakville, was reportedly going around the valley telling growers to sell their Cabernet to him, not to these East Coasters who didn't know wine from Alpo and Kentucky Fried Chicken.

Beckstoffer had an idea: start a big farming operation to supply Beaulieu with Napa Valley fruit. He went around to various growers and tried to convince them to tear out their old Carignan and French Colombard and replace them with Cabernet, Pinot Noir, and Chardonnay. The growers didn't relish the idea. For one thing, Cabernet produced only about three tons of grapes an acre, while Carignan produced eight. The growers didn't drink Cabernet and Pinot Noir and so weren't sympathetic.

All this he reported to Hartford; Watson told him, "Get vineyards!"

The Keig ranch — five hundred acres of pasture and potential vineyard in the heart of prime Cabernet country known as the Rutherford Bench — could be had for $2 million. Beckstoffer advised United Vintners to buy it. The Keig ranch could be planted in Cabernet, lots of Cabernet, and the grapes used to supply Beaulieu, which might then increase its production and make more money for Heublein. It was as simple as that. The truth was that all the land was not suited to grapes — there was a reason it had remained in pasture — as André Tchelistcheff and others told Knowles. But Knowles was not invited to take part in the decision made by Beckstoffer, Watson, and Solari.

The Keig ranch was officially purchased by the Vinifera Development Corporation, a shell for Heublein's land acquisitions. VDC also bought other vineyardland in Napa and in Mendocino County that had belonged to Petri and the Cellas and their associates. With VDC, Heublein could quietly bank land without people thinking Hartford was buying up the entire North Coast. Included in VDC was Beaulieu's vineyard operations, and heading VDC was the boy from Richmond.

Beckstoffer began the transformation from corporate executive to corporate farmer. He was living now in Atherton, down on the peninsula south of San Francisco, with its broad lawns and sprawling houses, but his attention was focused on the undeveloped regions north of the bay. He was on the road most of the time. Instead of annual reports, spreadsheets, value added, and the usual pop wines, Beckstoffer had to learn about rootstock, grafting, trellising, pruning, soil compaction, and the basic differences between, say, Cabernet Sauvignon and Thompson seedless.

He also had to learn about labor contracts, soon to be a hugely contentious issue in the Napa Valley. As the head of Vinifera Development, he had to deal with the union that became the United Farm Workers, a powerful force in California agriculture and one with a broad following, indicated by a successful national boycott of lettuce. The union's founder, Cesar Chavez, had led a strike of Mexican and Filipino workers in Delano in 1965, and since then his power had grown. The UFW had more than a hundred contracts in California and Arizona and claimed a membership of thirty thousand. The union's demands affected not just individual growers but also giants like Coca-Cola, United Fruit, Tenneco, and, as things turned out, Heublein.

The UFW flourished in the San Joaquin Valley, which is sixty miles wide and two hundred miles long, the greater southern stretch of the Central Valley and a natural incubator for a labor movement. He switched from lettuce to fruit and grapes, and singled out the 1,700 members of Allied Grape Growers, former owner of United Vintners and the major supplier of United Vintners' grapes. United Vintners now belonged to Heublein, and so the UFW planned a boycott of Heublein products as part of a broader strategy to get at the big Central Valley growers. The problem fell right into Andy Beckstoffer's lap.

Chavez wanted Heublein to bring pressure on Allied to accept the UFW as the representative union in the Central Valley. Other Heublein brass met with Chavez's representatives and tried to convince them that Heublein had no control over Allied. In the original sale, Allied had simply acquired 18 percent of United Vintners. Heublein had agreed to buy all its grapes from Allied, but was not responsible for Allied's labor practices and supposedly had no influence on Allied's collective decisions.

Chavez remained unconvinced and called for the boycott of Heublein products. Heublein executives were puzzled by this new phenomenon that had arisen among political groupies and even housewives. In Chicago and New York — all over — people were walking into supermarkets and liquor stores and *not* buying what they were supposed to buy. They were turning up their noses at products, and that meant loss of revenue.

The previous boycotts had made Cesar Chavez a celebrity and, ironically, everybody at Heublein wanted to meet him, including Stuart Watson and Jack Martin. Then things got nasty. Some union people camped out on Heublein's steps; others interrupted speeches of Heublein executives. The loss of sales of Hamm beer and Italian Swiss Colony wine was bad enough, but when Smirnoff began to suffer, Hartford panicked. Watson had seen what bad publicity had done to the stock of Dow Chemical Company, a major supplier for the Army in Vietnam and now a new American dirty word. As Beckstoffer told him, "We're talking imagery here."

What if Heublein acquired a similar reputation as an oppressor of the downtrodden? What if Smirnoff and Kentucky Fried became, in the public's mind, consumer versions of napalm?

Beckstoffer advised Stuart Watson to tell Allied to give in to Chavez. The big California growers had resisted reform for decades and were hostile even to the idea. Many believed Chavez had less interest in the farm workers than in his own organization and, ultimately, in political dominance. But living and working conditions of laborers in the Central Valley were abysmal.

In Napa, things were quite different. The valley was relatively insignificant in the larger picture of California agriculture. Even during crush there were no hordes of migrant laborers. The wines produced were much better than those from the Central Valley, so quality and scenic views — nature and those Victorian piles — attracted tourists, what was becoming an important industry in itself. Napa's overall fruit production was tiny compared with the mountains of grapes harvested out beyond the Sacramento and San Joaquin rivers.

Chavez didn't really care about Napa but wanted Heublein's leverage and so had decided to go after all Heublein products, not just wine. In some places the goods were off the shelves for as long as six months, and the corporation was looking at its first down quarter since it went public.

Beckstoffer decided to give Heublein's leverage to Chavez. Brand protection, he called it. He knew his bosses' fear of Chavez was rooted in ignorance of farming and farm management problems, amounting at times almost to paranoia. Once again the boy from Richmond found himself in the right position. He reasoned that Heublein and the Vinifera Development Corporation had nothing to lose in settling with Chavez: their production in Napa was relatively small. They didn't need mechanical harvesting, a pivotal issue in the Central Valley. Heublein couldn't care less if the lumbering picking machines were banned from the entire state of California.

And if the United Farm Workers got a real toehold in Napa, so what? Christian Brothers had signed with Chavez in 1967, giving him everything he wanted. Beringer was in its death throes. Robert Mondavi was still struggling. People in Napa Valley were treating Beckstoffer and his minions like lepers. Beckstoffer figured Heublein and the Vinifera Development Corporation were on their own.

He devised a strategy: treat Chavez's people, if not as associates, then as friends. The UFW had made headlines all over the country, and its leader was celebrated as a champion of the downtrodden. Beckstoffer would recognize these things and deal with the union officials as equals. Chavez himself was beyond Beckstoffer's reach, but his lawyer, Jerry Cohn, was not. Cohn struck Beckstoffer as smart, foul-mouthed, and sometimes reasonable. Beckstoffer invited him to a baseball game, and Cohn accepted. Then he invited Cohn to his house in Atherton. Jerry Cohn came, and what was better, he brought Dolores Huerta with him.

Huerta, Chavez's right hand, was tougher than Cohn, and as smart. Beckstoffer considered her the soul of the union. He wanted to get on her good side and offered her a Hamm's as an ice breaker. Apparently she thought this amusing, and drank the beer, a small triumph for the boy from Richmond. But there wasn't a lot of banter. Beckstoffer could see that Huerta considered Heublein and Allied the same bunch of bastards who were exploiting the pickers, and he set out to differentiate between the two. They weren't the same, Beckstoffer said, and he could prove it. He brought out Heublein's contract with Allied and showed it to her. He pointed out that Heublein did not own the cooperative and so could not make the concessions Chavez and Huerta and Jerry Cohn wanted. Heublein was powerless when it came to Allied. However, he added, Heublein could make its own concessions. Beckstoffer was ready to do that on behalf of Heublein if the boycott was stopped.

The next day, Beckstoffer went down to San Jose to meet Chavez. He found Chavez in bed with a bad back — and two guard dogs to protect him, named Huelga and Causa. Beckstoffer carefully shook Chavez's hand, but the real negotiating took place in a nearby motel room. Cohn was there, and some other UFW officials, all crowded in the small, unadorned space. A few Heublein people were present, too, but Beckstoffer ran the show. He agreed to union representation in the vineyards of Inglenook and Beaulieu, and to a ban on mechanized harvesting for four years.

That gave Chavez's people obvious pleasure. Cohn promised to name a street for Beckstoffer in the town of La Paz, the union's headquarters, for making that concession, which was of little importance for Heublein and of great significance for the union.

Beckstoffer wrote it all out on a yellow legal pad and signed the agreement on top of the television set. They all read it. He brought in bottles of Inglenook Chardonnay and everybody had a glass. Then they all signed the labels in an atmosphere of cautious festivity.

Chavez arrived in the back of a pickup, driven over to give his official blessing. He bestowed it on the gathering, but he told Cohn, "Well, Jerry, I guess we sold them out again."

Beckstoffer could take credit for ending the boycott — and incidentally for sticking Heublein's competitors in the valley with some real problems.

16

MEMBERS OF the United Farm Workers drove up Highway 29 in 1971, dropping in on Mondavi, Martini, Krug, Kornell, and others who had not signed, demanding to see the owners and threatening boycotts of anyone refusing a union contract. It was a moment the wineries had anticipated and feared. The owners convened at the Napa County Farm Bureau to plan some resistance. They knew Chavez didn't represent the majority of the workers in the valley — his people had not even consulted with them — and the owners did not intend to cave in.

Chavez was a potent force even in the abstract. He had temporarily shut down the Central Valley's grape and lettuce business, Christian Brothers had given him a toehold in Napa, and then Heublein had flung open the door. Now the wineries fell back on an organization that had grown out of a previous, unrelated struggle with the state, over an attempt to build a four-lane highway up the middle of the valley. Then, vintners, growers, members of Upper Napa Valley Associates, and free-lance conservationists had gone head-to-head with the California Department of Transportation and won. The organization was revived and expanded to include people from Sonoma and Mendocino counties and the Livermore Valley, and a lawyer from the California Farm Bureau, brought in to give them advice.

They called themselves the Winegrowers Council. They collected some money, put together a letterhead, and sent out spokesmen. One of these was a bearded, soft-spoken former carpenter named Rennick Harris, known as Ren, son-in-law of Andy Pelissa, who had sat on the Napa County Planning Commission when the ag preserve was created. Harris had been chairman of the committee that fought the highway. Before that he belonged to the carpenters' union in San

Francisco, and he had some ideas about workers' benefits that might apply to vineyard labor. But before those could be discussed, the Winegrowers Council had to deal with the Farm Workers boycott of North Coast wines.

The growers agreed that the vineyard workers needed to be represented. They began to publicly advocate a secret ballot to let the workers themselves decide who would represent them. The election could be supervised by the National Labor Relations Board. The Farm Workers had expected the small North Coast wineries to be a pushover, as Christian Brothers and Heublein had been. Union officials didn't want to wait for government intervention to arrive on creaking wheels. They also didn't want, in Ren Harris's opinion, an alternative to themselves to be made available to the workers.

Harris started traveling around the state to counter the boycott of fine California wine. He talked to the press and to the wine retailers, restaurateurs, church and temple congregations, even the American Civil Liberties Union. Why would the Farm Workers oppose a secret ballot? he kept asking. Meanwhile, the growers filed complaints in seventeen different judicial districts, seeking restraining orders against the boycott, and the NLRB finally ended it. But the fight over who would represent the workers was just beginning.

Harris was driving north on Highway 29 when a car — a blue Valiant, he remembered, full of screaming people — pulled alongside, then veered toward him. Harris wheeled onto the shoulder of the highway and jammed the brake pedal, putting his car in a spin. He took off in the opposite direction, leaving his pursuers in a cloud of dust.

The incident didn't bother him at the time; it was, he thought, an independent act of intimidation. Then someone followed him all the way to Alturis, three hundred miles away. Strangers started hanging around his house in Yountville. So he bought a .357 Magnum, got a concealed-weapon permit, and began to carry the pistol wherever he went.

Harris thought the growers had more to offer the vineyard workers than the union did. He wanted to take a page out of his past experience in the carpenters' union, when he had been allowed to float from contractor to contractor while keeping his benefits. Why couldn't the field workers have the same arrangement?

He proposed the idea to the membership of what had become the Growers Foundation, a more formal organization than the Winegrowers Council, and still growing. Even Louie Stralla had joined. The foundation would set aside 17.5 percent of the gross payroll in the vineyards and allot 2.5 percent of it to workers' pensions, 6 percent to vacations, 7 percent to health and life insurance, and 2 percent to run the foundation. They would establish a minimum wage of $3.50 an hour and allow the workers to move from job to job without losing a thing — a better deal than the one offered by Chavez and the United Farm Workers.

The growers needed somebody to sell the idea to the workers, not just in the North Coast counties but all over California. They needed someone closely associated with the vineyards, someone able to speak Spanish who was respected and willing to undertake a dangerous assignment. Harris wasn't sure such a person existed.

Rafael Rodriguez had managed Inglenook's vineyards for Solari and United Vintners, and went on managing them for Heublein. There were changes. He had been told to plant some new Cabernet and for the first time to use chemical spray to control parasites. John Daniel had always let the land lie fallow, to cleanse itself naturally, but the new owners didn't want to wait.

They didn't want to listen, either. Strangers gave the orders, and inquired often into Rafael's qualifications. He had an important job and no formal training, a Heublein man told him. The implication was that experience was not enough, yet Rafael was given the adjacent Beaulieu vineyards to tend in addition to Inglenook's. The acreage under vines that was Rafael's responsibility jumped from 100 to 250, a very large planting by Napa standards, but his pay remained the same.

Despite the workload, he found himself drawn beyond the rows of vines and into valley life. The 1960s were coming to an end, but the emotions and the discontent the decade had spawned showed no sign of abating. Rafael was himself confused by many things in America. His son was in Vietnam, but Rafael had some doubts about that war. He had doubts about the federal government, and sometimes found himself comparing it to Heublein — distant, autocratic, without regard for the individual. The workers had begun to complain of their treatment at the hands of the growers and the wineries all over California. Abuses existed and should have been addressed years before, but Rafael did not trust the union organizers.

The superintendent of the St. Helena schools came to see Rafael, and told him, "The Mexican students are out of the mainstream," as if Rafael did not already know that. There was little housing for Mexicans in the valley, no places for them to socialize, no regular festivals. The jobs most Mexicans held were seasonal and their lives migratory; the ones living year-round in the valley made very little money, so it wasn't surprising that their kids were out of the mainstream.

The superintendent was a good man willing to face the resentment of some in the community who might not want a Mexican on the school board. "There are lots of good Mexican students," he said. "They need some representation. I want you to run."

"You're talking Anglo," Rafael told him.

The superintendent offered to coach him in campaigning and in board-room behavior. "The community knows you, Rafael. You won't have any trouble."

Rafael was elected. He started attending the meetings, trying to acquaint himself with this democratic process. He discovered that it wasn't so difficult. Some of the members seemed genuinely concerned with the plight of the students, including the Mexicans, while others wanted to go through the paces of assimilation just to get the funds the schools needed. This disgusted Rafael, but he kept going to the meetings.

He had been raised to think that gringos were no good, that America was no good. But he was learning something different. In many ways — not just economics — Mexico was no better. Being discriminated against in Spanish was just as bad as being discriminated against in English. In America you could speak out. Rafael often spoke his mind and found that people listened.

The word came down from the head office at Inglenook that he was to cut down the almond trees. They had lined the drive for as long as Rafael had been in the valley but now were supposedly too old. Rafael did not agree. No one asked his opinion, however, because that was not the way Heublein operated, so he had them cut.

Looking east from the front porch of the little clapboard house he and Tila had lived in for half a dozen years, he no longer saw the green leaves of the almonds. Instead, he saw squat grapefruit trees he had been told to plant in their stead, with oleanders in between. No one had asked his opinion about that, either. The oleanders were host to many insects and eventually had to be pulled out, and the grapefruit trees all died of the frost.

Rafael grew increasingly dissatisfied with the vineyard operations at Inglenook and Beaulieu. Teamwork had gone out with the old management, and so had the proven practices of the past, like hand watering and careful pruning. Rafael was told to move the pruners faster, to do thirty vines an hour, minimum — too many to do it right.

Then Heublein brought in the union and things got worse. Rafael wasn't even allowed in the vineyards during pruning; consequently, the vines were going to pot. The union activities distracted the workers, who were required to picket elsewhere during their time off. It seemed they were always getting fined by the Farm Workers. This led to bad feelings and further difficulties on both sides. Through all the changes, the production increases, and the union headaches, Rafael's pay stayed the same.

Rafael received a baffling telephone call. A gringo he barely knew invited him to the house of another gringo in the valley. Rafael didn't know him, either, but when he arrived he recognized several faces: big growers and winery owners, not just from Napa but from Sonoma and even farther away. They all sat in a room and talked about a plan to provide benefits for the workers who refused to join Chavez's union. That interested Rafael.

The men wanted to know what he thought about the Farm Workers. He told them of the problems with supervision and quality control. They asked how many acres of vineyard he oversaw, and when he said 250, they were clearly impressed.

One of the men said, "Rafael, we need a face. If we try to present this thing to the workers, it'll be called a gringo trap."

He thought about it: these men might be gringos but they had a good idea. And the salary they proposed was three times what he was getting from Heublein.

The next day he walked up to Beckstoffer in the lobby of Inglenook, and told him, "I think I'm entitled to an increase."

"You're living in one of the best houses in the county," Beckstoffer said, as if that answer sufficed.

Rafael gave him two weeks' notice and walked away.

As president of the Growers Foundation he had to move from the property where his children had been raised and where he and Tila had been content. He would have to find a house in a valley with few Mexican-American neighborhoods, and high rents, and that's what Rafael set out to do.

He encountered Louie Stralla on the street in St. Helena. He didn't really know Stralla, and assumed he was a wealthy grower like others in the valley. Stralla seemed to know him, however. "Rafael," he said, "it's a shame you don't have a house of your own."

Rafael wanted to say, "How the hell do you expect me to buy a house on a field worker's pay?" Instead, he smiled and nodded.

Stralla took him into the bank and introduced him to the manager. "Give him a mortgage," Stralla told the man.

Rafael was told to find a house he liked. He did, off Zinfandel Lane, a bungalow with a carport, a lawn, lots of windows, and a fine, broad kitchen. There were trees out back. Tila agreed that it was a beautiful house and unfortunately fell in love with it, for when Rafael went back to the bank, he discovered he needed to put down $10,000 to get the mortgage. Rafael did not have that kind of money.

He ran into Stralla again, who said, "Did you get a house?"

"No," said Rafael, and started to explain. Stralla took him back into the bank. He told the manager to make some calls, and after more discussion Rafael got his mortgage.

Rafael was president of the Growers Foundation but his job lay in the field, selling the organization to the workers. They were mostly Mexicans and Mexican Americans who regarded him with a mixture of resentment and curiosity. Many workers did not even know they had a choice of who would represent them. Rafael pointed out to them, in groups and in private, the advantages of the foundation's program, and took heat from members of the United Farm Workers. They and their allies called his home when he was there and when he was away; they cajoled, then threatened. His family was frightened but would not admit it, and Rafael never discussed the dangers with them. That was part of his new life.

Police protection was offered but he turned it down; he traveled unarmed. In the field he was asked repeatedly, "Why are you doing this? Why are you siding with the Anglos and not with the workers?"

Over and over again he explained that he *was* on the side of the workers, that he wanted them to get a better deal than the union offered. They had a choice. His mission was to make them understand that, if nothing else.

In the speeches he gave he found himself talking often about his own life in Mexico City, about the hardship and discrimination. Patronage was the real problem, he realized — a system that made workers dependent on a small class or group of people, who extracted concessions, and even thanks, from them in the process. "You're falling under the patronage and the ideology of the union," Rafael said, his words making the union representatives more unhappy.

But the workers listened. They talked about their own lives — in town halls, in restaurants, on the dusty streets of little Central Valley towns. Often they wept and Rafael felt like weeping, too. The stories were so similar to his own, the circumstances little changed from those he had encountered in the Watsonville barrio and in the Zócalo in Mexico City.

The most difficult trips were those he made down to El Centro and Calexico, at the bottom of California, where the legals and illegals came by the thousands, looking for work. Every day before dawn they converged at El Hoyo, the Hole, swarming in the gritty darkness, hoping to be chosen by the labor brokers and assigned to trucks and buses that trundled them off to distant fields. It was here, amidst the smoke, the noise, and the threats, that Rafael moved among the men, explaining, entreating, sweating. He did not upbraid his opponents; he smiled and shook their hands, and when they refused to shake hands he did not take it personally. He argued the issues — pay, benefits, dues — and never once lost his temper.

Before daybreak the last of the supplicants would be gone and Rafael would find himself alone in the cold dawn, wondering if he could get back to his car safely. He was not afraid; he had eaten rotten banana skins off the floor of La Merced thirty years before, and that had been worse than threats from the union men in the dusty immensity of El Hoyo.

He did lose his temper with the growers. There were some members of the foundation who were willing to make changes for the workers' benefit — better pay, better housing, better hours, better toilets — and then there were those who only promised or pretended while life in the fields and vineyards went on as before. These men Rafael denounced to Ren Harris and the foundation's board of directors. Eventually they were forced to abide by the new standards, but it took time and it undid much of the work Rafael had accomplished in the field.

He came to represent 1,500 workers in three counties. In Napa, the UFW was still strong, and obstreperous. A few barns and hayfields were burned. After Christian Brothers and Heublein, Krug and Trefethen Vineyards signed up with the UFW. Things were happening in Napa: more plantings, more big companies spending more money, more tourists who had no idea what went on behind those winery façades and out in the vineyards. Each time Rafael passed through Rutherford his eye would pass over the vineyards of Inglenook and those of Beaulieu across Navalle Creek. It seemed he had worked there long ago.

Heublein had managed to offend almost everybody in the valley. They had further undermined Inglenook's reputation and begun the degradation of Beaulieu's. They had created an agricultural unit large enough to attract the attention of the union and then capitulated to it. They had let good people go, from the winemaker to Rafael. When at last they found themselves in virtual control of the valley, they began to sell off their most valuable vineyards to other outsiders. They discouraged their employees from taking part in politics and valley life. The list went on.

The biggest insult, the collective sign of corporate hubris, was the storage facility that went up in front of Inglenook, spoiling the view of the winery from Highway 29. To build this common warehouse, this hulking eyesore, Heublein had despoiled some of the best Cabernet vineyardland in the valley, sacrosanct since the days of Gustave Niebaum. The structure squatted there at the base of the Mayacamas like a permanent obscene gesture offered to the natives by a bureaucracy sequestered on the far side of the continent.

17

ANDRÉ TCHELISTCHEFF had seen thirty winters in the Napa Valley. The vines looked like black, spindly troops regimented by the cordons. Beside them glowed masses of wild mustard, first green and then a vibrant yellow after flowering. Splintered ice edged pools of water in the vineyard roads in the worst years, and frost on the shed roofs retreated before rays of the rising sun. In February, plumes of blue smoke from burning vine cuttings stood straight in the motionless air.

Spring was the most dangerous time. Cold air collected on the valley floor, threatening the new buds. André had spent many nights in the vineyards, mucking about with smudge pots. In theory he was the winemaker for Beaulieu, but in fact his duties were much broader and included helping out when frost threatened, when burning kerosene filled the darkness with smoke from the smudge pots and the huge propellers on stanchions roared.

Dorothy, a secretary at Beaulieu, called the men into the vineyards on those nights, and took sandwiches and coffee around to the different stations. She had come later to the valley, married to a schoolteacher; younger, taller than André, she had full, dark hair and a good laugh. Together they watched the men haul the smudge pots into place along the ends of the rows, through mud like gumbo, the air gelid. It seemed adventurous to her.

One frosty night she and André drove up the Oakville Grade together and looked back at the valley. The glowing fires reminded her of candles, and him of an encampment of Napoleon's army.

Both André and Dorothy divorced their spouses and got married. People said it was a rash act, but they were in love and could imagine no alternative.

André had retired from BV twice already and then allowed himself to be lured back again. Mme. de Pins said, while presenting him with a gold watch, "This man has cost me millions of dollars." Despite their differences, he liked Mme. de Pins, and pitied her. She cried for more than a year after the sale of Beaulieu and still couldn't bear to visit the winery or to talk about it. Since then, the value of BV had risen dramatically. Selling it was the worst business decision in the valley's history.

Legh Knowles considered himself the protector of Beaulieu's reputation. To do that he had to go along with some of Heublein's suggestions. He told André and Dick Peterson, "You guys are pros and can move around in the industry. I can't. I'm just a trumpet player. Resisting commercialism isn't in my personal interest."

As general manager, he had to be loyal to the corporation; it wasn't easy. Heublein subjected him to a plethora of corporate and subsidiary officials. At one point he figured he had eight bosses. Larry Solari, at the head of United Vintners, had an ally in Beckstoffer, who didn't like Knowles any more than Solari did. Beckstoffer asked why Legh Knowles needed two Cadillacs; he cut Knowles out of the negotiations over the Keig ranch — and those vineyards were for Beaulieu! — telling Knowles, "We're handling this on the corporate level."

The Keig ranch turned out to be pretty much a disaster. Beckstoffer insisted on planting 100 percent Cabernet instead of figuring out which grapes would be best for each spot. The vineyards were developing every disease known to grapes.

Knowles had heard about the formation of Vinifera Development Corporation while in Beverly Hills, not in Rutherford. Supposedly it was all done to provide good grapes to BV. Beckstoffer's associate in Vinifera Development wanted to send grapes to any BV fermenter that wasn't being used at the moment. Knowles objected, and was told those decisions were made at the chairman's level. That meant Beckstoffer was flying over his head, clear to Hartford.

The Heublein brass tried to get Knowles to take bad grapes. When Knowles refused, he was told to put them in the altar wine.

"Like hell," he said. Knowles was a Catholic and wasn't putting garbage in altar wine.

Ten minutes later the phone rang again. It was Hartford, telling him to accept the bad grapes.

•

The fact that Beaulieu belonged to the Smirnoff division of Heublein meant that Solari was off Knowles's back, but he still had several bosses. Stuart Watson wanted him to produce a lot more of the very expensive Georges de Latour Private Reserve, and Knowles refused. Watson came to lunch, and Knowles said, "I hear somebody's been calling me an idiot for refusing to jump production."

Knowles explained why that couldn't be done. All grapes and all wines were not the same. Private Reserve Cabernet had been carefully developed for thirty years. The grapes came from special vineyards. The concept shouldn't be tampered with. Et cetera.

Watson told him, "You don't have the confidence to run a winery." He wanted Knowles to sell two million cases, including a second, cheaper line of wine, like the Mondavis did.

"It'll hurt our image," Knowles told him. "You can't carry water on both shoulders."

But the executives didn't get it. They flew him to Hartford every weekend, to convince him to take over something called Heublein International. That job would get him out of Rutherford and out of the West Coast's corporate hairdo. Then they could do what they wanted with Beaulieu. He refused and became the symbol of the poor team player. At management meetings somebody would say, "Don't expect a piece of the action if you don't give us something," and stare at Legh Knowles.

One morning Larry Solari walked up to him on the porch of the Silverado Country Club and threw down a copy of the *San Francisco Chronicle*. "What do you think of this?" he asked contemptuously.

Solari hated him because Knowles talked about playing trumpet for Glenn Miller and promoted BV as a class act. Solari thought fine-wine talk was all bull. At luncheons and dinners attended by Heublein brass, Solari would tell the waiter to take the cork from the wine bottle over to Legh Knowles so he could sniff it. "He used to work for *Gay-lo*," Solari would say.

In the newspaper was an interview with André Tchelistcheff. André said that his '46 Pinot Noir was the only good Pinot he had ever made. André also suggested that the grapes used in BV's Pinots were probably planted in the wrong place. Now, anyone who knew André and knew the evolution of wine in Napa Valley knew he was speaking as a scientist. He didn't mean that the Pinots were bad or that the grapes were inferior, only that they were not perfect. Scientists were expected to speak the truth and exchange information while seeking the truth. But try explaining that to Hartford!

André had been enthusiastic about Heublein in the beginning. Watson had told him that the corporation wasn't coming to Rutherford to make money; André and Dick Peterson would be allowed to do whatever they thought necessary to maintain quality. It was only later that André realized it was corporate policy to make promises and then not keep them.

So much had happened in the valley since he had stepped out of Georges de Latour's Cadillac that first day in 1938. No one could have foreseen the changes, the accomplishments — or the money involved. No one could have foreseen the boneheadedness of some of the new owners of prestigious Napa Valley wineries.

Dorothy told André that Heublein was using him, keeping him on as a consultant for his PR value while ignoring his advice. The little ol' winemaker. He should quit, she added, and André knew she was right. Legh Knowles's statement about the inevitable commercialism had been the first indication. Then came the interview in the *Chronicle*. In the old days, one could talk openly about grapes and wine; it was expected.

Legh gave André hell about the interview, and he wasn't accustomed to taking hell from Legh. Then Watson announced that all future discussions with the press would have to be conducted in the presence of a Heublein representative — an insult. André had no choice but to quit.

Dick Peterson had taken Andy Beckstoffer across Highway 29 to see BV1, the most famous Beaulieu vineyard. It still belonged to Mme. de Pins. Peterson wanted the boy from Richmond to understand what a good vineyard was, but Beckstoffer wasn't impressed. He wanted mechanization and told Peterson he'd like to see some D8 Cats in there, making long, deep rows.

The result, Peterson explained, would be compacted soil and declining quality. Beckstoffer sneered. He was going to save Peterson and the others from themselves. "A vineyard is a business," he said. "You have to have a businessman running it."

The theory of the janitor came more and more into evidence. Napa was Sleepy Hollow in the mind of Heublein; the residents of the valley didn't know what they were doing. Stuart Watson met with Peterson in Oakland one day and asked Peterson to be the technical director of all the wines under Heublein's mantle, even those made in Portugal.

"I would fail if I had to work in an office," Peterson told him. "I'd stop smelling the tanks, tasting the wines, all those things I do in the winery."

Watson couldn't understand. "I'm talking about forty million cases," he said. Not a piddling little 180,000 cases. "You don't know what we're offering you."

Peterson said, "You don't know what you have."

Stuart Watson told Legh Knowles that Peterson was overconfident. Watson sent him to Portugal to help Lancers make some new wines, which Peterson agreed to do on an interim basis. While there, he tried not to treat the Portuguese the way Heublein treated the Napans.

On the way home, Peterson stopped at corporate headquarters, as was expected. One of the chemists asked when he was moving to Hartford.

"I'm not."

"You're not moving to Hartford?"

The head of Smirnoff Beverage and Import Company had been telling everybody that a new laboratory was being built in Hartford and that Peterson would run it. When Peterson asked about it, the man said, "I just didn't have time to tell you," and went on to say that the new wine lab would be the best in the country. Everything made in the far-flung corners of Heublein's empire would be sent daily to Hartford for analysis and discussion. Peterson just had to be there. In Hartford. The center of the universe.

Peterson gave notice and prepared to move to the Salinas Valley. A group of big growers wanted Peterson to run their winery. It would not be BV, and Salinas was not Napa, but anything was better than living under the oppression of the theory of the Hartford janitor.

Andy Beckstoffer knew the sound of opportunity knocking. The Vinifera Development Corporation now owned or leased 800 acres in Napa. It farmed 3,000 out of a total of 22,000 planted acres in the valley, and controlled 400 additional acres up in Mendocino County.

Then Heublein decided that it had enough grapes for the long term, and wanted to sell its vineyards and its vineyard management company and divorce itself from the United Farm Workers. Hartford wasn't worried about making a profit on the deal. Vinifera Development had been set up only to provide quality grapes for Heublein's wineries, and had done that. Its value in relation to Heublein's overall holdings amounted to less than peanuts. Vinifera Development had become a headache to Hartford, like so many things, and a reminder of the uncertainties of farm prices, the unhappy experiences with the union, and the intransigence of California grape growers. Stuart Watson and John Martin longed to be rid of all that and told Beckstoffer to find a buyer.

First he approached Connecticut Mutual Life Insurance, a company that had bought a piece of the Keig ranch. But it, too, had become disillusioned with the soil. Beckstoffer knew these Connecticut Yankees had no interest in or talent for getting further into it, and so he made a unique proposal: he himself would take the Vinifera Development Corporation off Heublein's hands.

He had only $7,500 in cash. He figured Vinifera was worth half a million. He arranged a leveraged buy-out, with Heublein loaning him the money and making a commitment to pump another half a million dollars into vineyard development. Heublein would retain 15 percent of the package, and Connecticut Mutual 10 percent. Beckstoffer would own, in addition to two farming companies, 150 acres in Napa and the 400 acres in Mendocino. Heublein would pay for the planting of what was still raw land and provide him the money at a fixed rate — while the prime was jumping to 20 percent. If he couldn't meet the payments, Heublein would plow them back into the principal, increasing Beckstoffer's nut. He couldn't lose.

The deal was worthy of an M.B.A. who had decided, back in New England, to go as far into the free enterprise system as possible. Beckstoffer further figured that if he could hold on long enough, the money would come pouring in and he could pay off the debt, or trade Heublein some vineyards developed with its own funds to satisfy his obligation.

That is what happened. Beckstoffer instantly became one of the biggest growers in the valley, one of the biggest on the North Coast, with inside information about what was coming on the market and the financial clout to act on it. He claimed he had done Heublein a favor, but others said that Stuart Watson made the boy from Richmond a millionaire.

III

As Good As the Best

18

PEOPLE DIDN'T KNOW what to think as it began to go up in 1966 — the first new winery in the valley in many years. It spread laterally north to south on the far side of the Southern Pacific railway line, a great Moorish arch in stucco, complete with a light tower and an inner courtyard. The Spanish colonial style harked back to early California history but still contrasted sharply with the grand old wineries of the previous century — Inglenook, Beringer, Krug — which suggested a certain northern European restraint despite their size and frenzied detail. The Robert Mondavi Winery was something entirely different; it looked, despite its simplicity, overwrought. The arch was *too* wide, some people said, the tower too tall, the whole structure shockingly different.

No one denied that it was impressive, and no doubt expensive, and impossible to look at without having some sort of reaction. Everybody seemed to be talking about Robert's new winery, and if not that, they were talking about Robert's new name. He had, unabashedly and without apology, changed the pronunciation of Mondavi. He was no longer Robert Mon-*day*-vi, the Anglicization Cesare had used when he moved to Minnesota, to make him sound more American. Now Robert was a Mon-*dah*-vi, the real Italian pronunciation and one that conveniently distinguished him from his brother and the rest of the family.

It was a brash move, and amusing, and at first people joked about it. But gradually it caught on and then an amazing thing happened: Mon-dah-vi started to sound right to people, and Mon-day-vi old-fashioned. Those who had been using the old pronunciation for years suddenly couldn't abide it. Every time they said Mon-dah-vi they lent tacit support to Robert's new venture and Robert's new life, and every time one of the Mon-day-vis heard someone say Mon-dah-vi he felt slighted, even if he didn't admit it, even if he laughed out loud and, if he was a friend of Robert's, shook his head at Robert's folly.

When the winery first opened for tours, Robert's older son, Michael, would build a fire in the salesroom's fireplace and walk out to the highway and try to lure motorists in. One day they had only three visitors, the nadir of the Robert Mondavi Winery. Then things picked up; on a Sunday in spring the sales staff moved $1,000 worth of wine, and Robert showed his gratitude by taking everyone — including Margrit Biever, the blond Swiss — out for $3 Mexican dinners.

Robert and his wife, Marge, had been growing apart for years, a process encouraged by Robert's long absences. Marilouise Kornell, a close family friend, increasingly heard claims that Marge was an alcoholic. This made Marilouise angry, as it did Blanche Mondavi, Robert's sister-in-law. Marge liked to have a drink but she wasn't an alcoholic. If she was, then Robert made her that way, in the opinion of both women. They thought Robert could be very cruel. They noticed that he gave the same presents to Marge and to Margrit — matching furs, then matching emeralds. Gradually the role of hostess was taken away from Marge, and that was the end of it. The high school sweetheart from Lodi, who always had her eyes on Robert Mondavi, was too weak to be married to him, too small town to keep up.

Nobody owned Robert Mon-dah-vi, not Marge, not his children, not even Margrit with the plaited pigtail.

The secret of Robert's ongoing success, Margrit Biever knew, was his good relations with those outside his family. People instinctively trusted him. Margrit trusted him. Robert would come into her office at the winery and talk about his dreams. Margrit had her old portable Corona there, typing out letters to people wanting to visit the winery. She organized the tours, throwing all her energy into the job. Sometimes she swept out the dining room; she inspected the tablecloths before guests sat down to lunch. There were always four or five visitors to be entertained; a certain style was expected. She had plans for concerts, a Great Chefs program, perhaps a cooking school and wine seminars.

Margrit fell in love with Robert, and his children resented it. When Robert held a birthday breakfast for her at the winery and insisted that the boys attend, Michael arrived with two bottles of bourbon, of all things — Old Crow and Wild Turkey — an obvious comment on the relationship between her and Robert, but fortunately Robert missed the point.

Margrit saw herself as scapegoat, taking the pins the children might otherwise have stuck into Robert. Because of her, they blamed him less for leaving his wife.

Michael was the first to come around. He saw that it was inevitable that he and Margrit be civil or the winery would suffer. Tim was very hard to get to know, very resentful, but Marcia, Robert's only daughter, was the worst. When the topic of a job for Marcia came up, Margrit suggested that she be the head of public relations, but she refused as long as "that woman" stayed. In the end Marcia went off with her husband to live in New York and Margrit took over public relations.

Robert assured her that everything would eventually work out with the winery, with the family, with the two of them. Margrit trusted Robert; she believed in the old Chinese saying: If you wait long enough, the body of your enemy will float down the river.

Big things were about to happen in the valley. Robert couldn't put it into words, but some of this inchoate knowledge inspired others. He told himself that someday everybody in the valley would thank him, but some never would. Some, and not just the Mon-day-vis, saw Robert as representative of the social and professional tensions in what had been a close-knit community and was now showing the strains of growth and increasing sophistication. Before, couples had remained together even if they were unhappy; liaisons remained discreet. Families had adhered even if some members could not abide one another. Robert Mondavi was changing all that with a flamboyant courtship and a struggle over Krug's assets headed inexorably for the courts.

The wine industry itself had been a leisurely profession unblemished by too much promotion, and Robert was changing that, too. Napa Valley was coming of age, and in some vague way it seemed to be Robert Mondavi's fault.

❧

Michael Mondavi's earliest memories were of the heady aroma of fermenting grapes and the deep shadows thrown by the tanks in Krug's cavernous rooms. He grew up there with the cellar workers, his babysitters, since the family lived in the old Krug compound. He started work when he was ten, cutting weeds in the yard and tending the vines. He trailed his father through the vineyards on those rare times Robert was home, tasting from the tanks along with him, keenly aware that Robert would soon be leaving again. He could not remember, as a man, ever having a meal at home with his father when there was not a stranger present — a distributor, a retailer, a hotelier. The talk was of wine, wine, wine.

He went away to school in the sixth grade — the end of his childhood. He pushed through adolescence on his own, without his father's presence. Michael missed him in a basic, irreparable way; even when he came home on holiday, Michael missed him. They had no time together alone. Usually Robert was on the TWA Constellation to New York or on the train for another three-week tour of duty.

Michael transferred to the Jesuit prep school in San Jose. In the summer before his senior year, Robert took him to lunch at the Sutter Club in Sacramento with the famous Maynard Amerine, from the Department of Viticulture and Enology at UC Davis. Robert talked, as he always did, about wine and California, wine and the future, and finally got around to saying that he wanted Michael to go to Davis. Amerine, a quietly decisive man, said, "Michael will not go to Davis."

"Why not? He's been working in the cellars and in the vineyards all his life."

"Because you can teach him more than I can. His biggest job will be learning how to make a profit."

He advised Michael to study business at the University of Santa Clara. Later, Robert told Michael that he was surprised to hear such good advice coming from the ivory tower.

Michael worked in the winery that summer. His father told the cellar man to give him the dirtiest, most difficult job he had: scraping mold off the bottom of a 36,000-gallon redwood tank, flat on his back. The mold — rich, many-generational — fed on the sugar and alcohol from the aging wine. It came off in layers, like strips of raw liver. He had to scrub the tanks as well, the filthy water dripping from the undersides mixing with his own sweat; he sponged up wine that slopped over the side of the vats and trailed across the winery floor. Getting a date in St. Helena those summer evenings was difficult for someone who, even after a shower, attracted fruit flies.

He avoided harvest his first two years at Santa Clara because he played linebacker, but during his junior year he came home the first night of harvest, worked a day, and went back to school, then returned to the winery the following day. He kept up that routine for two months. Wine was still the subject of all conversation. For a time Michael considered joining the Air Force and getting away from it. But he and his father worked out a future he could not resist: after graduating, Michael would spend the rest of the year as a trainee at Krug. Then he would go into the marketing and sales department of a big wine merchant in London. After that, he would spend eight months at Château Lescombes or Cheval Blanc or one of the first growths of the Médoc, learning how a topnotch château operated. Then some graduate courses in business, and finally into the arms of Krug. Michael would work his way up through the organization and be running the place in five years.

That had all changed with the fight between Robert and Peter. Michael thought his uncle Peter deserved the beating he had received. Michael tried not to hate Peter even though he had deprived Michael of a glorious career that was to include stints in England and France. He imagined himself working for Beringer, Masson, or Almadén, showing the world how good he was, being invited back, and refusing the offer. He imagined calling Peter "Uncle Babe" at a family gathering and watching with pleasure as Peter got angry.

Michael married the black-haired Isabelle in June 1966, and a week later went into the Army Reserve. Less than a month later the bulldozers had broken ground for the Robert Mondavi Winery. His father planned to crush in September, which people said was impossible, but they did harvest and make wine. Robert hired Warren Winiarski, who had worked for Lee Stewart, to help, and a young student of winemaking, Ric Forman.

Robert was committed to a number of growers, having agreed to take all their grape production. He wanted to make only great wines, but some of the grapes were less than great, like Sauvignon Blanc. Robert wanted to tell the growers to send their Sauvignon somewhere else but knew he would lose some of them if he did, and that meant losing their Chardonnay and Cabernet supply as well. So he decided to treat the Sauvignon like Chardonnay, as an experiment, to see if he could develop complexity and elegance similar to that produced in the great white wines of France.

He had tasted the Pouilly Fumés and Blanc Fumés from the Loire Valley, made of Sauvignon Blanc, which were some of France's finest wines. They were not aged in oak casks, however, and Robert decided that his Sauvignon would be. Also, he would leave the juice in contact with the skins for a period after crushing the grapes, then ferment the wine in stainless steel tanks with temperature control — similar to the process he first used at Sunny St. Helena — and then subject it to some new French oak.

The new Mondavi Sauvignon Blanc showed such fine and complex flavors some people didn't believe at first that it was Sauvignon. Robert arranged to have the wine served at a PTA meeting in Lodi, where his mother-in-law was a teacher. If people standing around a gym in Lodi liked the bouquet and taste — and they did — so would people in the fancy restaurants of San Francisco and New York.

He didn't know what to call it. California Sauvignon Blanc was either a sweet wine or a coarse one that usually ended up in a jug blended with something else. Robert wanted a proprietary name that carried the French association and was also thoroughly American. He would call it Fumé Blanc, a clever reversal of the French name.

Mondavi, the wine critics said, had created a new product. Never mind that the French had been making a similar Sauvignon Blanc forever; it had not so far been made in California. Sales followed praise. The first batch, 2,500 cases, sold at $2 a bottle, expensive when Beaulieu was selling its Cabernet for $2.50. But pricing had its own built-in rationale: if you charged more for a wine than anyone had ever considered paying, it had to be good.

Robert had told his partners and the banks, the insurance companies, the glass company, and others he owed that his winery would find itself in the black in eight years. But two years after opening, he ran out of money and was forced to look for a single heavyweight backer.

Suntory sent seven men from Tokyo to talk about a possible merger. The Mondavis put them up in the Napa Valley Inn and agreed to see only two Japanese at a time, so they could keep track of who said what. Schenley paid a visit to Oakville, and Nestlé invited Robert and Margrit to Geneva to talk about a partnership. Nestlé put them up in an elegant hotel during one of the coldest Januarys in recent history and offered to buy Robert out. Robert said no.

He decided to team up with brewers. Rainier bought out his partners and ended up owning most of the winery and the vineyards, but Robert retained control, another triumph and a source of amazement for his brother, Peter. Robert stressed the importance of promotion and of borrowing large amounts of capital. Anyone who misunderstood those two things misunderstood the industry and would miss the brass ring — château status. He hungered for it.

Robert could promote forever, but finding sufficient capital was not so easy. He still owned a piece of Charles Krug but had no say in how the family business was run.

Peter told people that Robert might own a piece of Krug, but then he had gone off and started his own winery. He didn't do any of the work in St. Helena or out in Lodi for the C. Mondavi and Sons Corporation, which still bought and sold bulk grapes.

Krug made a lot of money in the late sixties and early seventies. Robert brought a representative of Rainier around, trying to buy Krug, but Peter and the others didn't want to sell. Robert, also a director, complained that he had no influence on the final decision, just as he objected to his mother Rosa's giving some of her stock to Peter's boys. Well, Peter said, Robert had a vote. The others just didn't agree with him.

Robert couldn't handle that, in Peter's opinion. He tried to bring his lawyer to board meetings, but the family wouldn't allow it, until finally Robert became so insistent that his lawyer got in. Of course Joe Alioto had always attended and sometimes ran the meetings. But Joe was Krug's counsel as well as an old family friend.

Robert resigned from the board in 1973, and Peter hoped that was the end of it. Joe Alioto would have become a director, but since he was already the mayor of San Francisco, the law forbade it. So his son John became a director instead. Same family, Peter thought.

Peter didn't pretend to be sorry that Robert resigned. He did many things that angered Peter, like using the Mondavi name and then changing the pronunciation, and always comparing Krug and Mondavi wines. When Robert was on the road promoting his Fumé Blanc and high-priced reds, he would get a bunch of fellows — distributors, restaurateurs, wine writers — around a table, open the wines, fill up everybody's glasses, and then proceed to say that his wines were better than Peter's, that they had more "fruit," more "oak" — more character. Peter had heard all about it. Why couldn't Robert compare his wines to BV's or Louis Martini's?

Rosa had transferred some of her shares to Peter's children as part of a new partnership, ostensibly to reduce estate and gift taxes. Robert claimed that he owned less of Krug than he had before and was cut off from all decisions and a lot of the profits. He hired a lawyer to file suit against his family and also against C. Mondavi and Sons, the old partnership. He filed against the trust set up by Cesare and against the new partnership. If Robert was going to sue, he was going to do it right.

Peter and the other defendants countersued, claiming that Robert had breached his fiduciary duties to Krug by seeking to compete with it, had tried to monopolize the wine business, had violated antitrust laws, and generally had laid "unclean hands" on the family and company affairs. What had been a family quarrel, was about to be exposed to the full light of day.

Peter hired Joe Alioto to handle the Mon-day-vis' side. Alioto was a good lawyer and knew as much about the business as anybody. Peter more or less left it to Joe, and later regretted that. Robert and his lawyer made some pretty strong charges, and the judge — brought in from Fresno, which supposedly meant he was impartial — listened to them.

The fight between brothers affected Rosa Mondavi. Marilouise Kornell went to have coffee and biscotti with her one morning and found Rosa exhausted and immeasurably sad. She told Marilouise that Cesare had asked before his death for Rosa to attempt to bring the boys together, but the prospects for that were no longer realistic.

Rosa had cancer of the liver and ended up in the hospital at the time Peter was to be deposed in San Francisco. Peter asked the other side for a postponement, but Robert and his lawyer refused. Peter said they were hard-boiled, heartless. When he talked about that time, years later, tears still came to his eyes.

As the trial went on, Peter noticed that Alioto was spending an awful lot of time in Boston. It seemed that every Friday a limousine would pick him up and take him to the airport, and he would fly off. Then he would call Peter on Monday and say he couldn't make it back in time for the trial but that one of his associates would handle things until he got back.

People encountering Peter in the valley saw the familiar cherubic face gone pale, the mouth drawn. He no longer looked like Babe; he looked like a man facing some embarrassing revelations, and maybe real losses. His wife, Blanche, went to court herself to see how things were going. She was not impressed with Joe Alioto's associates. She told Peter and her sister-in-law Mary, "They're Mickey Mouses."

The trial was ridiculous, she thought. Demeaning. Who believed all the stuff that Robert and his lawyer claimed? Nobody who mattered, that's who. Blanche decided that the best way to get through that time was to play golf every day, a stratagem that succeeded. Golf took her mind off the unpleasantness of life that some people took such pains to expose.

The judge made some changes at Krug. He took the winery away temporarily from the family and gave it to a trustee to run. Peter didn't think he could stand that humiliation. He considered the court-appointed manager incompetent, and said so. Living there on the grounds as the Mon-day-vis did, in their rambling houses with the beautiful lawns and plantings, and overhead the same towering oaks that had shaded the family of Charles Krug and overspread such changes in Mondavi fortunes, and having to watch some stranger make a lot of mistakes drove Peter and Blanche to distraction.

Toward the end of the trial, Robert stopped by Rosa's house. A family friend from Lodi who had grown up around the Mondavis sat with them in the kitchen, listening in amazement as Robert and Rosa argued in Italian. The friend did not know what they were saying but could clearly sense the height of their emotions. It was unsettling. Finally Robert said something that made Rosa fall off her chair. Her friend rushed forward to help her while Robert stood staring down at his mother as if at a stranger. He seemed dazed. Then he helped Rosa up and the two of them got her into bed.

After Robert was gone, Rosa said, "I have two sons. One has short legs and he is a saint. One has longer legs and he is a devil."

She died shortly thereafter.

The trial concluded in 1976. The judge, Robert Carter of the Superior Court of the state of California, issued a decision in such unequivocal language that no one could doubt who was at fault. Carter condemned the conduct of the Mondavis who had, in effect, tossed Robert into the street and sought to deprive him of his inheritance. This "long smoldering plan" was laid at Peter's feet. The judge blamed him for curtailing growth in the early sixties and trying to take profits out of Krug for the individual shareholders. He said Peter paid too high a price for grapes from the old family business in

Lodi. After Robert had been sent away, Peter proposed raising the salaries of all the officers except Robert, and consistently undervalued Krug when discussing buying out other family shareholders. "What had been envisioned as a business for the family *and their heirs*," the judge wrote of old Cesare's intentions, "suddenly became a business for Peter and his heirs."

Krug's value, the judge ruled, had caused Peter and the others to look around for ways to reduce profits, like raising their salaries and paying the old corporation more than the grapes it sold to Krug were worth. Anticipating the death of Rosa and huge estate taxes, Peter suggested that Rosa "gift" Peter's boys with part of her holdings. Meanwhile, cash had to be amassed from Krug to pay the taxes when the time came. But Robert would have gotten a percentage of the accumulated funds. A new limited partnership was formed that prevented Robert from participating fully in Krug's profits. He would be forced to sell out the remaining shares to the new partners at book value, about one fifth of their actual worth.

"Can there really be any doubt," Judge Carter asked, "that by reason of the fraudulent activities of Peter in depressing the corporate earnings . . . he became the father of two millionaire sons? In view of the wrongful diversion of corporate profits to the new partnership, and the fraudulent activities of Peter, Rose and Mary, this court squarely holds that under such circumstances, what might have originally been a valid stock restriction, in equity and justice is totally invalid."

The court was not unmindful "that this unfortunate litigation involves family rivalries and emotions. In spite of the defendants' assertions to the contrary, the court has been unable and is unwilling to accept the argument that Robert, during his thirty years as a shareholder in Krug, ever calculatingly tried to hurt the corporation or to act in derogation of the interests of all members of the Mondavi family. The court is simply unable to be so generous with respect to the conduct of Peter and Mary."

The judge blamed Peter for problems with growers in the valley as well. Andy Pelissa, Nathan Fay, and Ren Harris had all sold grapes to Krug and then stopped. Peter had tried to blame it on Robert, saying he enticed these men to sell to him. "Robert had absolutely nothing to do with their termination of grower-winery relationship," Carter wrote. Rather, it was "the result of a deliberate failure by Peter to abide by the terms of the purchase contract, namely to buy

their grapes at current market price. . . . The treatment of the growers, by Peter as general manager of Krug, in the view of this court
demonstrates another abuse of authority and mismanagement of the
corporation."

Krug would have to go on the block ("involuntary dissolution")
in order to pay Robert the millions of dollars he now had coming to
him. There were buyers clamoring: Hiram Walker, Norton Simon,
Quaker Oats, Anheuser-Busch, Coca-Cola, and Pepsico. Peter and
his sister Mary had to pay all Robert's litigation costs, as well as
hundreds of thousands of dollars to him in damages. Even Fred Ferroggiaro, John Alioto, and Robert's younger sister, Helen, couldn't
escape without paying Robert something.

Peter claimed that the judge was biased. Not that Peter read his
decision; the lawyers in Alioto's office read it and told him what was
in it. Peter threatened to appeal, but the wind had been taken out of
his sails. It was difficult to argue with such a sweeping indictment,
and within months he was talking about refinancing. Robert would
get his money and Peter would get a debt so gargantuan he would
never escape it.

᪥

The day of the judgment, Robert telephoned Margrit Biever and
said, "We've won."

She recognized the victory for what it was: a chance to buy out
Rainier with an eventual settlement of almost $5 million. When Rob-
ert had advertised in the *Wall Street Journal* for investors years before,
he had received 257 responses. Now he was done with outside partners — with all problems. The bodies of his enemies were floating
down the river.

Others did read the decision: newspaper reporters, people in the
wine business, and residents of the valley. One thing that amazed
and fascinated them — out of many amazing and fascinating personal details — was the real worth of Krug. A letter from a representative of Schlitz to Fred Ferroggiaro, a board member, revealed
that Schlitz had tried to buy the winery and seriously contemplated
paying $32 million. Then the judge put a value on Krug of $47 million. Suddenly the battle between Mon-day-vi and Mon-dah-vi took
on a new dimension. Inglenook, Beaulieu, and Beringer had all sold

for peanuts compared to that price. If Krug was worth $47 million, then those properties and the entire valley were worth infinitely more than people had supposed. This was not just a family quarrel; this spat was not just about a dead mother's affection. It was about money.

19

THE WINES OF Robert Mondavi Winery had won the plaudits of the wine critics; they had found coveted space on retail shelves and on the lists of respected restaurants. Robert continued to beat the drum for Napa and for himself but, ironically, recognition came through the back door, from a direction no one suspected, catching the valley's foremost and now wealthy apostle quite by surprise.

Mondavi was not the only one reaching for the heights in Napa Valley. Many wanted to make wine as good as any they had tasted or read about, to compete with the châteaux of Burgundy and Bordeaux. To be as good as the best. They had been in the valley in most cases for only a few years, and found themselves up against centuries of tradition. France, for instance, had been producing wine for more than two thousand years. There the supreme grape species, *Vitis vinifera,* had arrived from the wilds of the Transcaucasus by way of the Euphrates Valley, Egypt, and Greece. Probably the Phocaeans, colonizers from ancient Ionia, first grew grapes at the mouth of the Rhone, but it was Enotria — Italy — and its emissaries that imposed *vinifera* on the sprawling interior of the barbarous France. The Romans, wine enthusiasts as well as arbiters of taste, established the best and most enduring vineyards in Burgundy, Champagne, the Loire Valley, and Bordeaux — that low, sometimes miasmic spit of gravel, limestone, and clay between the Atlantic and the Gironde where fresh water mixes with salt and the ocean tempers the winter gales and the heat of the southern sun.

Bordeaux grew up as a curious stepchild, open to outside influences, among them the English, who owned it until 1444 and in essence created the wine trade. The English shipped vast amounts of "claret" to London — and to Edinburgh, Dublin, Amsterdam,

Brussels, and Copenhagen — in cask, fueling the taverns and dining rooms of country squires and inspiring a class of foreigners who knew more about French wine than the French did. In Bordeaux, a vinous subculture extended from the quaysides to the cavernous cellars of *négociants,* who purchased wine in bulk for shipping, to the coopers, vineyardists, cellar workers, winemakers, professional tasters, and finally the proprietors themselves, often ruling in absentia and in various stages of prosperity or ruin.

Cabernet Sauvignon, the grape now most closely associated with Bordeaux, proved to be the greatest asset. It reached the region in force only in the early nineteenth century but there developed into the finest expression of the variety. Cabernet in that climate — governed by the proximity of a large, deep body of water — was wonderfully versatile; often blended with Merlot and Cabernet Franc, it produced wines ranging from watery to inkily complex. The English merchants encouraged the autonomous systems of production in Bordeaux governed by plots of land and reigning châteaux that sat on them.

Many French bankers and entrepreneurs built or rebuilt their Bordeaux palaces for the simple reason that there was no room left in the Loire Valley for the grand release of pent-up wealth. Many of the structures in the Médoc, north of the city of Bordeaux, were designed to enhance the wines, or, more specifically, the wine labels — an early instance of architecture as public relations — to give weight and solemnity to what were often shaky financial endeavors.

The most enduring of these, not surprisingly, were the châteaux making superior wine and selling it for the highest price. The French government's own official classification of 1855 picked as the four "first growths" those with the highest-priced wine over an extended period: the châteaux Lafite, Latour, Margaux, and Haut-Brion. The remaining hundreds of châteaux were ranked downward accordingly, through fourth growth to something called *crus bourgeois* — a descending order of worth.

Château Lafite sat quite literally at the top, on a hill in the north of the Pauillac district. The name was said to be a variation of an ancient local expression, *la hite,* meaning the height. Lafite provided wine for the tables of Sir Robert Walpole and Mme. de Pompadour; the property belonged to, among others, the Marquis de Ségur, also the owner of Latour and Mouton, who was guillotined during the revolution. The Rothschilds, Parisian bankers, bought it in 1868 and it remained in the family, a paragon of virtue in a landscape supposedly full of them, shaded by an enormous cedar and sought after by connoisseurs and amateurs everywhere.

Napa Valley had no Château Lafite, it had no first growths, but it had some remarkably good wine made by those whose regard for the French was tempered by healthy New World audacity. Some of them had worked for Robert Mondavi. Ric Forman had learned a lot from him and, that first crush, just how much they didn't know. Robert would say, "What do we do next?" and Ric would answer, "Well, let's pump over," and Warren Winiarski, also a Mondavi cellar rat, would pick up a hose and direct the stream of fermenting Cabernet juice over the cap. Basically they had all stumbled over hoses together, reinventing the wheel.

Forman had seen, through some inexplicable example set by Robert, what wine might be and what it could mean to a person's life. As inarticulate as Robert was, he conveyed an ardor that burned its way into the ambitions of the younger winemaker. Forman wanted to make the best. Since his name did not end in a vowel, he had been distinctly in the minority when he came to Napa, a tall, athletic, determined young man from the hills of Oakland who had gone on to UC Davis to study chemistry and ended up in the Department of Food Science. He got interested in wine only in his last year, becoming what came to be called a born-again — a person with another career in mind who finds himself converted to wine in the twilight of his studies. Forman worked first at Stony Hill, doing grunt work for Fred McCrea, then at Mondavi's. After that first crush, Robert had asked Ric, "Are you coming with us or not?"

Forman wasn't. Robert's winery was a family enterprise, closed at the top; Forman wanted unlimited possibilities. He joined Peter Newton, the British financial journalist, entrepreneur, and partner in a vineyard and winery south of Calistoga. Newton had big plans for both of them, and plenty of land and money. For a Brit, Newton was remarkably open and positive about the future of California wine. He intended to plant the right vines in the right places, and planned to build a dramatic winery, called Sterling after the paper products company that had made Newton rich.

One of his plans was to send Forman to France. He came out of college thinking there was only one way to make wine and was astounded when he arrived in Bordeaux. The traditional methods were totally different from those taught at UC Davis, not so heavily dependent on modern technology. The Bordelais and the Burgundians believed in letting some air get to the wine while it was being made and aged. They fermented in oak barrels instead of steel tanks. The wine picked up character in a process not concerned solely with cleanliness and chemical balance. Often they didn't filter or fine their reds; they didn't centrifuge the whites — centrifugal force could remove flavor as well as so-called impurities. Sometimes, in Burgundy, they let their Chardonnays stay cloudy right up until bottling time. At UC Davis, the emphasis was on mass production: everything had to be air-tight, squeaky clean. They had taken Pasteur's theory of microorganisms to the point of absurdity.

Two other men who had worked for Mondavi would go on to surpass him, in the short run, in a contest held in Paris, of all places, a contest that would turn the wine world on its head and bring Napa Valley to the forefront of minds that had never even dimly perceived of its existence.

One of these men was Warren Winiarski. After leaving the Robert Mondavi Winery, Warren had worked for a time as a consultant and a kind of vinous handyman around the valley. He moved from Dago Valley to Howell Mountain, higher and colder than what was commonly considered suitable for viticulture, into a farmhouse above an old Italian olive press. The grapes grew reluctantly on their fifteen acres, after frost claimed most of the first planting.

Warren bought grapes from Nathan Fay, in the shadow of Stag's Leap, lower and farther south, and coveted the old shingled house on what was called Parker Hill, a basalt knoll overlooking vineyards on one side, the Silverado Trail on the other. The day it came up for sale, Warren felt his pulse race. He put together a partnership that might allow him to live in the house while tending the vineyards and making wine, what the Davieses and some others had done before him. He had looked for partners everywhere, among old school chums, former associates, near-strangers. The story went round the valley that Warren — reader of great books, assiduous discusser of detail, a man who could discern the universe in a handful of Stag's Leap dust — had even encouraged his babysitter to invest in his Stag's Leap winery.

In 1970 he planted ten acres of Cabernet Sauvignon in view of rocks reminiscent of the storm scene in *King Lear*. The vigor of this alluvial land pushed the vines toward a precocious adolescence and then to a full crop only three years later. The Winiarski children went into the vineyards with pails of ladybugs, bought by the thousands to prey on harmful insects, and tossed them into the warming air by the handful.

Warren studied the soil composition. He attributed the fast growth to the "uniformity," a factor missing in Bordeaux, where the vineyards took longer to reach maturity and supposedly produced a superior wine. Warren didn't believe it. People were always talking about the secret French ingredient that would forever prevent other countries from producing wine as good; Warren came to think of it as the "hunchback in the winery" theory. No matter what Americans did, the French would always make better wine because they had a mysterious power Americans lacked.

He discussed French wines and French viticulture with André Tchelistcheff. Clearly there were differences between Napa and Bordeaux. The soil in Bordeaux had been farmed for thousands of years and was depleted; the vines were planted closer together, which meant more competition for available water and nutrients. The French insisted that a new vine could not produce grapes capable of making fine wine in less than seven years.

Warren disagreed. The Winiarskis harvested the '73 Stag's Leap Cabernet crop with friends and neighbors. The individual grapes, dark and lustrous, might have been sold by a jeweler. Warren subjected them to what he considered a modest winemaking regimen, using André now as his consultant. Not too much contact with the grape skins, which can make a wine too dark and tannic; they wanted to preserve the freshness of the fruit, as Lee Stewart might have done at the old Souverain.

Fermentation was complete by Thanksgiving. They introduced secondary, or malolactic, fermentation to soften the wine and give it greater depth. That lasted into the spring. Warren blended the Cabernet with a little wine made from the Merlot grape and put the blend in Nevers oak barrels. He clarified the wine by adding a touch of gelatin, causing solids to cling to it and fall out of solution, although some winemakers derided this as academic. Warren thought it got rid of the "green olive" smell. Then he left it in the barrels, tasting it periodically, not bothering to keep good records, remembering something the French said: Put the wine in the barrel like bread in the oven. Take it out when it's done.

His cooked along for fifteen months. The '73 satisfied his ideas about balance, suppleness, complexity, duration of finish, intensity of fruit. It had persistence, structure, magnitude. He knew it was good, but as yet he didn't know how good.

The other man hired by Mondavi was Mike Grgich, a Yugoslav immigrant who had first worked at Beaulieu. Grgich had left, as Forman and Winiarski had, because he wanted a winery of his own.

Some people had trouble distinguishing, in the early seventies, between Grgich and André Tchelistcheff, who had trained him. Both were short. Both had worked for Beaulieu. Both had difficult names and thick accents. Fortunately Mike Grgich (pronounced *Grrr-gitch*) wore a beret and André never did, and Grgich was younger. He had grown up on a farm outside Zagreb and vividly remembered the end of World War II, when the Germans withdrew and the resistance took over, backed by the Soviets. Grgich considered the partisans liberators until he saw these liberators separating people from their property.

The misery that followed the war had been greater than the misery during it. The Grgich family, obeying government directives, planted cotton year after year, never leaving the ground fallow, until nothing would grow. There was little to eat and no money. A dozen positions opened up at the agricultural university in Zagreb. After work, Grgich walked the six miles into the city and found an early place in a line that the next day contained hundreds of students. He got into the viticultural division and studied more or less constantly — in the park in good weather, in the city library, in cheap, unheated rooms built for maids in the big, ramshackle houses of the once-wealthy. At night he drifted from hotel lobby to hotel lobby, ordering a glass of mineral water if he ordered anything at all and reading until the waiter moved him along.

Grgich got out of Yugoslavia through an international exchange program for students. He went first to West Germany and then to Canada. He advertised for a job in California through the Wine Institute, and in 1958 Lee Stewart agreed to sponsor him. Grgich moved to Napa and into a modified state of servitude for the valley's foremost maker of white wines and its most celebrated skinflint. His first night at Souverain, Grgich was served a '51 Cabernet and a '54 Zinfandel. He liked the latter and thought the former heavenly. Stewart was winning medals for his wines, and Grgich decided that someday he would do something special, too.

Grgich and Stewart were compatible because both worked relentlessly. Grgich's father had told him to try to do something better each day and not to worry about the future, that somehow he would succeed. That first harvest he picked fruit all day and crushed in the evening; it was like being on another planet, without outside influences or normal considerations. Once he returned to his room after midnight and couldn't remember if he had eaten that day. He put on two eggs to boil, went to sleep, and woke up hours later in the midst of dense smoke.

He moved to Beaulieu. Inglenook made the best Cabernet, he thought, but BV was a close second. The quality control insisted on by André Tchelistcheff impressed Grgich; it sank into his blood. André taught him other things he would never have picked up on his own. They both attended meetings of the Napa Valley Technical Group at the Copper Chimney; there were so few people some nights they didn't even need to push two tables together.

Grgich finally left Beaulieu because he saw André's son, Dimitri, as André's logical successor. Grgich moved over to Mondavi, who wanted to make wines as good as the very best, but there again, the way to the top was blocked by family. Then Grgich got an offer from a real estate lawyer from Los Angeles that he couldn't refuse.

The lawyer was Jim Barrett. He had come to think of his profession as the equivalent of selling frozen chocolate bananas, full of idiot savants. Barrett wanted to do something with *soul*. He came to Napa looking for property and stumbled on Château Montelena, just north of Calistoga, one of the valley's preeminent white elephants. Château Montelena was a concoction of towers and parapets built by Alfred Tubbs in the previous century and reworked by a subsequent owner, a Chinese engineer who had built the Manchurian railroad. He had wanted to construct a moat around it, but had to settle for a lake with an island and an elaborate Oriental bridge.

It was for sale when Barrett found it, full of ghosts and spiders. He put together a partnership, and $1 million, and was in the wine business. What Barrett needed most was proven winemaking ability and began to look around for it, just as John Trefethen, Bill Jaeger of Rutherford Hill, Peter Newton, and others had done before him. He found Grgich and offered him, as Barrett liked to recall, "a piece of the action."

The following year, 1973, was crucial to Grgich's career and to Barrett's new venture, although neither would know it for a while.

The significance lay, appropriately, in grapes and the wine that came of them. The '73 Chardonnay from two vineyards in Napa and one in Sonoma, the Bacigalupi, arrived late in the harvest, hauled in a gondola behind an old Volkswagen that struggled up the hill to Château Montelena. The grapes had the radiance of pearls when Grgich held them up to the sunlight, and he danced as he watched them tumble into the crusher.

The technical director (*régisseur*) of Château Lafite in the mid-twentieth century, André Portet, took his fourteen-year-old son through the cellars, dipping tannic young Cabernet from the oak *barriques* with the "thief," a long glass tube with a handle at one end that is inserted through the bunghole and emerges dark with wine. He offered it to Bernard to taste. He was struck by the complexity of this beverage and later came to describe the flavor in great detail; generally, the wine seemed "round," meaning complete, and "elegant," a combination of nuance and enticement. Two years later, he and his father tasted the same wines again; Bernard began to understand the evolution of a substance that had seized the human imagination millennia before.

He enrolled in the Toulouse School of Agronomy and went from there to the agronomy school at Montpellier, France's equivalent of UC Davis. In part to avoid pushing a broom through the courtyard of some army barracks, he worked on an experimental farm in Morocco and then for John Goelet, the American cousin of the head of public relations for Lafite, who wanted his own vineyards. He sent Bernard around the world in 1968 to find the best place to grow Cabernet — the best place other than Bordeaux, of course — to South Africa, South America, Australia, and North America.

Chile was the best, in Bernard's opinion — his wife was Chilean — but the political atmosphere was definitely unpalatable. The state of Victoria in Australia offered fine prospects and a long history of wine production, and his brother, Dominique, eventually became the winemaker at a winery there called Taltarni. But Bernard liked the Napa Valley. He knew fine Cabernet was possible in northern California because he had tasted some old Inglenook wines and approved of everything but the high alcohol content, a product, he decided, of too much heat. So he looked beyond Rutherford, to the southeastern portion of the upper valley, below Stag's Leap, where the soils were deep and various, and the closer proximity of San Pablo Bay and the deep, frigid Pacific Ocean beyond it moderated the climate of south-central Napa much as the Atlantic did that of Bordeaux.

Bernard spoke no English but his brother did, and so Dominique came to Napa in 1971 to help him start Clos du Val, a Burgundian name for a California estate making the wine of Bordeaux — Cabernet Sauvignon — but destined to add Zinfandel and Chardonnay to the list. Bernard rented a shack behind the Cuvaison winery and poured a concrete slab to put up his tanks. He used Cuvaison's equipment, and during crush he and the Cuvaison workers stood in the gondolas and pitchforked grapes into the crusher like a bunch of kids having a good time in the California sun.

On a trip back to France he vowed he was through with the United States. All they ever talked about there was wine! He would spend two weeks a year in America, and that was it. But when he returned, he telephoned his wife in France and told her he would be a bit longer in the States. She arrived with a suitcase. They moved from a motel to an apartment in the little city of Napa. They bought some furniture. There was nowhere decent to eat in what Bernard called coffee-shop country. And heavy Italian cooking. No one took time to drink an apéritif; dinner was eaten at a different time in every house. Life was so unregulated!

In Bordeaux, the rigid social structure divided people into groups: cellar worker, *maître de chais,* enologist, owner. In California, everybody mixed. More amazing, there were no limitations. A cellar worker could become the owner of the winery, and often did. In Bordeaux, the banks would never lend money to such a person. Regularly, Bernard would say, "Just one more year." Then he would visit France again and feel confined, as if in a narrow place.

Back in Napa, he bought a barbecue grill.

The remarkable thing about the valley was the enthusiasm and ready acceptance no stranger could expect in France, which contributed to the rapid development of California wines. People shared everything, from crushers to fermenters to glycol for refrigerating one's tanks, meanwhile discussing techniques with an openness that would have amazed a French winemaker. Both Robert Mondavi and the Trefethens offered Bernard the use of their crushers until he could buy one for himself. If he had gone to a château in the Médoc seeking to use the equipment, the proprietor would have laughed in his face and kicked him off the property. In France, the proprietors all made exaggerated claims for their wines, and condemned those of their neighbors. In Napa, people seemed proud of their neighbors' accomplishments, as if every achievement contributed to the success of all.

In the beginning, Bernard's French friends and former colleagues did not tease him about his California experience. They viewed it as an adventure from which Bernard would return, broadened and chastened, to Bordeaux. But the burgeoning success of California began to threaten them, and the tenor of conversation changed. His countrymen derided California Cabernet whenever the opportunity arose.

There were stresses in California that didn't exist in France, the cult of personality being the most prevalent. So much was expected of the winemaker in America, not just making good wine but also performing as a public relations agent, standing up in front of groups of amateurs and receiving adulation. The French let the *négociants* handle sales and promotion; the winemaker was just another cellar worker. But in America he was becoming a celebrity. Many winemakers were beginning to live a high life on money made from the wine, and developing inflated personalities to go with it. Big fatheads, Bernard thought. Taming the winemakers' egos was going to be a problem in the Napa Valley.

Meanwhile — he realized it too late — the Portets had become Americanized. Their children, when they visited Bordeaux, complained of the rain; Bernard and his wife still spoke to them in French and Spanish, but the children answered in English.

20

IN 1975 WHAT appeared to be a tasteful military bunker went into a hillside above Highway 29 just west of Yountville. This amalgam of concrete and glass belonged to Frenchmen, but the man in charge was American, and his habitual attire included tennis shoes and shapeless corduroy trousers. The tortoiseshell glasses and air of distraction seemed more suited to a college professor than a self-created troubleshooter for an ambitious, unique, and thoroughly unlikely enterprise.

When he worked as a management consultant for Arthur D. Little, Inc., John Wright put forward a peculiar view of capitalism: business should be fun. Profit should not be a goal but a restraint. The point of business was to make just enough money to keep going, not to create a monster of productivity that chained a person to the wheels of power and stifled all creativity and imagination. Business should not be profit-driven; it should be idea-driven.

This quirky view had been put forward in New York and in Brussels. Wright told ADL clients — one of them the government of Algeria — not to worry about the bottom line, not to listen to the bean counters. You don't want to run a tight ship, he said. You want looseness. "Loosey-goosey" was a favorite expression of Wright's. That such a person would find himself working for the most profit-driven, tightly wrapped, tradition-bound promoter of a glamour product, champagne, was happenstance of the most remarkable sort.

The chairman of the board of Moët-Hennessy, Count Robert-Jean de Vogüé, came to America with his son in 1968 and, in a San Francisco hotel, stumbled into a meeting of California winery representatives. He tasted a few of the wines and decided Moët needed a facility in California, one of those grand gestures made on the basis of excess profits, a good mood, and what was then considered fantasy, at least in Champagne. People in America did not drink champagne, his advisors told him; they drank Cold Duck. Kornell and Korbel made good California sparkling wine in hefty proportions, and something called Schramsberg had appeared as a tantalizing suggestion of how good it could be. But no one knew if there was a real market for a native sparkler, and no other Champenoise seriously considered California worthy of consideration.

Moët was already making sparkling wine in Germany and Argentina, in addition to Moët & Chandon champagne, which included the famous, expensive Dom Pérignon. Moët-Hennessy also marketed cognac and perfume. Count de Vogüé considered himself a salesman, and according to his own calculations, he would not have sufficient sparkler to sell in the years ahead. Champagne was a finite product from a small, heavily regulated, precious salon in the mansion of French wine production, itself tightly controlled by the government's official classification system, including the ultimate Appellation d'Origine Contrôlée. Increasing stocks of good wine was not like turning on a spigot; there were only so many grapes — Pinot Noir, Chardonnay, and Pinot Meunier — grown within the official confines of Champagne. So additional sparkling wine had to be produced elsewhere.

It would not be *champagne,* of course, but it would contain bubbles and at least the suggestion of the finesse that had been actively discussed and lavishly promoted from Épernay, in the northeast corner of France, for two hundred years.

John Wright made his way to the portals of Arthur D. Little in San Francisco. His secret agenda as a management consultant was wine; he liked it and he liked the idea of growing grapes. He began driving around Napa Valley on the weekends, looking for property. One day he picked up two hitchhikers who lived in the Mayacamas range and knew of a place for sale on Mount Veeder. Wright and a partner bought it and planted Zinfandel and Merlot, dipping into the labor pool of a nearby commune.

Meanwhile, Wright was completing a marketing study of wine in America, along with Lou Gomberg, the journalist and occasional real estate agent. They concluded that the consumption of good wine was bound to rise and that sales of the best could increase 15 percent a year. ADL sold the study to several European clients, and shortly thereafter Wright was summoned to Paris by the Banque Nationale to explain it to some French businessmen. Among them was Moët's secretary-general — champagne houses sometimes comported themselves like duchies — and he asked Wright to meet with two other Moët executives when they traveled to Napa.

Wright realized that he could make a living consulting and run his vineyard on the side. He could be idea- rather than profit-driven, and he resigned as a full-time ADL employee when he got back to California.

He did play host to visiting Moët brass, including Alain Chevalier, Moët's director-general — Wright was moving inexorably up the protocol list — whom he took for a walk on the Silverado golf course and found himself questioned about the feasibility of a sparkling-wine facility in Napa, with the suggestion that he might run it. Wright's habitual gestures — cocked head, raised eyebrows — could not completely cover his surprise: he was a relative newcomer to wine, and surrounded in the valley by people who knew infinitely more about it than he.

In Brussels again, he was introduced by the director-general of Moët to the chairman of the board of Moët, Kilian Hennessy. Finally Wright met the chairman, Count de Vogüé, in Épernay, where Wright was put up in a palatial former hunting lodge and exposed to the legendary hospitality of the big champagne houses, including — this time — a tentative offer to become chairman of the board of a new California venture.

The management consultant had been idea-driven into the position where he would someday have to make a profit. Meanwhile, he decided he would do nothing that was deliberately outrageous. After all, the French had committed themselves solely on the basis of personality. Wright did speak a little — very little — French, and some German. He was not ethnocentric; he got along with the French because they thought of him as a crazy American, with qualities they could never have accepted in one of their own countrymen. In their view, Wright was a raging left-wing socialist, but he was a raging left-wing *American* socialist. He wore casual clothes and had hippies working in his vineyard, all very amusing.

When the French talked about elections and moon shots affecting champagne sales, Wright kept quiet, knowing such things had no real effect on the market. Champagne sales were booming, elections or no. Champagne stocks had sunk lower than at any time that century, and Robert-Jean de Vogüé had made the gut decision to export some expertise at a time when land in Napa was inexpensive. The steep parts could be had for only $1,500 an acre. Wright was not interested in the dearer, more fertile valley floor. He wanted the cooler slopes and "stressed" grapes, those having to work for their water and nutrients, giving them more character.

Wright was convinced that Napa could produce grapes as good as Champagne's, a suggestion that brought Gallic chortles from his new colleagues. They often used the word "*climat,*" the rough French equivalent of what some Americans were calling "microclimate." But what the French were forever discussing, what they appeared to believe in, was soil. Wright thought climate really made the difference.

Moët bought his Mount Veeder property, and then land in Carneros. Wright oversaw the planting, operating out of a cinderblock garage, an unlikely address for a successor to Dom Pérignon and two hundred years of transcontinental effervescence. Early results were dismal. Moët sent over its director of viticulture, known colloquially as Mr. Disaster. He looked at the vineyards and shook his head. "Even the morning glory won't grow," he said, and wrote a devastating report describing the Americans as well-meaning amateurs.

Wright thought, We'll show those bastards.

Word had gone round the valley that the French had arrived with money; people sought out Wright's cinderblock cave, not just hippies but those with ideas and even experience in promotion and viticulture. Wright hired them. Fortunately Chevalier kept his French underlings away most of the time. The French technical people were tinged with chauvinism — that was the polite way to put it — and Wright found himself dependent on his own research — mostly Dr. Albert Winkler's *General Viticulture* — and the advice of locals.

Wright threw a party for Count de Vogüé, who was in the valley to play golf. Among the locals who came was Katherine Trefethen, wife of Gene Trefethen, the president of Kaiser Industries, who had invested in vineyardland when the ag preserve went through. The next day Wright and his consultant, Will Nord, went to lunch at the Trefethens' "villa," a house with a pool just north of Napa, surrounded by vineyards and backed by a cavernous redwood structure, an out-of-use winery with a dirt floor, designed by the legendary Hamden McIntyre, builder of Inglenook and Far Niente. Wright and Nord were looking for a place to crush experimental lots from the upcoming harvest and this seemed a likely prospect: the old winery was bonded and, better still, the Trefethens had mature grapes to sell.

A loosey-goosey arrangement sprang up between Moët-Hennessy and Trefethen Vineyards. The French paid for equipping the winery and Wright was to use it until Moët's facility could be built in Yountville. He worked with John Trefethen, Gene's son and the manager of Trefethen, and his wife, Janet; together they got the place in shape for the harvest, using equipment prescribed from France. Within months Wright and his staff were putting together experimental batches of wine for the French technicians to try.

The property in Yountville had belonged to developers wanting to put up houses, but the county killed that project. Moët-Hennessy picked up some of the 350 acres of scrubby hills and vineyards for $1,100 an acre, 20 percent down and 6 percent interest, with an option to buy more.

The first design put forward for the winery looked like a Moroccan mosque, according to Jim Hickey, director of the Planning Department. A second drawing, for a lower structure of glass and native stone built into the hillside, gained approval. It was to contain the winery, offices, a visitors' center, and a tasting salon. Eventually it came to include a restaurant. Some citizens of the county complained that the plan was too ambitious and that the complex was sprawling beyond the original guidelines. Wright just shuttled his eyebrows, but later told a friend, in private, "You have to go back to Aquinas. He said, 'It's better to seek forgiveness than ask permission.'"

Domaine Chandon — that was to be the name of California's bold new sparkling wine, made according to the honored precepts of Champagne and produced in quantity — rose on stone and concrete walls poured horizontally and then hoisted into place with a crane, riveted with steel, circumventing the big oaks and creeping laterally across the hillside. The office seemed to hunker down, the long common room lit by a sloping wall of glass and full of potted plants, oak furniture, boxes, and other clutter; it resonated with a dozen overlapping conversations, reflecting Wright's informality. A panel of cubbyholes reared above his desk, stuffed with papers, for Wright had a theory about mail: if he let it sit unopened for three weeks, most of it would take care of itself.

Increasingly, there was Napa Valley wine to be sold. Fine wine, even fine sparkling wine made by Frenchmen, found itself competing with foreign and local products. Few things were proving as important in selling it to Americans with a budding interest in an Old World institution — wine — as the presence of the person who had made it. Or the person who had hired the person who made it and who owned the building in which it was made, as well as the stainless steel tanks and all the expensive French cooperage. Customers didn't want just a bottle of wine. They wanted a face to go with it, and a story: a few organoleptic inferences, a hint of struggle and glamour — a persona.

Lee Stewart, of the old Souverain, had said, "Any jackass can make wine, but it takes a super jackass to market it." That sentiment no longer amused vintners who spent more and more time on the road telling people why their wine was good and pouring it at luncheons and dinners, following the trail blazed by Robert Mondavi. If California wine was good, then there was nothing wrong with standing up and saying so. Particularly if *your* wine had been officially rated above others at a tasting. And it was a poor wine indeed that could not win a medal somewhere in the sea of local and state competitions, set up to provide marketing tools and given legitimacy by visiting experts, including wine writers. These itinerant critics had become increasingly important to the success of California wine.

After the sales slump in 1974, California wine crept up the slope of public awareness. But it remained far from the peak of recognition occupied by the Europeans. California vintners still faced the humiliation of being laughed at in New York and Boston when they made justifiable claims about their product. California wine was okay, people said, but it would never equal the French.

California needed official recognition, something momentous and singularly unexpected, to impress the trade, the public, *the world,* with what had become, in less than two decades, a real American phenomenon. California needed the equivalent of a continental shift.

21

WARREN WINIARSKI received the most important telephone call of his life early in 1976. A wine writer in San Francisco, Robert Finigan, whose *Private Guide to Wines* was widely read by wine drinkers and collectors, said, "I want to tell you about Patricia Gallagher."

Patricia Gallagher was an associate of Steven Spurrier's, a British wine merchant and publicist in France. Together they ran L'Académie du Vin, a school of wine appreciation in Paris. "Patricia wants to come to California, taste some wines, and get acquainted," Finigan added. There was a second reason for her visit: to choose some wines to take back to Paris that might possibly be used in a tasting, part of the bicentennial celebrations there. "Would you be interested in having her visit Stag's Leap?"

American wine critics often claimed that California wines were underrated abroad and that some were as good as the French. But convincing Europeans of this was impossible. "California wines are reminiscent of those of Provence" was a common saw, referring to *vin ordinaire* of southern France and usually based in ignorance of both West Coast and Provençal wines. Such debates turned on condescension and the inevitable incantations about unique French heritage, soil, and *climat*.

Warren and Barbara received Patricia Gallagher in the brown shingled house they had bought on Parker Hill. It was rough, with no real front door. The 137 acres they owned ran from the Silverado Trail down the backside of the hill and out into the vineyards. They hoped someday to build a modern winery facing the trail and maybe a new house. Oaks grew thickly. The views on all sides were spectacular, but the one to the east provided a sublime diversion from the rudiments of the Winiarskis' domesticity. First Warren poured her a glass of his Gamay Beaujolais, made from a grape similar to the one used in France. She tasted it, and said pleasantly, "*Fleurie!*"

Comparisons with French wine were unavoidable. Warren had learned to let these pass without comment; he was happy to be compared with one of the best Beaujolais, however, and next poured the '73 Stag's Leap Cabernet. Gallagher seemed to like it, and Warren suggested that she take a bottle back to Paris.

"I'm afraid," she told him, "of sensitive feelings."

She was followed to California by Steven Spurrier, a slight young expatriate whose wine shop in a mews off the rue Royale, close to the Madeleine, was one of the best in Paris. Most Parisians assumed Spurrier was French, but in fact he was part of a long tradition of Britishers smitten with wine and existing in more or less permanent transition among wine-related billets. Hugh Johnson, the wine critic, wrote of Spurrier in the introduction to Spurrier's book about regional French wines: "Ask him where he lives and he will hedge. Is it London or Paris? No answer. Neither would be accurate. . . . He is always somewhere else. Where? In a cellar, a vineyard, a tasting room. . . ."

Spurrier's academy attracted young chefs and sommeliers from the French Restaurant Association. He had a reputation as a teacher and promoter of wine who knew everyone in the French trade but remained relatively unencumbered by the classic French myopia concerning the wines of other countries. In California, he tasted up and down the state, and returned to Paris determined to test California's best Cabernets and Chardonnays against reputable French palates. Cabernet Sauvignon and Chardonnay were the logical categories, since those grapes predominated in France, and Bordeaux and Burgundies had served as paradigms for the Californians' efforts.

The tasting, of reds and whites, would be "blind," and the results broadcast to demonstrate the noble link between France and America on the two hundredth anniversary of American independence. Vines across the sea. Thomas Jefferson, the United States' first and foremost enophile and an admitted French partisan, would undoubtedly have approved. Over the past decade the discussion of California's technical achievements had reached into the heart of European winemaking, even into France. Frenchmen had a reluctant interest in what these Californians might be up to — and precious little knowledge.

Later, wine critics and the owners of châteaux would accuse Spurrier of sensationalism and, worse, of stacking the deck. The event, known forever after as the Paris Tasting, would say as much about the official wine world as it would about the wines themselves.

The Cabernets Spurrier chose were the '72 Clos du Val made by Bernard Portet, the '70 Heitz Martha's Vineyard, the '71 Mayacamas Vineyards, the '71 Ridge Monte Bello from the coast range south of Palo Alto, the '69 Freemark Abbey, and Winiarski's '73 Stag's Leap.

From the large cast of California Chardonnays he picked the '73 Château Montelena made by Mike Grgich, the '73 Spring Mountain, the '72 Freemark Abbey, and the '72 Veedercrest Vineyards, all from Napa, the '73 David Bruce from the Santa Cruz Mountains, and the '74 Chalone Vineyards from an isolated winery in the Santa Lucia range high above the Salinas Valley.

Spurrier made arrangements with the Hôtel Inter-Continental and began assembling a panel. Anyone could compare Cabernets and Chardonnays from France and the New World, and many had, in fact, countless times — in kitchens, wineries, and ballrooms throughout California and the United States. But the Paris Tasting was to be held in France with French, not American, tasters. And not just any French, but those schooled in evaluating wine and blessed with a sensorial acuity that had brought them fame, led by Pierre Bréjoux, inspector-general of the Institut National des Appellations d'Origine Contrôlée, whose job it was to travel France tasting wine and assuring that it met the legal standards of French quality.

Also to be included was Michel Dovaz of the Institut Oenologique de France. The Bordelais and Burgundian estates would be represented by Pierre Tari, proprietor of Château Giscours and the secretary-general of the Syndicat des Grands Crus Classes, and by Aubert de Villaine, codirector of the Domaine de la Romanée-Conti, one of the most renowned winemaking estates on earth. Also invited to swirl, sniff, and perorate were the director of the respected *Revue du Vin de France,* Odette Kahn, and Claude Dubois-Millot, a director of the widely read gastronomical review *Le Nouveau Guide.* Rounding out the panel would be the owners of two restaurants given three-star ratings by the Michelin guide, Le Grand Véfour and Le Taillevent, and the sommelier from the thrice-starred La Tour d'Argent.

There could be no doubt: these people knew what they were doing. Their findings might fall harshly on American ears, some of them suggested, for there would be no softening of judgment when the sanctity of great wine was involved. But they would help the Americans *learn* by providing sound appraisals of wines made in imitation of Bordeaux and Burgundies heavy with the accumulated glory of two thousand years.

Spurrier did not tell them that they would also be blind-tasting French wines alongside the American ones.

☙

In May 1976, André Tchelistcheff led a group of wine enthusiasts to France, part of a venture called the Tchelistcheff Wine Tours International. He was asked to take along three cases of California wine for delivery to Spurrier, and he readily agreed. André was proud of California wine.

The Cabernets and Chardonnays were parceled out to friends and colleagues on the tour that included Louis Martini, Bob Travers, owner of Mayacamas Vineyards, Arthur Haley, the popular writer who owned a home in Napa Valley, and Jim Barrett, one of the owners of Château Montelena. The wine went through customs without incident, not illegally but a shade surreptitiously, and was handed over to Spurrier. Then the tourists went off to the French countryside and more or less forgot about it.

The patio at the Inter-Continental was crowded with press, industry stalwarts, and not a few tourists. On the table before the arrayed wine glasses stood a legion of anonymous bottles, wrapped and numbered. There were note pads, pencils, sliced bread for clearing the palate, and utensils in which to spit wine after it had been evaluated.

Spurrier told the tasters as they arrived that the event would also include French wine. They seemed unaffected by the revelation. The outcome of such a comparison was a foregone conclusion in their minds. After all, to be tasted alongside the American Cabernets would be the '71 Château Léoville-Las-Cases and the '70 Château Montrose, and two first growths, the '70 Château Haut-Brion and the '70 Château Mouton-Rothschild.

The French Chardonnays were no less impressive: the '73 Meursault-Charmes of Roulot, the '73 Bâtard-Montrachet of Ramonet-Prudhom, the '72 Puligny-Montrachet "Les Purcelles" of Domaine

Leflaive, and the '73 Beaune Clos des Mouches, from the renowned shipper Joseph Drouhin.

The tasters made no objection to the public forum. The assembled press drank its champagne and prepared to gather bons mots scattered by the savants as they exposed the wines to their palates' pitiless erudition. "Finding these Californians is easy," said one expert, working his way through the whites. "You don't even have to taste. One sniff is enough. Smell this one. Almost no nose. Nothing in the mouth. Definitely Californian."

"Ah, back to France," said Raymond Oliver, owner of Le Grand Véfour, after sampling another Chardonnay.

"Nervous and agreeable . . ."

". . . a good nose."

Moving on to the reds, the tasters were reminded of "the magnificence of France. It soars! . . . Certainly a *premier grand cru* of Bordeaux."

They took notes, scoring each wine on a scale of one to twenty points. When they were done, the glasses partially filled before them, the table alitter with bread crusts and the dark circles left by the Cabernets, Spurrier and his associates began to remove the wrappings from the bottles.

ॐ

Jim Barrett had enjoyed the visits to the châteaux with André Tchelistcheff and the other Californians, including the wine talk, the walks through damp cellars with the racks of oak barrels, the confusion of rural roads, the fine dinners eaten in the light of guttering candles. Better than doing real estate in L.A.!

Barrett considered himself lucky: to have hired Mike Grgich, to have won some awards early, to be able after each harvest to roast a pig and drink a lot of *cerveza* with the winery crew. Now he was trying to understand these French winemakers and make friends among them. At Château Lascombe he and his wife were two of eighty people for lunch, seated at a long table — Frenchman, gringo, Frenchman, gringo — everybody smiling and trying to communicate. He wasn't doing too shabbily, Barrett thought.

Then he received word that somebody wanted him on the telephone, and thought, Not good. Very few people knew how to reach him. The news was bound to concern either his children or the winery, and to be catastrophic.

It wasn't. The caller identified himself as a writer for *Time* magazine in Paris, and asked, "Do you know you've just won the Paris Tasting?"

Years later, Barrett would remember wanting to say, "Hot damn!" But he was on French turf, and so he said, "Not bad for kids from the sticks, eh?"

He returned to the table knowing that his Chardonnay had just bested four of the most famous Burgundies. It was close to incredible, but Barrett told his wife, "No big deal."

❧

The telegram read: STUNNING SUCCESS IN PARIS TASTING ON MAY 24 STOP TOOK FIRST PLACE OVER 9 OTHERS WITH LE PREMIER CRU WINE STOP TOP NAMES IN FRANCE WERE THE BLIND TASTERS STOP. . . .

Mike Grgich, back in Napa Valley, read the telegram again. He hadn't even known that his Montelena Chardonnay had been entered in a tasting. The Barretts were still in France, and the old winery outside Calistoga reflected the indolence of spring: recent vintages maturing in cask, and an agreeable silence.

Fewer than two thousand cases of the '73 had been produced, all of it sold except for those few cases the winery kept for its own use. Grgich found a bottle, pulled the cork, and poured himself a glass.

Barbara Winiarski received the telephone call from Dorothy Tchelistcheff, just back from France, while sitting in the dining room, the winery's office. Dorothy told her in a rush that the '73 Stag's Leap Cabernet had won the tasting of reds at the Académie du Vin in Paris, besting some of the world's most famous wines, including the first-growth Mouton and Haut-Brion.

Barbara didn't know exactly what to make of it. Warren was on the road selling wine, and when he called that night, she said, "Do you remember Steven Spurrier coming here and taking some wine for a tasting? Well, we won."

"That's nice," said Warren, and he began to talk of other things.

Within a few days a letter arrived from Spurrier confirming the fact that the '73 Stag's Leap had received highest marks from the panel of nine French judges. The '70 Mouton had run a close second, the Haut-Brion third, the Montrose fourth, the Ridge fifth, the Léoville-Las-Cases sixth, the Mayacamas seventh, Bernard Portet's Clos du Val eighth, the Heitz ninth, and, finally, the Freemark Abbey.

Among the Chardonnays, the Montelena had amassed the most

points. The Meursault-Charmes came in second, the Chalone third, the Spring Mountain fourth, the Beaune Clos des Mouches fifth, the Freemark Abbey sixth, the Bâtard-Montrachet seventh, the Puligny-Montrachet eighth, the Veedercrest ninth, and the David Bruce last.

The story appeared in *Time,* under the headline "Judgment of Paris." The magazine seemed to enjoy tweaking the collective French nose with the assertion that the judges were "high priests" of the cult of French enology, and that "the unthinkable happened: California defeated all Gaul."

The next day the Winiarskis' telephone started to ring, and it never really stopped.

The details of the tasting emerged gradually, and with them the realization of just what had taken place on the patio of the Inter-Continental that warm day in May. Not only had California wines finished first in both categories, but six of the eleven most highly rated wines were Californian.

Some shocking details concerned the behavior of the judges once the labels had been revealed. After successive moments of disbelief — a farrago of blows to French complacency — at least one judge tried to upgrade the ranking of the French wines, but Spurrier managed to collect the cards before the results were undermined. Some judges refused to give up their accompanying notes, and one complained that he had been forced into traitorous activity. The wine that had reminded one judge of "the magnificence of France . . . certainly a *premier grand cru* of Bordeaux" was in fact a Napa Valley Cabernet. The wine that had brought Raymond Oliver "back to France" was Californian. The wine that had prompted another to claim that finding the Californians was easy, and to deride the bouquet and taste, turned out to be a white Burgundy.

The '73 Montelena, before its identity was revealed, had been described as "fruity and elegant . . . *très complet,*" and the '73 Stag's Leap Cabernet as "tender, with a lot of stuffing . . . a fine balanced wine that will open with much charm."

Members of the French wine industry immediately proclaimed the tasting unfair, even "a direct attack" on the indisputable notion of French supremacy. A campaign began to find the most acceptable explanation for the inexplicable. Some of the French and California wines were from different vintages, the critics pointed out. California wines show better when young than do French wines, said others. The justifications took on a frenzied quality: there were slightly more California than French wines in the tasting: the wines had not been uniformly chilled; the crowd on the patio of the Inter-Continental distracted the tasters; the day was hot; the tasters were not accustomed to California wines; the order of wines tasted was biased against the French; the delicate French wines had been discombobulated on their journey to the hotel; comparative tastings are inherently unfair; statistically, the results were slightly different than reported . . .

A few hit upon the most logical explanation: that the California wines were as good as the French ones. The Bordeaux all belonged to the 1970 vintage, the best since 1966 and so far the best of the decade, but a hard, tannic one. They could not have been as discombobulated as the American wines, however, since the American ones had recently crossed the Atlantic Ocean.

The real problem with disavowing the Paris Tasting, the insurmountable, inexcusable, inexpressibly disgusting unavoidability of it all was the nationality of the tasters themselves. They were French. Therefore they couldn't be publicly accused of prejudice.

In private, the industry seethed. Baron Philippe de Rothschild, owner of Mouton, the resounding second wine in the Cabernet tasting, telephoned one of the judges in a state of near-apoplexy, demanding, "What are you doing to my wines?" Spurrier was denounced as a sensationalist, a secret agent — an Englishman — and an enemy of the country that had so kindly accepted him. Meanwhile, the *Time* piece had an electrifying effect on the relatively minuscule market in fine domestic wine. Customers in liquor stores on both coasts requested cases of Montelena or Stag's Leap. (A wine shop in New York City received four hundred telephone calls in one day.) Serpentine car lines nosed into the lanes leading to Stag's Leap and Château Montelena on the weekend, full of people searching for the winning wines. The rest of Stag's Leap's vintage was soon depleted, even though the Winiarskis would sell only one bottle to each carload and they kept the price at $7.

The valley waited to see what the *New York Times* would say. The *Times* wine critic, Frank Prial, probably the most influential wine writer in America, was considered a Francophile by the Californians. He wrote not one but two articles about the Paris Tasting, the first dealing with the whites and accompanied by a photograph of smiling

Mike Grgich, the genial anticommunist and accomplished wine-maker, dressed in tie and V-neck sweater and holding a glass of the '73 Château Montelena Chardonnay. Prial laid out the facts of the American victory, recalling similar tastings and similar results in New York, when "champions of the French wines argued that the tasters were Americans with possible bias toward American wines. What is more, they said, there was always the chance that the bur-gundies had been mistreated during the long trip from the wineries. What can they say now?"

But a week later Prial was back on the subject of the Paris Tasting and this time assumed a more judicious tone. The results, he wrote, "deserve closer examination." Only one judge had picked Stag's Leap as the best wine, whereas two judges had picked the Haut-Brion. Another judge had grouped Stag's Leap, Mayacamas, and Montrose for first, while a fourth paired the Haut-Brion and Montrose. "Be-yond that there was little unanimity. . . . Is such a tasting a valid judgment on the quality of the wines involved? Probably not."

He went on to recall another blind tasting, in which a nonvintage Cabernet from Sonoma County had outshown some first-growth Bordeaux. "Was it better than, say, the 1970 Haut-Brion? The French wine had only begun to develop." Where, Prial asked rhetorically, would the '73 Stag's Leap Cabernet be when the '70 Mouton peaked? "Obviously, the variables involved in this kind of tasting are incal-culable. Only the most naïve reader would conclude anything other than that on a certain day a certain group of French wine specialists agreed that California turns out some fine wines. . . . One would be foolish to take Mr. Spurrier's little tasting as definitive."

Reading the column, Jim Barrett decided that Prial was biased in favor of the French. He had contributed to the polarity of opinion rather than having resolved the argument. The column was most notable, Barrett thought, for its implications that the Paris Tasting was somehow unfair and that California wines were incapable of graceful aging. Not that it really mattered. Barrett could have sold six times the amount of Chardonnay he had on hand, for a lot more than $7 a bottle.

Barrett knew you were only as good as your last hit. The Paris Tasting was the best hit of all. He calculated that it was worth roughly $4 million in publicity.

Robert Finigan wrote that the results came as no surprise to him. After all, French and California wines had been professionally matched before with similar results, but they had been matched in California and New York and the tasters had been American. The California winemakers imitated the French, and used the same oak barrels to age wine made from identical grape varieties. Finigan wrote that he had "witnessed with considerable awe the exponential improvement in California bottlings." Given this progress, what did the French expect?

In America, the predominant professional reaction was one of extreme caution and, in some cases, hostility. Roy Andries de Groot, the blind wine critic who often traveled to California — and who asked to be led into the vineyards, where he would stand absorbing the smell of wild mustard and the sound of birdsong — characterized the tasting in the pages of *Esquire* as "a publicity stunt" perpetrated by "a Parisian liquor store." De Groot added, "In the stormy aftermath, it is generally agreed in professional circles that this tasting had been very poorly managed."

Another critic, John Movius, writing for the trade, declared in *The Wine Scene* that because the scores were not subjected to statistical analysis, the results were virtually meaningless. He added grudgingly that the contest had not been won by the Californians, as had been reported, that in reality the outcome of the tasting had been a tie!

The Californians had in fact achieved a stunning victory even if statistical analysis brought in the top-ranked wines neck-and-neck. "The sponsor should have been aware that reporters and wine 'beauty contests' are totally incompatible," Movius went on to complain, without saying why — that not only can judges be saved from distraction when closeted, but also that their remarks are not subject to exposure.

The supposed California partisan Nathan Chroman wrote a condescending, syntactically tortured review of the Paris Tasting. "There is much hoopla at the moment about the so-called victory. Yet there is great doubt in my own mind as to whether these types of odious comparisons really prove anything more than that people who should know better like to indulge in them."

The professional reluctance went beyond phobias about odious comparisons. Chroman was right: there had been innumerable blind tastings of French and American wines, but Spurrier was the first to bring together pedigreed French palates and formally subject them to California's wines, and then to subject their judgments to the eyes of the world. In being the first, Spurrier attracted attention that some critics resented.

Lurking in the doubts, in the innuendoes and denunciations on both sides of the Atlantic, lay a more general fear. The reputations of the *crus classes* were not the only things at stake; the entire industry could suffer by association. For if a panel of French experts in enology and wine tasting could be fooled, then who might not be?

The winners knew better than to crow. Having already reaped the benefit of so much publicity, they made only the most reasonable and generous statements. They did not consider the Paris Tasting a horse race or even a contest, they said. The French were not "losers" but merely coparticipants in the ongoing struggle for better wine.

Warren Winiarski wrote to the critic John Movius, saying, "I believe it was 'the fatal lack of knowledge' of what was happening in California wine-making . . . which led the tasters to fit the wines before them into so many procrustean schemata. One hopes the insights brought about by the outcome of the tasting, while perhaps temporarily embarrassing to some, will have the benefits that usually accompany the dispelling of dogma."

Robert Mondavi, whose wines had been left out of the tasting, told anyone who asked, "We knew nothing about it." It wasn't a bad position to be in. He could still take credit for some of the progress in California — and avoid the risk of having his wines put up against the others at the Inter-Continental.

As Legh Knowles of Beaulieu always said of wine tastings, "If you come in second, you've lost."

IV

Deluge

22

AT HOME, vineyards had replaced most of the orchards by 1976. Suddenly it looked as if the vineyards would survive. And with this plethora of vines and wines came people, not just winemakers but all the attendant staff of the flourishing new wineries, and all those on the periphery of this now world-renowned pocket of enological excellence. Many wanted simply to live and work in proximity to it. The population of Napa city and the towns to the north pushed at their borders, and new householders in the rural areas pushed at the limits of the agricultural preserve established less than a decade before. It seemed that California and the rest of America — like the French — had at last noticed the existence of a place called Napa Valley.

There were problems on the horizon, recognized by a relative few. Those who did notice them often acted alone to oppose what they saw as insidious and potentially harmful. For the most part they had little to do with wine or the burgeoning social life built around it; for a time they remained in obscurity, fighting little battles the sounds of which rarely reached the tourists, the aspiring householders, and the owners of the wineries themselves.

When Napa County offered Jim Hickey the job of planner back in 1970, he took it, along with a cut in salary. Napa wasn't on the way to anywhere professionally, or geographically, but planners like to build things and Hickey was no exception. He wanted to draw up a General Plan for the county that would preserve its special character and with it some of what human beings long for in their ever-broadening circles of exurban migration.

Hickey carried his ball-point pens in a leather scabbard attached to his belt under a blue blazer. His tie clasp was a cluster of little gold grapes. He moved deliberately through the county offices in Napa city, his resonant, thoroughly midwestern voice adding to the impression of authority.

The agricultural preserve, established just before he arrived in Napa, had been one of his reasons for taking the job. He came from an easterly direction, as most Californians did. Only after World War II, when he was stationed on the West Coast, did he understand that the sentence of a Michigan winter was not irrevocable. He went back anyway and graduated from Michigan State University, determined to do something to improve the world. Urban planning was a relatively new concept, tied to landscape architecture, but he was more interested in open space. He tried to put green belts around some industrial areas in Ohio, then heard that the Association of Bay Area Governments needed a regional plan for the San Francisco Bay littoral, which was growing in population as fast as any place in the country. Nine counties and a projected human mass of millions.

The Association of Bay Area Governments — ABAG was the unhappy acronym — had only $200,000 to spend, a ridiculously small figure for the task. During the course of completing it Hickey saw some strange things: Alameda County threw a party to commemorate the attainment of a million in population, as if that was something to be happy about; Santa Clara Valley celebrated the paving of its orchards. Everywhere houses took over meadows, woodlots, and mountainsides. Concrete towers imposed themselves between the people and the land and water, and most of the politicians cheered.

Only one county had a chance of avoiding that fate, he thought, and that was Napa. By geographical and political happenstance, Napa was not bisected by a major highway. Traffic between San Francisco and the state capital, Sacramento, shuttled to the east of what was sometimes called the Vaca Mountains; the coastal route up from San Francisco passed through Sonoma County, west of the Mayacamas. Those two ranges converged at the top of Napa, and the south of the county dwindled through marshy country — another problem for development — where the Napa River cut increasingly large loops until it merged with the shallow bay.

What Jim Hickey saw there was an isolated valley close to a big city, San Francisco, but with sides so rugged that the usual enticements to building did not exist except on the valley floor. The natural complexities of the area produced a crop, grapes, and an end product of exceptional quality and value. It was a special place, in an era when those words necessarily meant less and less, and dependent in part on luck.

"If Napa Valley can't be saved," he said, "no place can."

Hickey was just one of the people concerned. Others, with jobs and histories unrelated to wine, drawn to the valley and to its defense, included a lawyer, an academic, and the unlikely figure of a well-born Republican stockbroker, all representative of the general desires and commitments of a growing contingent of potential land-use combatants.

A banjo clock hung on the wall of Vic Fershko's office in downtown Napa, three minutes on foot from the county government building. Fershko went there often, carrying an old leather briefcase with floppy straps and an accordion file inside, wearing under his jacket broad, patterned suspenders. His straw-colored hair matched his mustache — an abundant soup strainer.

Fershko had no formal connection to Jim Hickey, the county planner, but over the years their paths had crossed in a strange, unpremeditated way. Like Hickey, Fershko arrived in California from the East, looking for work. He had grown up on the northeast border of Israel and Syria, and in Tel Aviv. He clearly remembered the crack of distant rifles as snipers took aim at his father, who was busy draining potential farmland. He remembered guns by the table at mealtime, and walking with his grandfather in the Tel Aviv market — the taste of hot garbanzo beans and the smell of syrupy black coffee in the Turkish shops.

His grandfather held him on his shoulders in the square the night Israel was voted into the United Nations, while people danced the hora and others waited for the results coming in over the loudspeaker.

Fershko came to America as a teenager, went to Brooklyn Law School, taught law for a while, and then took up his private exodus from the city in a beat-up car that broke down in Louisiana. It hobbled across the Southwest. He worked as the personnel manager for a janitorial service in Los Angeles until he passed the California bar. He heard of a legal-aid position in Napa and arrived for an interview the day before New Year's Eve, 1970, to find the room in the county building mobbed with applicants. He was asked if he was bilingual, and Fershko said yes.

"Spanish?" asked the interviewer.

"No, Hebrew."

The city offered him the job and he took it. He and his wife bought a house and two acres on the outskirts of Napa and equipped it with chickens, goats, and an uncontrollable zucchini plot. Then Fershko learned that a development was to go in next door, 270 houses on 100 agricultural acres, to be annexed by the city.

He read up on environmental law and discovered that annexation was subject to referendum. The Fershkos organized the neighborhood; they set up tables at the shopping centers. They had only thirty days to get 10 percent of the 24,000 registered voters signed up. Their placards said, "Vineyards or Subdivisions?" They amassed 6,000 signatures and the issue went all the way to the California supreme court, which ruled in their favor.

Fershko saw one thing clearly: politicians willing to vote for the creation of an agricultural zone will also vote, under pressure, for exceptions to it, eventually wrecking the land. The head of the Planning Department, Jim Hickey, aptly compared this process to a glacier composed of individual snowflakes that acquire an irresistible force. Enough exceptions to the ag preserve, and it wasn't a preserve any longer.

Napa Valley was one of the few places where the timing was right for opposition to development, Fershko thought. During the course of the subdivision fight he met others interested in land use who came together in coalitions that mutated or dissolved and then reformed for a similar objective. Often the same people resurfaced in different roles. Fershko was reminded of Claude Rains's line from *Casablanca,* "Round up the usual suspects." Fershko didn't like wine, or even approve of it. Wine was a snob's drink, in his opinion, and the land devoted to vineyards no more valuable because of them. The land was valuable because it grew *something,* and Fershko wanted it still to be there for whatever crop came next.

❧

One of the usual suspects had a beard and bright blue eyes. The California sun had otherwise obscured his northern European origins, but when he talked his sibilant enthusiasm was unmistakably

German. Volker Eisele could remember marches in the streets of his native Münster by the Hitler Youth; as a young man he regarded America as the destroyer of fascism and the refuge of decency. He sought and was granted a fellowship to study at the University of California at Berkeley and eventually became one of thousands of German intellectuals who sought citizenship and, with it, some expurgation of collective guilt.

He arrived in Berkeley in 1963. Student protest was about to transform the campus, and the war in Vietnam to move into the American living room. Vietnam changed everything. America lost its moral superiority; the concept of an ordered world fell apart. Volker joined "the movement." He heard Mario Savio, the apostle of free speech, and saw Joan Baez, the folk singer, march in a demonstration against the invasion of Cambodia. Governor Ronald Reagan called out the National Guard, and the Oakland police and the Alameda County deputies beat people and threw tear gas canisters into stores. Volker was shocked but he stayed on the fringes of civil disobedience.

He began to have doubts about the academic life he had envisioned for himself. Meanwhile, he passed the oral examinations for his Ph.D. in sociology and married a lovely landscape architect named Liesel. They spent more and more time in the open country north of the bay, and then decided to move to Sage Canyon in Napa County, to see if they could stand living in the country. Volker taught at the community college in Napa city. He wanted to write his thesis on ecology and politics, and traveled the county talking to ranchers and farmers. He found remote Chiles Valley, part of the watershed of the Napa River, which supported Swainson's hawks and bluebirds, chaparral, digger pine and valley oak, and grapes, where the setting sun acquired a roseate splendor, and he thought it was the most beautiful place on earth.

Unfortunately, the slopes above the road were used for dirt-bike racing. The machines filled the air with exhaust fumes and the scream of mounting rpm's. The Eiseles complained to the sheriff, who paid a visit to their house and asked why they wanted to interfere with a little harmless mechanized sport. Because the machines are disruptive, they said, and illegal. The sheriff pointed out that their dog had no tag and no collar, which was also illegal.

Volker and Liesel organized the neighbors in Chiles Valley in opposition to the race course. The county government refused to admit it even existed. The Eiseles tore down the sign on the road advertising the course, put it in their car, and drove to the city of Napa. They took the sign into the county government building, up the elevator, and into the county counsel's office. They put the sign on the desk. The county counsel had no choice but to admit that the sign, at least, existed, and by implication so might the illegal dirt-bike course.

Eventually it was shut down, but only after the fight had gone all the way to the board of supervisors. Volker learned two things from the experience: no natural place is safe from abuse, and political involvement is necessary to protect the land.

The environmental movement was in full swing in California, and its effects were being felt in Napa Valley. They could be read in the names of organizations that sprang up: Napans Opposed to Wasteland, Citizens Council for Napa Tomorrow, Citizens Against Urban Sprawl. Napans Opposed to Wasteland (NOW) helped elect slow-growth candidates to the board of supervisors in 1972, assisted by the Citizens Council for Napa Tomorrow, neighborhood groups, and the League of Women Voters. NOW was primarily a land-use group but, crucially, was based in Napa city, the real source of power in the county. In 1973 the slow-growth supervisors the coalitions had helped elect — John Tuteur, Jenny Simms, and Henry Wigger — voted to increase the minimum lot size in the hills to forty acres, a major victory in the eyes of their supporters.

A year later, another coalition opposed plans by the California Department of Transportation for a four-lane highway running up the middle of Napa Valley. That fight went to the state legislature in Sacramento, which passed a law precluding the construction of the freeway. The agricultural character of the valley was further strengthened, as were the ranks of "the usual suspects."

During the dirt-bike fight, Volker and Liesel Eisele had visited a neglected ranch in Chiles Valley directly across the road from the dirt-bike course. It was part of the original land grant to a Kentucky trapper, Colonel Joseph Chiles, called Rancho Catacula, where grapes were grown. It was bought in 1880 by Francis Seviers, a San Franciscan and a native of Schleswig in northern Germany. A former ship's captain, another German, built Seviers's farmhouse, which included a cupola, using thousands of square-headed nails. Seviers's son built a winery, Lomitas Vineyard, in the last years of the century and planted Zinfandel, Sauvignon Vert, and Berger. The old press and fermenters had fallen into disuse with Prohibition, and the property into general decline.

The Eiseles managed to buy it. They had discovered that they could actually live quite happily in the country.

23

RUMORS OF DEALS shuttled up and down the valley, some names foreign, some familiar. After Heublein had come Nestlé, the Swiss conglomerate predicated on chocolate and other delectables and a controversial baby formula peddled in Third World nations as a substitute for mother's milk. For Nestlé, Beringer, with the Rhine House mansion, grounds, and seven hundred acres of vineyards, was no more than a mote in the corporate eye. Moët made a success with Domaine Chandon by calling its product sparkling wine instead of champagne and by appealing to a market segment that would have spurned Cold Duck and other fizzy domestic wines.

The Paris Tasting brought more foreigners on permanent billet to Napa. They enrolled in UC Davis and could be seen wearing jeans and avoiding the sun that baked the university, all the while inhaling technical details that had fueled the rise of California wine.

Speculation heaved up the names of large American corporations plunging into the wine business without experience or knowledge. Pillsbury reached far beyond the mills of the Midwest to buy two wineries, one in Napa and the other in Sonoma, both called Souverain. (The original Souverain had passed to an airline pilot, Tom Burgess, who rechristened it eponymously.) Pillsbury lost millions and sold out, their Napa winery becoming Rutherford Hill.

There now arrived that symbol of American enterprise and global reach, the effervescent, optimistic, heavily monied maker of the ultimate beverage . . . Coke. The Coca-Cola Company of Atlanta, in an uncharacteristic act, had bought the Taylor Wine Company of New York. They began negotiating for an interest in Sterling Vineyards with Peter Newton, the journalist and financier. He had hired Ric Forman, the Oakland boy who had worked for Mondavi and then traveled to France, to learn to make wine as good as the best, and after that had turned raw flats south of Calistoga into prime vineyard. The grapes, including rare Merlot, and the wines had become bemedaled avatars.

Newton early on had seen the wide-open opportunity to buy the equivalent of land in the Médoc without having to pay for the *appellation*. Coke, of course, would have to pay him, and dearly.

Coke wanted to be the largest bottler of estate wines in the country. Sterling was already one of the world's most spectacular winemaking facilities, a white monastic vision on a firred lava knoll that was linked to the parking lot, and hence to the burgeoning lines of tourists, by a ski lift. Early in the deal making Coke representatives told Newton that the boys from Atlanta made lousy partners. They wanted it all, they admitted, and Newton agreed to give it to them — at a higher price.

Newton had learned a valuable lesson: that it is much easier and more lucrative to sell wineries than wine.

Coke also bought Monterey Vineyards in the Salinas Valley. Dick Peterson had gone to work there after leaving Beaulieu, to escape what he saw as Heublein's corporate idiocies and spearhead the new winery, a difficult endeavor. It was cold in the Salinas Valley, he had discovered, and the grapes tended not to ripen. They produced some funny flavors. The winery's finances had proved less than sound. Peterson took the problems personally and the stress affected his marriage, and then Coke came in with sabers rattling. It had big plans for something called Taylor California Cellars, the mass-marketing side of Coke's new interest in wine. Coke was going to flail the competition, it announced, the way it flailed Pepsi. With good value. With deodorant-type ads. With real comparisons of their wines with those of Almadén and Sebastiani. With competition!

Dick Peterson was embarrassed by the brashness of his new bosses — he was used to the measured cadences of Beaulieu's PR — but he had to admit they were on to something. The wine business, they said, was an old-boys' club, and they were right. The rest of the wine industry resented what Coke said and did, but Coke put good grapes into its wines and blew the whistle on competitors' sneaking sugary Central Valley fruit into their varietals. Peterson had to admit something else: Coke did not try to make over Monterey Vineyards or Sterling in its own image. Unlike other corporations, Coke asked for advice. It did not think that a janitor in Atlanta knew more about grapes than a Ph.D. in Gonzales.

Coke sought the advice of Ric Forman in its Napa expansion.

Forman was by now a minor legend for putting together Sterling out of brains, labor, and gall. When the boys from Atlanta came to Calistoga, Forman took them outside and pointed west toward Diamond Mountain, and said, "Buy it."

❧

Coke did buy a piece of Diamond Mountain, from an Okie with wheat-colored hair named William Hill. He would make a name for himself in Napa because he was among the first to see prime vine-yardland as real estate to be sold to outside investors.

Until his last year of college, Hill had never been west of Ama-rillo. Hill had gone on to get an M.B.A. from Stanford and to delve deeply into what he saw as the new play in the wine industry. Now when he stood up in front of business groups and wine enthusiasts, Hill didn't talk about stainless steel fermentation, French oak, and centrifuges; his calculated investment strategies seemed inimical to the romance of wine.

Hill revealed a curious preoccupation with hillsides. Winemaking in California was reaching the apex of its technological curve; the notion of wine as a kind of Pygmalion of the laboratory was chang-ing, and the best scholars and vintners were looking for the next advantage and finding it in the vineyard — the steep vineyard, Hill insisted — with proximity to water and good slope, aspect, soil composition, macroclimate, *climat*.

Not too many years before, Hill and his wife had been crawling around under the madroñas on Diamond Mountain, amidst poison oak and pine needles, looking for *climat*. They had a rope for mea-suring and a shovel for taking soil samples. Somewhere in there was a 320-acre parcel for sale. Few people thought the mountains were worth farming, but Hill did. He was convinced that in the old days the settlers had grown grapes there. Proof lay in old redwood stakes that had survived the century, and vines that clung to the fir trees, the vines being the many-generational progeny of some old immi-grant's efforts. The old-timers had known that the hillsides were frost free, since the cold ran down the mountain, and that difficult growing conditions produced more flavorful grapes and hence bet-ter wine.

He figured that one hundred acres were plantable. He went to a company that had put together real estate deals out in the Central Valley and persuaded them to form a partnership to buy the property and let Hill manage it. He didn't get a piece of the action because it was his first deal, the culmination of years of study and trips to Bordeaux that had convinced him of the overall importance of vineyards on the western coast of continents near deep, cold oceans. Because of the earth's rotation, the jet stream moves the ocean air over the vines, keeping them as cool as possible while still allowing growth. Mountainsides are best because rocky soil allows the vineyards to drain. Consultation with Tchelistcheff, the California state farm advisor, and the manager of the Martinis' Monte Rosso vineyard reinforced Hill's belief that the Mayacamas range between Mount Veeder and Diamond Mountain had the potential to be the best vineyardland in the world.

Hill had decided that America was slowly becoming a wine-drinking culture and that a wine boom was imminent. Higher prices for American wine would mean more money for deep-ripping the land, constructing reservoirs for drip irrigation, and all the other technology that had moved out of the lab and into the vineyards. Venture capital worked in high-tech start-up companies and it worked in commercial real estate, and there was no reason it wouldn't work in highly specialized agriculture. The secret was management, long-range planning, and an expanding market.

He farmed Diamond Mountain Ranch and looked around the Mayacamas for more land. He found five hundred acres on Mount Veeder with forty acres planted, and put together a multinational partnership that was to be the cornerstone of future deals. He bought and farmed Veeder Hills, then flipped the property to a wealthy Swiss named Donald Hess. Hill bought another, larger parcel and kept right on looking.

Dick Peterson had worked for Gallo as a rocket scientist, for Beaulieu as winemaker, and he had put Monterey Vineyards on the map. He longed to get back to Napa Valley, and saw the Coca-Cola purchase of Monterey and Sterling as a possible route. He was mentally on board the Coca-Cola ship, as he put it. He remained the enologist at Coke's Monterey Vineyards but was also technical director of the Wine Spectrum, Coke's umbrella for its wine interests. The Wine Spectrum might someday take him "home."

He threw himself into the wine-marketing battle; for a couple of years Coke tore up the competition. But Coke's executives were accustomed to obscene profits. When you can sell citric acid, water, and sugar for more than the price of beer, Peterson thought, you develop unreal expectations.

Then Coke brought in a new president to rev up Spectrum's profits. A hatchet man. He questioned all decisions, cut the advertising budget, and sales dropped for the first time. It was the janitor theory all over again. This time the janitors decided to sell. Coke's California dream came to dust, and so did Peterson's plans for returning to Napa.

The buyer of Coke's properties was Joseph E. Seagram & Sons, the whiskey distillers. From pop to booze — not a good sign for the industry. Peterson knew little about Seagram, only that it was owned by a Canadian family, the Bronfmans, who were, he had heard, unconventional.

The Bronfmans owned only 39 percent of Seagram, but that amounted to control of a billion-dollar colossus that encompassed value-added beauties like Canadian Club whiskey and a great deal of wine. Seagram's wine-marketing apparatus went back to the 1940s, when the late Samuel Bronfman bought Paul Masson Vineyards. He held on to Masson at a time when other distillers were getting out of the wine business, and established limited inroads for California wine abroad, spawning the eventual, global Seagram Classics Wine Company. With the purchase of Coke's Wine Spectrum, Seagram became second only to the Gallos as a major tributary of California's trend-swept wine lake.

The jewel in the Bronfmans' West Coast diadem was Sterling, bone white on its volcanic knoll, controversial visual Siren for tourists and possessor of fine vineyards. The consensus among Sterling's neighbors was that the wines had slipped a notch under the tutelage of Coca-Cola. Also, Monterey Vineyards should have laid claim to more of the low-end market. All this could be set right with money and will, but no one seemed to know what the will of the Bronfmans might be.

The current president, Edgar Bronfman, showed up in California and toured the properties, assistants in tow. It appeared to Dick Peterson at Monterey that the new owner had only the vaguest notion of what he was looking at. Later, the technical people came out, all wearing the same dark suits, minor versions of the president, all with what Peterson thought of as the jogger's moth-eaten look. He told his colleagues that Edgar turned them out with a cookie cutter.

Because the wines had been made one way under Coke's ownership, they had to be made another way under Seagram's.

Peterson complied. He considered himself so familiar with visiting brass that he did not argue and could anticipate many of the demands, even the most ridiculous. He designed a new label for Monterey Vineyards and went to New York to confer with the new president of Seagram Classics, Dick Maher, a former Marine who was forever popping up in different corporations: Procter & Gamble, Gallo, Heublein, Shakey's Pizza, Beringer. It was Maher who had been brand manager for Heublein's infamous Bali Hai and I Love You. At Beringer, he oversaw the winery operation in St. Helena, turning it into a factory, and headed Nestlé's wine group, Wine World.

Peterson assumed Maher would be in charge of his bailiwick within Seagram, but began to have his doubts as soon as he arrived in Maher's office and took off his coat. "Just throw it on the table," Maher told him. "That's what I do with mine."

Peterson asked why he didn't have a coat hook.

"Nothing goes on any door or wall without Mrs. Bronfman's personal approval," Maher said. "They've been designing me a coat hook for six months."

That told Peterson that Maher probably had no clout.

He got Maher's approval of the new label and went back to California. A consultant arrived from New York to redesign the label. He had never designed a wine label before and ignored Peterson's prototype and his advice. After wandering around for three days, the consultant came up with a label — one covered with seagulls.

Peterson complained to Maher, but the label appeared on the bottle anyway, proving to Peterson that Maher had no clout.

Edgar Bronfman's oldest son, Sam, was to take over Seagram's wine operations on the West Coast, a small slice of the family pie. When Peterson met Sam Bronfman he was pleasantly surprised. Tall, bespectacled, straightforward, likable, young Sam showed some knowledge of wine. Taylor California Cellars didn't interest him, and Monterey Vineyards had considerably less appeal than Sterling. Sam talked about quality and about creating a sparkling wine in Napa in conjunction with Mumm's champagne, also owned by Seagram.

Some notoriety followed Sam. While still at Dartmouth College, he had been kidnapped, and eventually was saved by his father and a bag of cash. Sam's face had appeared on the cover of *Time,* and there was the suggestion that Sam had arranged the kidnapping himself. Peterson did not believe this but could understand how a person might rebel against such a wealthy, powerful family. He felt sorry for Sam, whose father had announced that the leadership of Seagram would go to Sam's younger brother, Edgar junior, not to Sam.

Dick Maher described the Seagram head office in New York as "a goddamn jungle." Peterson wanted to tell Sam to leave and start his own winery, out from under the thumbs of the two Edgars, but of course he didn't.

The company was run by the spirits guys. Anything that contained alcohol they considered booze. They all talked about "beverage alcohol": whiskey, beer, and wine — it was all the same to them. The official position was that people drank Thunderbird and Château Pétrus for the same reason, to get high. Peterson refused to use the phrase "beverage alcohol," seeing it as a subtle put-down of wine by those committed to the gargantuan profits generated by spirits and resentful of wine's better "image." Even Maher insisted on using "beverage alcohol." When Peterson told him he was being dishonest, Maher said he was just being flexible.

The New York office told Peterson to develop a "wine cooler," an effervescent mixture of cheap wine, fruit flavors, sugar, and carbon dioxide that the sales department thought would become a big seller. As a former Gallo rocket scientist, Peterson knew how to blend. He came up with a wine cooler they liked in New York, and sent them the formula.

The technical people started showing up at Monterey asking how he had made the cooler; Peterson would say, "The way I told you." The words didn't sink in. It was as if they were speaking two different languages. He realized that the New Yorkers were out there to make a wine cooler just like Peterson's, but they had to do it themselves. They wouldn't use his formula. Seagram had bought Peterson, but he wasn't one of them.

The technicians in White Plains sent Peterson some samples of their wine coolers. They were all bad. The technicians tossed them into the market test anyway, alongside Peterson's cooler, and only his tested well. Finally they flew Peterson to White Plains for consultation, and *then* decided to use his formula.

Now he had a corollary to his janitor theory: "If you didn't do it here, it doesn't count."

White Plains asked him for ten more wine coolers but he didn't send them any. He returned no phone calls and accepted no invitations to technical conferences. The company asked him to defend the practice of blending wine from different years and doing away with vintage dating; he refused. Instead, he wrote letters making nonnegotiable demands for quality that went unanswered.

Secretly he hoped Seagram would fire him. The company seemed to bend over backwards to avoid letting people go who had accrued benefits; this was called the golden handcuffs. Peterson had been at Monterey for twelve years and would have gotten severance pay, at least. Dick Maher couldn't believe Seagram *didn't* fire him, but Peterson knew they needed his know-how.

Meanwhile, he looked for a way back to Napa. Wineries were sprouting there like toadstools, and sometimes Peterson wondered if there would be any land left for making a new Napa wine for the millennium.

24

ROBIN DANIEL LAIL had moved back to the valley after her father's death. Rutherford and Napa Valley — what a few years before had seemed merely a nice place to be from — had taken on a new dimension. Robin now cherished it. She wanted to accomplish something there, and went to work for a local agency that organized volunteers to help with the elderly, children, the injured, and shut-ins. She stayed for three years, working with a small grant and building the organization around her.

The couple that had bought her father's house and property from Betty, with the intention of developing it, opened it to visitors. Robin found herself giving guided tours through what had been her home — through her own childhood, in effect. She pointed out the richly paneled ceiling in the Niebaum dining room, the elegant detail of the broad front porch, and the closed door of John Daniel's study at the head of the stairs, all the while telling herself, "You have the finesse of an elephant." But she kept going back.

Once she took a friend to the house, which was about to be sold again, and together they made their way up to the attic. Robin looked out beyond the oaks, toward the pasture and Navalle Creek. She said, "Isn't it beautiful?" and began to cry.

Her friend said, "You can build your own estate."

One February afternoon in 1976 Rafael Rodriguez came home to find a stranger sitting in his living room. Momentous change for Rafael had always occurred in the early months of the year: he had left Mexico thirty-five years before and traveled north through the cold; he had gone to work at Inglenook in early winter, with the vines like dead things and the wild mustard greening up in the vineyard rows. Now the flowers had emerged in riotous strips of yellow after the rains, an unmistakable sign of the coming spring, but Rafael did not feel in tune with the new season.

The early excitement and sense of accomplishment at the Growers Foundation had given way to bickering. Politics had begun to infiltrate what had been a spontaneous response to big unionism, at least in Rafael's eyes and in the eyes of the founders. Most of the pickers had been won over, but with success had come an altered course. Now the board wanted to strenuously oppose "activism" by the United Farm Workers, still a force in the valley; there was less emphasis on the needs of pickers' families. Rafael thought the foundation was losing touch, and that he was just another face in an expanding crowd.

He was less than impressed with the appearance of the fat, bearded man in an old T-shirt, shorts, and steel-rimmed glasses, his hair in disarray. What, Rafael wondered, could he want? He had been brought there by a man Rafael knew only slightly and who introduced the stranger with some ceremony. The name meant nothing to Rafael. "He's just bought the old Inglenook place," the man explained.

"That's nice," said Rafael.

"He has the intention of keeping it as it is. I told him I knew someone who could help him."

Rafael noticed his wife peering from the kitchen, and his youngest daughter, Susanna, gesturing.

The stranger asked in a deep, oddly accented voice, "How would you like to come to work for me?"

"I would be delighted," Rafael said politely, "but I'm already employed."

The stranger talked on about the Daniel place. Rafael invited the two men into the kitchen. Tila served them tacos, and while they ate they continued to talk about the Niebaum estate. Rafael went into his small cellar and brought out a '52 Inglenook Burgundy, a rare wine that clearly pleased his visitors.

"Take your time in deciding," the stranger told Rafael, who had not even agreed to consider the offer, "but I would like to know as soon as possible."

When they had left, Tila and Susanna rushed up, their faces alight. "Don't you know who that is?"

"Who?" asked Rafael.

"The director of *The Godfather*. That's Francis Ford Coppola!"

Eleanor and Francis had heard about Napa Valley from friends in San Francisco, where they had moved from Los Angeles, to a big house in Pacific Heights. Before they visited Napa, Francis assumed it would be an Italian community with lots of little Italian restaurants. He wanted a cottage and an acre of grapes where he could go occasionally and make a little wine.

The Coppolas discovered instead a rather prim valley, a Waspy town called St. Helena, and a willing real estate agent. Their idea of what they wanted grew steadily. Finally the agent said, "Well, there's one big place, but I don't think you want that much home."

The Coppolas said they would take a look at it.

Eleanor was slight, with soft brown hair and a voice that seemed, in contrast to her husband's, deferential. But her words carried the weight of consideration. Riding up the long driveway, she looked out at vineyards, meadows, a beautiful white frame Victorian set on several hundred acres, all up for auction. Blond, suntanned Californians lay about the pool. Francis later told people the scene reminded him of *An American Tragedy* by Theodore Dreiser. It reminded Eleanor of paradise.

The house was like a ship, with a broad, decklike porch, smallish rooms, and exquisite woodwork. The windows were all stuck shut and there was no closet space; the Coppolas made a bid of almost $2 million.

That turned out to be low. The place went to a couple with development plans, and for a time the Coppolas put it out of their minds. Francis invested in a winery on Mount Veeder, and he and Eleanor got caught up in a new food and wine fad. They went to Chez Panisse in Berkeley and to other stellar restaurants in San Francisco. Along the way they heard that the development plans for the old Niebaum estate had fallen through — something about agricultural zoning — and the place was on the market again. This time they offered $2.5 million.

Eleanor had a window put in the kitchen facing north, and that was about all she had done. To her, the house was a work of art. She chose nondescript furnishings so the woodwork would stand out; she was grateful it had never been painted. Each room was different: burl maple in the sitting rooms, oak in the dining room, lots of mahogany, and inlaid floors and ceilings. Opposite sides of the sliding doors matched the wood they faced. She didn't alter the arches, and left the original windows — big sheets of rolled glass — open to the view.

Francis felt he was in over his head at a difficult time in his life. His new film, *Apocalypse Now,* into which he had put $16 million of his own money, had just been released to unenthusiastic and in some cases scathing reviews. He felt burned out, angry, reclusive. He intended to live in the country and make some wine, a subject he knew little about. Despite the fact that he owned cases of Romanée-Conti, his favorite beverages were lemon soda and ginger ale. Wine was what his father had made in the basement in New York when Francis was a child, what the relatives drank when they came to visit. Breaking the wine jug had gotten Francis into trouble more than once.

After moving west, he had started drinking good wine and had made a pact with himself: whenever he won money in Las Vegas — not a lot, a few thousand dollars — he would use it to buy wine. Something to leave to his children. His friend Bill Cosby poured Romanée-Conti at home like it was water; another friend served Château Lafite as his house wine. So Francis bought some Romanée-Conti and some first-growth Bordeaux but he didn't really know why they were good.

One day while the house was being worked on, a car rolled up under the centuries-old oak in the front yard, and a balding man and his blond companion stepped out into the dappled shade. They were Robert Mondavi and Margrit Biever, calling unannounced. Mondavi was not exactly a neighbor but a universal presence in the valley; the Coppolas welcomed them. Francis went down into the cellar and took a bottle of nineteenth-century Inglenook Cabernet from behind a wooden barrier. Together they decanted it into a peanut butter jar and the bouquet rose to fill the room.

Mondavi said, "See? See what's possible here?"

He spoke enthusiastically about the place, built by an old Finnish sea captain named Niebaum. Francis felt the force of its history and started to get excited. "Why," he asked, "couldn't we grow grapes here and make a Bordeaux-style wine? Just one wine, like they do at the great châteaux?"

"Of course," said Mondavi. "That's what should be done."

Slowly Eleanor filled the house with their things: portraits of Francis's grandparents brought over from Naples, a suit of samurai armor, a portrait of Napoleon, a double-barreled shotgun with a straight English stock. She enrolled their children in school in St. Helena. The house seemed to her a healing place, set far back from the road and manmade sounds. The air smelled clean and the stars burned with a new intensity. The vineyards all around reflected the cycle of life, things growing and dying, and would help her understand the forces they would soon have to live with.

They began to entertain the way Francis liked to, cooking pasta in the kitchen while others looked on. They thought of themselves as part of the Italian tradition, the family waiting until the father came home to sit down to dinner, even if Francis was shooting far away and didn't appear until nine o'clock.

Food was important, but so was wine. First Francis wanted to make fine wine and sell it in jugs, Italian fashion, but people talked him out of that. After making one vintage with the help of his father and brother, and all the kids up to their knees in grape juice, he knew he needed a winemaker. But before that he needed a vineyard manager.

❦

Rafael had his problems at the Growers Foundation. Some of the members did not treat the workers well, and wanted Rafael to disguise the fact. He told them they would have to change the way they did business, and some did change, but others resented what he told them. Rafael decided to leave. But since his departure would be seen as a victory for the United Farm Workers, he agreed to keep it confidential.

The Coppolas were all in the pool the afternoon he drove up to the house. Francis came over to him, and Rafael said, "I think I have an answer for you."

"Good. If it's positive, talk to my business agent here."

The man, a lawyer, took Rafael aside and they talked about the job. Rafael would have to oversee not just the vineyards but the entire property, the lawyer told him. He would have to keep it up to the standards set by John Daniel. For that, Rafael's present salary would be doubled.

"Choose any location you like," the lawyer added, "so we can build you a house."

Rafael felt he had come full circle. The salary alone would have been hard to turn down, but he loved the place, too. He thought of all the men who had helped him: Emmolo, Sousa, Stralla, and now Coppola. Because of them, he was where he was and, in some ways, what he was.

Tila did not want to move again, and Rafael agreed with her reasoning: if they lived on the property, he would have no time of his own, so he took the job on condition that he commute the two miles. Coppola and the lawyer agreed, and the cottage next to the winery, once Rafael and Tila's living quarters, became an office where the new proprietor of the old Inglenook estate worked on movie scripts while glancing across Navalle Creek at horses gamboling in the meadow.

❧

Betty Daniel returned from New Zealand unhappy with the experience of living there, most of her money gone. She moved for a time to Silverado and then went into Queen of the Valley Hospital, with complications arising from age and too many pills. Robin went regularly to see her. One day she found Betty cradling two imaginary infants in her arms, singing to them. Robin realized that her mother was hallucinating and that the imagined infants were herself and her sister, Marky.

Betty died in Robin's arms.

Marky found that she was able to let the unhappiness go at last. She could feel affection for her mother dead that she had not experienced while Betty lived. She remembered once in writing class reading a poem dominated by the fierce, Old Testament image of Betty, and being asked by her instructor if she loved her mother. "It depends on the day," Marky had said.

Marky had always bent before her mother's will, to minimize the pain. Now she saw that Betty had not been entirely responsible for her own behavior. She had surely needed psychiatric help at a time when that was not a common or an acceptable admission. People around her had suffered, but so had Betty.

Marky didn't mourn Betty as she mourned her father, but she came to see her in a more kindly light. Betty had given her things of real value: a love of books and literature and flowers, and at least a semblance of religion. Marky did not accept all the tenets of the Church of Jesus Christ of Latter-day Saints, but she did count herself among the believers. There was comfort she would not have had but for Betty.

After the house on Niebaum Lane had passed to the Coppolas, the woman who sold it to them sent Robin Daniel Lail a package. Robin had gotten to know her over the years, and when she opened the package she found the key to John Daniel's study.

25

ROBERT MONDAVI offered Robin a job, not in the tasting room but in the office. She was to be his administrative assistant. Robert had been a friend and an admirer of John Daniel's; Robin's father had bought the first case of Mondavi Cabernet made in Robert's new winery. Despite her heritage, Robin knew little about the wine business. She could certainly learn from Robert Mondavi, the most successful, visible, and controversial vintner in the valley. He had praisers and detractors; anyone working for Robert took on both. He was said to drink deeply from the cup of life, to consider that his right. More beautiful women worked at the Robert Mondavi Winery than at any other in the valley; a certain style was required for the inner circle. Robin was attractive and had a good tennis game, as well as some real experience in business. She also had energy and drive. She would probably have to put up with innuendoes if she worked with Robert, but then all women close to him did.

She admired Robert Mondavi and sympathized with him. His family had rejected him. Most people would not have recovered from that. Robin understood the pain Robert must have felt, and where the drive to succeed came from.

Robert's strength lay, she soon realized, in his lack of vindictiveness. He did not try to get even. Neither was he greedy. Money was simply a means, if the most effective one, for getting what he wanted. He did not believe in frugality for its own sake, having proved that spending money makes money. His contributions to the home-grown wine business were simply incalculable.

One of Robin's first outings as a Mondavi understudy was to San Francisco, to a wine tasting at an elegant and highly regarded restaurant. Robert had coached her in the essentials of wine appreciation, but she felt uneasy in the group of proven enophiles. She knew she was expected to master the arcane techniques: holding the glass against the white background of the table cloth to assess the depth of color; determining whether a wine's meniscus, or surface, indicated proper concentration; flicking the glass so that the wine rode up the sides and then watching it seep down, revealing in the rivulets, or "legs," its viscosity; thrusting your nose into the glass and inhaling a bouquet that might contain any of a thousand descriptors — like butter, oak, toast, nuts, raspberries, citrus, coffee, black tea, tar, truffles, peaches, vanilla, yeast, cigar box, earth, eucalyptus. Then tasting the wine, rolling it around in your mouth, breathing air in over it with a slurping sound that contravened decent table manners, following the wine's progress as if in a military campaign — "assault," "middle palate," "finish" — all the while searching for the proper sensory adjectives: "prickly," "tannic," "mouth-filling." Also mouth-watering, full-bodied, honeyed, raw, burnt, bitter, youthful, alcoholic, mature, faded . . . The variables were infinite. That was, Robin came to realize, one of the great attractions of wine.

Large stemmed glasses stood before them, containing young, deeply purple wine. The tasters tilted the glasses in the light, just as they were supposed to; they swirled the wine with cunning twists of the wrists; they thrust their noses over the rims and inhaled provocatively, gazes fixed on the middle distance, uttering occasional grunts and sighs of indecipherable portent. Robin joined them: she looked and swirled and thrust her nose into the glass. Unfortunately, she thrust it into the wine as well, and inhaled a generous portion of Robert Mondavi Reserve Cabernet Sauvignon.

What goes up, she later thought, was bound to come down again. It did, all over the front of her white dress.

She excused herself and walked into the rest room with as much dignity as she could muster. Once there, she broke into tears. She would not go out there again; she would simply die and be carted out later. The more she cried, the more she realized that dying was not a real alternative; instead, she would stay in the bathroom for the remainder of the evening, perhaps for the remainder of her life.

She stripped off the dress and stood before the sink and mirror, washing Cabernet out of the cloth and steeling herself for what came next. She matted the dress with towels, put it back on, and — with

a large mauve spot where before there had been only virgin white —
walked back to the tasting room. She took her seat. Robert Mondavi, she had noticed with gratitude, never even blinked.

Robin proved to be capable of making decisions. She rerouted all
Robert's private telephone calls through her desk, knowing that he
was temperamentally unable to resist answering the phone. Rerout-
ing his calls saved him and others time. When the company attorney
protested, Robin pointed out that Robert answered the telephone
even in the middle of management meetings. They should all be
shielded from that.

To prove her point, and to make the decision more acceptable to
Robert, she had his phone removed when he was out of the office
and a pay phone installed on the wall. She put a roll of dimes on the
shelf. Robert didn't get the joke at first, but when he laughed the
others laughed, and Robin kept screening his calls.

People objected to her access to power. Margrit, in charge of
public relations, had brought with her great style and great ideas.
The concerts had become the hallmark of the winery, as were the
cooking classes, both Margrit's suggestions. At first she seemed
doubtful of Robin's ability to oversee Robert's affairs. When Margrit
and Robert were out of the country, which was often, Robert would
often call the winery with specific, sometimes difficult questions for
Robin; the sound of the international operator's voice would make
Robin's palms sweat.

One morning she woke up with a job, a husband, and a child asleep
upstairs — all that was required in life according to the theory of
horizontal planes. It wasn't enough. Maybe, she thought, she should
forget Napa and her family's legacy, dismiss the memory of her father, get a divorce, move away, and strike out in an entirely different
direction. Instead, she followed the example of Anne Morrow Lindbergh, whose books she had been reading, and took a week off.

In Carmel, she lay on the beach where she had played every summer since she was a child. The sea had a powerful effect on her; she
felt like a newborn colt, pushing out one leg, then another, gradually
unfolding, standing, then galloping. She headed back to Napa at
night. The highway stretched ahead, empty in the starlight. She
drove fast but not too fast, the radio on; she would clearly remember
strains of Mozart in her time capsule before the remarkable thing
happened, before she was no longer in the car but in a ballroom in a

French château, wearing a taffeta gown of water-silk blue with gold sleeves and dancing with a man she had never seen before. She became a ballerina, making the most amazing leaps . . .

A few months later she went to France with a group of Mondavi employees. If they were to make wine as good as the French did, Robert said, they should know something of the culture. They toured the châteaux of the Loire Valley, and as Robin stepped down from the bus in the driveway leading to one, she felt an inexplicable rush of adrenaline. The feeling of familiarity — she had never before been there — was almost suffocating.

She entered the château in search of some connection but didn't find it in the drafty rooms. She climbed to the ramparts, where she thought she heard carriages in the courtyard and horses' hooves on the cobblestones. When she looked over the edge she saw nothing but rotund tourists with cameras.

She started down the stairs and came upon three busts arranged on the landing. In the middle stood the statue of the man she had danced with in her daydream, driving back from Carmel. She stared into the stone eyes, thinking, Come out. I know you're in there. . .

Robert Mondavi had the succession all set up at his Oakville winery. Michael was to be president, Tim president of production and vineyard operations, and Robert chairman of the board. The problem was, the boys were quarreling, just as Robert and Peter had quarreled.

Tim's blond hair and beard contrasted with Michael's dark complexion and the brush of black mustache. Tim was slight and ascetic looking, clearly not the former linebacker Michael had been. People described Tim as "inwardly directed," and some said thwarted. He gave recitations in minute detail about the wines he made, verbosity having become a Mondavi trait after Cesare's death. With Tim, the words came out with a greater intensity, in a higher register, different from his father's inarticulate rush of ideas, slogans, aspirations, and sales figures, and from his brother's hale regard for the product. Tim was more artist than corporation man. He took his job so seriously that even the most ardent Napa viticulturists felt their eyes glaze over when he described his wines. Some winemakers dreaded sitting on judging panels with Tim because he took so long to make up his mind.

Tim resented Michael's title; the differences between them invaded the business. All decisions had to be jousted over. The arguments were not really about sales strategy, rotating fermentation tanks, centrifuges, or whether to buy a new winery in Lodi; they went much further back, in the opinion of those who knew the Mondavi boys, to who put mashed potatoes in whose hair thirty years before, in the days when Robert was on the road so much.

They still vied constantly for their father's attention. The winery and sales staff divided into pro-Michael and pro-Tim factions, with more splintering between pro-Margrit and pro-Marcia, Robert's daughter, living in self-imposed exile on the East Coast. The similarity between Robert and Peter's old relationship could not be escaped. To make matters worse, occasionally Robert inadvertently referred to Tim as Peter.

This Balkanization of the Robert Mondavi Winery forced Robert to reconsider his strategy: Michael would become managing partner and Tim would become managing partner/winegrower. Some other executives — the sales manager, the attorney, and the financial analyst — joined them in a management council. When a consulting firm that Robert brought in to look over the company told him he could not run his business by committee, Robert said, "By God, I have two sons, and they're going to learn to get along."

Marcia was simply named partner. Robert remained in charge as senior partner, although the absoluteness of his rule, if ever challenged in court, might have been difficult to defend. Robert told people that Michael had accepted the change in principle, if not in fact. He and his brother were coming together. They were learning to share and to meet their individual responsibilities, Michael's in marketing, Tim's in winemaking.

A vice president of the Robert Mondavi Winery told prospective employees to read *King Lear*. He also suggested that they look up the definition in the dictionary of "Italian hand" (". . . with reference to Italian diplomacy in the sixteenth century, subtlety, craftiness, artfulness in intrigue, etc."). Things were not always what they seemed in Oakville.

თ

In the early seventies Robert had met a representative of Baron Philippe de Rothschild's in Hawaii; the man had spoken of the possibility of a cooperative deal between the baron and Mondavi. Even this vague suggestion excited Robert beyond what words could convey. The baron was the product of two hundred years of accumulated wealth and social grace. That he was considering Napa as a suitable place for expansion would carry great weight. A film commissioned by the baron about Château Mouton-Rothschild, called *A Rothschild and His Red Gold,* had dismissed California weather and wines as predictable and uninteresting; apparently the baron had changed his mind.

Three years later — the day after Mouton had been reclassified and officially elevated to one of the five *premiers crus* of Bordeaux — Robert and his sons called at Mouton on a swing through France. They tasted wine with the estate's manager, the formidable Philippe Cottin, and with Mouton's winemaker, Lucien Sionneau, but the possibility of a cooperative effort did not come up again.

Robert was reminded of the baron when in the Paris Tasting Mouton came in second to Warren Winiarski's Stag's Leap. Napa wine had proved itself to be not so predictable, and definitely interesting. Then in 1978 Robert received a call from the Mouton representative, who said the baron wanted to meet with Mondavi in Pauillac. Robert didn't know what he had in mind, but Robert was always willing to talk, and to go to France.

This time he took his daughter, Marcia. They had not spent much time together, and Robert hoped to atone for this and get to know her better in the natural grandeur of France. Good wine, good food, green country, opulent châteaux.

Mouton was the finest, and the life of the baron touched by all the drama and romance of the last sixty years, as Robert explained to Marcia. An aviator and a yachtsman, the baron had won the Coupe de France twice and raced Bugattis in the Monaco Grand Prix at San Sebastian and Le Mans. He had translated Elizabethan English poetry, written for the theater, made a movie, and pursued women, including the Comtesse Lili de Chambure, wife of a Belgian baron, by whom he had a daughter, Philippine, before marrying the comtesse. He had fought with the Free French and was imprisoned in Casablanca when his wife died in Ravensbruck, the concentration camp.

The baron's family was one of the most renowned in Europe. Five Rothschild brothers had left the Jewish ghetto of Frankfurt at the end of the eighteenth century and established separate fortunes in Austria, Germany, France, Italy, and Britain. The baron's great-grandfather, Nathaniel, an Englishman, bought Mouton in 1853 as a diversion. The baron's grandmother disapproved of wine as a "corrupting product," and the estate was neglected during the lifetime of Philippe's parents. The baron had reluctantly agreed to take it over in the early 1920s. After the war, he commissioned Cocteau, Dali, Braque, Chagall, and other artists to design labels for Mouton, considered pure sensationalism in the very conservative Médoc. He paid them in cases of wine.

The baron then undertook the signal achievement of his privileged life: the sanctification of Mouton. For almost four decades he sought to have it reclassified from second growth to *premier cru*. He believed the official 1855 hierarchy stigmatized Mouton, one of the finest, most expensive, and long-lived Bordeaux, and his label stated as much: "First I am not, second I disdain, I am Mouton."

The classification had never been altered, despite more than a century of discussion and some clear discrepancy between rank and quality; the baron lobbied in Paris, and promoted not just Mouton but with it all of Bordeaux. When the reclassification came in 1973 it was hailed as a personal triumph, and one for the Médoc, a timely idea that, once identified and broadcast, proved irresistible. The baron — the *poète-vigneron* — changed the new Mouton label, designed by Picasso, to read, "First I am, second I was, Mouton does not change."

The chauffeur was waiting in a big black Mercedes when Robert and Marcia got off the plane in Bordeaux. He drove them north, through the Médoc, so venerated and so important in its way to the development of Mondavi wine and the Mondavi name, which had been built on the tradition of French viticulture. An artful gateway opened onto a long gravel drive leading to simple white monumental architecture offset by statuary both classical and modern. Every pebble seemed in place. The baron met them in the courtyard, dressed in a Mexican serape given to him by Harry Serlis, president of the Wine Institute, who had first mentioned the name Mondavi to Baron Philippe and who would soon be a member of the Mondavi board — it was in the living room of Serlis's Palm Springs home that Robert and Margrit would finally be married — and the baron addressed him fondly, in heavily accented English, "Bob, I want to show you what I'm doing here."

All Robert could think of was that a man whose family had figured highly in European finance for two centuries, who had himself done more for wine in France than any living man, *had come to Robert*. He was about Robert's height and had an open, honest face, and a bald dome, as Robert did. They had some other things in common, if you looked at their lives. Circumstances were very different, of course, but they both had vision. They both wanted the best! Walking across the gravel, Robert thought back to the early days at Sunny St. Helena when he worked alone, and let the wine run through the filter while he walked into town for supper. He hadn't known then that he could make fine wine in Napa, and had wondered if the soil and climate in Bordeaux were unique, or if the methods of winemaking were very different. Now he might have the opportunity to find out.

They visited Mouton's famous *chais,* where the barrels sat in absolute formation like lines in a Dali painting, in the soft light of sconces on blemishless white walls. In the wine museum the baron had brought together the foremost collection of wine-related artifacts going back to ancient China and Egypt, and an admirable collection of seventeenth-century Dutch and Flemish still lifes and paintings by Juan Gris and Picasso.

They entered the studio where artists applied their talents to Mouton's and other labels. The baron emphasized detail, insisting on perfection — just as Robert did! Rothschild accompanied them to their rooms, small, beautifully furnished, with huge down pillows and silky sheets and graceful, old-fashioned bathing facilities. The servants took away the Mondavis' clothes to wash and iron them, and Robert and Marcia dressed for dinner. Also dining with the baron were an author ghostwriting the baron's autobiography and a music critic — both charming, witty women — and Philippe Cottin. With the elegant spitted quail came a thirty-five-year-old Mouton, and dessert with a forty-five-year-old Château d'Yquem that the baron had ordered almost frozen, the precious, icy, sweet wine having lost none of its flavor and only a bit of bouquet. The baron asked Robert not to tell the owner of Yquem that he served his wine that way, so he would not be offended. Not one word relating to business had been spoken.

After dinner, the baron approached Robert and asked if he would care to meet with him the next morning in the baron's bedroom.

Back in their rooms, Robert said to Marcia, "Would you look at the simplicity of that meal. The meticulous detail! The servants did precisely what the baron wanted — were proud to do it. They had to do it, or else!"

The baron's social ease impressed Robert as much as the style of his life. "It's amazing how he can keep a man like Cottin at a distance, yet close."

Robert thought he was dealing with royalty. What the Rothschilds represented was really the ultimate in acquired wealth, the ease and opulence new money assured after two centuries. The leatherbound, mostly unopened books rising on shelves, the paintings, sculpture, furnishings and fine cuisine, the army of servants, all belonged to a member of a family that had brought itself up on a grand scale, to emulate kings and eventually to be made honorary members of the court. Robert Mondavi would later puzzle over the phenomenon, would ask more than one person in his ever-broadening travels, "How do you achieve that sense of elegance and tradition?" At times he seemed almost disheartened by the amount of time required for such a transformation.

The next morning Robert and Marcia were ushered into a bright room, where the baron sat propped in a vast four-poster, a tray on his lap and a servant and a telephone at hand, surrounded by cut flowers, dogs, and papers to be read, signed, or discarded. The business discussion proved genial and to the point: the baron wanted a joint venture in Napa Valley with Mondavi, to produce a new wine of great quality. "You take fifty percent," the baron said, "and I'll take fifty percent."

He had mentioned Robert's name first.

"You should put your name on the label," the baron went on, "and so shall I."

A Mondavi next to a Rothschild!

"Do you think we should do a red and a white?" asked the baron.

"We should make just one wine, a red — Cabernet."

That was it. They agreed to a small production, five thousand cases, and to purchasing vineyardland and eventually building a winery. "Since you're in California," the baron said, "you should make the wine. But would you mind if my winemaker came over occasionally?"

Robert would not mind. He saw this as possibly the most momentous development the valley had witnessed, a potential coup of such magnitude that the trade — the world! — would be changed. Everything else would fall into line, the Mondavis, with the help of the baron, leading the column of America's new *noblesse* into the next century. And all on the basis of a conversation lasting less than two hours, without a contract or anything signed, just good will between like-minded men.

They committed themselves to secrecy while the lawyers harried the details, a process that could take months. That night, in celebration, they drank a one-hundred-year-old Mouton, followed by the de rigueur frozen Yquem — the most enjoyable meal of Robert Mondavi's life.

26

SMALL WINERIES had emerged in the clefts and canyons of the
valley, and new ones continued to rise from the valley floor. In
1979 the minimum acreage required for building within the ag
preserve was doubled, from twenty to forty acres. In the next four
years at least twenty old Napa wineries would come back into production, riding on the cash and optimism of corporations and individual investors. No less than eighty new wineries would soon go
up in a valley that Lee Stewart had said, ten years before, might
possibly support half a dozen.

An early exemplar of success, Joseph Phelps Vineyards, stood
just down Tapling Road from the Heitz winery. Joe Phelps, a Colo-
rado highway contractor, had built the rough-hewn Wagnerian lair
from the timbers of old bridges. Joe Heitz had come to the dedication with a bottle of 1864 Madeira, which he opened and sprinkled
over Phelps's unfinished plywood floors for good luck before they
drank the rest. The ceremony seemed to have affected the entire valley.

The boutiques — the word grated on the owners of those wineries offering a specialized, stylish, and expensive product — bought
French oak barrels and raised their wines like vinous crown princes.
The upbringing might be strict, the wines oak-riven and alcoholic,
but they usually won the competitive tastings. Their prices reflected
not just good equipment and great attention but also the high interest
rates charged by the banks. A boutique's monthly nut could provide
a fine tax break for those who required one; it could also be financially ruinous.

Sales of the best — that is, the most expensive — Napa wine
went up 20 percent in 1979 and continued to rise by almost that
much annually. The same year, the value of the dollar began to fall

on foreign markets, making domestic wine a better buy in America. Americans were drinking more wine — up to 450 million gallons by the end of the seventies — an increase that far exceeded the rise in adult population. While the price of wines like Georges de Latour Private Reserve and Mondavi Reserve Cabernet would continue to go up, and to be paid, the price of Gallo's Hearty Burgundy would soon be headed south. Those premium winemakers who could hang on stood a good chance of someday being quite comfortable.

Most of the new wineries belonged to entrepreneurs and refugees from previous lives and professions. Competition grew among them, and with it the size of the required investment. An acre of raw land needed at least five years to be transformed into productive vineyard, at a cost of thousands of dollars. Grapes had to be bought in the meantime, and space leased for the winemaking, until a winery could be built. Many got into the business with only the dimmest idea of what sort of wine they would make and how they would sell it. Some prospered and some failed.

A collection of former Berkeley fraternity brothers put up $125,000 in 1978, borrowed as much again, and bought ten acres and some old buildings on the Silverado Trail. The manager was Dan Duckhorn, a short, comedic banker who had worked for the Crockers in San Francisco, ran a small railroad for them in the Sierras that went under, and then managed a nursery in Napa, his nose turning strawberry red under the sun and his acumen with money providing an advantage.

Duckhorn and his wife, Margaret, worked seven days a week for a meager wage, and sometimes no wage at all, but the operation lost $125,000 the first year and the same amount the second year. They raised another $160,000 and went back to the bank for a smaller infusion. They brought in more partners, raising another $100,000, and still had not sold a bottle of wine because it hadn't aged sufficiently, a typical predicament. It took a large fortune to make a small one, people said.

At the end of three years the winery owed the bank $300,000. The Duckhorns had concentrated on a single grape variety, Merlot, and had signed long-term contracts with several reputable growers. Fortunately Duckhorn wine won medals; eventually the money would come rolling in, as it did for so many others. Their names sounded like notes in an unending carillon: Chappellet, Burgess, Cakebread, Anderson, Pecota, Smith-Madrone, Shafer, with an antiphon of place names used by wineries like Caymus, Mayacamas, Spring Mountain, Diamond Creek, Carneros Creek, Conn Creek, Rutherford Hill, alternating with natural phenomena — Silver Oak, Stonegate, Pine Ridge, Quail Ridge, Flora Springs — until the valley rang with their collective success.

To put in vineyards and build wineries at great cost, knowing they are in part experimental, racked the nerves of many responsible for them; such ventures eroded the Edenesque qualities that brought these people to the valley in the first place. Ric Forman had to admit he was one such person. His early success with Mondavi and then with Peter Newton at Sterling had placed him at the apex of winemakers. From that vantage point he marveled at the naïveté of the newcomers. They didn't understand that starting up a winery was not relaxing. You have to move fast and make most of the decisions without advice. It had been *he* who had to choose which tanks to buy for Sterling, which crusher and how big it should be, where to put the valves, the cooperage, the new equipment, without any real experience, all of it quite scary.

After the sale of Sterling to Coca-Cola, Forman went with Newton — the British paper entrepreneur was now a very wealthy man — into the hills behind St. Helena, where a winery was to be built on a spine of the mountain and steep vineyards put in under the gap in the Mayacamas range that served as a funnel for cool air and fog from Sonoma County. Forman would do pioneering viticulture amidst the manzanita, oak, and Douglas fir of those wild but accessible slopes, and his name would go on the label — the ultimate recognition.

Forman had 49 percent of the deal, Newton had 51 percent. Forman liked Newton and trusted this brilliant Oxonian: Newton was amusing, shrewd, and knew how to operate in the world of business. He gave Forman a lot of room to maneuver, and Forman poured his life into the new venture. What he had learned at Sterling helped but did not alleviate the heartache: the steepness of the hillsides made grading and planting extremely difficult; once in, the vines were still subject to frost. When a batch of wine went wrong, Forman blamed himself. He wanted to create something special, something that would last. It took up all his mental and physical energy, and he found that he had less and less time for his wife and young son. He assumed, without ever really admitting it to himself, that his family would still be there when he finally emerged from the tunnel of his own ambition, holding a bottle of wine with the Forman name on it.

Newton's second wife, a tall, angular Chinese named Su Hua, provocative in microskirts and sometimes outrageous in appraising wine and human history, became a force in both Newton's and Forman's lives. Su Hua had social ambitions that, in Forman's opinion, were bound to clash with the needs of the winery. He got on well enough with her. Su Hua told Forman, as she did many people, that her great-grandfather had started the Opium War and that her grandfather had been a first cousin of the husband of the dowager empress. Forman thought that if everyone who claimed to be Chinese royalty really was Chinese royalty, then the last emperor would have thousands of grandchildren. He didn't care. What he worried about was the effect Su Hua had on his partner. It seemed she worried more about having the right cars than the right grape varieties. Su Hua and Peter were always going to the opera in San Francisco, it seemed, or traveling, or having stylish house guests. "They got poncier and poncier," Forman complained.

Su Hua did not want Newton Vineyards to be confused with the white, monastic Sterling, she said, which had been designed as a marketing statement. Newton, by contrast, would blend into the hill with a minimum amount of earth moving and construction — the equivalent of a Rothko minimalist canvas. A garden would be built over the cellars, and a pagoda above the fermenting tanks. At harvest time the deck could be taken up and the wine pumped over and then the whole thing reassembled after crush.

The Newtons' house, built farther up the hill, was designed in hexagonal form, with slatted windows arranged to provide uninterrupted views through the house. The door was constructed of brass in the shape of a lotus flower. When the Formans went there to be entertained, Ric's wife hated it, or seemed to. That made Forman more unhappy with the situation. Also, he had to make decisions on his own while the Newtons were away, only to have Peter later ask why he had planted a particular variety on a particular slope, and why he had bought a certain tank. They began to argue.

Forman worked harder. "Driven" did not adequately describe his state of mind; "closed up" was better. No one, including his wife, could get in there with him. He intended to be reborn as the partner in a successful winery that might look like a Chinese pagoda but was still *his,* or at least partly his, and the hard life would be behind them.

Then one day he looked up and his wife and half-grown son were leaving him, and he realized he needed help.

The psychiatrist considered Forman's marriage typical of those of ambitious corporate executives: stressed by absence, by lack of communication, by an inability to enjoy what little time the couple had together, and by a resentment of the product — in this case, wine. The psychiatrist lived in the valley and knew many couples in the wine business. The successful ones had gotten beyond the territorial concerns and were tolerant of the separation. They talked about something other than wine at night. The wives had learned to fit into the system, taking over the entertainment, the marketing, and sometimes the management in what was still very much a man's world.

If a woman had insufficient self-esteem, things got worse rather than better. She became a "crush widow," nagging at the vintner when he was home, preferring negative attention to no attention at all. She attacked wine or the winery because it was convenient just to have a target. The husband misunderstood, thinking he was building something and that his wife did not appreciate it. The cycle tended to repeat itself, growing worse each time.

A compulsive, self-made man like Ric Forman reminded the psychiatrist of a heat-seeking missile: he was going to get what he wanted. It took a mature, determined woman to live through the effort, avoiding the slow burn that often consumed such marriages. The psychiatrist knew because he and his wife, a psychiatric social worker, had come to Napa to live in the country and ended up owning a winery, like everybody else.

Forman felt as if he were on a bicycle and couldn't get off. He and Newton split up, and then his wife divorced him. He would later have trouble remembering the details, so deep was his depression. He eventually sued Newton, adding to the lengthening list of court actions in the valley. Although Forman received damages covering at least part of the effort he had put into the project, $30,000 worth, he felt cheated and misled. He had given everything, including his personal life, to a dream, and he still had no winery.

Forman could have lived well enough by consulting, as André

Tchelistcheff and others did, but he didn't want that. He wanted his own label. He blamed himself for the break-up of his marriage and found no solace in the fact that he was not the only burned-out case around. The wine business was not conducive to marriage, or to much else. He wanted a more balanced view of life, to think less about wine and to avoid people who talked about it all the time.

He owned some land directly across the valley, in the hills above the new Meadowood resort. Forman knew his work wasn't finished, that he had to make one more stab at his ambition. He borrowed money and laid out a vineyard on the steep hillside, and all one year the valley reverberated with dynamite blasts. He watched vineyards take shape once more where God never intended vineyards to be, and then a house and small winery in the same building where before there had been solid rock, and a swimming pool like a lagoon, and a redwood deck looking out over the valley and the town of St. Helena that resembled in the distance the Burgundy he so admired, dominated by vineyards and church steeples. Among the prominent landmarks he could see were the vineyards he had put in under the brow of the Mayacamas for Peter Newton.

Forman made wine, rolling the little crusher and press out onto a concrete pad under his bedroom window. His name would go on a label at last; he would have no trouble selling the tiny three-thousand-case production, split equally between Cabernet and Chardonnay, at a very high price. He became what he wanted to be, a success, and took up gardening and bicycling. He stayed lean and healthy with a rowing machine, sometimes screwing the resistance control down all the way and hauling on the handles until his body was laved with sweat. He swam in his beautiful pool.

Ric Forman often wished that his former wife would drop by and see how happy they might have been together. Sometimes he imagined them starting over again, together, but she had remarried and begun a second family. Ironically, her new husband decided to get into the business; he was building a winery, putting in vineyards . . .

27

THE VALLEY had changed in a basic way. The old cattle- and horse-ranching culture, like the prune and walnut orchards, was gone, and with it the dominance of people who rode western and considered themselves down-to-earth, without interest in social advancement. Some of them noticed the change when they saw that men at the top of the valley were wearing mink and raccoon coats to Mondavi concerts and other up-valley gatherings. It was a sign that Napa had moved from farming backwater to something grand, and that the vintners were separating themselves from the rest of humanity.

Parties in Napa Valley acquired an exclusivity missing even at the old social square dance. At first the natives were amused: people who in relative terms had just arrived in the valley now considered themselves its essence. But this became galling. Old families without fancy wineries or imported social pretensions found themselves in the shadows. Those who lived in the city of Napa were further removed from the nimbus of wine-related grace. They were referred to by some up-valley people as "Napkins," affected by "napathy." The fact that André Tchelistcheff was a Napkin, as were many winery workers, did not soften the notion of up-valley superiority.

Wine, so recently the symbol of the immigrant experience, had become the imprimatur of material success. It wasn't just the fur coats on a few men; it was their willingness, their eagerness, to be identified as vintners.

In the old days, a person's profession had remained more or less invisible. A vintner had no more cachet than a rancher or a prune farmer until the concurrence of two trends: the highly personalized wine selling and the recognition of vintners by San Francisco society. That happened when some imported people began giving lavish parties in the valley with guest lists dominated by vintners. People with money and standing in San Francisco then began putting vintners on their guest lists, making over them as if they were stars, and suddenly they *were* stars.

After the Exciting Wave had come something entirely different, an influx that included foreigners, developers, clothes designers, interior decorators, and others seeking a safe haven for their money. They found in the valley great beauty and a unique but as yet undefined status. It involved the *idea* of wine rather than the reality of producing and selling it. Now one might be simply social, as the old Boring Crowd had been, but without being considered boring. It was acceptable to be rich and socially ambitious — a category that began to include some once-struggling, even Italian, vintners. One might be part of the broad service stratum that increasingly kept it all afloat; one might permeate upward as vintners acquired younger versions of first wives and first wives acquired improved versions of work- or travel-obsessed husbands, and opportunities increased exponentially with the valley's ever-expanding horizons.

Among the lavish parties staged in the valley were Pat Montandon's, on Rutherford Crossroad. She was married to Al Wilsey, a wealthy businessman, and had a varied career herself. She wrote two books, *How to Be a Party Girl* and *The Intruders,* described in the blurb as "the extraordinary incidents and phenomena of [Montandon's] encounters with the forces of malevolent hatred and unrelenting evil, occasioned by the curse of a slighted tarot reader." Pat Montandon was also a television talk-show host and the organizer of "literary" discussions involving some unlikely participants.

Mostly she gave parties. Each year there were several, with restricted guest lists that included vintners and their friends, and entertainers as illustrious as Benny Goodman. The parties caused comment, not all of it positive. The feeling was that certain people might be accused of putting on airs and that maybe some of the energy ought to be harnessed for the general good.

Robert Mondavi, asked to raise money for the St. Helena Hospital, invited Pat Montandon to lunch at the winery. He counted on her and Al Wilsey to make a substantial contribution, and on Margrit Biever to assist in convincing them. Robin Lail was also at the table in the airy conference room, hung with original art, the glass walls facing vineyards and framing outdoor sculpture and the cadres of well-behaved tourists constantly plying the edges of the lush courtyard. Each group found the other comforting. The tourists liked the sight of a few privileged people dining in style, sipping wines produced on the premises, because it affirmed their notion of the leisurely, glamorous vintner's life; the diners liked the sight of the tourists because it assured them that the public cared enough about the product to stand in the sun.

During the course of the conversation Margrit suggested having an auction of Napa Valley wines and donating the proceeds to the hospital. Robert seized on the idea. There was a great precedent for it in Burgundy, he said. The Hospices de Beaune, founded in the fifteenth century, had been auctioning wine for hundreds of years. It drew not just Burgundians but also wine lovers and the press from all over the world, part of the annual Les Trois Glorieuses — gala dinners and general merry-making. Napa could do the same thing under the California sky. Wineries would provide special tours and other events; the donated wine would sell for much more than its market value, adding more positive publicity. In Beaune, the auction was used to set the price for the current vintage. Here, the event would provide a showcase for older wines, for the wineries, and for the Napa Valley name.

"Do you know," Robert said, turning to Robin, "that your father and I had been looking for something like this to promote the Napa *appellation* since the forties?"

Pat Montandon wanted to organize it and followed up with meetings at her house. Robin helped her at Robert's request, directing the charge from the distant promontory of the Robert Mondavi Winery. Everyone who attended liked the idea of an auction. The Napa Valley Vintners Association, an increasingly potent group with a burgeoning membership, decided to run it with the help of the locals. Volunteers might come from outside and inside the ranks, but the vintners would call the shots.

As chairman of the host committee, Robin took part in preliminary planning and watched others move into positions of influence. First of all, they needed a setting. The most obvious place would once have been the Silverado Country Club, but that was far down-valley and a bit old-fashioned. The newer, smaller resort, Meadowood, seemed a more likely choice. It lay in a narrow, beautifully landscaped valley just east of St. Helena. The contemporary, under-stated architecture, the golf course, tennis and even croquet courts fit elegantly into the land's contours. Meadowood belonged to the Pacific Union Company, a San Francisco developer with a fat com-mercial portfolio and a heterodox approach to the profession. One of the principals, Bill Harlan, wanted to get involved in the dynamics of the valley and to provide a home for the Napa Valley Vintners. That made him a real contender for the auction.

The trouble was, Harlan had bought the Meadowood property out from under Robin's husband and a partner, who had had their own plans for development. When Robin first met Harlan by the Meadowood pool, in the shade of pines and oaks untouched by his bulldozers, she was ready to thoroughly dislike him. But Harlan confounded those assumptions, as he would later confound his ad-versaries on other fields: Bill Harlan was cunning, but once he started talking, it was difficult not to get caught up in the tale.

Harlan looked a bit like a conquistador if you forgot the pleated khakis and the black four-door Jaguar sedan. Thin beard, pointed nose, eyes like blue marbles. Harlan *looked* at you. He had once been more at home on a motorcycle than inside a svelte import. He had traveled through Africa in the sixties on a Matchless motorcycle, and ended up surfing at the southern tip of the continent. Back home, he learned to fly, and sold airplanes until he got bored. He worked on Stanford University's research and training vessel, a 132-foot schooner that commuted between Monterey and Panama. It was dif-ficult finally to get off, but he had to make money.

Harlan had no business training. He did have what he thought of as "people skills." That meant marketing of some kind, and so he applied to a small San Francisco securities firm and showed up for the interview in the beard and hair that hung to the shoulders of his one worn suit. He didn't get a job but, being Harlan, kept trying. He shaved, got his hair cut and bought a new suit, and finally was hired by the same firm that had originally rejected him.

He didn't know the difference between a stock and an insurance policy but became a trader anyway. After six months he joined a real estate firm, more to his liking although he still had to wear a suit, and shoes. Land in northern California was hot. He learned to ag-gressively sell lots in the middle of nowhere. He got in on a nine-thousand-acre development in Tahoe and at the end of his first year, when he was just thirty years old, made $115,000. The next year he made $120,000. It took so little time to make that kind of money, so he moved into a casino in Tahoe and started gambling eight hours a day. At the private poker games upstairs he made up for what he lost downstairs at blackjack. He knew all the entertainers and was treated like a VIP, but he learned that the elation he felt at winning wasn't worth the pain he felt at losing — a valuable lesson.

The market for land slumped in 1972. Harlan was sent to Lake County to troubleshoot an image problem on a development there. Several times a week he passed through Napa, and liked it. He started checking out the wineries, checking out the land. He was living now on a houseboat in Sausalito harbor he had gotten in trade for a car that he had been given in lieu of a debt. The houseboat leaked but it was a great life, and Harlan saw an opportunity in floating real estate.

Domestic barge building turned out to be a small bonanza, the last free ride in California — unregulated, no requirements other than buoyancy, a great way to fulfill your architectural fantasies. Redwood decks, stained glass, anything. Eventually he had fifteen houseboats built and himself lived in a replica of a sixteenth-century Islamic palace with Moorish arches, called the Taj Mahal.

He decided he had to exercise more control over his destiny. He had to be active, not reactive. He didn't want to be a guy who only sold; he wanted to *create value*. That meant a quantum step up in the numbers game. He tried to get a job in the mortgage business but all they wanted was M.B.A.'s. The people who would hire him, Harlan wouldn't work for. Catch-22. He started his own mortgage business without knowing anything about it. He called up the insurance companies and told them he had some reputable developers that wanted to borrow money, then he called up some developers and told them he had some insurance companies that wanted to get involved. He made himself a mere vice president so he wouldn't have to make decisions, and called the new business the New England Mortgage Company, which sounded as if it had been around for years and so gained instant credibility. But the bottom really fell out of the market in 1974 and Harlan lost a huge fee on a pending deal. He had an option on six hundred parcels in Incline Village in Tahoe and thought he had it sold to some Japanese, but some Arabs claimed to have the rights and the whole thing ended up in court. Another big hit gone.

One of his competitors, Peter Stocker, had some new ideas about real estate, including condo conversions; he and Harlan teamed up and formed the Pacific Union Company, and the tide turned again. They took in a third partner, an investment banker named John Montgomery, and eventually Pacific Union had a billion dollars' worth of development projects in and around San Francisco.

Harlan had been looking in Napa for years, for what he wasn't sure. His friend Carl Doumani, owner of Stags' Leap Winery — next door to the Winiarskis' Stag's Leap Wine Cellars — told him about a foreclosure on a ramshackle country club outside St. Helena.

"No," Harlan told Doumani, "I'm coming to Napa to get *away* from business. I want to plant vineyards and build a winery and appreciate a certain quality of life."

Doumani said, "Let's just go sit on the deck and have a drink."

That was on a Sunday. They drove into a narrow wooded canyon that opened onto a funky golf course next to the old clubhouse. Harlan saw the intrinsic value he had been trained to see. This was his chance to *create* value in a beautiful hideaway, built within the larger Shangri-la of Napa Valley.

He bought the place the following Tuesday.

It had taken Robert Mondavi less than two hours in Baron Philippe's bedroom to cut a deal — and a year and a half to get a contract. The lawyers on both sides of the Atlantic quibbled, in two languages. Finally the baron's lawyers agreed for him to put up the money, and Robert's lawyers agreed for him to provide the grapes. Robert would crush them; the baron would pay for the cooperage. Robert would make the wine, but the baron's winemaker would regularly visit Oakville to advise and instruct. Robert would pledge the fruit from forty of his best acres west of Highway 29 and later sell them to the "joint venture." The joint venture would buy another one hundred acres east of the highway, and there a winery would be built. Robert and the baron would share the costs equally, and the profits, if there were any.

The joint venture hired an artist for $50,000 to design a label. Everyone agreed that the silhouettes of both men should be on it, but there was disagreement about positioning them. Also about whose name would appear highest on the label. After eighteen months the artist showed a sample to the baron, who said, "Too many zigwigs." The artist had tried to make Robert and the baron seem dynamic by surrounding them with vibrant Z's but had over-done it.

Some of the Z's were removed, and the silhouettes jockeyed slightly so that the baron's head was ever-so-slightly elevated over Robert's, but Robert's name was scrawled above that of the baron — a power trade. Both men seemed locked into a kind of Siamese eno-philia, back to back, protecting their derrières from a public that was almost certainly going to be surprised and maybe outraged when it saw the price of the bottle.

Still they had no name. "Joint Venture" was hardly suitable. But what moniker could possibly sum up the tradition of Bordeaux and the élan of California, the celebrity of Rothschild and the energy of Mondavi?

One morning the baron telephoned Robert from Paris, and said, "I've got it. We'll call the wine Opus."

"I know what you have in mind," Robert said, thinking of a grand composition, "but music bothers me a little." He liked to think of wine as an art form in its own right.

Two days later the baron called again. "I've got it. Opus *One*."

That was it. Number one, the grandest composition.

They signed the agreements and the word went out, and people marveled at Robert's tenacity and good fortune, and at Rothschild's acumen in choosing the very best way to export some capital from a politically unstable France and at the same time break new ground in what had become a global vineyard. All Californians, particularly those making wine in the Napa Valley, would share in it. Hands across the sea were in turn to be laid upon them all.

Behind the congratulatory din were heard first wry comments ("What about a magnum Opus?") and then dissent. California had for twenty years — for a century, in fact — struggled to establish its identity as a producer of good wine. Now, after the Paris Tasting and other victories, one of Napa's foremost vintners was fawning over the French for the public relations benefit, tacitly acknowledg-ing their superiority.

Such "cooperation" amounted to capitulation in many eyes. War-ren Winiarski spoke out against his old employer in a bit of public discourse uncharacteristic to the valley. California and French styles of wine were different, Warren told a reporter for a California business journal. So were the soils and microclimates. "Robert Mondavi is a marvelous winemaker," he added. "Why he needs the baron to do all that he has already been doing all these years is beyond me."

The first Napa Valley Wine Auction occurred as assiduously planned, in June 1981. The underwriters had put up $5,000 apiece and the charter sponsors $2,000 for the privilege of being forevermore listed as original supporters. Robin and her sister, Marky, agreed that their jointly owned vineyard, Napanook, inherited from their father, should be a charter sponsor.

The chosen chairman of the auction was Louis Peter Martini, son of old man Martini, who had started the Napa Valley Vintners Association forty years before, in the company of John Daniel. Robin helped choose the committee heads, including the head of the crucial visuals committee. Appearances would count for so much at the first Napa Valley Auction. The head of the visuals committee, Molly Chappellet, went regularly to Meadowood for a year just to observe the progress of sunlight across the greensward next to the creek, where she intended to set up tables for the luncheon. The colors chosen were all coordinated and encompassed the grape-related spectrum: purple, burgundy, green, and gold. There were baskets woven from grapevines, and flocked balloons like gigantic grape clusters hung from atop the poles in the brilliant white auction tent.

On the big day Napa Valley wine brought in $140,000 for the Queen of the Valley and the St. Helena hospitals, a resounding success. Guests sat in the shade along the creek and ate and drank in celebration. Robin watched one of the balloon clusters break loose from its mooring and cross the golf course on the breeze with slow, gazellelike leaps, the afternoon sunlight slanting lavender through the flocking and drawing all eyes to that languid passage.

Robert Mondavi spent much of his time in the air. He plied the six thousand miles between Oakville and Pauillac, home of Mouton; he was in Bordeaux for the 1981 harvest, and met with Christian Moueix, son of Jean-Pierre Moueix, the owner of Château Pétrus, across the Gironde in Pomerol. Pétrus was becoming the most expensive red wine in the world, and in addition to that estate, the Moueix family also owned the châteaux Trotanoy, La Grave, and Magdelaine. Christian had even broader ambitions. He had attended

UC Davis and was looking to expand the family's holdings beyond the confines of France — in Australia. Now, Robert knew plenty about Australia. He had been involved in a venture in the Margaret River area, in the west; the antipodes had much to offer. But California had more — and more to gain if it could attract Pétrus on the heels of Château Mouton-Rothschild.

"Why not Napa?" he asked.

"Too expensive," said Christian.

Robert pressed. He explained how he and the baron had structured the joint venture; Christian and his father could arrange a similar one. "You have a great name," he said. "It will push up the value of any land you buy. You can figure on getting a dollar or two extra on any bottle of wine, which will more than meet your costs."

Christian said he would consider it. He asked where Robert was staying in Paris, his next stop; a few days later Robert received a call there from Christian, who asked him to stay on another night so Christian could fly up and talk further. They met in the dining room. Christian asked if Robert knew of anyone with good vineyardland who might consider a joint venture, and Robert said, naturally, "Yes, Robin Daniel Lail and her sister, Marcia Daniel Smith. They own one hundred and twenty-four acres of vineyard. It's called Napanook."

Robin heard later that Christian had tried to call her then, from Paris; she was playing in a tennis tournament at the time. She had met him while traveling with Robert, and had originally been struck by Christian's formality. When Robert told her of Christian's interest, Robin was both excited and skeptical. She saw this as a way of picking up her family tradition and moving forward, although her sister and her sister's husband were reluctant. Robin would have to convince them, that was clear, if she convinced herself.

A partnership with a great château like Pétrus would reflect well on the Daniel daughters and on the judgment of their father, who had cherished Napanook and kept it intact and productive. But large questions remained. Robin had dreamed of starting her own winery, and a partnership meant diluted authority. A foreign partnership introduced more imponderables. Everyone in the valley was talking about foreigners taking over. Count La Doucette from the Loire Valley and Jean-Claude Boisset of Burgundy had both bought prime land for planting. Donald Hess, heir to a Swiss sparkling-water fortune, now owned William Hill's piece of Mount Veeder. Another Swiss, Stefan Schmidheiny, had bought Cuvaison, and the West German company Peter Eckes owned Franciscan. Representatives of Romanée-Conti and Château Lafite-Rothschild were sniffing around. Over in Sonoma County, Buena Vista had gone to the German concern A. Racke, and Firestone Vineyards down south belonged in large part to Suntory of Japan.

The possibility of a deal really depended on Christian's needs and on how well he and Robin got on.

They met again in Robert's office in December. The tall, dark Bordelais seemed less formal now, eager to plunge into the wilds of north Yountville and prepared for the occasion, as if from the pages of L. L. Bean, in canvas jacket with a corduroy collar, lumberjack shirt, a Gallic version of Top-Siders, and mirrored sunglasses. His beard was fashionably trimmed to a mere shadow, his heavily accented English equal to American idioms and humor, and when it was not, his smile made up the difference. Most of all she was struck by his intensity and what she saw as a fortuitous arrival. It was such moments that suggested to her the very real possibility of predestination. Later, deep in conversation, she and Christian came up with a hundred and fifty coincidences that had brought them together.

They talked of combining two great traditions, Napanook and Pétrus, and making one of the finest wines in Napa Valley. That had always been Robin's intention. The venture would be split fifty-fifty between Christian, and Robin and Marky. Eight thousand cases of wine a year, sold at a sufficiently lofty price, would make the venture profitable. All Robin had to do was convince Marky and her husband, Jim. He was in the electric sign business — large electric signs — and he took a dubious view of this Frenchman.

Marky had made it a point to stay out of the decision making. She and Jim lived in Yakima, and while Napanook was in estate she let Robin, as executor, deal with most of the unpleasantness concerning lawyers and bankers. At one point the latter had suggested tearing out the precious Cabernet Sauvignon and Cabernet Franc at Napanook and replacing them with Chenin Blanc because one of the banker's wives liked white wine! She and Jim had not kept up with the wine business, either. Now this proposal from the Moueix family caught them unawares. The only way to appraise the situation properly, they decided, was to go to Bordeaux.

Christian met them at the airport. Marky would never forget his bright yellow scarf, or that he was late and running. There began a series of meetings both confidential and not exactly candid. She thought that Christian, though charming, played his cards close to the vest. Her father would have done it the same way, of course. Christian said he didn't want to make a California wine but something that was both French and Californian. He had set up a tasting at his office in Libourne to show what he considered typical of both places — big, "jammy" fruit from California, a "stemminess" from France. They tasted many examples from Fronsac, St. Émilion, and Pomerol — but no Pétrus.

They went on to his home. Marky, too, felt the power of coincidence. Already Christian seemed to be part of her family. Then they passed through gates and approached a house that reminded her of Inglenook — Georgian, pale yellow with a red roof, wine colors — and for a moment she thought she would burst into tears. She put on sunglasses. Inside, she was introduced to Christian's three-year-old daughter and felt she was looking at herself. She knew precisely what the girl's life was like. The bells just kept ringing and she was grateful Jim was there to handle things.

During the next thirty-six hours they drank a '71 Pétrus and a '62 Magdelaine with simple, elegant food — pâté, roast pork, confit. Christian took them through the vineyards. It was early spring, the earth ready to explode. Christian talked, talked about the land. The rows at Magdelaine were so rocky the workers had to use a plow to cultivate; in the middle of the Pétrus vineyard — only about twenty-five acres of mostly Merlot, so valuable that the bunches were harvested by hand according to individual ripeness by pickers with scissors — he spread his arms, and said, "This is Pétrus. You can't make great wine without great soil."

He pointed out where the Romans had planted. Land, he said, really belongs to no one. God gave it to you to be the steward and, like the parable of the five talents, you must increase what the land yields.

Christian's father, Jean-Pierre, was skeptical of this California venture, but also charming. He brought out a magnum of Bollinger champagne for the three of them in the middle of the afternoon, and

Marky thought, I'm in trouble. Jean-Pierre had an amazing art collection: a brass dancer by Degas, a couple of Picassos, lots of Dufys. Also Warhol, Motherwell, Rothko. France was on shaky ground politically, with a Socialist government abhorred by these propertied Bordelais. The wealth tax had just been introduced. They felt nervous with all their eggs in one basket.

Quite suddenly, the deal seemed inevitable.

28

SINCE THE CREATION of the ag preserve in 1968, making residential and commercial development more difficult, Napa County had grown more slowly than the rest of the Bay Area. In 1975 a land-use provision included in the county's General Plan clearly distinguished between urban and nonurban uses of the land. This was more important than it seemed at the time. The land-use "element" in the county's blueprint for the future provided a written underpinning for what the land-use advocates in the valley wanted all along: enduring protection against development within the ag preserve that could not easily be overturned by hostile county officials.

The supervisors crucial to the evolution of the General Plan included slow-growth advocates like John Tuteur, Jenny Simms, Sam Chapman, and Dowell Martz. But the ag preserve was still subject to the will of the board, and the board remained politically volatile. The forty-acre minimum lot size for the watershed — the hills above the valley floor — was reduced to twenty acres in 1976, then raised back to forty for both the hills and the valley floor three years later.

The 1980 election threatened to change the complexion of the board. The loose collection of slow-growth advocates seemed destined to be replaced by a majority favoring more houses, businesses, and people. The political term "balanced growth" was a euphemism for counterrevolution in the eyes of people like Vic Fershko, the lawyer raised in Israel, wearer of suspenders and the soup-straining mustache. The real argument of the pro-growthers was, in his view, "No radicals, no elitists, and our children have the right to live here and find jobs." And the real objective was development.

Fershko wasn't alone. The usual suspects came together under the old umbrella Citizens Council for Napa Tomorrow, basically a land-use group that had picked up members from Napans Opposed to Wasteland. The council had organized a popular conference called, intriguingly, "How Many People Can You Mix with Wine?" It included members of the various alliances: Citizens Against Urban Sprawl, Citizens Against the Destruction of Napa, Upper Napa Valley Associates, League of Women Voters, other ad hoc organizations, Democrats and Republicans. There were a few oddballs with their own agendas — fear of crime, a dislike of minorities, pure aesthetic and environmental concerns — but most of the people had the common desire for restrained growth.

Their biggest job was always lining up support in those areas that had nothing to do with agriculture — Napa city, Yountville, and St. Helena. This time the objective was a voter initiative — a proposal to be placed on the ballot — that would establish absolute limits on the amount of development allowable in the unincorporated parts of the county.

One of the usual suspects working for this was Volker Eisele, the sociologist from Berkeley trying to support himself and his family as a grape grower. Fershko admired his determination. Volker belonged to People for Open Space and had helped elect one of the slow-growth supervisors, enrolling college students in Angwin — Seventh-day Adventists! — in the cause.

Volker, Fershko, and many others from various groups formed Citizens for Growth Management and launched the voter initiative. If successful, the residents of the county would be able to vote directly on the issue of growth and to send a clear message to elected officials. The initiative's objective, no more than a 1 percent increase in population every year in the unincorporated areas, would bind the elected officials whether or not they favored slow growth. They would have no alternative but to restrain development.

The initiative came to be known as Measure A. Fershko drafted the proposal. Citizens for Growth Management set up tables outside the polls during the May primaries and collected signatures. They needed 5,000 names to get the initiative on the fall ballot, and collected 7,000 without too much trouble.

Measure A passed in 1980, and the new board had nine months to adopt it officially. By now most of the supervisors were progrowth; they thought Measure A was being stuffed down their throats. During those nine months they did what they could to thwart its effect, approving more residential development at Silverado, next to the old country club on the outskirts of Napa city, and entering into an agreement with developers to expand American Canyon, at the bottom of the county, the valley's stepchild. American Canyon was a bedroom community close to the freeway leading to Sacramento. It had risen in a welter of subdivisions and tacky roadhouses that had more in common with Solano County and Mare Island than with comely Napa. Many up-valley residents did not even know that American Canyon was in the county. Those who did didn't care what went on there, just so long as the people in the new bungalows — flags flapping at the project offices to lure more low-budget home buyers — stayed in the south end.

Fershko was more concerned with strip development along Highway 29 north of Napa city. Measure A might limit population growth, but the board could still grant zoning variances to builders of shops and hotels in what should have been vineyards.

Volker had learned never to let up. He had gotten his injunction against the motorcyclists; he had helped elect one of the slow-growth supervisors on the current board. Now that supervisor planned to retire at the end of his first term, and Volker wanted him replaced by someone sympathetic to the land. The question was, who?

Volker might have run himself but he was not yet a naturalized citizen and, even if he had been, probably couldn't have won. He had a German accent; his house was filled with volumes of Brecht, Goethe, Schiller, Rilke, Mann. He read German newspapers and followed German politics as closely as he did those in his adopted land. He would never sound like a native, but he would have liked to sit with the supervisors and vote against townhouses, traffic lights, malls, creeping asphalt, householders — and tourists. On weekends, cars backed up along Highway 29 in front of the big wineries. The side roads were overrun. During the summer months it was hard to attend to the business of the valley, which was agriculture, for all the cars and bodies.

Volker's agenda was simple: use the isolation of Napa Valley and its sound economic base as a model for the preservation of open space. To accomplish that, he needed time, and politicians willing to hold the line against development.

The hardest part was finding candidates who understood the issues. Volker and his friends discussed the problem and proposed as a candidate a member of the St. Helena City Council, a certified public accountant named Mel Varrelman. He seemed bright, and concerned about the issues. Volker convinced some potential backers in St. Helena that he was the right candidate, and invited Varrelman to a meeting that included the likely supporters: a local real estate agent, a publicist, a geologist and a physics professor, and the retiring supervisor, Dowell Martz. Together they had contributed about $7,000 for a campaign.

Varrelman had been raised by a poor foster family in Salinas; he knew what it was like to be on the outside looking in. He had taught school and gotten his CPA accreditation by going to night classes. His philosophy, he told the group, was to preserve what already existed in the valley and to otherwise try to help people. In stressful times he wrote poetry, which his wife collected in a big scrapbook.

Varrelman and the others at the meeting discussed the continuing threat of development, the burgeoning problem of tourism, the requirements of a proper candidate, and the need to find one. Finally Volker said, "Mel, we're talking about you."

ﾗ

Another "suspect" was about to appear.

To say that W. Robert Phillips, Jr., was a Republican was redundant. His mother was a Biddle and his father a member of an old and socially prominent New Orleans family. He moved to Burlingame, where Phillips grew up to be a Stanford man and a Marine. He fought in the South Pacific during World War II and later in Korea, but his bearing, trim gray head, and his voice belonged to a born chairman of the board.

As a senior vice president of Paine Webber in San Francisco, Phillips made a lot of money *mano a mano* with his competitors, taking what he could within the law. He often said, "That's what it's all about."

His wife, Alexandra, was the great-great-granddaughter of Claus Spreckels, the German immigrant who in the middle of the previous century cornered Hawaii's cane production and then the world's sugar market, producing a huge fortune contested by subsequent generations. Alexandra's parents built a house in Napa Valley that was capacious and reminiscent of the South, with slatted shutters and magnolias, breezeways, a wisteria arbor, and a private view of the benign landscape beyond shrubbery and a sequestered pool. The Phillipses, part of the Exciting Wave, came up every weekend and eventually moved into the house, and Bob became a grape grower.

People in the financial community said he was nuts, but he liked the life and what he recognized as a place unique in the country. Then some developers from the outside proposed building a hotel just off Highway 29 not far from his property. The hotel would be called the Vintners Inn and would include meeting halls, parking lots, and all the appendages of a technological oasis — right in the middle of the agricultural preserve.

Phillips's neighbor, a grower from an old Italian family, protested. His name was Joe Taddei and he stood by himself in opposition to the county while it proceeded with the developers' application. At first Phillips was incredulous, then annoyed, and finally outraged. The Vintners Inn threatened his repose, but he could have lived with that. Phillips believed in the sanctity of free enterprise and private property. A loyal member of San Francisco's chronic minority party, he had voted for Ronald Reagan every chance he got. But he now had doubts about laissez faire. The more protected the land is, the more valuable it becomes. He was willing to give up some rights under the ag preserve for that increased value, but the developers, with money to spend and much sophistication, were trying to cash in. They lied about their intentions and their support, and cast a shadow over the whole valley.

He decided to join Taddei in the fight. Phillips got a few of his wealthy friends involved, like the Mays, owners of Martha's Vineyard, but those making the hard tactical decisions and contending with the county and the developers' hired guns belonged to a different social set. They were people Phillips would ordinarily have avoided, men with beards and mustaches and political backgrounds that Phillips considered extreme. For instance, the lawyer fighting the Vintners Inn, Vic Fershko, had been involved in various noisy protest groups down in Napa city. And Volker Eisele, from Berkeley, had a lot of radical opinions about open space. The idea that Phillips would align himself with such people was once unimaginable.

Phillips invited them to his house, with the breezeways and wisteria and murmuring pool overlooking a hundred green acres, for a glass of wine. He had them over for a meal. Not only were they on the right side, Phillips thought. He *liked* them.

In the end they all decided to sue the county instead of the developers, a brilliant ploy. The county's General Plan, required to spell out land use, did not contain all the elements specified by law, so Fershko argued that no development should occur until the General

Plan was complete. Jim Hickey, director of the Planning Department, which was working on the plan, tacitly backed the strategy. The Napa County Farm Bureau, to which Volker belonged, joined the suit, making the cause thoroughly respectable.

The judge agreed with their argument; he ruled that for a year nothing could be built in the ag preserve. And Fershko recovered all the legal fees from the developers. The idea for the Vintners Inn went up in smoke, sending a signal to other developers that in Napa they faced opposition and would not be able to roll over local ordinances and local officials.

During the victory celebration, one of Phillips's new friends pointed out that the fight should not have been necessary. The idea of enduring farmland in the valley was supposedly inviolable. Phillips, the Republican social lion, came to see the episode not as a coda to legal land preservation but as a warm-up for other, more serious battles to come.

V

In the Eye of the Beholder

29

As the lines of the future were being drawn by advocates and opponents of development, the valley's overall success took on increasingly curious manifestations. The outside perception of Napa as a unique, romantic place surpassed even the reality; at home, some disillusionment replaced the ideals of the sixties and early seventies.

The idea of wine as something more than a beverage continued its organized assault on the public consciousness. Wine was coming to be seen as a social determinant, something one drank as much for status as for pleasure, a notion tacitly advanced by the industry. The old family winery as symbol of honest toil and other agrarian values was replaced with associations of privilege, consumption, even creativity.

Falcon Crest, the television series, struck Mike Robbins as an unfortunate reflection of life in Napa Valley, one dominated by greed, lust, and violence. He could hardly complain, though, since it was Robbins's home that flashed across the screen one night a week — at an hour sufficiently late to avoid the eyes of most schoolchildren — a looming, white, gabled Victorian on a mountainside, shaded by palms and hedged by vineyards, symbolic of wealth and exclusivity. In fact, his place was so overrun by tourists looking for the *real* Falcon Crest that his neighbors complained of being unable to get up and down the road on weekends.

Sometimes Robbins had trouble getting into his own driveway. He put up signs saying the house and some of the grounds were off limits, but the tourists wandered around anyway, looking at his olive trees and at the pool beyond the box hedges, peering through the windows.

"Can't you read?" Robbins would ask, and the visitors would just smile and look at him in a funny way, as if this rotund middle-aged man with a cannonball head and a Ralph Lauren polo shirt did not exist and that the remembered scenes on television were reality.

His winery, including the big house and the shops, rest rooms, and parking lot, was called Spring Mountain. The Spring Mountain Chardonnay had come in fourth in the Paris Tasting, ahead of three famous white Burgundies. Mike Robbins was somebody and Spring Mountain was something, yet it had been superseded in the popular mind by its fictional counterpart. Signs all over St. Helena directed the untutored to Falcon Crest, not to Spring Mountain. So ubiquitous was the Falcon Crest name that Robbins finally began to sell a much cheaper line of wine with the name of the TV show.

About that time an odd thing happened: he found himself losing interest in the wine business and in the valley. The money was rolling in and he didn't have to work nearly as hard as he had years before, when he and his first wife started little Spring Mountain down on the valley floor. But life had gotten complicated and the valley had filled up with people, many of them unhappy with the boob-tube version of Napa and the physical presence of its mentor. Suddenly all Robbins wanted was to sell out, buy a fifty-two-foot sloop, and sail away.

He had once dated Grace Kelly, the movie star. Robbins was a cadet then at the naval academy and she a student at a finishing school. They met at the Phi Gam house in Philadelphia, and after that she used to ride the train to Baltimore and the bus to Annapolis, and he would meet her at the bus stop. Grace stayed in a little bed-and-breakfast used by young women dating the middies. She was a stand-up girl, he thought, and would become a stainless steel great lady. In four years he never laid a glove on her. Years later, when Grace's daughter was married in Monaco, Robbins sent her a case of wine — Spring Mountain, not Falcon Crest.

After the Korean War, Robbins went to work for Coldwell Banker and then got into California real estate. By the mid-sixties he was making substantial bucks, as Robbins put it. He started Spring Mountain down on Highway 29, in what became St. Clement, and meanwhile sold condos and leased towers in the Century City project in Los Angeles. He ran the winery by phone, and commuted between L.A. and Oakland. People were very helpful:

Robert Mondavi loaned him equipment; André Tchelistcheff and Joe Heitz gave him advice.

He moved his family to Napa and the kids worked in the winery and went to school in St. Helena. It was a good life. Napa was old-style America, rural but not stifling. One day you could be up to your knees in mud and the next day having lunch with a baron.

In 1974 the old Parrott place came on the market. Robbins knew real estate and he knew some history, and this was a deal. Tiburcio Parrott had been a friend of the Beringer brothers and something of a character, the bastard son of a banker and rake who moved to the West Coast before the Civil War. Tiburcio's house above St. Helena, influenced by the architecture of Rhine House below it, included a wraparound veranda, towers, and double doors with stained glass, and on the landing a famous stained glass panel portraying a parrot, but which in the television series was said to be a falcon. Tiburcio called the house Miravalle.

Robbins bought and had it gutted and restored, and a brass plaque placed next to the front door that read, "Beware of Occupant."

One day a man introduced himself to Robbins, and said, "I'm from Lorimar and we want to film a television series here."

Robbins said, "Beat it."

The man was very persuasive. The series sounded as if it would be a California version of *The Waltons*. Lorimar would build a set and pay Robbins a lot of money for using Miravalle for only a few days each year. His name would be in the credits as a technical advisor. What more could he ask?

He agreed. Then the shows began to air and Robbins discovered they had more in common with *Dallas* than *The Waltons*. Dramatically, wine was to Falcon Crest what oil was to the Ewings. The characters spent much more time squabbling and feuding over inheritances and fast deals — mostly real estate — than making wine; they seemed to spend a lot of time in the hospital, or in bed with one another, or lunching in fancy restaurants and glowering at enemies and former spouses, or running rivals off the road. Once a winery was even blown up on television.

Also, Robbins cringed at the technical mistakes in the programs. Finally he told the people at Lorimar, "Hey, guys, run the scripts by me or take my name off the show." They took his name off.

People in the valley started making snide remarks. Robbins knew they knew he wasn't responsible for the content of *Falcon Crest,* but he still felt culpable.

By then he had split up with his wife. Now Miravalle/Spring Mountain/Falcon Crest was worth, in Robbins's opinion, $20 million. He tried to sell it. There were plenty of prospects, even at that high price, but he noticed something strange about the people, something he associated with the notoriety from television. In California, Robbins said, they tipped the dish and we got all the nuts.

An effeminate man from Santa Fe looked and sounded rich, and Robbins put him up in the guest house while he absorbed the "energy" of Spring Mountain. He bought cases of wine, and trinkets, and his check bounced. Then there was the industrialist from Milan, who arrived in a helicopter. He said he wanted to buy the place, and how soon could Robbins move? Soon, Robbins said. The industrialist pinched all the women in the tasting room, and took them up in the helicopter, always holding a glass of Chardonnay. He left assuring Robbins he would buy; over the weekend he called twice, collect, to assure him that he was serious.

When finally Robbins talked to the real estate broker on Monday, the broker said, "You won't believe this, but that guy stiffed the helicopter company for four thousand dollars, and he just tried to steal my car."

❧

At the far end of St. Helena from Spring Mountain sat Sutter Home Winery, a simple name for such a glossy edifice and another example of radically altered perception. Sutter Home represented sudden — almost cataclysmic — good fortune based on the boom in national wine sales and a kind of fluke. One family was remade in much the same way that it remade the red grape Zinfandel into a white wine, one that sold in quantities beyond their imagining.

The old clapboard Victorian house next door to the winery had been there for a hundred years, but its common phase hadn't included the formal walkways, rose bushes from the Orient, Roman statuary (*The Four Seasons of Bacchus*), monumental wooden wine press screws from Europe, intercom-locking iron gates, and spotlights that plucked the house out of the shadows and made it a landmark. And few neighbors could ignore the main Sutter Home winery a mile away — on, appropriately, Zinfandel Lane — where tank trucks trundled along the chain-link fence with great frequency, loaded with out-of-county juice bound for what was a factory in the middle of the ag preserve.

Sutter Home's output of white Zinfandel had risen from twenty thousand cases annually to millions. Zinfandel had been one of the prizes of California, a grape of mysterious origin that produced dark, flavorful wine, good as a blender and superb alone. Its status had improved with the skill of California winemakers, going from a simple red for any table to a complex one brought up in French cooperage, occasionally developing a brawn beyond the appreciation of all but connoisseurs. Some Zinfandels took on the alcoholic concentration of port, but the best and most versatile stood comparison with Cabernet Sauvignon and represented a unique native accomplishment. Then, thanks in large part to Sutter Home's success, people ordering Zinfandel in restaurants all over the country started sending back the bottles, saying, "Don't you know Zinfandel's *white?*"

In the mid-seventies red wine was drunk at most American tables where wine was drunk at all. White wine soon began to elbow its way forward because newly converted wine drinkers favored whites, which were less demanding of palates accustomed to soft drinks and beer, and because the industry wanted them in the vanguard. Most winery owners preferred making white wine because it could be released for sale sooner. White wine was acceptable both as an apéritif and as an accompaniment to food. People tended to drink more of it, and so campaigns were launched suggesting that white wine was more genteel and the traditional choice of Americans, when historically the opposite was true.

The claim proved to be self-fulfilling. By 1981 three bottles of white wine sold for every one of red. Many of those bottles contained wine made from red grapes but barely tinted with pigment from the grape skins, producing a wine ranging in color from off-white to neon pink. This had once been widely drunk as rosé, but "blush" became the popular marketing term, a semantic degradation mirrored in the product itself: sweet, cloying, and relatively inexpensive.

The greatest, unblushing benefactor of the blush phenomenon was undoubtedly Sutter Home. Some people in Napa Valley saw its white Zinfandel as a paradigm of the valley's triumphs, others as a grotesque example of Napa's craft and an indication of deeply rooted problems.

•

The Trinchero family bought the little rundown winery on Highway 29 in 1947 but could not afford the $12,000 extra that would have gotten them the house as well. Mario Trinchero, from Asti, had moved to Napa from New York with his son, Bob, a streetwise West Side kid of twelve. Bob experienced a ringing in the ears that the doctor finally diagnosed as a sudden lack of noise in Napa. Bob wore a white shirt and tie to school, where the students appreciated his New York accent. ("Say something, Bob!") After high school he went into the Air Force, and then started making wine with his father and his uncle at Sutter Home — jugs from purchased Napa, Sonoma, and Solano County grapes, sold directly to bars and retail shops.

In 1960 Mario and Bob bought out the uncle, and three years later Mario died. Bob borrowed money to expand. By then Sutter Home was selling fifty-two wines, some kind of record, including table wines, sparklers, white ports, sherries, angelica, four "burgundies," six vermouths, and a red they would prime with sugar and carbon dioxide and call chianti. They sold gallons, half gallons, even tenths. Also two vinegars and three salad dressings. Bob Trinchero wasn't getting rich but he was making a living, far from the cacophony of West 66th Street and Columbus Avenue. Then the price of North Coast grapes started going up, and he complained to Darrell Corti, of Corti Brothers, professional wine purveyors. Corti said, "Ever hear of Amador County?"

Amador lay to the east, in the foothills of the Sierras. Trinchero tried an Amador Zinfandel and liked it. He bought twenty tons of Amador grapes and made an alcoholic red by fermenting out all the sugar and putting the wine into old French barrels. He was thinking Cabernet but using Zinfandel. The wine was dynamite. He sold eight hundred cases in a flash, and people demanded more; every year the volume and the price rose. Trinchero thought he saw a way to solve the conundrum of the fifty-two labels. He told Corti, "I would like to make just this one wine. But I want a white, too."

Corti suggested making a white from the Zinfandel also, by running the juice off the skins right after pressing. That way it would pick up just a bit of color. "You can call it Eye of the Partridge" or, Corti said, something equally fancy.

Trinchero made 200 cases the first year and met some resistance in the marketplace. "A white wine from red grapes?" the liquor store owners would say. "That's weird." Some insisted there was no such thing, and others wouldn't even hear him out. No one knew how to sell it but that didn't matter, since the wine sold itself.

Trinchero made 350 cases in 1974 and called it white Zinfandel. He made 700 cases in 1975, and after that doubled the volume every year except for one, when he tripled it. By 1980 he knew something was up. He told his friends to cash in on this anomaly known as white Zin, but they were slow to follow. By 1982 white Zin was a major component in the total mix of California sales, and Sutter Home sold more than anybody else. Red Zinfandel had fallen out of favor and Trinchero had in a way saved the varietal. He had also created a new category that was only now dawning in the minds of the big producers, Gallo included, but had already made Trinchero rich.

The first thing he noticed was that people he didn't know came up and shook his hand. They treated him like a combination guru and movie star. He was invited to lunch. Somebody threw a catered party for three hundred with a ten-piece rock 'n' roll band, and guests came from embassies, the California Agricultural Commission, and the Wine Institute. To do what, he wondered. To see Bob Trinchero? Suddenly he realized that the small-town, mom-and-pop winemaker didn't exist anymore.

Next came invitations to join things, like the Napa Valley Technical Group and the Republican party, neither of which had been too eager to recruit the producer of fifty-two versions of cheap wine. People came out of the woodwork, wanting his opinion, his presence, his money. He bought a Mercedes. He bought his wife a Mercedes. It took her a long time to pay a hundred dollars for a dress but she got comfortable with it. She had always worked — on the bottling line, as the bookkeeper, in the tasting room. The Trincheros had once gone five years without a day off, with the kids corralled in the playpen and both parents selling the fifty-two wines. Trinchero realized that to spend money well, you have to be born to it. After he had bought a nice big home and a big car, and had gone to Hawaii, what?

The house next to the old winery was to be restored and used as office space. Trinchero liked to say that he told the decorator there was no spending limit and the decorator exceeded it. The couch in the foyer, for instance, cost $13,000. The rugs were all Persian, and old, and the brass fittings cast in Italy. The oval portraits were medieval, and the Italian screen upstairs from the seventeenth century. Trinchero asked the artist doing the decorating — a woman with a cigarette holder in her teeth — if she could make the walls of his office look like the walls at Pompei. She said, "You got it."

The cracks came out real, the patina ancient. Grape leaves and Bacchus heads all around the molding. A lot of money went to buy some antique pages of the Bible, in Latin, but even more money went for the frames. The high-backed chairs came from England, the conference table from the Philippines — one piece of wood five feet in diameter. There were four kinds of camellias impossible to find outside the Orient, planted by the patio, in front of the rose trellis. The seeds came in through Los Angeles and the Trincheros were the first to get them. Also a complete lily technology. The cost of it all was $2.6 million, and then the decorator went to work on the Trincheros' home.

Every afternoon when Bob left the office, as his brightly dressed receptionist was opening the iron gate by remote control, he would glance at the couch beside the ornate front door, and think, That couch cost more than the whole house cost in 1947.

30

RAFAEL RODRIGUEZ had a new pickup in which to make his way around the 1,500-acre Niebaum-Coppola Estate, as the old Daniel place had been rechristened. He knew it as well as any piece of land in the valley: canyons back in the Mayacamas, high meadows, and 83 acres of vineyard — Cabernet Sauvignon, Cabernet Franc, Merlot, and some Zinfandel and Chardonnay. Rafael had been involved with those grapes in one way or another since 1953. Now, more than thirty years later, the two Cabernets were blended in a "big" — powerfully flavored and complex — red wine made under the supervision of André Tchelistcheff.

Coppola did not know wine and vines as John Daniel had, but he was more approachable. And the old Niebaum house had been flung open, it seemed, to the world. Rafael had never seen so many visitors, not just movie stars and directors but also ordinary valley people. The Coppolas had invited the winery and field staffs to a harvest party held right there in the house, with silver service, plenty of wine, and a Spanish singer. Rafael's older daughter's wedding reception took place right on the Niebaum-Coppola lawn.

Francis Ford Coppola's debut as a vintner had not been auspicious. One year he made a dense, alcoholic wine for himself and his friends, from all the grapes left over at the end of harvest, and called it Vinoforte. He put his grandfather's picture on the label and gave cases to associates at his Zoetrope Studios in San Francisco, founded in partnership with his friends George Lucas, Carroll Ballard, and other Hollywood Young Turks looking to remake the industry. They came up with the slogan for Vinoforte: "One glass is worth two."

In the beginning he had wanted to bottle his excess Cabernet Franc in gallon jugs and sell them for $50 apiece. Some new friends in the valley talked him out of it. That was no way to market wine, and besides, he could sell the excess to Inglenook, who hungered for the grapes after they lost the estate to the Coppolas in the bidding.

Relations between Francis and his conglomerate neighbor — Heublein had been bought out by R. J. Reynolds, which in turn would be swallowed by Grand Metropolitan of London — were not good. Like most Napans, he hated the sight of the barrel cellar in front of the old Inglenook winery, Heublein's legacy. Coppola's first winemaker and the Inglenook winemaker were said to be acting out their bosses' latent hostilities by throwing rocks at each other's pickups, passing on the narrow lane.

Coppola wanted his commercial wine to be the biggest and the best in the valley. His winemaker liked the idea. They would cellar the wine for eight years before releasing it, unheard-of in wine marketing and financially impractical. Francis didn't care. He let the man have his head, and the first vintage, the 1978, became a huge, tannic monster with great character and shoals of sediment. Francis wanted to call it Claret, after an old Inglenook label, but used Rubicon instead, an Italian word meaning red river.

He wanted a beautiful label like a stock certificate, and he went to Tiffany & Co. in New York. Tiffany told him the store didn't print labels, only personal stationery. Francis said, "Do it as a calling card. Instead of printing 'bar mitzvah' on it, print 'wine.'" That was the look he wanted on a bottle of Rubicon.

While Francis was away filming, the winemaker bought barrels and expanded the space taken by the "cellar" — the upper floors of the old Niebaum coach house and winery. Francis respected the winemaker's energy and determination but found himself in competition with him. Francis wanted to transform the top story into a recording studio and projection room, but the winemaker felt possessive. Is this a winery, he asked, or a film studio?

Francis let him go. The studio was built, complete with screen, comfortable seating, and all the marvels of modern moviemaking. Racks of film in bright metal canisters sat in the adjacent barrel room — with the Rubicon aging in French oak — enjoying the cool and the dark and, like the wine, hoping someday to be shown.

Francis faced financial disaster, not with wine but with the film *Apocalypse Now*. Its reception and Zoetrope's problems threatened to drag him under. At one point he figured he owed $50 million. He could have declared bankruptcy but would have lost the house and winery, and so decided to pay off the debt. He made money on more conventional projects, like *Peggy Sue Got Married*. Thirty-seven million in the first nine weeks. Receipts from *Apocalypse* started trickling in, and gradually he climbed out of the hole.

At home, he hired a winemaker away from Joe Phelps and enlisted the aid of Tchelistcheff, who advised a more modern winemaking regime, with some fining and filtration for a subtler, better-balanced Rubicon. Francis agreed to sell Inglenook his excess Cabernet Franc, which would go into a fine new Inglenook wine called Reunion, and he felt a softening of the discontent that had brought him to the valley in the first place.

His oldest son, Gian-Carlo, by-passed college to work with his father. He shot some scenes in *Cotton Club,* worked on 3-D films for Disney, and promoted rock concerts. He took a scriptwriting course and made a rock video. He was associate producer on *The Outsiders*. He drank Rubicon to accustom himself to the product of his family's château while trying to break into the movie business.

Francis took him to the East Coast for the filming of *Gardens of Stone;* there Gian-Carlo was killed in a freak boat accident in an estuary off the Chesapeake Bay.

The sorrow Francis and Eleanor felt was mitigated by where they lived and by the natural cycle of life about them she had spoken of but had not expected to become so utterly real so soon. The estate proved to be a healing place. In the house they hung a portrait of Gian-Carlo opposite the sitting room window. In the painting, a serious, black-haired young man rendered in a style more befitting a Medici than a twentieth-century scion stands next to a table, his hand resting on a super 8 movie camera. Beyond the painted window can be seen the old oak and in its shade Gian-Carlo's lustrous red roadster.

⤜⤏

Robin met Francis at the Mondavis'. He told her to come by the house any time she liked. "I know what it means to you," he said. "If we're not there, just go on in."

Robin Lail considered Eleanor one of the strongest women she knew. Robin had no real intimates among women — that was

Betty's legacy. She liked Eleanor but thought that she and Francis had retreated into themselves after Gian-Carlo's death. Francis went through people and things, she thought, like any artist, but he was generous. She wished him well. But during his financial difficulties she couldn't hold back the fantasies: if the Niebaum-Coppola place came up for sale again, maybe she and her husband, Jon, could put together the capital to buy it.

Robin had developed into a more forceful woman than the one returning to the valley a few years before. The straw-colored hair clipped close, the khaki skirt, and the bearing had not changed, but she had clearer ideas about what she could accomplish. She still lived in St. Helena but every day drove into San Francisco, where she had gone to work for Pacific Union, doing for Bill Harlan what she had done for Robert Mondavi: organizing, screening calls, acting as a sounding board. Robert had been very good about letting her go. She had found herself well prepared for the pressures of a big company like Harlan's. She didn't see as much of her two daughters as she would have liked, but she found the work fascinating.

At home, the partnership with Christian Moueix became a reality. Robin was proud of that. She and Marky formed the John Daniel Society, as a business entity and as an umbrella to cover their share of the deal. The society not only paid tribute to their father but also had an active, ongoing part in what Robin hoped would someday be the preeminent Napa Valley château. The partnership had come about because Robin pushed, but it went to credit John Daniel. He had preserved and passed along Napanook Vineyard; he had said of the Yountville property, "It's good, and uncluttered. Don't ever sell it."

Now all they had to do was produce a great wine from it.

The creation of the John Daniel Society struck some people as excessive, a kind of ancestor worship. Napa Shintoism. The society gave Christian Moueix a powerful entrée in the valley and instantly made him part of local lore. It neutralized some of the unspoken resentment felt about the succession of outsiders investing in — "buying up" — the valley. At first Christian's enthusiasm for the place had known no bounds. He arrived as if on an expedition and set out to learn everything about Napanook. He spoke of the grapes there as if they were people. They don't like dust, he said, and Napa was incredibly dusty. They like a light rain before harvest, and it rarely rained in the county at that time. So he intended to have the grapes *washed* before being picked, an idea that astounded and amused some of the natives.

Christian announced that he planned to sleep in the vineyard. It was the only way to feel at one with the vines, he said. Then someone mentioned rattlesnakes. Sometimes the snakes lay up under the grape leaves, hunting for frogs' and birds' eggs. The workers would fling dirt onto the vines before picking, to dislodge them. Napa rattlers were a shy species, out mostly at night and no real danger. A dozen were killed a year, but ground breaking for new vineyards on the adjacent property of Domaine Chandon had sent dozens more into Napanook. After Christian heard that, there was no more talk of sleeping in the vineyard.

For a time he stayed at the Lails'. Robin took him everywhere, introducing him to people, making him feel at home. What people often saw was a lean young man with a severely trimmed beard and dark glasses. He seemed to like the valley. Robin was as forthcoming as she could be about a project wrapped in secrecy, for mysteriousness was Christian's way. People wondered aloud what sort of wine he and his winemaker would come up with — what blend of grapes and how much it would cost. Christian just smiled and spoke in elliptical, broken English.

One day she took Christian to Stag's Leap, to talk to Warren Winiarski and to see his vineyards. Warren told Robin that he was happy she had succeeded in putting the venture together with the Moueix family, that her father would have been proud of her.

"You don't know how happy it makes me to hear you say that," she told him, and Warren was surprised to see tears in her eyes.

Harlan had liked Robin from the beginning. She had a lot of history, he thought. She explained the valley to Harlan and his partners. She knew so much: where the best wineries and vineyards were, who was who, what was fitting and what wasn't. He wanted to know what the valley needed and how his organization might complement it. Robin's work on the first auction had so impressed him that he hired her away from Mondavi. She was organized, disciplined, good with people. When Meadowood was finished, and they went through the transition from development to an operating property, Harlan asked her to become the general manager.

Robin came back home to work, making decisions. Harlan

moved to the valley, which had gotten a hold on him, as had wine. There was so much opportunity. On a trip to Italy he had visited several regional schools and wine libraries, and decided Napa needed something similar. An idea began to take shape: build a complex south of the city of Napa where visitors to the valley could go and be introduced to wine, get a feel for the valley, learn where the different wineries were, and decide which ones to visit. A hotel and convention center could be built — alternatives to smokestacks. All good synergy, one of Harlan's favorite words.

He discussed the idea with his partners. They owned a boat together, a 106-foot ketch built in 1910. Harlan had traded a dozen parcels of land for it back in the seventies, when he was always trading things — planes, oriental rugs, anything of value. They kept a crew on the boat who moved it around the world, and Harlan and his partners took turns flying into various ports. They planned for southern Napa what they would call the Gateway Project, and meanwhile Harlan had more ideas.

He and some other investors, including Robin, started a little joint venture called Merryvale, without a winery or vineyards, using purchased grapes and know-how. They hired a consultant to make the wine, and rented space in a small winery north of St. Helena, Rombauer, owned by an airline pilot. It was known as custom crushing. But Harlan also wanted something real, something of his own.

His favorite name in the valley was Sunny St. Helena; it was bright, optimistic, and the winery was for sale. Harlan wanted to buy just the name. He had this other idea for a kind of marketplace at the town's south end, in the heart of up-valley. It would be made up of all these synergistic parts, including a good restaurant and a common tasting room. Those wineries without direct access to Highway 29 would have representatives in Harlan's market, to talk to tourists. "Roadies" wouldn't have to drive all over the hills, searching for individual wineries.

There would be some retail space, some office space. He could use the business people as resources: soil engineers, water engineers, consultants for vineyards, winery managers, packagers — foils, labels, and bottles — landscape architects, outdoor furniture suppliers. Businesses that complement and service the wine industry. And tourists could come and see these professionals doing what they did.

The more he thought about it, the more possibilities Harlan saw. Maybe there would be some residential development. It was something the valley needed. The Sunny St. Helena parcel wasn't large enough for all that, but there was another parcel directly across Highway 29 that was. The architecture would be what Harlan thought of as straightforward, authentic "country." Something to fit the scale and the colors of an agricultural community. A day-care center and a farmers' market. Also a flea market. They could move the town hall there, and have exhibitions. Just as Meadowood was the common ground for the vintners, the complex in the south of town would be common ground for the growers.

When Harlan found he couldn't buy just the name Sunny St. Helena, he bought the whole winery. Robin would run it for him. In August 1986, while the deal was still in escrow, he leased a concrete pad where some purchased grapes could be fermented, and they were in the wine business. Bill Harlan became what some people began to call a lifestyle vintner.

31

MEN WHO a few years before woke up every morning thinking about the weather now woke up thinking about market share. Everyone needed an advantage in a business that had grown competitive and dollar-hungry while the price of land, bricks and mortar, expertise — and money — continued to rise.

Wine tastings, those large celebrations of small differences, occurred almost without surcease around the state and the country, elevating the winemaker and winery owner in the minds of the cognoscenti and the general populace. The only implacable foe of the comparative tasting was Legh Knowles at Beaulieu. He had no patience with them or with wine talk. "People should just drink wine," he said, "and forget about acid and malolactic fermentation and all that bullshit."

You didn't need reasons for listening to Glenn Miller, he said, or Rachmaninoff. Why did you need them for drinking wine? "Why," Knowles asked, "do winemakers smell wine with just one nostril? One's not better than two. They do it because it looks good! Like Harry James playing trumpet with one shoulder hunched."

He saved his greatest contempt for wine writing. He remained friendly toward the writers, but was a scathing critic. His favorite illustrations of the pretentiousness of wine-related prose were "prismatic luminescence" and "Episcopalian in its predictability."

Even the most resolute craftsman of wine, with the degree of reclusivity that often went with it, could not avoid wine tastings. They seemed a waste of time to Joe Heitz, who had an idiosyncratic wine, Martha's Vineyard Cabernet, but after someone asked him for his autograph, Heitz was seen more often in the midst of swirling, sniffing devotees of the ultimate beverage.

Most wine writers were not journalists in the traditional sense. Often they were professionals in other fields, feeding an obsession or, having stumbled into writing about wine, unable to break the habit. Even though the pay was poor there was something addictive about the hearty salutation that a wine writer received from vintners, the sumptuous meals provided for him, the free bottles arriving with the post, the private tours of cellars, the barrel tastings, parties, awards, free travel, and the suggestion of privilege that went with it all — most of it illusory.

Wine writers were often the only link a winery had to a public that was wine-ignorant or wine-indifferent, if not wine-averse. The mention of a Chardonnay or a Sauvignon Blanc in a column added legitimacy to the label glimpsed later on a shelf, and an enthusiastic review could catapult a wine to the top of the market. No wonder the stroking of writers became an art form in itself, one with bona fide historical precedent. A century before, Napa Valley vintners banded together and invited out the New York press. A resoundingly favorable article appeared in *Harper's Weekly,* the first successful bit of public relations that contributed then, and subsequently, to the valley's preeminence over neighboring Sonoma and other North Coast counties in the public mind.

The acerbic Heitz and his wife, Alice, had taken up the tradition early in Napa's renaissance. The Heitz house, it seemed, had become a kind of hostel for writers from California and the East Coast. Heitz was a good, salty source for stories about the valley. His best Cabernet, from Martha's Vineyard, was said to taste like eucalyptus because of the presence of a eucalyptus grove nearby. Heitz had first bottled the wine separately, not because he thought it was startlingly good but because he wanted to give credit to the grower, Tom May, and the Heitz Martha's Vineyard Cabernet had created a stir in the wine press. Heitz said eucalyptus smelled to him like nothing but cat piss, but if the critics wanted to attribute the wine's mintiness to eucalyptus, and wine drinkers to pay an arm and a leg for it, that was fine with him. The year Martha's Vineyard Cabernet reached $12 a bottle, Heitz opened a bottle on impulse, standing outside the winery and drinking Cabernet off the hood of a local's pickup, laughing and laughing at the absurdly high price.

The importance of wine reviews had grown with the competition. The best writers about wine were real journalists, among them Frank Prial, Dan Berger, and Alexis Bespaloff. Most of the others were divided between the old, erudite swirl-and-sniff school and the new proselytizers who raved about their chosen wines and wine-makers, and occasionally condemned those they considered unworthy. Some gained influence not with reporting or imaginative use of descriptors, but with numbers. Digits replaced adjectives as the ultimate accolade. Eventually two men — a lawyer in Maryland and a bicoastal media entrepreneur from the suburbs of New York City — came to dominate wine criticism in the United States.

When Robert Parker began to taste wine and rate it on a scale of 1 to 100 in his buying guide — called, appropriately, *The Wine Advocate* — few people in California noticed. Parker was a government lawyer with a strictly local audience, a regular in the liquor stores and wine shops of Baltimore and Washington, D.C. He had not tasted wine until he graduated from college and followed his girl-friend to Alsace for the summer. Parker drank Coke. But Coke was too expensive in France, so he turned to wine.

His lean years as a critic ended with the coincidence of a strong dollar and the big, luscious '82 harvest in Bordeaux. He judged the '82s to be one of the best vintages of the century, and wine devotees as well as young, upwardly mobile professionals flush with Reagan prosperity, desiring to expand their sensory experiences and to acquire the accessories of wealth and sophistication, began to buy. With *The Wine Advocate* they could chose the best wine by the numbers, without having to read the prose that went with them, just as they chose cars and tape decks. With the favorable exchange rate, even the modest investor could get a piece of the heralded '82s, and they moved by the container load. Merchants pasted the Parker ratings next to the racks of Bordeaux — and his ratings of California wines next to the West Coasters — and his mailing list expanded exponentially.

Parker had his detractors. He assigned numbers to wines arbitrarily, they said. He had too much power. He tended to overwrite, deepening the blush of an already purple genre. His favorite '82 Bordeaux, the Mouton-Rothschild, rated a rare 100, "offers a gustatory and olfactory smorgasbord of heavenly delights . . . oodles of celestial aromas: blackcurrants, oak, toasted almonds, exotic spices, and mineral scents . . . one of the legends of this century." Parker's critics claimed that the '82 Bordeaux wines were grotesquely fruity and out of balance and would not last. The community of wine writers split

over the issue; the debate went on for years. From the standpoint of
Parker's popularity, the ultimate quality of the '82s was not that important. By then his reputation was established, and he continued to
enhance it with an amazing array of wine tastings and sound evalu-
ations.

Another, greater source of influence was *The Wine Spectator,* a
tabloid combining reporting about wine with much of its élan. It
was owned by Marvin Shanken, who had made some money in the
wilder years of investment banking, in the early seventies, and had
tasted some good California wine. When he tried to buy older vintages of Krug and BV, the retailers in New York just laughed at him.
French wines were the only ones worth keeping, they said, but Shanken knew better. He suspected that something was going on Out
There, and wanted to invest but was unsure as to how.

There was no hard information about the drinks industry, no
Moody's for wine, no Standard & Poor's for liquor. He paid $5,000
for a drinks industry newsletter, *Impact,* in 1972; he got two hundred
subscribers and a metal drawer full of filing cards and started asking
questions. He traveled through Napa Valley, among other California
locales, journalist now instead of go-go banker. The story went that
Joe Heitz was the only person who would buy Marvin Shanken
lunch in those days. Soon there was not a vintner in the valley who
would have passed up the chance.

Shanken recognized trends, like the white wine cocktail boom;
the industry wanted access to his research. In 1979 he bought *The
Wine Spectator* for $40,000, moved the editorial offices from San
Diego to San Francisco — to Opera Plaza, developed by Pacific
Union — and added *Market Watch* and *Impact International* to a media
conglomerate based in Manhattan. Shanken spent a lot of time in the
sky over America's hinterland, plotting the *Spectator*'s "mean, hard,
and ugly" course. Swirl-and-sniff journalism was dead and something else had arrived, not just wine by the numbers but also wine
as social credential. Its glamorous aspects had so far gone underreported in a new age characterized by designer dresses and boutique
Chardonnays in the White House. The egalitarian spirit of the sixties
and seventies, when some of the best wineries had gotten their start
in California, disappeared in the rush of black-tie galas, vertical tastings of precious vintages, and spectacular events.

The *Spectator* did not just cover these. Shanken used the glitter of
the wine world to create some of his own, and became the first per-

son in America to make a success of a mass-circulation wine publication. The Wine Experience, held alternately on the West and East coasts, brought together recognized experts from two continents, wine and food personages, and was mobbed by an industry that had never felt absolutely at home in America. Vintners clamored to stand behind tables in evening dress, to pour their wares at their own expense; the wine and liquor conglomerates underwrote "theme" tastings of wine and food, with elaborate decor and elbow-pinning crowds. The money poured in, much of it going to a scholarship fund, but so did ads for the *Spectator*. Some vintners considered themselves above rank business, and Marvin was all business. They criticized his style of promotion, and then sent in their checks.

The broad failure of small wineries predicted in the early eighties did not occur. The ailing ones found ready buyers among foreigners and the conglomerates. Although national consumption of wine began to decline after the cheering gains of the previous decade, the sale of boutique wine rose, part of a general trend toward buying less but more expensively, whether the product was Cabernet, chocolates, or cars.

Duckhorn Vineyards, able to launch itself ten years before on a few hundred thousand dollars, would have needed close to three million by the latter half of the eighties. Land was selling at $35,000 an acre and the price still levitating. A good and necessarily tasteful small winery, with Vaslin press and other equipment, required a huge cash outlay. Buying quality grapes and hiring a winemaker put another $50 or $60 into the cost of every case produced by a small winery. In addition, a budding vintner needed a house in the valley, which meant spending $400,000. And no major marketing operation was considered viable without a guest cottage for wine writers and visiting Frenchmen, who had come to expect luxury in the dispensing of wine and information. That was another $250,000.

Americans drank an average of only 2.5 gallons of wine apiece a year, and 40 gallons of soft drinks. The French drank 21 gallons of wine, and the Italians close to 23. But the quality and price of wine drunk in America continued to go up.

By 1985 Napa had close to 200 wineries. The state of California had 675, and the United States about 12,000. The domestic wine business was worth almost $3 billion, and contributed twice that much to the national economy. The export of 17 million cases of wine coolers the following year helped retard the trade deficit. Indeed, the sale of coolers in the United States did much to conceal the decline in consumption of jug and other cheap wines, while the boutiques' market share improved.

A San Francisco investment firm, Hambrecht & Quist, undertook a study of opportunities in American wine that included an index of prices over the years of Gallo's Hearty Burgundy and Beaulieu's Georges de Latour Private Reserve. After inflation, the jug price stayed the same from 1977 to 1985, but the Private Reserve increased at least 60 percent. Volume growth in the premium wine sector was rising as much as 25 percent a year, and even E. & J. Gallo had noticed.

Gallo got into the lower end of the premium business late and unspectacularly, and bought five hundred acres of land in Sonoma County's Dry Creek district and began to develop it. The company transformed a small mountain with colossal earth-moving equipment, bought secondhand from the builders of the trans-Alaska pipeline and brought south on barges. The topsoil was stockpiled, the mountain reduced to terraces, swales, roads, and reservoirs, then the soil returned, the slopes planted with Cabernet and other high-class varietals, and the lakes stocked with black bass.

The Hambrecht & Quist study affirmed what many vintners already knew: premium wines were doing well but competition was fiercest among the "fighting varietals" — those priced in the low single-digit category — and unrelenting everywhere. There were other problems. The market for wine was highly fragmented. Distributorships were drying up. Marketing was growing more and more expensive, as was the practice of aging wine before release. Good grapes were scarce and wineries with grape contracts but no vineyards of their own were in trouble. The decline of the dollar had wiped out foreign competition, but that wouldn't last forever.

Investment opportunities lay in premium wines, good vineyards, new growing areas capable of matching the quality of North Coast fruit, and "marketing-based strategies." This, said Hambrecht & Quist, "is the only way to establish a defensible brand position. In the long term, brands allow price premiums and hence above-average profitability." In other words, those brands recognized — for whatever reason — could be marked up, while equally good wine without brand position was doomed.

Another possible problem was the sentiment in America against alcohol in any form. Hambrecht & Quist did not perceive this as a large, immediate threat, but many vintners did.

The pursuit of good health affected the wine industry in two ways. Since Americans were drinking less but also better, the boutiques profited from the national stretching of tendons and laving of pectorals, the jogging, swimming, playing at tennis, and the consumption of only those foods conducive to the perception of physical perfection and unblemished character. White wine replaced vodka and tequila as the cocktail of choice. When sporting people did not drink Perrier or anemic beer, they increasingly drank good wine. There emerged the "food wine," a redundancy devised by some promoters to emphasize the compatibility of wine with food — and to excuse some remarkably inept winemaking.

The temperance movement had its dangers. Abstinence was an old enemy of wine in America, a social and ultimately a political force that appeared under the new guise of consumer rights and protections, known in the trade as neo-Prohibition. The word had an ugly, if not readily decipherable, connotation, one that frightened even the owners of successful boutiques, cut increasingly into the national consciousness, and called up the specters of past "drys," who had very real counterparts in late-twentieth-century America.

Alcohol had been a godsend in the eyes of most colonials. The enormity of the American landscape, the inhospitality of the natives, the lack of comfort and of culture, the appalling roads, numbing work, loneliness, and the threat of starvation and violent death lent a certain urgency to drinking. Raw alcohol was considered positively healthful. Supposedly a dram warded off chills and aided digestion of frontier fare; it certainly made the prospects rosier. Local brandies made from any fruit available gained popularity in New England. Homemade beer was used as a substitute for drinking water, as it had been in the mother country. Cottage breweries sprung up everywhere, as did cider houses fed by flourishing apple orchards.

Wine posed more problems: it traveled badly and tended to spoil in kegs and poorly sealed bottles; it was expensive and so only the wealthy could afford it. Even their supply was spotty and uncertain. The contradiction was that grapes grew wild in the colonies, and in great abundance. American grapes were, in fact, the hardiest and most prolific on earth. Leif Ericson had been inspired by the prodigal American grape to call the continent Vineland seven hundred years before the landing of the Pilgrims. But the wine produced from these purple, pitty grapes — identified in 1763 as *Vitis labrusca* — had a distinctly feral taste often characterized as "foxy." Even when fortified with spirits it lacked the appeal of a jug of applejack or a tumbler of mint-flavored brandy.

Liquor prevailed, particularly rum, a uniquely American taste. Columbus had brought sugar cane to the West Indies on his second voyage. The liquor distilled from it was a regular ration for British sailors, as an antidote to scurvy, but it was America that embraced rum as its own. America's first distillery, opened in Boston in 1700, converted cheap imported molasses into rum, what became a significant New England export. Paul Revere was no stranger to it, and George Washington was elected to the Virginia House of Burgesses after distributing seventy-five gallons of rum to his future constituents.

Farther inland, grain whiskeys abounded. The Reverend Elijah Craig of Bourbon County, Kentucky, brought lasting fame to his neighborhood at the end of the eighteenth century with his version of corn whiskey. By that time drinking spirits had become an American tradition diligently observed at all times, and sustained. Toddies were often customary before breakfast. Throughout the day men, and often women and children, indulged in a broad range of grogs, flips, slings, juleps, punches, and other concoctions. Liquor was an accepted, even mandatory, activity at town meetings, civil occasions, church ceremonies, legislative convocations, and as a palliative and an encouragement to labor in American fields and factories.

The man who thought he saw an alternative was an eccentric Virginia planter, scientific dilettante, and brilliant statesman who became the third President of the United States. Thomas Jefferson drank wine and used it on the local gentry. His own cellar at Monticello was built of brick, when less expensive fieldstone went into the rest of the foundation. He had installed a dumbwaiter with which to hoist bottles up to the dining room, so he could fill glasses without having to interrupt conversation. He discussed wine with any guests willing, and ordered, at great risk and expense, cartons filled with fine European wine to be sent across the sea and then, if they arrived at Richmond, over tortuous Virginia byways until they arrived at

Charlottesville, after months of exposure to heat or cold, light and constant discombobulation. He served the survivors in gilded cups and cooled them in a large porcelain bowl with a scalloped rim.

As special envoy to Paris, Jefferson traveled widely, in considerable discomfort, just to taste wine. He visited the reaches of Bordeaux and wrote home of Lafite, Haut-Brion, and Yquem, of Burgundy, and Montepulciano. Jefferson may have been the most celebrated colonial wine bore, but he was also an agrarian visionary, convinced that Americans could make as good wine as Frenchmen. He imagined a prosperous rural land with orderly rows of vines as common as corn, and the American yeoman farmer at home with his drink, his work, and his family.

Jefferson imported European *Vitis vinifera,* runty little sprigs wrapped in rotted cloth, which he had inserted into the Old Dominion soil and even tended by imported Italian vineyardists. That went beyond dilettantism, as the height of either folly or conviction. That he failed was as much a setback for succeeding generations of Americans as it was for the always nascent, always struggling, and apparently doomed American wine industry. For Virginia fungus and Virginia frosts blighted the fruit and killed the vines, and the noble experiment was abandoned.

"No nation is drunken," he wrote, "where wine is cheap." In America, the excesses of spirits could readily be seen on plantations and in crossroads taverns at any time of the day.

The early apostle of temperance, Dr. Benjamin Rush of Philadelphia, a signer of the Declaration of Independence and surgeon general in the Continental Army, had warned of the dangers of liquor in his *Inquiry into the Effects of Ardent Spirits on the Human Mind and Body.* Like his confederate Jefferson, he assigned wine, beer, and cider to the temperate category, ascribing to them the salubrious properties of "Cheerfulness, Strength, and Nourishment, when taken only in small quantities, and at meals."

As early as 1840, towns and counties had begun to vote themselves "dry" in the South and Midwest. By then beer and wine were lumped with whiskey as "the subtle poison of the devil," a gross generality that would reverberate through society for generations. Temperance became a popular cause among women who suffered most at the hands of addled husbands whose trip home from work had included a stop at the tavern. But the admonition to abstain from alcohol was not limited to groups like the Woman's Christian Temperance Union; it came also from the pulpit and from politicians. The movement acquired class overtones, the avowedly responsible elements of society seeking to control the masses by imposing tee-totalism. A sober nation meant better productivity and fewer battered wives and children.

By 1880 whole states were going dry, and active prohibitionists sought to remove mention of alcoholic drinks from textbooks and to change the interpretation of "wine" in the Bible to unfermented grape juice. The fervor was popularly represented in the figure of Carry A. Nation, a temperance agitator and religious hysteric. Cartoons of the period show a determined middle-aged woman in a black duster and poke bonnet, holding a hatchet. The steel-rimmed glasses and lantern jaw reflect a messianic will that made her an emblematic figure of late-nineteenth-century America. Around her lie the ruins of that celebrated male domain, the saloon: broken mirrors, smashed whiskey bottles, upended cuspidors, and the terrified, boozy faces of men hiding under tables attest to her power as reformer and the incarnation of woman's wrath.

Born to a kind but shiftless Kentucky landholder and his unstable wife — she thought she was the queen of England — Carry Nation grew up with slaves as nurses and playmates, an ailing child deprived of parental affection. Revealed religion was a strong and sometimes terrifying presence in her life. The country resounded with the cries and ardor of the tent revivalists, who at that time swept through the South exhorting tens of thousands to accept a real and vengeful God. Carry was baptized by immersion in an ice-fringed stream while too sick to walk, an experience she would never forget. Temperance was a cornerstone of those revivals.

Carry lived in the more or less constant presence of strong drink. Her grandfather, a deacon in the Baptist church, mixed a brandy toddy every morning before breakfast and shared it with other members of the family, including infants. Carry saw the ill effects of the tavern on both her father and her first husband, a doctor and Free-mason who died an alcoholic. She hated the protective male exclusivity of the lodge and the saloon. Her second marriage, to an older widower named David A. Nation, a Civil War veteran and feckless newspaper editor, continued what had become transitory poverty and extreme domestic unhappiness. She found solace in religion and in the WCTU, launched in 1874 as a general reform movement with prohibition as the guiding light.

Her standard salutation was "Do you love God?" She made a

practice of snatching cigars out of the mouths of men on the street, and goading them to avoid alcohol, at a time and in a place where violence was casual, fatal, and often condoned. But hardened saloon keepers were greeted with, "Good day, you donkey-faced bedmate of Satan." In 1899, in Medicine Bow, she and a fellow WCTU member carrying an accordion walked into Strong's Saloon singing hymns and demanded that the joint be closed, in accordance with Kansas law. Carry was six feet tall and weighed 170 pounds, but Strong was able to throw her out. The women moved on to a drugstore that sold whiskey, rolled the keg into the street, and destroyed it.

Newspapers gloried in the idea of a woman attacking men and male institutions. Six months later she loaded her buggy with rocks and bits of brick and set out for neighboring Kiowa, Kansas. She went to Dobson's Saloon with rocks and brickbats neatly wrapped in newsprint and lined up along one arm. The few men at the bar were nursing hangovers with hair of the dog and the bartender polishing glasses. Singing "Who Hath Sorrow? Who Hath Woe?" Carry broke glasses and bottles behind the bar with her wrapped missiles, demolished a rocking chair, and marched up the street to a similar encounter.

The Kiowa smashings brought her national publicity and a mass of letters and telegrams, but it was the raid on the Hotel Carey in Wichita that provided the proper symbolism. There the bar, the finest in the West, not only dispensed strong drink to men but also provided them a constant view of the painting *Cleopatra at the Bath,* which included the representation of pubic hair. Again Carry's foray was matinal, her armaments a cane and an iron rod as well as stones. One of these was hurled through the *Cleopatra* canvas before the others brought down the huge mirror and an array of bottles, decanters, and gilded signs. She was arrested.

During subsequent smashings Carry was in turn smashed, both by men and by prostitutes, wives and women friends of barkeeps armed with clubs and whips. She took up the sharpened hatchet, hallmark of the committed. Lecturing all over the United States, she gained a celebrity that blunted her violence. Some said she did more for beer and whiskey than any contemporary, for men discussed her endlessly over drinks. She helped inspire the saloon wars of the first years of the century and focus attention on the temperance issue.

Ironically, she was kept at length by the leaders of the WCTU and other temperance groups who considered themselves paragons of civic virtue and did not want to be sullied by Carry's extremism.

The drys remained a relatively small group of zealots with disproportionate power during Prohibition, until Repeal in 1933. It took the country half a century to get over the drys' influence and now, in the 1980s, they were back again, on the National Council Against Alcoholism, at the Center for Science in the Public Interest, and in the ranks of Mothers Against Drunk Driving and Students Against Drunk Driving. Wherever people spoke of the health benefits of a glass of wine, of its religious heritage, historical provenance, organoleptic subtlety, and cultural significance, there were others to talk about rotting livers and ruined lives, an alcoholic past and an abstemious future in which tiny particles would be scientifically traced through the human body and all possible ill effects broadcast with a zeal as old as fermentation.

If neo-Prohibition ever caught on, the palatial aeries of Napa would look out over condos, not vineyards, and the agrarian dream of a few — from George Yount to Niebaum to John Daniel, the Davieses, the Rodriguezes and the Eiseles — would be as dust to the desert wind.

32

VINEYARDS STRETCHED like muffling corduroy over the valley, but beneath this prime commodity lay a certain contentiousness, due in part to the geographical constrictions of Napa, where people could not avoid one another for long, and in part to the powerful self-esteem of some residents. That some vintners had big egos was by now evident. They had been fitted in great numbers into the valley's narrow confines as if with a golden shoehorn. Many were self-made; others were accustomed to commanding either large work forces or large assets, or both, and grew litigious in the new environment. Still others had expansive visions, and unyielding notions of how those visions would be realized.

Lawsuits touched a disproportionately large segment of the populace and involved property lines, easements, water rights, soil run-off, grape quality, noise from wind machines, sulfuring, broken contracts, and the names ascribed to remote corners of the land.

Warren Winiarski and his neighbor Carl Doumani had both claimed the name Stag's Leap. The battle over it lasted a dozen years, cost them at least $100,000 apiece, and revealed the fractiousness of geographical claims, for real estate had become more than location in Napa; it was essence.

Doumani had owned Duke's Barbecue, near the University of California at Los Angeles, and done some southern California home speculation. He had never been north of the No Name Bar in Sausalito when a friend invited him to a wedding reception in Napa in 1970. He stayed at Meadowood and drank sparkling wine at Schramsberg, and by the time the weekend was over had decided to buy a ten-acre home site.

The real estate broker kept talking about Stag's Leap, an old ranch with a white elephant for a house, and four hundred acres, some of them planted with vines. Too big, Doumani said. But the broker took him by the place, and they stood on the porch, under the rocky palisades so romantically named, looking down the narrow valley softened by the late afternoon sun, and Doumani said, "You son of a bitch."

Six months later he owned it. The abandoned house had been built by the Chase family, from Chicago, in the 1880s, and the property had included a coach house, greenhouse, and all the amenities of a country estate, including the winery, the original Stag's Leap. It was Chase who chose the name, claiming as Indian legend what was probably his own invention, but the name stuck. The house itself passed through a succession of failed commercial enterprises, including a temporary billet for military wives with husbands stationed at Mare Island. It was from the field in front of the house that Alexis Klotz, the brass-assed pilot and friend of John Daniel's, had flown a bag of cash to southern California as a favor to Louie Stralla. The reputation of Stag's Leap Manor had grown quite seedy by the time it closed for good in the early fifties.

Doumani moved with his family into the guest house and tried his hand at destroying the rudiments of those less-than-glorious days. Demolition became his hobby, he said, although Doumani was not known for physical exertion. Give me a five-foot wrecking bar and a nail puller, he said, and I can bring down anything.

Eventually a dozen makeshift bedrooms and the turret were removed. The looks of the place improved, but his relations with his neighbors did not. He got into an argument over a fence. He sued Winiarski, who had filed for use of the name Stag's Leap Wine Cellars on his label. Doumani figured that name belonged to his property, although no wine had been made there in years. His lawyer told him their case was a cinch. Doumani didn't even bother to go to court, and the judge ruled that the name Stag's Leap was a geographic entity — anybody could use it.

Doumani told the lawyer to appeal, but the lawyer waited until the deadline had passed. Meanwhile, Doumani had begun to make wine at Rutherford Hill, planning to build a winery of his own. He preferred Petit Sirah to Cabernet. When he started marketing it under the name Stag's Leap Winery, Winiarski sued *him*. Winiarski claimed that he now had exclusive rights, and the judge agreed.

That ruling was overturned on appeal. During each stage of litigation people in the valley took one side or the other, on grounds of principle or personality. Doumani wanted to develop Stag's Leap Ranch into a hotel or, at best, a bed-and-breakfast, restoring the house to a grandeur it had never known. The state supreme court finally declined to hear the case, so Doumani and Winiarski found themselves right back where they had started. They decided that they would both use the name but with subtle variations, one in the placement of the apostrophe: Stag's Leap Wine Cellars (Winiarski); Stags' Leap Winery (Doumani).

The fight became part of a broader struggle over appellations. No one wanted the Napa Valley name debased by cheap wine made from foreign — that is, out-of-county — grapes. Not even those importing them, big wineries like Sutter Home and Beringer. To be able to put "Napa Valley" on a label was clearly an asset. For years import limits and narrower definitions of vineyardland had been heatedly discussed. In France, the term "Appellation d'Origine Contrôlée" was used primarily to classify according to geography, grape variety, and vineyard practices. "Appellation" is defined as "the act of calling by a name," or "a designation," but in France it really meant quality, and could delineate as precisely as a plot of ground between two stone walls.

In America, the interpretation was broader and much more lenient. The Bureau of Alcohol, Tobacco and Firearms ruled that there would be a formalization of appellations in America, and the addition of new ones, known as American Viticultural Districts. But the procedure was sloppy and the BATF's purpose unclear. The agency did not make quality distinctions, as in France, but simply sought to divide up the land. Wary of lawsuits, the BATF tried to please everyone, and ended up with appellations that were often meaningless.

Napa Valley's appellation was granted in 1981. Two years later, within Napa, came Howell Mountain and Carneros, leading to the controversial inclusion of both Napa and Sonoma counties in the Carneros appellation. Growers in the farther reaches of Napa County fought to have themselves included in the official Napa Valley appellation, even when the claim seemed irrational.

People began to ask, "What is Napa Valley?" It appeared to be a narrow, fertile plain extending south from Calistoga to the city of Napa, with small, steep mountains as sides. But some saw "the valley" as a kind of market basket, with pockets in unrelated stretches of the county. It was decreed that any geological crease was officially Napa Valley and any grape coming from those environs Napa Valley fruit, regardless of how undistinguished. This enabled the growers to get higher prices for their grapes, and those making wine from them to charge more.

That different spots within Napa produced very different results was known to the old-timers long before anyone heard of "micro-climates." Back in the thirties, André Tchelistcheff had described a taste found in certain Beaulieu Vineyard Cabernets as "Rutherford dust." He was not discussing what blew across Highway 29 during harvest in and around the town of Rutherford, but the sensory impression left by a mouthful of Cabernet produced between the southern boundary of Oakville and Zinfandel Lane to the north, east of the Mayacamas range and west of Highway 29.

The "Rutherford Bench" was a largely arbitrary classification of a geological phenomenon not apparent to the eye and not necessarily apparent at all geologists, although there were those willing to attest to it. Later, it would require more lawyers than geologists to prove its existence, and that of other mostly arbitrary distinctions made by landowners around it. The "Bench" was in fact a gravelly outflow with roughly the same boundaries as denoted by the dusty-berry taste.

Geography took on olfactory characteristics. It was theoretically possible for the knowledgeable palate to amble around the Rutherford Bench and, using successive bottles of Cabernet from the different vineyards, to encounter the tastes of cranberry, cassis, cherry-mint, blackberry, currant, red raspberry, black cherry, Bing cherry, and herbs. These distinctions, real and fanciful, involved not just soil but an additional matrix of sun, elevation, exposure, and heat. The celebrated team of UC Davis professors, Maynard Amerine and Albert Winkler, had devised a system in 1944 for measuring the heat to which vines were exposed in various regions, but the system was only a rough measurement.

Climatic and viticultural distinctions were more subtle. Many small, quality operations were not satisfied with a "macro" view of the valley. They wanted definitive boundaries to separate them from the rest and to pay tribute to the particular character of their fruit and the wines made from it. They wanted the federal government — the omnipotent and sometimes capricious Bureau of Alcohol, Tobacco and Firearms — to recognize officially these viticultural districts, also referred to as "sub-appellations."

The Napa Valley Vintners Association and the Napa Valley Grape Growers Association got together to form an appellation education committee. Viticultural districts quickly became the new measure of quality, as well as a new marketing device; everyone wanted his own.

The Stag's Leap area was warmed during the day by afternoon sunlight reflected from the overhanging rocks, and cooled at night by fog and cool air rolling north out of San Pablo Bay. One theory was that the moving air encountered the knoll in the center of the valley — owned in part by Robert Mondavi — and increased in speed, further cooling the adjacent vineyards. Whatever the explanation, grapes in the narrow confines of Stag's Leap did have their own characteristics, good quality being an important one.

Gary Andrus, a former developer with an interest in the nearby Pine Ridge Winery, decided to put "Stag's Leap Vineyard" on one of his Chardonnay labels, having put together some purchased grapes from the area with common characteristics. Warren Winiarski and Carl Doumani took Andrus to court to prevent this. It cost Andrus's partner $150,000 — the price of fighting these battles had gone up — but the judge ruled in his favor and then called the principals and their lawyers into his chambers. The judge told them to go outside and settle. Later, Andrus called Winiarski to make amends, having earned the right to put "Stag's Leap" on his label. "You'll always be the Château Margaux of the district," Andrus told him. "Why don't you turn this around, take hold of it, and be the leader?"

In other words, champion the Stag's Leap sub-appellation. But Warren bitterly opposed what he considered the exploitation of his winery's name and reputation.

A Stag's Leap committee was eventually formed among the neighboring vintners. It included not just Andrus, Dick Steltzner, John Shafer, Bernard Portet, and Joseph Phelps, but also Robert Mondavi's family. Their vineyardland along the Napa River, comprised of heavy soils utterly unlike those on the other side of the Silverado Trail, was suited to Sauvignon Blanc, not Cabernet. But they wanted a piece of the sub-appellation deal, and so did Silverado Vineyards to the north, owned by the widow of Walt Disney, as did Chimney Rock, Altamura, and others so far removed from the real

Stag's Leap as to barely qualify as satellites. A retired dentist from Los Angeles, Stan Anderson, maker of sparkling wine on Yountville Cross Road, also wanted in and eventually had to be included.

The committee redrew the boundaries, and redrew them again. The American appellation system had been rendered meaningless by making the BATF the judge and jury, when the bureau didn't care about quality, used a cumbersome set of regulations, and quaked at the prospect of a lawsuit. Instead of being exclusive, the viticultural district was inclusive; rather than denoting quality, it broadcast geography. Something for everybody.

The Mondavis later put forward to the BATF a plan to divide the valley into blocks named after the towns — Napa, Yountville, Oakville, Rutherford, St. Helena, Calistoga — as well as after mountains and other landmarks. These names would appear on wine labels as distinct viticultural districts, although wines produced within these districts were quite various.

Many vintners objected to the fact that towns like Rutherford and Oakville had more natural allure because of their association with historic properties. The petition, known as the Township Plan, included a proposal to create a separate viticultural district for the so-called Rutherford Bench, still barely discernible amidst the creeks and alluvial fans at the eastern base of the Mayacamas Mountains.

In some eyes Tim Mondavi was also tacitly assigning superior status to his family's vineyards and others within the Rutherford and Oakville appellations. The proposal included not just a Rutherford Bench, but also an Oakville Bench. People willing to accept the notion of a Rutherford Bench, even if it didn't exist but had been talked about by the old-timers for decades, rebelled against an Oakville Bench.

In both cases, the Benches were really outpourings of little creeks that had created fans of soil on the valley floor as they interlaced with the Napa River. In the case of the Rutherford Bench, there was a single fan of sandy soil over what is known as the Franciscan Formation, a marine sedimentary conglomerate. Logically, "Rutherford Fan" should have appeared on a wine label, but the words were not as marketable.

The Oakville Bench was a larger problem. No one had ever talked about an Oakville Bench before people started looking for it, among them a member of Dickenson, Peatman & Fogarty, the same Napa city law firm that represented the Robert Mondavis in other matters pertaining to real estate. The fact that the Benches of Rutherford and Oakville seemed at least partly imaginary did not escape critics of the Township Plan. One pointed out that the only bench he had ever seen in Oakville was on the porch of the Oakville Grocery.

33

A N EARLY ADVOCATE of the Howell Mountain appellation was
Randy Dunn, owner of Dunn Vineyards and something of a
maverick in the valley. At a time of grand winery designs,
"philosophies," and the apotheosis of the vintner, Dunn represented
something else: an older inclination to perform the tasks of his profession himself and to avoid those things everyone said you had to
do to be a star in Napa.

Paradoxically, Dunn's wine became one of the costliest and most
sought after in the valley in less than a decade. His story served both
as a primer on the basics of a craft many vintners had altered to
produce less demanding wines and as proof that early allegiance to a
specific place and a specific grape was very important.

The spine of Howell Mountain is two thousand feet above the floor
of the valley. Dunn owned a tiny piece of it. He had unruly red hair
that swallowed the stems of his aviator glasses, and a beard streaked
with gray. His house, designed by him, was built of cedar along
clean, contemporary lines, but the sprawl of Dunn's enterprise suggested a working homestead elsewhere in the West, except for the
gnarled stumps of Cabernet Sauvignon pulled from the vineyard and
piled near the house, to be used as fuel for barbecuing. The corru-
gated iron barn roof was held in place by large round rocks. An old
green flatbed truck with a towering hood was backed into a tangle
of blackberry bushes. Machinery of obscure function sat under the
shed roof, and wooden pallets were stacked in the shade of big pon-
derosas. The land beyond the barn descended through blond stubble
to the stock pond. One of the horses, a bay mare, drank from a
discarded bathtub in the paddock the morning Dunn left the house
to deal with the crush of 1987.

His winery, formerly an old olive press and storage facility, was overhung with wisteria and backed by a ruined orchard. A famous football player once drove all the way up Howell Mountain to buy some of the Cabernet made there. Dunn liked the remoteness of his place and the runty, flavorful grapes it produced. The winding road down to the valley floor required between fifteen and thirty minutes to descend, depending on how hard Dunn pushed his pickup.

The first load of grapes arrived at 8:30. It had taken the pickers more than an hour to fill the gondola, a heavy metal tub on two wheels, bought secondhand and repainted. Dunn's Mexican worker, Raul, uncoupled it from the back of the pickup and attached the tongue to the front of the forklift. Dunn maneuvered the gondola onto the concrete pad in front of the winery, the staging area. He had poured the concrete himself, with the help of his stepson, Mike. On the pad sat stainless steel fermentation tanks, including two that had once been used for holding milk.

To the unaccustomed eye, the concrete pad did not suggest the birthplace of a fine wine but the site of some ingenious industrial improvisation. A worn plastic shovel lay to one side, and a rubber squeegee for pushing spillage off the pad. A nitrogen tank was lashed to one of the fermenters, to be used for cleaning bottles. Coils of electrical wire lay beneath hoses varying from the garden size to two-inch transparent plastic pipe for moving the must. The bottom of an empty beer keg supported stainless steel nozzles, nuts, and bolts. The beat-up refrigerator stood by, and a plastic garbage can, an apple press, some wooden platforms, and an old trailer for hauling away the stems.

The metal hopper that separated the grapes and crushed them, known as a stemmer, had been wheeled into place and fitted with a plywood collar to cut down on spillage. The collar had been further adapted with a piece of tarpaulin held in place by a broom handle and bungee cord, to catch the grapes before they hit the concrete.

The stemmer began to rattle and shake. It was attached by wires to a remote electrical switch that Randy had rigged up earlier that morning. The red Nicolini pump moved the thick must from the stemmer toward the metal tanks. Dunn had performed all the electrical work himself, journeyman mechanics being part of the romance of the modern winemaker who made only 2,500 cases of Howell Mountain Cabernet a year, a minuscule output compared to that of other wineries. The ton of grapes in the one teetering gondola, based on the retail value of the bottles it would eventually fill, was worth thousands of dollars.

Young Mike, blue-eyed and muscular, climbed up and began to fork the grapes into the stemmer. "The secret of pitchforking," Dunn told Mike, "is to keep your feet in one place. Some guys waltz around and end up with a gondola full of juice."

The berries were beautiful — blue-black, glossy, with deep green leaves. Stems piled up on the concrete; the must, moved by the sighing pump, turned the hoses purple. Stray grapes rolled about. Dunn picked up a broken bunch and his fingers adhered with the sweet, sticky juice. Within minutes it had also anointed tools and boots, and its fragrance hung in the air.

Dunn stirred the must with a metal rod, then with his hand urged it toward the pump. He could figure the sugar content by the stemmer's arthritic behavior: the more sugar, the less liquid he got. The pump labored. Finally he shut it off, disconnected the hose, got down on his knees, and shoved a bare arm up into some of the best Cabernet in the county.

He forked out the second gondola himself, a job that would have gone to Raul, but Raul had no rubber boots and Dunn didn't want him to mess up his pale yellow calfskin ones. Dunn wore a baseball cap to block the sun; printed above the bill were the words *Santa Rosa Stainless Steel*. His black T-shirt was full of holes, festooned with chest hair. A wrench protruded from his back pocket.

He finished in ten minutes and Raul hauled the gondola back up the road to the vineyard. Dunn lifted the cover on the milk tank and peered in at five hundred gallons of juice — a bog of skins, pips, and some leaves, fearsome in its inkiness. He had paid the crew $90 to pick that last ton, $10 more than the day before. The grapes were small and the bunches scattered. He told the pickers not to worry about the leaves, and that made them smile — removing leaves meant more work.

Later, he would add a couple of buckets of prepared yeast to the must, to get the fermentation going.

Mike was wetting down the horses with the hose. The hayfield below looked white in the sun, the pond sky blue. Dunn's wife, Lori, in fresh white shorts and a sleeveless blouse, was hanging out clothes on the porch. Dunn picked an apple from a tree next to the winery and walked up to the house to get a drink, past the room that served as Dunn Vineyards' office, and on into the kitchen, leaving his boots outside. "We sure won't have to buy twenty new barrels this year," he told Lori. The crop was short.

The house had oak floors and airy rooms with tongue-and-groove ceilings and big windows. A butcher block stood in the middle of the kitchen floor. Before, Dunn had worked as the winemaker at Caymus Vineyard down in Rutherford. While a UC Davis student interested in bugs, not wine, he had come to Napa to pick Caymus's second crop of Cabernet for an incidental course he was taking in winemaking. The first Dunn vintage, fermented in two plastic garbage cans in the black of his Econoline van, tipped over when he stopped suddenly on the highway, and poured out when he opened the van's sliding door.

He had met Lori in the office of the Department of Entomology. She worked as a secretary, and he invited her to go flying in his 1946 Aeronca Champ, one of the old tail-draggers. He took her to the plane on the back of a Norton motorcycle he had to push to start. Lori had serious doubts when she found herself sitting in the back seat of the Aeronca, holding the brake while Dunn spun the propeller, but it was too late to get out. They had flown west, toward Napa, and landed on a deserted island in the middle of Lake Berryessa that was covered with wild flowers.

They were married four years later. The old house over the cellar was home when they first moved to Howell Mountain — the same house the Winiarskis had once rented. Their neighbors were all Seventh-day Adventists. The Dunns borrowed from the bank to buy land, vehicles, cooperage, bottles. Randy kept his job at Caymus while building his own brand, with Lori doing the office work and taking care of their two daughters. It seemed they drove the oldest car in the valley, an El Camino with a door that stuck.

Randy now heard the pickup on the road above. "Doesn't sound like he's pulling anything," he said, still listening. "Oh, yeah, he's got a load, all right."

After that load was crushed, Dunn drove up to the vineyard. The ridge offered views of the cedar roughs off to the east, toward Berryessa, beyond the undulating tops of the row of olive trees. He could see a bit of the Napa Valley floor through haze to the southwest. The breeze came from that direction. "We're going to run out of sugar," he told the crew boss, whose face was covered with sweat and grime. "Things are cooling off."

Overnight, the sugar content of the grapes would drop as the vines pulled moisture from the soil. The harvest was staggered because the grapes didn't ripen uniformly. Some of the runty ones had been left by the young men hustling along the rows of vines. "You have to pick these, goddamn it," Dunn said, but he smiled as he tossed a few into the gondola.

The crew hadn't made much money on this mountaintop. Dunn was sympathetic. Picking was hard work, and only the Mexicans were equal to it. In a decade of winemaking he had seen only two white men and one black one try to pick grapes, and none of them lasted.

He left a six-pack of cold Budweiser in the shade of a ponderosa for the pickers.

"*Cuántos dólares?*" the foreman asked, indicating the gondola.

"We'll call it full," said Dunn.

Driving down, he passed a discarded gondola at the foot of the vineyard. It had been given to him after it broke loose from a pickup on the Oakville Grade and killed a man. Dunn used it for burning vine cuttings; the Mexicans called it El Diablo.

Four months later, in January, Dunn drove up the hill armed with hand clippers and a pair of long-handled shears. Dealing with the dormant vines would surely warm him up, he thought, parking the pickup next to the metal gate. The dogs had beat him there; they raced through the vineyard. The vines had spread in riotous senility since harvest, and he put on sunglasses to protect his eyes from the canes that always flailed at him when he pruned.

Each vine posed a little viticultural problem; Dunn enjoyed solving them. He had to determine which canes to leave and which to cut, and whether to train the shoots along the metal wires; he used a combination of pruning methods, depending on the individual vine. The object was to get rid of dead wood and give the new growth direction and opportunity. He left a spur behind each cane, so there would be something to grow the following year. He clipped a small vine and trained a larger one along the metal. He wrestled with bull canes, switching from the pruning shears to the long-handled ones. Soon he was unbuttoning his denim jacket.

The truth was, he liked to prune. It was a vacation from paperwork. The bank, the state of California, and the feds all had their forms and questionnaires. How many ag reports, he often wondered, should a small winery have to file? Why should a person who crushes only thirty tons of grapes have to bother with all that? The county wanted to know exactly how much property he owned. The feds wanted monthly reports on how many cases of wine he had in storage, how much in cask. They wanted to know how much bonded wine he had, and how much he paid taxes on. Every month!

The bankers were no better. They agreed to lend him money based on the value of his inventory. Not the real value but their notion of it. They said his less expensive Napa Valley Cabernet, a blend, was worth $4.50 a gallon, and they would lend him half of that. Dunn pointed out that he was paying more than $8 a gallon just for the grapes. The banker said, "Well, we're not in the wine-selling business."

Dunn wanted to say, "You're not in the winemaking business, either."

Dunn Cabernets had climbed steeply in the estimation of wine reviewers. They were intensely flavorful and had lots of tannin, at a time when many California Cabernets were made in a lighter, less interesting style. They sold long before Dunn officially released them.

After six years of labor, with Lori in the makeshift office and Dunn in the cellar, Lori had come out on the porch one afternoon and called down to him, "I want to go out to dinner."

He had stopped forking stems into the old trailer. "Call Mustard's," he said, "and make a reservation."

"We'll never get in there."

"Tell them who you are."

"Really?"

She went back into the house, and in a few minutes reappeared. "We got a table!"

Lori made a wooden sign. She put white paint in the grooves so their friends could read *Dunn* in the dark, coming across Howell Mountain. Then strangers started arriving, wanting tours. She and Randy thought it was a fluke, but the cars kept coming. Lori painted black in the grooves where the white paint had been, to obscure their name, but still people found the place. Finally Lori went out with a sledgehammer and knocked the sign down.

One day she came back from driving the girls to school and found a big Lincoln Continental waiting in the driveway. Lori had just had knee surgery and so didn't want to get out of the car just to explain that tours weren't offered at Dunn Vineyards. She talked through the car window, and the people drove away, and she felt guilty about it. She had to bang on the door of the old El Camino for five minutes to get it to open. When Randy came home he found her sitting in the kitchen crying, crutches in a corner. "You're going to put up a sign saying we don't do tours," she said. "I can't stand it any longer."

Once Tim Mondavi telephoned from his car and asked permission to bring up some visiting French winemakers. They arrived in the heat of the day and Randy took them up to the vineyard. The Frenchmen all wore black shoes and didn't want to leave the shade of the vines. Tim seemed stunned by the austerity of Dunn's operation; he called it "folkloric."

Dunn had not joined the Napa Valley Vintners Association. The initiation fee was $300 and the annual dues another $1,000, the price of three or four hours of flying time a month. He figured he didn't need the Vintners. Most people joined just to be part of the Napa Valley auction, but he didn't approve of the organization's rules. When a friend of Dunn's tried to donate several vintages of Dunn Cabernets to the auction, the offer was rejected because Randy didn't belong to the Vintners. The auction was supposed to be a benefit, he thought, not a test of solidarity.

The '85 vintage of Dunn Vineyards' Howell Mountain Cabernet rested in mixed cooperage two and a half years after it was made. Most of the barrels were stacked near the cellar door. With the beam of a small flashlight, Dunn checked the dates chalked on the barrels, then knocked the rubber bungs free with a wooden mallet, inserted the long glass thief, and withdrew columns of densely purple wine. He emptied the thief repeatedly into small bottles, eyeballed the wine for clarity and depth of color, marked the bottles, and set them aside. He made occasional entries in a battered ledger with a pencil. His records were slightly better than they used to be, when a woman working for the Bureau of Alcohol, Tobacco and Firearms called and said she was coming up to look at them. Dunn told her he wasn't prepared. "How long would it take you to get prepared?" she asked.

"About ten years." There was a pause. Dunn added, "My forte isn't paperwork."

He closed the cellar door, to keep the cats out. The '87 vintage had been in barrel half a year and had yet to be racked (moved from barrel to barrel). Some winemakers racked every three months. Dunn had never worried about racking schedules until his Cabernet got such good write-ups and became so valuable, and then he started worrying.

The third batch of the '85 vintage he kept in a separate place, in new Nevers oak, as an experiment. He clambered over the barrels, taking samples. There were three separate vintages in barrels in the cellar, which was a rarity. Dunn released each vintage a full year after most of his competitors released their wine. One of his biggest expenses was inventory, and taxes he had to pay on it. He had enough wine for 1,800 cases of the '85 — about average for the Howell Mountain Cabernet — and would bottle it within the month. The retail value of that tiny output was more than half a million dollars.

The two other vintages were also being kept for release later. Collectively, it represented a great deal of money, and Dunn tried not to think too much about it. Good wine required time. So far he had been unable to hasten the process of aging before sending his wine to market.

The "lab" was under the office, next to the main basement, where stacked cases of wine already sold waited for the deliveryman. In the cubicle stood a secondhand spectrophotometer — he wasn't sure exactly how to use it — and a device for measuring pH, calibrated glass tubes, various wines in bottle, a tape measure, a toolbox. Dunn took four bottles of the experimental lot up to the kitchen and poured them into four wine glasses and warmed the glasses individually with his hands. The "nose" came up with the warmth. The first two were similar, but the third definitely had the aroma of new wood.

He took a mouthful, drawing air in over the wine to get the molecules up into his nasal passages. The first wine had good body, a taste of berries, and powerful tannins — the mouth-puckering element that seemed to fur his teeth and would preserve the wine for decades. The second one had a touch of vanillin, from the barrel staves, and the third was woodier still. The fourth sample had a slightly "green" taste likened to bell pepper. He would rather not be doing this today because he was getting a cold, but decisions needed to be made, and the blending done. He had thirty new barrels in the cellar, at a cost of $400 apiece, and could put half the '85 in them and later make the blend and bottle it.

·

The next morning, 1,400 cases of bottles arrived before dawn. By 6:30 A.M., a boxy white van was parked in the narrow passage leading to the concrete pad, and the itinerant bottling crew was ready to start. Raul had cut back the blackberry bushes to make room. The van was plugged with hoses and electrical wires. The Dunns used to bottle themselves, with help from friends, but it took longer and there were mishaps. One day they accidentally pumped a barrel of Howell Mountain Cabernet into the garden.

By nine o'clock the line was rolling. Bottles on the conveyor belt were fed into a big vertical wheel called the orbit, where air was blown in and then the bottles sparged with nitrogen, a protection against oxidation. The bottles moved into a horizontal wheel that aligned them with valves; they descended into the necks and flooded the bottles with Cabernet. The corker, a Bertoloso bought second-hand from Stag's Leap, thwaped a cork in every two seconds. A stack of metal foils stood nearby. The line squealed as the bottles were shuttled along, an endless, lurching snake.

Full bottles were fed into the waiting cases and the cases shuttled down the metal ramp to Raul, who stacked them on the pallet, mounted the forklift, and took the cases to the house.

Lori came down to watch; it was the weekend and she wore a fresh shirt. "I'm all showered and ready for the tourists," she said, laughing, knowing they would arrive unannounced. The Dunns still offered no tours or tastings but found it impossible to keep enthusiasts away, and Lori refused to be rude.

Dunn wore his usual outfit, jeans and boots, with the addition of a big jackknife in a scuffed holster. He had planned to take a flying lesson for an advanced rating but couldn't pull himself away from the activity, even though the owners of the bottling line knew their job. The Dunns were paying a dollar a case for the use of this traveling circus. The labels of wines the crew had bottled in the past were plastered to the side of the van: Sunrise, Frog's Leap, William Wheeler, Ravenswood, all small outfits. It had been as far north as Ukiah, as far south as San Luis Obispo.

A tourist couple did arrive, wide-eyed. They had ordered a case of wine months before, and Dunn fetched it for them while Lori found the bill. Then Dunn stood around and talked to them, watching wine dripping from the filler into a plastic bucket.

Lori warmed up smoked Cornish game hens for dinner from a box of two dozen, plus two dozen pheasants, that they bartered for a case of Dunn Vineyards' Cabernet. Their daughters, Jenny and Krisi, fair and freckled, displayed the good humor of children raised in proximity to hard work and affection, while their parents talked business and drank some Howell Mountain Zinfandel made by a neighbor. One of the ironies of life was that the Dunns couldn't afford to drink their own wine because it was too expensive and there wasn't enough to meet demand.

A new rug had been laid in the office at the other end of the house and a Macintosh computer moved in. They had also bought an open-ended accounting program and paid a woman to set it up and include their mailing list, which had grown to 1,500 names. Now Lori was able to call the files up instantly, and speed-print the mailing labels. They decided that the price of the service was worth the trouble it saved.

The telephone rang. Randy took the call in the office while Lori did the dishes. A distributor in Oregon wanted to represent Dunn Vineyards and wanted to send a packet of forms. "Hey," Dunn said, "I don't do forms."

A retailer called from southern California. He had been sent a double shipment of Dunn Vineyards Howell Mountain Cabernet by mistake and wanted to keep and sell the extra shipment. "No," said Dunn. "If you sell any of that, you'll never get any more Dunn wine."

He felt the new carpet with his socked feet. The wood stove was still warm. The old filing cabinets, the student's desk, and the captain's chair originally in the office had been replaced with modular office equipment and a chair of brushed aluminum. The computer was a marvel, he thought. It produced a wrap-up of the month's finances and did a paper trail for the records. Lori had gotten up in the middle of the night to turn the computer off and run into their bedroom door.

Dunn wanted to put a recorded message on the answering machine saying there was no more wine available that year, but Lori wouldn't agree. She wanted to explain that there simply wasn't enough wine to go around. She had to deal with retailers who could be quite rude, men who in the beginning had never heard of Dunn Vineyards and were forced to call by their customers. They grew outraged when the Dunns wouldn't sell them any.

The telephone was still ringing. This time a distributor from New York said that the restaurant Windows on the World wanted to put Dunn Vineyards' Howell Mountain on its wine list. Dunn was reluctant. "A place like that could use up fifty cases a year."

"I know wineries that would give their left nut to get on the Windows list," said the distributor.

"Basically my philosophy is that I don't give a damn," Dunn said, not unfriendly. "All right, I'll send them five cases."

The distributor thanked him. "You've made me look good."

Dunn knew that if he made more wine, the quality would go down. There were only so many grapes from his vineyard, and they were unique. He wasn't going to take advantage of the prestige he had built up any more than he was going to hype what he already had. Besides, he *wanted* his wine to be hard to buy.

Before going in to watch television, he checked the messages that came in during dinner. A caller said, "I'd like to find out about buying some Howell Mountain wine . . ."

"Good luck," said Dunn.

∾

The airplane he ordinarily flew was a single-engine Cessna, tied down at the edge of the Angwin airstrip. It belonged to a friend who rented it to Dunn by the hour. He left his pickup next to a hangar and climbed into the cockpit, cranked up the engine, and taxied out to the runway. The plane lifted off in a tricky crosswind. Pope Valley lay on the right, dry and hill-locked, Napa on the left. Almost immediately Dunn was over his own vineyard, a tiny vernal patch on the ridge of Howell Mountain. He could see the Douglas firs, the house, the pond, and the pasture. The place was so small that, at a thousand feet, you had to know it was there.

He turned left, to avoid the white gliders being hauled up out of Calistoga. Mountains trailing off from the lowering mass of Mount St. Helena looked like firred, crumpled tinfoil with deep defiles, and the valley floor as formal as any European duchy, offset by Sterling's monastic white stucco. The big wineries at the top of the valley stood out like palatial afterthoughts: Krug, Greystone, Rhine House. The Mayacamas grew fatter and more stolid, full of little hanging vineyards and feats of landscaping, sequestered mansions with tennis courts like chevrons on sleeves of lawn. Inglenook sat massively in the lee of Mount St. John, the Coppola house behind, lost in the oaks.

Dunn flew on over Robert Mondavi Winery, Far Niente, Domaine Chandon, and turned left, passed over the Napa River, Wappo Hill, Stag's Leap, and left again, toward home.

Greetings to our customers, old and new,

Many things have happened since our last release letter. . . . One of the most obvious is that your address on the envelope was not hand typed.

Ah, yes the times have not completely forgotten us on Howell Mountain. . . . Lori was over-worked. Mailing lists, invoicing, check writing, financial statements, spread sheets and word processing are all a part of us now. . . .

Another new leaf that has been turned over is in the area of transportation — yes, that faithful 1969 El Camino of some 222,645 miles has been put out to pasture and replaced by a ¾ ton Ford pickup truck. This "new image" vehicle (folks still don't seem to recognize us in it) easily and safely hauls 100 cases of wine, 3500 lb, down the mountain to St. Helena. But, they're just not built the same. . . .

As you might imagine, one of the purposes of this letter is to announce the release of the 1985 Vintages. . . . If you want the HM it must be ordered, and paid for, now. Do not wait until December!

Our little girls are growing up fast. This year Kristina (a first grader) lost her first tooth, learned to jump rope, and to read. Jennifer (now 9 years old) has started to ride Lori's horse and occasionally even reads to her little sister. Michael graduates this June from UC Santa Barbara. . . .

Lori, while not hacking away at the Mac . . . is constantly beautifying our surroundings. If not by sun-bathing, it's by planting flowers, bushes or trees around our new house. . . .

It has been back to school for Randy — a lot of intense studying and flying. He is in the final stages of obtaining an instrument rating which permits piloting into clouds. . . .

Ah yes, I almost forgot "ole" Chewy, our fearless snake dog. She got bit again by one of those buzztail snakes. . . . We got the skin for a hatband, and Raul, our right-hand man, put salt and lemon on the meat and ate it. . . .

Dunn Vineyards is a working reality. It appears we have gained acceptance in the wine world, even if it is in a microscopic way. It has been a long haul. Our existence is directly dependent on our loyal customers, for which we thank you.

34

WINE HELD powerful sway over its devotees and those who knew little about it or its history. They did know that wine stood for something special, and they would drive a hundred miles to Napa on the weekends to discover what that might be, or, already knowing, to taste and somehow be part of it, willing themselves to sit in their cars in the middle of Highway 29, waiting for access to Mondavi, Beaulieu, or Sterling, dust from the tractors drifting across the view and the sun reflecting in dark glasses behind the windshields of "roadies" and latter-day pilgrims.

A century before, the Gold Rush had captured the popular imagination and had drawn people by the thousands to the continent's farthest edge. Striking it rich was only part of the appeal; equally important was the proximity of a dream larger than ordinary existence, capable of transforming common citizens into grand and independent beings.

Hollywood had been another version of that phenomenon, more radiant, more elusive. Now wine shared in it, having moved up from mere pastime to creator of personal wealth to social credential and then into a class of its own. What had before been merely romantic and sometimes lucrative took on the trappings of high civilization. Wine was no longer something to drink on a hot day or a mere accompaniment to bread and cheese; it was an accoutrement of culture. To drink it was to indicate an appreciation of the fine things of life. To make wine — better, to own the institution that made it, with its own "architectural statement" and "philosophy" — was to place oneself near the top of a privileged, learned order.

Wine had long been described as an artistic commodity. "The winemaker's art," in fact a craft, was a phrase repeated throughout history; winemakers realized early on that art is more marketable than craft, and more prestigious. Robert Mondavi and his family, on the release of Opus One, compared the different vintages of their elegant new Cabernet to Picasso and Cézanne — and charged an unprecedented $30 a bottle. They and other vintners began to talk about "sculpted" wines, as if each bottle were a piece of Carrara marble on a pedestal to be shaped by hammers and chisels.

Oils and watercolors graced the walls of the Mondavi and other wineries. Margrit Biever, Robert's wife, was no longer the head of public relations; she was Mondavi's vice president of "cultural affairs." Painting and sculpting became as common among the spouses of successful vintners as origami in royal Japanese households, and benefits for the opera and other arts in San Francisco ran with Napa Valley wine. Vintners who a few years before had been accustomed to discussons of the weather, Brix, pH, and then the all-important market share now also had to accommodate themselves to expressions of light, form, and technique.

If wine was art, the winery was perforce a studio. Some became unofficial galleries as well. By extension the owners, or those prospective owners with large plans and large fortunes, began to see the winery as a museum, an ideal place to entomb and appreciate art, edifices they said would be glorious tributes to wine but what others called vaunted monuments to ego.

The Sterling and the Robert Mondavi wineries had caused much comment and criticism when they were built. But this amounted to little compared to the latest architectural controversy. Rising out of the flats south of Calistoga was a pink and terra-cotta edifice resembling a Cretan palace. On the volcanic swell above it, simultaneously and in the same Mediterranean hues, appeared the rudiments of a house that promised to be more spectacular than Mondavi's redoubt on the oaky mound behind Yountville, the one with the indoor swimming pool, and the Newtons' Chinese pagoda above St. Helena. They might be kings of their mountains, but the owner of these new creations was leaving them far behind in audacity and cultural statement. The new winery was to be both a tribute to wine as art *and* a temple of myth.

Jan Shrem, its owner, had been inspired by the paintings of the nineteenth-century symbolist Odilon Redon, himself known as "the prince of dreams." Those encountering Shrem at receptions in the valley, and in the halls of the county government building in the city of Napa, were surprised to see a polite middle-aged man graying at the temples, not an overpowering industrialist or real estate hustler. Shrem, the son of a Lebanese dry goods merchant, came to New York City from South America in the forties, broke and alone, lived in a relative's apartment, rode elevators daily with armfuls of insurance forms to earn $110 a month, ate at Horn and Hardart, and studied at night. He took the Greyhound to Salt Lake City, sold encyclopedias door-to-door, studied international relations at the University of Utah, but maintained a passion for the opera, architecture, and the painted and the plastic form.

After graduation he kept going west, first Los Angeles, then Japan. He imported books to Tokyo and began to publish. English was replacing German in all technical journals, and these became his private bonanza. His employees rose in number from a few to two thousand. He married a Japanese artist and began to expand his acquaintances among artists and architects. One designed a building for him that was built on the outskirts of Tokyo. It was Shrem's good fortune that Tokyo boomed and, booming, moved in his direction, surrounding the building and increasing its value a hundredfold.

Shrem and his wife had moved on to Paris. There he successfully published coffee table books, still dabbling in real estate but pursuing art and architecture as both vocation and avocation. To this cultural accretion he added wine. When he was fifty years old he decided to create a kind of oasis for himself and his collection, one suited to a self-made millionaire, art *amateur* and enophile, and that conformed to an overarching vision.

His winery in Napa Valley would be a temple to art, wine, and mythology, with a sculpture garden and a ziggurat, waterfalls, and pavilions. He would call it Clos Pegase: Clos for the enclosed and highly prized little vineyards of Burgundy, Pegase for the mythic winged creature. Shrem owned the Redon painting, a winged stallion rearing against a nightmarish void, his favorite piece in a large and valuable art collection, and one that lent itself to his carefully constructed vision. In Greek mythology Pegasus, emergent from the neck of Medusa, had cracked the earth on Mount Helicon with his hooves and released water of such purity that it inspired the Muses — the perfect symbol.

Michael Graves, the postmodernist architect from Princeton,

New Jersey, presented the winning design in an international competition, one of such lavishness that it alarmed Shrem's neighbors on Dunaweal Lane. This monstrosity, they said, would sap the ground water and pollute what was left. Shrem's lofty vision was really a tourist attraction, a Cretan pyramid to lure Winnebagos from as far away as San Diego so their passengers would pay to gawk at expensive art and buy overpriced wine and other gimcracks as souvenirs of the San Simeon of northern California.

They filed suit against Shrem and against the county that approved his design, but the winery was built anyway. It proved to be more Knosson temple than Egyptian pyramid, without the sculpture garden, ziggurat, and waterfalls — the lawsuits prevented that — but with cupolas and narrow windows under the knife-edge shadow cast by an expanse of tile. There were two entrances, one for people, one for grapes. Two archaic columns symbolized the task of making wine and the pleasure of drinking it. The portico of the people entrance was open to the sky, to welcome Pegasus, whose water would irrigate the symbolic fields of Bacchus, formerly Dionysus, god of wine.

The house on the hill reflected the winery's classical motifs. But the sunken swimming pool outside looked up at Diamond Mountain, beyond an array of linear metal sculpture and the enormous conceptual thumb, created by the Florentine sculptor Cesar, on the patio. Inside, the same mahogany doors and window frames, and porcelain breasts and other contemporary art in carefully contained space hung with masterpieces. In an alcove beside the fireplace hung Redon's *Pégase,* near the extruded-plastic drool on the hearth known as *Expulsion.*

Shrem held an open house and served uncut noodles, symbol of hospitality in Japan. Not all the neighbors came. Standing on his patio overlooking his stunning creation and the firred slopes of Diamond Mountain, he was reminded of an ancient Japanese proverb: When you step outside your house, seven enemies await you.

Neither art nor myth could match the powerful draw of what had come to be known as nostalgia. This was not just a hankering after the past, which in some ways closely resembled the present — the valley had seen success among wineries in the previous century, before they were finished off by depressions, phylloxera, and Prohibition — but a specific yearning for the glories of an earlier, less crowded, more promising time. Much of the attraction of the wineries themselves was their age, the intimation of an earlier industry that the Davieses and others like them had sensed when they arrived in the sixties. This aura still hung in most views across the soft green furrows of Napa Valley.

To those views was added, in 1983 — in the imaginations of a Napa city internist and his girlfriend — one of America's most acceptable bits of nostalgia: a locomotive, running between the vineyards, its whistle lofting on the clear morning air.

Dr. Alvin Block thought the valley needed a commuter train. Once a train had run south to Vallejo, on the bay, where passengers boarded a ferry to San Francisco. The railway line still paralleled Highway 29, crossing and recrossing it, left from the days of steam locomotives and then the freight train that had ceased serving the valley when Southern Pacific finally pulled out. Passenger service could be viable again, Block was convinced. The Bay Area Rapid Transit system did not come close to Napa; the valley was clogged with traffic, and there were plenty of people who would be eager to take to the rails.

Block got together a group of potential investors. He went to see Southern Pacific's man in San Francisco, who told him that the idea of a passenger train in the valley had already been discussed by the company's executives, and rejected. Short runs were not profitable, he added. Southern Pacific was divesting itself of the Napa line.

Block began to amass information for his board of investors. He envisioned their train bringing people from Sears Point, south of Petaluma, across the top of the bay and then north to St. Helena, where the tracks ran right through the middle of Krug's property. Then he realized it was only twenty-three miles from the Kaiser plant south of Napa to Krug, a very short run that might lend itself to a special kind of train, one that would alleviate traffic on Highway 29 while offering a unique experience. A wine experience.

Block's final board was made up of two doctors, a newspaper ingénue, a raiser of Christmas trees, and the owner of a moving business. If they won the bidding, they would suddenly find themselves in possession of a railroad, one without trains and badly in need of repairs, extending twenty-odd miles from a decrepit warehouse at the south end to a weed-choked lot in the middle of vineyards at the north end. There were hundreds of crossings and rights-of-way, some derelict stations and platforms, and a great deal of money to be spent.

They needed a chief executive officer to raise funds, and advertised in the *Wall Street Journal*. Five hundred people who considered themselves perfectly qualified to run a Wine Train, whatever that was, applied.

Jack McCormack owned a house in Malibu. He had a salt-and-pepper beard and the easy laugh of a man who knows how to promote. He had been involved, he wrote in his résumé, in five major start-ups. He had helped launch American Honda, and after that U.S. Suzuki. He still carried the old business card that said, "You get more nookie on a Suzuki."

The idea of a Wine Train appealed to him; it was a good symbol. He often asked people, "What does Los Angeles have as a symbol?" He then pointed out that it didn't have one. There was nothing people could identify with. San Francisco had the Golden Gate Bridge, and Napa Valley would soon have the Wine Train.

After he applied for the job of CEO, Alvin Block invited him up. McCormack met with him and the rest of the board, and told them, "You're selling the same thing we were selling when we were pushing motorcycles, in an uphill image battle. You're selling *fun!*"

He was hired. Then Southern Pacific raised the price. There were other bidders, but Block's group got it in the end; they thought they would get the show on the road for $600,000, but McCormack told them, "No way. You need at least $3 million."

McCormack spent months on a feasibility study and hired a civil engineer who knew railroads. He tried to raise the money in the valley, without luck. People were afraid of what their neighbors would think if they invested. But outside the valley all the vibes were positive. McCormack got a brokerage firm with experience in public and private offerings interested. He wanted to sell individual shares for $40,000 and corporate shares for $100,000, and planned to raise as much as $5 million.

Potential investors wandered in and out. Money was slow coming in, and the organization badly needed a large infusion of cash. Someone suggested that McCormack call Vincent DeDomenico, a pasta magnate. McCormack didn't know DeDomenico from Adam but called him anyway. He sent him the packet of information and talked to DeDomenico again a few weeks later. DeDomenico said he would drop by, and drove up from some factory he owned in San Leandro, in a champagne-colored Mercedes, an old-style Italian with a hairline mustache, combed-back hair, and a dark suit. He looked around and asked a few questions, and left.

They met again, in Lyon's Restaurant in Napa city. DeDomenico said he was interested in investing. McCormack figured him for a $100,000 player, max. He called him later to ask if he had decided, and DeDomenico said, "Yeah. I think I might do four million and my daughter'll do one million."

McCormack almost dropped the phone.

Vincent DeDomenico's father started out selling vegetables, but his wife talked him into building a macaroni factory at the corner of 18th Street and Valencia in San Francisco. His father later regretted the decision: with vegetables, everything was cash. But with macaroni you had to make the product, keep an inventory, sell, and collect. You needed people on the road — all that worry.

Vincent, one of four DeDomenico boys, sold pasta from Sausalito to Eureka back in the thirties. He always came home through Napa, stopping at a couple of groceries and at the Miramonte Hotel in St. Helena. He liked the valley.

His father built another factory, and the family named the business Golden Grain. Vincent's responsibilities increased, his horizons broadening with success. He met Fred Holmes, who owned a home in Napa Valley and who sold Golden Grain beans from the Central Valley. Fred served DeDomenico good wine, and introduced him to Robert Mondavi and some others in the valley: old man Martini, Hanns Kornell, Barney Rhodes, who had sold Martha's Vineyard to the Mays. DeDomenico attended dinner parties in Napa before some of his later critics there were even born.

The DeDomenicos never became famous, but one of their products did, created after Vincent DeDomenico watched his sister-in-law mix a can of Swanson's chicken broth with vermicelli and rice. The dish that resulted, a kind of pilaf, was delicious. DeDomenico had eaten something similar at Omar Khayyam's, but so far no one had tried a commercial adaptation of pasta and rice.

DeDomenico experimented with the combination himself, adding dried soup instead of canned, and the results were equally impressive. From there the recipe moved through the offices of Golden Grain and emerged as Rice-A-Roni, "the San Francisco treat." Within a year it grossed $100 million and forced him to build another factory in Chicago.

Every year Golden Grain grew larger: Noodle-Roni, bread stuffing mixes, soups, drinks. It acquired Ghirardelli, the Hershey of the West, and built another pasta plant in Seattle, and then the largest yet, in San Leandro, across the bay from San Francisco. A 60 percent share of the national rice-mix market would more than support all the DeDomenicos, and there were many.

In the mid-seventies Vincent DeDomenico saw an ad in the *Wall Street Journal* for the old Daniel place in Napa Valley. He decided to buy it and bid $1 million, but it wasn't high enough. A couple with plans to develop bought the house, and then a few years later it was sold again to a movie director. The death of Fred Holmes erased DeDomenico's main connection with Napa, and he put the valley out of his mind.

The DeDomenicos sold Golden Grain to Quaker Oats for $275 million. Some of the family members stayed on to help run things, including Vincent, but he found that he had time, and money, on his hands. In 1986 he heard about plans to run a train from Napa to St. Helena.

His daughter dug up some research done on traffic there and learned some surprising things: 2.5 million visitors came to the valley every year, and 1.8 million of them went to only half a dozen wineries right on Highway 29. DeDomenico said to himself, "Christ, the train is a perfect way to deliver the visitors."

He talked to Robert Mondavi about it. He remembered Robert telling him, "If done right, it's a good idea."

DeDomenico trusted his judgment. He said, "Maybe I'll buy into this thing."

When Dr. Alvin Block heard about DeDomenico's offer, he said, "Let's meet Mr. Big Bucks."

A dinner was set up at Petri's Restaurant, where the investors assembled at a long narrow table and chatted with DeDomenico. He dropped a couple of bombshells. He intended to blend the concepts of elegance and transportation — in other words, to run one type of train for everybody, instead of making it exclusive, and to run it often.

Running many trains and catering to the lowest common denominator might be more commercially viable, Block said, but in so doing they risked losing the good will of the valley. DeDomenico made it plain that he didn't welcome unsolicited advice from doctors and others unaccustomed to hardball business. The Wine Train desperately needed an infusion of several million dollars, and the group at Petri's watched DeDomenico and McCormack take control of what had been Alvin Block's baby.

☙

Not everyone in the valley was in favor of a Wine Train. After the facts started coming out, it developed some dedicated opponents from very different segments of valley society.

Norm Manzer sold State Farm insurance out of a renovated stone building on a side street in St. Helena. Outside was a stone slab with an iron ring in it — a hitching rail put up in 1889 with the building. Manzer appreciated things like that. His office was crowded with restored artifacts: a spring wagon like the one used by Jacob Schram at the turn of the century, an old gumball machine, signs, bottles, milk cans, reproduction furniture, and a conductor's cap.

Manzer was a train buff. He took his family on train trips when he got the time. The old Southern Pacific tracks, unused, lay just across the street, on the far side of a stand of evergreens that blocked the intense afternoon sun. Most days of the year he left his door open, and came to work tieless. Selling insurance was a question of contacts, and most everybody knew Norm Manzer.

When he first read about the Wine Train, he knew it would be a success. People loved trains and they loved the valley; putting the two together was a natural. He tried to imagine a train running past his office, after all those years, and the pleasures it might entail.

The more he read about it, the more interested he got. The Wine Train was to stop at various wineries, and in Yountville and St. Helena. There was also to be a dinner train, passengers eating and drinking while taking in the scenery. The organizers intended to make six runs up the valley every day during tourist season, and maybe eight. That was really sixteen runs, since the train would have to return each time to Napa city. The Wine Train claimed that within four years nearly half a million passengers would be riding between May and October.

Manzer got out his calculator. Those projections meant 68,000 passengers a month, and 2,200 a day. Most of them would be disembarking in St. Helena, which had limited facilities. Where, Manzer wondered, were 2,200 people going to go to the bathroom?

The Wine Train backers said the influx of tourists would be good for the town because they would buy things. When people went to Disneyland, Manzer asked himself, did they also shop in Anaheim? They did not.

There were hundreds of little railroad crossings in Napa Valley — driveways, dirt roads, vineyard lanes, as well as major thoroughfares. According to the law, a train had to blow its whistle five times at each crossing. Using his calculator again, Manzer figured that meant about five thousand whistle blasts a day. The tracks wandered back and forth across Highway 29. He could foresee some traffic problems that made the present ones seem benign.

Manzer assumed the Wine Train investors would do some kind of study, an environmental assessment, and work out the problems and answer all the questions. The investors would limit themselves to what was generally acceptable. Then he read in the newspaper that, because of an anachronism in the old laws regulating railroads, the Wine Train — inheritor of the Southern Pacific's mantle — could do pretty much as it pleased. The backers were not undertaking an environmental assessment and were pushing ahead heedless of the objections.

The more he thought about it, the angrier he got. He found some others as angry as he. Gradually an organized opposition began to grow, including some wealthy people that Manzer had never met, with big houses tucked away in the valley and apparently with no need of insurance from State Farm. But they were determined and, like Manzer, convinced that the Wine Train was a cancer.

Betty Peters's ample white Victorian on the western edge of St. Helena was surrounded by the assets of Napa Valley: things growing — not just flowers and shrubs but also tomatoes and other vegetables that she and her Mexican gardener spent hours working with — and that fragrance of plants being watered that is so Californian. She had been coming to the valley from San Francisco for twenty-five years. She and her late husband had had nothing to do with wine but had been part of the Exciting Wave; now she played cards regularly with Alexis Klotz, the former pilot, and often had dinner with her friend Katie Spann, another professional woman and a valley resident. One summer evening the two of them were dining on the porch when they heard the blast of a whistle. Betty Peters asked, "What's that?"

"The Wine Train," said Katie Spann. On a trial run from the yard in Napa city.

Betty had read about the train, of course, but until that moment had never seriously considered it. She realized that the two miles separating her property and the railroad tracks were nothing to that whistle.

35

THE HAIR of Jim Hickey, the planning director, had turned white since he arrived in the valley twenty years before. The flesh around his waist had become such a concern that he rarely drank wine now. But he still towered above his colleagues, and his enemies, of which there were many. He still carried his pens and steel-rimmed spectacles on his belt in a leather holster. He still dominated the office of the Conservation, Development, and Planning Department, County of Napa, 1195 Third Street, Room 210, Napa, California, and he still saw the plans for every building, large and small, proposed for inclusion in the landscape.

What he saw after 1985 disturbed him. There were too many strip-zoned businesses sucking tourist dollars from Highway 29, and too many wineries in the valley engaging in activities that had nothing to do with the production of wine. They steadily encroached on the agricultural preserve, attracting with their success all the peripheral enterprises related to tourism and residential development.

Hickey still believed that Napa was the only suburban county in California close to a big city, maybe the only one in the nation, with a chance of preserving its rural character. That chance narrowed steadily. When he looked at the maps in his office, he still saw an isolated valley in the shape of a teepee, with sides too rugged, it would seem, to support ambitious, manmade structures. And yet houses had appeared in the watershed like mushrooms, and wineries and other commercial structures bloomed on the valley floor.

If you poke two hundred light-commercial holes in the fabric, he asked himself, is it still an ag preserve? What is the acceptable level of activity at a processing plant for the valley's prime commodity? Grapes were different from other farm commodities. Ordinarily people didn't care where their staples came from. Bread eaters didn't drive out to the country to see where the wheat was grown and the flour made. Likewise, wineries were different, but how different? What was a winery, anyway?

The question, when put to county officials, gave rise to the predictable response: Ho ho ho. A winery, they all said, was a place where you made wine.

Hickey pressed. If a winery made wine, then should it also sell T-shirts? Should it conduct tours and hold concerts? What about cooking schools, restaurants, gourmet shops, and art exhibits? If the county allowed wineries to do these things as nonconforming uses under the zoning ordinances — and it did — then the county could be sued by anyone prevented from opening a shop or a restaurant in the ag preserve who did not also happen to own a winery.

Hickey's analogy of the glacier was familiar by now: a snowstorm here, a snowstorm there, and once the glacier forms it can't be stopped. Hundreds of little decisions encroached on the ag preserve in the same way until their cumulative force became irresistible.

Little things, little conservings, had also contributed to the quality of life in Napa. Orchard and vineyard owners were no longer allowed to burn old tires, producing clouds of black smoke to ward off frost. Towering signs advertising wineries and other commerce had been forbidden. Forty-acre minimum lots in the hills — the watershed — had been created to limit building above the valley floor, to prevent the streams from silting up and other environmental problems. Older developments like Silverado, the Auberge de Soleil, and the original Meadowood wouldn't be allowed in the Napa Valley of today.

Enlightened land-use policies grew out of public awareness, and occasionally public outcries, like those over the Vintners Inn, the split-lot development that gave rise to the ag preserve, and the proposal by the state to build a major highway up the middle of the valley. A relative few banded together and defeated that, too, finally getting both houses of the state legislature to vote to remove the highway plan from the project book of the California Department of Transportation.

The valley could well have a major airport instead of the small, manageable one on the outskirts of Napa city. Once a back-up for Travis Air Force Base, it could have received any kind of aircraft, but the county added some asphalt to one end of the runway that would sustain only little executive jets. That automatically excluded the big planes and contributed to a better quality of life for the residents of the lower county.

Now everyone wanted to take credit for the ag preserve, even those who had opposed it. The ag preserve was a sacred cow, often invoked by the very people seeking to subvert it. Exceptions — the special deals people cut with the board of supervisors for their own projects — had become the real enemy. The legality of the ag preserve, with its minimum-lot zoning requirements, had never been ultimately tested in court. Hickey believed that John Daniel was pressing his suit against the county when he died, and wished that he had lived to take it to the state supreme court, or higher. If he had lost there, the verdict would have made it easier for elected officials to say no to developers.

He was tired of the argument that development creates jobs. Development also does away with jobs. He had raised five children in Danville and Napa, and had watched them all leave the valley. They had no connection with farming or winemaking and had sought their careers elsewhere. He didn't resent that. Agriculture was Napa Valley's reason for existence, and those who didn't like agriculture — the sound of the wind machines, the smell of sulfur, the curtains of dust — should live elsewhere.

Hickey wondered who was really responsible for what was to happen. Where did the maximum accountability lie? Upstairs in the board room, where the five supervisors sat? In the state legislature? If the state of California gained control of the valley, who in Sacramento would stick his neck out for Napa? With surrounding Contra Costa, Alameda, and Santa Clara counties having a million people each, and Napa only 120,000, Hickey worried about what the state would do to the valley.

There was talk of having it declared a national preserve, a treasure — a Yosemite with vineyards. But who in Washington would stick his neck out? And if Napa was declared a national treasure, it would be in the federal government's hands forever.

The answer had to be found locally. Some of Napa's citizens were no less committed than when they opposed the highway and helped create the ag preserve, but where was the leadership that existed then? Hickey didn't see it. The old leaders — Al Harberger, old man Martini, Robert Mondavi — were either gone or fading. Their successors sent their lawyers to the county board meetings instead of coming in person. There was too much money to be made, and too fine a life to pursue. The environmental groups like the Upper Napa Valley Associates used to field candidates and get them elected, but no more. The vintners and the growers represented different interests. People weren't pulling together; the cracks showed and things slipped through.

Since 1970, the county had acquired two hundred new wineries, eighty bed-and-breakfasts, and several hotels and restaurants, all in the unincorporated area, the ag.preserve. Some tourism was good, but how much? At some point the accommodations and amusements become the industry. They take over. Hickey didn't want Napa to go the way of Fisherman's Wharf, which no longer had any fishermen. He didn't want it to turn into a version of Disneyland, which some people said was already happening. The hot-air-balloon business alone was worth $1 million a year. The balloons were pretty to look at and fun to ride, but were they agriculture?

There would probably be a Wine Train. Was this in any way related to the idea of a valley devoted to growing crops and the kind of life that implied?

The more Hickey thought about it, the more convinced he became that the wineries were the central issue. The vintners served as exemplars, whether they liked it or not; they could set the agenda. Wineries provided 30 percent of the jobs in the valley and were generating about $600 million annually in "gross economic output."

A few years before, when the numbers question was raised, some vintners stood up before the board of supervisors and talked about winemaking as "the marriage of the grapes." Burgundy, they pointed out, had three hundred wineries. In those days they didn't even need to use a permit to build one in Napa. The storage facility that went up in front of Inglenook created the demand for some control — Heublein's inadvertent legacy — but now the number of wineries in Napa had passed two hundred and was on its way to matching, maybe surpassing Burgundy's. And there were not enough grapes grown in the county to supply those already in existence.

If the wineries were the issue, then a definition was essential; in a way it would also be a definition of the Napa Valley of the future. So it was important to get it right. The question, put to the board and then to the people, would create a storm exceeding even Jim Hickey's expectations, but he asked it anyway: "What *is* a winery?"

❧

North of the city of Napa, on Big Ranch Road, sits a red brick apparition that vaguely recalls a famous house in rural Virginia, Monticello, built by Thomas Jefferson. Monticello Winery was, when built, one of the more blatant attempts to capitalize on nostalgia and myth. The winery's owner, Jay Corley, sought to distinguish his winemaking and marketing operation from the competition in Napa, and in that he succeeded. Napa Valley's Monticello is a simplified, pygmy version of the real one, the home of the country's ultimate enophile. Monticello, Napa Valley, is not a home at all but an office with kitchen facilities for entertaining visitors in the wine trade and luring wine-loving tourists over from the corridor of Highway 29.

A plaque put up by Corley recognized Jefferson's espousal of wine and food. Corley told his visitors that Monticello, Napa Valley, continued in that grand tradition, and that he had distant relatives in Virginia. In some ways, Corley pointed out, he had improved on Monticello, Charlottesville. For instance, all the *Vitis vinifera* that Jefferson longed to grow in Virginia now thrived in northern California. So did the olive trees that Jefferson so admired. Shrubs and trees at Monticello, Napa Valley, replicated those on the other side of the continent. Corley liked to add, "I think Jefferson would be proud."

In 1985 Corley headed Napa County's Planning Commission, the five-member citizens' group appointed by the board of supervisors to review building and land-use requests and, under Hickey's guidance, to pass its recommendations along to the supervisors to be voted on. Serving on the Planning Commission was considered an honor. Over the years it included vintners like Corley, growers as various as Andy Beckstoffer, the boy from Richmond, and Andy Pelissa, whose family had been in the valley for generations, winery workers and others with no connection to the industry, salesmen, and even a retired airline pilot.

During Corley's tenure the Planning Commission and the Planning Department had dealt with, among other things, the General Plan. This was a blueprint for the county's future that outlined what was and what was not permissible under the law. The revised General Plan had been hastened along by the Vintners Inn suit brought a few years before. The introduction stated that the General Plan "establishes a balance between diverse, and in some cases, conflicting programs."

The summary of the overall goals contained in the plan was written in capital letters: "PRESERVE AGRICULTURE, AND CONCENTRATE URBAN USES IN EXISTING URBAN AREAS."

The guiding hand behind the General Plan was Jim Hickey's, but many people contributed to it. The great collective effort was finally finished. Corley figured he had done his civic duty by sitting on the Planning Commission during that period, and he looked forward to resigning from it and devoting more time to selling wine. Then Hickey formally asked his question — What is a winery? — opening up a whole new can of worms.

It came in the form of an official memorandum from the Conservation, Development, and Planning Department to the Planning Commission. The amusement it generated was short-lived. Hickey was serious. He stated the current zoning ordinance definition: "'Winery' means a building or portion thereof used for the crushing of grapes, the fermenting and processing of grape juice, or the aging, processing and storage of wines. It may include on-site disposal of winery waste generated on the site, bottling of wine, the warehousing and shipping of wine, plus related office and laboratory activities as accessory uses. Retail and wholesale activities conducted within the winery shall be limited to wines produced on the site or wines produced by the winery at other locations."

Hickey pointed out that wineries were generally considered agricultural processing facilities, the final step in dealing with a prime agricultural commodity. "The question before the Commission today is what activities beyond the actual making, bottling and selling of wine . . . are or should be recognized by the County as part of a normal winery's operations."

Hickey listed the things that a winery was not: a restaurant or delicatessen, a general retail store, a public theater or concert hall, a bed-and-breakfast, inn, or hotel, a bottling facility for something other than wine, a multiple-unit housing development, a hot-air-balloon launching or landing site, and a business office for activities unrelated to the winery.

He recognized that many vintners thought highly visible promotion was necessary to publicize their wines and winery, and that sales of items like T-shirts, wine glasses, and even concert tickets enabled them to stay solvent. "Reasonable restraint" had in the past enabled the county to wink at what was in fact not allowed. "However, based on the expanding list of activities taking place at many wineries today and in many agricultural zoned areas, it appears that the common sense–reasonable restraint approach is not working." Some wineries and landowners, Hickey added, "feel that there are no limits or constraints on their activities."

It sounded innocuous enough, but Jay Corley knew the issue was explosive. Hickey was not talking solely of restraints on commercial activity but also of a way of life. The vintners had always done pretty much as they pleased, and now they were being officially questioned. Many would resent it. Corley himself had problems with restraints being imposed on existing wineries. Like Monticello, for instance. He needed the kitchen there for promotion. But plans for some of the newer wineries struck him as either blatantly commercial, ripping off the Napa Valley name, or preposterous edifices only marginally related to wine. Specifically he thought of Peju Province, a new facility referred to as a "chain-link winery" because it contained not much more than a concrete pad supporting fermentation tanks surrounded by a fence. And, of course, Clos Pegase.

Hickey concluded that the answer to his question might also answer a larger one. "If the Commission's decision is that the future of agriculture is inseparable from the success of the wineries and the success of the wineries is inseparable from the adoption of a broad, permissive definition of a winery that allows individual wineries to expand their operations in almost any direction with little or no direct relationship to the wine-making process, then the future of the County's agricultural areas is limited. . . . The cumulative effect of all such changes will slowly but surely move the character, the quality and the future . . . from agriculture to tourist-oriented commercial development." The glacier theory all over again.

Corley recommended that public hearings be held to decide what, indeed, a winery was. Then he resigned.

Hickey received responses from the predictable sources and saw, in retrospect, that they framed the debate. The Napa County Farm Bureau, whose president was Volker Eisele, grape grower and former

Berkeley sociologist, supported the current winery definition and limited tours, tastings, retail sales, and social events. "Our current reputation for fine wines and hospitality has long been promulgated by people dedicated to making the finest wines possible," Eisele wrote to Hickey. "The surest way to lose this reputation and the market for our wines is to make hucksterism our main goal, relegating Napa Valley to the side show of the wine world."

The Napa Valley Grape Growers Association president, Bob Phillips, the former Marine and wealthy grower north of Yountville, wrote to Hickey to say essentially the same thing, though in greater detail. Phillips suggested "grandfathering" the less onerous winery activities "*unless* such uses were not permitted under specific restrictions within the winery's original or amended use permit." In other words, enforce regulations against food service, concerts, and unrelated profit schemes. "Further commercialization of our agricultural areas would be detrimental, and the opportunist who would abuse the county's nuturing attitude toward our industry by flying under the protective colors of 'winery' must be avoided."

That was one side. From the other came two letters, one bearing the logo of the Napa Valley Vintners Association, written by the executive director. He paid tribute to the agricultural quality of the valley, but pointed out that as the global economy had changed, "so must we to stay competitive. . . . Simply making wine is not enough. We must take strong steps to sell the product. . . . Efforts to curtail some of these marketing techniques would put the entire industry at a competitive disadvantage."

The most interesting letter Hickey received was signed "R. Michael Mondavi," president of Robert Mondavi Winery. Hickey assumed that the Mondavis' lawyer had written it. In the old days, Robert would have undertaken the task himself, but those days were gone, and besides, the letter contained the legal germ for what became the Vintners Association's official position.

Michael Mondavi suggested that a "winery district" zone be recognized that would include wineries, their activities permitted by the current use permit, and any other activities it had engaged in since before the time such permits were required. The winery district notion would go beyond grandfathering by formally sanctioning the status quo. Michael Mondavi wanted not only tours and tastings made legal but also gift shops, art galleries, kitchens and banquets, musical events, film festivals, and cooking seminars: "All the activities . . . permitted by the great wineries of France, Germany and Italy."

For a year Hickey waited for more specific instructions from the Vintners Association. The Agricultural Advisory Council, made up of vintners and growers, did not produce a definition suitable to the two groups, who drifted apart. Acrimony spread between vintners and growers over the issue; there was considerable grumbling, but no agreed-upon proposals. Finally Jim Hickey set up a public hearing on the winery definition issue, and said, "If we do nothing, we are jeopardizing the future of the valley."

That year, 1987, the Napa Valley Wine Auction became the signal event, drawing people from all over the country, all over the world. The wine to be auctioned was not just any wine but the best the valley had to offer, which in the minds of those who made and sold it, who tasted and talked about it at length, who lived by it, meant the best in California, equal to wine produced anywhere on earth.

This Napa wine didn't come just in ordinary bottles but also in beautifully etched glass bearing the names and vintages of Napa's most famous wineries and their imposing silhouettes. Some bore special labels designed by artists; others stood emblazoned with crests and vineyard scenes in bright enamel that would never fade. The wine came in generous quantities as well: magnums, imperials, jeroboams, and huge nebuchadnezzars, which required two men to open and serve, although these wines, modern heirlooms, had not been made to violate so soon but to contemplate from the far side of richly shadowed crystal. These bottles were not set in simple wooden crates but in elaborate cases carved from mahogany, walnut, and exotic woods, some the size of baby grand pianos and fitted with thick glass also etched, and with display racks and heavy brass inlaid locks and even thermostatic controls designed to carry this high craft, this art, into the next century and beyond.

They were to be auctioned not just as opulent containers for some of the best wine on earth but also as imprimaturs of taste, even of worth. The institutions producing the wine numbered in the hundreds and supported a new class, gently laundering fortunes made in less genteel expressions of American enterprise. The valley cradling them had remained a pastoral island in an ocean of industrial excess.

At the end of the century the forces that had made it had miraculously been put off here. But beyond the arrayed glass and its pricey contents, beyond the incredible *success* of it all, the final view down the valley's long, vernal corridor had yet to be decided.

The wine was worth hundreds of thousands of dollars if the value was determined by what people were willing to pay in the name of charity. The fact that money flowed in such abundance proved both the quality of Napa's prime commodity and the generosity of those who appreciated it. The auction might be indebted to the older one in Beaune, but Napa's cardinal event wasn't bound by the commercialism of the Burgundians. No wine prices were set at the auction; rather, it celebrated the valley's extraordinary twentieth-century renaissance, and provided enjoyment for Californians and their friends.

The auction fell during the summer equinox and drew enthusiasts of all sorts, for reasons less rational than sensory. The cast would have surprised the auction's founders just a few years before, and included not just wine fanciers, wine collectors, wine sellers, and wine pretenders but also artists, athletes, restaurateurs, gourmet chefs, computer entrepreneurs, scions from both coasts and abroad, politicians, doctors and lawyers with a vague dream of someday owning a vineyard and producing something of inherent value, promoters, day trippers, hustlers, and hangers-on without qualifications other than disposable income and a nose for celebrity.

The day before the auction, Highway 29 lay beneath hundreds of idling cars, most of the occupants having arrived from the south, drawn by the reputation of the event and by the wineries' dispensing the usual amenities: a glass of wine and a chance to gander. They contended with the cars belonging to the natives — the German imports and restored classics, pickups driven by the vineyard managers and suppliers, and the low-slung sedans of the migrants, with crosses dangling from the mirrors. All vehicles, no matter how recently washed and polished, had a second skin of dust that rose beneath the wheels of the tractors and drifted across the highway. Dust was the great equalizer in Napa. But it was also a measure of your worth: dust on the Mercedes, dust on the boots, meant you belonged to something far from the pavement of San Francisco, Mexico City, Manhattan, and Paris.

No winery, no monument, was to be outdone. They contended for the most imaginative soirees to attract the coveted amateurs of wine, with string quartets, rides in wicker baskets beneath hot-air

balloons that floated overhead like enormous netted melons in bright
pastels, and special tours of cellars dense with French oak, with noted
winemakers offering samples of Cabernet and Chardonnay from the
traditional glass thief.

Luncheon tables arranged in the shade were covered with produce, flowers, even ice sculpture, and on the ice arranged garlands
of seaweed and fresh fare from the docks in San Francisco and beyond: oysters, clams, cracked crabs, and steamed crawfish. Toasts
and testimonials were offered to the past and the future while eyes
strayed to the smoky green of Mount St. Helena beyond stands of
regal palms.

There was no better way to see the valley than from the air. Little
single-engine and larger planes took off in succession from the landing strip atop Howell Mountain, banked to the left to avoid the gliders rising out of Calistoga, and turned and headed down the valley.
The view to the south was instructive as well as moving: two mountain ranges moving apart, between them the precise patchwork of
vineyards punctuated with oaky knolls and bisected by the highway
and the swell of the up-valley towns of St. Helena, Rutherford, Oakville, and Yountville before the sprawling environs of Napa city. Beyond that lay the shimmering disk of San Pablo Bay; the distant
peaks of Diablo and Tamalpais floated on the extreme southern horizon. Below, houses lay in the folds of steep, wooded slopes or slot-
ted among the blocks of vineyard, swimming pools gleaming like
bits on a vast Parcheesi board, at the end of serpentine drives.

No stranger to the valley could have found his way easily to the
gala held at Meadowood the evening before the auction. One narrow
lane off Silverado Trail beckoned toward the fastness of the eastern
hills. Another lane bordered by vineyards let to a gatehouse and entrance to the lush, hidden canyon. Uniformed men touched the
brims of their hats as the first cars slipped past and entered the corridor of shade trees and stone walls. A sentinel pine stood at the edge
of the fairway. The most striking color was white — white clubhouse, white shorts worn by croquet players on a grassy surface as
smooth as a billiard table, the big white tent covering half an acre,
white blouses of waitresses preparing to pour Napa Valley sparkling
wine into eight hundred fluted glasses, a sea of white tablecloths.

Within an hour the lawn was crowded with the inheritors, either
through family or corporate fiat, of the great names of the valley,
and with new arrivals, in a medley of suits and gorgeous gowns.

The sun lost its withering heat to the ambient air, which became a breeze. In a climatic arabesque, the temperature fell while the setting sun retained its edge. Birds streaked low over the fairways. Shadows encroached. The grass acquired a coppery hue at odds with the dark green of the trees. The touch and the taste of white wine — the product of all that photosynthesis — pleasantly stunned and soothed those who had been working all day in the figurative vineyards of public relations. By dinnertime the bracketing hills glowed like mesquite coals.

The guests moved to their assigned places beneath the tent. They talked about the weather and the upcoming harvest, new endeavors, and travel in the interest of selling wine, and only occasionally of divorces and feuds. They were not by nature critical. But areas of deep concern remained: the neo-Prohibition movement that required warning labels on wine bottles, charges abroad of a Disneyland atmosphere that degraded them all, increasingly strident politics in the valley, and the gathering sentiment for restrictions and new taxes on their great industry.

Many of the vintners had the growers on their minds. Contracts had become complicated, with the importance of good grapes gradually outweighing the technological aspects of winemaking. Vintners and vineyardists were theoretically bound together by a common purpose, but any contract could be gotten out of. It was still a matter of a handshake. There had always been a few vintners and a few growers you would not shake hands with; their names didn't have to be spoken. Everyone knew who they were, and open criticism had an ill effect on the valley as a whole. Lately, however, the growers were being mentioned not as contract breakers but as a controlling, maybe dangerous force.

After dinner, couples danced to the rhythm of a big band, strains of another era. Servants struggled to put up plastic sheeting between them and what had become a wind, but the chill was unavoidable. Before midnight most of the guests were leaving, recrossing the lawn, riding back down the drive and out into the lane, the headlights of the cars illuminating rows of vines standing in the star-riddled night.

VI

Noah's Children

36

O NE BRIGHT MORNING in August 1987, as crush was getting under way in Oakville and tourists were gathering on the patio of the Robert Mondavi Winery, near the bronze statue of Saint Francis, a black Cadillac limousine pulled up to the entryway. The license plate read RM WINE. A black chauffeur got out, opened the doors, and stood by as a group approached along the colonnade, their words and laughter animated by the fine day and the prospect of an outing. It was a scene that, with some variations, might have been repeated on dozens of different thresholds in the valley. Some of those who had contributed to its success were now enjoying their final years, while their children and their contemporaries grappled with the problems and put forward their own visions — of wine as a generator of acclaim and fortune or as the staple of the Jeffersonian dream.

This group consisted of Robert Mondavi, his wife, Margrit Biever, and another striking woman named Nina, who had in recent months become the Mondavis' constant companion and a kind of surrogate hostess at many Mondavi events. They had entertained the sommelier of the Ritz hotel in Paris the day before, and were anticipating the arrival of the aging wine memoirist and member of the board of Château Latour, Harry Waugh, but now they were bound for the town of Woodbridge, outside Lodi in the Central Valley, where the Mondavis owned a wine-producing plant for the local grapes, one that put out wines much less expensive than those made at Robert Mondavi Winery in Oakville.

Robert was dressed for a casual, sentimental journey — striped shirt open at the neck and no jacket. He was going back to the neighborhoods he had known as a child; the contrast between what he had been then and what he had become could not have been starker, read

not just in the presence of the limo — one of two identical ones in
the Mondavi fleet — and the setting, but in his self-assurance and
triumphant optimism. There were others in the valley who, after so
many years, had been as successful in their way as Robert Mondavi,
but few who seemed to enjoy it as much.

The women had dressed more formally. Margrit's dress suggested colorful confetti against a black background. It might have
been designed by Miró, with pink shoes to match, a string of very
large imitation pearls, and a pink straw hat. The brim was wide
enough to ward off even the Central Valley sun. At Woodbridge, as
the second-tier Mondavi winery was called, bulk wine was bottled
under the RM label and referred to simply as a "commercial" product. In liquor stores and wine shops it was displayed on shelves different from those on which sat the prestigious Robert Mondavi line.
But the RM wines made money, and occasionally had to be treated
with fanfare.

Nina's business suit was fashionably broad of shoulder, but restrained compared to her usual attire in Oakville. Lodi was, after all,
the *interior*. Nina was a former art student and resident of Long Island
with many years experience abroad. She attended most functions at
the winery and beamed on Robert Mondavi a glorious smile for the
duration of his extemporaneous remarks, which came often. Nina
provided a steady complement of appreciative remarks to Robert and
to Margrit, and a sunny disposition for all events. Her enthusiasm
seemed at times nondiscriminatory, her energy inexhaustible. Some
of the senior officers in the company considered Nina a courtier;
others were quite fond of her.

The three stepped into the limo and the chauffeur, Jim, drove
toward Yountville to pick up a priest, an old friend down from Spo-
kane to bless the grapes at Woodbridge. The priest waited in a gray
mohair suit and a canary-yellow shirt that contrasted with the white
clerical collar. He was accompanied by a heavily dressed middle-aged
woman who had flown down with him. Together they carried a
valise containing holy water and utensils to be used in the blessing,
and a two-hundred-year-old robe from Hawaii made of pineapple
silk and emblazoned with pastels, which Jim carefully stowed in the
trunk.

They headed south, passed Napa city, and turnd east, away from
the sprawling bayside suburbia and into farmland. Mondavi sat on a
jump seat, in a fine mood. The success of the Woodbridge facility

was a personal triumph. In Lodi he had once put in twelve-hour days with his brother, Peter, nailing together wooden boxes for shipping vegetables and fruit, working with great speed. Each time Robert talked about it, it sounded like the first; Margrit had heard the box-nailing story many times.

Robert thought he owed Lodi something. The Woodbridge winery, in addition to making money, had shown the locals that Lodi fruit could be made into acceptable wine, that their fortunes didn't have to be decided by a few industrial wineries like Gallo. "We're bringing prosperity to the northern San Joaquin," Robert told the priest. "Dad would be proud. He came to me when I was a junior at Stanford, you know, and asked me what business I wanted to get into. He said he thought there was a future in table wine. My brother was a few years behind me —"

"The poor thing," said Margrit. "He's always been years behind."

"Now, Margrit . . ." Robert switched abruptly to his "mission," what had become a full-time preoccupation. He was personally going to make the world aware of the historical, cultural, and religious significance of wine, he said. To do that he had enlisted the help of Nina. Several hours a day Nina sat in her stylish office off the lawn and looked at maps of Mesopotamia, ancient Egypt, and Gaul. She perused books like *The Epic of Gilgamesh* and others with references to wine, going as far back as six thousand years, and books about art, of course. She viewed slides — of a Sumerian woman tending a vineyard, of a Roman being flogged with vinewood, of an alabaster relief from Assyria showing a king and queen under a vine pergola, with a kylix, the Greek wine cup, being handed to the king. So much cultural heritage, all of it to be organized by a production company in San Francisco for Robert's presentation, soon to be put on the road, with six projectors for high impact.

"We'll have our own symposium," Robert said. "We'll bring in anthropologists, historians, artists, priests, rabbis, doctors. I'm going to *sell* our mission. Our eighty marketing people are going to get behind it, they'll be our ambassadors."

Nina said, "We're not just selling wine . . ."

"That's right. We're selling American culture! I said that to Reagan at the Alfalfa Dinner, remember? I have a mission. I'm not very articulate but I'll get the idea across."

"Your sincerity and energy are so appealing, Robert," said Nina.

"People know we have integrity. They said we couldn't do it with wine, and we did it. They said we couldn't do it with food, and we did it. We brought in Julia Child. We'll raise the cultural level, too."

"Your foresight is amazing, Robert. You're able to look beyond the bottom line."

Robert wanted the wine industry to *prove* that wine was good for you, but that effort had run into problems. He had invited Ernest Gallo to lunch at Robert's mountaintop home. Ernie came with his wife, his son Joe, the heir apparent, and a bottle of E. & J. Gallo Sauvignon Blanc. Ernie kissed the bottle before pouring everyone a glass. Michael was there, too. Robert brought out a Mondavi Sauvignon Blanc and talked about how it was made. Gallo said, "You're willing to tell anybody what you're doing, aren't you?"

"Yes, if there's an exchange."

Joe Gallo had not said a word. In Mondesto, the Gallo executives trooped in for lunch and Ernie did all the talking and then the executives trooped out again.

Ernie and Julio had fought in the beginning, just like Robert and Peter, and Michael and Tim, but the Gallos had divided up the responsibilities and agreed not to disagree. If a conflict arose between them at a meeting, it was set aside until the next time. If they disagreed again, the same thing happened. After the third disagreement the subject was dropped. That was the way for brothers to get along.

Robert knew Gallo had to approve of the idea of a controlled study of the effects of drinking wine — something that had never been done — or the idea would get nowhere. No one had the Gallo financial clout or the Gallo facilities, including a laboratory where scientists worked on all imaginable manifestations and combinations of wine and spirits. For decades Ernie had sat up in his office in Modesto trying to anticipate every development in the business; the scientists were part of that strategy. Over lunch, Ernie had told Robert that the wine industry couldn't decide what conclusions it wanted and then hire the researchers. The research had to be pure.

There was another problem. The cigarette companies were paying large sums to people claiming to have contracted cancer from cigarette smoke. What if the same thing happened with wine? Already there were warning labels, the first assault. If someone sued Gallo over a perforated liver, that same person might try to subpoena the Gallo research files. If those files contained evidence that a product was harmful and the manufacturer knew it, the research could presumably be turned against him. It could be turned against the industry.

Robert didn't want that and so shifted the mission in the direction of culture, away from science. He wanted the Gallos' help, but Ernie had told him, "History doesn't do a thing for me."

The limo entered the outskirts of Lodi, lined with new bungalows. "This must be the site of the old co-op," Robert said, craning his neck. "It's all been built up. Look, there's the old Del Rio winery, it's closed. I have to find out where we nailed the boxes. Take this road to the right, Jim."

The limo bumped between two weedy lots, Margrit holding her hat in place, the priest's thin hand clutching a black leather handgrip. Nina, in the front seat, exuded interest in Mondavi roots. "This is *fascinating,* Robert."

"My God," he said, "I think I'm lost. Go left, Jim. Here it is. There was an old shed. This is the place Peter and I nailed the celery boxes. If we worked nonstop we could make twelve dollars a day. I studied the nailing motion, you see, and figured out the fastest way to do it . . ."

Nina said, "You're a genius, Robert."

At Woodbridge, a white tent had been erected on the grass in front of the winery, and round tables handsomely set for a sumptuous luncheon. The tables on the tarmac, next to the scales and the big automated crusher, had been spread with white cloths and Woodbridge wines arranged behind banks of glasses, to be used by the employees later, after the blessing. A group of Woodbridge brass stood respectfully in the parking lot, anticipating the limo's arrival. Gondolas full of Sauvignon Blanc were lined up at the crushers. "Look at these grapes," said Robert, leaving the car with a bound. He plucked one from the gondola and ate it. "Boy, they taste good. Gallo used to make wine from these grapes, but they didn't publicize it. We're proud of this area, proud of this fruit."

A long table on the tarmac had been spread with a white cloth, stemmed glasses, and an array of RM wines. Michael and Tim were waiting side by side, hands folded. The three Mondavi men headed for the winery, where the workers had assembled for an inspirational talk while a Mondavi public relations officer helped the priest on with his vestments.

The Mondavis reappeared, trailed by a newspaper reporter. Michael handed out glasses to the assembled workers. Robert stood with his back to the crusher, a glass of Woodbridge Cabernet in hand. "We're learning to harmonize our wine," he told the assembly. "We're making it with better balance, better taste. This wine will invite you to enjoy your meal with it. Let's get Tim in here."

Tim stepped forward. Slight, bearded, fair, he seemed determined to speak as fast as his father; his voice rose with the effort. At the same time he went up on his toes, as if trying to clamber up the slope of Mondavi rhetoric. "We're doing some things different. Leaf removal, for instance. And indirect sunlight, stress management by moisture. It used to be that the norm was to fertilize and irrigate. Well, we're stressing the vines and getting less herbaceous qualities. We're sculpting the wines."

Michael smiled, the picture of corporate assurance in a lavender Ralph Lauren polo shirt, teeth shining beneath the salt-and-pepper mustache, the blue eyes unfocused. "Our objective is simple," Michael said when his time came. "It's to produce the best wine possible. We're making world-class wines here. We're taking what we've learned in Napa and applying it here — a wonderful synergy. Our theme is that making good wine is a skill, and fine wine an art."

If the Woodbridge workers were interested in art, they gave no indication of it. Promotional themes seemed far from the reality of agrarian Lodi and the thousands of tons of grapes that the growers needed to get rid of each year. The fact that the wine was selling pleased them. They liked the taste of it, judging by their interest in the open bottles, and they were accustomed to the triple-barreled barrage of Mondavi information, company objectives, and family accomplishment that never really ended as long as the three men were together.

The priest handed Michael the silver bowl and container of holy water. Tim held the censer. As the blessing was about to start, Robert thought of something else and interrupted. "This is the Mondavis' fiftieth vintage! We started in thirty-seven but then we had a family feud so we've been on our own since sixty-eight. When we came back home a few years ago, our purpose was to make the finest popularly priced wine anywhere in the world."

The priest, diminished by the voluminous robe, began to speak of the harvest in a thin voice while men sat waiting on tractor seats in the line of gondolas. "This tradition goes back to the time of

Noah. One of his first projects after the flood was to plant a vineyard. At harvest time they picked the grapes, blended and blessed
the wine, and returned the best to God. That's what we will do today, symbolically."

Margrit stood close to her husband; Nina shot Robert repeatedly
with her Leica. The sweet smell of incense wafted across the yard.

The priest intoned, "May the many blessings of Almighty God
descend upon this family, and the workers. In the name of the Father,
Son, and Holy Spirit . . ."

Robert started to make another announcement, but Michael said,
"Just a second, Dad." The priest wasn't finished.

He picked a handful of Sauvignon Blanc and squeezed the juice
of the grapes into the holy water, to scatter over the assembly.

"You're a good crusher, Father," said Robert.

The Mondavis spread themselves among the tables, to talk to the
growers who supplied the grapes and to nibble on filet mignon and
sip RM Cabernet. Trucks started up continually in the background,
hauling the gondolas to the crusher. Michael got up and crossed the
tent to his father's table, knelt beside his chair, and told him that
some of the growers were concerned about the Mondavis' purchasing a large vineyard in Tepesque, on the central coast of California
in the Santa Maria range. They wondered if the family intended to
sell Woodbridge and maybe the Oakville facility and move operations down there.

Robert stood up. "I hope you growers understand why we
bought Tepesque," he said. "We're assuring our supply of grapes.
Tell them, Tim."

Tim stood up. "It's an important step forward. We're certainly
not going backward. We're seeking the ultimate, ultimate, ultimate,
from all over California." He bobbed up and down on his toes.
"Woodbridge has just opened our eyes to the possibilities. Let's keep
Tepesque in perspective — we're not going to put anything in the
back seat. We're demanding, but we're loyal . . ."

Nina murmured, "Oh, lovely."

The black limo slipped through the back streets of Lodi. Robert was
distracted by discussion of the wine museum he intended to build;
Nina, in charge of those preparations, was talking about slides of
early California wine artifacts that, as vice president for cultural af-

fairs for the Robert Mondavi Winery, she had put together. She hoped some of the works would be included in the collection that might someday be housed in a building in Oakville.

"I'm going to build a Byzantine chapel," Robert told the priest, who smiled wearily.

"It's going to be fabulous," Nina assured him.

"Turn here, Jim!"

Little bungalows lined the street, pickups and aging sedans in the narrow driveways. Clotheslines strung out back supported overalls and blue cotton shirts; dogs stood on the pavement, barking at the shiny black box with its tinted windows.

"We're looking for Walnut Street," Robert said. "My God, how things have changed. There's the house. The second one from the end. They've cut the tree!"

Jim pulled over and Robert leaped out of the limo in front of a clapboard house with a low roofline and a tiny front porch. The paint on the clapboards had curled under the Lodi sun. Metal awnings shaded windows behind which the blinds were drawn. The grass needed cutting.

"The back yard's much bigger," Robert said. "I had to mow it all the time. There was a chicken coop, too. I had to clean it out once a week. Come on."

The priest, his companion, Margrit, and Nina stepped warily among the tufts of Johnson grass, Margrit holding the brim of her straw hat. Robert led them through the side yard, watched by a man on the porch of a neighboring house, who was gripping a can of beer.

"This was my room." Robert indicated a window with a torn screen. He was surprised to find the chicken coop gone. Nina photographed the area where it had stood, and then photographed Robert, Margrit, and the priest next to the house. The neighbor gathered his courage and came across the yard, adjusting his baseball cap. Before he could speak, Robert told him, "I used to live here, all the way back to 1922. There was a tree right there. I wonder why they cut it down. Do you know? . . . Well, the old neighborhood's changed some, I guess, but then maybe it hasn't. This really is something to see . . ."

They climbed back into the limo. The neighbor's wife and children had come out to stand on the boundary of their yard; they looked at the mean little house that had once belonged to Cesare

Mondavi and then they looked at the limousine. They read the license plate. Others appeared on porches up and down the street, watching the Mondavi party roll away.

Robert said, "The Italian grocery was right over there, and up Sacramento Street was the pool hall where the pickers shot eightball. There's the movie theater, that's School Street." Where the Phantom drove the old Studebaker, emitting stogie haze. "Our second home was right up here, the one with the wisteria."

The second house had shrubbery and little concrete lions on the porch steps.

Margrit said, "You've come a long way."

Robert watched as the town dwindled into countryside and vineyards rose up. "That's Flame Tokay," he said, always instructive. "They're doing head pruning. Now, there used to be a fruit stand right up here. There it is! Pull over, Jim."

He bought melons, peaches, apples. Gallons of cider, bags of tomatoes. Onions. Jim backed the limo up to the stand and opened the trunk; he shoved aside the robe of pineapple silk and the priest's utensils and began to load the cavity with fresh San Joaquin produce. By the time they were done, the back of the Cadillac had sunk several inches.

They barreled toward Napa, into the setting sun. The air conditioner labored away but the car was warm and suffused with the smell of ripening Crenshaws. Robert began to talk again about the mission, the need to awaken the world to the heritage and the social importance of wine. He could devote himself full-time to it now that the winery was being run by Michael and the wine made by Tim.

First the priest fell asleep, then his companion, then Margrit. Her head drooped and she listed to one side, the brim of her straw hat bent on the priest's shoulder.

". . . The beginning of art is when the invisible starts to become visible," Robert went on.

"You're a visionary," said Nina, sitting upright in the front seat, facing straight ahead. Even she appeared to be drifting off.

37

S OMEONE WHO KNEW the valley as well as Robert Mondavi, someone who had arrived, as Mondavi had, on the heels of Prohibition, who had contributed as much to the reputation of Napa wines but who had not, paradoxically, ever put his name on a wine label, was André Tchelistcheff. Now in his eighties, André continued the work that had brought him to America and to the de Latour estate, amidst changes no one, André included, could possibly have foreseen. Napa was big business, not just wine but also tourism and all that came with it — restaurants, hotels, shops, promotional galas, and various diversions — and a new class of vintner who knew little about winemaking and treated the product as an indication of breeding. Increasingly André had doubts about the ability of people in the valley to reconcile their differences and ambitions, and about the valley's capacity to contain them all.

One afternoon in the early summer of 1987 he put on the tuxedo he had bought to attend a dinner at the White House the year before; Dorothy put on a gown. Together they drove across the county line, into Sonoma County. A party was being held at Buena Vista Winery to celebrate its 130th anniversary, and André had agreed to speak after dinner, despite the fact that he was ill. He and Dorothy had been in Italy when he suffered acute stomach distress that was difficult to diagnose. André had endured stomach problems since the ailment that almost killed him as a child. He had gone into the hospital when he got back to Napa, where the doctors couldn't tell him precisely what the problem was, only that his digestive system wasn't working as it should have and that his condition was precarious.

He had to rest every day and eat only selected foods. The doctor would not let him drink wine but would let him smoke a few cigarettes. André had been smoking for almost seventy years, since before the time he had gone to war and been rescued by the Cossack on the frozen battlefield of the Crimea. Nicotine was an integral part of his make-up. Once he had quit smoking and found his tasting skills altered; he had lost his sensory bearings and didn't entirely recover them until he started smoking again.

The throng in the shade of tents and eucalyptus trees at Buena Vista, outside the town of Sonoma, sweated discreetly and sipped sparkling wine and bottled Calistoga water brought round by young women in starched white aprons. The guest list included the most illustrious names in California winemaking, including Ernest Gallo. Buena Vista was now owned by the Moller-Racke family of Germany, distillers of spirits in huge quantities. They had done a masterly job of public relations since coming to California, at great expense. That morning, Buena Vista's sales and marketing force had been taken in hay wagons up onto a hill in Carneros to witness the release of a special wine produced to commemorate the occasion. A plane passed overhead, and five skydivers plummeted earthward, colored smoke streaming from canisters attached to their feet, a magnum of the new wine strapped to each of their chests. They landed in front of the astonished crowd and began to pour the wine, the bottles having already been opened and glasses distributed.

The assembled panel of experts addressed the question: the state of the wine industry in the year 2000. A trends analyst from a marketing research firm had some depressing things to say about Americans' general interest in wine, which seemed to be waning; a doctor predicted that the trend toward abstinence would develop into a powerful social movement. The wine purveyor and critic Gerald Asher commented that Americans will always drink anything that is pink, bubbly, and sweet. Someone else referred to wine coolers as a weapon of assault on the consciousness of lumpen America, forcing it to recognize the existence of wine.

Robert Mondavi, a panelist, spoke of his mission. Wine should be bought naturally by the populace, he said. It was not elitist — a difficult point to make here in the seclusion of Buena Vista's multi-million-dollar renovation, in the company of formal gowns, black ties, and the endless supply of cold sparkling wine.

André had participated in the renaissance of Buena Vista, the dream of old Agoston Haraszthy, importer of the first *Vitis vinifera*

in the late nineteenth century; a Haraszthy had made the first commercial sparkling wine, Eclipse, and the inspiration had carried over
into the present century. André had visited Buena Vista in the 1930s,
when it lay in ruins, a striking contrast to the wall of ivy that towered over the four hundred guests who took their seats and dined on
lobster mousse in tomato saffron sauce and on boned quail in phyllo
pastry. They sipped wine from nine different glasses and were sere-
naded by eight professional players of the German hunting horn,
flown in from Germany and dressed in hunting boots, green frock
coats, white gloves, and tricorn hats with gold piping, to simulate a
musical tradition going back to the Middle Ages.

André stood up and talked about the amazing success of wine in
California, his words coming slowly. Dorothy watched him, on the
edge of her chair. They left right after dinner. A few friends spoke
unhappily of André's condition: the great man was suffering. Some
didn't expect him to last the year.

Two months later, the harvest was well under way. In the early
morning, low-slung sedans lined the service road beside the Silverado Trail, their headlights illuminating dust drifting from beneath
the wheels of tractors pulling empty gondolas. The headlights died
and the darkness filled with staccato Spanish — shouts, songs, laughter,
imprecations. Men ran through the vineyard here just as they did all
over the valley, in a medley of shirts, jackets, hats, and bandannas,
plastic bins in hand. They waded into the vines with short, curved
knives with serrated blades, and their spoils began to collide with the
bottoms of the bins in a ragged drumbeat.

Within minutes the bins were being raced to the gondolas and the
grapes dumped. By full light the tractors were backed into the ocean
of vines and the pickers had almost disappeared. The slowest of them
plucked leaves out of the loads. By noon, picking was over and the
men back in the shadows of eucalyptus along the river or outside the
barracks of the bigger wineries, drinking beer, working on cars. The
coolness, the lavender sky streaked with clouds, fooled no one: it
was going to be another hot day in the valley.

In the wineries, the grapes were being crushed and wine made. This
was André's busiest time of the year. He parked his old yellow Dat-
sun roadster in the shade of a eucalyptus tree outside the Niebaum-
Coppola winery and carried his black enologist's case across the

driveway and into what had once been Captain Niebaum's stable. André inhaled the pleasant, heady aroma of fermenting Merlot. The winemaker, Steve Beresini, greeted André on his first stop on one of the busiest days of the harvest season.

"I want to smell the Cabernet Franc," André said.

Beresini obliged, drawing off a glass from the tank. He was in his thirties, and yet André seemed almost as young, a diminutive figure in a blue V-neck sweater and khakis, with a delicate step and deferential air. Only his face revealed his great age. He prized the Cabernet Franc, an important ingredient in the Rubicon blend. It had been innoculated with a yeast culture to stimulate malolactic fermentation, which transformed malic acid into softer lactic acid and made the resulting wine more supple. Malolactic was easily interrupted by too much heat.

He sat the black case on a bench. The handle was broken, mended with cord. Made in 1910, purchased secondhand in 1940, and carried through the portals of many wineries, the case contained the tools of the itinerant wine consultant: Bunsen burner, glass slides, a microscope wrapped in an old towel. André poured some alcohol into the burner and lit it. He sterilized a slide by passing it over the flame. "It's a very poor burner," he said apologetically.

He placed a drop of the Cabernet Franc on the slide and slipped it under the scope. What he saw when he peered through the lenses were little black dots, malolactic cells. The microscope had a magnification of only 650 and to see the cells clearly he needed 1,000. Pasteur had worked with only about 450, the maximum in those days. André said, "It's good."

He smelled the wine and added a guttural "Yah," more for emphasis than resignation. He could tell the grapes had gotten too hot on the vine. They were "jammy." The vineyards at Niebaum-Coppola received no irrigation, and since the soil was shallow, the vines got overstressed in the heat and the droughtiness. It was dangerous, but that same deprivation, that struggle to survive, produced intense, flavorful wines.

He smelled the Chardonnay after Beresini drew it from a barrel with a wine thief. "Smells good," André said. But they couldn't grow decent Chardonnay here. Too hot. The best place was still Carneros.

He put some wine on a slide, and the slide under the microscope. "Anything growing in there?" Beresini asked.

André nodded. He checked the Chardonnay's fermentation chart. Black marks showed declining sugar, red marks rising temperature. Everything was fine.

"Supposed to go to ninety again today," said Beresini. "We need to check the Zinfandel. I'll tell Rafael."

André didn't care for Zinfandel. It wasn't a serious grape. He shook hands with the winemaker and walked slowly back into the sunlight.

He drove out the lane, past Inglenook and then past the little schoolhouse where Dimitri had gone when the Tchelistcheffs moved to Rutherford in 1938. Fifteen students, two teachers. It seemed like yesterday. He remembered things in a rush: de Latour riding up from the city in a big black Cadillac, John Daniel flying over in his plane. Many other people younger than André, many long gone. His friend Marquis de Pins had been seriously ill and insisted on being taken to France. Hélène had traveled with him and placed him in the American hospital in Paris, where the marquis demanded to be taken on to the château, Montbrun. Hélène would not let him be delivered in an ambulance. She hired a limousine and propped the marquis up so he could arrive in the proper style. He died shortly thereafter.

Hélène had never gotten over the sale of Beaulieu. For a year she couldn't bear to visit the winery. After her death André had come to see clearly the futility of possessions. She spent her adult life worrying about inconsequential bits and pieces of the past and the disposition of the most minute portions of her inheritance. All for nothing. André was glad that he had lived an unencumbered life. He, probably the most enduring person in the California vineyard, had never bothered to start a wine cellar. He had none of the great BV Pinot Noirs from the forties, none of the old Georges de Latour Private Reserves, and it didn't bother him at all. The bottles of wine people gave to him and Dorothy they kept under their bed.

He stopped by a new winery just off Highway 29, owned by one of the Swanson heirs. The young winemaker stood outside, shirtless, directing the Australian cellar rat in the delicate process of dumping a gondola loaded with Chardonnay into the shiny new crusher. "See that brownish tinge?" André asked him. "The French dream about such color."

He and the winemaker discussed the balance of the fermentation. The pH was too high, André said, and advised adding tartaric acid. That is how they did it in California, although the French scoffed at the practice. The French didn't scoff at adding sugar, however, because they had to in order to get their wine's alcohol level up. And the Californians scoffed at that.

The winemaker, just out of school, wanted to ferment the Chardonnay in new, 130-gallon puncheons of Allier oak, medium toast. Until recently all the barrels used in the valley were fired and assembled in France, but now there was a good cooper in Napa city and vintners were having their barrels custom-charred. "It will be too strong," André told him. "The sap will make the wine bitter. First fill the barrels with hot water and rock salt, twenty pounds per thousand gallons. Leave it in for two days."

"I'll do what you say," the young man said, but he was skeptical. The barrels cost $600 apiece and he wanted to get as much flavor out of them as possible. Americans tended to make wine that was too flavorful, André thought, wine that did not invite people to drink it. André knew it was important to let the young have their enthusiasms but he could not let them make mistakes. There were so many winemakers about now, seeking to make their mark, wanting someday to own their own wineries; all but a very few would spend their lives working for someone else.

On Rutherford Cross Road he passed another new winery, this one without a roof but already in operation. Everyone was in such a hurry, and 20 percent of the small wineries operating on the edge of bankruptcy. The competition was incredible, but so were the opportunities. So much depended on public relations now. Promotion. No more honest discussion of the shortcomings of individual vintages and vineyards. No real criticism, just marketing. What André's friend Jack Davies called bullshitting.

André remembered when the Davieses arrived in the valley more than twenty years before, their enthusiasm and determination. The astounding success of Schramsberg had been earned. Recently Jack had telephoned André to inquire about his health, as so many people had, and André asked what he had been doing lately. Just bullshitting, Jack said.

André had one more stop that morning before returning home to sleep. Conn Creek, on the Silverado Trail, was owned now by a conglomerate but still producing good Cabernet Sauvignon. The winemaker and his assistant were waiting for him. They all went through the cellar, the assistant knocking the bungs out of the barrels and all three of them sampling. Of the young Chardonnay, the winemaker said, "This has a banana quality."

"Also white sage," said André, "like a Sancerre."

They tasted a Cabernet from Conn Creek's west-facing, early-ripening vineyard, fermenting on the skins for ten days. The winemaker said, "Very minty."

"Good color," said André, tilting the glass against the light. "The malolactic's in that silkiness. Very concentrated." He poured the wine into a bucket and thrust his nose into the empty glass. "That's what Cabernet should smell like — cherries."

They moved on to the Zinfandel. André took a single whiff of his sample. "Onions," he said, pronouncing it *oinyons*.

"Peppery," said the winemaker. "Loads of blackberry and cassis. Even strawberries."

"Oinyons," André repeated.

The winemaker laughed. "Can't you think of anything nice to say about Zinfandel?"

Older samples of Cabernet and Chardonnay sat in bottles on the patio. They tasted them in the sunlight, overlooking the Silverado Trail and the mountains. The young men spat over the wall into the shrubs, but André carefully expelled each mouthful into the little plastic bucket. He particularly liked the '85 Merlot, which contained 10 percent Cabernet Sauvignon. "Beautiful spine from the Cabernet," he told them. "Very good, very tender. It has oak, but just as a single ingredient. Fantastic."

André smoothed his hair and gazed up toward the Auberge de Soleil across the Silverado Trail. The hotel was expanding; below, Round Hill's winery was going up. "So many things being built," he said. "Soon we won't be able to move."

Dagmar de Pins Sullivan and her husband, Walter, spent much of the year in France, at her late father's estate, Montbrun. When in the valley they stayed in their house on the old de Latour estate, a modest place with redwood shingles similar to the other outbuildings. The cottage was lavishly done inside, however, with French provincial furniture, paintings, and art books by the dozen arranged in stacks on the tables, in shadows cast by the deep eaves. The main house across the drive was no longer lived in, and used only for special events, like the cooking school that Dagmar conducted a month or two a year, and for weddings and receptions.

Few people knew how Dagmar hated that. Money brought in by leasing the house for a few hours helped offset the costs of what was still a large estate. Beaulieu might no longer belong to the family, but the extensive vineyards and the gardens did, and had to be maintained. The people who temporarily rented the big house usually had little idea of what it represented; they didn't know that Georges de Latour, Dagmar's grandfather, created what was in his time Napa's most successful château. They could be very indiscreet. The doors to the interior rooms had to be locked or else people used the beds.

Dagmar had never really gotten over the sale of the winery to Heublein, agreed to by her mother and orchestrated by Walter. Sometimes when she looked at him she got mad all over again.

They sat drinking coffee in the living room of the cottage when Dagmar saw a stretch limousine creep across the gravel drive. She called in the groundskeeper. "Who are those people?" she asked.

"Diamond and Angel," said the groundskeeper.

"Diamond and Angel?"

"Rock musicians. They're getting married." He grinned, and added, "He's got a diamond in his ear."

Dagmar didn't say anything until the groundskeeper was gone. Then she turned and glared at Walter, who was reading. "Well," she said, "I never thought we'd come to that."

38

ROBIN RETURNED to Napa from a trip to Ireland in February 1988 to find her desk at Sunny St. Helena piled with directives. The little house next to the railroad tracks provided office space until the big house behind the winery could be renovated. As the troubleshooter for Sunny, and as Bill Harlan's representative in the valley (but no longer at Meadowood), Robin's tasks were unrelenting, if sometimes vague. In addition to the management of Sunny St. Helena, she had the tiny custom-crush operation, Merryvale, to worry about. Its wine was made from purchased grapes, with a hired winemaking consultant and rented space in another winery.

Harlan and his partners had various other interests around the valley, among them the building housing a smart new restaurant, Tra Vigne, and the ongoing plan for developing the southern end of the city of St. Helena, complete with his idea of a cameo rendition of professional valley life. Harlan was trying to raise money and putting his plans through the various governmental hoops. He faulted her decisions almost daily because he was feeling so much pressure. There was a saying among the office staff that you could tell what sort of day it had been by the number of times Bill Harlan made Robin Lail cry.

Yet it was Bill Harlan who had told her to stop acting like an administrative assistant in the first place and start being an executive. It was Harlan who had dragged her into the action, and for that she would always be grateful. She felt foolish, getting tearful, but understood why she did. It wasn't just the stress at Sunny St. Helena but also that Dominus was soon to be released. Everything she had attempted in her family's name rode on the reception of this new venture, of which she was a joint owner. The John Daniel Society would receive international attention and, more importantly, her father's legacy would emerge in the concrete form of wine, bottle, and vintage.

There were so many things to do to make sure that turned out right. And Robin's relations with Christian Moueix were not what they had once been. In the beginning they had counted 150 happy coincidences that had brought them into partnership; he had called Napanook vineyard "a jewel box, the best vineyard I had seen in California. I had never had such a feeling — a promised land!"

Recently Christian had sounded less sure of all that. Dominus's agricultural costs, including crop thinning and the washing of grapes before harvest, were twice the average in Napa. Pétrus's winemaker, Jean-Claude Berrouet, also flew regularly to Napa to give advice, which often did not conform to local conventional wisdom. And negotiations among Robin, Marky, their husbands, and Christian over winery and label design, marketing, and the very important element of publicity had taken its toll.

Christian could be a difficult interview. Journalists were generally enamored of the heir to Château Pétrus, but they tended to interrogate, and Christian didn't like direct questions. He considered himself a kind of mystic but had trouble explaining exactly what sort of mystic. He quoted great thinkers but was not so forthcoming with ordinary things. Inquiries about his family and his decision to invest in Napa annoyed Christian. Asked by a journalist over lunch at the Meadowood Grill if he had considered other vineyards in Calfornia before choosing Napanook, Christian responded, "This question is too precise for such a day," gesturing toward the blemishless California sky, "so early in the meeting. I always try to be honest but, you see, sometimes there is more than one truth. As Pirandello wrote . . ."

Finally he said, "Yes and no."

Robin was good with the press and with industry groups. But when she asked to be allowed to appear before a meeting in Dallas of Chateau and Estates, the marketing firm handling Dominus, Christian said the questions would be too technical for her to answer. "I run two wineries on a daily basis," Robin told him. "I know the technical stuff. And I'm a good speaker."

In the end, no one went to Dallas. Dominus's manager in Napa, a transplanted New Yorker named Daniel Baron, spoke to a similar group in Phoenix. Robin wondered if the decision had more to do with the fact that she was a woman than with her own ability to handle herself. Whenever she had a disagreement with Baron, Christian sided with him. Whenever she had a disagreement with Christian, Robin's brother-in-law, Jim Smith, tended to side with Christian. Marky had left most of the decisions up to her husband, and Robin found herself the only woman among strong-willed males.

The irony was that John Daniel would likely have behaved in the same way. Wine was a man's business in his day and remained one into the new age. While male bastions elsewhere collapsed thunderously, in the wine business they were subsiding with the speed of ivy-covered ruins. In the late sixties, when it all began, if a woman was seen in a winery, it was usually behind a typewriter. A few got behind sales counters, then into the labs. The most famous woman winemaker was probably Mary Ann Graf, or her successor at Simi, Zelma Long. Then there was Jill Davis at Buena Vista, Cathy Corison at Chappellet, and Dawnine Dyer at Domaine Chandon. But most of the winemakers were men, as well as the presidents. Eugenia Keegan, president of Château Bouchaine, and Carolyn Martini, president of the Louis M. Martini Winery, were exceptions. The same could be said of Eileen Crane, a former food nutritionist and social worker who had overseen the design and construction of two big wineries, Gloria Ferrer Caves, in Sonoma, and the latest French enterprise, Domaine Carneros, an $11 million joint venture of Taittinger of Champagne and the Kobrand Corporation that included a grandiose château rising from a sheep pasture.

Other women worked relentlessly in various jobs, willing to let men have the glory. The number of wineries whose de facto leadership was provided by wives of the owners, for instance, would have surprised a lot of people. Women were generally better at marketing and public relations than the men, and often at management, but recognition was spotty, and grudging.

A week later she drove down to Napanook. A cool wind blew off the Mayacamas but the sun shone brightly. There was no Dominus winery yet — the wine was made at Rombauer, the custom crusher — just the old shed used as an office, and vineyards sloping gently up toward the foothills. Her mother had tried to sell them after John Daniel's death, and Robin had forced the bank to put Napanook in the estate. Otherwise she and Marky would have lost it. Now, two weeks before the release of Dominus, she found herself wondering why she had so little control over it.

As she walked with Baron, the manager, between the vines and listened to his explication of plantings, pruning, and ground water, she remembered walking there with her father, at the end. John Daniel had approved of it all: the vines planted seven by seven feet, the head pruning, the St. George clone that had a long taproot ideally suited to conditions at Napanook. Looking up the valley, Robin could see Mount St. John and the high meadow behind Inglenook.

On the way back to her car, Robin stopped by Baron's office, where she spotted a cardboard box full of old photos and family documents. It was not the sort of thing she wanted lying around, and gathered up the box to take with her. Baron insisted on inspecting it first. Robin was used to people pawing over Niebaum and Daniel artifacts, a practice going back to the sale to United Vintners and Heublein, and so said nothing to this New Yorker who seemed unaware that a culture had existed in Napa before he and Christian Moueix arrived.

On the way home she touched the brakes and turned left at Whitehall Lane. She circled the old landing strip, Rutherford International, which still belonged to the family and had very little use other than for the yearly Chili Ball. The tattered windsock hung limply. Robin stopped at the base of a wooded rise beyond it, known as Mole Hill, the inspiration behind her father's droll little wine, Mole Hill Red ("A wine you'll gopher"). This was the site for a house she and her husband had been planning for years while living in St. Helena. A bulldozer had already cleared an entrance to the property, and when she and Jon had enough money the house would go up. The view would include the clay flats where her father had set down his single-engine plane more times than she could count.

A clutch of Swiss journalists slung with cameras emerged from the front door of the old Niebaum house, notebooks in hand. Eleanor Coppola escorted them out to the driveway, where her husband bade them goodbye and watched them pile back into their minivan. He took a few snaps with his new Fuji camera. Francis had shaved his beard ten days before and then let it grow again; his head looked similarly skinned. In a khaki safari suit that obscured his pendulous stomach he looked more like a deep-sea fishing captain than a movie director.

"They asked me about the mechanics of filming," he told Eleanor, his voice after years of living in California still riven with the guttural vowels of suburban New York. "That's the thing about journalists. They challenge you, and then you have to define something."

His teenage daughter, Sofia, and a friend emerged from the house, followed by a nurse holding a baby girl, the daughter of the late Gian-Carlo. Her name was Gian-Carla. Someone had placed a red dot on her forehead, and Francis touched her, and said affectionately, "A little Hari Krishna."

It was evening. The nurse and Eleanor took the child back inside, and Sofia and her friend rode off in a Saab convertible, leaving Francis under the big oak. The massive limbs had been wired up after one fell on a Rolls-Royce. He walked down the driveway and across Navalle Creek to his study. The little house was filled with the aids to writing: desk, pads, pens, a computer, telephones, clocks, radios, a television set, and various electronic devices for diverting a man who considered himself something of an inventor. The house had been many things over the years, including a home for Rafael Rodriguez, but now it was a sanctuary. Francis's most recent movie, *Tucker: The Man and His Dream,* was in the can. He was telling people it would be his last, but he knew it wouldn't be. *Tucker* was based on the life of the brilliant, unorthodox inventor of a new automobile and about the establishment's attempts to bring him down. Inevitably the critics would compare Tucker's career with Coppola's. He kept two of Tucker's creations under tarps on the property.

He put on a straw boater, part of the zany collection of improbables. He could see what was left of the old meadow, ripped and fertilized in preparation for planting. Cabernet Sauvignon, Cabernet Franc, and Merlot — the Rubicon blend — would soon go in there. The vineyard would be named for Gian-Carlo. Watching the land being plowed the month before, Francis had been amazed that men could withstand such dust. The vineyard would outlast him and serve as a memorial for his son. Francis also planned to build a little house for Sofia on the western rise, close to Inglenook's winery, where the old water tower now stood. Eventually the Niebaum-Coppola Estate would produce a sparkling wine named after his daughter.

He planned to set up an irrevocable trust so the property could never again be borrowed against and consequently lost. Someone in the family would have to carry on. Maybe it would be his granddaughter. In fifty years, Francis often told people, Rubicon could be the greatest wine in America.

Gian-Carlo's death had reminded him of his own mortality. There were two books being written about Francis; he had one of the manuscripts on his desk. In the old days he wouldn't have cared what the author said, but lately he wanted the record set straight. He began to read, and correct: his son had been twenty-two when he was killed, not twenty-three. Francis's mother had *not* been an Italian actress. His wife was *not* an Irish actress . . .

A cool breeze came up. The heat of the sun lingered in the room. He could hear the sound of birds preparing for the night. He couldn't see the big house but he could see the creek bank that Niebaum had so elaborately buttressed with coolie labor and mountain stones. Before, it had been quite wild along Navalle, and still was, back in the canyon. People had lived here for thousands of years, before the Romans, before the Greeks . . .

The release of Dominus in San Francisco was a success; it should have been, given the elaborate arrangements. Christian gave a party in Napa as well, and then flew on to Japan. Robin held another party, at Meadowood — paid for with her own money — and invited all the people Christian had cut from her original guest list.

In some ways the release of Dominus in New York was more important. Californians could be counted on to support California wine, but the East Coast was really an extension of France in the view of many California vintners. People there bought much more European than domestic wine; the arena was larger and the stakes were higher. Robin wanted to plan the New York event, but that duty had gone to Chateau and Estates.

The day before she left, Harlan thrust his head into her office. He said, "Well, have a good time." She wondered if he meant it.

She and Jon flew east. The night before the party at Four Seasons they attended a champagne reception at Seagram's townhouse and attended the opening of *A Walk in the Woods* with the other celebrants. The party moved to Sardi's, where it was joined by James Taylor, Roger Mudd, and Morley Safer, then moved on to the Rainbow Room for dancing.

The following evening Robin wore a black dress to Four Seasons. Marky wore red, a nice counterpoint. They sat at separate tables and sipped Perrier-Jouët poured from painted bottles and watched Christian, sitting next to Edgar Bronfman, officiate. Christian was the epitome of Gallic charm in his double-breasted pin-striped suit and the carefully hedged seven-day growth of beard, smiling steadily. The wine writers scattered among the tables clearly liked the '84 Dominus offered for their perusal. The '83 was being held back a year because it was too tannic. Robert Parker, who had also tasted the '85 and '86, would describe Dominus in *The Wine Advocate* as having "the ability to be California's most profoundly complex wine."

Chateau and Estates, which also handled Pétrus, would have no trouble selling all that Christian could produce at $38 a bottle, less than Opus One at its release but still a high price for a California Cabernet. Dominus had smaller, roughly equal percentages of Merlot and Cabernet Franc, and was made in the restrained Bordelais style. Almost all of it had already been spoken for.

Missing from the crowd was Larry Rivers, the artist who had designed the label for Dominus. He had been invited but no one had really expected him to show up. The label itself, a sketch of Christian seated in a chair, legs crossed, was bound to cause comment, not all of it favorable. In the beginning Christian had expressed nervousness about even allowing his initials to appear on the foil. That had progressed to the possibility of his signing the label, and from there to an artist's rendition of his likeness. Now a different famous artist was to be commissioned to portray Christian for each successive vintage. Some people thought it a clever idea and a public relations coup, others that it was the ultimate in hubris. Christian had one-upped Rothschild and Mondavi, whose Opus One label had silhouettes of the two men but not an annual reinterpretation of their personas.

The artist might be missing, but the architect of the future Dominus winery was represented. I. M. Pei, more renowned even than Larry Rivers, had been asked to come up with some design suggestions after Christian had looked at the competition in the valley. He considered obvious wine manufacturing plants, however original in appearance, to be gross; he hated Clos Pegase. But I. M. Pei was very expensive, and Robin questioned such extravagance.

During dinner the young architect from the firm, seated at Marky's table, spoke *sotto voce* about the prospective Dominus winery. "To put the winery in the middle of the vineyard is to recognize the role of agriculture. Crush, fermentation, bottling, and aging must all be celebrated for their primary purpose. We haven't yet decided how to celebrate the bottling line. And storage doesn't have the same spirituality as wood aging. . . ."

Christian stood up to speak. Slipping easily from English to French and back again, he thanked the people involved in Dominus in chronological order: first Robert Mondavi, then Daniel Baron, and *then* Robin. She heard him say, "One of the great opportunities of my life was to meet her at Mondavi's home. In the next few days we found the basis for our venture. She is dedicated to her father's memory. . . . Then I met Marky Smith, a poetess, so we established a family venture. We had some problems, as in any family. . . ."

The applause, although she expected it, caught Robin by surprise. This was a triumph, in a way the culmination of everything she had set out to do, however inchoate that notion, seventeen years before. She felt proud, grateful — and still on the periphery.

39

THE GAINS MADE by Robert Mondavi and the big corporations like Heublein, Nestlé, and Seagram, even the accomplishments of as disparate people as André Tchelistcheff and Robin Lail, had been exacted at a price. What they represented was of interest and value, but life could not return to the idyll of a few decades before. Every new arrival and every new edifice had to match, or outdo, what had gone before.

Atlas Peak looked more like Wyoming than Napa: mountainous, arid, with overhanging sandstone hoodoos. A few scruffy manmade structures sat randomly in a mostly empty landscape. The idea of growing grapes there would not have occurred to the early settlers, even to those who had set redwood stakes on the steep slopes of the Mayacamas across the valley. The mountains on this, the eastern side, known by various names, had less moisture and less relief from the sun and cold and were linked to the world by a single tortuous road.

Atlas Peak had been the inspiration of William Hill, vintner, manager by objective, and dealer in vineyard real estate with connections up and down the West Coast and abroad. Hill had sold the crucial piece of Diamond Mountain to Coca-Cola — before Coca-Cola sold out to Seagram — and taken the money with him across the valley, and south, to buy these 1,300 high acres. People thought he had overreached this time. There wasn't even enough water on Atlas Peak for the rattlesnakes.

The only way you could see it properly was from an airplane. Atlas Peak had been a cattle spread run by an absentee Central Valley rancher. Christian Brothers had considered buying it back in the sixties but concluded that it was frost-prone and too droughty. Hill had a different impression: the soil had to be good because of the size of the few trees — madroña, oak, and pine — in the pockets. Where trees would grow, so would vines.

Moisture was the key to making it on Atlas Peak. Solid-set sprinklers had been perfected, little nozzles capable of spraying the frost-threatened grapes with water; the water then froze on the bunches and, paradoxically, kept some heat inside and the grapes themselves from freezing. It was the best frost fighter available, but it required a lot of water.

First Hill had a lake built on the saddle between two slopes to collect run-off, and a deep channel carved down the little sloping valley with drain lines feeding off it. At the bottom was another artificial lake with a sump pump that would move the unused water back up to the top lake. It could be recirculated again, for irrigation or frost protection. Nothing was wasted, but the process was expensive. Land and the initial development cost Hill and his partners about $6 million, and then an unexpected thing happened: in 1984 the Bank of America pulled the plug on the project.

The bank was in trouble with bad energy loans and loans to Third World countries, and people like Hill were the casualties, not the big old borrowers like the Mondavis. Development loans in the wine business were always short-term, but there was a gentleman's agreement that they wouldn't be called. So much for gentlemen. The bank gave him four months to scrape up $1.5 million, and as soon as he handed over the check, told him he owed another $4.5 million.

He heard that Whitbread, the giant British brewer, was searching for a property in California. Whitbread North America owned the Buckingham Wile Company, and its marketer, Julius Wile Sons & Company, handled the wines of Piero Antinori, of Tuscany, and those of the champagne house of Bollinger. They all wanted into the Golden State — two more "class" foreigners (Bollinger and Antinori) and one more foreign moneybags (Whitbread). Hill told them he had 600 prime vineyard acres out of a total of 1,300 and that it was very difficult, almost impossible, to put together such a large, contiguous package in Napa Valley. This one had spectacular views, and he was offering it for the very reasonable price of $11.5 million.

Dick Peterson waited for his visitor inside a large, ornate metal gate that opened by remote control. Outside lay the wilds of Soda Canyon and Atlas Peak, and some enemies. Inside lay the rudiments of what resembled an armored invasion or a strip mine. The particulars of the development were kept close to the corporate vest of Whitbread and its troubleshooter, Peterson, who already had problems with the locals and didn't want them compounded. Some people living on Atlas Peak and along Soda Canyon Road objected to the huge machines rumbling past, the clouds of dust, the dynamite blasts, and the prospect of someday meeting a semi loaded with wine and out of control on those steep, serpentine loops.

Never had a job made Peterson so happy, and he had had many — with Gallo (Champion's Belt), Beaulieu, Heublein, Coca-Cola, Seagram. That was all behind him now. He had left Monterey Vineyards for a final triumph in Napa, on Atlas Peak, one that would take a decade to accomplish and would finally put a wine for which he was responsible among the stars. Peterson was accustomed to corporations that looked only three months down the road. But the Whitbread group understood long-range planning — a product of tradition. Whitbread had been established in 1742, which made it older than the United States. The Antinori estate was more than six hundred years old. Bollinger had been around for a century and a half, at least. A little time didn't bother Whitbread. It didn't expect Atlas Peak, for instance, to turn a profit for two hundred years. Now *that* was vision.

Whitbread also knew how to trust an expert in the field. The corporation let Peterson have his head. He had found his undergraduate engineering study of particular value, considering the scale of this operation and the sheer mass of earth that needed moving. He dressed more like a construction foreman than a winemaker: chinos, sturdy shoes, a hard hat in the back of his dusty station wagon, a beeper on his belt. The winemaking would come later.

A car pulled up on the other side of the gate. The driver seemed surprised to find such a fancy barrier in the middle of wild country. After some difficulty he got it to open and quickly drove through before the gate closed again. Peterson waved him over to his dusty station wagon, and together they set off on the tour. Peterson loved to give it to visiting corporation brass, friends, even the occasional journalist. He would have given more tours, but getting people to drive the miles up twisting Soda Canyon Road was not easy.

"Those are Dio Cats up there," Peterson said, pushing a large palm in the direction of the southern hills, where rose the clouds of dust. "This is a moonscape, but we're ripping it. We'll put terraces in there. . . . We'll fill that canyon with rocks the size of Volkswagens, then cover it up with some muck from the caves we're digging over there. . . . We're creating a swale here. We'll have about $30 million in it when we're through."

Masked men drove big dirt haulers past them, the crash of metal echoing over the air conditioner.

"The vineyard will cost about thirty thousand dollars an acre to develop. That may seem expensive, but if you want five hundred acres of vines now in Napa Valley, you have to create it. If we depended on private contractors, this would *really* cost a fortune. . . .

"Now this reservoir has a three-year supply of water just from run-off. Nine hundred and sixty acre-feet. We bought used equipment and built it ourselves."

Geometrically precise slopes ran down to brown water; a sailboat had been pulled up onto the muddy bank, tiny in the distance. "We bought the sailboat at an auction. We're bringing up some sand from Monterey. It'll be forty-four feet deep when we're done. . . .

"We built our own caves . . . I went to England, to a coal mine, watched how those machines worked, and bought one. Now we're digging our own thirty-thousand-square-foot cave."

They went up to see. A D5 Cat with a rotary drill hummed away, providing earth for the two muck trucks. Peterson led his visitor into the maze of tunnels that rang with the sound of heavy machinery. He had kept the walls rough on purpose — more natural looking. The floors were poured concrete. A laser beam had been used to guide the operators digging into the rock; when the tunnels broke through and met one another, they were never off by more than a couple of inches. Fifteen-foot steel bolts had been sunk into the rock face so it wouldn't crack. Epoxy plugs, Peterson said, held the bolts in place. "Twenty thousand pounds of pressure on the screw. Then we put Shotcrete on the face, an engineering marvel."

No other winemaker could have done what he was doing. You had to be confident with machines, for one thing. He had bought an extra Euclid earth mover, for instance, just to cannibalize, knowing how expensive new parts were. He understood foot-pounds of pressure, horsepower, hauling capacity, wattage, tensile strength. . .

"These walls were formed by two distinct mud flows," he went on, "moving ahead of the volcanic action." The efficiency of rock sorters, the power of pumps, the reach of short wave, the vagaries of dynamite. Peterson was so enthusiastic that he had insisted his new wife come up and get involved. She had told him, "I don't like loud noises," so he had parked the station wagon far enough away, with a view of the hoodoos beyond the blasting, and told her about rock displacement, muck yields, Shotcrete. This might not be a winemaker's dream, he had said, but it sure is an engineer's.

There had been some problems. The neighbors were suing Whitbread for refusing to do an environmental impact study. They had banded together and enlisted the aid of Vic Fershko, and tied up Whitbread in court. Peterson considered Fershko and his friends and clients to be troublemakers.

"We're putting in the irrigation pipes with a slip plow," Peterson continued. "It's really neat. We have a tractor with a boom that extends over six rows, with a hydraulic hose and an auger. Just about as production line as you can get. Then there's a guy on a Honda laying out the pipe, and another guy punching the holes and snapping in the emitters. Six acres a day, slickest thing you've ever seen."

The visitor asked what kind of wine Peterson intended to make, to pay for all this. Looking straight ahead, Peterson answered, "It isn't enough nowadays to have good wine. It has to be unique. We're going to have Cabernet, but we're going to put some Sangiovese in, too."

Sangiovese went into some fine Italian wines, as well as some distinctly ordinary ones. The Italian connection. Antinori had sent him five hundred olive trees, which were being planted at the end of every other row of vines. Symbolism. If Peterson had his way, an olive leaf would also appear on the label.

"This grabs my spirit of pioneership," he added. He would make wine better than Beaulieu's, better than anything his last nemesis, Seagram, could come up with. "I just have to make this sucker work."

The party Seagram threw the following spring to honor its latest vineyard acquisition, in Carneros, impressed even those up-valley people accustomed to such celebrations. They were greeted by the sight of wind surfers, driven across artificial Winery Lake by bay breezes in their pastel sails, and by Polynesian dancers on the island, under palms, swaying in time with the music, their many-colored lavalavas bright in the setting sun. Silhouettes of cows, painted orange and purple with green and blue polka dots, grazed on the bank.

There was a white tent containing beautiful watercolors by the wife of the vineyard's previous owner, and a barge with thick hawsers for railings, where Domaine Mumm sparkling wine was offered before dinner, and a skein of rose blossoms set adrift on the water.

The host, René di Rosa, wore a gorilla suit. He and his wife, Veronica, owned Winery Lake and the house above it, stuffed with contemporary Bay Area art, but no longer the vineyard of the same name. Di Rosa planned to turn the house into a museum so that the public could see such famous works as the "Rhinoceros Car" and other life-size sculpture and cultural accretions he kept in the basement, which he planned to spill out over the lawn and onto the lake and even *into* the lake. He would be able to pay for it all because Seagram had just given him more than $8 million for 170 planted acres.

Di Rosa had come to Carneros, southern Napa, in the sixties to escape San Francisco and the occasional demands of daily journalism. He had inherited money and had the desire, like several others who had gravitated to the valley, to write a novel. Only after he had bought an overgrazed sheep ranch did he realize that he could not write a convincing novel — shades of Lee Stewart at Souverain Cellars — and so cast around for some other pastime. Grapes were a possibility. Carneros was windy, foggy, or both, and cool, and produced the best Chardonnay and Pinot Noir in the valley, which was a general realization that dawned long years after Louis Michael Martini had planted there and Beaulieu, Buena Vista — and René di Rosa — followed.

He was one of the first Napa Valley growers to insist that his vineyard name appear on the label of the wines into which his grapes went. Mondavi and some other vintners obliged. Di Rosa's grape prices, and the reputation of his vineyard, rose steadily, and twenty years later Winery Lake Vineyard was recognized as a very good one. The sum of $8 million worked out to almost $50,000 an acre, a record. But some time after the sale had gone through, di Rosa stood at the window of his art-choked house, looking out at the vines with tears in his eyes, and told a friend, "They stole it."

Sam Bronfman, the man who bought Winery Lake Vineyard, sat at the head table in his blue blazer. The thick glasses and mustache added to Bronfman's preppy exemplum: he had gone to Deerfield and to Williams, where he played every sport he could play decently, particularly tennis. Nowadays, down at the San Mateo headquarters of the Seagram Classics Wine Company, he and his lieutenants sometimes shot hoops in the sunny noon hour, between strategy sessions and marketing reviews.

Bronfman had decided to put the office on the peninsula so he could be equidistant from Napa Valley and Monterey Vineyards, farther south. He and his wife had moved to California in 1987 and found that blue skies and warm days made up for the removal from the seat of power in New York, occupied by his brother and his father. Sam wanted to be independent and to a degree he was, having some of Seagram's financial clout without too much intervention.

On the wall of his San Mateo office hung a list of Sam's personal operating principles:

> Focus on solutions
> Practice Open, Honest & Direct Communication
> Listen, observe and learn
> Have fun
> Integrity always
> Be accountable
> Practice Mutual Trust, Support & Respect
> Focus as a Team
> Confront the Issues/Take risks
> Tell the Truth

Underneath the list was a photograph of his father playing solitaire, whiskey glass at hand. Next to it hung another photograph, of white Sterling on the hill, with the inscription "To my son Sam. A great shot of a beautiful jewel in our family crown."

Sam had some problems with the whiskey/wine tension. Seagram was primarily a maker and marketer of spirits; therefore one side of the company was in competition with another side, one that Sam Bronfman happened to have chosen as his life's work. Some of the decisions that came down from the top — like the "equivalency" ad campaign equating a drink of whiskey with a glass of wine, to offset claims that wine was a more healthful product — caused PR fallout and some personal anguish.

People in the valley hated those ads. He couldn't speak out against them without appearing disloyal and so said nothing. In fact, he loved wine and saw it as his personal salvation, but whiskey and stock transactions provided the wherewithal. Those, not wine, paid for Winery Lake Vineyard, the medaillons of lamb surrounded by baked oysters wrapped in sorel, and for the Polynesian dancers.

Life down on the peninsula had proved pleasant for Sam, if sometimes disconcerting. Seagram, a public company controlled by the
Bronfmans, was worth billions: it included a portion of Du Pont and
all of Tropicana. But Sam abhorred ostentation. He drove his Pontiac
to work for a year before he discovered, through the medium of his
household's au pair, that his old car was often the subject of dinner
party conversation. Two aspects of that revelation stunned him: that
babysitters in Atherton discussed such things, and that people paid
attention to Sam Bronfman. Not wanting to appear eccentric, he
sold the Pontiac and bought a BMW 750.

He was going to make a name for Seagram's wine. The Winery
Lake purchase was part of the plan; so was the very expensive par-
ticipation in the Domaine Mumm project on the Silverado Trail, yet
another California sparkling wine. Both entities complemented Sterling. Now Sam was on the lookout for a smaller, even more precious
jewel to add to the crown, a Duckhorn or a Diamond Creek.

His most controversial decision had been to represent Charles
Krug Winery. For years Krug had skated the edge of bankruptcy.
Sam went to see Peter Mondavi, and told him, "We're looking for
opportunity, and you're undermarketed."

Peter said, "If you're interested in marketing, fine. If you want
to buy us, get out."

They talked. Sam went back to his people and then took some of
them to a secret meeting at Peter's house on the Krug grounds. They
talked some more. The lawyers got involved. What they eventually
signed was an exclusive worldwide marketing agreement for the potentially profitable CK Mondavi jug wines, as well as the once-re-
spected Krug line, now not so hot but better than its reputation. And
the Peter Mondavis' financial situation was better than commonly
supposed: Krug was, in fact, paying taxes. That was the official line,
anyway. Some thought Krug wines were even worse than their reputation and that Peter remained a volatile man with large family
pride, impervious to suggestion. Sam had heard about the trial involving Peter and Robert but considered it ancient history; his people
didn't really check out Peter's estimates of annual case production
and didn't look over the winery as carefully as they might have.

Sam figured the agreement effectively blocked anyone else from
buying Krug, should further debt problems arise. That was a primary objective. If Peter ever tried to sell to someone else, that person
would have to pay back Seagram as well as cover Krug's other debts,
or accept Seagram as the marketing agent and give up those profits.

Sam reasoned that no one would want to do that. He assumed he had, in effect, the right of first refusal should Peter ever decide to sell. But if he had tried to have that right written into the contract, Peter would have rebelled.

After the deal went through, Ernest Gallo invited Sam to lunch in Modesto. Ernie told Sam, "It's nice you're doing this for Peter."

Sam's prime competitor in the eventual acquisition of Krug would be Michael Mondavi, official head of Robert Mondavi Winery and an empire builder. Michael thought Krug would someday be sold and was happy to be in a two-horse race. He told Sam, "If somebody has to market the brand, I'm glad it's you."

Michael always bid on the old Krug wines coming up at the Napa Valley Wine Auction. He saw them as family heirlooms. Two years earlier, Sam had bid against him, wanting to see how high Michael would go. Finally Sam took his hand down, thinking, "Is this what it's going to be like when we're both after Krug?"

He stood up at the Winery Lake party and said to the assembled guests, "Hi, I'm Sam Bronfman. My main claim to fame is that I talked René and Veronica into selling us a little piece of heaven."

40

THE FORCES FOR development were being felt in different ways. Tourism had its uglier aspects — people without manners, traffic and general congestion — but it also had the potential for great profits. This potential was not lost on the vintners themselves. Increasingly they came under pressure from others in the valley, many of them committed to the growing of grapes, to limit both the scale and the nature of subsidiary winery activities. Many wineries diminished the role of agriculture, or played off the reputation of Napa Valley, or both. This disagreement was becoming a major rift in the normally discreet, sedate Napa Valley.

Mike Martini, grandson of old Louis Martini, founder of the Napa Valley Vintners Association, was now president of that organization. He was also the winemaker at Louis M. Martini Winery. The morning he opened the door of the meeting hall at the Meadowood resort, during crush in 1987, his hands were stained purple with the juice of Cabernet Sauvignon. He wore jeans and a yoked shirt with a leather cigarette case in the pocket. Blond, blue-eyed, and large, Mike had to preside over his grandfather's legacy and eat the fine lunch in the Vintners Room before he could get back to work.

Martini belonged to what Dick Maher, now president of Christian Brothers, called the Napa Valley Lucky Sperm Club, a group that included all third-generation Martinis and Mondavis, as well as Robin Lail, Paula Kornell, and other inheritors of Napa money and land, and the tradition that people like Maher yearned for.

Mike Martini would not have ended up in the wine business if it hadn't been for his family's long involvement; he knew that. He had a reputation as a maverick. Some people considered him a throwback to a less sophisticated time. Mike liked to tell people that while a student at Fresno State he had majored in partying. During the Vietnam War he enlisted in the Air Force and became a weatherman in Germany. After the war he fell in love with an English girl and moved with her to the Nevada desert. One day she told him, "I never thought I'd be sitting in an outhouse at ten below with a goat to keep me warm."

Mike went back to school and eventually to UC Davis; he learned to make wine. His first harvest as winemaker at Martini was done alone. His father wanted to see if Mike could handle it and didn't even show up.

Mike argued with his sister Carolyn about everything, arguments being Italian conversations. They sorted out their individual turf and the turf of their sister Patty and, eventually, that of brother Peter. Suddenly the Martini kids — those Lucky Spermers — were running one of the oldest, biggest, and best-known winery and vineyard operations in California.

What Mike had noticed when he first returned to Napa Valley after his time in the Army and the Nevada desert was the gentrification. And the fences. Back in 1972 he had been able to ride horseback from Whitehall Lane to Spring Mountain Road along the base of the Mayacamas. Now he encountered the suburbs of St. Helena, locked gates, and strangers shouting at him.

"This isn't agrarian," Martini told his friends, "it's Carmel."

In 1984 the president of the Napa Valley Vintners Association, John Trefethen, called Mike up and said, "We need a big winery represented on the Vintners board." That was the beginning of Mike Martini's second education. He joined the board and got involved politically, something he never thought would happen. He became secretary-treasurer, then vice president, and finally president of the Vintners Association — the accepted line of progression. The Vintners had a lot of influence but was remote from the everyday life of the valley. It seemed to him that many of the members had a problem with elitism, perceived and real. He decided that as president he would do something about that. He proposed bringing up-valley together with down-valley in a celebration of the 150th anniversary of the planting of the grape vine, a reconciliation between the vintners and what he called the "six-pack community" of Napa city.

When he brought up the possibility, some vintners objected. They worried about a deterioration of their "image." That made

Mike Martini mad. He told them, "The down-valley people think you're snobs up here because you *are* snobs."

The pleasant Meadowood meeting hall had been built especially for Vintners Association meetings. It was airy, with pale gray clapboard walls, oatmeal-colored carpet, comfortable chairs, and continuous white desking on ascending levels of a well-lighted ellipse. Members filed in singly and in pairs and sat facing the podium. For the most part they were better dressed than their president; a few had hands stained, like his, with Cabernet juice.

The first business dealt with the Wine Train, as he thought it might. The train had made a run up the valley the previous week, and people from Yountville to St. Helena had complained about the noise and the disruption of traffic. The Wine Train was not a simple issue. Trains were generally considered good because they cut down on fuel consumption and traffic, and so most vintners would ordinarily have supported such a thing. But the Wine Train was not intended to alleviate traffic or to move large groups of people economically from one part of the valley to another. It was, in his opinion, to move a relatively small number of people dramatically, contributing to noise, pollution, traffic delays, and the carnival atmosphere that on weekends prevailed in Napa. Most of the sixty-seven vintners present opposed the train, but tentatively. They agreed, typically, that the organization should take a position on the Wine Train, although exactly what that position was remained unclear.

Their stance on a winery definition was equally vague. The issue had been around for a couple of years now and was coming to a head. There were two sides to the argument, the grape growers in the valley wanting controls placed on winery construction, expansion, and activities, and the vintners wanting none of these. Negotiations with the growers had been broken off; the Agricultural Advisory Council set up to help was moribund. The county Planning Department was moving ahead on its own after Jim Hickey, the planning director, had called for a formal definition. If the vintners didn't seize the initiative, someone else would, and they would have a definition imposed on them.

But achieving consensus within the Vintners Association was very difficult, as this meeting had indicated. The argument between the vintners and the growers didn't seem to amount to much, but something large and uncontrollable was about to grow out of it.

Martini had only a few more meetings to conduct before passing his responsibilities on to someone else. After the meeting, but before lunch, he and the other vintners gathered on the terrace and drank wine supplied by the members; they talked about the harvest. Mike enjoyed that part. From Meadowood's kitchen came the smell of roasting lamb. That and the taste of icy Chardonnay in the autumn sunlight made him realize just how hungry he was.

❧

The problem of the Wine Train came forcefully home to Carolyn Martini the day she received the Wine Train representative at the Louis M. Martini Winery. As president, she tried to deal with everyone equally, without prejudice or ceremony. Carolyn was a big woman with a direct gaze — another blue-eyed Italian. She carried her keys on a ring attached to the belt of her trousers. She had come to the presidency of the winery in an unusual way, by default, since her father had simply refused to decide who would succeed him. Neither would he tell his grown children what to do, and so they had to work it out for themselves. The wisdom of it struck her later, after she and her siblings had thrashed around for a while and then filled the necessary slots and taken over the management of their grandfather's legacy.

Carolyn's father would not issue orders because *his* father had done nothing but order people around. Louis Michael Martini, the colorful, talented tyrant, had believed that if he shouted loud enough people would automatically understand and agree with him. Carolyn had always been able to tell, when she visited her grandparents, which of them had won the latest fight.

Her grandfather had loved to spend money: he stayed at the Clift when he went to San Francisco but would buy his own fish and bring it back to the hotel wrapped in newspaper. He repeatedly embarrassed his son — Carolyn's father, Louis Peter Martini — by telling the chef how to cook it. Her grandfather had hired a seamstress to make Carolyn an opera dress when she was twelve — aquamarine, with a matching cape — and picked her up after school in a black Cadillac. He handed her an anthology of operas, and during the drive into San Francisco she read about the one she was about to see. Afterward, they ate ravioli at Fior d'Italia.

When she was fifteen, he took her to Europe aboard the *Leonardo da Vinci,* first buying her too many clothes and having them packed into steamer trunks. They stayed in big hotels; her grandfather would go out at midnight and come back with bread, prosciutto, and wine. She slept late. He insisted on ordering her American breakfast, corn flakes and sour milk. She met all the Martini relatives in Genoa and left half her wardrobe with those nice Genoese girls.

Carolyn was glad to have known the old man so well. Years later, when she went to the movie *The Godfather,* she saw in Marlon Brando's performance a composite of all her grandfather's friends. But she had known instinctively that any family member within his radius would never be truly free, and moved to New Jersey after graduating from college. She worked at Rutgers and got a degree in library science. Her grandfather wrote her long letters saying come home, come home. Anybody with any sense lives in California, he said. She ought to be there, too.

She wrote back: "When you were my age you traveled half-way around the world without speaking the right language. I speak English, and I only went to New Jersey."

Her father had spent years in military school, at UC Davis, and in the Army thinking about how to get along with his father. Louis junior, as he was known, or Louis Peter, had decided to treat his father as a general, and he, Louis junior, would be the staff officer, making recommendations but not allowing himself to be drawn into disputes. A lot of good ideas would go by the boards because it wasn't his father's nature to accede to others' suggestions. But it might save Louis junior from an ulcer.

When Louis junior took over the winery, he bought used equipment, cash-and-carry. He didn't like borrowing money. Every year he tried to get the debt down to zero. He couldn't understand how people could operate heavily in the red and sleep at night. Owning their own vineyards and paying their own way, the Martinis managed to keep prices low. They didn't need to be first in sales; they didn't have to compete with the hypesters. Louis junior could honestly say that the wines he made were sound. He was unable to say they were the best in the world, but he noticed that other vintners had no such inhibitions.

Now it was Carolyn's turn. She was closest to her younger brother, Peter. Mike was tight with their sister Patty. Carolyn and Mike struck sparks; it came to seem natural, if inconvenient, since she was the president and he was the winemaker. Then she took a management course and during a discussion of personality types thought she came to understand the conflicts in her family. She went home and made every member write down what made them happy and what they expected from their jobs.

Carolyn proved to be a dominant personality, according to the test, results-oriented and impatient, while Mike was dominant but people-oriented, trusting, not much interested in the bottom line. Carolyn's type found it difficult to hand out compliments; Mike's type needed to be accepted. So there were bound to be sparks. Both had weaknesses that could be overcome.

She considered management by objective really management by dictator. In a family business, you do what works. She gave her father, still chairman of the board and an analytical type, lots of facts, and time. Drop a stone in the water and walk away. The Martini winery picked up some talented refugees who had come to realize that corporate America didn't care about them. She told them they could call themselves whatever they wanted, except president. As soon as they went up a rung on the ladder they were going to run into a Martini, anyway. That was the reality.

She wouldn't buy a corporate jet even if she wanted one; peer pressure wouldn't allow it. The Martini winery had to make expensive changes, to prepare for the global competition. In a few years the pressure to consolidate, to sell out, would be tremendous. There were once many car and gun manufacturers in the United States, and now all but a few had been absorbed. She didn't want that to happen to the Martini winery.

She kept the old Italian sayings in mind: never invest in something you can't hold in your hand; never own property you can't drive by on your way home to lunch. The Martinis did have far-flung vineyards in Sonoma, Pope Valley, up in Lake County. They used their own imported grapes in the best blends, but she knew that some limitations had to be imposed on winery expansions in Napa Valley or people and buildings would displace grapes and other good things that came with agriculture.

The Wine Train was a separate issue, but linked. When Vincent DeDomenico first proposed it, he and Jack McCormack came up to the Robert Mondavi Winery with a scale model. Most of the wineries sent someone to hear them out. DeDomenico said the train would be a tasteful operation. Carolyn got the impression he wasn't interested in hearing objections; he wanted to know which wineries wished to be included as Wine Train stops and he wanted to know within two days. She said to herself, "Time to go home to din-din."

Later she wrote a letter to McCormack and listed her objections, safety being a big one. Tourists would be spilling out of trains. What were the wineries supposed to do with them after they got them disentangled from the barbed wire? Hundreds would wander across Highway 29 to Sutter Home, endangering themselves and the drivers of all those cars. And what about Napa's children and dogs? They didn't understand trains and some would undoubtedly get run over. Finally, what was the advantage for a working winery to have the Wine Train stop, when the sort of tourist disembarking wouldn't be interested in buying wine?

She sent a copy of the letter to the *St. Helena Star,* which published it. Martini was the first winery to publicly raise objections; that caused some rumblings. McCormack responded, but not in enough detail. Carolyn thought the questions should be fully answered.

Some others came out against the train, Sutter Home, Beringer, and Peter Mondavi among them. The Wine Train's right-of-way ran directly through the Krug property, between the winery and the sales office. The ultimate example of chaos would be the simultaneous arrival of the Wine Train, buses, free-lance tourists, trucks hauling loaded gondolas, semis packed with outbound cases of wine, government inspectors for the BATF and OSHA, a hot-air balloon, and a couple of stray mutts.

The woman hired by the Wine Train to sign up participating wineries asked Carolyn point-blank: "Are you going to take these people or not?"

"We would accept them under the same conditions as other tourists," she said. No special arrangements, no deals.

"Well, do you want to be on our map or not?"

"Draw your own conclusions," Carolyn told her.

Opponents hoped that the Interstate Commerce Commission would force the Wine Train to comply with local zoning and other laws and to conduct a study of its overall effect on the environment through which it was to make its daily runs. But the commission ruled the other way. Because it was a train, it did not have to comply with local ordinances, including a requirement to study the possible effects of the train on valley life.

One of the communities objecting loudly was St. Helena. The mayor threatened to lie down on the railroad tracks in protest, not a practical step but one that got some attention. St. Helena was afraid the Wine Train would disrupt what was a very pleasant place to be. St. Helena had the reputation for being the safest city in California. In the weekly newspaper readers were as likely to find ads for grape knives and refractometers as those for dog food and light bulbs. St. Helena had good schools, an excellent library, a hospital, a bakery, an all-night supermarket, and ten churches. "St. Helena is a clean city," the chamber of commerce correctly observed, "and climatic conditions are attractive to persons who are interested in modern outdoor living. Beautiful homes, tree-lined streets, attractive shopping facilities, excellent schools make St. Helena an ideal place in which to live, work and play."

With a population of only five thousand, it hardly qualified as a city, although it had some big-city problems: heavy traffic (and only two traffic lights), insufficient water for projected growth, a strained sewage-treatment plant, a shortage of rental units, and too many skateboarders. It had adopted what the elected officials called a slow-growth plan, inspired by the county's plan to restrict growth to about 2 percent a year. That was actually not slow growth; India's growth rate was only slightly higher. But the Association of Bay Area Governments had recommended an even faster rate of growth for St. Helena. A water shortage and lack of sewage facilities had prevented St. Helena from complying with even its own plan, but relentless pressure from the state and from developers continued for more houses and everything that houses brought with them.

Now this proposal to bring crowds of people to St. Helena, then haul them to various wineries and create additional traffic tie-ups, and develop the moribund depot into another tourist attraction. DeDomenico owned the depot, too. St. Helena didn't want him using it as a dumping ground for tourists. The city of Yountville had similar feelings about the railside site within its boundaries; so did Oakville and Rutherford. But the old Southern Pacific had shared in favorable legislation passed in the previous century to encourage railroad building, including an imperviousness to citizens' objections. These were the enticements that had drawn Leland Stanford and his friends into transcontinental gandy dancing, making them rich and unaccountable. The Wine Train was to share in that grand tradition — a further mockery, since the round trip would be less than fifty miles and there was no connection to the outside world.

The Friends of Napa Valley, organized by Norm Manzer, the State Farm representative, and others, fought the Wine Train in the pages of the *St. Helena Star,* the *Napa Register,* and other newspapers. Manzer took heart from letters regarding the Wine Train that seemed to blow across the editors' desks: "We are being used in the most cold-blooded and inconsiderate way, and it makes me angry as hell that they are trying to slip this project through a loophole in regulatory statutes governing transportation. . . ."

He was encouraged by a ruling of the California Public Utilities Commission that differed with that of the Interstate Commerce Commission. The PUC, with jurisdiction over intrastate passenger service, wanted an environmental study done. So a legal battle took shape between two bureaucracies, one in Washington and one in Sacramento, both riven with political considerations that had little to do with Napa Valley, and both distant from it.

Vincent DeDomenico was annoyed with Jack McCormack. DeDomenico lived in Burlingame, on the peninsula, and didn't get up to Napa much. He counted on McCormack to take the pulse of the community and troubleshoot the train, and McCormack had either underestimated local resistance or underreported it to DeDomenico, who started getting the newspaper clippings in the mail from friends and strangers; almost all of them were antagonistic. If he had known how much trouble he was destined to have in the valley, he would have stayed out of it, but he already had more than $4 million invested in the Wine Train and would have to put in another $1 million if there was a cost overrun. The old railroad yard in Napa was alive with welders and mechanics revamping the old coaches he had bought around the country. The big engine ready for use cast a majestic shadow across the siding there. It was too big for the task, but impressive, painted burgundy and forest green.

DeDomenico started going up more often. He bought some wine at the 1987 auction; when people asked him for particulars about the Wine Train, he said, "I'm not a train man, I'm a spaghetti salesman."

Questions about an environmental impact report irked him. Why should he invest yet more money in a study that was not required by law? Why should he encourage more delays in a business venture that had already been delayed too often?

He made some inquiries of his own. The Friends of Napa Valley was a misnomer, in his opinion. Its membership comprised only 1 percent of the population. What about the other 99 percent? At the county fair in Napa, close to one thousand people had signed a piece of paper indicating they favored a revival of a train in the valley. What about them?

He noticed that declared opposition among the wineries had grown considerably by the beginning of 1988. In addition to earlier disavowals came new ones from Burgess, Caymus, Chappellet, Montelena, Duckhorn, Girard, Kornell, Heitz, Phelps, Rasmussen, Pocai, Mayacamas, Napa Creek, Newton, Pecota, Pepi, Saddleback, Sage Canyon, Schramsberg, Shafer, Silver Oak, Spottswoode, Sterling, Stonegate, and Stony Hill. There were more than two hundred wineries in the valley, DeDomenico thought, and most of them were *not* on that list.

St. Helena's city council filed a complaint with the Public Utilities Commission protesting the Wine Train. By the spring of 1988, St. Helena had been joined by the county, the cities of Napa and Yountville, the Napa Valley Vintners Association, the Napa Valley Grape Growers Association, and the Napa County Farm Bureau. The mayor said — and DeDomenico read the words in another clipping — "If Mr. DeDomenico has a train to nowhere, it won't be very profitable."

41

A STUFFED wild turkey, shot purposely through the head, set the decorous tone of the headquarters of Bob Phillips's Vine Hill Ranch. There were also two posters from wineries to which Phillips sold grapes, Pepi and Duckhorn, and an old desk, a swivel chair with an ailing spring, and a telephone. Some crucial work went on in that dusty cubicle, more like a tack room than the office of a former vice president of Paine Webber.

The slatted shutters on the big house beyond the garage, more reminiscent of New Orleans than the ranchos of the mission days, had been closed against the sun. The table under the wisteria arbor was set for lunch. A low-pressure area out over the San Joaquin Valley had pulled cool air in from the Pacific Ocean, and some of it found its way up the Napa Valley, but not enough.

A few nights before, Phillips and Tom May had found themselves together at Meadowood, talking about the probability of another early harvest, and then about the Wine Train. They agreed that something should be done. The train would, among other things, block the railroad crossings during crush, preventing growers like Phillips and May from getting their grapes to the wineries on time. It would bring in more tourists rather than control the masses already there. It was not the good thing its promoters claimed it to be, not an environmentally sound people mover but another tourist attraction.

Yearly estimates of the hordes visiting Napa Valley had now reached four million — in a narrow space with slightly more than 100,000 residents. Half a million were expected to board the Wine Train, if it ever pulled out of the new station down in Napa city. Now two vintage diesel engines stood ready, plus a steam locomotive and twenty Pullman cars done up in flocked velvet. The Wine

Train spokesman was still talking about six round-trip excursions a day on a twenty-one-mile track.

When Phillips got angry his voice took on an uncharacteristic flatness. He had been a Marine but also a businessman; he liked to think of himself as a compromiser. A few months before he would not have believed it possible that an entire community in America could be slighted for the sake of a single individual — Vincent De-Domenico, creator of Rice-A-Roni — but that was precisely what happened. The Interstate Commerce Commission refused to hear complaints against the Wine Train, thereby suggesting that De-Domenico would not have to produce an environmental impact report on the train's effects on the valley. Mel Varrelman, the up-valley supervisor, had written to President Reagan, pointing out that local governments wanted the study done and were being ignored. The irony was that Republicans dominated the ICC, which was thumbing its nose at an overwhelmingly Republican constituency.

The more Phillips talked about it, the madder he got. When Southern Pacific first announced it would sell its Napa line, Phillips had gone to a meeting with Alvin Block and a number of potential investors, including Phillips's friend Charles Crocker. Crocker had owned one railroad and didn't want another. He told Phillips afterward, over lunch, "You may be missing something here. If the ICC has sole jurisdiction, then the railroad sites can be developed without any local controls." DeDomenico could do whatever he pleased.

Phillips had written to the county, urging it to buy the right-of-way. It would have made a fine bicycle path or a simple walkway, and now the county was faced with unending tourist trains, whistles, automated railroad crossings and the cost of building them, and maybe high-rise hotels as well. The Vintners Inn, a few years before, had been blocked by simply invoking the law against construction in the ag preserve. But railroad law was arcane, even irrational, written to encourage railroads and frustrate the citizenry, and consequently hard to get a handle on. There were dozens of different land parcels involved, county and city zoning requirements, state environmental laws, and a contemptuous federal agency.

Now outsiders like DeDomenico were taking advantage of a reputation built up with a lot of effort and hardship. Parasites were feeding on the valley's success. Only recently had Phillips come to think this way. Laissez faire had suffered another blow in his mind.

The valley had also attracted some wealthy people who gave parties and flitted around without understanding the issues. They were basically harmless. There were others with the cash and the will, or at least the inclination, to oppose DeDomenico. Phillips wanted to bring them together for a show of entrenched opposition to the Wine Train. Such a demonstration might ameliorate the train's impact, and could possibly kill it.

At noon he left his office and went out to welcome his guests. The first was Betty Peters, owner of a bank in San Francisco and a long-time weekend resident of the old Bourne estate on the outskirts of St. Helena. Next came Tom and Martha May, he a du Pont heir and a former schoolteacher who, like Phillips, wore jeans. Katie Spann arrived in big, dramatic sunglasses and a summer smock, and Clark Swanson in pink trousers more common at beach weekends on the East Coast. An heir to the frozen food empire, Swanson had recently bought a house and vineyards in the valley and was having a winery built. He and his wife spent the balance of the year in London. Finally came Barney Rhodes, sweating in seersucker, eager for water from the tall carafe. He had sold Martha's Vineyard to the Mays, owned Bella Oaks, and had been investing in Napa land and wines since his early days as a physician for Kaiser Permanente.

They all took seats at the long, shaded harvest table, where Alexandra Phillips had laid out cold artichokes, seafood pâté, marinated herring, dark olives, three kinds of chèvre, French bread, and two bottles of Duckhorn Sauvignon Blanc. Places had also been set for Andy Beckstoffer and Michael Mondavi, who did not show up. The Mondavis' position on the Wine Train remained opaque. They seemed to be waiting for the political and legal wrangling — the dog and pony shows, as they called them — to be over. Then they would step forward either to take credit or to prosper in some canny way. Robert Mondavi had originally encouraged DeDomenico without impressing on the pasta king the importance of decorum and accord in the valley. Michael Mondavi had in private expressed misgivings about the Wine Train, but the Robert Mondavi Winery was not on record as opposing it.

The Mondavis' behavior was generally explained by the "Italian connection," the tendency among some Italians not to criticize one another, and by the profit motive. The Mondavis owned extensive property along Highway 29, including the corner in Oakville where the Oakville Grocery stood. Mike wanted to develop the parcels —

how extensively was a matter of speculation — and more tourists would presumably enhance whatever enterprise sprang up there. But the Mondavis had joined the chorus in favor of an environmental impact report by the Wine Train.

Phillips offered a brief toast and then reviewed the status of the train. An administrative judge for the Public Utilities Commission had just opined that the Wine Train must show cause why it shouldn't come under the PUC's jurisdiction. The PUC itself was expected to rule the same way in a few days. That would mean that the Wine Train and DeDomenico would, in the eyes of the state of California, not be protected by the Interstate Commerce Commission and would have to comply with the California Environmental Quality Act. And that would mean an official study of the train's contribution to noise, pollution, and traffic. The Wine Train, which had already delayed its launch two times, would have to put it off again for at least a year.

"DeDomenico intends to appeal this to the highest court," Phillips said. "He's got ten million dollars invested and there's no way he's going to back off. Now we have a little window of opportunity."

Phillips had been to Sacramento to discuss the Wine Train with Napa's representatives in the state legislature. They wanted a stronger show of opposition before they got involved. "Frankly, they'd like to see a little public outrage down here. They want marches and press conferences to bring national attention. They want to put pressure on the PUC to hang in there if the ruling is appealed, but they know that will cost money."

"Norm Manzer will provide the outrage," said Betty Peters.

Money was a larger problem; the various groups opposing the Wine Train had not raised much. Yountville and St. Helena had filed injunctions against the train to prevent the development of station sites without the towns' approval. But Yountville had no funds to sustain the fight, and St. Helena had already spent more money than some citizens thought it should spend. The Napa Valley Grape Growers and the Napa Valley Vintners had joined the towns in the suit but had not put up a significant amount of money. The Vintners was capable of a big contribution, but with such a diverse organization consensus was practically impossible. Many vintners had a potential stake in the Wine Train's success, like Bill Harlan, who owned land on both sides of the highway in south St. Helena and had recently built a handsome new sidewalk in front of Sunny St. Helena, next to the railroad tracks.

Another problem was the upcoming election for the county board of supervisors. The incumbents, both challenged by candidates in favor of more development in the county, needed money for their races. They feared coming out against the train because they might lose votes, and their reelection was crucial.

"Damn right," said Barney Rhodes. "If they're not reelected, the Wine Train won't matter because the whole valley will be subdivided."

"If it comes down to losing on the Wine Train," said Tom May, "or losing the ag preserve, we'll lose on the Wine Train."

Phillips wanted to separate the two issues and then raise money for the Wine Train battle. It could cost as much as $250,000.

"That's a small contribution," said Swanson, "from twenty-five people who really want to preserve the lifestyle of the valley. What do they pay for a picture on the wall? How much for a piece of jewelry? Ask them how often they spend ten thousand dollars, and then ask them how much their home is worth."

"Lay it on the line," agreed Rhodes.

"We may have a constitutional issue here," Phillips said, "if the ICC tries to preempt the PUC. Then what do we do?"

They would have to hire a good lawyer. The many environmental groups in Washington dedicated to changing the views of bureaucracies might agree to help the valley. After all, it was a national treasure. "If things got bad enough," he added, "with enough publicity, the ICC would have to respond."

The Sauvignon Blanc tasted very fine and retained its chill in the terra-cotta receptacles, but water was in greater demand. It was hot out there on the lawn, and the breeze barely discernible.

Alexandra brought up the possibility of tax deductions for money given to a legal fund; someone else thought of tracking DeDomenico's contributions to the opposition candidates for the supervisorial seats and then publicizing the fact. Rhodes suggested appearing before the present board and explaining that, twenty-five years before, a teenage boy had been killed by a Southern Pacific train colliding with his car at the Zinfandel Lane crossing. Someone else would be killed unless the study was done and the number of Wine Train excursion runs greatly reduced. "Maybe we can shut this thing down for a while," he said — at least until the election was behind them and all the guns could be trained on DeDomenico.

The Wine Train prospect had been around for years. There was in this opposition, however well meaning, a sense of tardiness, a leisurely approach to a phenomenon that had moved well beyond the realm of possibility. Sauvignon Blanc, even fine Sauvignon Blanc, and three kinds of goat cheese would not facilitate the demise of the Wine Train. The group didn't constitute the main opposition, made up of several organizations that had worked for many months, led by the Friends of Napa Valley and the State Farm rep, Norm Manzer. The men and women dining under Phillips's wisteria were just better connected to other money receptacles. Phillips reasoned that the effects of real money had yet to be felt in the struggle.

His wife said, "It's high time people in the valley realize it costs something to have what we have here. It's time to pony up."

"We all voted down the bond issue for the valley to buy the line in the first place," said Betty Peters. "God, was that dumb. We should have bought fifty-one percent and then scuttled it."

"Let's find out how deep DeDomenico's pockets are," suggested Swanson.

The harsh light overexposed the shrubbery and trees and threatened to vaporize the mountains across the valley. No sound of terrestrial traffic reached this recess of Vine Hill Ranch, but the hum of a light aircraft carried over from Mount Veeder. The group further decided to formally ask Charles Crocker and Andy Beckstoffer to join, and two prominent vintners, Michael Mondavi and Carolyn Martini, to state publicly their opposition to the Wine Train, part of the broader issue of development and tourism in the valley. It had been written about in the *New York Times* and *Newsweek*. The Wine Train was a national symbol of the same commercial excesses committed by the wineries; the vintners were in the awkward position of deploring DeDomenico's opportunism while refusing to impose restraints on their own. Phillips didn't want the Wine Train to be seen as a grower-vintner issue, however, because it would acquire class overtones. Then the people of Napa city and the general population wouldn't join the fight.

Betty Peters had one final bit of news: DeDomenico intended to buy a private railway coach for himself and hitch it to the back of the Wine Train.

Phillips's sudden anger showed. He said, "It had better be armor-plated!"

42

THE DEBATE over wineries — how they were to be defined and required to behave — had grown acrimonious by the late spring of 1988. The Napa Valley Grape Growers Association had formally proposed to the Napa County Planning Commission that new wineries in the valley be required to use Napa Valley grapes for at least 75 percent of their wine production. The proposal was picked up by the press and became known as the 75 percent solution.

Andy Beckstoffer made the announcement of the growers' stand. This did not help win over some of the vintners who might have been in favor of the 75 percent solution, for Beckstoffer was not universally liked. Reverdy Johnson, who became president of the Napa Valley Vintners Association when Mike Martini's term expired, called Beckstoffer's proposal "extreme" — a fighting word in the valley. He accused the growers of attempting to monopolize grape production at the expense of the wineries.

The hard feelings, even hatred, that had surrounded the creation of the ag preserve twenty years before now began to gather about the winery definition. Wherever one looked in the valley, one saw the causes of the controversy — in the brash new structures thrown up against the backdrop of trees and sky, in the commercial enterprises pushing at the corporate limits of Napa, Yountville, St. Helena, and Calistoga, in the frenzied marketing activity that took vintners and their representatives up and down the valley, and, of course, in the press of tourists and residential development.

Napa's creation of the ag preserve in 1968 had been highly unusual, combining the efforts of a relatively few people outside local government and a remarkable unanimity among county staff and elected officials. Since then, Napa had fluctuated between slow-growth and pro-growth supervisors, each side heavily dependent on urban voters. City dwellers had the most influence and would ultimately determine the character of the rural areas of the county. If "the city" ever completely lost sympathy with the look of "the valley," the zoning would change and the ag preserve would be lost.

Napa Valley contained the most valuable farmland in America. The county had been, in a curious way, both an inspiration to other regions and a laggard. The creation of the ag preserve had come at a time when Marin County was also working on a plan to limit development in the western part of the county. Napa set an example for Marin, proving that the zoning battle could be won, and Marin had followed with its own zoning requirements, over the objections of the farmers and ranchers.

Marin had maintained a majority of supervisors interested in land preservation, assisted by the powerful Marin County Conservation League, which bought development rights from farmers and created permanent easements. About 10 percent of Marin had been removed in this way from possible development. Napa County's environmental and conservation groups, however, lacked a unified voice. The county's electorate was not as sophisticated as Marin's. At least a third of Napa County's work force commuted south to jobs in the shipyards of Mare Island or to Travis Air Force Base. They rarely got a glimpse of the top of the valley. They had views of the hillsides and distant mountains, but there were no county parks, and relatively little access to country away from paved roads.

The residual value of an acre of Napa Valley land — the value of what it could produce, with grapes as the primary crop — was about $10,000. This relatively high yield kept the grape growers and vintners in favor of limited development. But a collapse of the wine market could put them in the developers' camp. There was the additional problem of large corporations owning the land, without a long-term commitment to it.

Neighboring Sonoma County, compared to Napa, was in worse shape. Because the county had waited too long to address the problem of development, and because Sonoma contained both an interstate highway, 101, and a major city, Santa Rosa, much of the prime land had already been built on and the pressures for continued growth were almost irresistible. The city and the politicians favored development, and Sonoma's General Plan lacked the teeth in the plans for Napa and Marin.

In the past twenty years many groups had sprung up around the country dedicated to the preservation of rural and wild places. They sought generally to revamp the attitudes of Americans as well. Recently the call among many such groups had been for "regionalism" — an attempt to preserve an area's natural character while providing for the needs of those living in it. Agriculture was one "partner" in such a landscape, which might include other human endeavors, but in a way that did not wipe out the natural setting.

Regionalism grew from a general knowledge that land was not, after all, inexhaustible. Citizens with automobiles and access to an extensive network of good highways could not forever leave behind ruined cityscapes and cluttered suburbs in their search for tranquility at the far edge of development, where they then created more of the same problems. Human activities — housing, commerce, industry — had to be concentrated in specific areas, and fields, woodlands, wetlands, prairies, and other natural environments allowed to flourish around them, free or relatively free of human encumbrance. Although farming was just one aspect of the total regional environment, it was an important one. The worth of rural land was measured in both productive capacity and the contribution to people's happiness. Napa's countryside obviously pleased those who lived in it and those who visited; the danger was that it could be taken for granted, and then exploited.

One such group in favor of regionalism, the Greenbelt Alliance in San Francisco (formerly People for Open Space), developed a map showing the impact of proposed development on the nine counties around the bay. The area contained almost four million acres of ranches and farmland, vineyards, parks, and open space that looked deceptively abundant in the abstract.

Other regions in the United States had begun to use more creative zoning to assure the survival of this type of rural land. Purchasing or trading for easements that lock up development rights was being done in Montgomery County, Maryland, on the northern edge of Washington, D.C., one of the fastest-growing communities in the country. In 1980 a plan had been adopted to preserve agriculture and rural space with new zoning and subdivision regulations that reduced residential density in rural areas from one unit on five acres to one on twenty-five, affecting a third of the county.

Speculators, developers, and some farmers loudly objected because the county was essentially taking the speculative value out of the land. It did this by creating "sending" zones, "receiving" zones, and transfer rights. A farmer in a sending zone was assigned a development transfer right for every five acres, and allowed to sell the right rather than the land to developers. The developer could then use the right in a receiving zone approved for residential development, allowing him to build one additional housing unit for each such right. The farmer's land was permanently taken out of residential development, and growth directed to a suitable, planned environment. Montgomery County would use 27,000 transfer rights and preserve almost 14,000 rural acres by the end of 1989. The county has lost only a thousand rural acres to development since passage of the law, whereas before the law the county lost 3,500 rural acres every year.

Few landowners in Napa Valley had given up their development rights for compensation. An organization known as the Napa County Land Trust had systematically preserved a fraction of the valley by either purchasing the rights or receiving them as grants. The Land Trust had been started in 1970 by June and Francis ("Si") Foote, a former IBM executive and entrepreneur who sold his computer-related business and retired to Napa. He and his wife bought a large hill in Stag's Leap and set about building a house on top with a 360-degree view and a remarkable isolation. Foote figured that he personally hauled a million pounds of rock up the hill — 500 pickup loads — and worked as the hod carrier for his Mexican stonemason.

Since the Land Trust was established, 1 percent of Napa County had been removed from the possibility of development. The Footes hoped to double that figure by the end of 1990. They set an example in the county. Si Foote once told a friend, "Rich people don't realize that giving money away is more fun than making it."

The argument heard during the debate on a winery definition, that Bordeaux and other French viticultural districts had a seemingly infinite number of wineries, ignored the fact that, in France, the government had long-range plans for land use and exercised strong control. Each department in France had the right to prevent development of farmland by blocking sales or by condemning the land, purchasing it, and selling it to another farmer. That idea was anathema in America.

Oregon, New York, and Massachusetts all had plans for removing rural land from development, what former Senator Paul E. Tsongas called "the dominant issue in the next decade" — the nineties.

⚬

In Napa, something had basically changed in the two decades between the creation of the ag preserve in 1968 and the struggle over a winery definition in 1988. The cohesion of the old Boring Crowd, the stimulation provided by the Exciting Wave, the welcome diversity of the foreign arrivals and new money looking for acceptable furbishings, even the determination of young, university-minted winemakers still pushing into the valley, were all lost in a broader sea of individual ambition and a blatant desire for power — a relatively recent trend.

Few people who had come of age with Napa Valley had escaped without scars. Success had brought compromises, and disappointments. Now some old scores were going to be settled and the vestiges of accord and common purpose lost.

One person not marked, one person whose existence proved that the valley could have unqualifiedly good effects on people, was Rafael Rodriguez, vineyard manager for the Niebaum-Coppola Estate, naturalized American citizen, grandfather, and labor leader emeritus.

The wedding of Rafael's youngest daughter, Susanna, had been scheduled and then postponed a couple of times. She was to marry a cellar worker at Inglenook named Carl; the date was finally set in June. Rafael wanted to have the reception at the Coppolas', as he had with his older daughter, but the Coppolas had already scheduled a trip to Italy (Francis planned to take forty cases of Rubicon with him), so Rafael called the Clarion Inn in north Napa city to book the banquet room.

Susanna had lived with her parents for thirty-five years. The last of Rafael and Tila's children, she was such a constant in the house that Rafael feared the effects of her leaving. Would he and Tila be able to adjust to her absence? Would Susanna be able to take care of her husband, and he of her? Several times Rafael had asked his prospective son-in-law, over a table liberally spread with chiles rellenos, enchiladas, and various other examples of Tila's prowess in the kitchen, "Carl, are you sure you know what you're getting into?"

Carl was, in Rafael's opinion, a solid young man. He and Susanna had met at Inglenook during crush, in the scale house. The big gondolas would be hauled onto the scale for weighing and a sugar scan — a funnel shoved into the grapes by the state inspector and the contents analyzed for sugar content, and the figures recorded and the price set. Susanna had been the one making the computer entries; she looked up and saw a handsome young man with a black mustache.

They dated for years after that. Susanna moved into a much better job, as an assistant to a wine marketer on Spring Street in St. Helena who represented several good vineyards in the valley and who imported some of the best European wines, among them Biodi Santi and Romanée-Conti. Being single and living at home, Susanna could afford to drive a little BMW with a sunroof. She had not learned to cook nearly as well as her mother because there had been no need. She was a mommy-and-daddy's girl — the phrase was laughingly hers — and the fact didn't bother her at all. She wanted to be what they were: strong, principled, reticent. She wanted to stay forever in the valley, which she loved, where she could not remember, on the eve of her wedding, ever having experienced an act of overt hostility or discrimination.

Her parents' lives had been very different. She had heard about the dirt floor in the house down in Brawley where her mother had grown up, and her father's difficult passage out of Mexico. But they never recalled those hardships. Her father did not talk about the past — and often not about the present. When he worked for the Growers Foundation, when there was union trouble and a lot of uneasiness, the subject was never raised at the table.

Then one night in April, when Carl came over for dinner and Rafael brought out an old bottle of Inglenook Charbono, the subject of children came up. Susanna believed that women should get away from the idea that they can have it all, a full-time job and a family. Children need their mother, she said. Then she heard her father speaking of his childhood in Mexico City, of hunger and other deprivation, of slaving in the market, of pushing a cart across town, of making shelves out of old fruit crates and seeing on the labels and the little tissues spread on the floor the bright, idealized scenes of California fields and California orchards. Finally Susanna said, "Oh, Daddy, you're going to make me cry."

The Catholic church in St. Helena filled slowly. The day was overcast and cool, more strange weather in a strange year, but ideal for a wedding. Rafael stood outside in his formal suit, greeting people. There were almost as many fair heads in the gathering congregation as dark ones, an indication of the diversity of Susanna's and Carl's friends. No fewer than four video cameras had been set up inside the church, recording the bridesmaids, who walked one by one down the center aisle in their glistening gowns, and the young men in white jackets.

Susanna emerged from the car in a white dress with a long train. She seemed frail but quite beautiful, smiling, remarkably composed. Tila wore green; she too seemed composed but Rafael knew there would be some tears. As he led Susanna up the aisle, he himself felt a rush of gratitude and sadness: he would have to be careful when he spoke at the reception.

Carl waited in his white jacket, smiling. Susanna released Rafael's arm and took Carl's. They turned to face the priest, looking like movie stars. "You are surrounded by those who mean the most to you," the priest said, "family and friends."

Later, he said, "Happiness is not something that happens," and Rafael thought about that.

After the Ave Maria, Susanna and Carl walked up together and placed a bouquet of flowers at the feet of the Virgin. They took their vows, loud and clear, a loving, slightly amused pair who seemed more at ease with each other than many people who had been married for years. Then they embraced and it was over.

Outside, drifting clouds over the eastern mountains were turning a radiant pink, building like the defiles of some higher range. It was probably raining over in Wild Horse Valley, but to the west the sky was clear, promising a hot day. The traffic was backed up all the way to Zinfandel Lane. The vineyards still showed the subtle reds and yellows of wild flowers between the vines, thriving on the unusual moisture. Such things concerned Rafael as the manager of the Niebaum-Coppola vineyards, but they would not concern him as much in the future. He planned to retire in a few years. He would take Tila to see Washington, D.C., the Congress and the monuments, but beyond that his plans were vague.

The guests were waiting at the Clarion Inn and the ten-piece mariachi band was ready. Four white doves moved restively in their cages, and the tables had been elaborately set up around the dance floor. After everyone had gone through the receiving line the band struck up, not fast music in the beginning but a ballad, to which

Susanna and Carl first danced alone and then were joined by others. A rock band waited to take over when the mariachis were done, dinner served, the speeches made, and the crowd ready for some basic American bump and grind.

Rafael stood up and the music and conversation ceased. He raised his glass of sparkling wine, and said, "I am an emotional person. Do not be surprised if you see champagne running out of my eyes. . . . If my life was a book, it would be twenty-four thousand pages long and would record all the hopes and tragedies. This is one of the truly happy days of my life."

VII

The Tragedy
of the Commons

43

S EEN FROM the air — there were often planes overhead in the spring of 1988 — the valley retained its stunning beauty. The towns had grown up considerably since Robert Louis Stevenson viewed them from the slopes of Mount St. Helena more than a century before, and vineyards had displaced woods and pasture. The long, unmarked vistas the Davieses had encountered in 1964, the lightless nights that the McCreas, the Winiarskis, the Eiseles, and others had confronted in the remoter hills, had been marked and kindled by the growing population and all the manmade amenities it entailed. But the overall impression was still rural, even timeless.

The foothills, because they were protected under the provisions of the agricultural preserve, did not support the tiers of houses encountered elsewhere in California; the valley floor had kept the soft contours of the "edible" landscape, a place where things grow, rather than one supporting rigid forms on a plain of macadam and concrete. The accord between natural process and man-driven designs was tenuous, however. The strains could be seen in the slow but steady expansion of structures already in existence, in the appearance of new ones, in the roads and parking oases — macadam and concrete — and the stream of cars attracted to them. The closer the viewer got, the more apparent the strains became. From Sterling's chair lift, from the dormers at the top of Greystone, from the Oakville Grade and the crests of the Silverado Trail, from the wooded swales on the Mondavi compound above the Napa River, you could see buildings, driveways, and gates — lights and more lights — that had not been there just a year or so before.

The suggestion of agrarian simplicity was just that, and fading. The visitor sipping sparkling wine on the deck of the Auberge de

Soleil no longer looked out over a land reminiscent of Burgundy or Champagne. He saw instead an expanse of roofs in the foreground, and the skeleton of yet another winery putting on prefabricated flesh.

Andy Beckstoffer's ranch on Zinfandel Lane sat far back from the road, shaded by trees. A long driveway lined with shrubbery led to the expanse of lawn that encompassed tennis court and swimming pool. Glass walls on both sides of the house flooded the interior with light. The living room contained porcelain figurines on shelves and those leather-bound volumes traced with gold leaf that adorn so many tasteful American homes, designed as much for viewing as for reading; the commissioned portrait of the Beckstoffer children over the mantel completed the impression of solidity and comfort. Except for the palm trees, the house might have sat in a well-to-do suburb of Richmond, Virginia.

Beckstoffer, suntanned and healthful, emerged from his house in polo shirt, pleated khakis, and dun-colored bucks, carrying a tray of glasses and a bottle of Napa Valley Chardonnay for his guests' enjoyment. He saw around him the lush blessing of a well-watered California existence, unless he looked in the direction of Sutter Home's white Zinfandel factory just to the east. There millions of cases were annually churned out, from grapes trucked in from the Central Valley and beyond. The complex vaguely resembled an oil refinery.

When Beckstoffer first arrived in the valley in 1969, as the brash young troubleshooter for Heublein, he had no idea how things might turn out. The other guys from Hartford were long gone, but Beckstoffer had endured. He now owned or managed close to 1,500 acres of vineyards in Napa, probably more than any other independent grower. He figured he was worth upwards of $10 million. He belonged to the Northern California Young Presidents Club, was a contributing member of the Republican party, a founding director of the Napa Valley Grape Growers Association, and probably had more enemies than any resident of the upper valley.

He had come forcefully into the argument for responsible land use. He did not want houses, new wineries, and expansions of existing ones cutting into the ag preserve and its value, and had put his well-earned corporate skills and energy into the effort to prevent this. His adversaries accused him of self-interest; Beckstoffer liked to think of his involvement in the valley as an enlightened form of it.

He had found natural allies, like Bob Phillips, past president of the Napa Valley Grape Growers, and a Republican. Beckstoffer and Phillips collaborated politically. Both had southern roots — Beckstoffer had not managed to get into Stanford, as Phillips had — and both were wealthy. Then there were the unnatural allies, like Volker Eisele and Vic Fershko. Eisele was a Democrat, and Fershko a Republican, but both were activists in antidevelopment causes Beckstoffer would once have scorned. Fershko, the lawyer with the most flamboyant mustache in the valley with the possible exception of Stu Smith's, had consistently opposed subdivisions and other expressions of untrammeled free enterprise. Volker, the bearded champion of open space, had with the help of some like-minded growers and the staff of the Farm Bureau transformed that sleepy county agency into a potent political force, with a land-use committee and a real agenda.

Beckstoffer had nothing to do with the Farm Bureau, but he was an active member of the Napa Valley Grape Growers Association, along with Volker. Beckstoffer recognized talent when he saw it. He also recognized common cause. The valley was devoted to agriculture; growers represented, at least theoretically, the greater good. The ag preserve allowed only two uses other than agriculture, and those two were houses and wineries. Ideally, the former contained farmers and their families, and the latter existed solely to enhance agriculture. If houses were built for commuters, and wineries just for tourists, then they didn't belong.

A winery was a processing plant for Napa Valley's prime commodity, grapes. If it transformed Central Valley grapes, or those from Sonoma, into wine, then it did no more for Napa agriculture than an orange-packing plant.

That argument greatly annoyed the vintners. They wanted no restrictions on what they called "marketing," a catchall for any activity that might sell wine, like tours, T-shirt sales, concerts, cooking schools, and what amounted to operating restaurants. The vintners wanted the government to assure them the right to engage in these activities in the ag preserve, even though the activities weren't related to agriculture. In free enterprise, Beckstoffer argued — in board meetings, before the Napa County Planning Commission, and occasionally while socializing with vintners — that government shouldn't be involved in marketing, whether of wine or automobiles. Marketing was an activity to be conducted by businesses, within the zoning laws. Beckstoffer didn't object to wine tastings at the wineries, but he did object to the people and the traffic — the sheer numbers — that were inimical to agriculture.

The livelihood of the growers as well as the vintners depended not just on the price of grapes but also on the good reputation of Napa Valley. If Napa wines came to be viewed as the bounty of a kind of Disneyland North, or the valley as just another bedroom community for San Francisco, people would be less willing to pay $20 for the kind of Napa Valley Chardonnay that Beckstoffer poured with a deft twist of the wrist and a discerning eye. The grapes grown in the valley might no longer fetch such a high price. If the price ever fell dramatically, Beckstoffer's house would soon be surrounded not by vineyards but by the sort of development that would make even Sutter Home look benign.

Volker Eisele spent a larger percentage of his time working on land-use issues than did Beckstoffer or most of his other allies. Volker's wife, Liesel, often said to him in exasperation, "You're a walking contribution!"

With two children of college age, a vineyard, a house in Chiles Valley, and the standard relationship with a bank, the Eiseles didn't have money to spare for worthy causes. The option was obvious: work.

Volker did, for the Greenbelt Alliance, for the Farm Bureau, for the Napa Valley Grape Growers, and for various political candidates. He had helped to elect Mel Varrelman to the county board of supervisors and to tilt the five-member board away from development and toward slow growth. As vice president and then president of the Grape Growers he had participated in the push for a winery definition that included a requirement that Napa Valley wineries use mostly Napa Valley grapes. Beyond that, if the wineries imposed some restrictions on themselves, then future planning commissions, boards of supervisors, and even businessmen would be encouraged to respect the integrity of the ag preserve. But the minimum grape requirement was the real issue.

Volker had worked for two years with the vintners, trying to get a compromise definition. During that time, relations between vintners and growers had steadily worsened. The Napa Valley Vintners Association was fifty years older than the Napa Valley Grape Growers Association, and much more influential, not by virtue of age but

economic might. Many of the vintners also owned their own vineyards, so the growers had no monopoly on grapes. But the growers
were the official voice of agriculture, and lately that voice had grown
stronger. The close relationship between the Farm Bureau and the
Grape Growers, and more forceful personalities in leadership positions, had greatly added to the authority of agriculture. Surely that
was the primary activity in the valley — growing, not selling, not
catering to tourists, not putting up houses. The growers were better
organized than the polyglot, highly individualistic vintners, and had
moved into the vacuum created by the vintners' inaction. Vintner
"approach avoidance" of the winery definition issue had created a
unique opportunity for farmers.

The Eiseles worked on their house when they found time. The steps
to the front porch were being rebuilt and a stylish landing put in at
the foot. The front room, with tall doors opening onto the porch,
served as a combination parlor and library, the walls packed with
books, most of them written in German. A wood stove sat in the
hallway. Fresh fruit and vegetables were set in bowls on the kitchen
counters beneath dangling fly tapes. The skin of an enormous rattlesnake killed in the driveway hung from a board above the door, a
reminder of the perils of country life. In the dining room were a
fireplace, chairs and table, and a big window overlooking a raised
terrace designed by Liesel. Beyond the terrace stretched the vineyard, and beyond it steep hills covered with oak and digger pine. A
linden tree grew at the northern edge. Sometimes the Eiseles sat out
in canvas chairs and drank their own Cabernet, made on the property, and felt the splendid isolation of Chiles Valley.

They passed hours alone in their cars and on the telephone. The
answering machine was a lobby in its own right, and Volker spent a
lot of time communing with it. Some of the voices he heard would
have surprised him back in his Berkeley days, particularly the voices
of Republicans. He viewed himself as a social democrat in the tradition of Germany's Willy Brandt. He would accept any assistance
in the struggle for open space; he had found it among people much
more conservative than he. Volker discussed national politics with
Andy Beckstoffer and Bob Phillips, and found that they were usually
on opposite sides, but aligned on local issues. Beckstoffer was easy
to get along with, but sometimes Phillips had trouble with Volker's
outspokenness. Phillips would say, "Volker, don't be so radical."

At Berkeley, Volker had been accused of being not radical

enough. Still, in the eyes of some vintners he was a dangerous left winger. Volker considered himself a rationalist, a believer in the Enlightenment, opposed to excess — too much ease, too much asphalt, even too much wine. He lacked sympathy for certain vintners in Napa Valley, those whose prosperity had left them manipulating, immutable, hostile to criticism and sometimes to ideas. But his primary objection to them was their disregard for the long-term use of the land.

The idea of requiring a percentage of Napa Valley grapes in Napa Valley wine first surfaced in discussions of a winery definition between the Napa Valley Grape Growers and the Farm Bureau. It was not, on the face of it, a radical notion, but some vintners viewed it as such. Better grapes made better wine, the vintners said, and wineries would always pay well for quality fruit. They didn't have to be coerced by the county government.

The growers thought things were more complicated than that. Every year huge tonnages of grapes and grape juice were "imported," trucked in from the Central Valley and outlying counties, and turned into mostly mediocre wine. It sold for much less than wine made from Napa grapes, but for more than it would have fetched if it had not been made in Napa, despite the fact that it had no real connection to the valley. Martini used out-of-county grapes in its best blends, as did Hanns Kornell. But other vintners used their Napa Valley address cynically.

Beringer had capitalized on the valley's name in a second brand of low-cost wine called Napa Ridge, made of imported grapes. Hundreds of thousands of cases of Napa Ridge were produced every year at Beringer's plant at the north end of St. Helena. Many people, including some of Beringer's own employees, considered Napa Ridge an outrage. Beringer was the inheritor of the earliest winemaking traditions in the valley, symbolized by the ornate stone and timber Rhine House and the lines of lovely, sheltering elms along Highway 29. Beringer's Swiss owner, Nestlé, had been praised for doing things right since it came to the valley, and cited as the antithesis of the corporate brashness of Heublein. Beringer had bought good vineyards and improved the quality of its best wines. Then Napa Ridge appeared. At first the natives had been amused: there were many ridges in Napa, but no Napa Ridge. It was to Beringer what Falcon Crest was to Spring Mountain, a cheap knock-off. Marketing it through the Nestlé network brought in an inordinate amount of money and made Mike Moone, Beringer's president, look good on his visits to Vevey.

Some vintners who detested the name Napa Ridge defended the practice of using imported grapes. There was a chance they might someday want to do the same, and some already had, to help defray the expense of making premium wine. Caymus Vineyards had a second line; so did Stag's Leap Wine Cellars. Warren Winiarski had made it plain he was willing to move the production of his Hawk's Crest out of the ag preserve and the ag watershed if it was seen as an encroachment or as a detriment to the Napa Valley name. Other vintners were not willing to move or to cease making wine from imported grapes.

Many vintners as well as growers thought expansion of wineries to process out-of-county fruit did encroach on the ag preserve. Imported grapes required new facilities for producing the wine, and with them came more people, office space, waste water, cars, parking lots, and retail sales of T-shirts and the like. Wine "theme parks" would be next. Entrepreneurs would truck in Central Valley grapes and sell the wine made from them to naïve tourists at inflated prices, without using a single Napa Valley grape.

So the question officially arose among growers: could Napa wineries be required to use a certain percentage of Napa grapes? Volker, as a ranking member of the Napa Valley Grape Growers Association, put the question to Vic Fershko, the lawyer. Fershko feared such a requirement might violate antitrust laws, so when the Grape Growers first met with the Vintners Association's representatives, Jay Corley and Reverdy Johnson, he didn't press the issue. They talked around it. But the idea of a minimum grape requirement continued to be discussed among the growers.

Then the winemaker for Domaine Chandon appeared before the Farm Bureau's board of directors, at some risk to his own livelihood, and urged them to seek a minimum percentage of valley grapes to stop the degradation of the Napa Valley name. Finally Andy Beckstoffer, at a meeting of the board of the Napa Valley Grape Growers, said, "Let's try it and see what happens."

Volker had the idea of tying the grape percentage to the Napa Valley appellation. In other words, adopt the same requirement used by the Bureau of Alcohol, Tobacco and Firearms for wines using the Napa Valley name on the label. According to the labeling law, 75 percent of the grapes used in a bottle of "Napa Valley" wine had to come from Napa. The same requirement could apply to all new wineries in the valley and to expansions of existing wineries. Present operations would not be affected, but any additional winemaking ventures would be bound by the 75 percent requirement.

It seemed a reasonable proposal. In France, the wineries were required to use 100 percent of grapes grown within the appellations. But the question would further separate the growers and vintners, bring to light some old animosities, and in the end split the valley like a fault.

44

REVERDY JOHNSON, the new president of the Napa Valley Vintners Association, steered his aging Alfa Romeo up the drive to Meadowood for the July meeting. Reverdy was a vintner but also a lawyer — an appropriate profession for the leader of the association in these troubled times. Jim Barrett, owner of Château Montelena, had invited Reverdy onto the board several years before in part because he was a lawyer. Reverdy's fellow officers on the board — men like Mike Moone, president of Beringer, and Dick Maher, president of Christian Brothers — ran huge wineries and were good at corporate politics, but it was Reverdy who had to face the general membership and who had to maneuver in an increasingly contentious regulatory environment.

Reverdy smoked a pipe with a flat bowl and a short, crooked stem. The pipe, along with the salt-and-pepper beard and steel-rimmed glasses, added to his contemplative mien. His Levi's and boots, however, were evidence of what he considered his affinity with the soil. He had grown up in New Jersey and graduated from Harvard, but he loved the land. That had led him to the heights of realty law in a firm with offices in San Francisco, Los Angeles, San Jose, Dallas, Newport, and Washington, D.C., and into a vineyard and winery partnership.

Reverdy prized his ability to analyze problems, part of his law school training. Today "appellation education" was on the Vintners' agenda, but the winery definition was the big issue. After many months of fruitless negotiations between vintners and growers over land use, Reverdy had nothing definitive to tell his colleagues except that the growers had rejected the vintners' proposal for a winery zone — the so-called overlay plan, an idea put forward by Michael Mondavi in a letter to Jim Hickey. According to the plan, an overlay zone would be superimposed on existing wineries, legalizing many of the activities that were not now legal and giving them plenty of statutory room to expand. The overlay plan had never been officially approved by the Vintners board and certainly not by the whole membership, but still it had become the de facto vintner position, largely because Reverdy liked it.

The Napa Valley Grape Growers and the Farm Bureau, on the other side, wanted limits imposed on new wineries and on the expansion of existing ones, *and* they wanted a fixed percentage of Napa Valley grapes used by Napa Valley wineries. This would automatically limit expansion of existing wineries and the creation of new ones. There were risks involved for the wineries, like poor harvests that would make grapes hard to come by. But in France, when the harvest was poor, the French simply made less wine; they did not import grapes from other regions and try to keep up their production. A winery either believed in quality or did not. The market would eventually take up the slack by providing more money for the good harvests, and preserving the land in the meantime, but many of the vintners would not accept this argument — including Reverdy Johnson — because it meant less control and less profit.

He parked in the shade of the big ponderosa pines and got out. His vanity plate said C-RANCH, a tribute to a development project on the coast that he as an attorney had helped facilitate. Other vintners were climbing the steps; there would be a good turnout at the Vintners meeting today. In five years the group had advanced, in Reverdy's view, from a chowder and marching society to the status of real trade association. This was a response to the demands of the current marketplace. Appellations and land use were subordinate in his mind to the need for effective marketing.

Reverdy Johnson was often heard to say, "They don't understand the industry." When he said this he was referring to most of the world outside the "super-premium" end of the wine business, including the growers. The Napa Valley Vintners, whose members constituted many of the super-premium labels, was a highly diverse, idiosyncratic group driven by wildly different motives. Some of *them* didn't understand the industry either, he thought, but that was another problem.

Wineries were closely held companies, meaning no shares were sold to the public and information about them surfaced at the pleasure of the owners. Not all that information was real. The industry was viewed according to what was commonly referred to as conventional wisdom, and that fluctuated between extremes. Vintners were said to be either making a fortune or losing their shirts, depending on the nature of the information released. Some vintners were making a lot of money, and others were losing as much, but neither sort cared to admit it.

What most outsiders didn't understand was that fine wine did not sell itself. It had to be marketed. The vintners argued that any restraints on the marketing of Napa Valley wineries reduced the competitiveness of Napa Valley wine — and then used the argument as an excuse for cashing in on the tourist trade at the expense of land preservation. The growers favored limiting winery activities, and wanted a minimum requirement for local fruit, which was in the interest of preservation but would also raise the price of Napa Valley grapes.

The growers were a more homogeneous group than the vintners. They considered the vintners a bunch of egomaniacs too selfish and too removed from reality to understand what they were doing to the valley by expanding and by importing grapes to be made into inferior wine. The vintners considered the growers little more than yahoos led by a couple of wily men, Beckstoffer and Eisele, who were trying to create a monopoly and jack up the price of their product. But some vintners agreed with the growers' proposals to limit winery growth and activities. That made Reverdy's job more difficult, since he approved of new wineries, expansion, and the importation of grapes to keep the wineries prosperous and autonomous.

Surveying the group assembled in Meadowood's bright amphitheater, he realized that, in a way, the vintners had been *too* successful. Because they had created an industry that attracted people and notoriety, other people tended to lay problems at their doorstep. The flood of tourists was an example. John Wright, the president of Domaine Chandon — so slumped in his seat in the first tier as to be almost horizontal — had sponsored a study indicating that only 20 percent of the cars in the valley belonged to tourists. The rest of the traffic was locally generated, but the wineries continued to be blamed for congestion. Not everybody put credence in Wright's claim.

Another part of the problem was envy. The vintners were considered exciting, vibrant personages, with almost as many backgrounds as there were individuals. They pursued a combination of cottage industry and high-tech entrepreneurship that fascinated people; they had achieved a preeminent position in the world and occupied a distinct piece of geography that everybody wanted to look at and to live in. Some locals and some outsiders resented that.

The valley's history could be read in the assembled ranks: Eleanor McCrea, Roy Raymond, Louis Martini, Brother Timothy, who had represented Christian Brothers for half a century, Robin Lail, Tom Selfridge, who had taken over the management of Beaulieu from Legh Knowles, Chuck Carpy, Harvey Posert, sitting in for Robert Mondavi and perusing his usual stack of wine publications, Jack Davies, Warren Winiarski, Jim Barrett, Dick Peterson, Dennis Fife, president of Inglenook, Jan Shrem, Larry McGuire from Far Niente, Guy Kay, vice president of operations for Beringer, and many more. Seated in the front row, the only man wearing a tie, was Bob Dwyer, the Vintners' executive director, formerly executive director of the Napa Valley Grape Growers. The Vintners had been smart enough to employ Dwyer when he came after the job. Dwyer provided insight into the motives of the growers, who had become the vintners' adversaries.

After the meeting had gotten under way, Jack Davies stood up to urge the vintners to attend a public hearing on county zoning in Napa city. "People are calling for the county to be more liberal in allowing expansion of nonconforming uses," Davies said in his flat midwestern voice. "They're urging the county to change the former policy along Highway 29. If the zoning is weakened, this has the potential of a chain reaction that will hasten commercial development that conflicts with agricultural uses."

"Jack's comments lead us to the winery definition," said Reverdy. "This has been around a long time. It's no longer a question of just production but of what wineries may do and how they can expand."

He explained that he and Tom Selfridge had been discussing the issue with Andy Beckstoffer and Volker Eisele since April. Even the ambience of the Auberge de Soleil, where they met, had not helped. The growers had rejected the idea put forward by the vintners for a winery overlay zone exempt from the usual regulations. "There is a traditional distrust of the vintners," Reverdy said. "They think we're trying to haul a Trojan horse through the valley, to create new wineries. One thing coming up crystal clear is the 75 percent grape requirement for all new wineries and for expansion of existing ones."

A minimum grape requirement was, he admitted, a very appealing notion on the surface. After all, the ag preserve existed to preserve agriculture, and wineries existed only to augment it. "Unfortunately," he went on, "life is not that simple. This industry is organized in a somewhat more complex way" — he meant that the growers didn't understand it — "and making wine and marketing it well sometimes means not using Napa Valley fruit."

Being restricted to Napa Valley grapes meant making less money, in short. Louis Martini agreed, as did Justine Meyer, owner of Silver Oak Cellars, who had always depended on grapes from Sonoma County for making good wine. But not all wine made from imported grapes was good, or necessary — Beringer's 200,000 annual cases of Napa Ridge were ample testimony. And Christian Brothers was at that moment bottling a new wine of which half had been made from *French* grapes. Christian Brothers had spent a fortune on full-page color ads in *The Wine Spectator* praising Napa Valley's unique climate and soils, with an artist's rendition of the layers of geological significance, and then Dick Maher had gone clear to France as a publicity gimmick.

"I had hoped to be able to go into the winery definition hearing in two weeks saying we are in agreement with the growers," Reverdy said. But that was no longer possible. "If we give them the 75 percent requirement, we can do anything else we want. But remember, this doesn't just affect new wineries. And you're all going to want to expand."

The growers' representatives monitored as best they could the flood of bulk wine pouring into the valley. Most of it went to Sutter Home, Beringer, and other big operations. Everyone agreed this was an outrage, but other vintners wouldn't complain because those same vintners might all someday want to put out their own million cases of cheap wine. Meanwhile, the biggest properties had been taken over by corporate giants not particularly interested in the best land use — not just Beringer but also Grand Metropolitan, owner of Heublein and, incidentally, Inglenook and BV. There were Whitbread, Moët-Hennessy, and Seagram — owner of Sterling, much of Diamond Mountain, Winery Lake Vineyard in Carneros, and the marketing agent for Krug. Seagram had spent almost $1 billion to buy Martell, the cognac house, and could probably have bought all of Napa Valley if it chose.

The Mondavis couldn't prevent such a move by one of the big multinationals. They and the rest of the home-grown dynasties were no match for the new competition. Certain growers thought some old Napa families — Lucky Spermers — lacked harmony, drive, and intellectual rigor — part of a larger problem in the nation. Thirty years before, the Europeans and the Japanese were afraid to enter the American market. Now they were taking over. They seemed to look at America the way America had looked at Honduras at the beginning of the century, the way Britain had looked at India.

Ironically, other locals and recent arrivals sought to imitate the foreigners. They hungered after aristocracy, or the appearance of aristocracy, and owning a winery, a California château, was often as close as they could get. Wine's instant equation with culture left obvious discrepancies. Some vintners praised art without learning anything about it; they spoke of high civilization, had videos prepared on wine's role in its development, and made speeches about the cultural diversity of wine without bothering to open a book of history or literature. This task was left to experts who supposedly infused them with knowledge. Some vintners so yearned for nobility that they pursued barons, counts, and princes, entering into deals with them and otherwise celebrating the association. It was good public relations, good marketing. But their one opportunity for truly noble behavior — to protect the land absolutely — they squandered in ego gratification and profits.

Two days after the vintners met, the growers held a press conference at the Farm Bureau, in a utilitarian building on the outskirts of Napa city that could not have been more starkly different from Meadowood. The building also contained the County Farm Supply store, CalFarm Insurance, and the Napa Valley Grape Growers Association, which shared the staff of the Farm Bureau but had a different board and different officers. The sun bounced off the pavement outside, and just yards away traffic trundled between clotted Trancas Avenue and the first glimpses of open country.

A coffee urn had been set out and chairs and tables arranged. The handful of reporters gathered under the low ceiling were all local. Wilted by the heat, they sat facing Volker Eisele and Andy Beckstoffer, an obvious contrast in styles. Volker wore a work shirt, Andy a polo shirt with a representation of a horse and rider stitched on it.

Volker considered Beckstoffer a great triumph of the rational land ethic; Beckstoffer considered Eisele an excellent organizer and political tactician, and a workhorse for his cause.

Volker glanced one last time out into the hall. He said, "I guess KVON isn't going to show up."

"Let's do it," said Beckstoffer.

Volker passed around press releases containing the growers' proposal for a county ordinance defining a winery. He and Andy had worked out the details, and the board of the 240-member Grape Growers Association had unanimously approved it. "Look at this proposal," Volker began, "in terms of the preservation of the agricultural preserve. This is the twentieth anniversary of its creation. When I look back, I see it hasn't been touched. That's extraordinary, and unique in this country."

As always, he was acutely aware of the sound of his voice: precise and foreign, regardless of his command of American idioms. "Every time we have made a decision, we have looked toward the preservation of the ag preserve and the ag watershed. We have worked hard to come up with a recognition of the legitimate needs of the wineries."

The reporters read the press release. Volker and Beckstoffer had devised categories for the wineries — "heritage," "charter," and "estate" — an imposition of order on a disorderly enterprise. A heritage winery was one established before July 30, 1974, the date that use permits were first required for Napa Valley wineries. A charter winery was one established after that date but before the adoption of this new ordinance, and an estate winery was one established after passage of the new law. Estate — that is, new — wineries would be required to process at least 75 percent of Napa Valley grapes. They would not be allowed to conduct public tours, tastings, or promotional events, and only wines produced on the site could be sold there.

Heritage and charter wineries could continue their present practices if lawful at the time they were first undertaken. Any expansion outside the original "footprint" of heritage and charter wineries on agricultural land would require compliance with the rules regulating new wineries.

In other words, older wineries could get away with what they were already doing if it was legal at the time they started doing it. If not, the tours, sales, and culinary powwows would have to stop.

And any expansion of existing wineries was subject to the Napa Valley grape minimum, the so-called 75 percent solution.

"Let's go back," said Beckstoffer, "to understand how we got here. The county says the primary function of zoning is to protect agriculture. In the ag preserve and the ag watershed only three things are allowed: agriculture, houses, and wineries. Twenty years ago it was decided how the land could be split up; today we're finally deciding the uses."

"We're defining a winery like Webster might," Volker added, "but according to the zoning laws. We need to recognize that we are in 1988, not 1968. We need to recognize that Napa Valley is famous, important in the culture of the country and the concerns of the citizens. We want to preserve agriculture, give credit to the wineries already here, and take into consideration traffic and tourism."

The young woman who covered the wine industry for the *Napa Register,* Mary Beth Christie, asked why they, the growers' representatives, hadn't gone first to the Napa Valley Vintners Association with their plan rather than presenting it at a press conference. "We want to make sure the story goes to the people of the county straight," Volker told her. "The vintners are fully informed of every step, but we haven't heard from them. We have adopted this as an official position," he added.

Afterward, as he poured Beaulieu Sauvignon Blanc for the reporters who tarried — Volker had sold grapes to BV that went into the wine — he spoke candidly. "Something has to be done. . . . Talk to people door-to-door and you'll hear that they don't like the wineries. They think the vintners are arrogant, elitist, and cause the traffic. . . . The average person in the county can't afford a bottle of real Napa Valley wine. If something isn't done, we'll see a voter initiative passed that will shut down a lot of operations."

The growers' proposal for defining wineries was aired on local television that night and in the *Register* the next morning. But there was no immediate response from the vintners. Volker spent most of the weekend at his house up in Chiles Valley, working around the place and waiting for a call from Reverdy Johnson.

He heard Bob Dwyer, executive director of the Vintners Association and an old acquaintance of Volker's, on the radio. Dwyer spoke as the vintners' official representative. That was a bit of a problem for Volker — and for Andy Beckstoffer, Bob Phillips, and anyone who had dealt with Dwyer in the old days, when he worked for the Napa Valley Grape Growers. Dwyer had helped build up some credibility for the growers at a time when the organization was moving away from a mere farmers' lobby and toward a real political presence in the county. When Dwyer got the job with the Vintners, he told his old colleagues that he wasn't abandoning the cause of agriculture. Volker would never forget the day Dwyer left. They and some others from the Farm Bureau and the Napa Valley Grape Growers had gone up to the Red Hen on the frontage road off Highway 29, to commemorate the occasion. While they drank beer, Volker noticed that Dwyer had on new, expensive Italian loafers instead of his ordinary shoes. Volker said, poking fun at him, "Soon you won't even speak to us, you're so elegant." Dwyer protested, but had in fact gone over to the other side.

Now Dwyer was saying that the growers had put the 75 percent requirement back on the negotiating table, when it had never been taken off. He was saying that the growers and the vintners were still far apart, suggesting that it was the growers' fault.

Volker found it difficult to determine exactly what the vintners wanted or, more precisely, what they stood for. Egocentric, often reactionary, they defied systematic analysis. If they rejected the growers' proposal, they would appear selfish, but that didn't seem to bother them. Public sentiment was clearly running against tourism and the wineries; the whole world knew there was a problem out there, that if the wineries didn't regulate themselves they would be regulated, and much more harshly than what the growers proposed.

Bob Phillips called to say he had heard the vintners were abandoning their overlay proposal. What might replace it was anybody's guess. In the end it would be Jim Hickey's staff in the Planning Department that decided the issue, and Phillips wanted to make sure they were properly informed. The upcoming public hearings would be important, he said.

Volker hung up thinking that the real problem was the big wineries. Driven by short-term profits, they wanted total flexibility, total opportunity. Concerned only with their interests, they failed to realize that the county government also represented 110,000 people who didn't care about the big wineries and were increasingly hostile to them. The wineries imported vast quantities of grapes that in no way contributed to the livelihood of others in the valley.

Volker, Andy Beckstoffer, and some others had divided up the task of finding out just how much fruit was imported. Volker had sat down with *The Gomberg Report* in Andy's office, Beckstoffer House in St. Helena, to calculate the tonnage trucked in from the Central Valley and elsewhere. He estimated that between 50 and 60 percent of the cases of wine made in Napa was made from imported grapes. This harvest, 1988, it might well reach 70 percent. Grape production in the valley was static because most of the plantable land was already under cultivation, and because of drought and other adverse weather conditions. But the wineries kept growing.

45

R EVERDY JOHNSON wrote a letter to Jim Hickey, head of the
Planning Department, that began "Dear Jim" and went on
to praise Hickey for the "excellent" perspective of his report
on winery density. Reverdy repeated the Vintners' desire for an overlay zone that would allow existing wineries much leeway in expansion. "We have offered it as a means of changing the focus of the
dialogue from the trees to the larger forest."

In his report Reverdy referred to, Hickey had written, "One of
the major appeals of Napa County . . . is the feeling of open space
you experience when you are driving through the unincorporated
area. [Hickey was a planner, not a poet.] That feeling is enhanced by
the general absence of billboards . . . overhead utility lines, suburban
subdivision, shopping centers, multi-lane highways, freeways and
urban development. . . . Most people, residents and tourists see the
County and identify with it from the view they see through their car
or truck window. . . . The view begins at the highway and contin-
ues across the vineyards and open space until the eye is stopped by a
visual obstacle."

The public tended to think of those views as belonging to it,
Hickey added, and the visual obstacles were taking over. "Some feel
that the quality of the environment is being eroded by the number,
density, scale and the general appearance of new wineries."

Reverdy called a meeting of the Vintners board: Mike Moone,
Dick Maher, Tom Ferrell, Dennis Groth, Stan Anderson, Agustin
Huneeus, Steve Girard, and Warren Winiarski. Jay Corley was also
present because of his association with the auction and because Corley was an insider. They all gathered to hear what Reverdy had to

say about the growers' proposal for defining wineries, and Reverdy told them, "We'd better pay attention to these guys."

⌘

The elevators on the third floor of the county administration building in Napa city opened onto a narrow hallway and a pair of glass doors. Sometimes the doors were locked while, on the far side, the county supervisors and the county counsel and maybe the county planner hashed out some particularly ticklish bit of county business. Often these people were trying to avoid lawsuits by petitioners denied permission to build or expand some structure, lawsuits being expensive and the county counsel a kind of built-in antidote to litigious rulings by the county's lawmakers. But usually the doors were unlocked, as they were on that Tuesday morning at 10 A.M., when the zoning hearing was due to get under way.

Although it was just a zoning hearing, many people had lately become interested in the subject of development, and half the sixty public seats were already taken. The supervisors themselves sat at a slight elevation, behind an elliptical podium in five plush, high-backed chairs covered in buff-colored plastic. Behind them stood an American flag and one of the state of California. A mural depicted grapevines attached to wooden stakes like those used by the early immigrants — the only suggestion of the county's primary vocation in an otherwise contemporary, characterless government chamber.

Zoning requirements and the winery definition were both to be addressed. Hickey's report had brought responses not only from Reverdy Johnson but also from the Napa Valley Grape Growers. Volker Eisele had sent Hickey a copy of the growers' draft proposal for the winery definition that had been presented at the press conference the previous week. Those in the audience read Reverdy's letter, and the correspondence and reports that had been reproduced and laid out on a table for public perusal, but Reverdy was not present. The vintners were still reeling from the growers' proposal to categorize the wineries and limit their expansion, and had no real alternative to offer. Reverdy had at the last moment withdrawn the Vintners' overlay plan — which the members had yet to approve — to make more changes.

The wineries were unofficially represented by Joe Peatman, of Dickenson, Peatman & Fogarty, the preeminent Napa city legal firm and the automatic champion of any client seeking to expand his business within the ag preserve or to develop a new business. It was Peatman who had come up with the idea of a special zone for wineries — the overlay plan — that Michael Mondavi first presented to Hickey. Peatman had himself been a supervisor from 1969 to 1972. The photograph of Peatman on the wall of the chamber showed a fresh-faced young man wearing a white shirt and tie, black-rimmed glasses, and an expression of budding impatience. His law firm now occupied the corner suite just across the street from the county building. Peatman had walked the distance thousands of times in the intervening years, carrying a briefcase, taking on a florid complexion, and displaying the habit — almost a tic — of glancing over his shoulder during public hearings.

Peatman was present. So were Volker Eisele, Bob Phillips, Warren Winiarski, a number of other growers and interested citizens, and some businessmen petitioning for legalization of their activities in the ag preserve — a Fast Gas and a convenience store — represented by Peatman. He stood up, straightened his tie, glanced over his shoulder, and told the supervisors that the county had finally come down to the crunch. "I don't know how you could recognize these commercially developed properties as adversely affecting agriculture," he said. "Most of them are older than agriculture. If you vote this down, it will politicize the county and turn the subdivisions against the growers. You're looking at real long-range trouble."

Volker stepped up to the lectern and introduced himself; the five supervisors and the county counsel already knew him, since Volker had helped elect three of them. "I feel compelled to make some statement," he said. "Agriculture is the oldest use of the land. When George Yount settled here he didn't start a convenience store, he planted a vine."

No one wanted to harm the businessman, he added, but to protect agriculture. "The way to go about this is to allow the nonconforming businesses to exist, but don't allow them to expand."

The supervisor from District 4, Harold Moskowite, a thick-necked, buzz-cut landowner from the eastern part of the county, leaned toward his microphone and asked Volker, "How would you like for us to tell you you can't plant any more vines?"

"That's kind of silly," said Volker, "since I am in conformance with the law. *You're* one of the people who want to change this."

Moskowite had been defeated in the spring primary and would be out of office at the end of the year. Volker had helped organize that defeat. Moskowite now demanded to know if Volker represented the members of the Napa Valley Grape Growers or just the board. It was an old charge — that Volker's and Beckstoffer's views had nothing in common with those of the average Napa Valley farmer — and it was false.

Volker said simply, "Both."

Bob Phillips stood up. He said that the measure under discussion would, if passed, eventually allow strip zoning to extend virtually the length of the scenic corridor. "It would be regarded by outsiders as one of the stupidest things we could have done."

Several in the audience agreed with him, but Peatman told the supervisors that his opponents were speaking in platitudes. What they didn't understand, the lawyer said, was that a failure to pass the measure would put people out of business.

Several members of the audience laughed at him. Bob Phillips shouted, "Be honest!" and Peatman wheeled on him, flushed, half-specs riding down his nose.

During the lunch break Volker crossed the street to the Blue Plate Diner. He was discouraged by the reaction of the supervisors to Peatman's pro-development pitch, what Volker saw as a blatant attempt to compromise the General Plan. The supervisors' innocuous replies reflected the fact that a political campaign was in progress. The two supervisors up for reelection didn't want to antagonize voters with the contest only a couple of months away, and so tried to straddle the issue of commercial expansion.

The other problem was that the supervisors deferred to the county counsel, a lean, dispassionate presence in all deliberations, since the county feared nothing as much as a lawsuit. The session had provided a clear example of why local government no longer worked, in Volker's opinion. Power was divided among the five representatives — the supers — whose function mixed parliamentary and executive duties. And then there was this curious person on the side, the government lawyer, who had to give his opinion on all points, and various bureaucratic experts. The supervisors were expected to rule on things as varied as land use and tax policy, usually without experience. Moskowite, for example, was a rancher. The chairman of the board, Bob White, a man who could always be counted on to rule in favor of development, was a barber. At present, Moskowite and White were being overruled by the so-called slow-growth majority on the board: Mel Varrelman, Jay Goetting, and Kathleen McCullough. But Jay and Kathleen were up for reelection. If they lost, the board would swing the other way, toward growth and more development.

Jay Goetting had been a radio announcer before being elected to the board. Only Kathleen McCullough had previous political experience, as the mayor of Yountville. The county prided itself on its local government and the fact that the citizens could get close to their supervisors, but actually the system was inefficient. The salaries remained too low to attract real talent. The world was changing, and hard decisions had to be made and they weren't being made. And the supervisors' authority was constantly being undermined by state laws that superseded local ones.

The supervisors occupied the stage but the county counsel and the public set the tone. Volker wished for a strong executive, someone who would seize the moment and make a major pronouncement on land use, something to rivet attention. The board should declare what was necessary and then direct the county counsel to make it legal, not the other way around. Rather than openly vote against the ag preserve, the board allowed a string of little exceptions that would eventually kill it.

Land use was an esoteric subject. Politicians sometimes just didn't get the point, and let themselves be swayed by the likes of Joe Peatman. Volker wondered why Peatman behaved as he did. Why would he want to destroy the valley, to see it paved over, when he had to live here? Peatman had been on the board of supervisors when Volker and Liesel had the problems with the dirt-bike course across the road from their house; he had voted with the majority to get rid of the race course. But something had happened to Peatman since then. People said the process was a game to him — a lucrative game.

Volker went back after lunch, climbing the stairs instead of taking the elevator. He didn't get enough exercise tromping through the vineyards, checking sets and taking sugars. His shoes were covered with Chiles Valley dust.

Moskowite glared at him as the proceedings began. Moskowite was now championing a church that sought to build a school in the agricultural watershed, in contravention of the law, and the school was voted down. Bob White, the barber, deplored what he called political decisions.

"Does that mean our decisions are political," Varrelman asked, "because they don't agree with yours?"

There hadn't been so many sparks in a long time, Volker thought.

It wasn't until late afternoon that the supervisors got around to the wineries. The Planning Commission was called in for a joint session; they sat at a table facing the board, listening to an assistant to the director of planning, then to Hickey himself. The overhead lights glinted in the steel rims of his glasses. Hickey said that standards had to be established for new wineries in the unincorporated area, and limitations imposed. Since his report had gone out, the Planning Department had received twenty-nine applications for new wineries. There were already 205 in the valley, most of them on Highway 29. "The minute we adopt a standard saying we can have only so many wineries," he said, "someone will test it in court."

Therefore he was proposing a temporary moratorium on new wineries and a thorough environmental study that would prevent undue lawsuits. "As soon as we get a winery definition, we will have to set density standards." The door would finally be closed.

It didn't seem like much, but for the first time a ranking county official had publicly suggested that the valley's capacity to absorb its own prime industry was finite.

46

ON THE Fourth of July the Winiarskis — Barbara and Warren and their son, Stephen, their two daughters, Kasia and Julia, and Kasia's fiancé — all gathered on the beach next to the pond that had recently gone in at the base of Parker Hill. The new house above it bore no resemblance to the old one. Now there were many doors and broad windows offering a view of Stag's Leap and of a Japanese garden with a bowed footbridge and elliptical flagstones under the oaks. Warren and Barbara had spent many hours going over the details. Sometimes Warren had stood outside with a book of photographs of Japanese terracing, directing workmen.

The pond had been similarly conceived and executed, with washed stones brought in, and sand, and nozzles on the bottom to force the water upward to be aerated, and even a tankful of trout went in. Ideally, they would feed off insect larvae dropping from the branches of overhanging trees. It was all far removed from the little house in Dago Valley the Winiarskis had rented when they first arrived in the early 1960s. Warren had bought a fly rod, and he stood on the dam and flicked the line out across the surface of the pond. There was no fly attached to it.

The valley was now split, he thought, between those who wanted to make as much money as possible and those who wanted to preserve its character. The stress showed. Warren's son had recently told him, "The valley has really changed. This energy isn't my energy." Barbara spoke wistfully of the days when they could see only a few lights from the top of Parker Hill. The Winiarskis all agreed that something should be done about the number of people, but what?

Warren talked often of the Greeks. They had seen moderation as a virtue, one that he thought could apply to land use. Growth tempered by restraint. The Greeks had a theory about the size of a city, for instance: it should be contained within the human capacity to know it. Not so large that one side could fall to the enemy without the other side realizing it. But imposing limits on the ideal state was not part of the concept.

How could the people of Napa Valley say others couldn't live there? By raising the question of ornamental value. Vineyards provided not only a way of life but also a kind of healing; those who had nothing to do with vineyards profited by just looking at them. If the vineyards were destroyed by tourists and householders — by the paradox of their own allure — where then was the residual value? There had to be a point where even the Greeks would have said, No more! Even if it came down to a contest between old and new citizens, the old ones had already arrived and *there was no more room*.

The great modern experiment had begun with Descartes, to make man lord and master of nature. Now man lived in an age of material abundance, but it wasn't always so, and wouldn't always be so. The advantages of a few simply could not be bestowed on the billions inhabiting the globe at the end of the twentieth century. The rate of present consumption guaranteed the exhaustion of resources.

Warren — still flicking the fly line — favored limitations on growth, but he had to be careful. Speaking out too strongly would cost him his effectiveness in his community, which meant within the Vintners. The association was suspicious of change, glacial in movement. Any forward position could be disastrous for the person taking it. In the appellation discussions, Warren had tried to behave like an English parliamentarian, guiding the opposition away from the further bastardization of the Napa name. When the idea of vineyard districts first arose, Warren had to get the vintners to agree to study the possibility of producing a white paper, then to agree to produce it, and only then to agree to *consider* what the white paper said.

The winery definition had emerged as the crucial issue. Public pressure against the vintners was irresistible: people in the valley wanted limits. On his own, Warren had done some research on the county's land-use practices and on the idea of a mandated plan. He had decided that the General Plan resembled the Constitution of the United States; it was in its way a sacred, shrouded document. The needs of the past inherent in the General Plan related to those of the present.

He looked up at the rows of vines belonging to his neighbor. They seemed to roll toward him like breakers on a vibrant green sea.

The wineries, he thought, were straying from the General Plan and so becoming the greatest threat to the thing they had created, the agricultural preserve. They had become the enemy.

⟡

The extraordinary meeting of the Napa Valley Vintners packed the seats in the Meadowood amphitheater and filled the aisles with men and women hugging their knees in the chill of an overzealous air conditioner. Still they came, letting in sunlight through the open door, lining the walls. Reverdy had never seen such a turnout nor heard such bitter comments. The rarity of the moment was best exemplified by the presence of Michael Mondavi, who sat gripping a black leather pouch that was less than a briefcase but more than a purse, stuffed with papers and other things of importance to the inheritor of the mantle of Robert Mondavi. Michael's black Porsche was parked out under the trees; his black polo shirt lay like a brush stroke on the canvas of familiar faces to which Reverdy addressed himself on the issue of the winery definition.

The general membership had at last sensed a geologic shift in public opinion away from their immediate interests. The public wanted winery activities legislated. Reverdy told them, "This is a moving target. Don't expect an early resolution."

There were three things they had to consider about the winery definition. First, the overlay plan to legalize the wineries' extracurricular enterprises that Mondavi and Reverdy favored had come under sustained attack. The growers objected to any legal change in the ag preserve or the ag watershed (the hills), which the overlay plan would entail, and had come forward with their own definitions. He held up the proposal that Volker and Beckstoffer had presented at the press conference. "There are some marvelous names," he said. " 'Heritage,' 'charter,' 'estate' . . . What this really means is no new public wineries and no expansion."

The second thing to be considered was the 75 percent Napa Valley grape requirement for new wineries and additions to existing ones. Beckstoffer and Eisele were trying to restrict any conversion of the ag preserve into commercial use for the processing of out-of-county grapes. They had no problem with expansion within the existing "footprint" of the wineries in the ag preserve or the ag watershed, but they didn't want that print to grow in size unless the 75 percent rule applied to the expansion.

The third restriction dealt with activities conducted at the wineries — tours, tastings, concerts, benefits, cooking schools, serving meals to visiting groups. "Frankly," Reverdy admitted, "none of us knows what is or was lawful based on our use permits."

The old permits had been vague and open to interpretation. Now most vintners wanted to make their activities legal within the new winery definition eventually to be passed by the county board of supervisors. Many of those uses would be prohibited in new wineries; the uses could be grandfathered for existing wineries — deemed allowable exceptions to zoning, but not strictly legal. Grandfathering might not stand up to a court challenge, and so Reverdy thought a zoning change was preferable.

"Now we have to consider the problem of a conservative county counsel," Reverdy said. The county counsel would probably advise the supervisors and the Planning Commission that the growers' proposal was legally sound. "There's a receptivity to emphasizing Napa Valley grapes for wineries located here so as not to debase the Napa Valley appellation." The public seemed sympathetic to the 75 percent solution, implying that the public didn't understand the wine business.

Many people in the audience didn't want to even think about the 75 percent solution. The fact that it came from Beckstoffer hardened their resistance. Beckstoffer was the real problem; he had come to the valley with Heublein and gotten rich with corporate land and leases. He had grown into a power in his own right and he had, people said, political ambitions. He owned vineyards not just in Napa but also in Mendocino, and had put out his own wine there with his own label. Now he was trying to tell the vintners what to do.

"We are taking various steps to solve these problems," Reverdy said, "without understanding exactly what the problems are."

By "we" he meant the vintners, the board of supervisors and their appointed Planning Commission, Jim Hickey, director of the Planning Department, up-valley and down-valley citizens, and presumably even the growers. The situation required a master environmental report and assessment of the impact of wineries on the valley. Declaring Highway 29 and the Silverado Trail scenic roads was also needed, to give the county more regulatory power. Reverdy could go along with all that as long as the wineries weren't unduly restricted. "I propose that we as vintners strongly support what the county proposes."

If the vintners didn't go along, they would look like Neander-
thals. They should get involved in the study, respond to questions
when the time came, and give the impression that they *wanted* to
understand their impact on the environment.

People took notes as Reverdy spoke — Dick Maher, Guy Kay,
Beringer's vice president of operations, even Michael Mondavi.
Reverdy used a lot of "ahs," aware that many members in the hall
had very different ideas about all this. But it was no longer possible to ignore these questions. "People ought to realize," he said,
"that we're going to have a rough row to hoe in defending the idea
that anything we're doing not stipulated in the use permit is, ah,
allowable."

Mike Grgich spoke in the thick accent that had not changed appreciably since he arrived from Yugoslavia. "The county is telling us
who we are, the growers are telling us who we are, and we're not
strong enough to say who we are. We should accept no ropes around
us. I come from a Communist country and I know what ropes can
do. We need, as you say, to discover the problem and make our own
decision."

"In reality," Reverdy said, "we don't control our own destiny."

Reaction had so far taken the form of mutters, groans, complaints about Beckstoffer and Eisele, and occasional bitter laughter.
Now arose a general if muted denunciation of the whole state of
affairs: the idea of not controlling their destiny offended most of the
members.

Reverdy recognized a lean young man in the back of the room,
Alan Tenscher, the new winemaker at Schramsberg who had been
hired to replace the one lured away by Domaine Mumm. Tenscher
had been sent to the meeting by Jack Davies, and he spoke of "the
tragedy of the commons," the fact that each user of common land is
locked into a system that compels him to increase his output in order
to get ahead. Eventually this would destroy the land. Tenscher held
the attention of a group not accustomed to listening to winemakers
on any subject other than wine. "Without restrictions," Tenscher
concluded, "we are going to lose a valuable natural resource. We
need to go into this ready to work with the government agencies.
We need to submit to the environmental impact reports for the long-
term viability of our industry."

Guy Kay agreed with him. Kay's radiant good will was well
known. He pointed out that the argument over a winery definition

had been going on for two years and that in its innocence the Planning Commission had first asked the vintners what to do about limiting winery growth. The vintners, he reminded them, had not been responsive. If the wineries had accepted some restrictions in the beginning, things would not have come to this. They would be controlling their destinies. Now it was imperative that they leave the meeting with agreed-upon positions on the 75 percent solution, land use, the winery moratorium, and the notion of grandfathering winery activities.

Justin Meyer, thick-chested, florid, a voluble and at times amusing man, could not contain his impatience. "We give the growers too much credibility," he said. Formerly a member of the Christian Brothers, Meyer had gone over the wall to marry and then to found his own winery. "The Growers Association represents only one third of the county's grape growers. *We're* the growers. We own more than half the grape production in the valley, but they're drawing the lines of battle and trying to tell us how to run our business."

What they were talking about, Meyer added, was price fixing. "Don't let them take the position that they're champions of open space and we're trying to rape it."

Warren Winiarski said, "If we don't address the profound anxieties of the government and the people about the future of the valley, someone else will. We are beyond, Justin, a fight between the wineries and the growers."

Michael Mondavi agreed with Meyer. "If we adopted a 75 percent rule, somebody like Gallo could come in and buy a few tons of Napa grapes and drive up the price, knowing he's using 1 percent and we're required to use 75 percent. It makes us less competitive."

The president of Sterling, Tom Ferrell, disagreed with the 75 percent solution on principle. "Let's face the issue now, not later. We also have to deal with some limitations or the valley's going to change."

Tom Selfridge, so far a silent representative of one of the oldest wineries in the valley, Beaulieu, spoke in support of some limitations on outside grapes, adding, "We face the loss of the valley."

Reverdy suggested that the board of supervisors vote in a moratorium on winery permits — except those for private wineries without tours and tastings — to be in effect until after the completion of an environmental impact report. "We need to say that the concept of the overlay district warrants full investigation, but we're prepared to shape it to meet the county's concerns." But not to give up the idea of the special zone for wineries, as the growers wanted them to do.

"The growers will consider that a stalling tactic," said Justin Meyer.

"The rogue element," Reverdy said, trying to dramatize the problem, was the county planning staff under Jim Hickey's direction. "What will they decide?" he wondered aloud.

Dick Peterson, manager of the Atlas Peak development, opposed a moratorium on new wineries. "It's a devastating thing for those of us with a winery in the pipeline. We plan to crush grapes, for Christ's sake."

Mondavi said he would go to court to oppose the moratorium. Five years had gone into the design for the Opus One winery, part of the joint venture between the Mondavis and the Rothschilds, to make it a spectacular addition to the valley's architecture. The permit had not yet been formally issued, and the moratorium would further delay things. Mondavis didn't like waiting. "We'll see the county in court," he said.

Dick Maher, head of Christian Brothers, today wearing a fly-fishing vest, the only vintner who dressed in Bermuda shorts and knee socks for the Vintners' auction dinner, believed strongly in the power of public promotion. "We've been accused of running rough-shod over the land and altering the lifestyle of the valley," Maher said. "Quite honestly, ladies and gentlemen, we haven't done what we should have in the past."

"Dick's exactly right," said Dennis Fife, the general manager of Inglenook. "We've been out-PRed. It's as simple as that. We're people with great marketing expertise, and we've been clobbered by the growers."

"Don't confuse it with PR," Warren pleaded. "We're talking about the future of the valley."

Alan Tenscher went back to Schramsberg disturbed by what he had heard. Few in the meeting seemed to understand the issue. The real battle was for open space, and if they lost it, it was lost for good.

People could become too comfortable, he thought. When the stakes got as high as they had gotten in Napa, those already entrenched were reluctant to act. When they did act they stuck to narrow self-interest, and that could be fatal. By simply reacting to the growers, the vintners had taken a weak position that would almost certainly lead to further mistakes.

Tenscher had studied economics before switching to enology. Like other born-agains — those students who had come late to winemaking, only to become absorbed in it — he wanted a satisfying vocation and he wanted to bring some happiness to people's lives. In economic terms, he thought that he was creating *use* value as a winemaker, not *exchange* value. It was a humanizing craft, but winemakers were accustomed to the role of technician nonetheless. They looked over their shoulders a lot, since the competition for jobs was fierce. To enter the vintner-grower fray as an equal was rare and exhilarating.

Tenscher went into his own files and dug up the essay "The Tragedy of the Commons," written by Garrett Hardin. The author referred to Adam Smith's notion of the Invisible Hand, the force that supposedly leads a person pursuing his own gain to the promotion of the general good. That notion was no longer tenable. Self-interest was not synonymous with the public interest but tragically counter to it. Hardin quoted the philosopher Alfred North Whitehead: "The essence of dramatic tragedy is not unhappiness. It resides in the solemnity of the remorseless working of things."

Napa's tragedy, like that of any common ground, derived from the presence of too many human beings and the unending attempt by the individual to maximize his gains. "Ruin is the destination toward which all men rush," Hardin had written, "each pursuing his own best interest in a society that believes in the freedom of the commons."

The commons could well become a figurative parking lot.

47

THE CHILI BALL, organized by the Napa Valley Grape Growers Association, reflected none of the acrimony in the valley, but then the Chili Ball was supposed to be fun. Held every year on the grounds of old Rutherford International to raise money for the Agricultural Lands Preservation Fund, it was the closest thing to an up-valley/down-valley festival, with a Texas chili cook-off and a country rock band. Chili was not part of the dinner but a specialty concocted beneath the trees for the judges and spectators to taste. The cooking teams — wineries, commercial establishments, real estate firms — drank wine and even some tequila while they worked. A few contestants smoked something that left them dreamily recumbent under the trees at the edge of the old airstrip.

Carl Doumani, owner of Stags' Leap Winery, made the rounds of the cooking booths in a pith helmet, carrying a blender bucket full of margaritas, a symbol of apolitical merriment. He had planned to make rattlesnake chili from rattlers caught in the hills, but the snakes had not appeared that summer in sufficient numbers and Doumani had been forced to use beef.

There were other vintners in the crowd, but nonvintners prevailed. People drank beer and ate barbecued ribs, sitting on hay bales with paper plates, watching the hot-air-balloon concessionaires take people up and down for free in tethered wicker baskets. It was dark before the band struck up. Then the green, blue, and orange balloons shone brightly against the sky, the butane blowtorches slowly lifting them like inverted minarets toward the stars. The ropes grew taut, the torch blasts subsided, and the baskets drifted back to earth.

Robin didn't attend the Chili Ball. She had more than enough to occupy her with the Mumm Cuvée Croquet Classic, underwritten by Seagram, set at Meadowood and organized by her. The tournament was part of a plan to establish Meadowood as Napa Valley's preeminent watering hole. The purse totaled $25,000, a record. Meadowood now employed not just a croquet pro but also an assistant croquet pro. The Classic had attracted players from clubs all over America, a vintner or two, and Bill Harlan and his partner Peter Stocker.

There was much talk in the valley about Harlan. Just that week a story had appeared in the *San Francisco Chronicle* detailing plans for a $400 million project in the industrial area south of Napa city, to be done by Pacific Union. The development would include office buildings, restaurants, a shopping center, and an "air park" to allow private planes landing at the Napa airport direct access. Harlan's plans to develop the south end of St. Helena had not been so prominently aired, but they were no secret, either. Harlan had run into some opposition on the St. Helena City Council, one of whose members worked for Andy Beckstoffer. Harlan believed that Beckstoffer was jealous of his success in the valley, that he had tried to prevent Harlan from joining the Young Presidents Club and was now complicating his efforts to create a commercial microcosm of Napa Valley life next door to Sunny St. Helena.

Of course, having Beckstoffer as an enemy had its advantages, too: your enemy's enemies were your friends.

Robin had mixed feelings about these things. Her father had opposed restraints on businessmen and land reform by government fiat, and she shared some of those views. But she didn't want to see the valley strip-zoned and paved over. The contention among the various factions in the valley distressed her, as she knew it would have distressed John Daniel. He believed in accord among like-minded people and in conducting one's affairs in private. The light of publicity lately thrown on every disaffection would have saddened him.

In addition, Sunny St. Helena — at least its management — was having the usual problems associated with young wineries. The business was capital-intensive and there never seemed to be enough money. Harlan considered the successes his and the failures hers. She was always there and so bore the weight of unrealized, and unreal, expectations, but didn't have the power she felt she deserved.

After a recent Vintners meeting she had joined Mike Moone, Jack Davies, Guy Kay, Jay Corley, and Chuck Carpy for lunch, the only woman at the table. The talk was of Proposition 65, the state law that would require warning labels on wine bottles and other consumer goods; the men didn't like it. Robin said the wine industry should be more involved. The vintners should talk to restaurants and other businesses about the problem, and to politicians. They should stop considering themselves — and she included herself — so high-powered and removed. She went further and suggested that wine should team up with beer, even with spirits, in opposing restraints on trade. "We're going backwards," she said. "We need to be pro-active rather than re-active."

Mike Moone asked why she didn't get involved with the Wine Institute, the lobbying arm of the California industry. Robin said she was trying to get Sunny St. Helena off the ground.

"That's a weak-kneed excuse," Moone said.

That made her mad. Robin was not a confrontational person. Plant a seed and back off. Seek advice. She had once gone to see one of the men at the table, to ask his opinion of her prospects in the valley. He told her that working for Mondavi had been a mistake, that by becoming Robert's alter ego she had lost credibility. She had since gone to the president of one of the largest wineries in the valley for more advice; he had told her she was a ball ricocheting around the valley, trying to be the grande dame of wine. Why did she want to raise her family's name from obscurity? What difference did it make? This was California! Robin couldn't believe his crassness. He was himself a parvenu, having arrived in the valley on the wings of a corporation, setting himself up as an arbiter of taste, even tradition. She had left him feeling deflated, and telephoned Robert Mondavi, still the best source of good counseling. "Feed yourself," Robert had told her. Attend to your needs and the rest will follow. She knew that if she had been with him, Robert would have taken her by the elbow, and said, "Do you realize how lucky you are?"

She told all the men at the table that the Wine Institute was nothing but a power clique. That really set them off.

Sunday was the last day of the croquet tournament. The coastal wind had shifted to the east and the valley felt periodic blasts of hot, dry desert air. Robin wore a Panama with a trailing red scarf and whites, as everyone did, not just the contestants but also the spectators, seated at tables arranged around the croquet court, shaded by white umbrellas. They had paid a healthy fee and come from considerable distances to dine and to watch the Mumm Cuvée Napa Classic.

The manicured grass seemed to vibrate in the sun. Robin was accustomed to playing in the evening, when the wickets threw long shadows. Harlan showed up in his white pleated trousers, suspenders, and the battered straw hat. It was easy to imagine him in some British protectorate in the previous century, drink in hand, surveying the natives.

So far the tournament had gone off perfectly, except that both Harlan and his Australian pro had been eliminated before the semifinals, and this last day was even hotter than the one before. By lunchtime the thermometer had reached 105 degrees. The sweat quotient threatened even the most demure young women in their white gowns, Domaine Mumm visors, and sunglasses, their hands wrapped as often around little icy bottles of Calistoga water as around champagne flutes. They and their companions hunched forward to stay within the circles of shade; they dabbed spoons at cold but rapidly warming gazpacho while the finalists hammered wooden balls back and forth across the green. Next came cold salmon steaks with baby carrots, and Sterling Chardonnay, and a surprising number of people left both untouched. It was just too hot to eat.

The players hailed from Sonoma County, Arizona, Palm Springs, even Ireland. When the match was done, Robin took her turn at the microphone and thanked the staff at Meadowood for helping and the spectators for coming. Then she walked down to the pool and sat in the shade. The tournament had been a success, but already she needed another project.

Guy Kay's bow tie was a holdover from the years he spent in the East, doing product development for Nestlé. Soups and sauces. The company had sent him out west to start up a chocolate factory, in Salinas, in the sixties. From there he went to freeze-dried coffee in Ohio, then back to California to take over production at Beringer, in St. Helena. Kay was supposed to know something about vines because he had some in his back yard.

In 1972 the Napa Valley Vintners Association had still been a small group. Kay remembered Louie Stralla asking him, "Who the hell are you, you pot licker?" Kay was the thirteenth vintner to join and always sat next to Stralla at lunch. When it was your turn to be host, you brought a case of wine on your shoulder. If you had a problem with Pierce's disease or a stuck fermentation, somebody would tell you how to fix it. At the first Vintners harvest party, Bob Trinchero showed up with pasta and Chuck Carpy with a bagful of baguettes and a piece of roast beef. Jim Nichelini, an older vintner, played the accordion. By the time Nichelini died in the mid-1980s, the parties had themes and the party goers wore fancy costumes and the earthy Nichelini had been ostracized.

Some of the new, socially ascendant "lifestyle" vintners competed to be the most highfalutin. They included H. Gilliland ("Gil") Nickel, owner of a nursery in Oklahoma and now of Far Niente. His wines were successful even at, and perhaps because of, their extraordinarily high prices. The Chardonnay had what was supposedly the most costly wine label on earth, made with thirteen color passes. The back label explained why the front label was so expensive. In the carriage house Nickel had built on the property he kept a '51 yellow Ferrari, two classic black Bentleys, a '32 tangerine Ford roadster, a white Jaguar roadster, and a four-cylinder BMW motorcycle.

The Vintners had become an increasingly exclusive organization; at the same time it had lost credibility in the community. The growers enjoyed a somewhat better reputation. Kay thought of Napa County's agricultural community, which included growers *and* vintners, as a classic example of a minority. From the outside it was seen as homogeneous and referred to as the "wealthy, up-valley interests." However, it viewed itself as extremely heterogeneous and contentious. It existed in a place ruled by the laws of the majority, and would someday have to face up to that and try to become a more active part of the larger local populace.

The Napa Valley Wine Auction was a good example of something gone wrong. It was almost impossible for someone outside the organization to get on the board. A thousand local volunteers made the auction possible, but they had no say in how it was run. There were two boards, actually, one for the auction and one for the Vintners, but the same people sat on them. It was a closed shop.

As a member of the Napa County Planning Commission, Kay had a goal beyond civic duty: to pass the valley on to succeeding generations in the best condition possible. That meant that some money-making schemes had to be allowed to fail. It meant stricter rules governing processing facilities — that is, wineries. It meant that the Napa Valley appellation must not be prostituted. And it meant a land-use plan that protected the scenic corridors.

Kay put on his straw hat and headed for Napa city. He didn't think the 75 percent solution was unreasonable, but he did think the growers had complicated the issue. He didn't agree with some of the growers when they said that all the vintners were self-centered. He didn't agree with the vintners who said that Jim Hickey, director of the Planning Department, had usurped power. If you put everybody in one room, Kay thought, you would discover that they were not that different.

Hickey was looking for solutions within the restraints of the law, but because the vintners thought he represented restrictions, they didn't like him. Hickey resisted incredible pressures.

Guy Kay was one of five appointees on the Planning Commission; he had served for more than two years. But on the winery definition issue — the most important of his tenure, maybe his lifetime — he was not allowed to speak out or to vote. That was because Kay worked for Beringer. Neither were two other members of the commission allowed to speak or to make their feelings known with body language because they, too, had connections to the wine industry. It was all an outgrowth of the California Fair Political Practices Act, which had been invoked by a cautious county counsel fearful of lawsuits. So in the middle of its most important debate in two decades, the Planning Commission consisted of only two remaining members, a young engineer and a retired airline pilot, neither of whom knew anything about wineries, agriculture, or land use.

They had all dressed for the occasion. Volker Eisele had on a sport jacket. Andy Beckstoffer resembled the young corporate representative from the days of Heublein's arrival in the valley. Reverdy sat next to him in a tattersall shirt and paisley tie, and Volker sat on the other side. Bob Dwyer was present but kept his distance: today the growers' proposal was to be pitted against the winery overlay zone plan.

Volker spoke to most everyone in the room, but Reverdy and Bob Dwyer didn't seem to know many people. Volker saw that as indicative of the vintners' real weakness: being out of touch.

Warren Winiarski was there, and Robin Lail, Michael Mondavi, Carolyn Martini, a few other vintners, a few growers, and some of the county's more tenacious environmentalists. Jim Hickey sat solemnly at the table reserved for the planning staff while the Planning Commission sorted out what the nonvoting members could and could not do. One of the excluded members would be allowed to vote after all, so the commission could have a majority, but she would not be allowed to speak.

When "Stretch" Lewis, the retired airline pilot, opened the proceedings to public comment on the proposed winery ordinance, Volker stepped up to the podium. He spoke of the years during which the activities of the wineries — tours, concerts, and trinket sales — had existed outside the law. A winery definition was needed to address these and broader concerns, he said. "We want to preserve the agricultural preserve and conform with the General Plan. . . . We own the land and farm the land and consider ourselves stewards. Please look at everything we propose as a means of preserving agriculture." The overlay zone proposed by the vintners would guarantee almost unlimited expansion of wineries, he said. "The vintners' approach doesn't take into account the environmental needs of the valley."

Beckstoffer approached the microphone, smiling broadly. He said, "Thank you for the opportunity to speak," in his best Tidewater accent. "It *is* an opportunity. It has been twenty years since the ag preserve was placed in being. A lot has happened. Agriculture has been preserved, the quality of the wine has gone up, as has spending on technology and the vineyards. We've seen creative marketing." But there had been some disturbing trends, he added. Development and tourist promotion were encroaching on agricultural land. The Napa Valley Grape Growers and the Farm Bureau were therefore urging the commission to accept their proposal for winery definitions. It was time to act. No more delays, no more bickering. "Our desire here is not to harass wineries but to protect the land."

It was Reverdy's turn. He began by reminding the commission, and the audience, that fully one third of employment in the county depended on the wineries. "We are committed to agriculture," he added, "because we believe in it and because our survival depends on it. We are dependent on Napa Valley's reputation, and if we degrade that, we degrade ourselves."

He explained that the Vintners Association meetings resembled town meetings "and were just as effective." The joke, intended to explain why it had taken the vintners so long to reconcile their views — why they had yet to be reconciled — elicited no laughter. The vintners were aware of public concern over development and tourism, Reverdy went on. They thought some regulation of the scenic corridors was good. They supported the idea of an environ-

mental assessment, and thought the overlay plan still warranted serious consideration. But he warned that agriculture would not survive "without an economically viable wine industry."

That brought them to the 75 percent solution. " 'Napa wine from
Napa grapes,' " Reverdy said. "That has a homey ring, it's pleasantly
isolationist and simplistic — and fatally flawed."

Production of wine in the valley vastly exceeded the grape supply, he pointed out. Anyone wanting to expand had to react crea-
tively to a crop shortage. Since outsiders didn't understand the business, the government shouldn't tinker with supply and demand.
What he didn't say was that, in the end, the good harvests would
balance out the bad and that an increasing number of wineries were
bringing in grapes from outside the county not to counter bad
harvests — of which there were few in California — but to cynically take advantage of their Napa Valley address. And these huge
amounts of imported grapes required winery expansion that inevitably encroached on the ag preserve.

Volker didn't trust anyone with C-RANCH on his license plate.
He knew that Reverdy understood the intellectual argument for restricted growth and a minimum grape requirement, but Reverdy
didn't want restrictions. The Vintners board was not opposed to the
75 percent solution, but Reverdy wouldn't put it to a vote. He
planned to make Chardonnay from Sonoma grapes at the Johnson-
Turnbull winery, and it was possible that a tough board of supervisors might someday take that privilege away.

Michael Mondavi took his turn at the podium. He introduced
himself as "Robert Michael Mondavi," having lately changed not his
name but the emphasis on it. Formerly he had introduced himself as
"R. Michael Mondavi." Speculation had it that eventually he would
drop the Michael, transforming himself into . . . Robert Mondavi.
He pointed out that a century before there had been 166 wineries and
about 20,000 acres of vines. Those numbers had plummeted during
the phylloxera epidemic and Prohibition. Now there were more
than 200 wineries and 30,000 planted acres, the point being that
that was more or less back at the same level, and that the wine industry was highly vulnerable to nature and historical determinants
like neo-Prohibition.

The 75 percent solution was unfair, Mondavi said. It cut down
on competitiveness, as did the proposed restrictions on promotional
activities at the wineries. With the 75 percent solution the wineries

would be "significantly impacted and lose market share. If the growers' proposal is adopted, it will make a lot of non–Napa Valley wineries very happy."

Mondavi did not point out that his family owned extensive vineyards in other parts of California, including the one north of Lodi, in the Central Valley, or that he was concerned about obtaining a building permit for the Opus One winery, now threatened by the moratorium.

During the break, Andy Beckstoffer and Reverdy Johnson got together in the hall. Beckstoffer asked Reverdy, "Are we really that far apart?"

Reverdy said he didn't think so. They talked about a compromise. "Are you comfortable with the idea of their passing an ordinance without an EIR?" Reverdy asked.

Beckstoffer said yes. He feared that if the upcoming supervisorial election went against the slow-growth candidates, the growers might not get a winery definition that included a Napa Valley grape requirement, or any restrictions on development. But he didn't say that. Reverdy hoped to get a draft proposal approved that would legalize activities at the wineries. The existing definition in the zoning code said, in effect, that a winery was a facility to crush grapes and ferment and age wine, with some marketing to be done on the side. Virtually none of the extra activities now going on at wineries were included in the existing definition.

The new proposal put forward by the growers addressed three essential points. One was the 75 percent grape requirement. Another was the kind of direct marketing allowed, involving tourists and promotion, and limiting the marketing of wine made elsewhere. The third point was grandfathering. The attempt to do away with legal nonconforming uses had given rise to the overlay plan, which would have created special zones within the ag preserve for existing wineries, so their activities couldn't be challenged. If this extra "zone" was ever created by legislative act, it would be very difficult to attack it.

When the hearing resumed, Reverdy came forward to suggest that a winery definition be agreed to *in principle* and that the old overlay proposal be used as a standard for the EIR. While he spoke, Volker whispered to Beckstoffer that Reverdy had tried to trick him during the break. Volker urged Beckstoffer simply to call for an environmental study and a decision by the commission, and not get

involved in the grandfathering question, which could scuttle plans
for a meaningful definition. Beckstoffer followed his advice.

The two commissioners allowed to speak offered little comfort
to either side. One didn't care for government intervention in business but neither did he care for the overlay zone; the other one didn't
like the 75 percent solution and admitted that the whole question
seemed academic to him. "We get applications," he said, "and we
give permission to build, and then the applicant sells out to a gyne-
cologist. It used to be dentists. Next year it will be eye-ear-nose-
and-throats. We've already been through the lawyers."

Beckstoffer whispered to Volker, "This guy's off the wall."

Finally the commission agreed to recommend to the board of supervisors that an environmental study be done to determine the effect of winery expansion on the valley, and that a moratorium on
new wineries be enacted. Now it was up to the board.

Jim Hickey, sitting there listening, thought of the scene as one of
those rare intrusions of reality into politics. Both sides had gone as
far as they possibly could; they had exhausted the input. Suddenly
everybody was asking for action — an indication that the process
had run its course. The Grape Growers' position seemed the strongest to Hickey. Its members had voted on a winery definition, but
Reverdy was unable to say that the vintners had voted on the overlay
plan. Reverdy had never put it up for a vote because he knew it
would be defeated. The vintners were not all opposed to restrictions,
but it was the big wineries nowadays that called the shots, and
Reverdy went along. Michael Mondavi was one of them, too. He
was building an empire, in Hickey's view, one that had as much to
do with real estate as with wine. Robert Mondavi no longer even
came to the meetings. In the old days, you could call Robert and
he would answer the telephone, but his sons hid behind their secre-
taries.

Hickey saw it as a numbers game. Ten wineries were one thing,
a thousand wineries another. The process of limiting them reminded
him of wrestling: you look for any handhold. One handhold was the
environmental impact report, another the General Plan. Hickey was
approaching retirement age and still received offers from elsewhere,
but his work wasn't done in Napa County. The message he got,
talking to people, was that they wanted the valley to endure, and the
existence of the ag preserve was no guarantee that it would. The ag
preserve could be overturned by an unsympathetic board — three

votes and thirty days. The agricultural areas were losing influence in county government, with all the development in the south end of the county. The five supervisorial districts were rooted in Napa city and spread outward in a sunburst; up-valley had less and less clout.

Hickey stood up, and said, "This is indeed a momentous day. We have something we haven't had in two and a half years — an element of finality."

Volker headed back to Chiles Valley thinking that the real importance of the hearing was perceptual: the Vintners Association had been forced to go public with the overlay plan, and the commission had called for a study. Something had actually *happened*. The Vintners' overlay plan had no public support, that much was clear. Reverdy's real hope was the supervisorial elections coming up in November. The elections were terribly important. Now was the time for the growers to get a law, before the popular vote. The weak dollar had given domestic wine a large share of the market; the wineries were flush and couldn't complain about foreign competition. They could live with some restrictions better now than they might after the elections, which could upset all Volker's plans if the voting went the wrong way.

He drove his old BMW hard along the Silverado Trail. He liked German cars. When people joked about Volker's preference for such a prestige driving machine, he joked back at them: "Marx and Engels said the proletariat has just as much right to enjoy the fruits of its labor as the bourgeoisie."

48

THE DREADED east wind was known for its heat and aridity, a North Coast sirocco that crossed no sea and carried no desert grit, just Napa dust raised by field hands checking the drip valves on miles of plastic pipe. Everyone was mindful that water was scarce, and could become nonexistent if this solar conflagration continued. San Francisco saw its hottest day on record that summer of 1988. The temperature reached 114 degrees in Calistoga. Then late in July the fog rolled through the gaps in the Mayacamas and up from San Pablo Bay and left a strange clamminess in the air.

The weather had a direct effect on the grapes, sparse in comparison to other years. It would be another short crop, another early harvest. Ripening was uneven, yet some growers and some vintners, like their peers in Bordeaux, found themselves allies in declaring 1988 a great vintage before the fruit was off the vines. The shortage led to an early bidding war over Chardonnay in Sonoma County between Gallo and Beringer that pushed grape prices up. Napa growers hoped the war, like the fog, would cross the mountains to their vineyards, and it did.

Anyone with good Cabernet Sauvignon could have sold their supply five times over, for almost $2,000 a ton — an astronomical price by anybody's reckoning. A good vineyard could produce at least three tons of quality grapes an acre. From that income had to be deducted the cost of debt service, pruning, weeding, picking, smudge pots or wind machines, fencing, irrigating, replanting, and trellising, but still the growers were doing better than at any time in memory.

So were the vintners, although there were clearly problems ahead. Sales of even premium wines had begun to decline nationally, and at home the natives stirred, demanding changes in the way wineries did business and increased their hold on the land. The clever vintner looked beyond the mere making of wine, for a hedge against real and imagined disasters.

When Michael Mondavi moved into his father's old office from his cubicle beneath the stairs at the Robert Mondavi Winery, he brought with him his glass-top desk made of steel beams, the black leather chairs, black file cabinets, the black-framed print of an owl and the watercolor of Wappo Hill (his stepmother had chosen the name) with a black sky, and the fat black datebook containing the many events he had to attend as the Mondavis' managing partner and as chairman of the board of the Wine Institute.

There was much claim on Michael's time, but lately the winery definition had been shoved to the forefront. A million dollars had already been spent on the design and implementation of the Opus One winery, to be built across Highway 29, and now there was to be a moratorium on new wineries. The Mondavis would already have had the permit if the family had been interested only in meeting the county's building requirements. Instead, the Mondavis and the Rothschilds wanted a structure of which the valley would be proud — an antidote to the chain-link wineries. Time and money had gone into the design's perfection.

Part of the problem was Baroness Philippine, daughter of the late Baron Philippe, who had died in January. Philippine had to approve the plans, and she had dragged her feet until the political realities of Napa Valley had caught up with them.

Michael had originally planned for the winery to stand on the bank of the Napa River, but there were laws against building on the flood plain. A new site had to be chosen. The Mondavis were forced to jump through all the hoops any outsider had to jump through, and that galled him.

After appearing before the Planning Commission, Michael had gone to each of the five supervisors and told them individually of the merits of the Opus One design. He got on the telephone to the architect and the soil sample people and told them to speed things up. He didn't care about overtime; he wanted that winery application completed and on Hickey's desk the Monday before Tuesday's supervisorial meeting, when the moratorium on new wineries was expected to be officially voted in. If Hickey didn't approve the application, then Michael would have to ask for an extension and use some political persuasion.

A couple of days later an unusual thing happened: he received a call from two of the five county supervisors, asking for contacts in Washington, D.C. The winery definition and the Wine Train had been often on the front pages of the newspapers, but so had the water problem. There was not enough water in the West, in California, in Napa County. Water shortages could cause real hardship in the future, and the supervisors wanted more of the water from Lake Berryessa, a reservoir on the eastern edge of the county created by the Bureau of Reclamation in the mid-1950s. Napa had given up the rights to all but a fraction of the 240,000 acre-feet of water; the rest went to neighboring Solano County. Now Solano wanted to buy the dam from the federal government and with it rights to all the water. Napa wanted more than its current allotment. Negotiations were under way in Solano, but the final decision would be made in Washington, where the supervisors had no influence.

Michael did have some influence. He got on the telephone not to Capitol Hill but to a politician he knew in Solano County, one of Italian extraction who also happened to be a family friend. Michael and the politician discussed the problem of Lake Berryessa, and Michael asked if the negotiators from Solano might not be a bit more accommodating with regard to Napa County's needs. The politician said he thought they might. Michael later claimed to have called the supervisors, and told them, "I'll trade you ten thousand acre-feet of water for a winery permit."

In the end, Michael didn't have to use those "bullets," as he put it. The Opus One permit was approved anyway, the day before the board voted for a moratorium.

He wasn't through with politics, far from it. Michael opposed the minimum Napa Valley grape requirement as a blatant power grab by the growers, and blamed their leaders, Volker Eisele and Andy Beckstoffer. Eisele, for instance, didn't understand that the vintners were selling only two things: wine and image. The steak and the sizzle. Eisele wanted to take the sizzle away.

Beckstoffer was a larger problem. Michael thought Beckstoffer was using Eisele for his own ends — a clever opportunist manipulating an idealist. In Michael's opinion, Beckstoffer was driven by the basic emotion of greed. He owned a lot of vineyardland in Napa, and the 75 percent solution would boost the already steep price of his Napa Valley grapes. Michael would never do business with Beckstoffer, although they had been friends of sorts. They had jogged together a few times, but Beckstoffer wouldn't discuss his business affairs and the jogging ceased. Michael still saw him socially on occasion; this was a small valley and people had to get along, or appear to.

Beckstoffer's balls weren't just brass, in Michael's opinion. They were stainless steel. To understand Beckstoffer's motives in the winery definition fight, Michael cast back to the days of Heublein's arrival in the valley. Beckstoffer was one of *them*. In Heublein, the wineries had always been pawns of the liquor interests. The distilleries dictated the management of the wineries according to what was good for spirits; they didn't give a damn about wine.

Michael's plans in the valley included some building at the corner of Highway 29 and Oakville Cross Road, just south of the winery. The Mondavis owned everything there but the Oakville Grocery — owned by Joe Phelps — and a little house. Michael wanted to see the corner cleaned up; he wanted a good restaurant there. The Opus One winery would be in the vicinity, and maybe, someday, a wine museum just across the highway.

His plans weren't limited to Napa. The family also owned extensive vineyards in central California, where they weren't so restricted by local laws. They could promote wine any way they chose down there — big kitchens, concerts, and other events were no problem. Farther south, Orange County was the fastest-growing area in California, and the wealthiest, and the biggest market for Mondavi wines. People were a little more innocent about things down there; the Mondavis were still considered prophets. Michael liked southern California a lot.

The Mondavis were going to be the first family of California wine. Michael could launch new initiatives that went far beyond the activities of the Wine Institute. He wanted a joint venture with Angelo Gaja, the famous Piedmont producer. When the idea had come up, Michael had told his father, "Let's go home, Dad," meaning back to Italy. That was just the beginning of a new, larger push outward into the global theater of wine.

At home, Michael didn't get the strokes Tim got, Tim being the winemaker. But the directors of wineries received more press and public attention — more blatant envy — than presidents of multinational corporations. They were asked to speak, to sign autographs; they were minor deities in some circles.

Robert Mondavi was still competitive with his sons. Lately Michael spent a lot of time with investment bankers and accountants, trying to decide how to keep the winery in the family after his father was gone, for succeeding generations. He and Tim agreed that the company should stay private, but they didn't always agree on details.

There was a residual tension between the two brothers that others in the organization felt. Many thought that if a break ever occurred between Michael and Tim, some of the property could be sold off to satisfy Tim. He could take Vichon Winery, for instance, which the family had acquired. But if Michael ever decided to leave, it would be a disaster. Tim was no executive, and there was no one else to hold all the Mondavi enterprises together.

The prospect of a more immediate disaster lay in the growers' proposals for limiting winery activities and imposing the 75 percent requirement. As far as Michael was concerned, the only buffer between the vintners and the radical growers was the county board of supervisors. The supervisors were vitally important, not just to Michael and the Mondavis but also to the future of the wineries in a time of increasing competition and a growing distrust in the country of the product they sold. There were presently two pro-growth supervisors on the board, and three slow-growthers. Two of the slow-growthers were up for reelection, and Michael had decided to make sure that at least one of them didn't make it. He wanted a board of supervisors sympathetic to growth, and intended to get one.

The evening of the day the supervisors finally voted for the moratorium on new wineries, the Davieses had a dinner party. It was to honor Pru and Harry Waugh, the British wine critic, and the guests included Bernard Portet, the Burgesses, the manager of Meadowood and his wife, and the Davieses' youngest son, Hugh, who had come home after graduating from college to work at Schramsberg.

The party took place on the back patio; after dinner Jack stood up and welcomed his old friends the Waughs. In the twenty-four years since the Davieses had come to Napa, he said, the valley had changed in ways unimaginable. Schramsberg sparkling wine had been drunk by heads of state and royalty at the White House and in presidential palaces around the world. It, like the valley, had received a level of recognition that no one could have predicted in 1964.

While he spoke, Jamie watched a bat circle the tables and come to rest on the wall a few feet from her husband's head.

•

Jack's private view of life in the valley in the summer of 1988 was not rosy. The wineries were constantly whipped by events. If the vintners didn't come together and join with the community, they would be beaten to death by outsiders — environmentalists, real estate developers, legislators, journalists, and entrepreneurs. The fact that the Wine Train had not been derailed was tragic, in his view. A bigger threat was development in American Canyon, south of Napa city; if it became incorporated, there would be no limits to its growth. In a few years the county vote would be overwhelmingly weighted against the up-valley interests, including agriculture. Few vintners seemed to realize this, and trying to rally them was exhausting.

A few months before, the Davieses' boys had been home. They told Jack, "You've given up."

At the next Vintners meeting, Jack was asked to be chairman of the committee on tourism, a subject directly related to land use — the real issue — and he accepted. Visitors were good, he thought, but they should be treated pleasantly and informatively, and there were just too many bodies now to do that. Studying the problem might contribute to solving it.

Jack had prepared his report, but when he tried to present it at a meeting of the Vintners, he discovered that few people had read it. The winery definition, politics, and promotion of the product so occupied people's minds that the tourism report was put off.

Jack worried about the upcoming supervisorial election. Kathleen McCullough, a capable, principled woman in favor of slow growth and agriculture, did not convey the warmth needed in a successful politician. She didn't always listen to good advice and had hired a campaign manager who lived not in Napa but in Oakland. Jack thought Kathleen might well lose. If the other slow-growth supervisor, Jay Goetting, also was defeated, the county would be a very different place. The gains of the last twenty years could be lost.

Back in 1965 there had been two dozen wineries on agricultural land in Napa Valley, and a few more within the boundaries of the towns. By 1978, there were 54. Over the next decade the number of wineries increased to 204, an average of more than one new winery a month.

Since March 1988, the county Planning Department had received forty-one applications for additional wineries, an average of nine a month, and fourteen applications for expansion of existing wineries. Those applications were unaffected by the moratorium. When the new wineries were built, the total number in the valley's ag preserve would be 245. They would be processing far more grape tonnage than Napa Valley was capable of producing.

The moratorium was just a stopgap. The board of supervisors ultimately had to deal with the problem, acting on the advice of the Planning Department. Some of the language included in the proposal for an environmental impact report made Reverdy Johnson angry, however. Someone in the Planning Department wrote that tourists' "abilities to drive deteriorate with the progress of their tours from one winery to the next." That implied that they were all drunk! The proposed ordinance further implied that wineries were responsible for contamination of the air, water, and vistas of Napa Valley.

Reverdy managed to get the phrasing changed before the ordinance was to be voted on by the supervisors, but he saw the document as a warning. The fact that these charges could appear in a document for public review, prepared by county staff, was incredible and said worlds about the political situation in the county. It said that the wineries were not liked by the Planning Department and others in the community, and that the wineries did not have the support of the current board of supervisors. The election could change that if the vintners made their weight felt.

The growers submitted their revised proposal for a winery definition to the Planning Commission. Reverdy received his copy and got even angrier. The growers had made no concessions to the wineries for expansion, and continued to insist on strict limits for tours, tastings, and promotional events at the wineries. They wanted to do away with kitchens in the wineries that catered to the public *and* to get the 75 percent solution made into law. Reverdy had thought the growers might compromise on all of these points. After all, compromise was what lawyers thrived on; it was the lifeblood of politics.

He telephoned Andy Beckstoffer. Reverdy told him that he couldn't conceive of anything more calculated to engender animosity than this same old proposal from the growers, coming as it did after many months of negotiations between them and the vintners. Beckstoffer talked for a while, and although he didn't exactly say so, Reverdy understood him to mean that if the growers could get control of the source of grapes in the valley, Beckstoffer didn't care what the wineries did. If the growers couldn't get control of the grapes, they would tie up winery operations indefinitely.

Early on the Friday morning before Labor Day, Volker Eisele called Vic Fershko. He was to represent the growers at the next meeting of the Planning Commission, and Volker wanted to make sure Fershko gave nothing away. The battle lines were clearly drawn now. The real issues were the 75 percent solution and limitation on the wineries' accessory uses. In other words, how much Napa Valley fruit would be required, and what the wineries would be allowed to do to make money, other than producing and selling wine. Volker told Fershko to make sure those two questions were prominently addressed by the EIR.

Then Volker went around the house closing windows, to keep out the heat. He walked out to his Cabernet vineyard. The harvest was shaping up to be another difficult one — a natural reflection of the general state of affairs in the valley. A short crop of tolerance and good will. The white grapes had all been picked at the same time, the dust was as bad as ever, and tourists down on the valley floor were thicker than fruit flies. Only the pickers seemed free of the tensions, unruffled by the traffic, grueling labor, heat, dirt, wasps, and rattlesnakes. At night, the sound of cornets and Spanish guitars drifted up from trailers and cars parked behind wincries all over the valley, from the bunkhouses and the shade along the river, where the pickers slept on car seats and rose again at four in the morning.

Volker collected grapes from various parts of the vineyard and put them in a plastic bag. These vines were four years old and the individual berries looked good. Volker used a wide trellis system that opened the vines to air and sun; he was proud of his fruit. The old yellow and blue gondola sat in the shade, full of Chardonnay. He would hook it to his pickup and drive it down to Conn Creek in an hour. The Cabernet would eventually go to BV, Quail Ridge, and Monticello. He had once sold it to Vichon, which put out a vineyard-designated wine with Volker's name on it. After the Mondavis bought Vichon, Volker called Michael Mondavi and asked if he intended to continue using Eisele grapes. Michael said he and Tim would decide and call Volker back, but Volker never heard from them.

He fished a bunch of Chardonnay out of the gondola and bit into it, and the juice ran down into his beard. It was delicious — that was the way to taste grapes. He had sold them to Conn Creek, owned by American Tobacco. Volker's son, Alexander, blond, just out of high school, was working with the pickers who came up to the Eisele vineyard every harvest. Alexander had given up a job in a Calistoga restaurant. He was nineteen and had no idea what he wanted to do in life, a fact that bothered his father. Volker blamed it in part on Napa Valley. Life was too easy here, too secure, almost a feudal society. People with land, including the Eiseles, enjoyed unbroken green vistas and an almost inexhaustible source of labor. If Alexander had a car problem on the road, he had only to stand there and soon someone would happen along to help him.

Nearby Solano County was due to double in population in the next dozen years; if the Association of Bay Area Governments had its way, Napa County would be second in growth at the millennium. A voter initiative might be the only way to deal with the development problem: put power directly into the hands of the people. But first Volker and his allies had to deal with the supervisorial election.

Volker spoke to Alexander in German and to the pickers in Spanish. They expected to get almost four tons of Chardonnay from the acre plot. Volker needed to make $5,000 from it to break even and had just about reached that point; the vines were seven years old. He got only $800 a ton for his Sauvignon Blanc and was considering budding over to more profitable Chardonnay. But budding over was expensive.

He went back to the kitchen and put the grapes in a plastic tray and mashed them together to get a sample. The telephone rang twice; each time the caller's voice was recorded while Volker used the refractometer, a metal tube that resembled a miniature telescope. It had a hinged window at one end that he clamped shut over some captive juice. The sugar content bent the rays of light passing through it and the refractometer converted that to numbers. This Japanese refractometer — the Germans made one but the Japanese version was cheaper — told him that the grapes had reached 22 Brix, a simple measurement of sugar percentage. Volker's customers wanted the grapes at 22.5 Brix. That meant he would probably pick on Sunday, after the heat had driven the sugar up another half a percentage point. If he waited longer, the alcohol in the resulting wine would be too high.

He washed his hands and this time answered the telephone. It was someone from the Farm Bureau saying a reporter from the *Napa*

Register wanted to talk to Volker. The telephone rang again. The winemaker at Monticello was sending someone up to check the sugars tomorrow. Then Quail Ridge called, asking about the Cabernet Volker had just sampled. At last Alexander called from the home winery a few hundreds yards away, to say that the Chardonnay was ready to go down the hill.

⤬

At noon Bob Phillips left the office of Vine Hill Ranch behind the garage and went into the house. He had been gratified by the response to his fund-raising efforts to combat the Wine Train and was eager to share the news with his allies. Swanson wouldn't be there — he and his wife had gone back to London — and Tom May was busy, but his wife, Martha, had kindly agreed to provide lunch for another gustatory meeting of the ad hoc fund raisers. Barney Rhodes and Katie Spann joined them, and the foursome sat out on the veranda and dined on chicken salad, two types of cheese, strawberries, a fig and a chocolate confection in gold foil.

Bob poured some Chardonnay. After a discussion of speed walking and pulse rates, Bob got to the point. There were now eight participants in the suit to force the Wine Train to do an environmental study. They included the communities of Yountville and St. Helena, the Napa Valley Vintners Association, the Napa Valley Grape Growers Association, and the Napa County Farm Bureau, as well as the Friends of Napa Valley. At a closed session in St. Helena, they had found common ground. Within days the pledges of financial support had started coming in. So far Bob had commitments for $30,000. If he could find matching funds — and he would — the figure would be $60,000.

That was not a lot of money but neither was it negligible. A person down in the industrial zone of San Leandro, where Vincent DeDomenico still drove to work each day in his champagne-colored Mercedes, might at least notice the sum of $60,000 and imagine the legal wheels it could set in motion.

Bob was also trying to raise $50,000 for the campaigns of the slow-growth supervisors, Kathleen McCullough and Jay Goetting, a separate effort but part of the larger problem. The Phillipses and the Wilseys had sent a cosigned letter to dozens of friends and acquaintances, like Donn and Molly Chappellet, who had a large stake in the valley but were reluctant to become embroiled in public controversies. If Kathleen and Jay lost, the letter said, the future was bleak.

It was the Wine Train that concerned him now. So far, members of the Vintners Association had not pledged money. Bob hoped they would. He had not approached them, acting on the advice of Warren Winiarski, who had suggested giving them a chance to stand up and be counted. But the organization was still in the awkward position of wanting no restraints on its members' activities, while calling for restrictions on the Wine Train.

The order of business at the next Vintners meeting was the winery definition. In Reverdy's opinion the growers had pushed too far. Compromise did not figure in their plans, and Hickey and the Planning Department staff had joined the growers in what Reverdy angrily called "an indictment of the way this industry does business."

The vintners still had a choice, he said. They could be contentious or they could take a general position of support for the ag preserve and the early objectives of the Planning Commission, to bring some order to winery development. The final ordinance would be decided in "another arena," he said — the board of supervisors. Reverdy didn't have to say that the board's slow-growth complexion might well be changed by the November elections.

Other vintners were as angry as Reverdy. John Wright of Domaine Chandon called Jim Hickey "a would-be dictator, power-mad, who is finally getting what he wants — more power."

"Put that together with the leadership of the growers," agreed Reverdy, "and we have a cauldron that's bubbling over."

Members proposed various ways of getting rid of Volker Eisele and Andy Beckstoffer, who continued to jockey for political advantage behind the scenes. Dick Peterson wanted to start another growers' organization, so Beckstoffer and Eisele would have no constituency. Reverdy said, "Other than undermining their position, which bears thinking about, we should try to get the Planning Commission to look at our issues and put off the decision making for a future period of time."

By that he meant until after the election.

Jack Davies listened. Finally he said, "Things are ringing reminiscent." He recalled the fight over the ag preserve twenty years earlier, and added, "Wholly inside of these issues today — the winery definition and the Wine Train — is the possibility for this organization to say what we think is best, regardless of whether or not it becomes law. . . . Not a legalistic view, not what could we do, but what *should* we do."

He paused, and added, "I've known practically everybody in this room for a long time. It's hard to believe that anybody's without a long-term interest in the valley. We have to do what we think is right, and needed, not just what might become law."

But it was personalities that most interested the vintners. During the wine tasting, one turned to another to complain about the growers. "You can't deal with them. They're Vietcong!"

49

THE Napa Valley Coffee Roasting Company, on Main Street, Napa, two blocks from Vic Fershko's law office, had a big espresso machine and round, marble-topped tables with bowed-branch chairs where he could sit and drink Java or French roast and eat homemade pie. Burlap sacks of coffee beans lay in stacks on the old hardwood floors, and ceiling fans gently stirred the aromatic mix.

Fershko often took his coffee here in the morning, on his way to court or to the county government building at the corner of Third and Coombes, or after playing pickup basketball at the church gymnasium, something he did instead of eating lunch. Today, Wednesday, he dropped in before he was supposed to speak for the Napa Valley Grape Growers Association at the Planning Commission hearing — these hearings seemed endless — but still didn't know what he would say.

He felt dispirited. The judge in the Whitbread case, involving the Atlas Peak winery development, had just ruled against Fershko's client. Fershko hadn't expected that. He and his client wanted to force Whitbread to do an environmental impact report, which seemed both reasonable and lawful, and now Whitbread was off the hook.

The general environmental damage in the area was enormous. A woman who had grown up on Atlas Peak remembered being able to hear the church bells in distant Yountville; now all she heard was heavy trucks. A big corporation with a lot of outside money had come into a remote area and disrupted it. That wasn't right. The company had sent a Beverly Hills lawyer to the settlement conference who told Fershko, in effect, that he was going to ream him. He had only an hour, the lawyer added, before he caught a plane. What could they work out?

Catch your plane, Fershko had said, and walked out.

He planned to appeal. He did a lot of work at cost, like this case; he thought he could win in the San Francisco court of appeals but it would take time and, meanwhile, Whitbread would be in business.

After coffee, Fershko walked over to the county building, carrying the floppy leather satchel. His father had fought against Rommel in North Africa as part of the Palestinian brigade, and had returned to Israel to join the underground, to kick out the Brits. The authorities had torn up the house looking for him but his father harbored no bitterness. And Fershko thought he had problems with Whitbread!

Fershko said hello to people in the elevator. He found Mary Handel, executive director of the Farm Bureau and the Napa Valley Grape Growers, waiting in the board room. She had some advice for Fershko, who was representing them: state our philosophy. Stick to the points. Don't give anything away in the huddle.

Reverdy arrived, representing the vintners, the other side. Somebody asked him, "Cabernet in?"

"Almost done," said Reverdy.

They both waited in the front row, to do their bits. Then the hearing was put off for an hour, so Fershko, Mary Handel, and a member of the United (formerly Upper) Napa Valley Associates named Francine all went down the street to a deli. Fershko again read over the proposed ordinance for a winery definition.

Walking back, Fershko said, "These things are a waste of time. The decision is really made up in the supervisors' offices. We should go straight there rather than discuss these philosophical questions and waste the afternoon." He wanted to go wind surfing.

Beckstoffer had arrived. They all sat together while Jim Hickey reviewed the history of the winery definition issue and tourism, yet again. He and the Planning Department favored the growers' winery definition and intended to use it as a basis for their proposed ordinance.

Reverdy didn't like that. The requirement that 75 percent of the grapes used by new wineries come from Napa Valley was not enforceable, he said. It shouldn't be included in the environmental study. "Where our fruit comes from has nothing to do with environmental impact."

People yawned and looked at their watches. The assistant county counsel nodded off to sleep. Fershko decided to keep his presentation short. "Many of my clients are picking grapes and so can't be here," he began, stroking his mustache. The commission's concern about new processing plants on agricultural land was shared by the growers. "The 75 percent solution should be included in the EIR," he said, and then quoted Reverdy: "'Simplistic. Draconian.' These same things were said about the ag preserve twenty years ago. The sky didn't fall in then, and it won't this time, either. There are over two hundred wineries and we have to do something to stop it."

∼

Supervisor Kathleen McCullough's wedge-shaped office in the same building displayed a poster from the California women's suffrage movement next to a drawing of a woman in a bandanna, feeling her biceps, and the inscription "We can do it." Kathleen considered herself a feminist, but her enthusiasm was for politics in general. At fifty-four she was tall and slightly schoolmarmish, with short blond hair going to gray and big rimless glasses. Born in southern California, she had studied English at Berkeley; she belonged to Volker's generation but not necessarily to his world.

She and her husband lived in Yountville, where they had moved from Marin County a dozen years before, preferring country to city life. When they bought their house the seller had told them the twenty acres of vineyard next door lay in the ag preserve. Three weeks later bulldozers came and tore out the vines for a subdivision, and Kathleen was shocked more by her naïveté than by the seller's lie.

She worked as a tour guide at Beaulieu and began to attend town meetings. Politics had always been an interest — she had walked for Adlai Stevenson years before and worked briefly for John F. Kennedy and George McGovern — but small-town politics was different. There you could get your hands on the issues, like zoning and sewage treatment, but the only way to have real influence was to hold office. She had run for mayor as a long shot and beat her opponent three to one.

The job taught her something about land use: housing, hotels, and shopping centers should all be in the population centers, not in agricultural areas. The spill-out of commercial development onto the land was hard to resist but well worth the effort. The county was advised by the Association of Bay Area Governments to accept a large increase in population, so great care had to be taken. As mayor she had a hand in creating low-income housing. Yountville convinced a developer to donate an acre of land, and then built eight single-family homes and obtained a federal grant for self-help housing. The buyers worked thirty hours a week as a team and in return got equity and a strong sense of neighborhood. Opponents of the plan said she was trying to import blacks from Oakland, but most people liked that modest social experiment.

She ran the city — Yountville was really a town — in strict accordance with the General Plan. While still mayor she was approached by Mel Varrelman and asked to run for supervisor. She was more in favor of slow growth than the incumbent, Mel told her. Kathleen thought about the possibility for a long time. Her two daughters were grown and gone, and her husband retired; she liked the idea of being a supervisor, but friends discouraged her. Her opponent had been in county politics for many years. "It would be great," they said, "but you'll never win." Kathleen told them, "Any incumbent can be beaten," and she was right.

Now *she* was an incumbent supervisor. Kathleen saw the upcoming election as a crossroads. Her opponent, Fred Negri, had amassed far more campaign money than she, most of it from developers. He had already spent $48,000. Kathleen had only $26,000, total. Her biggest supporters were women professionals, schoolteachers, growers, and wineries that valued her strict views on land use. The list of contributors including the Winiarskis, the Stuarts at Silverado Vineyards, the Phillipses, John Shafer, Al Wilsey, René di Rosa, Guy Kay, Tom Ferrell at Sterling, Gil Nickel, and Tom Selfridge, who donated a case of '68 Georges de Latour Private Reserve to Kathleen's fund raiser.

The vintners opposing her included Michael Mondavi. He had supported her until the advent of the winery definition, and discovered that Kathleen was no rubber stamp. She opposed the sanctioning of illegal activities at wineries. She believed in a strict formula for growth, and that, she further believed, would step on Mondavi toes. She assumed Michael had plans to develop the corner of Highway 29 and Oakville Cross Road, and that he shifted his support to Negri in return for assurances that his plans wouldn't be hampered.

Kathleen thought Michael had problems with women politicians. So did some others, including the membership of a shadowy group of vintners known as the GONADS. Kathleen knew about the GONADS only by rumor; it was an informal, all-male eating and drinking society that included Mike Moone, Justin Meyer, and Carl Doumani. GONAD lunches sometimes lasted half a day. She knew some of those men opposed her reelection.

Kathleen had so far been unable to counter her opponent's direct-mail campaign, comprising what she thought of as "fluff." Kathleen tried to stick to the issues but found herself dealing instead with personalities. Negri used the fact that he had been born and raised in Napa as a prime qualification for being supervisor. He tried to cast Kathleen as an outsider. Negri bragged about working for the same company, Syar, for twenty-five years. Syar supplied rock, asphalt, sand, and gravel for road and other construction, was one of the few big industrial plants in the county, and was rooted in development. Negri intended to keep working for Syar if elected, which seemed to bother none of his supporters. He talked vaguely of the need for building a new superhighway up·the east side of the valley, right through Stag's Leap. He had no objection to legalizing activities at the wineries or to expanding them. He said land use was a red herring, that the real objective of the growers was to raise grape prices.

Bob Chelini, the winemaker for Stony Hill, had been up since 6 A.M. making pork scaloppine, fettuccine, and osso buco for the September meeting of the GONADS. It was his turn to be host. He had found a huge bottle of 1972 Ruffino chianti that he planned to serve with lunch, but there would be no shortage of wine. Four bottles of Stony Hill Chardonnay from four different vintages stood on the kitchen table, and the first arrival, Dan Duckhorn, set two bottles of Merlot near them. Chuck Carpy added Freemark Abbey wines of various vintages, and Justin Meyer a '75 Christian Brothers Cabernet and a bottle of his own Silver Oak.

All were opened. The breadth and longevity of the collection grew as more members came up from the driveway: Jay Corley of Monticello, Carl Doumani of Stags' Leap Winery, Mike Moone of Beringer. They pulled chairs into the shade of the eaves and began to sample the wine. Under an umbrella sat a slab of cheese and a big Italian sausage, copa, to be hacked at with a butcher knife and eaten with the reds and the whites as preparation for the feast to follow.

There were twelve GONADS in all, including a couple of what had been termed, for lack of a better category, "half-GONADS," meaning they didn't have time to participate every month. Mike Moone was a half-GONAD. He told the first of the jokes, one about deer hunting and sodomy, which served as an ice breaker.

Justin Meyer asked, "Why are the gays all going to vote Democratic in the presidential election? . . . Because they *Dukakis,* but they don't *do Bushes!*"

Carl Doumani could never remember his jokes. He wrote them on bits of paper and kept the papers in the pocket of his safari shirt. Sometimes these men took the slips away and then he was left joke-less but unrepentant. Doumani, known as "the Ayatollah," had been one of the founders of the GONADS. The acronym stood for the Gas-tronomic Order of the Nonsensical and Dissipatory. The group had grown out of the original Napa Valley Vintners Association, once an eating club that had degenerated into a marketing organization, in Doumani's view. Anybody who made and sold wine could join the Vintners; they didn't even have to be nominated, and they couldn't be blackballed. Well, the GONADS was exclusive.

In the old days, the Vintners meetings had taken less than an hour. A member could go into a back room for a swig of cognac. People talked about wine, crops, budwood. Doumani had quit be-cause all the talk turned to politics. His friend Meyer had written to a few men who knew how to enjoy themselves, saying that a place had to be found for "Brother Carl" to eat and drink once a month. That was the genesis of the GONADS, utterly subservient to the rule of stomach, palate, and the blackball. Each month a member pro-vided the place, the food, the wine, and the transportation. Doumani held his last meeting in Zihuatanejo, Mexico, better known as Zee-wat. Neither politics nor business could be discussed, and only death could free up a membership.

Anyone asked to join the GONADS had to be a particular sort of man. The members had a hard time defining what that sort was.

Bob Trinchero, owner of Sutter Home, arrived in dark glasses. He poured himself a glass of '83 Stony Hill Chardonnay and joined the others in the shade. Stu Smith came down the mountain from his winery in old cap and jeans; with that fierce beard he looked like a character out of some sourdough romance. Smith and Chelini were the only two members who actually made wine. Stu retained some of the old countercultural impulse that had brought people to the valley in the early seventies; he did very little marketing, not wishing to stand up and talk about French oak or malolactic fermentation, preferring to let his wines hang out there — the antithesis of an ex-alted salesman like Moone. Yet they were both GONADS.

Steve Girard arrived and Moone rose and pretended to knee him in the groin, the GONADS' salute. Moone shouted, "How're they hanging?"

The roar of engines drew their eyes upward. Two silvery props dived in out of the east, almost topping the pine tree, and the plane peeled up and out, the pilot grinning down at them. "Koerner!" said Doumani.

It was Koerner Rombauer, who owned a custom-crush operation on the other side of the valley and flew for a commercial airline. Now he had to land, get into his car, drive down Howell Mountain and across the valley and up Spring Mountain, so he wouldn't be eating and drinking for another half hour, poor fellow.

Talk turned to harvest. Trinchero said he was buying land up north, far from Napa Valley, and putting in vineyards. Chardonnay, he said, was where Sutter Home's next million dollars was coming from. Carpy turned his large face toward Trinchero and asked without expression, "Are you now going to make Chardonnay out of red grapes?"

Trinchero said he was thinking of making a white wine out of a red grape other than Zinfandel, one called Grenache.

"White Grenache," mused Moone. "Sounds like a disease of the crotch."

Justin Meyer told another joke. "What do eggs Benedict and blow jobs have in common?"

No one knew.

"You hardly ever get either one at home!"

A haziness from autumn fires hung in the distance. On the deck, Chelini spread white cloths on two picnic tables and put out the silverware and white plates. The men cut more copa and cheese, and free-ranged among the many wines. The collection had grown to include an '82 Newton Chardonnay, a '78 Forni Cabernet, a '78 Cabernet made by the couple who had once owned the Niebaum house.

Conversation came around to grape prices. Neither business nor politics was supposed to be discussed, and grape prices involved both nowadays. Someone predicted a 40 percent price rise in contracts over the next two years. Dan Duckhorn said, "Nothing in the valley shows the change as much as the value of grapes. In the early seventies there was one price for Cabernet — eight hundred dollars a ton, at twenty-three sugars. Now there are a hundred and twenty-five different prices."

Rombauer arrived to a raucous welcome. Chelini waved them to the tables. They helped themselves to the scaloppine, fresh tomatoes, and marinated bell peppers, and dug in. Within minutes the sun had driven Justin Meyer and Koerner Rombauer out of their shirts, exposing their substantial stomachs to the sun. Justin draped a napkin over his head.

Chelini appeared with hats and Justin selected a tinfoil derby but kept the napkin in place under it, so that he resembled an albino Indian chief forking in homemade Italian grub, red nose protruding from the napkin's folds. Moone wore a pith helmet, dark glasses, and a gold chain. Similarly covered, the rest welcomed the sun and the splendid food and wine; they were out of the fishbowl of Napa, at least for the afternoon.

The jokes continued, emblematic in some way of the men who told them. Duckhorn's tended toward screwy impersonation. He flapped his hands and turned his face toward heaven and covered his head with a paper bag. By the time the punch line came, barely audible, he was being roundly booed for pantywaistedness and intellectual obtuseness, funnier than the joke itself.

Doumani, the Ayatollah, took out a box of small colored pellets that when thrown exploded on impact. He distributed them among the five other diners at his table. "Okay," he said, "let's get those bastards."

They unleashed their battery on the other table. The tiny bombs went off against plates of scaloppine, priceless bottles of Napa Valley Cabernet, and a hat or two. The air filled with the smell of burnt gunpowder. The table retaliated with chunks of fresh-baked bread. Then the Ayatollah's table attacked in a body. Stu Smith lunged at Doumani, and in the struggle that followed two bottles went over and vintage Cabernet poured onto GONADS' laps. Doumani shoved Smith off the deck and into the bushes, where his back came to rest solidly against the stone wall. There was a momentary pause. Stu sucked air, and Doumani helped haul him back up, and they turned to the osso buco, chastened by the friendly violence.

"This is a lot of food," said Carpy. That didn't stop him from attacking it.

The Ruffino was poured. The next GONADS lunch was to be in Hawaii, someone said. Movable feasts were popular but problematical. In Zcc-wat, Duckhorn had gotten sick and required five days to recover; Trinchero had had similar problems. Eating at home in Napa was best when one ate as much as the GONADS ate.

After lunch, Chelini uncorked a '55 port and decanted it on the banister. Discourse took a more philosophical turn. "Tourism's down at Beringer for the second year in a row," said Moone, suggesting that claims by the growers and county officials that Napa was overrun by winery visitors were false. "What we need is some good PR. The real word just isn't getting out."

Stu Smith shook his head. "PR is not what we need, Mike. What we need is a strong board of directors of the Vintners that will force the president to bring up in the meetings the things decided by the board. The membership needs to know what's going on."

"We need better public relations," Moone repeated.

"You're talking like a big producer," said Duckhorn.

The GONADS' rule had been violated: they were talking both business *and* politics. There was no accord on the issue of public relations versus limitations on the wineries. These men were all supposedly friends and couldn't stay that way if the question was put in such stark terms. They needed common cause but so far had avoided mentioning the name Beckstoffer.

Girard and Doumani were throwing dice at their table; Girard quickly won $40 but then lost it, and $40 more. The subject of the St. Helena City Council came up. Most of the men present disliked one of the members, closely allied with a prominent grower. The council member was difficult to deal with. "He's never been laid," said Moone.

"We need to run Justin against him."

Justin said, "Let's run Carpy."

"Don't run me," he said. "I'd tell them they're all full of shit."

Someone suggested that the county get rid of Jim Hickey. "Hickey's not the problem," said Duckhorn. The problem was the character of the overall population — increasingly urban and unsympathetic to agriculture, which included wineries.

Finally "Beckstoffer" was heard. That brought them to the 75 percent solution. They agreed that eventually a law would be passed limiting the amount of outside grapes allowed into the valley. There would then be a sizable lawsuit and the big wineries would win, or wear down the county government, which didn't have the funds or the will for protracted litigation, just as big developers did when their construction plans were thwarted. Trinchero would be the ideal vintner to take on the county, Sutter Home being the most obvious beneficiary of imported grapes.

But first would come the supervisorial election. If the slow-growthers, Kathleen McCullough and Jay Goetting, were defeated, such legal action might not be necessary. Suddenly the election was on everybody's mind.

The men walked up to the pool and swam, and drank more wine. It had been a fine lunch but less freewheeling than in years past, more sober — a mark of the times. At dusk they went off in twos and threes, leaving Mike Chelini with a great mound of uneaten salad.

50

O NE EVENING in late September Warren Winiarski received a telephone call from Reverdy Johnson. Reverdy was barely coherent. The board of supervisors had voted for a winery moratorium and then extended it for four months. The bad part, Reverdy said, was that Supervisors Mel Varrelman and Kathleen McCullough had agreed that the 75 percent solution should be considered in the environmental impact report being done by the county, when the Vintners' overlay plan was not being taken into account.

That meant, in the shorthand of Napa Valley politics in the latter part of 1988, that the minimum Napa Valley grape requirement for new and expanding wineries would be an official part of the political debate after the study was done. It would give a big boost to the 75 percent solution, and certainly to grape prices, and ignore the vintners' needs to expand and to legitimize their activities.

Choking back his anger, Reverdy said that Kathleen McCullough had gone directly against the interests of the wineries. He cast the vintners as Christians fighting the lions. Reverdy had always been pulled two ways as president of the Vintners, toward those members who favored limiting development, like Warren, and toward those who wanted unlimited opportunity, the big boys like Christian Brothers and Beringer. Warren hung up convinced that Reverdy had now gone completely over to the other side.

Warren was reminded of what Thomas Hobbes had written about the life of man as he existed in a state of nature: "solitary, poor, nasty, brutish, and short." Self-preservation was the motivating force. Some vintners thought they were fighting for self-preservation, but really they were defending their way of life, their happiness. Hobbes had defined happiness as the freedom from death or from the fear of death, and John Locke had added the notion of *comfortable* self-preservation. A man could ameliorate his condition — exist more comfortably — by continually acquiring property and subjugating nature. The ascendancy of the individual and of individual rights was an outgrowth of that need.

In Locke's day the only limitation on the individual was his ability to acquire, but by 1988 the environment could no longer accommodate unbridled acquisition. Untrammeled individual expression was no longer feasible; the greed and imperial fervor that had driven people out of the eastern states to conquer the American West, with its vast dangers and threats of death, were no longer justified. Then, the only limits were those preventing an individual from impinging on another. Man could once ameliorate his condition by endlessly exploiting nature, but no more. Some of the accepted practices of business and government had to change. There was something in the wind: limits had to be imposed on individual conduct and on the bastions of individualism, like large corporations.

The next day Warren read an account of the supervisors meeting in the newspaper. In it, Mel Varrelman said that interfering with the free market didn't bother him in the case of the minimum Napa Valley grape requirement. There was a bigger issue at stake, Varrelman said: the preservation of the ag preserve.

ᔕᕝᕝ

The October meeting of the Napa Valley Vintners Association at Meadowood reflected Reverdy's black mood. Bob Dwyer, the executive director, took notes and later wrote that the members, "one after another, expressed their frustration, anger and concern" over the fact that the growers' proposals for limitations on wineries and a fixed percentage of Napa Valley grapes were being included in the environmental review, and the Vintners' overlay plan was not.

Reverdy and the other leaders of the Vintners had agreed among themselves that the political situation in the county was just not acceptable. Their only recourse was to change the fundamentals, as someone put it, to rid themselves of the two slow-growth supervisors, Kathleen McCullough and Jay Goetting. That meant publicly backing their opponents. Some vintners expressed reservations about endorsements during the meeting, but the consensus, according to Dwyer, was that a winery definition had to include the Vintners' proposals "if the industry, as we know it, was to survive."

Reverdy attacked the supervisors for including the 75 percent solution in the EIR. It was time, he said, for the vintners to assert themselves. The board of directors, therefore, intended to interview the candidates running for the two supervisorial seats, and for the first time in its history the Vintners Association would endorse candidates. That wasn't all. Reverdy wanted a rally sponsored by the Vintners to bring together all winery employees, their families and friends with the candidates, to help them understand what was in the best economic interests of the valley — that is, what was good for the wineries was good for them.

Mike Moone made a motion that wineries be allowed to expand without nonconforming-use status, and that all existing operations be grandfathered. There was no mention of minimum Napa Valley grape requirements. Moone had been telling people in private that if the 75 percent solution ever went into effect, Beringer would buy up all the available vineyards, regardless of the price. The motion carried.

Then Koerner Rombauer, fellow GONAD, moved that the rally be held. That also carried. Moone and Rombauer would cochair the event; winery employees would be paid for a full day's work even if they attended. Dwyer later told a reporter for the *Napa Register,* "We have 4,000 votes out there. We are going to get them politically involved. This is a vote for their jobs." He told another reporter, "The sleeping giant has awakened."

The rally was scheduled for the end of the month at the Clarion Inn. There would be free wine, beer, hot dogs, and a Dixieland band. Bob Dwyer appeared on television to say that winery employees would be organized and registered to vote. The impression was that the Vintners had not yet decided whom to endorse, but in fact they had. Reverdy selected vintners to interview the candidates, matching Rombauer with Kathleen McCullough and Dick Peterson with Jay Goetting. To no one's surprise, both found the candidates unacceptable.

Reverdy wanted to invite only the pro-growth challengers, Negri and Mikolajcik, to the rally, but some vintners simply wouldn't accept that. So he drafted a letter to be sent only to the members saying that the Vintners leadership had interviewed the candidates for the two supervisorial seats, assisted by Moone, Rombauer, Corley, Peterson, Mike Martini, and Roy Raymond, and had come to a decision.

"Kathleen McCullough is clearly an intelligent, sensitive person with a strong commitment to the preservation of the physical character of the Valley," Reverdy wrote. "Jay Goetting is equally knowledgeable and articulate." However, both favored including the 75 percent grape requirement in the environmental review. "At the risk of being overly simplistic, McCullough and Goetting seem quite comfortable with regulatory activism" and therefore all vintners should support their opponents.

Fred Negri worked for an industrial supplier of building materials in Napa city, Syar; John ("Mickey") Mikolajcik was a nurseryman from American Canyon, in the county's south end. "They, together with Supervisor Bob White," the barber, "will constitute a majority on the Board, and will afford us the assurance of fair treatment on this critical matter."

For the first time in its history, the Vintners was aligning itself with forces favoring development — a watershed. What was supposed to be a confidential communiqué to the members was promptly leaked by Dwyer to a reporter for the *Napa Register* and another in San Francisco. By leaking the letter, he made the Vintners' choices in the election clear, without having to deal with the strife and possible embarrassment of a formal endorsement. It was another unprecedented move in the history of the Napa Valley Vintners Association, and an indication of the determination of the current leadership to control the political debate. It was also bound to split the membership if word ever got out that Reverdy's letter had been purposefully shoved beneath the nose of the media.

The story duly appeared in the *Register* under the banner headline "Vintners Back Mikolajcik, Negri." Corley and Martini loudly objected during the subsequent meeting of the Vintners board. Dwyer did not admit to leaking the letter. When asked how reporters had obtained copies, he said, "They have their ways." Afterward, he publicly denied that the letter was an endorsement. "This is an in-house recommendation," he told reporters.

If someone wanted to infer that the Vintners would like to see changes on the board of supervisors, and wanted the winery employees to vote against Kathleen and Jay, so be it.

Tom Burgess did not believe that the majority of the members of the Napa Valley Vintners Association supported the endorsement. He decided to poll them. He had been in the valley many years, after taking over the old Souverain winery owned by Lee Stewart. Burgess was something of a loner, a former airline pilot and owner of the fastest single-engine plane flying out of Angwin. Burgess usually attended Vintners meetings and tried to parcel out some of this time to the organization, but was not enamored of its politics. This endorsement seemed wrong to him.

Barbara Winiarski helped him write the letter and get it out to members to be polled. She told people, "We're not going to abandon the destiny of this county."

She and Warren held a breakfast meeting that included Burgess, John Williams of Frog's Leap Wine Cellars, Guy Kay, and the Davieses. They decided to buy a full-page ad in the *Register* and print the names of vintners in favor of Kathleen and Jay, supervisors for responsible land use.

There were so many half-truths in the air. Mike Moone had helped stampede the Vintners by arguing that the 75 percent solution would drive grape prices up to ruinous levels; at the same time he and others stated that vintners already owned 65 percent of the vineyards. They claimed that tourism was down, whereas Jack Davies's report clearly indicated that it wasn't. They were coaching Negri to say he favored strip development along Highway 29 if it obstructed the view, *but not elsewhere*. They asserted that Beckstoffer and Volker didn't speak for the growers in the valley, and then the Vintners leadership rammed through an endorsement by leaking Reverdy's letter to the press. All these things obscured the real problem: the Vintners was backing pro-growth candidates when it should have been backing the opposite.

Barbara had to hop that morning to get down to Napa and reserve the space in the newspaper.

Everywhere he went in the valley, André Tchelistcheff heard jarring words about the upcoming election; he also saw red ribbons tied to trees, signs, and mailboxes, and anti–Wine Train stickers in windows and on car bumpers. These protesters were misguided, in his opinion. If someone — even a pasta manufacturer in San Leandro — wanted to bring more publicity to the valley, why object? The valley should be open to all. If people thought of it as Disneyland, so what? Disneyland embodied the energy and creativity of America.

André had survived his latest illness and actually had seldom felt better. The stomach pains had abated and he was back on the road, advising clients during the 1988 harvest. He still drank wine, and a cigarette still graced his wrinkled fingers after meals. Now he fretted over what he considered the tragedy of his career, the fact that wine and social superiority had become equated. Wine was simply a beverage to be consumed, not an emblem of rank. Wineries were places wine was made, not social and political implements. Some vintners used the Wine Train to divert attention from their own unsavory practices, like the importation of grapes from other counties.

André supported the idea that Napa Valley wineries should use a high percentage of Napa Valley grapes. On the other hand, he believed that the wineries should be allowed to expand, free of restrictions. That, too, was essentially American.

A young reporter for the *Register* called and asked his opinion of all the controversy. André told her the real problem was not the 75 percent solution, winery restrictions, or the Wine Train; it was self-adoration, "the disease that brought down Rome." Growers and vintners had, in their collective success, forgotten their own origins, and the origins of wine. They were taking extreme positions out of self-interest and an overweening pride. "We are so proud of ourselves," he said.

Before the political rally could begin on the scheduled day, Reverdy Johnson had to break up the three-hour lunch with Dwyer, Moone, Corley, Meyer, Michael Mondavi, and Guy Kay. The subject of the perceived endorsement had gone back and forth, Reverdy pushing to make it formal, Guy Kay resisting. There was no final agreement.

Six hundred people waited in the meeting room in the Clarion Inn adjacent to the one where Rafael Rodriguez had held the wedding reception for his daughter. They sat in low rows of metal chairs or stood against the walls, waiting to hear the questions put to the politicians by Mondavi, Meyer, and Moone, who took their seats with the ease of men in the presence of their own employees.

The four candidates were not so fortunate. It was up to Dwyer to introduce them, and up to Reverdy to provide the perspective. This he did with legal conciseness that obscured his residual anger, although a discernible edginess remained. "The reason we are here," he said, "is because nobody knows what a winery is."

The amusement the words provoked didn't faze him. The problem was a serious one, he added; it reflected the fact that outsiders did not understand the industry. Then he invited the candidates to address the issues, starting with Kathleen McCullough.

Those in the audience who knew her, Barbara Winiarski among them, could sense her uneasiness. Kathleen thanked the vintners for inviting her and praised them for the taxes they paid, adding, "I need to speak for the public interest as well as the number one industry in our county, which is agriculture and the wine industry."

She said the board of supervisors was attempting to define a winery in a way that not only regulated the proliferation of wineries but also related them to the preservation of the land. She implied that the question was bigger than the wineries; it concerned the entire valley.

Her opponent, Fred Negri, shorter than Kathleen, with blow-dried hair and bright, eager eyes, had made notes while Kathleen spoke. "I have worked for Basalite Block Company for twenty-seven years," he said when his turn came, "and now with Syar Industries. I am familiar with the manner in which the free enterprise system works and what it's driven by. I respect it very much and I think it's something that makes this country great. I think for local government to jump to control the way a company produces and markets its product interferes with that free enterprise system." He supported grandfathering all the winery activities.

While Negri spoke, the incumbent from District 5, Jay Goetting, stared at the ceiling. It was a habit that did not serve him well. The whites of his eyes were exposed to the audience, conveying an impression of boredom. His years as a radio announcer had given him a resonant voice, however. "For a group of self-proclaimed political neophytes," he said, "this is probably the biggest and best political rally I have ever seen occur in Napa County."

He admitted he had trouble distinguishing between a political recommendation and a political endorsement by the Vintners. The wine industry could be headed for chaos, he said. It was a mistake to rally employees to vote for particular candidates only on the basis of how they might vote on the issues of tourism, development, and home-grown grapes. He had met with the leaders of the Vintners, Goetting said. "While they wanted a firm commitment from me on several key issues, including the 75 percent rule, at this crucial point just days before the election, I couldn't give that."

Goetting's real constituency lay south of the city, in American Canyon, where residents wanted to incorporate and turn the development into another city, without county-imposed restrictions. He had been less than enthusiastic in support of those ambitions. He desperately needed whatever support he could find. So he attacked his bemused opponent and one-time supervisor, Mickey Mikolajcik. "He is strongly opposed to the control of growth. . . . He supported special-interest zonings." Besides, Goetting said, Mikolajcik was lazy.

The sight of Mikolajcik's high forehead and gap-toothed grin did not inspire confidence among those leading vintners who had invited him to the Clarion and endorsed him. But Mikolajcik's looks were preferable to his words. "I come from that southern end of the county," he began, "down in American Canyon." He lauded free enterprise and recalled the lean years when winery owners had to entice people in off the highway. "Them days are gone. Thank God them days are gone."

The audience's laughter seemed to surprise him. "I want youse to know I travel up and down this valley, Silverado Trail and Twenty-nine, many times. Every week, as a matter of fact. I own a hundred and sixty acres in Pope Valley. Not in grapes — too many bears . . ."

The continuing laughter posed a problem for the vintners sharing the program with Mikolajcik. If they, too, laughed, it might be taken as a sign of disrespect for a candidate they had publicly endorsed. Glum expressions, on the other hand, might be interpreted as a sign of disapproval. They settled for wry, mandarin smiles.

"We all love Mother Nature, but she can turn a mean hand," Mikolajcik continued. "If you had a freeze and you didn't have the grapes, and the 75 percent limit was there, what would happen to the small wineries? . . . You have to make sure your valley is preserved. Your valley floor will be there forever. You have to make *sure* it's there. You want to be sure your customer wants Napa Valley wine. You have to be nice to them . . ."

When Mikolajcik was done, Reverdy invited questions from the panel. Mike Moone, Beringer's master salesman, who had found himself at the head of one of the valley's oldest and biggest wineries, was accustomed to commanding the floor. He began with a rambling claim that tourism was decreasing, not increasing. The winery definition under consideration left no opportunity for wineries to attract more tourists and wine buyers, he said, which is what they should be doing. He asked the candidates for suggestions "for helping wineries to be competitive in this arena."

Kathleen had to deal first with what amounted to a denunciation

of the current board of supervisors. She asked Moone to repeat the
question. The second version was even less friendly than the first.

Kathleen pointed out that no one really knew where the traffic in
the valley came from, and that the moratorium was needed until a
proper study could be done. "When the moratorium is lifted and we
consider allowing new wineries to establish here, we would have the
data necessary to make intelligent decisions."

Mikolajcik took a desperate stab at Moone's question. "I have
checked out different places, people talking to different people about
the winery business and the traffic. All right." He broke off to tell a
story about Sunday drivers in the thirties. Then he said, "It's hard to
believe that the people do love their car, but we all do. My wife loves
hers. I like my truck. It's still on the road. I don't want to make youse
laugh about it . . ." But laugh people did.

Negri praised tourism as proof of "the kind of class act we really
are in the Napa Valley." Goetting spoke of traffic as a problem common in the Bay Area, one that needed to be addressed. Its relation
to marketing would, he hoped, be included in the environmental
study. No one had answered Moone's question.

Justin Meyer asked about the proposed forty-acre minimum lots
for wineries. His Silver Oak Cellars had been built on only twenty
acres a decade earlier, he said. Would it be grandfathered into the new
requirements or classified as nonconforming?

Goetting said no one knew yet what the rules would be and so
the question couldn't truthfully be answered.

Negri said simply, "You would be conforming," which was the
answer they all wanted.

Mikolajcik began, "Nonconforming use is a terrible word. I
asked a guy where he worked. He told me. I told him he made too
much money. The man didn't like me . . ."

When Kathleen's turn came, she said, "If I can remember your
question, Justin, it's about your particular winery. . . . I don't believe
the new regulations refer to anybody who is established either as a
heritage or estate or vintage winery. . . . I don't know if I can absolutely answer that question for you this afternoon."

The answer was truthful, but Kathleen had used the hated words
— heritage, estate, vintage — put forward in the growers' proposal.

Michael Mondavi came last. Like Mike Moone, he told the candidates "to think as a business entrepreneur or business owner, a
vineyard owner, winery owner. . . . Under the proposed restric-

tions, how would *you* operate a winery and how would *you* be able to build a company and compete in a more competitive world today than we've had in the past twenty-five years?"

"That's a very difficult question for me to answer," Kathleen said. "About the only thing I can say is that a county is only as strong as its industrial base, and I respect that and have always supported agriculture in this county, and the wine business. I've done that by being a county supervisor who has, on every issue affecting agriculture and land use that has come before me in the last four years, always voted to restrict urban uses out in the agricultural area, if not totally eliminate them. That means housing. I have supported the ag preserve to keep out any kind of attack on the twenty-year-old experiment. . . . Without that understanding on the board of supervisors of the land-use issues, the wine industry could not have gone as far as it has."

Mention of the twenty-year-old experiment elicited no sympathy from the audience. When Mikolajcik said, "I don't believe in restricting wineries in the method of advertising or selling their products," the crowd applauded.

The election lay only weeks away. Sitting in the back of the room, little noticed on the floor, was Robert Mondavi. He hugged his knees. This was not his forum; it was in part his son's. Robert said nothing then, and very little during the clamor for beer and hot dogs afterward. But he later told a friend that he was bothered by the confrontational, even disdainful tone of the meeting. It appeared that the vintners had lost all the grace accumulated since the days of old Louis Martini and John Daniel.

51

TOM BURGESS had to sit for half an hour outside the next Vintners board meeting before he could tell Reverdy about the results of his survey: a majority of vintners in the valley did not support the endorsement of Negri and Mikolajcik.

Shortly thereafter, Reverdy announced at the meeting of the general membership that he, Reverdy, sensed a "polarization" within the association. He wondered aloud if "a critical error" had been made in supporting Negri and Mikolajcik on the single issue of the winery definition. It was backpedaling, it was late, and it changed nothing.

Guy Kay reported that he had been told by the county counsel that the Vintners Association had shot itself in the foot. Mikolajcik, if elected, would push for the incorporation of American Canyon, and the county would lose control of the south end. Mikolajcik's and Negri's supporters, including the developers, would want their due, which would mean altering the General Plan and eventually loosening up restrictions on building in the ag preserve. A three-to-two pro-growth majority on the board could further lead to redistricting, meaning an additional loss of power by agricultural areas and the entire up-valley. Guy Kay concluded, "We're making a deal with the devil."

Then the *Napa Register* carried a story saying that the Vintners had overruled Reverdy. The organization would not support *any* candidate in the supervisorial race. According to the official statement from the Vintners, progress in negotiations between vintners and growers over a winery definition — negotiations that had been going on for years without producing a document — had caused the change of mind. The growers seemed capable of at least some compromise. The leadership of the Vintners encouraged members "to support the supervisorial candidate of his or her choice."

John Williams, quoted in the story, said, "It is a retraction of a position we never really took. There are a lot of people with egg on their face."

In the same issue, on the page with the heading "Wine Industry Supports McCullough & Goetting," appeared almost fifty signatures of vintners collected by Barbara Winiarski.

The Friday before the election, Mike Moone called Warren on his car phone on the way to the airport. He said, "Let's cool the rhetoric," indicating that even he had perceived some ill will toward the handful of men running the Vintners, of which he was one.

"You haven't cooled it," Warren said. "Don't you realize that Negri and Mikolajcik will chew us up if they get elected?"

"Oh, we'll handle them later," Moone replied, and hung up.

Barbara was up before dawn on election day. She turned on the television. Some early results were coming in from the East Coast, from the presidential election. George Bush was expected to take the South and the West, and probably California; prospects for Dukakis were dim. There was nothing about Napa County that early in the morning.

Barbara worried about the weather. Dense clouds hung over the valley. A good turnout was needed for Kathleen and Jay. Barbara had signed up at the Farm Bureau as a driver for the elderly and disabled, to get them to the polls, but that might not be enough. She knew Kathleen had worked door-to-door up until the last moment; with a little help, she and Jay might make it.

Barbara opened the window to let out the cigarette smoke, and thought, Please don't rain. The land was a sea of gold, with some ruddy grape leaves as well. Against them were arrayed, up and down the valley, Negri's blue posters and Kathleen's smaller green ones, and all the red ribbon left over from the Wine Train protest.

Warren appeared, dressed and ready for breakfast. Barbara served him his bowl of oatmeal. "The question is," she said, "what to do if we lose."

Warren thought about it. Whatever the outcome of the election, it offered a chance to reform the Vintners. Backing down from the endorsement had been a triumph for moderation. If the pro-growth candidates won, Reverdy and Moone would use that as an excuse to get out of a verbal compromise between the vintners and the growers that they had recently agreed to. In principle, the vintners' representatives had swallowed the minimum grape requirement, but nothing had been put on paper. If the pro-growthers backed by the Vintners leadership won the election, then Reverdy et al. would see that as a vindication of their rule. But opposition to them within the Vintners would be galvanized.

Volker Eisele called. He had been in New York for a promotional event involving the appellation education committee, of which he was a member. Barbara filled him in on what had transpired in the past few days. She asked, "What do we do next?"

"Maybe a referendum," he said, assuming the worst.

"I had a feeling last night Jay would win," Barbara said. "I will feel bad if he does and Kathleen doesn't. One's better than none, of course." She paused. "I have this feeling Kathleen might lose . . ."

She returned to the breakfast table. Warren held up his empty glass.

"Tea!" said Barbara. "That's politics. You don't get your tea!"

Kathleen McCullough had showed up at the Veterans Home at 6:30, to greet the men as they went in to breakfast. She wore a white dress with a colorful scarf and gold loops in her ears. She felt relaxed and cautiously confident about the voting. Things were breaking in her direction. The push by the Vintners to endorse Negri had brought some people around to her side; they saw her as the candidate standing up for the public interest.

The turnaround on the Vintners endorsement had won over more votes. The rally, she thought, had been a public hanging. The tone had been set by Reverdy Johnson when he chose the panelists. Michael Mondavi had been the worst, asking her to put herself in the place of a vintner, and she had decided not to play his game. Kathleen knew land use was important to the vintners, as well as to other citizens, and she had stuck with it. Taking Michael Mondavi seriously was not easy for her. He acted as if he had pulled himself up by the bootstraps, but really he had been born with a silver spoon in his mouth. He had his own agenda, commercial development, and in her opinion would go to any lengths to get it, even at the expense of the ag preserve.

From Yountville she drove into Napa for the supervisors meeting. Low clouds hung over the city, and by the time the meeting was under way, fine rain needled the windows. Kathleen wasn't going to let that distract her. She voted against allowing the church to build a school in the agricultural watershed. That afternoon she planned to bring up the subject of Napa's homeless. Then she would go home and stay there until around 9 P.M., when she would come back to campaign headquarters and sit with her supporters while the returns came in.

Bob Phillips had gotten permission to erect a large sign at the edge of his property on Highway 29. It urged people to join the alliance seeking an environmental impact report by the Wine Train. He would have to take the sign down in sixty days, but maybe something would be decided by then. If the California Public Utilities Commission capitulated to the Interstate Commerce Commission, the train's opponents would continue their suit — all the way to the Supreme Court if necessary.

He had been heartened by the response in the county against the Wine Train, but was troubled by the supervisorial campaign. The local election was really about tourism, like everything else in the valley. He had helped raise $50,000 for Kathleen, some of it coming from vintners, but it might not be enough.

Phillips hoped the Vintners would discipline its leadership. The winery owners had to be hit in the face with a fish to realize that something was wrong. He had many friends among them, but sometimes they made him angry. Until a few years ago, their organization hadn't even seemed aware of the fact that there was a board of supervisors. Half the vintners were away from the valley at any one time, promoting their wine and soaking up the adulation of consumers, developing huge egos.

One problem with big-headed vintners was that you couldn't talk to them. They were always right. They spoke of the nobility of wine and then made the crassest sort of political choices. They talked about the necessity of drinking fine wine with fine cuisine and then backed somebody like John Mikolajcik for supervisor. Sometimes when Phillips heard all the talk about wine, art, and elegance, he wanted to say, "That's bull. People drink wine to get drunk." He didn't really believe that, but would have loved to see the vintners' faces if he had said it.

That afternoon he went into town and voted for Kathleen Mc-Cullough and George Bush — irreconcilable choices anywhere but in Napa Valley. Then he went back to Vine Hill Ranch and sat in his expansive study, the telephone at his elbow, watching the results come in.

It was Volker's day to clean the house. He had worked for hours, taking time off to deal with the telephone. The trip to New York had been interesting but not very fruitful. The vintners had tried to exclude the growers from the event beforehand. Moone had told him, "We don't want to stand next to guys trying to wreck our business." Volker had decided to go to the opera instead. He had argued with the cab driver about the lack of seat belts, but Volker liked New York.

The mopping would have to wait. He opened a bottle of his '82 Cabernet. The national elections, according to news reports, were going to the Republicans. His daughter, Christiane, was upset by this. Volker spoke to her in French, English, and German, trying to distract her, but his mind was on the local elections. It seemed to him that the men at the top of the Vintners had screwed up, regardless of the outcome. If Kathleen and Jay won, Dwyer was probably in trouble, but it was far from certain that they would win. Volker had tried to advise Kathleen against using an outsider as campaign manager; after a while he had to stop talking about it or lose what influence he had. He had raised money for her and kept his fingers crossed.

Christiane went into the other room where the radio was and then came back. She said, "Bush has won two hundred and seventy-nine electoral votes. We're all going under."

She went out again and slammed the door.

The old county courthouse in Napa city — Election Central — was crowded by the time Volker arrived. Boy Scouts were selling Cokes and hot dogs on the sidewalk outside in the cool autumn air. Volker said hello to Barbara Winiarski and her daughter Kasia, and Kasia's fiancé, Jim. So far the results were good for Kathleen, Barbara said, and not so good for Jay. At 8:45 it was too early to tell what might happen.

Volker crossed the street to the campaign headquarters shared by Kathleen and Jay, two little rooms at the top of a steep staircase with green cinderblock walls and torn carpeting. A small group stood at the table supporting the coffee urn and bottles of wine donated by Stag's Leap and Silverado. Volker shook some hands. He could feel the tension.

Kathleen arrived in her white dress, carrying a tray of vegetables and dip, followed by her husband with a plate of cold cuts. Faces brightened. Kathleen looked confident and relaxed, as if this were a social occasion and the dip and veggies her only stake in it. Jay Goetting came in from the next room, sipping white wine from a plastic cup. He patted Volker on the shoulder, but it should have been the other way around. Jay had received 650 votes and Mikolajcik 769. Kathleen had 1,090, Negri 1,166. The trend was not good.

Negri had rented the hall of the Native Sons of the Golden West, a block from Election Central. Volker decided to walk over. He found the big, ornate room crowded — almost as many people as in the courthouse — and hung with bunting. A buffet had been set up; Negri had booze, Volker noticed, a sign of confidence and full campaign coffers. Well-dressed men and women with elaborate hair styles stood in groups on the thick red carpet, obviously enjoying themselves. They seemed to know something Volker didn't.

He saw Dick Peterson there, winemaker and supervisor of the Atlas Peak project, with the thick-necked Harold Moskowite, the man Volker had helped defeat in the last election. He avoided them.

Going back up the stairs at Kathleen's and Jay's headquarters, Volker felt someone take his arm. "Kathleen's slipping," the man said.

She sat against the wall, in a line of supporters, making conversation and smiling. Her husband did the same. Volker thought that if Kathleen and Jay lost, then the county would get what it deserved. The press had done a good job covering the campaigns; the issues had been aired, and the *Register* had endorsed Kathleen and Jay. If people could still vote for Mikolajcik and Negri, knowing what they represented, then there was nothing else to be done.

A young man in a T-shirt arrived from Election Central and began to tape the lastest results to the wall. It was almost eleven o'clock and Kathleen was still trailing by 100 votes, and Jay by almost 700. Paul Battisti, the man who had defeated Moskowite in the spring primary, leaned toward Volker, and said, "This is sad. If Jay and Kathleen lose, we're going to have some long-range problems."

Beckstoffer showed up in cords and a Windbreaker, the collar turned up. He poured himself a glass of Stag's Leap Cabernet. Mel

Varrelman, the supervisor from St. Helena, tried to look cheerful. Volker poured a glass of the Silverado Cabernet and sat against the wall. This was the real hard core, the same organizers and volunteers who had worked on campaigns for years. There was not one vintner among them, and no grower other than himself and Andy Beckstoffer.

Jay's opponent had amassed 3,447 votes and needed only 4,000 to win. Jay's wife, acknowledging defeat before he did, began to sob. "Maybe he'll get a real job," she said. "I don't think two people should have to go through this. I have been cursed, spat on. Dogs have bitten me."

There was something disconcerting about Kathleen's composure in the face of what looked like defeat. It was 11:30 and she was down by 230 votes.

Beckstoffer told Volker, "I think I'll take off. It's going to be hard to change those figures."

At a few minutes past midnight, Jay called everyone into the room, and said, "I just want to thank you for yeoman service. You've done a hell of a job. I've had a hell of a time serving the county. It's not easy to say this, but it looks like the numbers just aren't there." He paused. "God help Napa Valley."

Kathleen's campaign manager, the one from Oakland — a determined woman who had so far mirrored her candidate's composure — began to weep silently. But Kathleen said brightly, "That should be about all the vote."

Volker raced across the street to Election Central, to see if a wave of late, sympathetic votes had broken over the tired officials on the phones. It hadn't.

The television crew arrived at 12:30 for interviews. Kathleen smiled. "It's still too close to call," she said. "It was an excellent campaign. We got out there and talked about the issues. . . . Now we have to wait for the absentee votes to be counted."

She thanked people and left. Volker descended the stairs after her. The sound of cheering carried all the way over from Negri's headquarters. Kathleen might not be conceding, but Negri was giving a victory speech and the media were all there to cover it. The race was over and everybody on the side of slow growth had lost.

This was Volker's eighth supervisorial race. He had pushed hard for sixteen years and helped to get good land-use policies in place, acting as an officer in the Grape Growers and the Farm Bureau. Now the candidates he and the others had worked for so diligently were dead politically. Negri and Mikolajcik had many IOUs out there among the developers and potential despoilers of the ag preserve. Even if they proved to be reasonable men, they were going to have a hard time resisting pressures from those celebrating in the hall of the Native Sons of the Golden West.

A handful of the McCullough-Goetting supporters stood on the pavement in the dark. Volker joined them, and said, "Let's move to Oregon."

It was very late when he got back to Chiles Valley. Liesel and the children were asleep. The kitten was stranded on a shelf in the kitchen and Volker lifted it to the floor and then he poured himself a glass of home-grown Cabernet. The day had been a disaster, locally and nationally. He blamed Kathleen for not listening to him, for being so cool. There was no connection between her and the constituents; she was the Napa Valley equivalent of Michael Dukakis.

He blamed himself for not being more assertive; he feared that grape growing would cease to be the main source of activity in the valley during his children's lifetime, if not in his own.

52

BOB DWYER'S office in the little clapboard building on Meadowood's southern frontier faced the driveway, which was as far as one could get from the clubhouse and still be within the resort's perimeter. The guardhouse stood on one side and the septic system on the other. On hot days the chemical balance in the aerating tanks was occasionally upset; then Dwyer, the executive director of the Napa Valley Vintners, bore the brunt of olfactory evidence that too many people in a narrow space adversely affect the environment.

The morning after the election, Dwyer sat in his office and telephoned the two victorious candidates, Mikolajcik and Negri, and reminded them that the Vintners had helped. He hung up thinking the association was going to have a very good relationship with those two gentlemen. He had called them a week before, after the Vintners voted to rescind the endorsement, to warn them. Dwyer had told Mikolajcik and Negri, "I've done all I can." Now he was convinced that the candidates' forum at the Clarion Inn had given credibility to the Vintners, despite the perceived retraction of the perceived endorsement.

Dwyer lit a cigarette and leaned back in his desk chair, legs crossed. He wasn't gloating over the outcome of the election, but in his opinion Andy Beckstoffer and Volker Eisele were dead meat. With the election the growers had lost all influence in Napa, and the vintners could move forward without confusing land use with winery activities. The vintners were no longer businessmen confronted by a bunch of growers trying to regulate them.

The winery definition still had to be addressed. It wouldn't be wise to bring up the overlay zone right away; that would wait until the new board had been sworn in and gotten used to their new chairs. Growth in the county was essential, in the view of the Vintners' small group of de facto leaders, which included himself, Reverdy, Moone, Maher, and Corley. The time was gone when the local government could sit around ignoring the wishes of the Association of Bay Area Governments and the economic boom in the rest of the state. Dwyer agreed with Michael Mondavi: the county had to let the pressure off somewhere. Napans were jealous of up-valley elitists making money out of the ag preserve. Joe Six-pack wanted in on the action. The elitists had held the line against growth for ten years, and now the whole place was about to break open like a piece of rotten fruit.

๛

Warren decided that what the Vintners needed was a stronger board and responsive leaders for a more complicated, maybe disastrous time ahead. When John Trefethen had been president, the board had sipped sherry and informally discussed problems. President Joe Phelps used to say, "Gentlemen, what's your pleasure?" That seemed a very long time ago.

It was a matter of custom that past presidents of the Vintners were asked to nominate new board members. Mike Martini had been president before Reverdy Johnson and therefore should be called, but Martini was publicly associated with the dissidents. If Mike didn't get a call from Reverdy, they would all know that something was wrong.

Warren didn't want them to nominate *him*. He didn't have time for any more politics. He intended to propose that a committee be appointed within the Vintners to study decision making and then ensure that the right people got on the committee. Moone and Dick Maher would try to pack it, but the committee must come up with the proper finding — that the executive had sought in the past year to by-pass the membership and should be restrained in the future, to prevent such an upheaval as the one that had just taken place.

Barbara called Mel Varrelman and they discussed the possibility of a recount in District 2. Fred Negri led Kathleen McCullough by only 167 votes. Some absentee ballots were left to be counted; the prospects weren't good, however. The *Register* had already given the victory to Negri. Kathleen was in seclusion and probably wouldn't request a recount.

Barbara tried to control her outrage over what had happened. She leaned toward decisive, even devisive action now. Everyone had to wake up! She was no longer content with what passed for diplomacy in the valley. The big question was whether the people committed to responsible land use could still work within the system.

Tony Soter called her. He was the winemaker at Spottswoode, and he suggested a splinter group within the Vintners for political purposes, a kind of rump organization. Keep the association together for trade purposes only. They both questioned the worth of the Vintners to the small wineries. It was the boutiques that lent prestige to the big ones. The Burgesses, the Stag's Leaps, and the Spottswoodes didn't need the corporations. The Napa Valley Wine Auction would prove to be an embarrassment if the small wineries all pulled out and left only wines from Beringer and Christian Brothers on the block.

Barbara hung up and began to draft a letter to all signers of the full-page ad that had endorsed Jay Goetting and Kathleen McCullough. "No doubt," she began, "winery endorsement of the pro-development candidates seriously endangered the future of agriculture in the valley . . ."

Outside, beyond the footbridge, she could see the welter of buildings, roads, and vineyards — of life — southwest of Parker Hill. When she had arrived in the valley twenty-five years before, she had been stunned by the beauty, isolation, and parched wildness of it all. Now she thought, There is a pernicious tendency to see the people on the other side as evil. This is not helpful.

Stu Smith, bearded GONAD and owner of Smith-Madrone Vineyards, told his wife, "We won the battle and lost the war."

The vintners had negotiated an unofficial compromise with the growers over the 75 percent solution back in October. But they had also helped bring in Mikolajcik and Negri. The new supervisors would side with Bob White, the other pro-growth supervisor, forming a majority. The ag preserve was closer to extinction; the old saw "Three votes and thirty days" had a new relevance.

The pro-growth endorsement had amounted to a palace coup. The Vintners' general membership no longer had a say. The problem, Smith thought, went back to Jim Barrett, owner of Château Montelena, who had packed the board in the mid-eighties with people he could control. He had done away with keeping specific minutes, blurring accountability. He had brought in Bob Dwyer and tried to use auction funds to pay for Vintners events. The beginning of decision by fiat.

Smith would stick around for a year, to see if the leadership improved. If not, he was out of there.

In the view of Guy Kay, Napa had officially stopped being a rural county the day the votes were cast. The *perception* of the ag preserve was now under attack. Outmoded language describing wineries as processing plants had been used to justify wine factories like the one outside his office window; the county planning staff had recognized the need for a better definition, and moved responsibly to come up with one, but all that was bound to change with the new board. It was going to be much more difficult to protect agricultural land in the future. Kay could easily imagine pressure from the state for Napa to grow ever faster, and that pressure being used politically to justify development and more state revenue.

Before the election, Kay had gone down to Napa, to the county building, to listen to the tape of the joint meeting of the board of supervisors and the Planning Commission, when the winery definition was opened to public comment. He decided that the Vintners had overreacted. Astounded by the endorsement of Negri and Mikolajcik, Kay had called up Mike Moone and told him it was a mistake. Moone reacted as if Kay were one of the enemies.

Kay had then tried the impossible: he called Michael Mondavi, to get him to add his name to the full-page ad endorsing Kathleen and Jay, to admit making a mistake. Mondavi said he couldn't.

"What about Tim?" Kay had asked. Tim could sign his name to the ad.

"I'll see," Michael had said, but Kay never heard from either of them.

Jack Davies was tired. The demands of marketing had reached a new high; with the phenomenal success of Schramsberg over the last quarter century had come a loss of personal liberty. It was impossible to delegate marketing — the customers wanted *him*. Just that morning he learned he would have to miss the traditional Christmas dinner at the Bohemian Club to make an appearance in southern California, which he had left twenty-five years before to move into a bat-infested old house in a little canyon off a valley full of Italians and prune orchards.

The outcome of the election saddened him. It was silly for vintners to assume that politicians, once elected, could be controlled. The wineries didn't have the influence the Vintners Association claimed; no effort was under way to develop a constituency. The association had no real political expertise, as the endorsement debacle proved, and no prospects for strong leadership. Jack didn't want the job and didn't see any likely candidates.

There was something about the wine industry that he had never been able to understand. Vintners were willing to spend hundreds of thousands of dollars — millions! — ten years before any profit was possible, but they would not invest in good communications and good policies. Why they couldn't take a similar long view would always be a mystery to him.

The agenda of the new supervisors was inimical to everything the Vintners should stand for. They would regret what had happened. The new county board of supervisors would go along with development plans in the ag preserve, and if you broke the line somewhere, you broke it everywhere.

❧

Volker had risen at 8 A.M. the day after the election, with only five hours of sleep, and driven back down to Napa. There he submitted a proposal to the Agricultural Lands Preservation Fund for a $3,000 grant, to have a legal study done of the Association of Bay Area Governments' so-called housing requirements. If the research showed that the requirements were not legal, then Volker would present the study to county and city governments trying to alleviate population growth pressures. If the requirements were within the law, at least opponents of growth would know what tactics to take.

The big battle would be the voter initiative. Whether to declare a moratorium on development within the ag preserve should be put on the next ballot. First Volker needed to round up a core group that would include Vic Fershko, Bob Phillips, Mel Varrelman, and a few others. The usual suspects. Volker believed that land-use battles were easier to win directly; people will vote for preservation when they won't vote for preservation candidates — a paradox.

The effort would require $70,000 and a dedicated group to work the shopping centers and collect the necessary signatures. The initiative was the riskiest ploy yet. He had to be sure the vote would carry, once the proposition was on the ballot. If it did not carry, a clear signal would be sent to the politicians that the residents of Napa Valley didn't care what happened to open space. Then there would be no defense against the bulldozers.

Volker didn't talk to Kathleen that day; he saw no point. The election was over and it was time to move on to the next thing, but the election results rankled. The Vintners had won, at least in the short run; it was the crowning of Dwyer's transformation. Volker laughed out loud when he thought of the derogatory comments Dwyer had once made about members of the Vintners when he worked for the growers. He wondered who among them might now lead. Warren was sufficiently intelligent but too cautious. Tom Ferrell, president of Sterling, had good impulses but was ultimately under the thumb of Sam Bronfman. Tom Selfridge would make a good president but was subordinate to Heublein, which was answerable to Grand Metropolitan. Tom Burgess had the guts, but did he have the political ability? Steve Girard was young and brash and made some of the right noises, but he had opposed the 75 percent solution and was a member of the GONADS. So was Stu Smith, and Dan Duckhorn, who always seemed to show up on the side of the winner.

Moone was next in line, but Nestlé reportedly had other plans for Moone; he wasn't in the running. That meant Dick Maher, ex-Marine and corporate survivor, would be the next president.

That weekend, Volker and Liesel went for a hike in the hills behind their house. Some friends went with them. The air was cool and the sky cloud-covered. Volker pointed out the different varieties of oak and the chestnuts that dangled big, pouchlike fruit from otherwise bare branches, and acorn woodpeckers, even a falcon. Overgrazing had destroyed much of the leafy understory of the big trees. The steep climb brought them to the spine of hills that ran the length of Chiles Valley. To the east lay the cedar roughs, to the north Mount St. Helena, and to the west, beyond the hills, Napa Valley proper, visible through breaks in the mountains, furred with chaparral and digger pine. The valley's natural isolation impressed itself upon what might have been a group of early westering migrants in another century.

One of the hikers peeled an orange and tossed the skin among the weeds. Volker snapped, "Hey, don't do that."

Liesel said gently, "It's biodegradable, Volker."

Back at the house, they settled in for dinner. Volker had never mastered the barbecue and so left that chore to one of his guests. He opened a bottle of his own Cabernet Sauvignon, the '83. He poured everyone a glass and sipped from his. He said, "I love this wine."

Newspapers lay on his chair. Volker intended to read the German ones after reading the American ones about the presidential election. There were messages waiting on the answering machine, including one from a reporter in Napa wanting Volker to talk about the future of the valley. Before returning the call he would have to determine what to say, how much to reveal and how much to withhold.

53

LOOKING BACK, many remembered no more vivid detail from the election's aftermath than the cutting of the big oaks, an event not directly related to the issues that had been fought over for three years but symbolic of the sacrifices success entails. The gnarled trunks and huge limbs of more than seventy majestic trees near Highway 29, across from the Old Bale Mill, collided with pastureland on the last undeveloped parcel on the valley floor, bought by a wine-marketing firm in Bordeaux — part of the internationalization of Napa Valley — and subjected to the bulldozer.

In the preceding two years eight foreign corporations had bought land and well-known wineries; the pasture was to be planted with vines that would eventually provide grapes for the firm's prefabricated winery, which had risen south of St. Helena, under flapping flags, its architectural anomie matched by the winery's exploitative name, Château Napa Beaucannon.

The objections of neighbors who had looked at the old oaks for many years were based not on the facts that the owners were foreign and that they had paid almost $3 million for 117 acres of graze. The three-hundred-year-old trees were being toppled to make way for yet another medium-priced Cabernet in an already glutted market.

The county could not prevent the cutting, since the land was zoned for agriculture. A spokesman for Le Begue Wine Company pointed out that vines and oaks are mutually exclusive, because vines can develop root fungus from the trees, and the ripping of the earth with blades pulled by giant Caterpillars to prepare the ground would certainly cut the roots, strangling whatever oaks remained.

A woman who watched the felling of the trees later said, "I felt like they were cutting people."

New faces and more new buildings would soon be appearing on the southern horizon, the direction from which the fog had always come, out of a bay whose littoral teemed with the industry of man. That industry was bound for Napa Valley in unprecedented force now that growth, made acceptable by the election, was seen as inevitable.

The developers' favorite lawyer, Joe Peatman, made plans to expand the offices of Dickenson, Peatman & Fogarty, across the street from the county's administration building. Much of the new business coming to Peatman was based directly on the flow of money into the valley. Real estate and the high value of Napa Valley wine had created a big demand for estate planning and all the incidentals that went with accrued wealth.

Significantly, Diamond Creek Vineyards was about to release a Cabernet for the unprecedented price of $100 a bottle. Vineyardland would be worth $100,000 an acre in a few years. That kind of value created a dynamic all its own. There was also a lot of growth south of Napa city. The industrial park had attracted some of the big wineries — Beringer, Mondavi, Sutter Home — seeking alternate sites for large-scale grape processing and commercial development. All that meant business, in addition to plans for development within the ag preserve and for the incorporation of American Canyon.

Mel Varrelman, the incumbent supervisor, advocate of slow growth, and the only member of the new board to live north of the city of Napa, felt the hot breath of a challenger for his seat in the next election. Warren Winiarski spoke publicly of "a difficult and dangerous time," and Mike Martini, always blunt, told a reporter, "I hope we still have an agricultural preserve in a couple of years."

The winery definition had yet to be resolved, although money for the master environmental assessment had been approved and talks continued between vintners and growers. But the suggestion that the acrimony had diminished was belied by expression on both sides. Bill Jaeger, an owner of Rutherford Hill Winery known for espousing untrammeled free enterprise — he was referred to as "the Manchester capitalist" — bought a page in the *Napa Register* and published an open letter: "The Growers Association is an undemocratic organization representing a relatively small amount of the total vineyard acreage in the Valley. It is an organization driven by greed and intent on acquiring the power to dictate grape prices for all Napa

Valley grapes. Masterminding the illusion that the group is public-spirited is sweet-talkin' Andy Beckstoffer. . . ."

Still, Beckstoffer and Volker Eisele met with a delegation of vintners in early December 1988, in Beringer's corporate compound across Highway 29 from Rhine House. This was significant because for the first time both sides, growers and vintners, seemed eager to arrive at a compromise. The power of the joint committee lay in the recommendation they would make to the county planning staff and the board of supervisors, for rules regarding wineries that might finally be made into law.

Mike Moone, Reverdy Johnson, and Jay Corley exuded confidence, fostered by the election results and sustained by the public pronouncements of the supervisors-elect that growth in the county was necessary. Beckstoffer took out the list of points that he and Volker had drawn up, including the 75 percent proposal. Only Reverdy opposed that. Furthermore, everyone agreed that winery expansion had to be regulated in some way. They also agreed on the maximum size of wineries, at least in principle — a surprise to the growers' representatives. The committee would recommend that winery growth be tied to available acreage; in the future, no winery could cover more than twenty acres, or 10 percent of the total parcel, whichever was less.

That was a real accomplishment, Volker thought. But this agreement, coming after more than two years of wrangling and political turmoil, would in the end amount to very little.

The new board of supervisors for Napa County was seated in January 1989, and immediately they dismissed the members of the old Planning Commission, the one that had dared to back the moratorium on new wineries, the study of the viability of a 75 percent grape requirement, and limits on commercial development in the ag preserve. The vote was three to two, the dissenters being Varrelman and Paul Battisti. The three voting in favor of the dismissal — over loud objections of six hundred citizens who had signed a petition urging that the commissioners be kept — were the new supervisors, Fred Negri and John Mikolajcik, and the incumbent Bob White, still board chairman.

Varrelman asked why, if the new board was in favor of responsible land use and the preservation of agriculture, they were dismissing a Planning Commission dedicated to those things.

White said, "The people have spoken. They want change."

Reverdy Johnson left the office of president of the Napa Valley Vintners Association to a literal round of applause. He had done a great deal of work during his year's tenure — and left a deep division between those members who saw the valley as an agricultural community and those who viewed it as primarily a marketing tool. He still opposed the 75 percent grape requirement; he still drove his old Alfa Romeo with the c-RANCH license plate up from San Francisco at least once a week, commuting between the jobs of lawyer for a big real estate firm and overseer of a Napa Valley boutique winery, wearing boots and smoking his pipe and viewing the world from the epicenter of Johnson-Turnbull Vineyards.

He had no regrets about his role in the recent political battles. In thirty years, Reverdy expected his children to look out over a valley floor covered with hundreds of mostly small wineries; many of them would not be pleasing to behold, in his opinion, much less paragons of architecture. But the sheer numbers envisioned for the valley bothered him not at all.

Reverdy's successor as Vintners president, Dick Maher, also president of Christian Brothers, was the corporate survivor with a past that included the U.S. Marines, E. & J. Gallo, Shakey's Pizza, Heublein, Nestlé, and Seagram. Now when he stood behind the podium at Meadowood, Maher was distracted by the extraordinary demands of his real job: Christian Brothers was unofficially for sale and soon to be acquired by a multinational conglomerate, casting the valley into another period of turmoil that recalled a similar transition twenty years before.

The $3,000 grant that Volker had obtained from the Napa Valley Agricultural Lands Preservation Fund, the day after the supervisorial election, had gone into research. He had discovered that the Association of Bay Area Governments' so-called requirements for more people and houses in Napa Valley were really not requirements at all but merely guidelines. Communities were expected to abide by ABAG's recommendations or risk losing state funding, but there was no law saying Napa had to grow. So ABAG could not be used as a compelling argument for development. There was already enough housing on the books to accommodate the county's projected growth for the near future, most of it in the incorporated areas. The county could resist pressure from the state to increase those projections — if the county had the will. The people had to force the county supervisors to stop granting exceptions to the current zoning laws and nibbling away at agricultural land.

Volker discussed the idea of a voter initiative with the usual suspects. The question always arose: Is it the right time? The effort was not only expensive, it was also highly symbolic. They didn't want to undertake an initiative and then lose. But the loss of the supervisorial elections told Volker it was time.

They all gathered in Fershko's office in Napa city. The group included Mel Varrelman and political allies in Napa city, including a current and a former member of the city council, the slow-growth supervisor Paul Battisti, a doctor, a member of the new county Planning Commission, and others. Volker thought the best political brains in the county had gathered in that room, under the banjo clock. They discussed the idea of an initiative backward and forward, and everyone present approved of going forward with it.

They needed a name. Organizations with real influence were not easy to form. Volker wanted to use the old Citizens for Growth Management, but others thought it sounded too stuffy, associated with the past. Someone suggested 2020 Vision, a reference to a year in the future. If the initiative got on the ballot for the June 1990 elections, and if it passed, no exceptions could be granted by the board of supervisors to the zoning of agricultural land and the agricultural watershed between then and the year 2020.

Ruth von Uhlit, an orchardist and an aging but vital woman, agreed to chair the organization. Harold Kelly would serve as treasurer. Volker wanted to stay out of the limelight; he had become a political lightning rod. Instead, he would work behind the scenes to raise money, not just for the initiative but to field a candidate in the next election who could effectively take on Bob White, chairman of the board, and to help Mel Varrelman in his fight against a pro-growth candidate soon to be fielded.

The initiative remained a large risk, but the precedents were heartening. Measure A, freezing growth outside the cities of Napa County, had been voted in by the county residents, most of them living in the cities. As Volker knew, people tended to vote for land preservation even when electing officials who talked about growth. Direct action appealed to different instincts in the voters, and 2020 Vision was counting on that.

Ballot initiatives had an impressive history in California. In the early years of the century Governor Hiram Johnson, a Progressive, managed to curtail the influence of the Southern Pacific Railroad with an initiative and statewide referendum. Direct action by citizens enabled them thereafter to bring any issue before the public by simply collecting a sufficient number of signatures to get the question on the ballot. Public dissatisfaction with taxes led to the passing of Proposition 13 in 1978, which cut government spending. By the national elections of 1988, as many as twenty-nine statewide grassroots measures had been included on ballots across the country, and hundreds of local issues. In California, the voters by-passed the politicians and directly decided a dozen complicated questions, including car insurance, tobacco taxes, care of the homeless, the AIDS disclosure requirements.

Volker thought the entire effort — the initiative and the general election — might require as much as $200,000. He talked to the Winiarskis and discovered that they, too, were thinking of forming a political organization. They had held another of their breakfast meetings on Parker Hill, attended by Tom Burgess, John Williams, Tom Ferrell, and Dan Duckhorn, now the unofficial dissidents within the Napa Valley Vintners Association. They wanted to effect political change and champion the right causes. Volker told Warren and Tom Burgess that the initiative was the most important thing, and they agreed to make a contribution to 2020 Vision.

The dissident vintners met subsequently at Duckhorn's house, on the road to Meadowood, and decided to model their organization on the political action committees, or PACs, that played crucial roles in the affairs of Sacramento and Washington, D.C. They would call theirs NAPAC, the Napa Agricultural Preservation Action Committee. Warren began to make the rounds of vintners, large and small, seeking pledges of financial support. One of the things he wanted to do was to educate people, so that eventually no one would even think of building in the ag preserve, just as it was unthinkable to build in a national park.

Volker raised $6,000 in January and put with it NAPAC's $3,000. He went to a law firm in San Francisco, Shute, Mihaly & Weinberger, and asked them to draft the initiative proposal, the same firm that had defended the suit against Measure A several years before. The firm was a recognized authority on land-use law, with a conservationist bent; the other San Francisco law firm with equally good credentials, but on the development side, happened to be the one for which Reverdy Johnson worked.

Gone were the days when such documents could be short, heartfelt, and to the point. Now it was technically an amendment to the General Plan, and lengthy, because it had to conform to new, often complex regulations, and it had to be able to stand up to a court challenge. When the proposal was ready and the groundwork laid, they would go public — on September 1, 1989. Then they would file the document with the Napa County clerk of court and start collecting signatures. If they got enough, the question would go on the June 1990 ballot.

☙

Meanwhile, the new board of supervisors was acting on the campaign promises of its newly elected members. Some of those promises applied to Jim Hickey, director of the Conservation, Development, and Planning Department.

Hickey was now sixty-three and had worked for the county for almost twenty years. Prior to coming to Napa, he had spent almost as much time studying and working on land-use and open-space problems. He had received awards from many groups, including the Napa Valley Grape Growers Association and the Farm Bureau. His contribution to the county's General Plan had brought praise from many quarters. Critics of Hickey and his department were numerous, however. He had controlled the county staff for two decades, and those who wanted to be excused from the rules, or wanted their clients to be excused, didn't like the rigorous procedures, the dog and pony shows. Hickey had taken sides politically, a dangerous position for a staff member. But no one could say that he hadn't done his job.

The three supervisors comprising the majority on the board individually assured Hickey that they wanted him to remain as county planning director. They would never dismiss him, they said, the way they had dismissed the Planning Commission in January. Since then, the board had appointed a developer to head the new board, and given other indications of the direction they intended to take the county, but Hickey believed the supervisors when they said they wouldn't seek to get rid of him. He was deeply involved in preparing the Master Environmental Assessment, authorized by the board at a cost of $160,000. It was to be a benchmark study of both scenic development and the impact of wineries on the county. The work had to be completed that year so ordinances could finally be passed dealing with these very important questions. They had occupied the county government and staff for years, and some sort of resolution was at hand.

On June 20, 1989, the board met in closed session, which wasn't unusual. After about an hour Hickey received word that his presence was requested in the board chamber. He went in thinking they wanted his advice, as they so often did. Instead, Bob White, supervisor from District 1 and chairman of the board, told Hickey he would have to resign and move out of his office by 5 P.M.

Hickey was jolted. This rotund little man, White, and the two others who had voted to get rid of him, Fred Negri and John Mikolajcik, all sat behind their microphones and stared down at him. They had told Hickey they would never do such a thing and now they were doing it.

Hickey told the board he didn't intend to resign. They would have to fire him. A discussion took place involving the county counsel. In the end, Hickey was told that he would have to step down as director of the Planning Department, but that he could stay on and work on special projects, including the environmental studies already in the works, until his retirement in June 1990.

Hickey said to himself, "One minute you're in and the next minute you're out."

It was not the way he had envisioned wrapping up thirty-eight years of professional life. You live by a majority of the board of supervisors and you die by it, the same thing he had always said about the ag preserve. Three votes and thirty days was all that legally separated Napa Valley farmland from asphalt and concrete; three votes was all that was needed to overturn the ag preserve, just as a three-vote majority was all that had been needed to create it.

Three votes separated Hickey from his desk in the Planning Department and put him into a narrow room down the hall from the county counsel's office.

He went to lunch with the deputy director of the Planning Department, who would take over temporarily, to work out the transition. Then he went back to his office and packed up. When he got home, Hickey opened a bottle of wine. His doctor had taken him off alcohol of all kinds, for his health, but that night he sampled some of the local product.

The editorial appearing in the *Napa Register* condemned the board of supervisors for the way in which Hickey had been dismissed. "Hickey, a longtime defender of the Agricultural Preserve and other zoning laws designed to ensure slow, carefully-planned growth in the Napa Valley, had clearly become a political target of pro-development interests."

The *Napa Record* editorial said that "something strange [is] happening week after week at the County Board of Supervisors. Over and over, when the votes are cast, statistical probability goes bellyside up and another motion is either passed or denied by a three to two split — invariably with White, Negri, and Mikolajcik voting one way and Varrelman and Battisti the other. . . . People who watch the board on a regular basis refer to it as the 'soap opera,' and White, Negri and Mikolajcik as the 'gang of three.' . . . Is there a hidden political agenda being enacted in the county of Napa? . . . The big picture in this county is that we have one of the jewels in the world's crown. We have the soil and the climate to create wines that match the very best. We are one of a dwindling number of counties in California where you can look out the window at night and see the soft shadows of the hills untouched by the vast parking lots and subdivisions."

The next meeting of the board of supervisors occurred less than a week after the closed session. The room was packed. Protesters of the dismissal of Hickey took up the "gang of three" characterization; one after another they stepped to the podium and attacked the board for its action, demanding an explanation. One man called Negri a simple front for development interests and pointed out that Mikolajcik owned property in American Canyon and would profit from incorporation there, something Jim Hickey had always resisted.

Mikolajcik shouted, "Liar!"

In the audience, Barbara Winiarski listened to testimony in favor of preserving agricultural land and to Chairman White's pledge that there would be no changes in the ag preserve. She considered this a red herring. The most immediate threat was not to the ag preserve but to the ag watershed, the land in the hills that was not planted in grapes and onto which the developers cast the most covetous gaze.

One of those testifying was a young man with big eyes and an earnest manner. As he spoke he rested a clenched fist on the podium. He represented, he said, some young people in the county concerned about the environment, and they had lost confidence in the board of supervisors after the dismissal of Hickey. The young man was Hugh Davies, the youngest son of Jack and Jamie, who had come back to Napa Valley after graduating from college to work in the winery. He had been born while his parents were still rebuilding the old Schram house and the winery. They had worked hard for the creation of the ag preserve while Hugh Davies was still an infant. Hugh's testimony that day represented a kind of passage, although few in the audience knew or remembered.

Mel Varrelman suggested that the board's three-man majority had violated the law in deciding beforehand to get rid of Hickey. Varrelman said that White had brought up the subject of dumping Hickey as if it were a "done deal," before the vote took place. "I believe there was a breach of the Brown Act. When I arrived at the board meeting . . . I had not one bit of knowledge that this was going to happen. . . . The purpose of the Brown Act is to protect the public from those abuses. I suggest an independent investigation. There's been a serious breach of the public trust."

He referred to the California Open Meeting Law, also known as the Ralph M. Brown Act, which prevented a majority of elected officials from meeting privately. It was illegal for members of an elected majority to have sequential conversations relating to government business, trying to reach consensus. An investigation was a potential threat to all those involved in Hickey's demise. If the Brown Act had been violated, charges might be brought against the supervisors and other county officials.

Hickey got some gratification from the testimonials, and from letters to editors. But in his mind's eye he saw a rising tide of development coming north from Vallejo, with investors wild to get in on the action in American Canyon, building housing tracts and shopping malls. He saw disarray, even panic, in the wine industry, brought on by neo-Prohibition and warring interests of the big corporations, crippling a constituency that might otherwise have been able to thwart the ruination of its own habitat. He saw tremendous pressure for residential development everywhere in the valley after the limitations imposed by Measure A expired. The voter initiative whispered about in the halls, 2020 Vision, was in his view a popularity contest. Even if it got on the ballot and passed, it would be challenged in court with the greatest legal muscle the building industry could muster, and that was considerable.

The General Plan was coming up for review in a county dominated by the likes of White, Negri, and Mikolajcik. Hickey was glad he would not have to deal with all the problems on the horizon. He would be gone by summer. Meanwhile, he sat alone in the office down the hall from the action, working on his special project, listening to the proceedings in the board room — meetings in which he had once played such an integral role — transmitted electronically through the little speaker on his desk.

54

THE NINTH Napa Valley Wine Auction, in June 1989, raised almost a million dollars and set a new record in the amount bid for a single bottle of American wine. A Dallas hotelier paid $30,000 for a six-liter imperial of Robert Mondavi's '85 Reserve Cabernet.

The Mondavis broke ground for the Opus One winery across Highway 29, not far from the river, the following month. It was the culmination of four years of planning, secret negotiations with architects and builders, and sparring with the county. The Mondavis had won the dog and pony show, only to discover a more basic problem, one related not to politics but to the make-up of the valley itself.

The design for the daring new winery — another advance in valley architecture — revealed a hemispheric structure to be partially buried, preserving the natural view and taking advantage of the cooling capacity of the earth. Berms in the shape of fans would stretch out from a squat peristyle topped with a redwood pergola, with colonnades on two sides. The architect said the design represented a "seamless blend" of two cultures, Californian and Bordelais, but the architectural model looked more like a mixture of Egypt and Crete.

The problem lay in the ground, not in the design. The winery was to be "one with the earth," but after the plans had been drawn and the site chosen and preliminary work begun, the builders found that the earth was extremely wet and that a deep drainage system would have to be installed under the winery. Then they discovered that subterranean hot springs pushed up the temperature of the soil, so that instead of cooling the cellars it would heat them. Insulation would have to be placed underneath the structure. The Opus One winery would bob in Napa's geothermal stew like a comely cork, with 15,000 square feet of storage for young wine and rows of unstacked new French oak barrels stretching away, à la Mouton, into the distance.

⤫

The railroad yard on Soscol Avenue in Napa city resounded with the work of carpenters and welders revamping seventy-year-old rolling stock belonging to the Wine Train, some of it bought abandoned in lots and pastures as far away as West Virginia and hauled west. Each lounge car weighed eighty tons and required about $250,000 in fittings, including carpets, Honduran mahogany panels, and modern machines for dispensing Napa Valley wine by the glass. The galley cars contained six-burner ranges and convection ovens, where venison and pheasant entrées were to be prepared, and the sauces to go with them, all of it hauled by thirty-year-old diesel locomotives emblazoned in green and burgundy.

The estimate of $5 million required to launch the train had so far been doubled. The Wine Train had not run in February, after all: the old Pullman cars just weren't ready. Part of Vincent DeDomenico's continuing expenses as owner of a nonoperational train were for legal squabbles with the local opposition groups and the demand by the Public Utilities Commission for an environmental review. A superior court judge ruled that the train had to abide by local zoning and building laws in erecting stations, but the overall jurisdication had yet to be determined.

Bob Phillips and Norm Manzer negotiated with Wine Train representatives and the PUC for a tradeoff: an environmental review in exchange for limited train service. In August 1989 the PUC finally agreed to a compromise whereby the Wine Train would agree to finance an environmental impact report, to be completed within a year, and in return could run as many as fifteen excursion trips a week. The trains would go to St. Helena and back, and passengers would be served meals, but they would not be allowed to disembark.

Within minutes of the PUC's decision, made down in San Francisco, the secretary who worked for Jack McCormack, president of the Wine Train, picked up her telephone in Napa and told a friend, "We're a train!"

That same morning another action took place, in the Napa County courthouse across the street from the county administration building, less than a mile from the Wine Train depot. Volker Eisele, Ruth von Uhlit, and Harold Kelly arrived to file the petition for the Agricultural Lands Preservation Initiative with the clerk of court. Volker had the papers, duly prepared by the attorneys, and a press release written by a veteran volunteer, Duane Cronk.

The legal committee of 2020 Vision, as the group sitting on the bench outside the clerk's office called itself, handed out the appropriate papers to local reporters. Kelly told the press, "The election last fall sort of set off the initiative. . . . The current board made us feel a need for locking in the requirements of the General Plan. The board is pro-development and will otherwise slowly eat away at the agricultural preserve."

The county counsel would have to prepare a title and a summary of the petition within fifteen days; the supporters would then have to publish it and collect four thousand signatures by the end of December — 10 percent of the vote cast in the last general election. Then the initiative would go on the June 1990 ballot.

The first shot in the next battle had been fired, but Volker Eisele wasn't there to witness it. He had slipped out of the building before the reporters arrived.

෴

Robin Daniel Lail had left her job as manager of Sunny St. Helena Winery that spring. She called it a leave of absence but in fact she was quitting, having dealt with Bill Harlan's quixotic moods and the uncertainty of Sunny St. Helena's finances for years. She realized that she should have left much earlier.

Being associated with several strong men, including John Daniel, had taken an emotional toll on Robin, but it had also taught her a great deal. There were other job possibilities in the valley, some closely associated with her past, some unrelated to it, and she was capable of dealing with them all.

Francis Ford Coppola, the man living in the house in which Robin had grown up, had mentioned to Robin's husband that he needed someone like Robin to organize his professional life. Coppola had gone from a repudiation of big box-office moviemaking to plans for the filming of The Godfather, Part III. Filmmaking fascinated Robin, but joining that world would mean leaving behind the one to which she belonged.

She wanted to wait a while before leaping into any new endeavor. She believed in ending things well, completely, so that real beginnings were possible. She had agreed to organize the croquet tournament at Meadowood for Harlan again, as a paid consultant, and she did that. Then she was free.

She would travel and think about her options.

⟡

The owner of her lost birthright, Inglenook, was still Heublein, part of the British conglomerate Grand Metropolitan. But a decision was made in Hartford and in London that had broad implications for the valley. Grand Met, which also owned Beaulieu and Quail Ridge, now bought another big Napa Valley winery with historic ties, Christian Brothers.

For 107 years the property had belonged to the Catholic church. Its sale brought $125 million to the Brothers' teaching order, and more than a thousand acres of Napa vineyard to Grand Met and Heublein, in addition to a huge, overly mechanized winery and an industrial brandy operation.

The losing bidder for Christian Brothers, Hiram Walker, the British distiller, had reportedly offered more than $125 million, but Heublein triumphed in part because Dick Maher, president of Christian Brothers, was an old Heublein man. One of the vice presidents in Hartford had been hired by Maher back in the salad days of Heublein's wine experiments; he and Maher had been the brand managers for I Love You and Bali Hai. Now they were making bigger decisions.

Heublein owned more historic properties and more vineyards in Napa Valley than any other corporation. Maher took over all the Napa properties, ruling from his old desk at Christian Brothers, where he kept a sawed-off howitzer shell filled with ice, to cool his soft drinks. The staff at Christian Brothers was cut, followed by a fall of the ax on the general manager of Inglenook, Dennis Fife, Legh Knowles's former assistant and the one person in Heublein's organization who had worked steadily and effectively to improve Inglenook wines. The firing of Fife recalled the beginning of the era of Inglenook's and BV's ownership by Heublein, when good people had been let go and bad management decisions made.

Then Tom Selfridge, president of Beaulieu, who had spoken up for limitations on wineries and a minimum grape requirement, was pushed out; much of BV's staff went, too.

The land owned by Grand Met/Heublein had become more valuable. Problems lay ahead for the wine industry, including the possibility of punitive taxes, more restrictive labeling laws, gathering neo-Prohibitionist sentiment, and declining sales. It was rumored that Grand Met was looking for a buyer for all its Napa real estate — the collective crown of the valley — maybe Hiram Walker or one of the Japanese conglomerates.

There was other speculation: Grand Met was trying to buy Whitbread, the huge British brewer. If that came about, Grand Met would then own Atlas Peak, in addition to all the other Napa Valley property. The company might keep Christian Brothers for its brandy operation, the only real moneymaker, and sell off the other parcels individually.

Inglenook had been reduced to fewer than one hundred acres of vineyards around old Niebaum's enduring edifice, as apparent and immovable in 1989 as it had been a century before. People wondered what sort of enterprise might be carried on there that would prove profitable. Those close to Francis Ford Coppola imagined him buying it both in the interest of symmetry and as an outlet for a long-held dream of moviemaking. Coppola wanted, these friends insisted, a studio similar to that of his friend and fellow director George Lukas in Marin County, a place where films could be shot and edited, with special effects. Coppola had already built a small studio at the rear of the property, transforming an old dilapidated barn, where the screen tests were reportedly done for *The Godfather, Part III,* drawing actors like Al Pacino and Madonna, who moved unrecognized through the valley. What if he bought Inglenook and transformed the storage facility built by Heublein in front of the winery into a full-fledged movie studio? Hollywood would have come in force to the banks of Navalle Creek.

More substantive were the negotiations undertaken by Walter Sullivan, husband of Dagmar and son-in-law of the late Mme. de Pins. Sullivan tacitly admitted that selling Beaulieu Vineyard almost twenty years before had been a mistake, and now sought to buy it back — when its value had increased tenfold. Sullivan rounded up potential backers and arranged a meeting with Grand Met in London, for early 1990, to try to recapture at least a semblance of the legacy of old Georges de Latour. One hundred million dollars was not an easy sum to raise, and his role and that of the de Latours' descendants would be greatly diminished, but partial ownership would be better than none at all. It might restore some of the grace to Napa Valley that he and Dagmar felt had been lost in the headlong rush for profits.

༄

In early December 1989 the Wine Train pulled out of the station in Napa city, bound for up-valley on its first trip of the day, the so-called brunch run. Most of the seats had been sold. To the price of the ticket would be added another $20 to cover the cost of fresh juice, Danish and muffins, and a choice of torta baked with Smithfield ham and shiitake mushrooms, grilled veal sausage with polenta and Fontina, or canneloni stuffed with ricotta. With this also came assorted fruits and jellies, steaming coffee from silver pots, and a glass of Napa Valley sparkling wine.

The passengers sat at tables covered with starched white cloths, each planted with a single fresh rose in a vase, and looked out first at the industrial environs of Soscol Avenue — warehouses, repair shops, the little Demptos factory where custom-charred barrels were made for wineries from imported Limousin and Nevers oak — and at the backsides of little houses lining the tracks. The sumptuous carpeting inside the train, the imitation gas lamps, and the smiling waitresses in white jackets with black piping wielding bottles wrapped in white napkins couldn't entirely distract the passengers from the bleaker world outside. They expected vineyards, not seedy neighborhoods and a broad intersection where morning drivers sat behind barriers and stared up at them while the big green and burgundy locomotive hauled them across Trancas Avenue and on north, past the dwindling Napa suburbs.

The morning fog had burned off, revealing the red and gold leaves of vines. The passengers sat high enough to ignore the cars on Highway 29 and to imagine themselves entering another era. Clusters of distant trees stood like islands, and the houses like old ranchos framed against the mountains. On the other side of the train, the broad valley floor stretched toward the river. Clusters of oak, eucalyptus, and pecan bracketed the train at times, then fell back to reveal new vistas.

The train was capable of touching everyone in the valley with the shriek of its whistle — barely audible inside the Pullmans. It provided a thread, often an unwelcome one, stringing together friends and adversaries, allies and competitors, and people who did not know one another but who were part of the industry of the valley.

Few passengers recognized the low brow of Domaine Chandon —
the bunker of the hillside above Yountville — or the late John Daniel's Napanook. Vine Hill Ranch and the house owned by Bob Phillips and his wife could be glimpsed off to the left. The train passed
a shop, Mustard's Restaurant, and a bed-and-breakfast backed by
vineyards with wild mustard blooming between the rows.

Pepi's stone winery lowered on the right side of the highway,
Far Niente on the left. Passengers being served their torta saw bee-
hives, the Oakville Grocery (*two* benches on the porch), the sprawling stucco Robert Mondavi Winery. Then came the Johnson-Turnbull winery with its fundamentalist profile, Cakebread Cellars, and
some of Beaulieu's vineyards. Peju Province, known as the chain-
link winery, had raised metal pylons around the concrete pad where
walls were about to go up at last. The sight that caused the most
interest was a massive stone structure with a red roof and a cupola
on top, set far back from the road. A seller of photocopiers from
Long Island, dressed in coat and tie, asked his waitress, "What's
that?"

She said, "Inglenook."

The de Latour estate lay next to it, obscured by trees. The train
rolled on, past Grgich Hills Cellars and across Bale Slough. It was
only ten in the morning, and there were few cars on the side roads
to spoil the illusion of travel through the America of Tarkington and
Twain. Then a motorcyclist streaked past, hand raised, his upthrust
middle finger an indication that everyone in the valley was not enamored of the Wine Train.

The house of Andy Beckstoffer lay off to the east in a welter of
trees. Just past Zinfandel Lane, the train passed the back yard of Rafael Rodriquez. The wooden tables set outside the Sattui Winery had
not yet attracted the flock of picnicking tourists. Next, the Louis M.
Martini Winery sat stolidly behind its metal fence, in contrast to the
gentrified Sutter Home Winery across the highway. Sunny St. Helena Winery hugged the railroad tracks; on the porch of the cottage
next door stood a man holding up a small boy and waving to the
engineer — Bill Harlan.

The Wine Train crept into St. Helena. Brunch was over and the
passengers would soon be moved to the lounge car, to make room
for those in the lounge car who would eat their brunch on the way
back to Napa. The photocopier salesman looked down at a man in a
red shirt standing beside the tracks, holding a sign on which were

painted the words "Wine Train" in a red circle with a slash mark through it. The man was smiling.

"Some people don't like the train," the waitress explained. "They think it's bad for the environment."

"Can't stop progress," said the salesman's wife.

Her husband stared until the man — it was Norm Manzer, the State Farm rep — was out of sight.

The supporters of 2020 Vision filed eight thousand signatures with the Napa County clerk of court, twice the number required to get the initiative on the June 1990 ballot. If the initiative was voted in during the election, development within the ag preserve and the ag watershed would be stopped for thirty years; if it was defeated, the future looked bleak.

The moratorium on new wineries would expire in January, in less than a month. The board of supervisors would have to pass an ordinance defining a winery, taking into account the environmental assessment and the demands from the supervisors' loudest constituents; what that ordinance would be was still unclear. The 75 percent solution seemed destined to become reality, but its opponents were quite capable of making a last-minute proposal that could upset the tentative accord between vintners and growers.

A few days before Christmas, Rafael Rodriguez left his office in the old Niebaum stable, now a sound studio as well as a winery, and drove out the back lane, along Navalle Creek. It was a beautiful day. An overnight freeze had left the sky an immaculate blue; although the air in the shade of the big eucalyptuses was frigid, the shafts of sunlight warmed.

Rafael left his pickup and walked to the top of the knoll separating the Coppola property from that of Grand Met/Heublein. Inglenook's massive frame reared on one side, and on the other lay the vineyard Rafael had planted for Coppola, the bright yellow leaves indicating that the vines were not yet dormant. That would mean late pruning and a busy spring, no problem for him. He had few worries of late. Twenty-five years before, Rafael had worried about death; he never thought then that he would reach sixty-seven years of age, and now that he had, he was unbothered even by that. In retirement, he planned to take up carpentry, the craft his father had practiced in a rudimentary way in Mexico City.

What did bother him was a sense of time's destruction. He had seen so many people, apparently inviolable, come to nothing. He had once thought that families lasted forever but knew now that they did not. He saw his own grown children pulling away from him and Tila, which was natural, even desirable. They had to make their own way. But he wondered, when he was dead, would they keep up the old way of life and the old connections? Would the Rodriguezes prevail?

He thought of these things whenever he thought of John Daniel. No family had seemed more fortunate than the Daniels, and yet in the space of a few years the members had dispersed and the property had slipped away. Rafael had heard that the winery and some vineyards were again for sale. He did not know if this was true, but if it was, he hoped that Robin Lail would find a way to buy them.

It seemed to Rafael that the land really did endure, whereas people and their projects passed on. The old water tower just over the Coppola line had been built at the time Inglenook went up. The tower had been fed by the spring high on Mount St. John; the two 5,000-gallon redwood tanks had supplied the whole winery in those days. Rafael remembered Marky and Robin playing there as children, racing up and down the stairs and peering out over miles of vines and trees under the same clear sky. Now one of the tanks had fallen in and the other sagged, and the little cupola on the roof was covered with lichen.

He hoped the structure would be restored before it collapsed entirely. He had built a fence around it, to keep the tourists away who wandered up from Inglenook and stumbled on what was for them just a curious ruin, one with little columns and gingerbread latticework. Rafael wondered about a man, old Niebaum, who could demand such perfection in a mere water tower. What vision did he have, and could he possibly have imagined what came to pass in all directions? No one would ever know the answer to that question, but in the elaborate, broken trim lay something truly extraordinary, dense with history, yet elusive — the suggestion of a fabulous dream in a broad, unspoiled valley.

Epilogue

ON JANUARY 17, 1990, the board of supervisors of Napa County at last addressed the winery definition. The controversy had been going on for four years; the public hearings during the last few weeks had been crowded and occasionally raucous. It had taken the board three days of wrangling, parliamentary maneuvers, and some comedic moments under the leadership of the board's new chairman, the recently elected Mickey Mikolajcik, to pass an ordinance laying to rest the most controversial question in two decades.

The new law would powerfully influence the valley's future for years to come. It included the minimum Napa Valley grape requirement — the so-called 75 percent solution — for new wineries and expansions of existing ones, and forbade new wineries to have public tours and tastings. This was seen as a triumph for the growers. But the tradeoff had been enormous, for the ordinance also amended the General Plan, legitimizing food service and other winery activities that were promotional, profitable, and not directly related to winemaking.

Many feared that new wineries would demand the same privileges as those enjoyed by existing ones. A legal challenge to the law might well mean more tourists and more encroachment on agricultural land in the future. Worse, new businesses unrelated to winemaking might also claim the right to build in the ag preserve, using the amendment of the General Plan as a precedent and breach through which more commercial development would flow.

Watching the final proceedings, Barbara Winiarski had the impression that the growers and the vintners, after so much bitter fighting, had agreed no longer to disagree. Andy Beckstoffer got a guaranteed price support for grapes; Reverdy Johnson got the right for existing wineries to do pretty much what they had always done. Shaking hands at the end, growers and vintners seemed to her indistinguishable.

The voter initiative, 2020 Vision, which would have taken future decisions affecting agricultural land entirely out of the hands of the county supervisors, suffered a setback: the signatures collected by volunteers were disqualified on a technicality. The initiative would not be on the June 1990 ballot, after all. The organizers announced that they intended to gather the signatures again and to have the question put on the November 1990 ballot instead — the beginning of big land-use battles over annexation and the inevitable spread of the cities.

Whatever the outcome, Jim Hickey's words still resonated: "If Napa Valley can't be saved, no place can."

ACKNOWLEDGMENTS
AND SOURCES

This book could not have been written without the assistance, shared knowledge, and recollections of hundreds of people. I want to thank them all, and to express my admiration for those who spent hours looking deeply and often painfully into their own lives.

I am also particularly indebted to my editor, Dick Todd, who provided encouragement and crucial guidance. Also to the staff of the St. Helena Public Library, fine professionals all. There I drew from the oral interviews collected in the Napa Valley Wine Library and from those collected by the Bancroft Library.

❧

The following is a list of the books I used, which may be of interest to readers:

Adams, Leon D., *The Wines of America*. New York: McGraw-Hill, 1973, rev. 1985.

Archuleta, Kay, *The Brannan Saga*. St. Helena, California: Illuminations Press, 1977.

Asher, Gerald, *On Wine*. New York: Random House, 1982.

Balzer, Robert Lawrence, *Wines of California*. New York: Abrams, 1978.

Beard, Yolande S., *The Wappo*. Banning, California: Malki Museum Press, 1979.

Bespaloff, Alexis, *New Signet Book of Wine*. New York: New American Library, 1985.

Birmingham, Stephen, *California Rich*. New York: Simon and Schuster, 1980.

Brewer, William H., *Up and Down California in 1860–1864*. Berkeley: University of California Press, 1966.

Broadbent, Michael, *Complete Guide to Wine Tasting and Wine Cellars*. New York: Simon and Schuster, 1982.

Carosso, Vincent P., *The California Wine Industry, 1830–1895*. Berkeley: University of California Press, 1951.

Cocks, Charles, *Bordeaux and Its Wines*. Bordeaux: Feret et Fils, 1854; English translation, 1986.

Dunne, John Gregory, *Delano: The Story of the California Grape Strike*. New York: Farrar, Straus and Giroux, 1967.

Ensrud, Barbara, *American Vineyards*. New York: Stewart, Tabori and Chang, 1988.

Finigan, Robert, *Essentials of Wine*. New York: Knopf, 1987.

Fisher, M. F. K., and Max Yavno, *The Story of Wine in California*. Berkeley: University of California Press, 1962.

Forbes, Patrick, *Champagne: The Wine, the Land and the People*. London: Gollancz, 1983.

Gilliam, Harold, *San Francisco Bay*. Garden City, New York: Doubleday, 1957.

Holliday, J. S., *The World Rushed In: The California Gold Rush Experience*. New York: Simon and Schuster, 1981.

Hyams, Edward, *Dionysus: A Social History of the Wine Vine*. New York: Macmillan, 1965.

Johnson, Hugh, *Modern Encyclopedia of Wine*. New York: Simon and Schuster, 1987.

————, *Vintage: The Story of Wine*. New York: Simon and Schuster, 1989.

Jones, Idwal, *Vines in the Sun*. New York: William Morrow, 1949.

Kerr, K. Austin, *Organized for Prohibition*. New Haven: Yale University Press, 1985.

Laughridge, Jamie, *Rising Star, Domaine Chandon: A Decade of Sparkle*. New York: Hopkinson and Blake, 1983.

Lawrence, R. de Treville, *Jefferson and Wine*. The Plains, Virginia: Vinifera Winegrowers Association, 1976.

Lembeck, Harriet, *Grossman's Guide to Wines, Beers and Spirits*. New York: Charles Scribner's Sons, 1983.

Lender, Mark Edward, and James Kirby Martin, *Drinking in America: A History*. New York: The Free Press, 1982.

Menefee, C. A., *Historical and Descriptive Sketch Book of Napa, Sonoma, Lake and Mendocino*. Napa, California: Reporter Publishing, 1873.

Morton, Lucie T., *Winegrowing in Eastern America*. Ithaca, New York: Cornell University Press, 1985.

Muscatine, Doris, *Old San Francisco: The Biography of a City*. New York: Putnam, 1975.

————, Maynard A. Amerine, and Bob Thompson, *University of California/Sotheby Book of California Wine*. Berkeley: University of California Press and Sotheby Publications, 1984.

Myers, George Jourdan, *Tiburcio Parrott*. Deer Park, California, 1987.

Parker, Robert, *Bordeaux*. New York: Simon and Schuster, 1985.

Pellegrini, Angelo, *Americans by Choice*. New York: Macmillan, 1956.

Ray, Cyril, *Robert Mondavi of the Napa Valley*. London: Heinemann/Peter Davies, 1984.

Robinson, Jancis, *Vines, Grapes and Wines*. New York: Knopf, 1986.

Saintsbury, George, *Notes on a Cellar-Book*. London: Macmillan, 1920.

Schoonmaker, Frank, *Encyclopedia of Wine*. Revised by Alexis Bespaloff. New York: William Morrow, 1988.

Starr, Kevin, *Material Dreams: Southern California Through the 1920s*. New York: Oxford University Press, 1990.

Stevenson, Robert Louis, *The Silverado Squatters*. London: Stone and Kimball, 1895.

Taylor, Robert Lewis, *Vessel of Wrath*. New York: New American Library, 1966.

Taylor, Ronald B., *Chavez and the Farm Workers*. Boston: Beacon Press, 1975.

Teiser, Ruth, and Catherine Harroun, *Winemaking in California*. New York: McGraw-Hill, 1983.

Thompson, Bob, *Notes on a California Cellarbook*. New York: Beech Tree Books/William Morrow, 1988.

Wagner, P. M., *Grapes into Wine: The Art of Winemaking in America*. New York: Knopf, 1982.

Wait, Frona Eunice, *Wines and Vines of California*. San Francisco: Bancroft Co., 1889.

Winkler, A. J., et al., *General Viticulture*. Revised edition. Berkeley: University of California Press, 1974.

Younger, William, *Gods, Men and Wine*. Cleveland: World Publishing, 1966.

INDEX

Abate, George: and ag preserve, 86,
    89–90, 91
Abruzzini, Fred, 45–46, 47
Adams, Leon, 118–19, 120
Agricultural Advisory Council, 328,
    371
Agricultural Extension Service: and ag
    preserve, 84, 86, 90
Agricultural Lands Preservation Fund,
    427, 482, 488
Agricultural Lands Preservation Initia-
    tive, 498
agricultural preserve: creation of, 82–
    92, 93–94, 254, 385; in 1970s, 205,
    206, 210, 254, 323; minimum acreage
    in, 236, 254, 322; effects of, 254,
    385–86, 389, 396, 407; in 1980s, 320,
    385–86, 389, 397, 407, 421; future of,
    436–37, 480, 482, 486, 492, 493–94,
    503; vintners and, 448
airport project: for Napa Valley, 321–22
Alameda County: development in, 206
Alaska Commercial Company, 70, 72
alcohol: American attitudes toward,
    284–89, 345 (see also Prohibition);
    warning labels, 338, 429
Alexander, Paul: and ag preserve, 84,
    85, 89, 92
Alicante Bouschet grape, 26, 110
Alioto, Joe, 24, 25; and legal battle of
    Mondavi, 169, 170, 171
Alioto, John, 169, 173
Allied Grape Growers, 79, 80; sale to
    Heublein, 131–33, 140; UFW and,
    143–46

Almadén, 78
Altamura winery, 294
Amador County, 268
American Canyon: development plans
    for, 256, 443, 466, 470, 486, 493, 494
American Society of Enologists, 127
American Viticultural Districts, 292
Amerine, Maynard, 18, 43, 50, 127,
    166, 293
Anderson, Dewey: and ag preserve,
    85–86, 87, 89, 92
Anderson, Stan, 295, 413
Anderson Vineyards, 237
Andrus, Gary, 294
Antinori, Piero, 361, 362
Apocalypse Now, 223, 272, 273
appellation: French laws, 292, 402; con-
    flict in Napa Valley, 292–94, 401–2,
    403–4; sub-appellation issue, 294–95
Asher, Gerald, 345
Assembly Bill 80, 89–90
Association of Bay Area Governments
    (ABAG), 206, 376, 446, 452, 479,
    482, 488–89
Atlas Peak, 360–64, 450, 475, 500
Auberge de Soleil, 395–96
Australia: winemaking in, 182, 250
awards: regional, 190, 236, 237; and
    Paris Tasting, 191–201

Bacardi, 137
Bacigalupi vineyards, 182
Baez, Joan, 209
Bale, Dr. Edward, 14
Bali Hai (wine), 140

Bank of America, 361
Baron, Daniel, 353–54, 355, 359
Barrett, Jim, 181–82, 194, 195–96, 199, 403, 406, 480
Basalt Rock, 83
Bâtard-Montrachet (Ramonet-Prudhom), 194, 197
Battisti, Paul, 475, 487, 489
Beaulieu Vineyard, 9, 10, 16, 20, 21, 27, 35, 44, 48, 53–54, 79, 103–16, 364, 365, 445; founding of, 103; and Prohibition, 105–6; Cabernet of, 107, 110, 111, 112, 125, 181; Tchelistcheff at, 107–12, 115–16, 127, 128, 155–56, 158; unsanitary conditions at, 109–10; Georges de Latour Private Reserve, 111, 157, 237, 283; Mme. de Latour manages, 111–13; burning of winery, 113; high reputation of, 113; Mme. de Pins manages, 113–16; Knowles joins, 116, 125–26; acquires Carneros vineyard, 126; Dick Peterson at, 126–28, 129, 140–41, 156, 158–59, 215; sale to Heublein, 129, 134–38, 140, 351; unionization at, 129, 134–38, 140; sparkling wine of, 140; under Heublein management, 140–41, 156, 158–59, 499; Pinot Noir of, 157–58; valuation of, 173, 500–501; Grgich at, 181
Beaune Clos des Mouches (Drouhin), 195, 197
Beckstoffer, Andy: background of, 129–30; joins Heublein, 130–33; acquires Allied Grape Growers for Heublein, 131–33; and Heublein's purchase of Beaulieu, 134–36; management of Heublein's Napa properties, 139–46, 156, 158–60; and Heublein acquisition of vineyards, 141–46, 156, 158–59, 396; acquires Vinifera Development for himself, 160, 396; and Planning Commission, 324; and Wine Train, 381, 384, 502; and 75 percent solution, 385, 401, 421, 440–41, 444, 451, 464, 487, 505; and vintner-grower conflict, 396–97,

399, 405, 406, 408–12, 416, 432, 435, 448, 458; and supervisor election campaign, 475–76, 478
Bella Oaks winery, 381
Beresini, Steve, 347
Berger, Dan, 279
Beringer Brothers, 14, 15, 21, 71, 78, 107, 144, 173, 212, 292, 375, 400, 407, 460
Berrouet, Jean-Claude, 353
Berryessa, Lake, 440
Bespaloff, Alexis, 279
Bianchi, Adam, 45
Biever, Margrit. See Mondavi, Margrit Biever
Block, Dr. Alvin: and Wine Train, 313–14, 316, 317, 380
Blumen, Jimmy, 50, 51
Boisset, Jean-Claude, 250–51
Bollinger, 252, 361
Bonnet, Leon, 107
Bordeaux: winemaking tradition of, 175–77; 1855 classification, 176; winemaking methods in, 177–78, 183–84; and Paris Tasting, 194, 196–99; reclassification of growths in 1973, 231, 232; reception of '82 vintage, 280–81
Boring Crowd, 36, 243
bottling, 305
Bouchaine, Château, 354
bourbon, 285
boutique wineries, 236–38
braceros, 57–59
Brannon, Samuel, 45
Bréjoux, Pierre, 193
Brewer, William H., 14
Bronfman, Edgar, 216
Bronfman, Edgar, Jr., 218, 357
Bronfman, Samuel, 216
Bronfman, Samuel, Jr., 365–68; takes over Seagram wine properties, 217–18; and Winery Lake Vineyard, 365, 367; dedication to wine promotion, 366–68
Bronfman family, 216
Brown Act, 494

Bruce, David, 193
Buckingham Wile Company, 361
Budweiser, 137
Buena Vista Winery, 13, 251, 344, 345, 346, 354, 365
Bundschu, Carl, 42–43, 48
Bureau of Alcohol, Tobacco and Firearms (BATF): and wine appellation, 292, 293–94, 295
Burgess, Tom, 212, 442, 463–64, 470, 483, 490
Burgess Cellars, 212, 237, 378
Burgundy: and Paris Tasting, 194, 196–99; wine auction, 244

Cabernet Franc grape, 176, 273
Cabernet Sauvignon grape, 29, 36, 37, 47, 49, 50, 110, 141–42, 156, 183, 184, 297, 298, 349–50, 364, 438, 445; in Bordeaux, 176
Cabernet wines: of Inglenook, 51, 181, 223; of Robert Mondavi, 51, 181, 223; of Beaulieu, 107, 110, 111, 112, 125, 181; of Stag's Leap Wine Cellars, 178, 179, 192, 193, 196, 197, 198, 199; California competitors in Paris Tasting, 193; and Paris Tasting, 193, 194–95, 196, 197; Dunn's, 297, 302, 303–5
Caen, Herb, 51–52
Caiocca, Julius: and ag preserve, 91–92
Cakebread Cellars, 502
California: international recognition for wine, 113, 190; and Paris Tasting, 191–201
California Environmental Quality Act, 382
California Fair Political Practices Act, 432
California Land Conservation Act (Williamson Act), 84, 85–86, 91
California Marketing Order for Wine, 119
California Open Meeting Law, 493
California Public Utilities Commission: and Wine Train, 377, 378, 382, 473, 497

California State Fair of 1943, 43
Calistoga, 45; and appellation conflict, 295
Carignan grape, 26
Carneros, 47, 188, 347, 365; appellation, 292; Seagram vineyard in, 364–65
Carneros Creek winery, 238
Carpy, Chuck, 36, 406, 428, 431, 454
Carter, Robert, 171–72
Catacula, Rancho, 210
Caymus Vineyards, 238, 378, 401
Cella family, 28, 45, 77, 78
Center for Science in the Public Interest, 289
Central Valley: unionism in, 143, 147; Napa use of grapes from, 397, 400
Chalone Vineyards: Chardonnay in Paris Tasting, 193, 197
Chambure, Comtesse Lili de, 231
Champagne, 185–86, 188–89; *see also* sparkling wine
Champion's Belt (wine), 122, 126
Chapman, Sam, 254
Chappellet, Donn, 447
Chappellet, Molly, 447; and Napa Wine Auction, 249
Chappellet Vineyards, 237, 354, 378
Chardonnay grape, 9, 21, 29, 47, 49, 140, 167, 178, 182, 183, 347, 365, 438
Chardonnay wines: and Paris Tasting, 192, 193, 194–95; California competitors in Paris Tasting, 193
Charles Krug Winery. *See* Krug, Charles, Winery
Chase family, 291
Chateau and Estates, 353, 358
Chavez, Cesar, 142–46, 147
Chelini, Bob, 454–58
Chenin Blanc grape, 9
Chevalier, Alain: and Domaine Chandon, 187, 188
Chevalier, Château, 3
Children of Sanchez (Lewis), 56
Chile: winemaking in, 182
Chiles, Colonel Joseph, 210

Chiles Valley, 209–10
Chili Ball, 427
Chimney Rock winery, 294
Chinese Exclusion Act of 1892, 15
Christian Brothers, 21, 48, 360, 406, 407, 460, 488, 499; and UFW, 144, 147, 154; Grand Met acquires, 499, 500
Christie, Mary Beth, 410
Chroman, Nathan, 200–201
Churchill, Randolph, 103
Churchill, Winston, 103
Citizens Against Urban Sprawl, 210
Citizens Council for Napa Tomorrow, 210, 254–55
Citizens for Growth Management, 255
CK Mondavi (wine), 30, 367
climat, 188, 214
climate: in Napa Valley, 10, 155, 188, 293
Clos du Val, 183; Cabernet in Paris Tasting, 193, 196
Clos Pegase, 310–12, 326, 358
Coca-Cola Company: invests in winemaking, 212–14, 215–16, 238, 360; Wine Spectrum, 215–16; sells to Seagram, 216
Cohn, Jerry, 145
Cold Duck (wine), 130–31, 140, 186
Comstock Lode, 69
Conn Creek Winery, 238, 349–50, 446
Connecticut Mutual Life Insurance, 160
Coppola, Eleanor, 221, 222–24, 273, 355
Coppola, Francis Ford, 355–57; and Niebaum-Inglenook estate, 221, 222–24, 316, 498, 500; problems as vintner and director, 271–73
Coppola, Gian-Carla, 356
Coppola, Gian-Carlo, 273, 356, 357
Coppola, Sofia, 356
Corley, Jay, 324, 326, 401, 413, 428, 454, 462, 463, 479, 487
Corrison, Cathy, 354
Corti, Darrell, 268
Corti Brothers, 268
Cosby, Bill, 223
Cottin, Philippe, 231, 233

Crabb, Hamilton, 14
Craig, Elijah, 285
Crane, Eileen, 354
Crawford, Charles, 121
Crocker, Charles, 380, 384
crush, 11, 49, 335, 346, 379
Cuvaison Cellar, 251

Daniel, Elizabeth (Betty): background and marriage of, 40–42; hostility to winemaking, 42–43, 53–55, 76; relations with Strallas, 46; marital problems, 53–55, 64–66; eccentricities of, 68, 75–76; sells remaining wine properties, 97–100; death of, 225
Daniel, John, 28, 30, 37–38, 348, 355, 428, 504; background of, 39–40; friendship with Strallas, 42–46, 52–53, 94–95; inherits and restores Inglenook, 42–55, 66–67, 76–77; and Napa Valley Vintners Association, 47–48, 249; and Wine Institute, 50; friendship with Klotz, 51–53, 54–55; marital problems, 53–55, 64–66, 67; and Niebaum history, 68, 73; and future of Inglenook, 76–77, 139; sells Inglenook, 77–81, 126, 134; as consultant at Inglenook, 80; opposes ag preserve, 84, 85, 88–89, 91, 92, 93–94; retires from consultation, 93; dropped from Vintners Association, 94; death of, 96–97
Daniel, John, Sr., 39–40, 41, 77
Daniel, Marcia. See Smith, Marcia Daniel
Daniel, Robin. See Lail, Robin Daniel
Daniel, Suzanne, 39–40, 48
Daniel family, 21
David Bruce: Chardonnay in Paris Tasting, 193, 197
Davies, Hugh, 442, 494
Davies, Jack, 3–5, 11, 16, 41, 82, 349, 395, 406, 423, 428; and creation of Schramsberg, 3, 4–5, 7–9, 21–22, 77; background of, 6–7; first vintage, 35; as newcomer, 35–36; marketing wine, 36–37, 38, 83, 481; and ag preserve, 82–83, 87–88, 448–49; and

growth issue in Napa, 442–43, 464; and vintner-grower conflict, 448–49

Davies, Jamie, 3–5, 11, 16, 82, 395, 464; background of, 6–7

Davis, Jill, 354

Davis, University of California at, 10, 43, 50, 178, 212

DeDomenico, Vincent: and Wine Train, 314–15, 374, 376, 377–78, 380, 384, 497; background of, 315–17

de Groot, Roy Andries, 200

de Latour, Georges, 348, 351; and founding of Beaulieu, 103, 104, 105–6; background of, 105; death of, 111; celebrity of, 113

de Latour, Mme., 105, 111–13

de Latour, Richard, 106

de Latour family, 21, 44, 53

de Pins, Dagmar. *See* Sullivan, Dagmar de Pins

de Pins, Hélène de Latour, 79–80, 111, 348; marriage of, 106, 138; marital conflicts, 112; manages Beaulieu, 113–16, 125; and sale of Beaulieu, 134, 135, 136, 137, 138, 156; and BVI vineyard, 158

de Pins, Marquis Henri Galcerand, 106, 111, 126, 349; discontent of, 111, 112, 114–15; represents Beaulieu, 111

de Pins family, 44, 53, 79

Deuer, George, 48, 62, 67, 76, 80, 81

development transfer right, 388

Diamond Creek Vineyards, 238, 486

Diamond Mountain, 214–15, 360, 407

Diamond Mountain Ranch, 215

Dickenson, Peatman & Fogarty, 296, 414, 486

di Rosa, René, 365, 463

dollar: fluctuation of, and wine market, 236–37

Domaine Carneros, 354

Domaine Chandon, 354, 401, 405, 502; creation of, 185–90, 212; design for winery, 189

Domaine Mumm, 365, 367, 423

Dominus, 352–53, 354, 357–58; release of, 357–59

Dom Pérignon, 186

Doumani, Carl, 247, 290–92, 427, 453, 454, 455, 457

Dovaz, Michel, 193

Dow Chemical Company, 143

Draper, Jerry, 22

Dubois-Millot, Claude, 193

Duckhorn, Dan, 237, 454, 456, 457, 458, 483, 490

Duckhorn, Margaret, 237

Duckhorn Vineyards, 237, 282, 378

Dunn, Lori, 299, 300, 306, 308

Dunn, Mike, 298, 299

Dunn, Randy: winemaking by, 297–308; background of, 300

Dunn Vineyards: winemaking at, 297–308

Dwyer, Bob: representing vintners, 406, 410–11, 432, 461, 462, 463, 474, 478, 483; shifted loyalties, 410–11

Dyer, Dawnine, 354

Eckes, Peter, 251

Eclipse (wine), 13, 346

Eddington, Lowell: and ag preserve, 83–84, 85, 88–89

Eighteenth Amendment, 16

Eisele, Alexander, 446, 447

Eisele, Christiane, 474

Eisele, Liesel, 210–11, 398, 399, 417, 483

Eisele, Volker: background of, 208–9, 256; and environmental movement, 209–11, 255, 256–57, 326–27, 397, 398–400, 482–84, 489–90, 497; and Lomitas Vineyard, 210–11; and winery definition, 326–27, 416–18, 421, 487; and 75 percent solution, 401, 421, 435, 440; and vintner-grower conflict, 405, 406, 408–12, 415, 432, 433, 435, 445–46, 448, 464; and supervisor election campaign, 474, 475, 476, 477, 478

El Real Restaurant, 83–84

Emmolo, Salvator, 61–62

environmental concerns: Napa Valley, 205–11, 254–59, 263, 317–19, 320–31, 364, 369–78, 379–84, 395–402, 446, 485–95; Wine Train, 313–15,

environmental concerns (cont.)
317–19, 323, 371, 372–78, 379–84,
497 (see also Wine Train); winery definition and, 385–89 (see also wineries); NVVA pro-development stance,
463, 464, 478–79
Ericson, Leif, 285
Erskine, Dorothy, 82
Exciting Wave, 35–36, 243

Fabrini, Aldo, 116
Falcon Crest, 263, 265–66, 400
Far Niente, 72, 406, 431
Fay, Nathan: and Mondavi conflict,
172; and Winiarski, 178
Ferrell, Tom, 413, 424, 453, 483, 490
Ferroggiaro, Fred, 24, 173
Fershko, Vic: background of, 207–8;
environmental concern of, 208, 254,
397, 450–51, 482, 489; and Vintners
Inn battle, 258–59; and 75 percent
solution, 401, 445; and Atlas Peak
case, 450
Fife, Dennis, 406, 425, 499
Finigan, Robert, 191, 200
Firestone Vineyards, 251
Flora Springs Wine Co., 238
Foote, Francis, 388
Foote, June, 388
foreign investment: in Napa Valley,
250–51, 485 (see also specific investors)
Forman, Ric: works for Robert Mondavi, 167, 177–78; visits Bordeaux,
177–78; and Sterling Vineyards, 212,
213–14; dedication and success of,
236; collaboration with Newton,
238–41; break with Newton, 240–41;
family problems, 240–41; acquires
own vineyard, 241
Forman Winery, 241
Forni, Charles, 45, 47
Fort Ross, 70
France: winemaking tradition and
methods in, 175–77, 178, 179, 183–
84; competition with California in
Paris Tasting, 191–201; appellation
laws, 292, 402
Franciscan Vineyards, 251

Freemark Abbey, 3, 36; Cabernet in
Paris Tasting, 193, 196; Chardonnay
in Paris Tasting, 193, 196
freeway project: defeated in Napa Val-
ley, 210
French Colombard grape, 9
Friends of Napa Valley: and Wine
Train, 376–77, 384
Fumé Blanc (wine): Robert Mondavi
creates, 167–68

Gaja, Angelo, 441
Gallagher, Patricia: and Paris Tasting,
191–92
Galleron brothers, 89
Gallo, Ernest, 20, 28, 45, 77, 79, 117–
24, 338, 345, 368
Gallo, Joe, 338
Gallo, Julio, 20, 28, 119, 124, 338
Gallo Co., E. & J., 9, 20, 21, 78, 117–
25, 132, 216, 237, 283, 337, 338, 339
Gamay Beaujolais grape, 141
Gamay Beaujolais wine, 192
Gardens of Stone, 273
General Plan, 205–7, 254, 258, 324–25,
416, 420–21, 436, 453, 470, 491, 495,
498, 505
General Viticulture (Winkler), 188
Girard, Steve, 413, 455–56, 458
Girard winery, 378
Gloria Ferrer Caves, 354
Goelet, John, 182
Goetting, Jay, 417, 443; reelection cam-
paign, 447–48, 459, 461, 463, 466–
67, 468, 471, 474, 475, 476, 481
Golden Grain, 315–17
Gold Rush, 69, 309
Gomberg, Lou, 77, 78, 80, 81, 132, 186
GONADS, 453, 454–58
Graf, Mary Ann, 354
grafting, 35, 61
Grand Hotel, San Francisco, 69
Grand Metropolitan of London, 272,
407, 499–500
Grand Véfour, Le, 193
grapes: growers (see growers); varieties,
9, 10, 13, 15, 21, 26, 27 (see also specific
varieties); crush, 11, 49; phylloxera and,

14, 15; in San Joaquin Valley, irrigation, 50; picking, 50; prices for, 56, 438, 456; harvest, 346, 445; origin of, 385 (*see also* 75 percent solution); 1988 harvest and prices, 438

Graves, Michael, 311–12

Greenbelt Alliance, 387, 398

Greystone Cellars, 45, 72

Grgich, Mike, 180–82, 193; at Mondavi, 180, 181; venture with Barrett, 180–81, 195; apprenticeships of, 180–81; background of, 180–81; at Beaulieu, 181; and winning of Paris Tasting, 196, 199; and winery definition conflict, 423

Groth, Dennis, 413

growers: NVGGA (*see* Napa Valley Grape Growers Association); conflict with vintners, 323, 328, 331, 385–89, 397–402, 403–26, 444; and 75 percent solution, 385, 398, 400–402, 406–7, 409–10, 421, 422, 444; press conference at Farm Bureau, 408–10; and zoning hearing, 414–18

Growers Foundation: and unionism in Napa, 24, 148–54, 221

Haley, Arthur, 194

Hambrecht & Quist, 283–84

Hamm beer, 133, 143

Handel, Mary, 451

Hanns Kornell Champagne Cellars: and unionism, 147

Hanzell Winery, 20

Haraszthy, Agoston, 13, 15, 345–46

Harberger, Al, 322; and ag preserve, 86, 87–88, 91

Hardin, Garrett, 426

Harlan, Bill: and Pacific Union Company, 245, 247, 274, 428; background of, 245–47; and Wine Auction, 246; Robin Lail works with, 274, 275–77, 352–55, 357, 428, 498; and Wine Train, 382–83; and croquet tournament, 428, 430, 499

Harper's Weekly, 279

Harris, Ren: and Winegrowers Council, 147–48, 153; and Mondavi conflict, 172

Harvey's Classics, 131

Haut-Brion, Château, 176; and Paris Tasting, 194, 196, 199

Hawk's Crest, 401

health: and wine consumption, 284, 338–39

Heitz, Alice, 279

Heitz, Joe, 9, 19–20, 21–22, 36, 77, 193, 236, 378; and wine reviews, 278, 279

Hennessy, Kilian, 187

Hess, Donald, 215, 251

Heublein, 360, 407, 441; acquires Inglenook, 92, 93, 95, 98, 132, 133, 134, 323, 499; acquires Vintage Wine Merchants, 130–31; Beckstoffer joins, 130–33; acquires Allied Grape Growers, 131–33; acquires Beaulieu, 134–38; antitrust suit against, 137; management of Napa properties, 139–46, 156–60, 212, 217, 396, 422, 499–500; Vinifera Development Corporation, 142, 144, 156, 159–60; UFW and, 143–46, 147, 151, 154, 160; sold to R. J. Reynolds, 272

Hickey, Jim, 189, 320–21, 322–24, 403, 422, 506; and Planning Department, 205, 208, 320, 371, 411, 432, 448, 492; and General Plan, 205–7, 259, 324–25, 436; and winery definition, 323–24, 325, 326–28, 371, 422, 432, 436, 451; and winery density, 413, 414, 436; supervisors board dismisses, 491–93

Highway 29: traffic congestion and, 313, 406, 422

Hill, William, 214–15, 251; and Atlas Peak, 360–61

Hobbes, Thomas, 460

Hollywood, 309

Holmes, Fred, 315, 316

Hospices de Beaune: wine auction, 244

Howell Mountain: appellation, 292, 297

Huerta, Dolores, 145

Huneeus, Agustin, 413

I Love You (wine), 140

Impact, 281
Inglenook Vineyards, 10, 14, 21, 27, 28, 37–38, 39–55, 64–81, 502; winemaking at, 48, 50–51, 62–63, 72–73; Daniel inherits and restores, 48–55, 66, 67, 76–77; and Napa appellation, 50; Cabernet of, 51, 181; success of, 66–67; founding of, 71–73; building of winery, 72–73; Daniel sells, 77–81, 126; Heublein acquires, 93, 132–34, 139–40, 499; United Vintners acquires, 93, 132, 134; Beckstoffer's management of, 139–40; unionization at, 145; storage facility built at, 154, 323; valuation of, 173; under Grand Met, 499, 500
Interstate Commerce Commission: and Wine Train controversy, 375, 377, 380, 382, 473
irrigation, 50
Italian Swiss Colony, 20, 78, 118, 120, 132, 140; Heublein acquires, 132
Italian vintners and growers, 7, 11, 21, 26, 27–28, 45–46, 47, 78–80, 117–25, 381–82; *see also specific families*

Jaeger, Bill, 181, 486
Jefferson, Thomas: as enophile, 192, 285–86, 324
John Daniel Society, 274, 352–53
Johnson, Hiram, 490
Johnson, Hugh: on Spurrier, 192
Johnson, Reverdy: and winery definition issue, 385, 403, 406, 421–22, 424, 425, 433–34, 435, 436, 444, 479, 487, 505; president of NVVA, 385, 401, 403, 406, 413–14, 448, 451, 460, 461, 479, 488; background of, 403, 491; and overlay plan, 404; and 75 percent solution, 451–52; and winery moratorium, 460; and supervisor election campaign, 461–63, 465, 467, 470, 471, 472; and winery employee rally, 462
Johnson-Turnbull Vineyards, 434, 488, 502
Joseph Phelps Vineyards, 236
Julius Wile Sons & Co., 361

Kahn, Odette, 193
Kaiser Steel, 83
Kay, Guy, 406, 423, 428, 430, 431, 432, 453, 464, 465, 470, 481; and Planning Commission, 431, 432
Keegan, Eugenia, 354
Keig ranch, 142, 156, 160
Kelly, Grace, 264
Kelly, Harold, 489, 498
Kentucky Fried Chicken, 133, 143, 144
Klotz, Alexis, 51–53, 54–55, 65, 291, 318
Knowles, Legh, 406; comes to Beaulieu, 116, 125–26, 127; at Gallo, 117, 118, 120–21, 123, 125; and sale of Beaulieu, 134, 137, 138; and Heublein management of Beaulieu, 141, 156–58, 159; on Paris Tasting, 201; disdain for tastings and wine reviews, 278
Kobrand Corp., 354
Kolb, Ted, 134, 137
Korbel & Bros., 186
Kornell, Hanns, 20, 94, 315, 400
Kornell, Marilouise, 94, 164, 170
Kornell, Paula, 369
Kornell Champagne Cellars, 186, 378
kosher wine, 16, 106
Krug, Charles, 14, 15, 21, 71, 107, 130
Krug, Charles, Winery, 23, 28–34, 45, 313; Mondavis acquire, 28–29, 45, 165–66; and unionism, 147, 154; legal battle of Mondavis over, 169–73; court valuation of, 173–74; Bronfman and, 367–68; financial difficulties of, 367–68; and Wine Train route, 375

labor contracts, 142–46; in Napa Valley, 142–46, 147–54
L'Académie du Vin, Paris, 191
La Doucette, Count, 250–51
Lafite-Rothschild, Château, 176–77, 182, 251
La Grave, Château, 249
Lail, Jon, 76, 357; interest in winemaking, 76, 95
Lail, Robin Daniel, 52, 54, 64, 66, 68,

74, 76, 360, 369, 406, 504; interest in winemaking, 76, 95; marriage of, 76; and death of father, 96; disinheritance by mother, 99, 100; and heritage of Inglenook, 139–40; returns to Napa, 220; and Coppola purchase of Daniel home, 225; works for Robert Mondavi, 226–29; visits French vineyards, 229; and Napa Wine Auction, 243–44, 249; collaboration with Moueix, 250, 251–53, 274–75, 353; and Coppolas, 273–74, 498; works with Harlan, 274, 275–77, 352–55, 428, 498; and Dominus wine, 352–53, 354, 357–58; and sexism in wine industry, 354; and Croquet Classic, 427–28, 429–30, 499; and vintner-grower conflict, 432

Lancers (wine), 130, 159
land preservation movement, 82–94, 205–11, 254–59, 263, 320–31
Larkmead (wine), 28
Latour, Château, 176
Latour, Louis, 137
Le Begue Wine Company, 485
Léoville-Las-Cases, Château, 194, 196
Lewis, Oscar, 56
Lewis, "Stretch," 433
liquor making: profits in, 130; American tradition in, 285
Locke, John, 461
Lodi: Robert Mondavi visits, 337, 341–42
Lomitas Vineyard, 210–11
Long, Zelma, 354
Lukas, George, 500

Magdelaine, Château, 250, 252
Maher, Dick, 140, 403, 407, 413, 423, 425, 479, 483, 499; and Seagram management, 217, 218, 219; on old vintner families, 369; president of Vintners Association, 483, 488
Manzer, Norm: and Wine Train, 317–18, 376–77, 382, 384, 497, 503
Margaux, Château, 176
Marin County: development in, 386
Marin County Conservation League, 386

Martell, 407
Martha's Vineyard, 36, 258, 278, 279; Cabernet in Paris Tasting, 193, 196; cost of Cabernet, 279
Martin, Jack: UFW and, 143
Martin, John, 135
Martini, Carolyn, 354, 370, 372–74; as president of winery, 372–74; and Wine Train, 374–75, 384; and vintner-grower conflict, 432
Martini, Louis Michael, 365, 369, 372
Martini, Louis Peter, 21, 30, 77, 194, 322, 372–73, 406; background of, 47; and ag preserve, 86, 88; and unionism, 147; and vintner-grower conflict, 407
Martini, Michael, 373–74; and Napa Wine Auction, 249; and Vintners Association, 369, 370, 372, 385, 479; as winemaker, 369–70, 400; and gentrification of Napa, 370; and supervisor election campaign, 462, 463; on overdevelopment in Napa, 486
Martini, Patty, 370, 373
Martini, Peter, 373
Martini Winery, Louis M., 354, 369, 372, 375, 502
Martz, Dowell, 254, 257
Master Environmental Assessment, 492
May, Martha, 36, 258, 381, 447
May, Tom, 36, 88, 258, 279, 315, 447; and Wine Train, 379, 381, 383
Mayacamas Mountains, 14; vineyards on, 215
Mayacamas Vineyards, 9, 18, 238, 378; Cabernet in Paris Tasting, 193, 196, 199
McCormack, Jack: and Wine Train, 314, 315, 317, 374–75, 377, 497
McCrea, Eleanor, 9, 88, 395, 406
McCrea, Fred, 9, 21, 77, 177, 395
McCullough, Kathleen, 417, 443; reelection campaign, 447–48, 452–54, 459, 461, 463, 466, 468, 469, 471, 472–73, 475, 476; background of, 452; and 75 percent solution, 460; reelection campaign, 474, 477, 479, 481, 482

McGuire, Larry, 406
McIntyre, Hamden, 71, 72, 189
Meadowood, 244–45, 247, 275; and
  Wine Auction, 244–45; and Mumm
  Cuvée Croquet Classic, 427–28
Measure A, 255–56, 489, 491, 495
Merlot grape, 176
Merryvale, 276, 352
méthode champenoise, 21–22, 35, 186
Meursault-Charmes (Roulot), 194, 197
Mexican farm labor, 56–60
Mexico: economics of, 56–57
Meyer, Justin, 407, 424, 425, 453, 454–
  55, 456, 457, 458, 465, 468
microclimates, 188, 293
Mikolajcik, John, 462, 463, 467, 470,
  473, 475, 477, 478, 480, 481, 487,
  492, 493, 495, 505
minimum acreage lots, 91
minimum wage, 149
Miravalle, 265, 266
Mission (Criolla) grape, 13, 105–6
Modesto: Gallo headquarters and labo-
  ratories at, 117, 120, 121–23, 124–25,
  126
Moët-Hennessy: and Domaine Chan-
  don, 185–90, 212, 407
Moffitt family, 45
Mole Hill Red (wine), 48, 355
Moller-Racke family, 345
Mondavi, Blanche, 33–34, 164, 170–71
Mondavi, C., and Sons Corp., 169,
  170
Mondavi, Cesare, 24, 25–26, 28–29, 31,
  32, 163, 342–43
Mondavi, Helen, 173
Mondavi, Marcia, 24, 230; and father's
  marital relations, 165; visits Roths-
  childs with father, 231, 232, 233–34
Mondavi, Marge, 24, 29, 33, 34
Mondavi, Margrit Biever, 34, 173, 223,
  228, 335, 337, 339, 341; responsibili-
  ties at new winery, 164–65; romance
  with Robert Mondavi, 164–65; mar-
  riage to Robert, 232, 310; and Napa
  Wine Auction, 243–44
Mondavi, Mary, 24, 31

Mondavi, Michael, 22, 23, 340, 368;
  and new Mondavi Winery, 164;
  resentment toward Margrit Biever,
  165; studies and early training of,
  165–67; as president of father's winery, 229; conflict with brother, 229–
  30; and winery definition, 327–28,
  421, 423, 424, 425, 434, 439–42, 453;
  and Wine Train, 381, 384; and overlay plan, 403–4, 415, 434, 479; and
  moratorium on growth, 425; and
  vintner-grower conflict, 432, 436;
  opposes 75 percent solution, 434–35,
  440; and supervisor election campaign, 453, 465, 468–69, 472, 481
Mondavi, Peter, 22, 27, 29, 337, 375;
  conflicts and fight with Robert, 22,
  23–25, 31, 32, 33, 34, 167; training
  of, 27; as winemaker of Krug, 29,
  31–33; as manager of Krug, 169,
  367–68; legal battle with brother,
  169–73
Mondavi, Robert, 22, 27, 315, 322,
  337, 359, 365; conflict with family,
  22, 23–25, 31, 32, 33, 34, 167; training of, 27; and acquiring of Krug
  winery, 28–34; tastings, 30–31; and
  Heublein intrusion into Napa, 141;
  and unionism, 144, 147; and pronunciation of family name, 163–64;
  opens own winery, 163–64; dissolution of first marriage, 164; bringing
  change to Napa community, 165,
  360; creates Fumé Blanc, 167–68;
  commitment to quality production,
  167–68, 175, 178; seeks backer, 168–
  69; ownership of Krug stock, 169;
  legal battle with family, 169–73; wins
  family suit, 172–73; buys out backer,
  173; and Bernard Portet, 183; on
  Paris Tasting, 201; visits Coppolas,
  223; hires Robin Lail, 226–28; plans
  for sons at winery, 229–30; collaboration with Rothschild, 230, 231–34,
  247–49, 358, 439 (*see also* Opus One);
  marriage to Margrit, 232, 310; and
  Napa Wine Auction, 244–45; and

Christian Moueix, 249–50; and sub-
appellation conflict, 294, 295; and
winery at Woodbridge, 335, 336,
339–41; sense of mission, 337–39,
345; and Wine Train, 381–82
Mondavi, Rosa, 23–24, 25, 26, 28, 29,
32–33, 169, 170, 171
Mondavi, Tim, 24, 340, 341, 441, 481;
and father's marital relations, 165; as
winemaker, 229, 411; conflict with
brother, 229–30, 441; and appellation
conflict, 295; and Dunn Vineyards,
303
Mondavi Winery, Robert, 335–36, 502;
opening of, 163–64, 167, 310; quality
commitment, 175; Grgich at, 180,
181; Robin Lail joins, 226–29;
Reserve Cabernet of, 227, 234, 237;
division of responsibilities at, 229–30;
and multinational competition, 408;
perpetuating family ownership of,
441–42
Montandon, Pat, 243
Montbrun, Château de, 106, 350
Montelena, Château, 3, 181–82, 378,
403; Chardonnay in Paris Tasting,
193, 195–96, 197, 198
Monterey Vineyards, 213, 216, 217,
362
Monte Rosso winery, 47
Montgomery, John, 247
Monticello Winery, 324, 326, 445
Montrose, Château, 194, 196, 199
Moone, Mike, 401, 403, 413, 428, 429,
453, 454, 456, 462, 464, 465, 467,
468, 471, 479, 481, 483, 487
Mooser, William, 72
Moskowite, Harold, 415–16, 417, 475
Most Happy Fella, The, 113
Mothers Against Drunk Driving, 289
Moueix, Christian: contemplates win-
ery in Napa, 249–50; and collabora-
tion with Daniel daughters, 250,
251–53, 274–75, 353, 355, 357–59;
and release of Dominus, 357–59
Moueix, Jean-Pierre, 249, 252–53
Mountain Red (wine), 121

mountainsides: Diamond Mountain,
214–15, 360; vineyards moving to,
214–15, 360–61; ag preserve acreage
on, 254; Atlas Peak, 360–64
Mouton-Rothschild, Château, 231–34,
235, 280; and Paris Tasting, 194, 196,
199, 231; reclassification in 1973,
231, 232; labels of, 232, 233
Movius, John, 200, 201
Mumm Cuvée Croquet Classic, 427–
28, 429–30, 499
Mumm's champagne, 217
Muscat grape, 26

Napa Agricultural Preservation Action
Committee (NAPAC), 490–91
Napa Beaucannon, Château, 485
NAPAC, 490–91
Napa (city), 11; and land development
in valley, 255; and appellation conflict, 295
Napa County Board of Supervisors:
and ag preserve, 85, 87, 89, 92; and
vintner-grower conflict, 416–17, 442,
446, 481; election for seats on, 442,
452–54, 461–69, 470–77, 478, 479;
and moratorium on wineries, 460;
agenda of new majority, 482, 487–88,
491–93
Napa County Farm Bureau: and unionism, 147; and environmental movement, 259, 326–27, 397, 398, 399,
404; and Wine Train, 378, 447; and
growers' press conference, 408–10;
and winery definition, 433
Napa County Land Trust, 388
Napa County Planning Commission:
and ag preserve, 84, 86, 87, 91–92; in
1980s, 324; and Wine Train, 371; and
75 percent solution, 385; and vintner-
grower conflict, 397–98, 418, 422,
424, 431, 432–37, 448; Kay and, 432;
and winery moratorium, 439, 443–
44; and winery definition, 444; supervisors board reshapes, 487–88, 491
Napa County Planning Department:
Hickey and, 205, 208, 320

Napanook Vineyard, 42, 55, 99, 249, 251, 274, 353, 502
Napans Opposed to Wasteland (NOW), 210, 255
Napa Record: on Hickey dismissal, 493
Napa Register, 96; on Hickey dismissal, 493
Napa Ridge, 400–401, 407
Napa River, 3
Napa Valley: revival in 1960s, 3–4, 77; winemaking origins in, 3–4, 13–16; fogs, 10; climate, 10, 155, 188, 438; soil, 12, 14, 179, 293; geology, 12; Wappos and, 12–13; etymology, 13; failure of nineteenth-century vintners, 14–15; appellation conflict, 50; ag preserve movement, 82–92 (see also agricultural preserve); minimum acreage lots, 91; unions and labor contracts in, 143–46, 147–54; new commitment to quality winemaking, 175, 177; and marketing of wine, 190; and Paris Tasting, 191–201; General Plan for, 205–7, 254, 258–59; development and environmental concerns, 205–11, 254–59, 263, 317–19, 320–31, 369–78, 379–84, 395–402, 446, 485–86; freeway project defeated, 210, 321; new wineries of 1970s, 236; wine snobbery and exclusivity come to, 242–43, 370–71, 408; land values and, 247, 282; concern over foreign investment in, 250–51, 485; number of wineries (1960s–1980s), 282–83, 418, 443; litigiousness comes to, 290–96; appellation conflict, 292–94, 401–2; air view of, 307–8, 395; traffic congestion in, 313; Wine Train controversy, 313–15 (see also Wine Train); airport project, 321–22; 75 percent solution, 385, 398, 400–402, 409–10, 411–12, 421–22; residual value of land, 386; regionalism and, 387; zoning hearing, 414–18; water problems, 440
Napa Valley Grape Growers Association: and appellation, 294; and winery definition, 327, 398, 404, 433;

and Wine Train, 378, 382, 447; and 75 percent solution, 385, 398–99, 401–2, 404; Beckstoffer and, 396, 397; extent of representation, 424 (see also growers); Chili Ball, 427
Napa Valley Lucky Sperm Club, 369
Napa Valley Technical Group, 32, 181
Napa Valley Vintners Association: founding of, 47–48, 249, 430–31; membership in, 85, 94; and Wine Auction, 244, 245; and appellation, 294, 401, 403–4; and winery definition, 327–28, 371, 385, 398–99, 404, 421–25, 448–49; Mike Martini and, 369, 370; and Wine Train, 371, 378, 382, 447, 448; and 75 percent solution, 401, 434, 461; overlay plan, 403–4, 413, 461 (see also overlay plan); exclusivity of, 431; and supervisor election campaign, 461–69, 470–72, 478–79, 480–83; pro-development stance, 463, 464, 478–79; dissidents within, 490
Napa Valley Wine Auction, 243–45, 249, 328–31, 368, 431, 480, 496
Nation, Carry A., 287–89
Nation, David A., 287
National Council Against Alcoholism, 289
National Labor Relations Board (NLRB): and union conflict in Napa, 148
national preserve: status for Napa Valley, 322
Navalle (wine), 93, 133–34
Naylor family, 40–41
Negri, Fred, 453, 454, 462, 470, 475, 476, 477, 478, 479, 480, 481, 487, 492, 493, 495
neo-Prohibition, 284, 289, 331, 494
Nestlé, 360, 401; and Robert Mondavi, 168; and Beringer, 212, 400
Newton, Peter, 177, 181, 212–13, 238, 239–40, 378; and Sterling Vineyards, 177, 212–13; collaboration with Forman, 238–40; home of, 239; marriage of, 239; break with Forman, 240–41
Newton, Su Hua, 239

Newton Vineyards, 238–40
New York Times: and Paris Tasting, 198–99
Nichelini, Jim, 431
Nickel, H. Gilliland (Gil), 431, 453
Niebaum, Gustave, 14, 15, 46, 48, 68–73, 107, 223; wine library of, 50, 71; background of, 68–70; founds Inglenook, 70–73
Niebaum, Tante, 39–40, 43, 46, 48, 74, 77
Niebaum-Coppola Estate, 221, 222–24, 271–73, 346–47, 355–57; Cabernet of, 271, 272; Rubicon wine, 272, 347, 356
Nord, Will, 188–89

oak barrels, 20, 30, 33, 51, 168, 178, 236, 304
Oakville: and appellation conflict, 295; and Wine Train, 376; Mondavi development plans at, 381–82
Oakville Bench, 295, 296
Oliver, Raymond, 197
Opus One, 248–49, 310, 358, 435, 439, 496; and winery moratorium, 439–42
Oriental labor, 69
overlay plan: of vintners, 403–4, 413, 415, 421, 424–25, 432, 433, 434, 435, 437, 460, 478

Pacific Union Company, 245, 247, 274, 275, 428
Paris Exposition of 1889, 73
Paris Tasting, 191–201, 212, 231, 264
Parker, Robert, 280–81, 358
Parrott, Tiburcio, 14, 265
Patchett, John, 13–14
Paul Masson Vineyards, 78, 216
Peatman, Joe, 414–15, 416, 417, 486
Pecota winery, 237, 378
Pei, I. M., 358
Peju Province, 326, 502
Pelissa, Andy: and ag preserve, 86, 147; and Winegrowers Council, 147; and Mondavi conflict, 172; and Planning Commission, 324
People for Open Space, 82, 255, 387

Pepi winery, 378, 502
Peters, Betty, 318–19, 381, 382, 384
Petersen, Vera, 84
Peterson, Dick, 406; at Gallo, 122, 126, 215; comes to Beaulieu, 126–28, 129, 215; and Heublein management at Beaulieu, 140–41, 156, 158–59; quits Beaulieu, 159; at Monterey Vineyards, 213, 215–16, 217; Seagram tells to prepare wine coolers, 218–19; and Whitbread's Atlas Peak project, 361–64; and moratorium on growth, 425; and vintner-grower conflict, 448, 462; and supervisor election campaign, 462, 475
Petri, Angelo, 78, 125
Petri, Louis, 28, 77, 78–79, 120, 126, 132, 134, 135, 137
Petri Wine Company, 78–79
Pétrus, Château, 249, 251, 252, 353
Phelps, Joseph, 236, 273, 294, 378, 441, 479
Phillips, Alexandra, 257, 383
Phillips, W. Robert, Jr.: background of, 257; and environmental movement, 257–58, 397, 399, 447, 482; and winery definition, 327, 410–11, 415, 416; and Wine Train, 379–84, 497, 502; and supervisor election campaign, 473
phylloxera, 14, 15, 39, 105
Pillsbury, 212
Pine Ridge winery, 238
Pink Chablis (wine), 122, 126
Pinot Blanc grape, 9
Pinot Noir grape, 21, 47, 49, 110, 140, 157–58, 365
Pocai winery, 378
Ponti, Joe, 45, 109, 110
Portet, André, 182
Portet, Bernard, 193, 294, 442; comes to Napa, 182–84
Portet, Dominique, 182, 183
Posert, Harvey, 406
Prial, Frank: and Paris Tasting, 198–99
Private Guide to Wines (Finigan), 191
Prohibition, 5, 11, 16, 27, 39, 40, 41, 105, 106, 289; neo-, 284, 289, 331, 489

Proposition 13, 489
Proposition 65, 428–29
pruning, 63, 301–302
Puligny-Montrachet "Les Purcelles"
 (Leflaive), 194–95, 197

Quail Ridge winery, 238, 445, 447, 499
Queen of the Valley Hospital, 249

Racke, A., 251
racking, 303–4
Rainier: and Robert Mondavi, 168,
 169, 173
Rains, Claude, 113
Rasmussen winery, 378
Ray, Martin, 7, 18, 112–13
Raymond, Roy, 406, 462
Reagan, Ronald, 209
Redon, Odilon, 310, 312
red wine: white outselling, 267
regionalism, 387
restaurants: wineries as, 324–25
Reunion (wine), 273
Revere, Paul, 285
Reynolds, R. J., 272
Rhinegarten (wine), 122
Rhine House, 14, 15, 212, 400
Rhodes, Barney, 36, 315, 381, 383
Rhodes, Belle, 36
Ridge Monte Bello: Cabernet in Paris
 Tasting, 193
Riesling grape, 9, 29, 49
Rivers, Larry, 358
Robbins, Mike, 263–66; and *Falcon
 Crest*, 263, 265–66; background of,
 264–65
Rodriguez, Rafael, 56–63; background
 of, 56–62; comes to Inglenook, 62–
 63, 67; manages Inglenook, 81, 97–
 98, 149, 151; manages Beaulieu, 149,
 151; and Growers Foundation, 149–
 53, 221; quits Heublein, 151; obtains
 own home, 152; works for Coppola,
 221, 224–25, 271, 356; marriage of
 daughter, 389–92; reviews changes in
 Napa, 503–4
Romanée-Conti, 251
Romans: winemaking among, 175

Roma Wine Company, 28, 120
Rombauer, Koerner, 456, 457, 462
Rombauer winery, 354
Rossini family, 18, 19
Rothschild, Baroness Philippine de,
 231, 439
Rothschild, Baron Philippe de: and
 Mouton, 198, 231, 232–34; Mondavi
 collaboration with, 230, 231–34,
 247–49, 358 (*see also* Opus One); per-
 sonality of, 231–32
Rothschild, Nathaniel de, 232
Rothschild and His Red Gold, A, 231
Rothschild family: and Lafite, 176–77
Rubicon (wine), 272, 347, 356
rum, 285
rural land: preservation concerns, 387
 (*see also* agricultural preserve; envi-
 ronmental concerns)
Rush, Dr. Benjamin, 286
Russian American Company, 70
Russian River, 70
Rutherford, 9, 42, 71, 108, 126; and
 appellation conflict, 295; and Wine
 Train, 376
Rutherford Bench, 293, 295, 296
Rutherford Hill Winery, 181, 212, 238,
 291, 486
Rutherford International, 99, 355

sacramental wine, 16, 105–6
Saddleback winery, 378
Sage Canyon winery, 378
St. Helena, 9; and land development in
 valley, 255; and appellation conflict,
 295; and Wine Train, 375–76, 378,
 447, 497; concerns over overdevelop-
 ment, 376; City Council, 428
St. Helena, Mount, 14
St. Helena Hospital: and Napa Wine
 Auction, 243–44, 249
sales: of Napa Valley wines, 236–37,
 306, 308
Salmina brothers, 28
San Francisco: in nineteenth century,
 68–70
*San Francisco Merchant and Viticul-
 turist,* 73

Sangiovese grape, 364
Santa Clara Valley: development in, 206
Sattui Winery, 502
Sauvignon Blanc grape, 29, 71; and Mondavi Fumé Blanc, 29, 71, 167–68
Savio, Mario, 209
Schenley Corp., 120
Schmidheiny, Stefan, 251
Schram, Jacob, 5, 6, 15–16, 40, 41, 71
Schramsberg Vineyards, 82, 88, 186, 349, 378, 442; creation of, 3, 4–5, 7–9, 21–22; first vintage, 35; marketing, 36–37, 38, 83, 481
Seagram, Joseph E., & Sons, 360, 364, 407; buys Coke's wine properties, 216–17; management style, 217–18; value of, 367
Seagram Classics Wine Company, 217, 366
Sebastiani family, 106
Seeger, Pete, 82
Ségur, Marquis de, 176
Selfridge, Tom, 406, 424, 453, 483, 499
Seneca Ewer Winery, 106
Serlis, Harry, 232
Serra, Father Junípero, 13
75 percent solution, 385, 398, 400–402, 406–7, 409–10, 421–22, 424, 432, 434, 435, 445–46, 451, 458, 460, 462, 463, 464, 466, 480, 487, 488, 503, 505
Seviers, Francis, 210
sexism: in wine industry, 354
Shafer, John, 294, 453
Shafer Vineyards, 237, 378
Shanken, Marvin, 281–82
Shrem, Jan, 310–12, 406
Shute, Mihaly & Weinberger, 490–91
Silverado Squatters (Stevenson), 5–6
Silverado Trail, 11, 422
Silverado Vineyards, 294, 453
Silver Oak Cellars, 238, 378, 407, 468
Simi, 354
Simms, Jenny, 210, 254
Sionneau, Lucien, 231
sirocco: North Coast, 438
slow-growth advocacy. See environmental concerns

Smirnoff Beverage and Import Company, 135, 159
Smith, Adam, 426
Smith, James, 75, 251–52, 354
Smith, Marcia (Marky) Daniel, 52, 54, 64, 65, 74, 75, 95, 97, 504; marriage of, 75; disinheritance by mother, 99, 100; and mother's death, 225; and Napanook, 249; collaboration with Moueix, 250, 251–53, 274, 353, 357, 358, 359
Smith, Stu, 455, 457, 458, 480–81, 483
Smith-Madrone Vineyards, 237, 480
soil: composition in Napa Valley, 12, 14, 179, 293
Solano County, 440
Solari, Larry, 78, 79, 80, 93, 142; management of Inglenook, 93; and Heublein acquisitions, 132, 133, 134–35, 137, 138; and sale of United Vintners, 132, 133, 140; as head of expanded United Vintners, 140, 156; relations with Knowles, 156, 157
Sonoma County, 11, 15; development in, 386; Napa use of grapes from, 397
Soter, Tony, 480
Sousa, Joe, 49–50, 64, 67, 68, 75, 81
Southern Pacific Railroad, 313, 314, 318, 376, 378, 490
Souverain Cellars, 9, 18, 179, 212, 365, 463
Spann, Katie, 318–19, 381
sparkling wine, 21–22, 140, 185–86, 212, 365, 367; see also specific vineyards
spirits: profits in, 130; American preference for, 285; versus wine, 366
Sporting Wine, 122, 126
Spottswoode winery, 378, 480
Spreckles, Claus, 257
Spring Mountain Vineyards, 238, 264, 266, 400; Chardonnay in Paris Tasting, 193, 197, 264
Spurrier, Steven: and Paris Tasting, 191, 192, 193, 194–95, 196, 198
Stag's Leap: conflict over appellation, 294–95
Stag's Leap Wine Cellars, 247, 401, 419; Cabernet of, 178, 179; opening of,

Stag's Leap Wine Cellars (*cont.*)
178–80; '73 Cabernet wins Paris
Tasting, 192, 193, 196, 197, 198, 199,
231; conflict over name use, 290–92
Stags' Leap Winery, 247; conflict over
name use, 290–92
Stanford, Leland, 69, 72, 376
Stelling, Carolyn, 46
Steltzner, Dick, 294
Sterling Vineyards, 177, 212–13, 214,
216, 217, 238, 239, 310, 407
Stevenson, Robert Louis, 5–6, 8, 10,
65, 395
Stewart, J. Leland (Lee), 9, 18, 21, 77,
179, 365, 463; and Grgich, 180–81;
and wine marketing, 190
Stocker, Peter, 247, 428
Stonegate winery, 238, 378
Stony Hill Vineyard, 9, 19, 177, 378
Stralla, Fontaine (Fon), 44–46, 53, 75,
94–95, 100
Stralla, Louie, 44–46, 48, 52, 64, 65,
75, 78, 94–95, 100, 149, 152, 291,
430; rents Krug winery, 45; opposes
ag preserve, 84, 85, 87, 89, 91–92
Students Against Drunk Driving, 289
subscriptions: for Napa wines, 206, 308
Sullivan, Dagmar de Pins, 125–26,
350–51, 500–501; marriage of, 114,
138; and sale of Beaulieu, 134, 135,
136, 137, 138
Sullivan, Walter, 79, 114, 125–26, 350–
51; and sale of Beaulieu, 134–38,
500–501
Sunny St. Helena Winery, 27–28, 502;
Harlan and, 276–77, 352–55, 383,
428, 498
Suntory, 168, 251
Sutter, John, 70
Sutter Home Winery, 266–67, 268–70,
292, 375, 396, 407, 458, 502
Swanson, Clark, 381, 384, 447
Swanson family, 348
sweet wines, 27, 120, 132
Syar, 454

Taddei, Joe, 258
Taillevent, Le, 193

Taittinger, 354
Taltarni winery, 182
Tari, Pierre, 193
tastings. *See* wine tastings
Taylor California Cellars, 213, 217
Taylor Wine Company, 212
Tchelistcheff, André, 18, 30, 104–5,
107–10, 111–13, 115–16, 142, 194,
195, 241, 242, 273, 344–45, 346–50,
360; meets de Latour, 104–5; comes
to Beaulieu, 107–10; corrects conditions at Beaulieu, 111–12; working
relations with Mme. de Pins, 115–16,
128, 156; and Carneros vineyard,
126; hires Peterson for Beaulieu,
126–28; remains as consultant to
Beaulieu, 127, 155–56; marriage to
Dorothy, 155; relations with Heublein, 156, 157–58; quits Beaulieu,
158; and Winiarski, 179; and Grgich,
180, 181; and quality control, 181;
and microclimates, 293; outlook on
future of Napa, 344, 348; health of,
344–45, 346, 464–65; works for Niebaum-Coppola, 346–48; unencumbered life of, 348; and vintner-grower
conflict, 464–65
Tchelistcheff, Dimitri, 107, 108–9, 127
Tchelistcheff, Dorothy, 155, 344
Tchelistcheff Wine Tours International,
194
temperance movement, 286–89
Tenscher, Alan, 423, 425–26
Tepesque vineyard: Mondavi purchase
of, 341
Thompson grapes, 140
Thunderbird (wine), 120
Time: on Paris Tasting, 197
Timothy, Brother, 406
To Kalon vineyard, 14, 25
Tour d'Argent, La, 193
tourism, 11; conflict over exploitation
of, 256, 411, 444; and *Falcon Crest,*
263–64, 265; and Napa mystique,
263–64, 265; Wine Train and, 313–
15, 317–19, 379, 473 (*see also* Wine
Train); winery definition and, 325–
26, 405, 467; Davies report on, 443

Township Plan: and appellation conflict, 295–96
Trader Vic's, San Francisco, 37, 38
"Tragedy of the Commons, The," 423, 426
Travers, Bob, 194
Tra Vigne Restaurant, 352
Travis Air Force Base, 321
Trefethen, Gene, 188
Trefethen, Janet, 189
Trefethen, John, 181, 189, 370, 479
Trefethen, Katherine, 188
Trefethen Vineyards, 183; unionization at, 154; relations with Moët-Hennessy, 189
Trinchero, Bob, 268, 431, 455, 457
Trinchero, Mario, 268
Trinchero family, 268–70
Trotanoy, Château, 249
Tsongas, Paul E., 389
Tubbs, Alfred, 181
Tucker: The Man and His Dream, 356
Turgenev, Ivan, 104
Tuteur, John, 210, 254
2020 Vision, 489–90, 495, 498, 503, 505–6

unionism: in Napa Valley, 142–46, 147–54
United Farm Workers, 142–46, 147–54, 160, 224
United Napa Valley Associates, 451
United Vintners, 78, 79, 132; acquires Inglenook, 80–81; and Inglenook sale, 93, 132, 134; Heublein acquires, 93, 132–34, 140; acquiring vineyards, 142
University of California at Davis, 10, 43, 50, 178, 212
Upper Napa Valley Associates (UNVA), 323, 451; and ag preserve, 83–84, 88; creation of, 83–84

Vallejo, General Mariano, 13
Vanderschoot, Felix: and ag preserve, 86, 87, 92
Varrelman, Mel, 256–57, 380, 398, 417,

418, 453, 460, 461, 476, 479, 482, 486, 487, 489, 494; and 75 percent solution, 460
Veeder, Mount, 186, 188, 251
Veedercrest Vineyards: Chardonnay in Paris Tasting, 193, 197
Veeder Hills, 215
Vichon Winery, 442
Villaine, Aubert de, 193
Vine Hill Ranch, 379, 502
Vineland, 285
vineyard labor: wages of, 56; migrant, 56–57; unionization, 143–46, 147–54; minimum wage, 149
Vinifera Development Corporation, 142, 144, 156, 159–60; Beckstoffer acquires, 160
Vintage Wine Merchants, 130–31
vintners: NVVA (see Napa Valley Vintners Association); founding families, 4; 1960s arrivals, 9–10, 17, 35–36, 77; nineteenth-century, 13–16; new quality commitment, 175, 177, 297–308; marketing concerns of, 190, 325, 397, 405, 435, 445; 1970s boutiques, 236–38; marital relations among, 240; snobbery and exclusivity among, 242–43, 309–10, 370–71, 408; concern over foreign investors, 250–51, 485; Randy Dunn's approach, 297–308; at odds with growers, 323, 328, 331, 385–92, 397–402, 403–26, 444; sexism among, 354; and Wine Train, 371, 375, 377–78; and winery definition, 371, 385–89, 420–26; use of second line, 400–401; overlay plan of, 403–4, 413, 415, 421, 424–25, 432, 433, 434, 435, 437, 460, 478; and zoning hearing, 414–18; GONADS and, 455; and supervisor election campaign, 470
Vintners Inn: battle over project, 258–59, 321, 380
Virginia Gentleman, 135
Vitis labrusca, 285
Vitis vinifera, 15, 175, 286, 345–46
Vogüé, Count Robert-Jean de: and Domaine Chandon, 185–86, 187, 188

Volstead National Prohibition Act of 1920, 16
von Uhlit, Ruth, 489, 498

Wagner, Charlie, 60–61
Wappos: and Napa Valley, 12–13
War Prohibition Act of 1918, 16
Washington, George, 285
water problem: in California, 440
Watson, Stuart: and acquisition of United Vintners and Inglenook, 132, 133, 134, 135; acquires Beaulieu, 134, 135, 139; and Heublein acquisition of vineyards, 142, 160; UFW and, 143; and management of Beaulieu, 157, 158, 159
Waugh, Harry, 42, 335
Waugh, Pru, 442
Weinberger, Casper, 88–89
Wente family, 106
whiskey, 285
Whitbread North America, 361, 407, 450, 451
White, Bob, 416, 417, 462, 487–88, 489, 493, 495
Whitehead, Alfred North, 426
white wine: outselling red, 267
Wigger, Henry, 210
Williams, John, 464, 471, 490
Williamson Act, 84, 85–86, 91
Wilsey, Al, 243, 447, 453
Wine Advisory Board, 79, 117, 119
Wine Advocate, The, 280, 358
Wine and Food Society, 50
wine appreciation, 227
wine auction: Napa, 243–45, 249, 328–31, 368, 431, 480, 496; Hospices de Beaune, 244
wine consumption: and Prohibition, 5, 11, 16, 27, 39, 40, 41, 105, 106; in 1970s, 237; French, Italian, and American, 282
Wine Experience, 282
wine glamour, 281–82, 309–10, 337
Winegrowers Council: founding of, 147; and unionism, 147–49
Wine Institute, 28, 43, 50, 119, 429, 441

winemaking: history of, 3; origins in Napa Valley, 3–4, 13–16; Prohibition and, 5, 11, 16; crush, 11, 49, 335, 346, 379; oak barrels, 20, 30, 33, 51, 168, 178, 236, 304; at Inglenook, 50–51, 62–63; pruning, 63, 301–302; new commitment to quality in Napa, 175, 177; evolution in France, 175–77; in Bordeaux, 177–78; by Randy Dunn, 297–308; racking, 303–4
wine marketing, 190; volume and value of American wines in 1980s, 282–83; tourism and, 321; and definition of winery, 321–31, 397, 405
wine prices, 236, 279, 283, 486
wine rating systems, 279–80
wineries: irrigation in, 50; Napa Valley growth in 1970s, 236, 323; cost of, 282, 486; number in Napa (1960s–1980s), 282–83, 418, 443; number of American, 282–83; architecture of, 310–12, 358, 496–97; definition issue, 321–31, 371, 385–89, 397, 398–99, 408–12, 414–18, 420–26, 433–37, 439–42, 448–49, 451, 461, 466, 467, 468–69, 470, 478, 481, 486, 487, 505; on-site marketing activities of, 325, 397, 405, 435, 445; grandfathering activities of, 327, 409–10, 422, 424, 435–36, 466, 468; competition and failures, 349, 360; sexism in, 354; grower classification for (heritage, charter, estate), 409, 421, 468; zoning hearing, 414–18; moratorium on, 424, 425, 436, 439–42, 442, 443, 460, 468, 503; employees of, and supervisors election campaign, 462–63
Winery Lake, 364, 365
Winery Lake Vineyard, 364–65, 367, 407
wine sales: of Napa, 236–37, 306, 308
Wines of America, The (Adams), 119
Wine Spectator, The, 281
Wine Spectrum, 215
wine tastings, 30–31, 49, 236, 278, 398; Paris Tasting, 191–201
Wine Train, 313–15, 317–19, 323, 371, 372–78, 379–84, 440, 443, 447–48, 449, 471, 473, 497, 501–3

wine writers, 118–19, 278–82, 345, 358
Winiarski, Barbara, 17–19, 395, 419,
    464, 466, 471, 474, 479–80, 493, 505;
    and Paris Tasting, 191, 196
Winiarski, Stephen, 419
Winiarski, Warren, 35, 77, 275, 395,
    406, 413, 419; arrival in Napa, 17–19;
    apprenticeships, 18–19; works for
    Robert Mondavi, 167, 177, 178;
    Cabernet making by, 178, 179; opens
    own winery, 178–80; studies soil
    composition, 179; and Paris Tasting,
    191, 196–97, 201, 231; on Mondavi-
    Rothschild collaboration, 248–49;
    conflict over Stag's Leap name use,
    290–92, 294; and second line wines,
    401; and winery definition, 415, 424;
    and growth limitation, 420, 486, 490;
    and vintner-grower conflict, 432;
    448; and supervisor election cam-
    paign, 453, 471; and winery morato-
    rium, 460; and leadership of
    Vintners, 479
Winkler, Albert, 43, 188, 293

Woman's Christian Temperance Union,
    286–87
women: in wine industry, 354
Woodbridge: Mondavi winery at, 335,
    336, 337, 339–41
Wright, Jim: Mount Veeder vineyard,
    186, 188
Wright, John: and Domaine Chandon,
    185, 186–87, 188, 189–90, 405, 448

Yount, George Calvert, 13
Yountville, 9; and land development in
    valley, 255; and appellation conflict,
    295; and Wine Train, 376, 378, 447
Yquem, Château d', 233, 235

Zapple, 140
Zinfandel grape, 13, 26, 47, 183, 266,
    267, 268, 348; white (blush) wine
    from, 266–67, 269, 396
Zoetrope Studios, 271, 272
zoning ordinances, 255–59; and winery
    definition, 325, 386

The Far Side *of* Eden

New Money, Old Land, and the
Battle for Napa Valley

AN EXCERPT

A DECADE LATER, James Conaway picks up his story of the Napa Valley, the premier American wine country and a place synonymous with the good life, in his new book, *The Far Side of Eden*.

Awash in dollars generated by the boom economy and the social ambitions it inspired, Napa is now beset by too much of a good thing: new arrivals determined to have a vineyard of their own, cult wines that few locals can afford, established families wishing to hold on to the old ways, and camp followers caught up in the glamour of it all. What has transformed a natural and agricultural beauty spot into a coveted global destination has left inevitable scars, and a small, impassioned band of environmentalists strikes back in a way that deeply divides the valley between those in favor of unbridled economic development and those insisting on limits.

In this excerpt from *The Far Side of Eden*, James Conaway once again takes us to the frontlines of America's ongoing conflicts over money, land, and power, and spins a tale that has ramifications for us all.

The Far Side of Eden • hardcover • $28.00 • 0-618-06739-6
Available from Houghton Mifflin Company, October 2002

AT THE SOUTH END of the valley, the Carneros hills roll in great earth swells down toward San Pablo Bay, and at the north end the lowering presence of Mount St. Helena sits like a cork in a bottle of opaque green glass.

The Napa River between these two points covers just thirty miles, and the valley floor is only a couple of miles wide at its most commodious, yet here, under skies oceanic in depth and color — a blue impossible in most of the world's climes — there occurred over the course of the twentieth century something truly remarkable: agriculture withstood the assault of development that overwhelmed the rest of this coveted bit of California, and the product of that effort — wine — was made into a symbol of privilege.

Meanwhile the valley, as is often said, became the envy of the world. But in the last quarter century some of the idyllic character has disappeared, and the valley, like the rest of the country, felt the pressure of opposing views about what it should be and what it should look like. In the 1990s those tensions came forcefully into play here, and I was drawn to the struggle in the belief that it embodied rudiments of the American character and held clues about the future of the American landscape.

I had not been to Napa Valley for many years, not since the late 1980s, when I had done research there in preparation for my book

Napa: The Story of an American Eden. When I did return I was surprised to find many additional vineyards, more traffic, new mansions high in the rugged but not inviolable hills, and a heightened sense of glamour; I also heard on all sides contending views and strongly expressed expectations that each view must prevail. Some people wanted only material prosperity, others only to capture the moment in time, and these were clearly on a collision course.

I moved back for a time, the highway drawing me in like memory, past the outskirts of the city of Napa in the south, into those broad expanses of vineyard like unfurled bolts of corduroy planted also with houses and recent manifestations of the booming tourist trade. I actually live on the other side of the continent but here felt, in a way, that I was home, too, or at least in some approximation of it: more than a tourist, less than a citizen.

I knew something of the valley's history and topography, having hiked in the bracketing, north-south–trending mountains that to the unknowing eye are secure in their ruggedness and isolation — the Mayacamas range on the west, dense with redwood and Douglas fir, separates Napa and Sonoma valleys, and the Howell range on the east, droughty, with a denser mix of chaparral amid the conifers, walls off the farther reaches of Napa County — and I knew that the valley supported great biological diversity. In addition to some of the finest *Vitis vinifera* on earth there was a good complement of California's native oaks, steelhead trout, deer, black bears, and a few spotted owls.

The valley's story, like California's, is essentially one of success, but in my absence some volatile elements had been added to the human mix, and they were potent indeed. The engines of commerce and electronics had carried the country into the greatest hegemony in human history, producing unimaginable new wealth, and a disproportionate amount of it had found its way into the valley. At the same time, there had flowered a school of protest with no roots in the commodity that had made the valley famous and was in fact hostile to it. These two elements were new, and already on the way to a showdown.

I found a place to live, in St. Helena, one of four "up-valley" towns: a room with a bed and table, windows shielded by mock orange trees, a sun-washed kitchen and a deck. There was a good restaurant just down the block, but I used it infrequently. I listened to the sprinklers each night, and awoke each morning to a fresh world, the exuberance of roses and mallows lining the fence replaced by the smell of baked earth that is so Napan. A few steps led to vineyards that surrounded the town and made available to the lowliest visitor open, matchless vistas of mountains and sky.

The months I spent in that little house were happy and productive, and I am grateful for them. It was the end of the nineties, that lost decade so full of hope and opportunity, and it seemed to me, in that place, at that time, that the future lay out there, just beyond the garden.

I still believe that what happened in Napa Valley is relevant to the rest of the country, however altered now are our interior landscapes. How people living in a contained, beautiful part of America dealt with threats to established order is in large part what this book is about. The account is factual, and it is important to note that the story isn't over yet. In this new century ideals share equal space only if they are lucky with hard global reality; meanwhile, the valley's fate is being fixed in the long weave of ambition and desire, wealth and restraint, vines and the wildness of chosen places.

Something had happened, something momentous, something involving money, lots of it — what didn't at century's end? — but more complicated and subtle. It pervaded the lives of Americans considered blessed by any standard, with houses close to some of the best restaurants on earth, the value of their property on a near-vertically ascending plane, their views of a gorgeous pastoral dream: mountains, agriculture as old as human history, wild mustard blooming in the spring and, in autumn, the air perfumed by fermenting wine as precious as that of Bordeaux, Burgundy, and Champagne.

San Francisco lay just across a sparkling inland sea, but the finest things could be had right here, too, at stations of the new cross — truffles at Sunshine Market, demi-glace at Dean & DeLuca. Appetites were enhanced by the best weather in a state famous for it, and the proximity of visiting Hollywood and other sorts of stars imbued existence with a certain *frisson*. And even if there were five million tourists a year to deal with, well, those already here in the Napa Valley were the envy of all who weren't.

Yet something was wrong. People disagreed over when "it" had happened, and why, but not about the effect: a real, and growing, sense of loss.

They felt it while sitting in a long line of cars on Highway 29, looking up at once pristine slopes dense with conifer and chaparral, studded now with "steroid houses," "muscle houses," "McMansions," all contemptuous names for places built not to live in but as monuments to finance, visited by absentee owners. The locals felt it overhearing conversations about vanity vineyards, "cult" cabernets, and gardens with "water features" to cover the traffic noise.

If they wanted to buy a house to actually live in, or to trade up, they had to listen to sales pitches not about the valley's illustrious history, its neighborliness, schools, and churches, all the old-fashioned values, but about the proximity of Tra Vigne and the French Laundry. If they owned a house already, they had to wait for a carpenter or a plumber because these tradesmen worked for the owners of the muscle houses or redone Victorians, and then the locals had to pay fees often inflated by the presence of so much outside money.

Worst of all, they had to listen to the stories. Many of these featured limousines but were otherwise interchangeable. "I was pruning my roses when this couple gets out," began one such account. "He's got on wraparound shades and a five-hundred-dollar shirt with not enough buttons, bought in Beverly Hills, and she's wearing haute safari from wherever."

The visitor might also be driving a new Lexus and looking nerdy in pressed jeans and granny glasses, sure sign of a Silicon Valley weekender. These were the young beneficiaries of the computer boom, and realtors referred to them as "the children."

The procedure was much the same: "He says, 'I'll give you . . . ,' " and here the figure varied among the millions, but was never less than one. "I tell him the house isn't for sale. He doubles the price. I have to go inside to get away from him." Later, the visitor calls and triples the offer.

The problem was, many of the stories were true, like the one about the house that sold for one-point-three, already an amazing sum for such a modest place, and then the new owners "tweaked" the landscaping — added some exotics and a stone wall — and sent to France for a containerful of furniture. They put the house back on the market for two-point-nine-five and received three instant offers for more. During escrow, an unsuccessful bidder offered the buyer point-five just to step aside — half a million dollars to get out of the way.

There was the house listed for four, bought by a venture capitalist who had seen it only once. Upon seeing it a second time, he decided he no longer fancied it and resold the house at a half-million-dollar loss to a thirty-five-year-old working in the acquisitions department of a major bank. And there was the cottage in the town of St. Helena, listed for point-nine-two-five, bid up to one-point-three. After that, everybody with a three-room Victorian guesthouse with one and a half baths thought it was worth one-point-three, and it was.

Houses that were not for sale were auctioned off without the knowledge of the owners, who were presented with offers as faits accomplis. Weekend guests bought their hosts' residences. One such couple reportedly paid millions, first stipulating that everything had to be left as it was, right down to the terrycloth bathrobes, since they didn't want to be bothered with purchasing their own things or didn't know what was required. Not that it mattered. Experts materialized to perform that function for the newcomers, many of them living in San Francisco and tripping up on commission. They advised on the creation of cunning archways, the buying of period settees or Mayan urns, the planting of herb gardens "with a culinary bias," the buying of wines from the Oakville Grocery, the joining of Meadowood Country Club, the ordering of cut flowers from Tesoro's, the hiring of chefs and the vetting of maids and valets and the planting of the ultimate symbol of success, more important even than a house — a vineyard of one's own.

Everybody who mattered suddenly had to have one. This link to ancient tradition was the latest, best way of transforming money into status, though what the newcomers really wanted was a vineyard *and* "a cabernet" made from its fruit that would be highly ranked by the critics and set them miles ahead of other merely wealthy people. The locals couldn't afford these wines but had to listen to weekenders talk about them.

And they had to listen to the story about the woman with a vineyard of her own who sold her mauve Bentley because it had no rack for holding lattes, and the story about the couple building a glass house containing smoke machines, and the story about another couple with monogrammed toilet paper, each square resembling an illuminated manuscript. You laughed at the stories, but they had an effect.

Life began to feel like a lottery, or like Renaissance Spain, the gold ships coming in and their sails overshadowing all past custom and convention. Their modern equivalent was the stretch limo, the pilot fish of the nouveau riche lurking in restaurant parking lots and in the shade of olive trees on landscaped lawns. Much of this bullion had been mined down in the Santa Clara Valley, once lovely orchards since paved over and rechristened with that unlovely moniker Silicon, symbol of the greatest economic expansion in human history, a chemical that transmitted electronic impulses and churned assets, changing the world, spinning off money to computer whizzes and venture capitalists, dot-commers, "IPO sluts," entrepreneurs, investment bankers, retailers, media- and consumer-related accumulators of capital, all belted to the marvelous economic engine of the fading American century. And not a few of them were disciples of personal gratification, and self-serving.

And there were the speculators, a category to which every winery owner and, in fact, many householders now belonged. That fact alone was galling. With the acceptance of it came another realization, even sadder, that in a few short years many longtime residents had gone from being members of a community to serving as its adjuncts. So many of the big old houses now belonged to outsiders the locals were unlikely to get to know, and so eventually, it seemed, would all the valley. These old-timers would be performing some service for the new people, if they weren't already, even though the locals were relatively rich on paper. If one of them sold a house or a little vine-yard, he couldn't afford to buy another, not "up-valley." He couldn't compete at the wine auctions that raised money for the schools and hospitals, couldn't get a new kitchen countertop put in, couldn't get a table at Bistro Jeanty or even at Green Valley Café because of all the tourists drawn by the celebrity.

Things were out of whack, not just in the real estate offices but also in the hills. Out of sight, larger muscle houses were being built, and caves dug to gargantuan dimensions to contain activities not related to wine, and outlandish embellishments put in. There was the per-sistent story of a canal built on a high dry ridge, complete with an operating lock and a barge that could be boosted up and down, this in a fragile place where water was scarce. Some people thought this a charming diversion, and others thought it disgusting ego gratifica-tion and bad taste, but they didn't say so because for the most part people in the valley were accepting souls, polite, reluctant to criticize.

This was just another story, no worse than the one about the woman who moved from the Midwest to a house in the hills cost-ing millions so she could make cheese and sell it to the CIA — the Culinary Institute of America. Thus a substance once the byproduct of mere agriculture had been elevated to a symbol of culture. For the first time in human history, people were spending fortunes to make chump change and in the process be associated with the most basic sort of enterprise — agriculture — which in this incarnation had become glamorous. It made no more economic sense than the mus-cle houses and vineyards on steep land where forest had stood, and people marveled at the cost of it all. Planting those steep slopes cost upward of a hundred thousand dollars an acre just to get the vines in, not counting the purchase price, unjustifiable on the economics, not arrived at by trial and error, as in the old days, but simply or-dained, bought, and written off.

There was no space left on the valley floor for such "vanity" vine-yards, but they had to go in somewhere, for the social and financial enhancement they promised, and that meant the hills. The visible new vineyards and muscle houses amounted to a fraction of what was going on out of sight, or so it was said; in the rainy season, development high in the Mayacamas and the opposing range to the east tinged the reservoirs of drinking water and turned the Napa River murky. There was too much happening up there for most people to keep track of and still live their lives. More and more of them worried about what it all meant, where it was all going, what was being lost.

James Conaway, the author of nine previous books, is a contributor to *National Geographic Traveler, Smithsonian, Worth, Food and Wine,* and other magazines.